Herman Vandenburg Ames

The proposed amendments to the Constitution of the United States during the first century of its history

Herman Vandenburg Ames

The proposed amendments to the Constitution of the United States during the first century of its history

ISBN/EAN: 9783744748704

Printed in Europe, USA, Canada, Australia, Japan

Cover: Foto ©ninafisch / pixelio.de

More available books at **www.hansebooks.com**

ANNUAL REPORT

OF THE

AMERICAN HISTORICAL ASSOCIATION

FOR

THE YEAR 1896.

IN TWO VOLUMES.

VOL. II.

Proposed Amendments to the Constitution, 1789 to 1889.

WASHINGTON:

GOVERNMENT PRINTING OFFICE.

1897.

THE PROPOSED AMENDMENTS TO THE CONSTITUTION OF THE UNITED STATES DURING THE FIRST CENTURY OF ITS HISTORY.

Prize Essay by HERMAN V. AMES, Ph. D.,
UNIVERSITY OF PENNSYLVANIA.

[At its Washington meeting, December 26, 27, 1895, the executive council of the American Historical Association voted to offer a prize of $100 for the best monograph, based upon original investigation in history, submitted to the council in the course of the year 1896. The committee of award, Profs. A. C. McLaughlin, of the University of Michigan; Moses Coit Tyler, of Cornell University, and James Harvey Robinson, of Columbia University, gave the prize to Prof. Herman V. Ames, of Ohio State University, for his elaborate monograph on "The proposed amendments to the Constitution of the United States during the first century of its history."— From Secretary's Report.]

CONTENTS.

CHAPTER I.

A GENERAL SURVEY OF THE ATTEMPTS TO SECURE AMENDMENTS.

CHAPTER II.

PROPOSED AMENDMENTS AFFECTING THE FORM OF GOVERN-
MENT—LEGISLATIVE.

CHAPTER VI.

PROCEDURE AS TO CONSTITUTIONAL AMENDMENTS.

APPENDIX.

This work is based upon the results of a careful search for proposed amendments in the Government documents covering the first century of the history of the Constitution. In many instances, especially during the last quarter of the century, the text of the proposed amendment is not given in either the journals or the Congressional Globe or Record, and in some cases the subject of the amendment is not even stated. In nearly all these cases it was possible to secure the text by consulting the file of the original printed drafts of resolutions and bills, which are to be found in the Senate document room in Washington.

It is probable that some amendments proposed by the various State legislatures have not been found, owing to the fact that some of these proposed amendments were not presented to Congress, and hence were not included in the Government records. Some cases of this kind have been found through an examination of the circular letters from the governors of the States proposing them directed to the governor of Massachusetts, which are on file in the Massachusetts archives in the State house at Boston. A complete list of such propositions would necessitate an examination of the journals of the legislative bodies in all the States, most of which are still in manuscript form only, but it is believed that the most important propositions of this class have been found. It is scarcely possible that all the proposed amendments presented to Congress have been included, although care has been taken to reduce the omissions to a minimum.

Acknowledgments are due to Mr. Amzi Smith, superintendent of the Senate document room, Washington; to Mr. Andrew H. Allen, Chief of the Bureau of Rolls and Library, Department of State, Washington; to Mr. S. M. Hamilton, of the same Department, and to Mr. L. B. Proctor, secretary of the New York State Bar Association. All of these gentlemen courteously extended to me every facility for the examination of documents placed in their charge.

Above all I desire to express my indebtedness to Prof. Albert Bushnell Hart, of Harvard University, at whose suggestion the investigation of this subject was first undertaken, and to whose aid and encouragement its completion is in large measure due.

PHILADELPHIA, PA., *October 7, 1897.*

THE PROPOSED AMENDMENTS TO THE CONSTITUTION OF THE UNITED STATES DURING THE FIRST CENTURY OF ITS HISTORY.

By Herman V. Ames, Ph. D.

Chapter I.

A GENERAL SURVEY OF THE ATTEMPTS TO SECURE AMENDMENTS.

1. ORIGIN OF THE AMENDING POWER IN THE CONSTITUTION OF THE UNITED STATES: PROCEEDINGS OF THE FEDERAL CONVENTION.

The "fathers" of the Constitution were not sanguine enough to suppose that the organic law which they had framed was so perfect that it would never need to be altered.[1] The experience of the Government under the "Articles of Confederation" had produced the conviction that there was need of a system of amendment by which the Constitution could be made to conform to the requirements of future times.

The specific provisions of Article V, which defines the manner of securing amendments to the Constitution, were not so much the result of institutional growth—as is true of so many of the provisions of the Constitution—as of mature deliberation and the spirit of compromise which characterized the work of the Convention. An examination of English and colonial precedents and of the State constitutions in force in 1787, as well as of the debates in the Federal Convention, proves the truth of this statement.[2] The framers were here entering

---

[1] See Mr. Iredell's speech in North Carolina convention. Elliot's Debates, IV. 177. Report of New York State Bar Association, vol. XIII, p. 138.

[2] However, the idea that provision should be made in the instrument of government itself for the method of its amendment is peculiarly American. Provision for the regular and orderly amendment of an instrument of government first appears in The Pennsylvania Frame of Government of 1683. A similar provision reappears in the Act of Settlement of 1683, The Pennsylvania Frame of 1696, and The Pennsylvania Charter of Privileges of 1701. Each of these documents provides that it shall not be altered, changed, or diminished "without the consent of the governor" "and six parts of seven of the assembly." No other colonial charter contained any provision for amendment. For text of above charter see Poore, Charters and Constitutions, II.

upon a comparatively new field. The colonists, although familiar with the English system, which enabled Parliament to effect fundamental changes in the constitution in the same way as in the statute law, were not inclined to follow this precedent.[1] "Their constitutions, purporting to define the power of the several branches of the government, in no case permitted definitive amendments by the legislature."[2] With few exceptions the State constitutions first framed contained no provison for their future amendment.[3] By 1787, however, eight of the State constitutions contained such a provision. Three gave the amending power to the legislature,[4] "but under restrictions which reduced it far below the power so familiar to our fathers in the Parliament."[3] Five, under various restrictions, reserved the power for conventions.[5] Not one made provision for amendment through the agency of either a convention or the legislative body. It was reserved for the Federal Convention to embody both methods in the draft it sent out to the States for adoption.

The desirability of some provision for amendment was admitted early in the session of the Federal Convention. Difference of opinion, however, developed later in regard to the method to be employed. Should the National Legislature or a convention called on application of the States propose amendments? Should a general convention, or conventions in the States, or the legislatures thereof, ratify the same? Further, what majority should be necessary to secure the adoption of an amendment? The matter first came before the Convention, May 29, 1787, through one of the articles of the Randolph plan, which read as follows: "Resolved, that provision ought to be made for the amendment of the Articles of Union whensoever it shall seem necessary, and that the assent of the National Legislature ought not to be required thereto."[6] The Pinckney plan, which was presented the same day, contained the first detailed suggestion of the procedure to be followed.

---

[1] It is true the legislatures had assumed power to declare their independence of Great Britain.

[2] Jameson, Const. Convention, p. 547. Story, ii, p. 576.

[3] Maryland, 1776; Delaware, 1776; Pennsylvania, 1776 Georgia, 1777; Vermont, 1777. Jameson, p. 550, note 1.

[4] Maryland, 1776; Delaware, 1776; South Carolina, 1778.

[5] Pennsylvania, 1776; Vermont, 1777, 1787; Georgia, 1777; Massachusetts, 1780; New Hampshire, 1784. Only in Massachusetts and New Hampshire during this early period were the constitutions submitted to the people for ratification. See Davis Am. Const., Johns Hopkins Univ. Studies, vol. iii, p. 472. Schouler, Const'al Studies, pp. 47-50.

[6] Elliot, Vol. v., pp. 123, 190.

It provided either for the calling a convention for the purpose
of amending the Constitution whenever two-thirds of the
legislatures of the States apply for the same,[1] or for the proposal by Congress, with the consent of two-thirds of each
House, of amendments which should be ratified upon the
agreement of two-thirds[2] of the legislatures of the States.[3]

The Convention evidently desired to reserve this very important subject for subsequent consideration, for it reached no
other conclusion before the committee of detail were instructed,
beyond a declaration "that provision ought to be made for
amending the Articles of Union whensoever it shall seem necessary."[4] The method agreed upon by the committee and embodied in the first draft of the Constitution was as follows:
"On application of the legislatures of two-thirds of the States
of the Union for an amendment of this Constitution, the Legislature of the United States shall call a convention for that
purpose."[5] This article, although agreed to on August 10, did
not give universal satisfaction.[6] Just a month later Mr. Gerry
precipitated a discussion by moving the reconsideration of the
article as adopted. His action was prompted by the fear that
"two-thirds of the States can obtain a convention that may
subvert the State constitutions altogether."[7] Hamilton also
favored reconsideration, but for diametrically opposite reasons.
He argued that the mode proposed was inadequate, inasmuch
as "the State legislatures will not apply for alterations but
with a view to increase their own powers. The National Legislature will be the first to perceive and will be most sensible
to the necessity of amendment and ought also to be empowered, whenever two-thirds of each branch should concur, to
call a convention." Madison also opposed the plan of the
committee on account of its vagueness. The article, in fact,
did not make clear whether "the legislatures were to propose
amendments and the convention was to adopt them, or whether
the convention was both to propose and adopt them, or only
to propose them for adoption by some other body or bodies not

[1] This provision may have been suggested by the article in the Massachusetts constitution (1780).
[2] Perhaps suggested by article in the New Hampshire constitution (1784).
[3] Elliot, Vol. V, p. 132. The genuineness of the Pinckney plan is now disputed.
[4] Ibid., 376. In the words of Randolph's resolution.
[5] Ibid., 381. The first constitutions of New Hampshire, New York, New Jersey, Pennsylvania, Delaware, Maryland, Virginia. and North Carolina had been framed and adopted
by conventions.
[6] Ibid., 498. Art. 19 of the first draft.
[7] Ibid., 530.

specified."[1] The force of Hamilton's and Madison's argument
was quickly seen by the reconsideration of the article. Roger
Sherman moved to add a provision to the same enabling Congress to propose amendments to the several States, but no
amendment should be valid without the consent of all the States.[2]
After an attempt to change this so as to read " two-thirds "
had been defeated,[3] a motion substituting " three-fourths" of
the States was agreed to unanimously. At this point Madison came forward with a substitute which, with certain modifications, to be referred to later, was substantially the same as
the article incorporated in the Constitution. It was agreed to
by a vote of 9 to 1.[4] Subsequently the provision which required the calling a convention to draw up amendments on
application of two-thirds of the States was inserted in deference to the desire that the people might have a more direct
share in the framing of amendments. Sherman, fearing that
"three-fourths" of the States might be brought to do things
fatal to particular States, as "abolishing them altogether," or
depriving them of their equality in the Senate, renewed his
attempt to secure a provision to prevent the ratification of an
amendment without the consent of all.[5] The failure to secure
amendments to the "Articles of Confederation," because of a
similar provision, was too deeply impressed upon the minds of
all to permit such a restriction meeting with general approval.[6]

In the course of the discussion the question whether certain
features of the Constitution should be exempt from amendment arose. Two such limitations were demanded, the one by
the Southern States, the other by the small States. Each of
these objects had been the subject of one of the great compromises of the Convention, and it was desired that the provisions
resulting from these compromises should be made irreversible.
The first limitation, providing that no amendment made prior
to the year 1808 should in any manner affect the clauses relating to the slave trade and the capitation or other direct taxes.

[1] Curtis, Hist. of Const., Vol. II, p. 475.

[2] Elliot, Vol. V, p. 530.

[3] Vote: Aye, New Hampshire, Pennsylvania, Delaware, Maryland, Virginia, 5; no, Massachusetts, Connecticut, New Jersey, North Carolina, South Carolina, Georgia, 6. Elliot. Vol. V, p. 531.

[4] Ibid., 531. Delaware, no; New Hampshire, divided

[5] Ibid., 551.

[6] "The Confederation," said Randolph in the Convention, "was made in the infancy of the science of constitutions." "The wisdom drawn from ten years of experience with the State constitutions and the Confederation shed a flood of light on their work." Davis. Am. Consts., p. 485.

was agreed to, to meet the objection of the slave States.[1] The
second limitation was suggested by Mr. Sherman, just before
the close of the Convention, after the failure of his motion
already referred to. It provided that "No State shall without its consent be affected in its internal police or deprived of
its equal suffrage in the Senate."[2] This was opposed by Madison on the ground that its adoption would be but the signal
for the application for special provisions from every State.
The measure only received the support of the three small
States represented in the Convention, namely Connecticut, New
Jersey, and Delaware. Having failed to secure the guaranty
he thought necessary, Mr. Sherman, determined to guard the
interests of the small States, moved to strike out the entire
article in regard to amendment, but this did not even command the support of all the small States. At this critical
moment Gouverneur Morris moved to add the provision guaranteeing to each State its equal representation in the Senate.
"This motion," says Madison in his notes, "being dictated by
the circulating murmurs of the small States, was agreed to
without debate or opposition."[3] Such, in brief, is the history
of the origin of the amending power as embodied in the Constitution of the United States.

The results of the deliberations of the Convention appear in
Article V of the Constitution, which reads as follows:

The Congress, whenever two-thirds of both Houses shall deem it necessary, shall propose amendments to this Constitution, or, on the application
of the legislatures of two-thirds of the several States, shall call a convention
for proposing amendments, which, in either case, shall be valid to all
intents and purposes as part of this Constitution, when ratified by the
legislatures of three-fourths of the several States, or by conventions in
three-fourths thereof, as the one or the other mode of ratification may be
proposed by the Congress; provided that no amendment which may be made
prior to the year one thousand eight hundred and eight shall in any manner affect the first and fourth clauses in the ninth section of the first
article; and that no State, without its consent, shall be deprived of its
equal suffrage in the Senate.

2. PURPOSE AND SCOPE OF THE MONOGRAPH: DIVISION OF
   THE PROPOSED AMENDMENTS INTO PERIODS.

Defects in the Constitution have revealed themselves from
time to time, and the amending power has often been invoked,

---

[1] Elliot, Vol. v., p. 531. See Rutledge's remarks.   [2] Ibid., 531.   [3] Ibid., pp. 551–552.

in a few instances successfully, as the fifteen amendments show. There have been voluminous treatises by eminent jurists and publicists, devoted to the discussion and interpretation of these fifteen amendments which have been incorporated into the Constitution, but very little has been written in regard to the manner of securing amendments. In fact, no attention has been paid, with rare exception, to the amendments which have failed, or to that numerous class of propositions which never went beyond the preliminary stages.

It is the purpose of this monograph to investigate this uncultivated field, and to endeavor to show, by means of a systematic examination of the records, what deficiencies have been felt and what remedies have been proposed. The material upon which this work is based has all been compiled from the records of Congress.[1] In this study of the proposed amendments only those have been selected which were actually brought to the official notice of Congress, either by its members, the State legislatures, or the Presidents, from the time of the adoption of the Constitution by the conventions in the different States to the end of the Fiftieth Congress, March 4, 1889.[2]

It is difficult to avoid the conclusion that it was the expectation of the members of the Federal Convention that a frequent use of the amending power would be made.[3] They doubtless thought that the plan adopted would secure the desired end whenever the popular will would justify a change. The action of the State conventions and the early amendment of the Constitution seemed to indicate that this view was correct. It will be of interest, therefore, to see to what degree their expectation has been realized, by an examination of the proposed amendments, and of the movements to secure their adoption. Before, however, passing to the consideration of particular amendments, it seems desirable to introduce a preliminary chapter which shall present a general view of the attempts to amend the Constitution, in order that the reader may have a comprehensive idea of this phase of the constitutional history of our country.

---

[1] Including an examination of the original bills, where text is not given in the Congressional Record, and circular letters of the governors of the States.

[2] No notice has been taken of petitions.

[3] See Hamilton's remarks in Federal Convention, Elliot, Vol. v, p. 530; also, the Federalist, No. 43, Hamilton's ed., p. 346.

It is the writer's purpose in this chapter to treat the proposed amendments chronologically by periods, aiming to give the general characteristics of each period, and in the subsequent chapters to consider the same topically.

Upward of 1,300 distinct resolutions, containing over 1,800 propositions to amend the Constitution, have been offered in the National Legislature during the first century of our history under the Constitution.[1] These naturally fall into four distinct periods: The first period embracing the years 1789–1803, and aiming at the perfection of details; the second period, including the years 1803–1860, and covering general alterations; the third period, comprising the years 1860–1870, and relating to slavery and reconstruction; and the fourth period, extending from 1870 to 1889, and proposing general emendations.

3. THE FIRST PERIOD: 1789–1803.

This period, which covers the early years of our history, is characterized by the passage of the first ten amendments, known as the Bill of Rights, in response to the spirit of dissatisfaction expressed by the series of 124 amendments proposed by seven of the States at the time of their ratification of the Constitution, and the general demand of the country for further limitations upon the powers of the Federal Government.[2]

The period is further marked by a number of amendments intended to correct the minor defects which had become apparent in the working of the Constitution. The provisions of some of these became crystallized in the eleventh and twelfth amendments.[3]

Of the one hundred amendments which have been suggested affecting the status of the judiciary, only one has been discovered which would nullify the provisions of the eleventh amendment. Although the twelfth amendment remedied the fault discovered in the electoral system, yet the system itself has given rise to more dissatisfaction than any other feature of our Constitution, as is shown by the fact that more amendments have been proposed on this subject than upon any other.

4. THE SECOND PERIOD: 1804–1860.

In this period, extending over a longer term of years than the other three together, were introduced upward of four hundred

[1] Down to the close of the Fiftieth Congress in March, 1889.
[2] Appendix, Nos. 1–124.
[3] App., Nos. 321, 358.

amendments covering a wide field of subjects.[1] Propositions contemplating changes in the election, term, removal, compensation, and duties of members of the legislative, executive, and judicial departments were the most numerous.

This being the period of conflict between the broad and strict constructionists, it is characterized by many attempts to confirm or prohibit, by amendment, practices established by custom. Of this nature were the amendments granting appropriations for internal improvements, and prohibiting or authorizing the establishment of a national bank; they were introduced periodically during the years 1813 to 1832, as the Congressional discussion or Presidential message or veto suggested. A closer examination of the scattered propositions shows that they are indices of the political struggles of the time; thus, it is evident that the trial of Judge Chase suggested the several propositions introduced during the years 1805 to 1809 in regard to the term and removal of judges. The resolutions proposing the apportionment of Representatives and direct taxes to the free inhabitants, and prohibiting the importation of slaves, introduced previous to 1808, were called out by the approach of that year when the agreement prohibiting amendments on these questions would terminate. As a result of the war of 1812 the members from Connecticut and Massachusets, acting upon the instruction of their respective State legislatures, introduced a set of interesting amendments, the work of the Hartford convention.[2] In 1833 Georgia offered a petition for the call of a convention to consider a series of thirteen amendments, the greater number of which were doubtless suggested by the recent nullification by South Carolina, and her own contest with the Federal judiciary, arising out of the Indian land question.[3] President Jackson's numerous vetoes, those of the national-bank and internal-improvement bills being especially obnoxious, gave rise to resolutions providing that a bill might be passed over the veto by a majority vote. The presence of a surplus caused Mr. Calhoun in 1835 and in 1836 to present a proposition providing for its distribution among the States. The crisis of 1837 led to the introduction of amendments prohibiting the issue of State bank notes. President Tyler's erratic course led to another flood of resolutions proposing amendments restricting the eligibility of the President to a

[1] App., Nos. 363–777.
[2] App., Nos. 424–431. 432–439, 440–447.
[3] App., Nos. 613–625.

single term, and enabling bills to be passed over the veto by a
majority vote, as well as to amendments preventing a pocket
veto.

The proofs are many of a widespread dissatisfaction on the
part of the country with both the existing method of electing
the President and the length of the Presidential term. At four
different times, between the years 1813 and 1822, an amendment proposing that the electors should be chosen by districts
was passed by one House of Congress.[1] During this period
forty-four amendments of a somewhat similar character were
offered in Congress. The failure of the electors in 1824 to
choose a President, and the subsequent defeat of Jackson by
the House of Representatives, gave rise to a very large number of propositions upon the choice of the Executive, so many
in fact, that one gentleman introduced a resolution that amendments should only be proposed decennially.[2] Some of these
stipulate that in no case shall the election devolve upon the
House of Representatives, and others, prompted by the alleged
bargain between Clay and Adams, provide that in case the
election should fall to the House, no member of Congress
should be eligible to the Cabinet. Various plans for the election of the President without the intervention of electors were
suggested. Some of these proposed a direct vote by the States,
more by districts, and twenty-two declared for a popular vote.
Among so large a number of propositions there were naturally some of a novel character. The most striking of these
were two suggesting the choice of President by lot. The first,
introduced by Senator Hillhouse of Connecticut, in 1808, provided that the Senators should hold office for three years, and
one-third retire annually, from the retiring Senators one should
be chosen by lot as President for the ensuing year.[3] The other,
brought forward by Mr. Vinton of Ohio, in 1844 and again in
1846, arranged that each State should by popular vote elect
from its citizens a candidate for the Presidency; from these
candidates one was to be chosen by lot.[2] The amusing details
of this suggestion were, that as many balls as there are Senators and Representatives from each State, inscribed with the
name of the State, shall be placed in a box. One ball shall be
drawn from the box and the candidate elected by the State the
name of which is upon the ball drawn out shall be President.

Various amendments were presented limiting the President to one, or at most two terms. An amendment making the President ineligible for a third term received the sanction of the Senate in 1824, and again in 1826.[1] During this period there were fourteen amendments proposed diminishing the veto power and two dispensing with it.

Amendments dealing with the relations of the Federal Government to individuals were few in number; so completely had the first ten amendments covered the field that nearly all dissatisfaction had been allayed. One of the few introduced, providing that anyone who should accept a title of nobility, or without the consent of Congress, a present, office, or emolument from any foreign sovereign or State, should cease to be a citizen of the United States and incapable of holding office therein, passed both Houses of Congress in 1810 and received the sanction of twelve States, failing of ratification by one vote only.[2]

The majority of the remaining propositions of this class aimed at the protection or abolition of slavery. As early as 1818, Mr. Livermore of New Hampshire introduced a resolution prohibiting slavery, which failed to receive the consideration of the House.[3] Again, in 1839, John Quincy Adams tried to introduce a series of amendments abolishing hereditary slavery after 1842, forbidding the admission of slave States after 1845, and prohibiting slavery and the slave trade at the seat of government. Shortly after the compromise of 1850 an unsuccessful attempt was made to still further protect the interest of the slavocracy by the introduction of an amendment providing that no amendment shall be made abolishing or affecting slavery in any State without the concurrence of the slave States.[4]

The most remarkable fact of the period is that not one of the four hundred amendments proposed during these fifty-eight years became a part of the Constitution. Six passed the Senate;[5] in addition, one only received the sanction of both branches of Congress.[6]

5. THE THIRD PERIOD: 1860-1870.

Toward the close of the second period there was a lull; during two sessions of Congress no amendments were introduced,

---

[1] App., Nos. 535, 545.   [4] App., Nos. 697-699.

[2] App., No. 399.   [5] App., Nos. 409, 485, 489, 505, 535, 545.

[3] App., No. 474.   [6] App., No. 399.

but at last an avalanche of propositions fell upon the second session of the Thirty-Sixth Congress (1860–61), nearly all dealing with some phase of the slavery question, prompted by the hope of preserving the Union. Some of these suggested very radical changes in the form of government, notably one proposing that the Presidency be abolished, and an executive council of three be established, each armed with the veto;[1] and another that either a dual executive should be created, or a division of the Senate into two bodies should be effected.[2]

Several States had already passed the ordinance of secession before anything had been done; finally upon the 2d of March, 1861, the so-called Corwin amendment prohibiting any amendment abolishing or interfering within any State with the institution of slavery passed Congress.[3] There was no chance for its ratification. The time for compromise had passed, and the question was transferred from legislative halls to the field of battle. For some months after this Congress was so occupied with the consideration of war measures that the amending power was scarcely invoked, but from 1864 on, the question of amendment became of the first importance. The political and social changes brought about by the war presented a new set of questions, so that the amendments relating to the legal status of individuals, which previously had been of the least, now became of the greatest importance.

From the large number of resolutions proposed during the reconstruction period, nearly all dealing with questions arising out of the rebellion, the thirteenth, fourteenth, and fifteenth amendments were ratified, registering the results of the war.[4] In this period the question of amendment received the most serious attention of Congress; hence it was the most productive in results. Besides the three now a part of the Constitution and the Corwin amendment, four amendments passed one House, but not the other.[5]

5. THE FOURTH PERIOD, 1870–1889.

The last of the reconstruction amendments was ratified in 1870. The last twenty years of the first century of the life of the Constitution form a period characterized by attempts to alter the Constitution in almost every particular. While in

---

[1] App., No. 804.   [4] App., Nos. 985, 1135, 1284.
[2] App., No. 795.   [5] App., Nos. 1055, 1079, 1250, 1308.
[3] App., No. 931.

this respect, not unlike the tentative efforts of the second period, the amendments considered in the fourth more generally contemplated substantial alterations than confirmatory enactment. About four hundred propositions have been introduced during this time;[1] two classes command attention, the one and the larger involving changes in the form of government, the other in its powers. Under the former the choice, term, composition, and duties of the legislative, executive, and judicial are considered; there being some one hundred propositions on the term and election of President alone. One of these—proposed by Mr. Maish of Pennsylvania, in 1877, and again in 1888—is worthy of mention. It provided for a direct vote by States, but the electoral vote should be distributed among the candidates in the proportion the electoral ratio should bear to the popular vote of each candidate.[2]

One noticeable feature is the increase in the number of amendments calling for the popular election of the President, Senators, and even such executive officers as postmasters and revenue collectors. The desire to reduce the number of members in the House of Representatives has led to the introduction, since 1880, of five amendments to accomplish this result, the last of these placed the number at two hundred and fifty.[3]

Two amendments have passed the Senate, the first in 1886, the second in 1887, changing the date of Inauguration Day to April 30, but both failed in the House.[4]

The second class, comprising amendments to the powers of the Government, covers a large variety of subjects. Many of these indicate a strong drift toward paternalism. Some are attempts to limit the powers of Congress as the State legislatures have been limited; others are intended to still further protect the civil and political rights of the individual; while others aim at the correction of abuses both of a social and political nature. A good example of this last group is the amendment introduced by Mr. Blaine, prohibiting the distribution of money to religious sects, which passed the House August 4, 1876, but received no further indorsement.[5]

During this period but few amendments received even brief consideration, and only four out of the entire number received the approval of one House.

---

[1] App., Nos. 1368–1736.
[2] App., Nos. 1438, 1705.
[3] App., Nos. 1507, 1530, 1553, 1585, 1716.
[4] App., Nos. 1676, 1691.
[5] App., No. 1401.

The prospect of almost certain failure does not seem to have diminished the number of amendments offered.[1] In recent years there has been a gradual increase in the number presented. During the fourth period there were over four hundred distinct propositions introduced, and in the Fiftieth Congress forty-eight resolutions, proposing amendments on twenty different subjects, were presented.

The detailed examination of the proposed amendments which follows shows that the importance of these propositions does not lie in their influence in effecting actual changes within the Constitution merely, but that they are indices of the movements to effect a change, and to a large degree show the waves of popular feeling and reflect the political theories of the time. It is believed that a study of the efforts to amend the Constitution will contribute to a fuller and clearer understanding of our history, both constitutional and political.

---

[1] "An examination of these reveals both the ingenuity and variety of the minds conceiving them, and the present futility of any ill-considered attempt to follow in their footsteps." Report of the committee of the New York State Bar Association, 1890. Reports of the Association, Vol. XIII, p. 142.

CHAPTER II.

PROPOSED AMENDMENTS AFFECTING THE FORM OF GOVERNMENT: LEGISLATIVE.

7. DISTRIBUTION OF POWERS AMONG THE THREE BRANCHES OF THE GOVERNMENT.

There seemed to be some apprehension among the members of the First Congress that the powers delegated respectively to each of the three branches of the Government might be usurped by one of the other departments; one department thus trenching upon the rights of another might disarrange the harmonious working of a system the success of which was supposed to be dependent upon the complete separation of the three branches of the Government. Accordingly an attempt was persistently made in the first session of Congress to reaffirm the doctrine in a formal manner. Mr. Madison included in the series of amendments presented by him early in this session a proposition,[1] which, as reported in a slightly different form and passed by the House, read: "The powers delegated by the Constitution to the Government of the United States shall be exercised as therein appropriated, so that the legislative shall never exercise the powers vested in the executive or judicial; nor the executive the powers vested in the legislative or judicial; nor the judicial the powers vested in the legislative or executive."[2] The Senate, however, either did not share in the apprehensions of the House or failed to see how this amendment could further insure the integrity of each department, and struck out the resolution. The next day, however, a motion was made in the Senate to add the following to the proposed amendments: "That the legislative, executive, and judiciary powers of the Government should be separate and distinct." Then follows a few phrases of political moralizing, to the effect "that the members of the two first may be restrained from oppression by feeling and participating

---

[1] App., No. 144. Very similar to famous clause in the constitution of Massachusetts (1780), Part 1, art. 30, and doubtless suggested by it. See also constitution of Kentucky (1792), art. 1.

[2] App., No. 230.

in the public burthens, they should at fixed periods be reduced
to a private station, returning into the mass of the people, and
the vacancies be supplied by certain and regular elections,"
etc.[1] This resolution shared the fate of that proposed by the
House, and was the last upon this subject which has ever been
suggested.

Experience has shown few cases of conflict between the
legislative and the judiciary,[2] or between the judiciary and
the executive,[3] but between the legislative and the executive
there have been several well-known instances of the attempt by
one department to encroach upon the prerogatives of the other.
The Executive has usually found his veto power an effective
weapon in protecting his powers from any encroachment of
the legislature.[4] The power of Congress over appropriation
bills has been supposed to protect it against aggression.

8. THE LEGISLATIVE DEPARTMENT: CLASSIFICATION OF AMENDMENTS.

The system of two Houses in the National Legislature was
to a large degree experimental. The Continental Congress and
the Congress of the Confederation had each contained one
House only. It is not surprising, therefore, that even in the
earlier years various amendments were proposed aiming either
to correct the imperfections which had become evident in the
working of the legislative department, or to introduce what
their authors considered desirable innovations; from time to
time in subsequent years various other propositions to change
the organization or powers of the legislative body have been
made. The class of amendments dealing with the organization
of this department will be considered in the present chapter.[5]
They may be conveniently divided into three groups; those
relating alike to both branches of Congress and those referring
distinctively either to the House of Representatives or to the
Senate.

---

[1] App., No. 271.

[2] The judiciary act of 1802 was not so much an attack upon the judiciary as on the Federal party.

[3] The decision in Marbury v. Madison (1 Cranch, 137) aroused Jefferson's hostility against the court. Jackson also refused to enforce the decrees of the court against Georgia. See post, par. 77. See also Foster, Com. on Const., I, pp. 303-305.

[4] Mason, Veto Power, par. 17-36. Davis, Am. Consts. Johns Hopkins Univ. Studies, 3d series, p. 465. Foster, Com. on Const., I, pp. 238 et seq.

[5] Those in regard to the powers of Congress in Chapter v.

We pass directly to the consideration of the first group. First in importance among the various attempts made in the early years to alter the Constitution, were those directed against the provisions relative to the regulation of elections, and the qualification and compensation of members of both branches of Congress. Other proposals were intended to prevent members accepting any other civil office, and still others to prohibit members from participating in such pursuits as would tend to prejudice their action and unfit them for service in Congress. In more recent years very few amendments which can be classed under this head have been presented, the only movement of importance has been the one directed toward a change in the time of the sessions of Congress.

9. REGULATION OF ELECTION TO CONGRESS

By the Constitution Congress may at any time by law make or alter the regulations prescribed by the legislature of the State for the time, place, and manner of holding elections for Senators and Representatives (except as to the place for choosing Senator)[1]. This clause created much dissatisfaction in some portions of the country; conventions in four of the Northern and three of the Southern States, at the time of their ratification of the Constitution, recommended substantially the same amendment to the Constitution, namely, that Congress shall not exercise this right "except when the legislature of any State shall neglect, refuse, or be disabled by invasion or rebellion to prescribe the same."[2] The South Carolina convention prefaced their proposition with the strong declaration "that the right of prescribing the manner, time, and place of holding elections to the Federal Legislature should be forever inseparably annexed to the sovereignty of the several States." The New York convention was willing to permit Congress to exercise the power of prescribing the time for the election of Representatives.

In the First Congress, in deference to this expression of opinion, several attempts were made to add to the series about to be recommended to the States an amendment on this subject, similar to those suggested by the State conventions. One was proposed by Mr. Sedgwick, giving Congress power to make regulations for elections, provided the States made improper

---

[1] Art. 1, sec. 4, par. 1.   [2] App. Nos. 3, 10, 16, 41, 49, 94, 105.

ones. Mr. Tucker suggested that the clause in the Constitution should be struck out, but all these attempts to amend failed. It is quite possible that the result might have been different had the Senators and Representatives from North Carolina and Rhode Island been present, for the conventions in those States recommended this change. [1]

10. REGULATIONS FOR PROVING ELECTIONS.

Only one attempt has been made to amend the provision of the Constitution in regard to the proving of elections. [2] This was one of the series of amendments introduced by Mr. Tucker of South Carolina during the discussion of the so-called "Bill of Rights" in the First Congress. It proposed that this clause should be amended so that instead of each House judging of the election of its members, "each State should be the judge, according to its own laws, of the election of its Senators and Representatives to sit in Congress." [3] The resolution failed to be referred, showing that in this case the House was unwilling to have the prerogatives of the Federal Government curtailed. In more recent years the tendency has been to assert the regulative power of Congress, and to supersede the system of regulation. [4]

11. QUALIFICATIONS OF MEMBERS OF CONGRESS.

One of the subjects which has greatly exercised the ingenuity of amendment framers is that of the qualification of members of Congress. Two groups of these propositions may be distinguished—those introduced between 1788 and 1815, and those introduced as a result of the civil war and applying to the disability of secessionists. [5] One of the classes which were to be excluded by some of the various propositions of the first group was that of debtors of the United States. Such a restriction was proposed during the general discussion of amendments in the First Congress. [6]

The opposition to the national bank during the Third Congress took the form of a prolonged discussion of an amendment proposing to exclude officers and stockholders of the

[1] See post par. 24, for propositions affecting Representatives.
[2] Art. 1, sec. 5, cl. 1.
[3] App., No. 197.
[4] See post par. 24. In the 52d and 53d Congresses there was a reaction against Federal control and certain laws were repealed.
[5] These are considered in par. 128.
[6] App., No. 204. Rejected September 7, 1789.

United States Bank from Congress.[1] The original motion was
so amended as to exclude only the officers of the bank, and
thus amended it was rejected by a vote of 12 yeas to 13 nays.[2]
The presence of contractors in the House led to the introduction of an amendment in 1806 to exclude contractors of the
Government from the House of Representatives.[3] Two years
later a similar resolution was offered, but included the Senate
as well as the House.[4] This may have been suggested by the
connection of Senator Smith of Maryland with a Baltimore
firm which had large contracts with the Government. A third
unsuccessful attempt was made in 1836 to secure an amendment making members of Congress ineligible to civil office and
prohibiting their holding or making any contract with or under
the authority of the United States.[5]

The exclusion of naturalized persons from Congress was
sought by another group of propositions. The New York ratifying convention and the Massachusetts and Connecticut legislatures in 1798 recommended an amendment making foreigners
naturalized since the Declaration of Independence ineligible
to the office of Senator and Representative in Congress.[6] The
political significance of these amendments is referred to elsewhere.[7] One of the amendments framed by the Hartford convention and recommended to Congress by the legislatures of
Massachusetts and Connecticut, through their Senators and
Representatives, stipulated that no person hereafter naturalized should be eligible to either House.[8]

12. INCOMPATIBILITY OF OTHER FUNCTIONS FOR MEMBERS OF CONGRESS.

No less than thirty-three resolutions have been introduced
proposing that members of the Senate and House of Representatives shall not be eligible to any appointment or office.

---

[1] App., No. 318.

[2] App., Nos. 320, 324.

[3] App., No. 374. See post par. 20 for further discussion.

[4] App., No. 387. The constitutions of some of the States had such a provision. See constitution of North Carolina of 1776, art. 27. For exclusion of clergy, see post par. 176.

[5] App., No. 655.

[6] App., Nos. 50, 330-333, 333a b.

[7] Post par. 36.

[8] App., Nos. 430, 438, 446. For replies of the various States, see post par. 22. The reply
of the legislature of Pennsylvania declares "the number of foreigners now in office does
not threaten any inconvenience. Out of 182 Representatives in Congress it is believed
that there are not more than four who were born out of the limits of the United States,
and in the Senate not one."

This proposition was first suggested by the conventions that ratified the Constitution in Virginia, New York, and North Carolina,[1] and the attempt was made in both branches of the First Congress to add such an amendment to the series about to be sent to the States for their ratification.[2] Amendments of this nature were also introduced in 1793, 1808, 1810, and 1818;[3] and from 1820 until the early "forties" similar amendments were submitted at almost every session of Congress. The last one proposing a general disqualification from all offices was presented in 1850.[4]

The amendment proposed by the legislature of Tennessee in November of 1825 is of especial interest, as it was evidently prompted by the utterances of Andrew Jackson.[5] When Tennessee, in the fall of 1825, nominated him as a candidate for the Presidency for the election of 1828, Jackson immediately departed from Washington, and in a speech before the Tennessee legislature resigned his office of Senator in order that he might not be open to the suspicion of using that office to promote his candidacy. At the same time he declared he would "impose a provision upon the Constitution rendering members of Congress ineligible to office under the General Government during the term for which elected and for two years thereafter," except in the case of judicial office.[6] "The effect of such a provision," said he, "is obvious. By it Congress would be free from that connection with the executive department which at present gives strong ground of apprehension and jealousy on the part of the people. If the change should not be obtained and important appointments continue to devolve upon Congress, corruption will be the order of the day."[7]

However desirable, theoretically, Jackson believed this change to be, in practice he did more to create the need of

[1] App., Nos. 29, 62, 81.

[2] App., Nos. 199, 275.

[3] App., Nos. 317, 387, 400, 401, 479.

[4] App., Nos. 493, 511, 516, 544, 546, 549, 569, 581, 595, 612, 642, 652, 655, 662, 670, 678, 680, 696, 715, 723, 727, 749, 755⁴, 763.

[5] App., No. 549. See also similar resolutions of the legislature of Tennessee of 1827, arraigning Adams and Clay, which were unanimously adopted by the house of representatives and only two dissenting votes in the senate. App., No. 581a. Niles' Register, XXXII, pp. 161, 183-186, 198. Counter resolutions of disapproval from the legislatures of Indiana, Ohio, and Maine. Ibid., XXIX, pp. 369, 429.

[6] Niles' Register, XXIX, 125, 155-157. Sumner's Jackson, p. 104, note 2.

[7] Ibid.

such an amendment than all his predecessors.[1] In this connection it is interesting to read what recommendation he made
in his first message, of December 8, 1829. Evidently having
in mind his previous recommendation, and conscious of his
own inconsistency, he writes: "While members of Congress
can be constitutionally appointed to office of trust and profit,
it will be the practice, even under the most conscientious
adherence to duty, to select them for such stations as they are
believed to be better qualified to fill than other citizens; but
the purity of our Government would doubtless be promoted by
their exclusion from all appointment in the gift of the President, in whose election they may have been officially concerned.
The nature of the judicial office and the necessity of securing
in the Cabinet and in diplomatic stations of the highest rank
the best talent and political experience should, perhaps,
except these from the exclusion."[2]

It is somewhat surprising to find Clay in 1841 presenting a
proposition similar to the one Jackson had been led to suggest
because of Clay's acceptance of office in Adams's Cabinet. But
times had changed. Clay was now attacking Tyler, the fear
of Executive encroachments having taken full possession of
him.[3] His State likewise indorsed his views, and presented to
Congress a resolution in favor of this restriction.[4]

The length of the period of ineligibility proposed varied
somewhat. A large number provided that a member should
be ineligible only during the term for which he was elected;
others assigned a more extended period, varying from three
months to two years thereafter. Still others provided that
the ineligibility should last until the expiration of the Presidential term during which a person shall have been a Senator
or Representative.[5] One even of a retrospective character was
introduced in 1822 by Mr. Blair of South Carolina, which
provided that "no one should be appointed by the President

---

[1] "Of his first Cabinet, three were members of the Senate and one of the House; and
Mr. Van Buren had been a Senator up to the 1st of January preceding. Many other
members of Congress received important appointments. During the first six months of
General Jackson's Administration more Federal appointments devolved upon members
of Congress than had before fallen to their lot from the commencement of the Government, in 1789, down to the 4th of March, 1829—forty years." Salmon, Appointing Power,
p. 55; Sargent, I, p. 164; Am. Register, V, 20; XXXVI Niles' Reg., p. 267. For protocol of original Jackson men arraigning him, see XL Niles, p. 387-389.

[2] Statesman's Manual, p. 702. See Benton's Thirty Years' View, I, p. 80, for comments.

[3] App., No. 715. Schurz, Henry Clay, II, p. 222.

[4] App., No. 727.

[5] App., Nos. 509, 655.

to any office who shall have been a member of either House of Congress in the last two years preceding the election of the President."[1] This was doubtless intended to prevent the President rewarding a member of the preceding Congress who had been especially active in working for his interests in the Congressional caucus of the party, which at this time usually made the nomination of the candidates of the different parties for the Presidency and the Vice-Presidency.

Some of these resolutions made exceptions in favor of certain positions, such as appointments in the Army or Navy, while others, similar to the one introduced several times by Mr. Underwood of Kentucky, permitted the heads of the Departments to be selected from Congress.[2]

The above propositions were of a very comprehensive character, some excluding members of Congress from all offices, both civil and military; the majority, however, applying only to the civil offices. There were in addition a few amendments proposed, the provisions of which were less stringent than the preceding. One, introduced in 1846 by Mr. Bagby of Alabama, to render members of both Houses ineligible to a Cabinet position;[3] also, a group of three amendments providing that no member of either House shall be eligible to the office of President or Vice-President.[4] The first of these resolutions was introduced by Mr. Bagby in connection with the above-mentioned amendment. It extended the time during which a member was ineligible to four years after the expiration of the term for which he was elected. One of the remaining two which were introduced in 1872, fixed the end of the period of ineligibility at two years after the expiration of the term.[5]

In addition, Mr. Turner of Kentucky has twice proposed, during the later seventies, an amendment prohibiting the appointment of any Senator or Representative, during the term for which he was elected or two years thereafter, "to any civil office of profit under the United States which was created or the emolument of which was increased during the said term."[6]

---

[1] App., No. 511.
[2] App., Nos. 549, 569, 612, 652, 678, 723, 755d, 763.
[3] App., No. 747.
[4] App., Nos. 746, 1347, 1351.
[5] App., No 1347.
[6] App., Nos. 1474, 1482.

13. COMPENSATION OF MEMBERS

The Constitution left the subject of the compensation of members to be regulated by law. In order to prevent members from arbitrarily increasing their own salaries, three of the State conventions included among the amendments they proposed a provision that no alteration of the existing rate of compensation should at any time take effect before the next election of Representatives.[1] In the First Congress, Mr. Madison also suggested a similar amendment,[2] which, slightly changed,[3] passed both branches of Congress, and was one of the twelve submitted to the States for ratification.[4] This proposition, together with that in regard to apportionment of Representatives,[5] failed to receive the approval of a sufficient number of States to secure its adoption.[6]

The modest per diem adopted by the First Congress as its salary did not arouse fears of extravagance. Accordingly no further amendment was proposed on the subject until 1816. In view of the increase of the revenue after the war of 1812, the Fourteenth Congress saw their opportunity to push through a new compensation bill, and did so, "with a haste altogether unusual," in the session of 1815–16. The new bill changed the compensation of members, which had been fixed by the First Congress at $6 per day and $6 for every 20 miles of estimated journey, to $1,500 a year, which was declared to be the correct equivalent of $6 per day. Others declared that it more than doubled that amount. The popular indignation aroused by this bill was something remarkable, and the entire country expressed its displeasure at the Congressional election that fall by failing to return an unusually large number of their Representatives, some of whom were leading members.[7] Upon the reassembling of Congress, Mr. Barbour of Virginia introduced a resolution proposing an amendment similar to that which failed to receive the approval of the States.[8] The popular disapproval did not disappear at once. A similar resolution passed

---

[1] Virginia, New York, North Carolina. App., Nos. 43, 58, 96.

[2] App., No. 129.

[3] App., Nos. 154, 216.

[4] App., No. 243.

[5] See par. 22.

[6] Ratified by Delaware, South Carolina, North Carolina, Maryland, Vermont, Virginia six States; rejected by five, See App., No. 243.

[7] "The Fourteenth Congress for ability, energy, and usefulness never had a superior." yet they received "the severest popular rebuke ever visited on a House of Representatives." Adams, Hist. of U. S., Vol. IX, p. 138. McMaster, IV, pp. 357–362.

[8] App., No. 458. In 1818 Congress repealed the unpopular act and passed a law fixing the salary at $8 per day and $8 mileage for every 20 miles.

the Massachusetts legislature by large majorities, and the legislature of Tennessee presented one of the same purport to the Fifteenth Congress, which aroused considerable discussion in the Senate over its reception.[1] Three propositions were presented in 1822. The first of these was similar to those previously introduced; the second went further and forbade fixing the pay of members of Congress at a greater sum than that adopted by the First Congress; the third provided that the compensation should be fixed decenially, after the new apportionment of Representatives.[2]

No amendment dealing with this subject was again presented to Congress until after the passage of the well-known "salary grab" act of 1873.[3] At the opening of the next Congress five amendments similar to the one sent out to the States by the First Congress were immediately introduced.[4] Instead of acting upon these resolutions this Congress repealed the obnoxious law, and with slight modifications revived the act previously in force, which has not been changed since.[5]

14 OATH TO THE CONSTITUTION.

To the clause in the Constitution providing for an oath,[6] only one of the States suggested an addition. The New York convention, evidently desiring some guaranty that the rights of the States should be protected, recommended that the Senators and Representatives and other officers of the United States should be bound by an oath not to infringe or violate the Constitution or rights of the respective States.[7] Another rather minute objection was phrased in an amendment suggested in the First Congress, which proposed to insert in the provision in the Constitution the word "other" between "no" and "religious."[8] The idea that the taking the oath was in itself a religious test seemed to find no favor.

---

[1] App., Nos. 458a, 473.

[2] App., Nos. 510, 512, 513. The legislature of Illinois in 1821 presented a resolution of disagreement to the proposed amendment. Annals, Seventeenth Congress, first session, p 35.

[3] United States Statutes at Large, Vol. XVII, p. 486. It was retroactive, and is sufficient proof that the precaution might well have been taken which the First Congress proposed. The act of 1873 raised the salary to $7,500 and actual traveling expenses.

[4] App., Nos. 1372, 1373, 1374, 1375, 1377. The senate of Ohio passed a vote, ratifying the amendment proposed by Congress in 1789, at this time. See post par. 180.

[5] The previous act was that of 1866. The new act fixed the compensation at $5,000 a year and 20 cents per mile mileage. Stat. L., Vol. XIV, pp. 333, 334.

[6] Art. 6, cl. 3.

[7] App., No. 76.

[8] Constitution reads, "but no religious test shall ever be required " App., Nos. 210, 238, 261. This suggests the case of Bradlaugh in the English House of Commons.

15. CHANGING THE DATE OF INAUGURATION DAY AND THE TIME OF THE SESSIONS OF CONGRESS.

The date of the expiration of the First and Second Congresses and of the first Administration was due to a vote of the Congress of the Confederation of September 13, 1788, fixing the date the new Congress was to begin. More than a score of resolutions have been introduced proposing a change in the commencement or expiration of the official term of Congress or the date of Inauguration Day. The inconvenience of the arrangement of the sessions seems to have been early felt, as Senator Burr of New York, in 1795, proposed that the date for the expiration of the term of Congress should be changed to the 1st day of June.[1] The amendment presented by Mr. Hillhouse, in 1808, to change the term of Representatives to one year, which is discussed elsewhere, provided that their term should expire on the first Tuesday of April.[2] With one unimportant exception,[3] no other change was suggested until 1876. Since that time there have been eighteen amendments proposed.[4] Several attempts have been made to set the date for the commencement of the Congressional term on the 31st day of December, or some day in the first week of January.

The desire to transfer Inauguration Day to a more favorable season of the year led to the introduction of a proposed amendment in 1876, fixing upon the 1st day of May.[5] In more recent years the above reason, coupled with the desire to bring the Inauguration Day upon the one hundredth anniversary of the inauguration of Washington, and thus appropriately round out the first century of our history under the Constitution, led to the presentation of several resolutions making provision for such a change. Two such resolutions passed the Senate unanimously; the first, introduced in 1886 by Senator Ingalls, designating April 30 as the commencement of the official term of the Executive and of the Congress; the second in 1888, presented by Mr. Hoar, fixed upon the last Tuesday of April, which in 1889 fell upon the 30th of the month.[6] The House,

---

[1] App., No. 327.

[2] App., No. 391. See post par. 26.

[3] Proposed in 1840 to fix the 1st of December as the day for the commencement of the term of members. App., No. 706.

[4] App., Nos. 1416, 1418, 1440, 1470, 1571, 1625, 1641, 1676, 1681, 1682, 1685, 1686, 1691, 1703, 1707, 1735, and 1672. The latter proposed to give Congress power "to establish the beginning of the Presidential and Congressional term."

[5] App., No. 1416.

[6] App., Nos. 1676, 1691.

however, failed to concur in either of these propositions. The
first was never reported from the committee to which it was
referred; the second gave rise to an interesting discussion. At
about this same time a resolution which had been introduced
by Mr. Crain of Texas three times since 1886, was reported
favorably.[1] It proposed an amendment to the Constitution
substituting the 31st of December for the 4th of March as the
commencement and termination of the official term of members of Congress, and provided that Congress should hold its
annual session on the first Monday of January. Mr. Crain now
wished to have the provisions of his amendment incorporated
in the Senate resolution, and advanced an interesting argument in favor of the change. He showed that under the
present system a Representative does not enter upon the discharge of his duties until thirteen months after his election,
and then frequently comes to his office to find that the issues
upon which he was elected have been determined and settled
by the second session of the previous Congress. Thus, Representatives who have been defeated at the polls defy the will of
the people by legislating in accordance with a policy that had
been adopted before their repudiation.

Mr. Crain further dwelt upon the fact that under the proposed plan there would be no election between the two sessions of a Congressional term; that there would be no short
term, and no necessity for extra sessions; Representatives
elected in November would begin to perform their duties early
in the next January, and thus would come fresh from the people and be in touch with the people. The necessity of a Representative's answering to his constituents after the second
session would tend to make him as faithful, zealous, and efficient as in the first session.

Some speakers questioned the need of a constitutional
amendment to change the date of Inauguration Day, as the
present date, the 4th of March, is fixed by law and not by the
Constitution. The greater number, however, considered this
necessary, but thought that the object desired by Mr. Crain
could be obtained by law.[2] It was further shown that by the
Senate amendment the short session would be made into a
long one, and thus give Congress more time to transact its
business. The House finally refused to suspend the rules and
pass the resolution by a vote of 129 yeas to 128 nays. Party

---

[1] App., Nos. 1682, 1686, 1707.
[2] See Manual of the Rules and Practice of the House of Representatives, p. 428.

lines were not drawn in the division.[1] Later in the same session Mr. Crain presented a resolution containing the Senate proposition coupled with his own, but the motion to suspend the rules and pass was rejected.[2]

Both the suggestions deserve to be incorporated in the Constitution. The great practical inconvenience of closing the second session of Congress on the 4th of March and the desirability of abridging the present long interval which elapses between the time of the choice of Representatives and the time of their entering upon the duties of their office becomes more evident from year to year. In addition to the sentimental reasons for changing the date of Inauguration Day to the 30th of April, the inclemency of the weather of early March often seriously interferes with the exercises of the day, which has become a gala day, thus exposing thousands to the dangers incident to that season of the year.[3]

Only one resolution has been submitted proposing to do away with the annual sessions of Congress. This was in 1878, and made provision for biennial sessions. The proposed change was doubtless suggested by the practice of the great majority of the States and the increasing fear of the danger of overlegislation.[4]

16. EXTRA SESSIONS OF CONGRESS: QUORUM AND VOTE.

Among the amendments proposed by President Grant in his annual message at the opening of Congress in December, 1873, was one providing that when an extra session shall be convened by Executive proclamation legislation during the continuance of such extra session shall be confined to such subjects as the Executive may bring before it.[5] There is no record to show that Congress ever considered the subject. The reasons which influenced the President in making this recommendation were evidently a desire to make the term of the extra

---

[1] For discussion, see Congressional Record, Fiftieth Congress, first session, pp. 1345-1353.

[2] App., No. 1719. Mr. Crain has proposed the same amendment in each Congress since. In the Fifty-second Congress it was reported favorably, but rejected. Record, Fifty-second Congress, second session, pp. 483-500. Some objected to this plan because it would bring in a new Congress before the new President, and thus they would canvass the vote for President.

[3] It is said that General Harrison's death resulted from a cold caught at his inauguration.

[4] App., No. 1470. Extra sessions were provided for. All of the States save five have biennial sessions. Bryce, Vol. I, p. 487.

[5] App., No. 1371. A common provision in State constitutions in eleven States. See Davis, John Hopkins University Studies, third series, pp. 479, 528.

session as short as possible and to guard against overlegislation, for he says: "One session in each year is provided
for by the Constitution, in which there are no restrictions as
to the subject of legislation by Congress. If more are required,
it is always in the power of Congress during their term of
office to provide for sessions at any time."

The constitutional quorum—a majority of all the members
in either House[1]—was larger than is usual in parliamentary
bodies, but no serious inconvenience was felt, and there has
been no effort to change the provision of the Constitution until
nearly the close of the first century of its history. In the
Fiftieth Congress, Mr. Wheeler of Alabama introduced a resolution to amend the Constitution so that "one-third of the
members of each House shall constitute a quorum," instead of
the existing requirement—a majority.[2] The need of some
change was suggested by the growth in the recent Congresses
of the practice of "filibustering," which has reached such pro-
portions as to seriously interfere with business. The claim of
no quorum has been one of the favorite means of "filibustering." Since the Fifty-first Congress, rules have been adopted
to check this practice in the House of Representatives.[3]

Another proposition, made by the ratifying conventions in
New York and Rhode Island, would, had it been adopted, put
an engine of irresistible power into the hands of the filibus-
terers, for the clause which provides that the yeas and nays
shall be entered on the journals at the desire of one-fifth of
those present was to be so changed that two members in either
House might require it.[4]

17. DISCIPLINE OF MEMBERS OF CONGRESS.

The Constitution adopted the English and Cabinet practice
of relieving members from responsibility for their utterances
in Congress before the regular courts, but it gave to each
House power to discipline its own members.[5] But one proposition has ever been presented to decrease that power. In
1789, Mr. Tucker of South Carolina moved that this clause
should be struck out.[6] The ground for his motion was not

[1] Constitution, art. 1, sec. 5, cl. 1.
[2] App., No. 1728.
[3] Manual and Digest, Fifty-first Congress, second session, Rule XV, cl. 3, p. 527.
[4] App., Nos. 59, 124.
[5] Constitution, art. 1, sec. 5, cl. 2.
[6] App., No. 198.

stated, but probably it was that a member should be responsible only to his State or constituency.[1]

18. PUBLICATION OF THE JOURNALS.

The clause in the Constitution which provides that the journals of each House shall be published from time to time[2] seemed too indefinite to some of the ratifying conventions. Four of the conventions, therefore, included in their series of proposed amendments one which required their publication "at least once in every year."[3] An unsuccessful attempt was made to add to the series of amendments recommended by the First Congress such a proposition.[4] Subsequent history has shown that the fear that the proceedings of Congress might be withheld for some time was groundless. The journals of each House have appeared annually, except that the proceedings of secret sessions have been made known only at the later discretion of the House concerned. In addition to the journals, the official debates of Congress since 1833 have been published by the Government.[5]

19. THE HOUSE OF REPRESENTATIVES.

The House of Representatives, as the most numerous of the two constituent elements of Congress, and as the branch which springs most directly from the people, has been the object of many propositions for amendment. Some 150 amendments have been proposed to the provisions of the Constitution relative to this branch of Congress. Many attempts have been made to alter the qualifications of its members, to change their number and apportionment, and to control their election.[6]

20. QUALIFICATION OF MEMBERS.

In addition to the resolutions proposing to alter the constitutional qualifications of members of either branch of Con-

---

[1] From 1789 to 1870 there were seventy-six attempts to discipline members of Congress. Of these twenty-six were cases of abusive language or disorderly behavior on the floor of the House and twenty-five for treason. Out of this number the actual censures for all causes in both Houses have been ten and the expulsions eighteen. Stated by Mr. C. F. Gottemy, a member of the Historical Seminary, Harvard University, 1890-91, from his research in the journals.

[2] Constitution, art. 1, sec. 5, cl. 3.

[3] Virginia, New York, North Carolina, Rhode Island. App., Nos. 30, 59, 82, 113.

[4] App., No. 274.

[5] The Congressional Globe, 1833 to 1873; the Congressional Record, 1873 to the present time.

[6] No proposition has been made to take the right of election from the people. See Story, I, p. 409.

gress,[1] two others have been introduced applying only to the House. In 1806, owing to the defeat of a bill[2] to exclude "contractors or any one participating in any way in the profits of such contracts" from the House of Representatives, because many believed it was not within the competency of Congress to add to the qualifications for members required by the Constitution,[3] an amendment with the same end in view was introduced.[4] It is evident from the references in the course of the debate that persons holding Government contracts were members of Congress. The danger and evil of this practice was urged by Randolph and others, but the only thing accomplished was the calling upon the Postmaster-General for a list of all persons holding mail contracts.[5] Two years later a somewhat similar provision was introduced, which applied to the Senate as well.[6]

One resolution has appeared bearing upon the qualifications of residence. By the Constitution the only limitation was that the member should be a resident of the State in which he was chosen[7]—a clause suggested by the parsimonious practice of the States in the old Congress of selecting persons who lived near the seat of government as their agents. The ratifying convention of New York proposed as an amendment a resolution to the effect that the legislatures of the respective States may provide by law that a Representative must have been an inhabitant of the district he represents for at least one year immediately preceding his election.[8] Congress does not appear to have taken into consideration the subject of this amendment, but some of the States have enacted laws requiring the Representative to be a resident of the district he represents. The constitutionality of such laws is so doubtful that the Massachusetts law was repealed. It amounts to the imposition by the States of a qualification not specified in the Constitution.[9] Positive law has in any case been little needed since both in

[1] Ante par. 11.
[2] Introduced by Randolph. Annals, p. 508.
[3] Annals, p. 880.
[4] By Mr. Newton. App., No. 374. The example of England (see 22 George III, c. 45) and possibly the presence of some of Burr's relatives may have suggested it. Mr. Newton, however, said "he would wish to see an American Congress composed of very different material from a British Parliament." Annals, p. 894.
[5] Annals, pp. 761, 828.
[6] App., No. 387. Ante par. 11.
[7] Constitution, art. 1, sec. 2, cl. 2.
[8] App., No. 77.
[9] Story, I, p. 447, note 1. Foster, Com. on the Const., I, p. 363, note 10.

the State and the national elections constituents usually
refuse to choose nonresidents. One case of the choice of a
Representative not a resident of the district occurred recently
in Massachusetts,[1] but in general the English practice in this
particular has not been favored.[2]

21. INCOMPATIBILITY OF OTHER FUNCTIONS FOR REPRESENTATIVES.

Various amendments excluding members of either branch of
Congress from civil appointment have been considered elsewhere.[3] The loss by Jackson of the election in the House in
1825, together with the alleged bargain between Clay and
Adams, by which Adams was given the Presidency and Clay
a position in the Cabinet, called out a proposition of a less
sweeping character.

In the following year Mr. Powell of Virginia introduced
the first resolution on this subject. It declared that no Representative, in the event of the election of President by the
House of Representatives, should be capable of receiving an
appointment to any office, where the power of nomination is in
the President, for the term of three years thereafter.[4] In the
next Congress two other amendments were presented to the
House, providing that under the same circumstances no member shall, during the continuance of that President in office,
be appointed to any office under the authority of the United
States.[5] All three of these resolutions were buried in committee, and no similar proposition has since been proposed.

22. APPORTIONMENT OF REPRESENTATIVES.

In order to insure the adoption of the Constitution by the
slaveholding States, it was found necessary to give to them a
partial representation for their slave population. Accordingly
it was agreed that " Representatives and direct taxes should
be apportioned among the several States" "according to their
respective numbers, which shall be determined by adding to
the whole number of free persons, including those bound to
service for a term of years, and excluding Indians not taxed,
three-fifths of all other persons."[6] The enumeration was to be

---

[1] In a by-election in April, 1893, William Everett, of the Eleventh Massachusetts district, was elected by the Seventh district.

[2] Bryce, I, pp. 482-438.

[3] Ante par. 12.

[4] App., No. 557. Except in case of war.

[5] App., Nos. 581, 593.

[6] Art. 1, sec. 2, cl. 3. Story, I, pp. 448-455. See Hinsdale's Am. Govt., Chap. XVIII for
methods employed. Foster, Com. on Const., I, pp. 393-397.

made once in every ten years, and the number of Representatives was not to exceed 1 for every 30,000, but each State was to have at least one Representative.

Dissatisfaction has, however, been expressed with these provisions at various times, and recourse has been had to numerous attempts to secure their amendment. The propositions to amend this section of the Constitution may be divided into four well-defined groups: First, the attempts made in the First Congress to establish a permanent ratio for the apportionment of Representatives; second, the few proposals, made with one important exception in the earlier years of this century, to strike out the clause granting partial representation for slaves; third, the attempt made in 1860-61 to incorporate into the Constitution a clause which should guarantee the slave States against any change in the method of apportionment without their consent; and fourth, the propositions growing out of the changes wrought by the civil war and culminating in the fourteenth amendment.

(1) The ratifying conventions of five of the States[1] were not satisfied with the simple provision in the Constitution, but desired that the ratio should be fixed in the organic law itself rather than left to the discretion or the caprice of Congress. All five propositions agreed in requiring 1 Representative to every 30,000 persons, until the whole number of Representatives amount to 200; three of the conventions suggested further, that above 200 the number should be continued or increased, as Congress shall direct.

In response to this general expression, Mr. Madison introduced in the First Congress an amendment which made provision for a fixed ratio.[2] The number placing a limit upon the size of the House was left in blank, to be filled in as the united wisdom of Congress should suggest. The resolution, as reported by the special committee to which it had been referred, provided that after the number amounts to 100 "the proportion shall be so regulated" "that the number of Representatives shall never be less than 175."[3] The resolution was considered for some days, and various attempts to amend were made.[4] It finally passed the House in nearly the form suggested by Fisher Ames. This made provision for the expected

---

[1] App., Nos. 2, 15, 27, 46, 79.   Massachusetts, New Hampshire, Virginia, New York, North Carolina.

[2] App., No. 128.

[3] App., No. 149.

[4] App., Nos. 150, 151, 152, 153.

growth in population, and was calculated "to prevent a too rapid increase of the number of members."[1] The Senate so amended the resolution that a greater increase in the growth of the population was required for additional representation.[2] A conference committee was appointed, and they reached a compromise which slightly changed the form of the resolution as passed by the House.[3] The necessary two-thirds majority was obtained. and the amendment went out to the States as one of the set of twelve.[4] It read as follows: "After the first enumeration, there shall be 1 Representative for every 30,000 until the number shall amount to 100, after which the proportion shall be so regulated by Congress that there shall be no less than 100 Representatives nor less than 1 Representative for every 40,000 persons until the number of Representatives amount to 200, after which the proportion shall be so regulated that there shall not be less than 200 Representatives nor more than 1 Representative for every 50,000 persons."[5]

Ten of the twelve passed the appointed ordeal. This article only lacked the indorsement of one State to make the requisite three-fourths necessary to secure its incorporation into the Constitution.[6] For some reason the Virginia legislature ratified this article nearly two months before indorsing the rest of the series.[7] It is an interesting fact that Pennsylvania, although ratifying March 10, 1790, all the amendments except the first and the second, subsequently reconsidered her action, for October 26, 1791, President Washington sent a message to Congress announcing the ratification of the first article by the legislature of that State.[8]

Delaware alone of all the States that took any action upon the amendments, refused to ratify this article.[9] The legislatures of Massachusetts, Connecticut, and Georgia do not

---

[1] App., No. 215.

[2] App., Nos. 241, 242.

[3] App., No. 295. It substituted "more" for "less" in the clause "nor less than 1 Representative for every 50,000 persons."

[4] It was article 1 of the series.

[5] The present ratio is 1 Representative for 173,901 persons. Cong. Directory, 54 Cong., 2 Sess., p. 207. App. No. 295.

[6] The following States ratified in the order given: New Jersey, Maryland, North Carolina, South Carolina, New Hampshire, New York, Rhode Island, Vermont, Virginia, and Pennsylvania. See App. No. 295 for list and dates of ratifications.

[7] Virginia acted on this amendment October 25, 1791, and on the others the 15th of the following December.

[8] App., No. 295. Article 2 was in regard to compensation of members.

[9] Ibid.

appear by the records to have ratified any of the series proposed by Congress. The assent of any one of them would
have made this article a part of the Constitution.[1] The failure
of Massachusetts to take decisive action upon these amendments is the more striking inasmuch as her constitutional
convention had been the first to propose a series of amendments, one of which was upon this very subject, the apportionment of Representatives.[2]

It has been the almost universal opinion of historians that
this amendment was most wisely rejected. The decennial
apportionment bill is usually settled aside from party grounds.
The last apportionment bill, which was passed by the Fifty-first
Congress without serious opposition, is a recent proof of the
truth of this statement.[3]

(2) The compromise which arranged the "three-fifths ratio"
was always a thorn in the flesh of New England, and after
the annexation of Louisiana made the admission of new slave
States probable, they felt that immediate action was necessary.
They believed that the influence of New England, already
immeasurably decreased, would soon be of so little weight
that her interests would be utterly disregarded, unless steps
were at once taken to do away with the existing basis of representation, which gave the South so large a voice in the
National Council.[4] Accordingly early in the summer of 1804,
the legislature of Massachusetts passed a resolution recommending that the Constitution should be amended in such
manner "that Representatives and direct taxes may be
apportioned among the several States according to the number of their free inhabitants, respectively." Later in the
same year Senator Pickering of Massachusetts presented
this amendment to Congress.[5] According to the custom the
resolution of the Massachusetts legislature had been sent to
the legislatures of the other States. All the States but two
answered immediately, and without exception condemned the

---

[1] No record in the State Department of their action. See post, par. 23.

[2] The Federalist opposed the "Bill of Rights" as unnecessary. This proposition was
disagreed to by both the Massachusetts senate and house of representatives on their
preliminary consideration, but final action does not seem to have been taken. Journals
of the Senate, Massachusetts. vol. 10, p. 192; Journals of the House of Representatives,
Massachusetts, vol. 10, pp. 209, 217, 218. See post, par. 97, final note.

[3] The proposed amendment would have enabled Congress to limit the number of the
House of Representatives.

[4] See Nar. and Critical Hist., VII, p. 547, note; Ames, Works, 1, p. 323; Quincy's speech,
Am. Orations, I, p. 145; Adams, Doc. of New Eng. Federalism, pp. 52-55, 77, 78, 148, 362

[5] App., Nos. 363-364. It was called the "Ely amendment."

proposition. "The joy of the Republicans rose as the reply of the States came in," for they claimed that the proposition had not been proposed in good faith as an amendment to the Constitution, but "was sent forth to gather public opinion on the fitness of dividing the Union."[1]

Again, in 1815, the similar resolution upon this subject included in the series of amendments proposed by the Hartford convention[2] was presented at the request of their respective State legislatures by the members from Connecticut and Massachusetts.[3] It is evident that this was prompted by the feeling that the declaration of war and other measures inimical to New England were carried through Congress by means of the additional representation given to the Southern States for their slave population.[4] None of the other New England States indorsed these amendments, and the legislatures of eight States at least passed resolutions of disapproval.[5] The return of peace rendered these propositions of no importance, and they were only recalled to reflect discredit upon their framers.

In 1843 the legislature of Massachusetts passed a resolution proposing the same amendment, which awakened great excitement not only in Congress, but also in the Southern States. Its introduction in the House of Representatives by John Quincy Adams[6] aroused a long and acrimonious debate over

[1] McMaster, Hist. of U. S., Vol. III, pp. 44–47, gives abstract of the replies of the other States. The resolutions of the legislature of Georgia declared "that the amendment proposed by the legislature of Massachusetts to the Constitution has its origin in injustice; and if adopted will disorganize the Union." "They therefore call upon the justice and magnanimity of the several States to oppose a measure having for its object the destruction of that Charter of Independence which was framed in wisdom and which they trust will receive the sanction of ages." Archives of Mass., House Misc., 5927.

[2] For other amendments proposed, see ante par. 11, post pars. 56, 93, 140, 157, 162.

[3] App., Nos. 424, 432, 440.

[4] No other State adopted these resolutions. For cautious action of Rhode Island and New Hampshire, see Niles' Register, Vol. VIII, pp. 37, 348; action of Vermont, ibid., VII, p. 167. See also Adams, New Eng. Fed., pp. 315–320, 322, 407, 408, 424.

[5] Vermont, New York, New Jersey, Pennsylvania, Virginia, Ohio, Tennessee, Louisiana. Niles' Register, Vol. VIII, pp. 16, 65–70, 99–101; Vol. IX, pp. 434, 451; Vol. X, 177; Vol. VII, Sup., p. 49; Annals of Cong., Fourteenth Congress, first session, pp. 89, 132, 365, 876, 932; H. J., pp. 278, 297, 672. Mass. Archives, 8157, 8161, 8181, 8184, 8187. The reply of the legislature of Pennsylvania declares the proportion of slaves to whites in 1790 to have been one-fifth, in 1810 as not quite one-sixth, and that the equal representation in the Senate more than compensates the North for the slave representation given to the South. It further declares "that any alteration in the basis of representation should be a complete one, such as would place the real power of the Government on the basis of its white population and render the number not merely of Representatives, but of Senators proportional to the free white inhabitants of the Union." Niles' Register, Vol. VIII, pp. 65–70.

[6] App., Nos. 733–734.

the question of its being received, which Adams characterized
in his diary as "the most memorable debate ever entertained
in the House."[1]   The resolution was finally received and
referred to a select committee.   In the meantime the new legislature in Massachusetts adopted resolutions proposing the
same amendment; thus two successive legislatures, "first when
the Van Buren party were in majority" and again "when the
Whigs were in the majority," had approved of this measure.[2]
The attempt was made to present the new resolution to both
Houses of Congress on January 23, 1844.[3]   The House thrice
refused to receive them.   In the Senate the motion to receive
and print was the signal for a fierce denunciation of the Commonwealth of Massachusetts by the two Senators from Alabama.   The one stigmatized it as the "Hartford convention
amendment," and inquired "if it were possible for such an
amendment to be made, could anyone believe that the Federal
Government would last twenty-four hours after it was made."
"Was Massachusetts desirous of dissolving the Government?
It so appeared, for she seemed to feel that there was contami-
nation by the union which existed between the two sections of
the country."[4]   Senator Bagby said: "If the legislature of
Massachusetts thought proper to lay the ax at the foot of the
very root of the principles which sustain our institutions, upon
it let all the responsibility rest."   He further declared that
they were now called upon " to give circulation to resolutions"
"the very character of which were seditions and incendiary."[5]
The Senate thereupon refused to print the resolutions by a
vote of 14 to 26.

A short time after this counter resolutions were presented
from the legislatures of Georgia, Alabama, and Virginia.   The
Virginia resolution, in part, declared: "That we can not regard
these resolutions as in truth a proposition to amend the Federal Constitution, but virtually one to dissolve the Union,"[6]
and "we regard this attack, by the highest constitutional

[1] Mem. of J. Q. Adams, XI. p. 455.   It would seem that a similar resolution had been
previously introduced from Vermont, but trace of it has not been found.   See remarks
made in debate.   Niles' Register, Vol. LXV, p. 349.
[2] Ibid., Vol. LXVI. p. 67.
[3] App., No. 734a.   Vote to receive in the House was yeas 74, nays 91.
[4] Senator King, Cong. Globe, pp. 179–180.
[5] Cong. Globe, p. 180.
[6] The petition of citizens of Haverhill, Mass., for the dissolution of the Union, presented by Mr. Adams the previous year (January 21, 1842), may have suggested this
answer.

authority of a sister State, as in the highest degree unjust,
unkind, faithless to the compromises of the Constitution, and
meriting the deepest condemnation of every patriot and friend
of the Union." The governor was especially directed by the
legislature to return the original resolutions to the governor
of Massachusetts.[1]   These resolutions were referred in the
House[2] to a select committee, which a few days later reported
having taken into consideration the several resolutions, and
that they agreed with the Virginia legislature that the resolutions of Massachusetts were "in truth a proposition to dissolve the Union," and that no such amendment ought to be
recommended by Congress, but ought "to be promptly and
decisively condemned." This resolution was agreed to by a
large majority.[3] Three days later Mr. Giddings presented his
declaratory resolutions which affirmed, "That the right of
amendment extends as clearly to that portion of said Constitution which fixes the ratio of Federal representation as to
any other part of the instrument. That every attempt to subvert this important right of the people should be promptly
condemned."[4] The resolution was tabled. In the meantime
the above-mentioned reply of Virginia, together with the original copy of the resolutions of Massachusetts, reached the
Massachusetts legislature. That body immediately replied,
unanimously, in part as follows: "Resolved, That the said
resolves of the legislature of this Commonwealth do express
the deliberate sentiment of the people of Massachusetts; that
they do, in truth and in good faith, propose an amendment of
the Constitution of the United States; that, so far from containing a proposition virtually to dissolve the Union, they
assert a principle which is essential to its stability and permanence, and to the assertion and maintenance of which, in
every constitutional way, the people of Massachusetts will
always hereafter, as they now do, firmly and conscientiously

---

[1] The text of the resolutions from Georgia, Alabama, and Virginia are to be found in the
Cong. Globe, pp. 243, 342, 360–361; Niles' Register, vol. 65, p. 382; vol. 66, pp. 13, 31. The Alabama resolution declared: "That the question of representation was adjusted by the convention upon equitable principles, and that Alabama will neither relinquish this right on
the request of one State nor at the bidding of any greater number." Mass. Arch.,
No. 11?83.

[2] For further proceedings in the Senate, on receiving and printing the various resolutions, and the apology of Mr. Bagby to Mr. Bates of Massachusetts, see S. J., pp. 106, 141,
142, 153, 334; Cong. Globe, pp. 179–180, 243, 342, 360, 361.

[3] 127 yeas to 41 nays. Cong. Globe, pp. 434–435.

[4] Cong. Globe, p. 432.

adhere." They further adopted a resolution, similar in purport to the "Giddings resolution," declaring "the right of the people, at their pleasure, to alter any or all the terms and conditions"—with "but a single restriction"—"upon which the Union was formed."[1] These resolutions were sent to all the States.

The action of the National House of Representatives upon the original resolutions of Massachusetts was completed when the select committee on the same finally reported that "the resolution ought not to be recommended to the House," and the report was adopted by a vote of 156 yeas to 13 nays, and the committee was discharged.[2] Thus closed an episode that clearly indicated the presence of an "irrepressible conflict."

(3) From this time down to the civil war the Federal ratio was accepted as a thing inevitable. In the upheaval of 1860–61, many attempts were made to reassert it, and thus to induce the slave States to remain in the Union. Fifteen resolutions were introduced in the second session of the Thirty-sixth Congress proposing an amendment declaring the clause fixing the "three-fifths" representation for the slaves should forever be unamendable.[3] This proposition was first made in the House on the 12th of December. On the following day Andrew Johnson introduced the same resolution in the Senate. In 1864 Senator Saulsbury included in his series of twenty articles, offered as a substitute for the thirteenth amendment, a similar proposition.[4] None of these passed, and the progress of emancipation of the slaves swept them away.

(4) On the other hand, the thirteenth amendment and the result of the war had now put an end to that class described in the Constitution as "all other persons," and the question immediately arose, How shall the apportionment of Representatives now be made to meet the changed conditions in the Southern States? Even before the close of the war amendments were introduced providing for a new method of apportionment of Representatives. Mr. Sumner, in February, 1864, proposed, as an amendment to the proposition which became the thirteenth amendment, additional sections, one of which

---

[1] Passed March 14, 1844, previous to the introduction of the Giddings resolutions. Niles' Register, Vol. 66, p. 67. In this same year the house of representatives of Massachusetts passed strong resolutions against admission of Texas. See post par. 93.

[2] Cong. Globe, p. 490.

[3] App., Nos. 810, 829, 833, 850, 852, 852b, 874k, 878, 894g, 917, 928, 939, 950, 964, 971g.

[4] App., Nos. 1006, 1021.

provided for the repeal of the clause in regard to the three-
fifths representation for slaves.[1] It was not acted upon, but
in the following December Mr. Sloan of Wisconsin moved in
the House a resolution that the Committee on the Judiciary be
instructed to inquire into "the expediency of so amending the
Constitution that Representatives shall be apportioned among
the several States according to their respective numbers of
qualified electors."[2] The motion was agreed to, but was reconsidered and tabled.[3] In the Senate the question was called up
again by Mr. Sumner introducing another amendment.[4] During the opening days of the next Congress nine propositions to
amend the Constitution in this particular were presented.
The first of these was by Mr. Sumner, who renewed his proposition of the previous Congress.[5] Messrs. Schenck, Stevens,
Broomall, and Orth followed with resolutions of a similar
character.[6] Another, introduced by Mr. Hubbard, proposed
to base the apportionment upon the qualified voters, and fixed
an educational qualification for all voters except soldiers and
sailors in the late war.[7] In these resolutions we note the
appearance of the plan for forcing the South to extend the
suffrage to the negro. On the 5th of January, Mr. Spalding
of Ohio, in a very earnest speech, suggested that a series
of guaranties should be extended to loyal men, among which
he named an amendment to the Constitution directing "the
apportionment of Representatives and direct taxes among
the States in such manner that 'people of color' shall not be
counted with the population in making up the ratio, except it
be in States where they are permitted to exercise the elective
franchise."[8] Mr. Pike immediately introduced a proposition
making this provision, and upon the reassembling of the
House, on the 8th, Mr. Blaine presented a resolution in these
words: "Representatives and direct taxes shall be apportioned among the several States which shall be included
within the Union according to their respective numbers, which
shall be determined by taking the whole number of persons,
except those whose political rights or privileges are denied or

---

[1] App., No. 986a. For other sections, see post par. 108, 122.
[2] App., No. 1039.
[3] Shortly after Mr. Sloan introduced an amendment of the same purport. App., No. 1040.
[4] App., No. 1046.
[5] App., No. 1047.
[6] Similar provisions to that of Sumner's amendment. App., Nos. 1048, 1050, 1053, 1071.
[7] App., No. 1059a.
[8] Cong. Globe, p. 133.

abridged by the constitution of any State on account of race
or color."[1] A week later Mr. Conkling offered a resolution
that an amendment to the Constitution be submitted to the
States in one of the two following forms: That the apportion-
tionment should be made according to the whole number of
citizens of the United States, "Provided, That whenever in
any State civil or political rights or privileges shall be denied
or abridged on account of race or color, all persons of such
race or color shall be excluded from the basis of representation;" or, "Provided, That whenever in any State the elective
franchise shall be denied or abridged on account of race or
color, all persons of such race or color shall be excluded from
the basis of representation."[2] These propositions of Messrs.
Spalding, Blaine, and Conkling foreshadowed the second section of the fourteenth amendment.

The Joint Committee on Reconstruction finally decided upon
and reported on the 22d of January an amendment declaring
that the Representatives and direct taxes should be apportioned according to the whole number of persons in each State,
with a proviso similar to that suggested by Mr. Conkling in
his second form.[3] The House immediately took the proposition into consideration, and there ensued a long debate, in the
course of which some twelve attempts were made to amend.[4]
These are indicative of the different views entertained on this
important question. One attempt was made to insert a proviso, "that the article shall not be construed to affect the
power of Congress to regulate the qualifications for electors
of the most numerous branch of the legislature of the several
States," thus implying that the Federal Government had such
a power.[5] This seems to have been an attempt to extend
unwarrantedly the power of Congress by this negative assertion. Other attempts were made to extend the scope of the
amendment. One such was directed against the requirement
by some of the States of a property qualification for the franchise.[6] It stipulated that "no State within the Union shall
prescribe or establish any property qualification which may

[1] App., Nos. 1068, 1069.
[2] App., No. 1072.
[3] App., No. 1077. For an abstract of the debate and legislative history of this amendment, see W. H. Barnes, History of the Thirty-ninth Congress, Chaps. XIV-XVIII.
[4] App., Nos. 1079-1103.
[5] Mr. Kelley of Pennsylvania. App., No. 1083.
[6] Mr. Ingersoll of Illinois. App., No. 1084; same by Mr. Baker, No. 1082a

or shall in any way abridge the elective franchise." An effort
was also made to secure the indorsement of woman's suffrage
in a negative form, by providing that the representation of any
State should be abridged for the exclusion from the elective
franchise of any person on account of "sex," as well as race
or color.[1] Another amendment substituted for the provision
fixing as a penalty the abridgment of the representation an
emphatic declaration that " the elective franchise shall not be
denied or abridged in any State on account of race or color,"
evidently assuming that Congress would have the power to
enforce the provision.[2]

Two other amendments received extended consideration, the
first of these, similar to a proposition introduced a short time
previously, basing the representation upon the number of the
electors,[3] proposed that representation should be apportioned
according to the whole number of male citizens of the United
States who are voters;[4] ultimately this proposition was rejected by a decisive vote. The other provided that "when the
elective franchise shall be denied by the constitution or laws
of any State to any proportion of its male citizens over twenty-
one years, the same proportion of its entire population shall
be excluded from the basis of representation."[5]

On the 29th of January the resolution, together with the
proposed amendments thereto, was recommitted to the Committee on Reconstruction;[6] two days later the proposition was
reported modified to read as follows: "Representatives shall
be apportioned among the several States which may be included
within this Union according to their respective number, counting the whole number of persons in each State, excluding
Indians not taxed : Provided, That whenever the elective franchise shall be denied or abridged in any State on account of
race or color, the persons therein of such race or color shall be
excluded from the basis of representation."[7] This amendment
was then carried by the House by a vote of 120 to 46. In the

[1] Mr. Brooks of New York. App., No. 1085.
[2] Mr. Eliot of Massachusetts. App., No. 1086. Also by Mr. Lawrence, Nos. 1086–1088.
[3] App., No. 1080.
[4] Mr. Schenck. Only 29 votes were cast in its favor. App., No. 1089. Three other proposed amendments based the apportionment on male citizens of the United States over
21. Nos. 1082b, 1101, 1102.
[5] Mr. Broomall of Pennsylvania. App., No. 1090. Also by Messrs. Sumner and Ashley.
App., Nos. 1103, 1123. This would have provided for such cases as the "Mississippi plan"
of educational qualification, as in the recent constitutions of Mississippi and South Carolina.
[6] App., No. 1079.
[7] Ibid.

Senate some fourteen attempts were made to modify the form
of the proposed amendment. Some of them proposed that the
words "male electors" or "citizens over twenty-one" should
be inserted in place of "persons."[1] Others, which are enumerated elsewhere,[2] anticipating the fifteenth amendment, contemplated conferring the franchise upon the negro or certain
classes of the African race.[3] The Senate failed to give the
amendment the necessary two-thirds vote.[4] A motion was
made to reconsider, but was never called up, for the same subject came up in a new resolution shortly after.[5]

Before the Committee on Reconstruction reported their new
resolution, eight other distinct amendments were proposed,
four in each branch of Congress.[6] The committee reported
to the House "the composite amendment," which contained, in
section 2, the provision for the readjustment of the basis of
representation. The amendment passed the House May 10 by
a vote of 128 to 37.[7] Nine amendments to the section on apportionment of Representatives were offered in the Senate;[8] only
one of them was accepted,[9] and the entire resolution now
known as the fourteenth amendment passed the Senate, and
received the concurrence of the House June 13, 1866.[10]

Only seven other amendments relative to this subject have
since been presented in Congress, all during the later "sixties."
The majority of them were offered before the ratification of the
fourteenth amendment, in connection with a series of amendments relating to subjects which were the outcome of the war.[11]
The last amendment, which was introduced by Mr. Ashley in
1869, proposed to give to the minority proportional representation in the House of Representatives.[12]

[1] App., Nos. 1091–1103.
[2] Post par. 130.
[3] App., Nos. 1094, 1096, 1097, 1099.
[4] 25 yeas to 22 nays.
[5] App., Nos. 1135–1140.
[6] App., Nos. 1104, 1108, 1117, 1118, 1123, 1126, 1132, 1134.
[7] App., Nos. 1135–1140. Amendments presented in the House Nos. 1141–1143.
[8] App., Nos. 1148, 1152, 1156, 1159, 1172, 1173, 1175, 1177, 1178.
[9] App., No. 1177.
[10] App., Nos. 1135–1140.
[11] Proposed by Messrs. Dixon and Ashley, App., Nos. 1194f, 1203, 1213c, 1219, 1227f, 1245.
[12] App., No. 1315c, for speech Globe 40th Cong., 3d Sess., App., p. 211. It provided that in
election of Representatives, whenever more than one Representative was to be elected
from a State, Congress shall "designate the manner in which such additional representation shall be chosen, and shall provide for securing to the qualified electors in such States
personal representation in Congress as near as may be." He advocated the "Hare system" of proportional representation. See post, par. 45, for schemes for proportional representation of the minority in elections of President and Vice-President.

We have seen that almost the whole difficulty of apportionment of Representatives arose out of the question of the status of the negro. The trouble manifested itself first in the Constitutional Convention itself, next in the early years of this century, and although on only one occasion from that time to 1860 were amendments introduced; still during all this period the additional power wielded by the white man in the South, owing to the partial representation given for the slaves, was one of the grievances of the North. The question was opened anew by the abolition of slavery, which had entirely changed the old relations. The second section of the fourteenth amendment was designed to meet this question, but it was only partial in its results, its provisions not affirming the right of the negro to vote. The fifteenth amendment completed the series of guaranties by forbidding in all cases the exclusion from the franchise of any person "on account of race, color, or previous condition of servitude."

It is significant that, just as the perplexing question of representation in Congress was settled by constitutional amendment, a new phase of the subject was opened, one which is likely to assume more importance during the second century of our history under the Constitution.[1]

23. LIMITATION OF THE NUMBER OF REPRESENTATIVES.

The early fear seems to have been of too small a House, as is shown by the action of five of the ratifying conventions in proposing an amendment fixing the apportionment at the ratio of 1 Representative to every 30,000 until the whole number of Representatives should amount to 200.[2] In the early years the increase in the number of Representatives did not keep pace with the growth of the population of the country. During the period 1790 to 1820, while the population rose from nearly 4,000,000 to about 10,000,000, or an increase of nearly 150 per cent, the House of Representatives a little more than doubled in membership.[3] By 1821 the evils of a numerous House of

---

[1] See Bryce, Vol. 1, p. 481; Hitchcock's Am. State Consts., pp. 33-34; Foster, Com. on the Const., Vol. 1, pp. 343-344; Commons, Prop. Representation, Chaps. IV, V, VI, and X, for instances of the trial of minority representation in certain cases. In the Fifty-second Congress Representative T. L. Johnson of Ohio introduced a bill for proportional representation. Mr. Buckalew, also, in 1867-1871, advocated a scheme for a cumulative vote for Representatives for Congress. Commons, pp. 114-115, 247-248.

[2] See ante par. 22, Part 1.

[3] Census of 1790, 105 Representatives, or 1 to 33,000; census of 1800, 141 Representatives, or 1 to 33,000; census of 1810, 181 Representatives, or 1 to 35,000; census of 1820, 212 Representatives, or 1 to 40,000.

Representatives appeared, and in that year Senator Barbour of Virginia introduced a resolution to amend the Constitution so as to limit the number of Representatives to 200.[1] He said: "There is a recommendation in favor of the smallest number consistent with the great principle of representation growing out of our peculiar form of government. As you multiply the number of the House of Representatives you give to it more the form and eventually more of the character of a National in contradistinction to a Federal Government." The author of the resolution asserted only his desire to counteract any tendency which might lead to a centralized government.[2] After considerable discussion the resolution was postponed indefinitely. In 1842 Mr. Underwood of Kentucky offered an amendment to the effect that "in the apportionment of Representatives, which is made based upon the census taken in the year 1850, the number of Representatives shall not exceed double the number of Senators." The resolution was referred, and the committee reported adversely.[3]

No other resolutions suggesting amendments upon this subject were presented in Congress until the early "eighties," when there were four amendments introduced, two of these at the time the bill for the reapportionment of Representatives was under consideration. They all proposed a reduction in the membership of the House as at present constituted, although they all fixed upon a different number. One provided that the House of Representatives should be composed of 300 members.[4] The others placed 325,[5] 350,[5] and 351, respectively, as the maximum number.[6] Two of these were presented by Mr. Herbert of Alabama. None of these resolutions were reported from the Committee on the Judiciary, to which they had been referred. The latest change suggested was in 1888, when an amendment was proposed to limit the House to 250 members.[7]

The desirability of reducing the size of the House of Representatives can not be seriously questioned, for it is a well-known fact that the House has become such a large and

---

[1] App., No. 504.
[2] This was the time of the beginning of the "Crawford machine."
[3] App., No. 725.
[4] App., No. 1507.
[5] App., No. 1530; 1553.
[6] App., No. 1585.
[7] App., No. 1716, with the proviso that in case a new State was admitted the representation to which it shall be entitled shall be in addition to the limit fixed until the next succeeding apportionment.

unwieldy body that the greater part of the business has to be
left to the committees. There is little prospect, however, of
effecting this change either by ordinary law or by amendment,
for there is a constant tendency to increase the number of
members more rapidly than the growth of the population
would call for.[1] The present House consists of 357 Representatives and 3 Territorial Delegates.[2]

24. ELECTION OF REPRESENTATIVES.

The Constitution provides that "the time, places, and manner of holding elections for Senators and Representatives shall
be prescribed in each State by the legislature thereof; but the
Congress may at any time, by law, make or alter such regulations, except as to the place of choosing Senators."[3] Congress
has always desired to assimilate its system to that of the States,
and this is almost the only case where the United States per-
mits the States to perform its functions. Thirty-four resolutions have been introduced in Congress proposing some change
in the provision quoted above in the case of election of Representatives. These for the most part were introduced between
the years 1800 and 1826.

The variety of methods in use in the different States, both
for the choice of electors and Representatives, suggested the
attempts made during the early years of this century to provide a uniform system.[4] These resolutions commonly proposed
amendments applying both to Presidential and Congressional
elections. The first resolution of the kind was offered by Mr.
Nicholas of Virginia, in the year 1800. It proposed a division
of each State into districts, the people in each district to choose
one Representative in the manner in which the legislature
shall provide.[5] In 1802 the legislatures of Vermont and North
Carolina presented resolutions of a similar character.[6] Again,

---

[1] The amendment sent out to the States by the First Congress would have enabled Congress to limit the House after the number had reached 200; see ante par. 22, Part 1.

[2] By the last apportionment bill the House was to consist of 356 members, the admission
of Utah as a State added one more Representative. The present ratio is 1 to 173,901.
For table of apportionments, see Hinsdale's Am. Govt., pp. 158-159.

[3] Constitution, art. 1, sec. 4, cl. 1. See ante, par. 9.

[4] In the early elections the following methods were in use: First, by districts in Massachusetts, Virginia, New York, Maryland, South Carolina. Second, by general ticket in
New Hampshire, Pennsylvania, New Jersey, Georgia. Third, in Connecticut a preliminary election was held to nominate a list three times the number to be chosen, from which
at a subsequent election the Representatives were selected. See also Story, I, p. 583.

[5] App., Nos. 339, 341. Jefferson favored election by districts and not by general ticket.
See letter of January 12, 1800, Works, Vol. IV, p. 308.

[6] App., Nos. 343, 347, 349.

after a lull of a few years, the legislature of North Carolina
renewed, in 1813, their resolution.[1] From 1816 to 1826 there
were twenty-two resolutions proposing the choice of Representatives by districts.[2] During the years 1816, 1817, and 1818
the legislatures of six of the States applied to Congress for an
amendment of this nature.[3] The earlier movement was championed by Mr. Pickens of North Carolina, the later by Senator
Dickerson of New Jersey, who offered an amendment regularly
almost every year from 1817 to 1826.[4] The Dickerson amendment passed the Senate three different times, namely, in 1819,
1820, and 1822, but each time failed to be brought to a vote in
the House.[5] The desire for local representation gradually led
to the general adoption by the States of the district system of
electing their Congressmen, and caused the introduction of
amendments on this question to cease.[6]

For a long time Congress made no use of its undoubted
power to regulate Federal elections.[7] Owing, however, to the
prolonged contest in the Twenty-sixth Congress, resulting
from the disputed election in New Jersey in 1838, which State
still adhered to the method of election by general ticket,[8] the
Whig majority enacted in 1842 a law making the election of
members of the House of Representatives by districts manda-
tory on all the States. The law was opposed by the Democratic party, and some of the States for a time refused to
comply with its terms, but after a few elections it was submitted to everywhere. Consequently, only once since has it
been proposed to amend the Constitution in this particular,
and this was in connection with a proposition to choose the
Presidential electors by districts.[9] During the reconstruction
period it was proposed to so amend the Constitution that it
should be the duty of Congress, at the first session after each

---

[1] App., Nos. 406, 408.

[2] App., Nos. 449, 452, 452a, 454, 459, 462, 468, 471, 481, 483, 486, 487, 490. 498, 499, 502, 505, 518, 525, 528, 533, 576.

[3] Massachusetts, in 1816; New Jersey and North Carolina, in 1817; New York, North Carolina, New Hampshire, New Jersey, and Connecticut, in 1818.

[4] Eight in all. App., Nos. 468, 486, 498, 499, 505, 518, 528, 576.

[5] App., Nos. 486, 596, 505. See choice of Presidential electors by districts, post, par. 39.

[6] At the same time the general-ticket system was adopted for Presidential election. See post, par. 40. In 1828, in the election for the Twenty-sixth Congress, only New Hamp-shire, New Jersey, and Georgia adhered to the old method of election by general ticket.

[7] Story, I, pp. 582, 583.

[8] See post, par. 25; Von Holst, II, pp. 336–340.

[9] App., Nos. 1247, 1248.

decennial census, to divide the several States into Congressional districts equaling in number the Representatives in Congress.[1] The purpose was to prevent "gerrymandering," but it is probable that this change would simply have caused bad districting on a grander scale.

Although Congress has refused to recommend any of these proposed amendments to the States for ratification, it has from time to time enacted additional laws extending its control over Federal elections.[2] In 1871 Congress passed a law requiring that all votes for Representatives must be by written or printed ballots,[3] and further made provision for the appointment of supervisors, who should supervise the registration and casting of the ballots for the election of members of the House of Representatives.[4] Again, in 1872, it exercised its authority by appointing a uniform day for the election of members of the House.[5] Since this last date in its apportionment bills Congress has prescribed that the districts shall contain as nearly as possible an equal number of inhabitants. These laws mark the extent to which Congress has gone in regulating the election of its members. The recent attempt made in the Fifty-first Congress to pass the "Federal election bill," which would have extended Federal supervision even further, is familiar to all.[6] Although there can be no doubt of the right of Congress to assume control over Federal elections,[7] there seems to be some hesitancy on the part of Congress to exercise this right. This undoubtedly contributed much to the defeat of the above-mentioned "Federal election bill," and led the Democratic majority in the Fifty-third Congress to repeal the statute of 1871 relating to the supervision of elections.[8]

---

[1] App., No. 1310.

[2] In 1866 it passed a law to regulate the procedure of State legislatures in electing Senators, 14 Stat. L., p. 243, c. 245, s. 1.

[3] February 28, 1871, 19 Stat. L , p. 440, c. 99, s. 19.

[4] To be appointed by the Federal courts in any election district upon the petition of a specified number of citizens. Ibid., p. 348, ch. 415.

[5] February 2, 1872, 17 Stat. L., p. 28, ch. xi. The law was modified to legalize elections in certain States on other days. All except Maine, Vermont, and Oregon elect at the stated time. An amendment, App. No. 1355, was proposed in 1872 authorizing Congress to fix a uniform day for State elections.

[6] During the debate the opponents of this measure threatened that if it became a law several of the States would return to the old system of electing their Representatives by general ticket in defiance of the laws of Congress.

[7] Ex parte Siebold, 100 U. S., 371; Ex parte Clarke, Ibid., 299; U. S. v. Gale, 109 U. S., 65; Ex parte Yarborough, 110 U. S., 651.

[8] Feb. 8, 1894, 28 Stat. L., p. 36.

25. PROVING ELECTIONS TO THE HOUSE OF REPRESENTATIVES.

During the turmoil and discussion in the Twenty-sixth Congress, connected with the settlement of the contested election of five Representatives from New Jersey—which led to a contest lasting several months, as the election and the control of the House depended upon the issue of the controversy—a resolution was introduced authorizing the Committee on the Judiciary to inquire into the expediency of amending the Constitution [1] so that the same shall define and prescribe the evidence upon which persons claiming to be members of the House of Representatives shall take their seats in the House and be entitled to exercise the privileges of members, until an investigation and decision by the House.[2]

Although the subject of determining the results of contested elections has continued to agitate the country at times ever since, there has been no further suggestion of an amendment to the Constitution. Party exigency has usually proved more powerful than considerations of right and justice, but no suggestion of adopting the English practice of a judicial decision has been made. The power of Congress, as the Constitution now stands, is incontestable.[3]

26. TERM OF REPRESENTATIVES.

At the time of the formation of the Constitution in all of the States but South Carolina the members of the lower branch of the legislature were chosen annually.[4] Many of the members of the Philadelphia Convention favored annual elections inasmuch as a longer term might make the Representatives independent of their constituents.[5] Others, including Madison and Hamilton, desired a term of three years or even longer, on the ground that in a short term new members could not become accustomed to their duties, and that too frequent elections tended to make the people indifferent to the election.[6] The two-years term was finally agreed upon as a compromise.[7]

---

[1] Const., art. 1, sec. 5, cl. 1.

[2] App., No. 703. This contest lasted from December, 1839, until March 10, 1840, when the Democratic contestant was seated. See ante, par. 24, for references; also Benton II, p. 159. Story, I, p. 585, note 1.

[3] In re Lonly, 134 U. S., 372.

[4] Story, I, p. 430. Robinson, Annals of Acad. of Pol. Science, I, p. 214.

[5] Gerry considered frequent elections the only defense of the people against tyranny. Elliot's Debates, vol. v, p. 184.

[6] Mr. Jenifer's speech. Elliot, v, p. 183.

[7] Triennial elections were first adopted by vote of 7 to 4, later struck out and two years substituted by vote of 7 to 3, one State divided; finally agreed to by unanimous consent. Elliot, v, pp. 184, 220.

There has been no general dissatisfaction with this term, and hence few amendments proposing a change have been presented. In the First Congress a resolution restricting the number of years in succession the same person could serve was presented.[1] It stipulated that no person should be capable of serving more than six years in any term of eight years.[2] Mr. Hillhouse, in 1808, offered, as the first article of his interesting series of radical amendments, a proposition that the term of Representatives should, after March 3, 1813, be but one year.[3]

No similar propositions appear until 1869, but since that date eleven resolutions, all to lengthen the term of service, have been introduced by members of the House. Eight of these proposed fixing the term at three years.[4] One of this group provided for the division into classes, so that one-third might be chosen every year.[5] Of the remaining three, two would have increased the term to four years, while one proposed to make the term of Representatives equal to that of Senators, with a similar division into classes.[6]

The lengthening of the term to three years, as well as the proposed division into classes, has much to commend it. There is little doubt that a longer term of service would greatly increase the capacity of the members for legislation. At present a new member is at a serious disadvantage.[7] A three-years term would not only afford a Representative a better opportunity to prove his worth, but give his constituency a better chance to judge of his competency.

27. THE SENATE: ELECTION OF SENATORS.

The Senate has changed less in the first one hundred years of its existence than its associated body, the House of Representatives. Although there are at present forty-five States in the Union, the Senate is still a comparatively small body. Inasmuch as it has been for the most part a dignified and con-

---

[1] Based on rotation rule of the old Congress of the Confederation. Art. of Confed., art. V.

[2] App., No. 194.

[3] App., No. 390. For other articles of series, see post, paras. 30, 34, 47, 57, 59, 60.

[4] App. Nos. 1425, 1440, 1499, 1534a, 1571, 1625, 1641, 1735a. Five of these by Mr. Springer of Illinois.

[5] App. No. 1425.

[6] App. Nos. 1313, 1360, 1548.

[7] By the present arrangement of sessions the election comes after the first session. This places both the Representative and his constituency at a disadvantage.

servative body, it has been the subject of less controversy than the House, which is more directly responsible to the people, and hence of a smaller variety of amendments.

The proposition most frequently presented has been that in regard to the choice of Senators by popular vote in each State.[1] Previous to 1872 there had been nine resolutions of this character, but since that date up to the close of the Fiftieth Congress this change has been urged some thirty times. This amendment was first proposed in Congress by Mr. Storrs of New York, in 1826.[2] In 1835 a similar resolution was introduced.[3] During the early "fifties" five propositions were brought to the attention of Congress.[4] Andrew Johnson, in 1860, when a Senator, and again in 1868 as President, advocated the same amendment which he had twice before in the "fifties" introduced when a member of the lower House.[5] The marked increase since 1872 in the number of resolutions proposing this change shows that it has a strong hold on popular feeling. Scarcely a session of Congress passes in which one or more resolutions are not offered to secure this amendment.[6] In the Forty-ninth and Fiftieth Congresses, respectively, there were six such resolutions proposed.[7] An examination of the journals of Congress for the years subsequent to March 4, 1889, which lie beyond the period of special investigation of this monograph, shows that the number of resolutions proposing this change is unprecedented. In the first session of the Fifty-second Congress alone twenty-five resolutions on this subject were presented.[8] The legislatures of at least fifteen States have, within recent years, recommended this amendment.[9] Congress has been so far influenced by the popular demand for this change that the House

---

[1] Wilson of Pennsylvania, in the Convention of 1787, made a motion to give the election of Senators to the people. Pennsylvania alone voted for it. The present system was agreed to by nine States to two. Pennsylvania and Virginia voting against it. Jour. Fed. Con., pp. 106, 147. Story, I, p. 504.

[2] App., No. 553. Tabled.

[3] App., No. 644.

[4] App., Nos. 756, 766, 769, 772. 775.

[5] App., Nos. 814, 1231.

[6] App., Nos. 1313, 1349, 1359a, 1366, 1370, 1375c, 1380, 1381, 1382, 1385, 1409, 1421, 1448, 1457, 1518, 1520, 1543. 1563, 1602, 1615, 1617.

[7] App., Nos. 1643, 1647, 1674, 1683, 1684, 1687, 1695, 1698, 1704, 1719, 1721, 1730. The preamble of No. 1643 gives as the reason for the change that "the Senate is now attempting to interfere with the power of the President to remove officials." See post, par. 60, note.

[8] S. R. 6, 8, 37, 99. H. Res. 2. 3, 6, 7, 13, 16, 18, 19, 20, 21, 30, 31, 34, 35, 37. 39, 47, 79, 83, 84, 90.

[9] California, Idaho, Illinois, Indiana, Iowa, Kansas, Kentucky, Louisiana, Minnesota, New York, Ohio, Oregon, Washington, Wisconsin, Wyoming.

of Representatives of both the Fifty-second and the Fifty-third Congresses have passed, by very pronounced majorities, a joint resolution to submit such an amendment to the States.[1] The Senate, however, has failed to advance either of these resolutions to a vote.[2]

Some of these proposed amendments provide for the choice by the people, if a State prefer it, but the great majority take away all option and make the election by the people imperative. Some propose to confer upon Congress the power to provide by law for the conduct of the election and the canvassing of the vote.[3] A tendency in the opposite direction, however, is seen in both the amendments recently proposed by the House of Representatives. Each contains a provision that "the time, place, and manner of holding elections for Senators shall be prescribed in each State by the legislature thereof."

Two of the recent propositions proposed to do away with the present basis of representation and substitute a system of proportional representation in its place.[4] The first of these provided that each State should have at least two Senators, but that for each million of inhabitants of any State in excess of two million, an additional Senator should be allowed such State. By the terms of the second each State would have one Senator, and an additional one for every million of population. There is little reason to suppose that the great compromise of the Constitution will be disturbed, for no State can be deprived of its equal representation in the Senate without its own consent, and it is not in the nature of things to expect that any one of the eighteen Commonwealths whose Senatorial strength would be reduced one half by the second proposition would consent to it.[5]

The principal reasons which have been urged in favor of the election of Senators directly by the people are as follows: First, that the method now in use is not in accord with our

[1] Fifty-second Congress, second session, Cong. Record, pp. 617–618. Passed without division. Fifty-third Congress, second session, H. J., pp. 398, 497, 499, 501. Vote 141 to 51.

[2] In the Fifty-third Congress, third session, reported adversely. S. Rep., 916; Cong. Record, p. 2152. In the Fifty-fourth Congress, first session, March 23, 1896, such an amendment was reported favorably, with an interesting report. S. Rep., 530; Cong. Record, pp. 3333, 3412–3415.

[3] As App., Nos. 1385, 1409.

[4] Bayne of Pennsylvania; App., No. 1543; Miller of Wisconsin; Fifty-second Congress, First session, Cong. Record, p. 201, January 17, 1892. The "Randolph plan," presented to the convention of 1787, made provision for proportional representation in both Houses.

[5] The following States would by this plan be reduced to one Senator: Colorado, Connecticut, Delaware, Florida, Idaho, Maine, Montana, Nevada, New Hampshire, North Dakota, Oregon, Rhode Island, South Dakota, Utah, Vermont, Washington, West Virginia, and Wyoming—18.

democratic system, and indicates a lack of confidence in the wisdom of the people; second, that the present method leads to the corruption of legislatures, and to the selection of men whose only claim to office is their great wealth or their subserviency to corporate interests. On the other hand, it is maintained that the proposed change would lead to the choice of deserving men, reflecting more truly the sentiment of the people. Again, it is urged that the proposed method would prevent the prolonged deadlocks which sometimes occur in the State legislatures in their effort to elect a Senator.[1] Further, it would take away one incentive for legislative gerrymandering of States. Finally, the advocates of popular elections claim that the evils of the present method, which tend to the introduction of national affairs into State politics and lead to the election of members of the State legislatures on national instead of local issues, would be diminished.[2] Still, it may be said in support of the present method that it has secured to the United States the only effective second chamber in the world.[3]

28. FILLING VACANCIES IN THE SENATE.

Only one of the ratifying conventions objected to that provision of the Constitution which gives the executive of the State power to make temporary appointments to vacancies in the Senate.[4] The New York convention included in the series of amendments which it proposed one to reserve this power to the legislature.[5] This would involve either a special session of the legislature in case of a vacancy or a continuance of the vacancy until the next regular session. The resolutions proposing the election of Senators by the popular vote usually made provision for this contingency. In general, the executive of the State was to issue writs for a special election,[6] although

---

[1] Recent examples: Illinois (1890); Montana, Washington, and Maryland (1893); Delaware (1894-95); Kentucky (1895-96). (1897.)

[2] References: In favor of the proposed change, John Haynes, Popular Election of United States Senators. Johns Hopkins University Studies, series XI, p. 547. S. Report 530, Fifty-fourth Congress, First session; Cong. Record, pp. 3412-3415. In opposition: Ex-Senator Edmunds, "Forum," Vol. XVIII. p. 270. Senator Hoar's speech of April 6 and 7, 1893; Cong. Record, pp. 101-110. Pro and Con, Publications of the Mich. Pol. Science Ass., vol. 1.

[3] "The election of Senators has in substance almost ceased to be indirect." See Bryce, I. pp. 100-101, note 1. Note provision in the constitution of Nebraska of 1875, which allows voters "to express by ballot their preference for some person for the office of United States Senator."

[4] Const., art. 1, sec. 3, cl. 2.

[5] App., No. 63.

[6] As App., Nos. 1360, 1543.

one provided that the vacancy should be filled at the next general election in the State, but that pending the election the executive might make temporary appointment.[1]

There is no need of an amendment. The period during which the office is vacant is short, and the legislature frequently chooses some other man than the one appointed by the governor and is not often influenced by the personal desires of the temporary incumbent for a reelection.

29. RECALL OF SENATORS BY STATES.

Among the amendments proposed by the ratifying conventions there was one which was advocated by two of the Northern States—New York and Rhode Island—providing that the legislatures of the respective States may recall their Senators and send others in their place.[2] The general doctrine of instructions received little adherence during the early years of Congress.[3] No resolution was brought before that body until 1803, when the legislature of Virginia proposed an amendment authorizing a State to recall its Senators.[4] Two years later, upon the acquittal of Judge Chase, Nicholson of Virginia, who had been associated with John Randolph in presenting the case for the House, and who was smarting under the sting of defeat caused by the failure of some of the Republican Senators to vote for the conviction of a judge impeached by their own party associates, sought revenge by trying to secure an amendment which would render Senators liable to recall by their State legislature.[5] Three years later the legislature of Virginia renewed its former resolution, which was presented to Congress by her Senators and Representatives. This amendment provided that Senators might be removed by a majority vote of the whole number of members of their respective State legislatures.[6] It called out in reply resolutions of disapproval from the legislatures of Maryland,

---

[1] App., No. 1687.

[2] App., Nos. 61, 121.

[3] Although the States early passed resolutions instructing their Senators (and requesting their Representatives) to favor or oppose measures. In the session of 1799–1800 the legislature of Virginia instructed the Senators to oppose naval expenses. Benton, II, p. 572. Griswold of New York, in 1803, made a speech against the doctrine of instructions of Representatives by State legislatures. Annals, Eighth Congress, First session, p. 664.

[4] App., No. 362a. Massachusetts legislature passed resolutions of disapproval. See Ibid.

[5] App., No. 367. Randolph presented an amendment for the removal of judges. Post, par. 71. Schouler, II, p. 78; McMaster, III, p. 182.

[6] App., Nos. 386, 388.

New Jersey, Tennessee, Georgia, Massachusetts, and Vermont.[1] This amendment, if passed, would have made the Senators directly responsible to the State legislatures. At first it would probably have resulted in the removal of such Senators as went counter to the supposed interests of their State, and it might have gone on until it would have led to the removal of all Senators who were not in harmony with the dominant party in the State legislature.[2]

It will be remembered that John Tyler, inasmuch as he believed in the right of instruction, resigned his seat in the Senate in 1836 rather than follow the instructions of the legislature of Virginia to vote for the "expunging resolution."[3] Likewise Senator White of Tennessee resigned his seat during the session of 1839–40 because the legislature of his State passed resolutions censuring him for having voted on certain measures with the Whigs and calling on him in the future to act with the Democratic party.[4]

It is worthy of note, in connection with the doctrine of instruction, that it is customary for the States in passing a resolution in favor of some amendment to prefix a preamble instructing their Senators and requesting their Representatives to urge its adoption, thus seemingly implying that the legislatures have the right to instruct Senators, but that the Representatives are responsible only to their constituents.

30. TERM OF SENATORS.

The term of Senators is abnormally long. With the exception of some judgships, it is the longest term of any of the elective offices in the United States.[5] It is not surprising,

---

[1] Annals of Congress, Tenth Congress, second session, p. 306. Ibid., Eleventh Congress, third session, p. 383. Ibid., Twelfth Congress, first session, p. 559. Archives of Massachusetts Legislature, Doc. 6845; Resolves of Massachusetts Legislature, Vol. XII, p. 365; Archives of Massachusetts, Misc. Doc., 6663.

[2] Richard Brent, in 1811, was censured by the legislature of Virginia for voting for the recharter of the bank contrary to its instructions. A bill setting forth its rights appears in the Laws of Virginia. See McMaster, III, p. 390.

[3] For letter of John Tyler, see Niles' Register, Vol. I., pp. 17, 25–27. Senator Leigh's letter refusing to resign, ibid., pp. 28–32. Resolutions of the legislature of Virginia asserting the right of instruction, S. J., p. 233 (Twenty-fourth Congress, first session). Mr. Rives of Virginia had resigned his seat in the previous year because he differed from the legislature on the deposit question, Niles' Register, Vol. I., p. 17. See also Niles' Register, Vol. XLVII, pp. 129, 161, 178, 313, 401–402, 445; Vol. L, p. 11.

[4] Benton, Thirty Years' View, II, p. 184. Webster expressed himself on several occasions against the binding force of instructions. Works, III, pp. 228, 356; V, p. 425. Foster, Commentaries on the Constitution, I, pp. 494–496, and notes for other instances.

[5] In the Federal Congress it was first fixed at seven years, then reconsidered and after a five and a nine year term had been rejected the six-year term was adopted. Elliot, V, pp. 203, 241, 245. Story, I, p. 508

therefore, that eight propositions have been presented to change the term of Senators, all within the first fifty years of the history of the Constitution. These all proposed diminishing the length of the term, some to one, others to three, and still others to four years.

Before discussing the separate amendments of this class, one amendment must be referred to, which was proposed by the ratifying convention of New York. It provided that no person should be eligible as a Senator for more than six years in any term of twelve years.[1] This would prevent a Senator succeeding himself. The advantage of the proposition was not evident, and it received no consideration in the First Congress.

One proposition was, however, presented in the First Congress affecting the term of Senators; this was the only resolution that has been offered proposing to reduce the term to one year. It further stipulated that no person should be capable of serving more than five years in any term of six years. The motion of reference was lost.[2] Three resolutions have been proposed fixing the term at three years. This suggestion first came from the legislature of Virginia in 1795.[3] Their proposition made provision for the division of the Senators into three classes, one-third to retire annually. The same amendment was next proposed by Senator Hillhouse, in 1808, as a necessary part of his plan for the choice of the President by lot each year from the retiring Senators.[4] This change was last presented in 1816, by Senator Bibb of Georgia, and after an extended discussion was rejected by an overwhelming majority of the Senate.[5]

Amendments were proposed in 1812, 1814, 1829, and 1839 reducing the term of Senators to four years.[6] The first two of these were resolutions from the legislature of Tennessee.[7] The last was one of a series of propositions introduced by Mr. Talia-

---

[1] App., No. 61. Similar restrictions proposed for Representatives in First Congress. Ante, par. 26. Another evidence of the fear of the creation of a ruling class and a desire for rotation in office.

[2] App., No. 391.

[3] App., No. 327c.

[4] App., No. 391, see post, par. 47.

[5] App., No. 451.

[6] App., Nos. 405a, 419, 594, 689.

[7] It would seem that Georgia had also proposed the same, for in 1816 the legislature of Louisiana, North Carolina, and Ohio passed resolutions disagreeing with an amendment proposed by Georgia. Annals of Congress, Fourteenth Congress, first session, p. 365. Archives of Massachusetts, Misc., 8105, 8183.

ferro of Virginia. It made provision for the division of the
Senators into two classes, so that one class should be elected
biennially. None of these resolutions were reported from the
committees to which they had been referred.

31. TRIAL OF IMPEACHMENTS OF SENATORS.

The ratifying conventions in Virginia and North Carolina
proposed as an amendment to the Constitution " that some tribunal other than the Senate be provided for trying impeachments of Senators."[1] The same amendment was rejected by
the Senate when presented in the First Congress.[2] Only one
attempt has been made to impeach a Senator. This was in
the case of William Blount of Tennessee, in 1798. Previous
to the trial he had been expelled from the Senate for violation
of the neutrality laws of the United States. He was acquitted
by the Senate for lack of jurisdiction.[3]

In 1795 the legislature of Virginia passed a resolution recommending "that a tribunal other than the Senate be instituted
for the trial of impeachments."[4] With the exception of the
propositions referred to in connection with the impeachment
of judges,[5] which were also presented during the early years of
the life of the Constitution, no other emendation of this clause
has been sought.

32. PRESENT STATUS OF AMENDMENTS RELATING TO THE LEGISLATIVE DEPARTMENT.

In the foregoing consideration of the various attempts to
change in any particular the form of the legislative department, we have seen, with the exception of the amendments
relating to the apportionment of Representatives and the popular election of Senators, that by far the greater number of
propositions were introduced in the earlier years of the century.
In recent years, with the exception of the above-mentioned
classes, amendments of this character have been comparatively
few. On the other hand, it is a noteworthy fact that there

---

[1] App., Nos. 44, 97, see post, par. 71.

[2] App., No. 286.

[3] Blount's counsel held that the Senate had no jurisdiction over him, first, because as a
Senator he was not a civil officer liable to impeachment, and, second, that since his expul-
sion he was no longer a Senator. The Senate sustained the first plea. Story, I, pp. 559–
561, 567, 568, note 4; Foster, I, pp. 529–531.

[4] App., No. 327b.

[5] Post, par. 71.

is a growing desire to place some restriction upon the exercise of certain powers by Congress.[1]

Among the amendments presented during the closing years of the first century of our history under the Constitution the following are the most important: The proposition to change the time for opening and closing the sessions of Congress; the attempt to increase the term of Representatives to three years; the effort to fix a limit upon the number of Representatives, and the growing movement to confer the election of Senators upon the people.

All of these amendments are evidently intended to reform Congress and make it a more efficient body. All of these proposed changes, it would seem, are worthy of being adopted, with the possible exception of the election of Senators by popular vote, the advantage of which may be questioned.

---

[1] See post, pars. 147, 149.

CHAPTER III.

PROPOSED AMENDMENTS AFFECTING THE FORM OF THE GOVERNMENT: EXECUTIVE.

33. EXECUTIVE DEPARTMENT.

More amendments have been proposed to change the provisions of the Constitution in regard to the executive department than upon any other subject, there being some five hundred amendments that can be classified under this head. Of these, by far the greater portion were relative to the choice and term of the Executive. Of the eighteen amendments that passed one branch of Congress during the one hundred years since the inauguration of the Government, one-half have contained provisions either affecting the method of electing the President or in regard to the duration of the term, and two have been presented to change the date of Inauguration Day.[1]

34. PLURAL EXECUTIVE: ABOLITION OF THE PRESIDENCY OR VICE-PRESIDENCY.

Two propositions presented at the same time in the trying days just previous to the civil war suggested very radical changes in the Executive office. The first was a resolution introduced by Mr. Jenkins of Virginia, calling for the appointment of a committee to inquire as to what changes are necessary in the form of the government for the self-preservation of the slave States, and suggesting the following for consideration: A dual Executive,[2] the division of the Senate into two bodies, or making a majority of the Senate from the two sections necessary for all action, or the creation of another advisory body,

---

[1] House 1, 1802, May 1, election of President and Vice-President, App., No. 345; House 2, 1803, October 28, election of President and Vice-President, App., No. 359; Senate 3, 1813, February 17, election of President and Vice-President, App., No. 409; Senate 4, 1819, February 3, election of President and Vice-President, App., No. 485; Senate 5, 1820, January 27, election of President and Vice-President, App., No. 489; Senate 6, 1822, March 11, election of President and Vice-President, App., No. 506; Senate 7, 1824, January 30, President ineligible to third term, App., No. 535; Senate 8, 1826, April 3, President ineligible to third term, App., No. 545; Senate 9, 1869, February 9, election of President and Vice-President, App., No. 1308; Senate 10, 1886, June 18, date for Inauguration Day, App., No. 1676; Senate 11, 1887, December 13, date for Inauguration Day, App., No. 1691; the twelfth amendment declared part of Constitution, September 25, 1804, App., No. 358.

[2] Under certain circumstances the McDuffie proposition would have resulted in two Executives. Post par., 50, 3.

a council.[1] The other, presented by Mr. Noell of Missouri, was a resolution authorizing the select committee to take into consideration the propriety of abolishing the Presidency, by amendment to the Constitution, and in its place to establish an executive council of three, the members to be elected by districts composed of contiguous States, and for each member to be armed with the veto power.[2] Once since has a similar proposition been made. . This was in 1878, when Mr. Southard of Ohio introduced a resolution proposing an amendment making full provision for the creation of an executive council of three Presidents, for their election and administration of the executive power.[3] The members were to be selected respectively from each of the three "prominent sections" of the country, "known one as the Western States, one as the Eastern and Middle States, and the other as the Southern States." The term of office should be six years, but it should be so arranged that one member should retire every two years. A majority vote should decide all questions in regard to the administration of the office. The preamble of the resolution declared as the chief reason for the proposed change that "the people of this country are opposed to monarchy or the 'one man power,' created by the accumulation of regal power in the hands of one person in the control and direction of their public affairs in their present extended and complicated relations and interests."[4]

The Vice-Presidency, especially since the passage of the twelfth amendment, has proved to be a comparatively unimportant office, and less essential to the successful working of our system of government than a single Executive. It is not surprising, therefore, that there have been seven attempts to abolish the office. The first of these was made by the Federalists at the time of their opposition to the adoption of the twelfth

[1] App., No. 795. The New Jersey plan presented in the Convention of 1787, favored a plural Executive chosen and removable by Congress. The desirability of a privy council appointed by Congress was also urged. Elliot, v, 192. See also Mason's proposition, ibid., 522. Dual Executive advocated by Calhoun as essential to the protection of his section of the country. Works, i, 393–396.

[2] App., No. 804. Possibly suggested by the Swiss Federal Council, first established in the constitution of 1848, and retained in the revision of 1874. Hart's Fed. Govt., pp. 65–66. This was reviving a proposition of Williamson's in the Federal Convention for a triple Executive to be chosen from the North, Middle, and South. Elliot, v, 358–359.

[3] To be elected directly by the qualified voters of all the States, but the ratio of the vote of each State was to remain the same as under the existing system. App., No. 1465.

[4] Other sections of the proposed amendment provided that no person should be eligible for a second term; for the keeping of a journal of the proceedings of the council, a copy of which should be sent to Congress at the beginning of every regular session; for their compensation, etc.

amendment. Mr. Dana of Connecticut moved to strike out all that portion of the amendment relating to the Vice-Presidency, the object being, as he frankly said, to abolish the office of Vice-Presdent.[1] The Federalists claimed that if the proposed amendment was adopted it would render the continuance of the office of Vice-President useless, and that true reform required its abolition. The effect of the proposed change upon this office was foreseen by several, but by none more clearly than Roger Griswold. He warned Congress that "the man voted for as Vice-President will be selected without any decisive view to his qualification to administer the Government. The office will generally be carried into the market to be exchanged for the votes of some large States for President, and the only criterion which will be regarded as a qualification for the office of Vice-President will be the temporary influence of the candidate over the election of his State."[2] Too often subsequent events have justified Griswold's forebodings. Although his views were shared by Randolph and some other Democrats, the dilatory tactics of the Federalists had aroused the Democrats so that they would brook no delay, and the proposition was rejected by a vote of 27 to 85.

This proposition was presented for the second time by Senator Hillhouse, also a New England Federalist, in 1808, in connection with his other amendments, changing to a considerable degree the legislative and executive departments.[3] The remaining five were suggested by Andrew Johnson's career. The first of these was introduced by Senator Poland of Vermont, in 1867, and the others in the years immediately following by Messrs. Ashley and Sumner, who maintained that the Vice-Presidency was not only a "superfluous," but also a dangerous office.[4]

---

[1] App., No. 358, Annals of Congress, Eighth Congress, first session, pp. 671–682. Dana had questioned the need of a Vice-President, in 1802, at the time the change which was later made by twelfth amendment, was first suggested. Annals Seventh Congress, first session, p. 1290.

[2] Annals, Eighth Congress, first session, p. 751. Gouverneur Morris, Senator from New York, wrote a letter to the legislature explaining his vote against the amendment. In it he says: "The Vice-Presidency would hereafter be but a bait to catch State gudgeons." Life of Gouverneur Morris by Jared Sparks, Vol. III. p. 173. Among the propositions suggested by Pickering for the consideration of the Hartford convention was one "to restore the original mode of electing the President and Vice-President to prevent the election of a fool for the latter." Adams, New Eng. Fed., p. 408. See also Niles' Register, Vol. XXIV, p. 411.

[3] App., No. 394. Ante, par. 26, 30; post par. 47, 56, 59, 60.

[4] App., Nos. 1205, 1227a, 1283a, 1352, 1369. In 1875 Garfield declared himself in favor of the abolition of this office. Record, p. 757.

35. FILLING OF VACANCIES IN THE OFFICE OF PRESIDENT OR VICE-PRESIDENT: ADDITION OF VICE-PRESIDENTS.

In recent years attention has been called to the fact that during the first century of our history under the Constitution, in addition to the death of four Presidents in office, there has been "over one-fourth of the time when the country has had no Vice-President," and "in the last forty years of the period this office has been vacant nearly one-half of the time."[1] It is not strange, therefore, in view of the frequent vacancies in the office of Vice-President, and the dissatisfaction with the old law in regard to the Presidential succession, that several attempts have been made to provide for this contingency by an amendment to the Constitution. These have been of two kinds, the one providing for the immediate filling of the vacancy by a new election, the other by the creation of additional Vice-Presidents.

What appears to be the earliest proposition of the first class was suggested by Senator Davis of Kentucky, in 1864, in an amendment in regard to the election of President and Vice-President, which provided that any vacancy in the office should be filled by the Senate from their own number.[2] By the terms of the amendments offered by Messrs. Ashley and Sumner on the same subject, vacancies were to be filled by a joint convention of both Houses of Congress, in which each member was to have one vote.[3] The same suggestion was renewed by Mr. Cravens at a later period.[4] Other propositions have provided that the colleges of electors should continue in office for the Presidential term, with power, in case of vacancies in both of the executive offices, to reconvene and elect a person to fill the same for the residue of the term.[5]

The amendments of the second class provided for the election of additional Vice-Presidents. Five such propositions have been introduced, the first by Mr. Hammond of Georgia,

---

[1] House Report No. 2493, Forty-ninth Congress, first session. Twenty-five years eight months and four days; eighteen years five months and five days. Vacancies occasioned first by the death of Vice-Presidents: Clinton (1812), Gerry (1814), King (1853), Wilson (1875), and Hendricks (1885). Second by the succession to the Presidency of the following: Tyler (1841), Fillmore (1850), Johnson (1865), Arthur (1881). Third by the resignation of Calhoun (1832).

[2] App., No. 1039d. See post, par. 46.

[3] App., Nos. 1104a, 1227d, 1283e, 1352, 1368.

[4] App., Nos. 1441, 1538.

[5] App., Nos. 1247-1248, 1539. The former only provided for a new election in case there remained more than two years of the unexpired term.

in 1881. This resolution provided for the creation of the offices of First, Second, and Third Vice-Presidents. The incumbents of these offices were to be elected by the same method as is at present employed in the Presidential election, and in the case of a vacancy in the office of President or Vice-President it was to devolve upon the next officer in order of the rank of his office.[1] Two similar resolutions have since been proposed.[2]

At the time the " Presidential succession bill" was before the Forty-ninth Congress, in 1886, Mr. Dibble of South Carolina proposed to the House a constitutional amendment, creating and defining the office of Second Vice-President. In the absence of the Vice President from the Senate this officer might preside, and in case of a vacancy in the office of Vice-President he should succeed to the same.[3] This resolution, slightly amended, was reported from the Committee on Election of President and Vice-President. The report of the committee, which is of considerable interest, claimed that the necessity of an additional officer in the line of succession was apparent from the experience of the past, but it criticised the " Presidential succession act" "as but a makeshift," and particularly objectionable in that it practically enables the President to designate his successor in case of his death or resignation.[4] The resolution was not advanced to a vote, and although introduced in the succeeding Congress, it was not again reported,[5] as the new succession act had met with the general approval of the country.

36. QUALIFICATIONS OF THE EXECUTIVE.

The amendments which have been proposed to the provision of the Constitution prescribing the qualifications necessary for President, for convenience of treatment will be considered in the four following groups: (1) Amendments to make the terms of the Constitution more stringent as regards naturalized citizens. (2) Amendments to make either Senators and Representatives or all officeholders ineligible, incidentally increasing the

---

[1] App., No. 1535.

[2] App., No. 1619, 1667.

[3] App., No. 1660.

[4] House Report 2493, Forty-ninth Congress, first session. " When the President appoints his Cabinet he at the same time executes a political will and testament, disposing of his unexpired term in case he cease to be President."

[5] App. No. 1706.

age qualification. (3) Amendments to make secessionists ineligible. (4) Amendments to remove the restrictions against naturalized citizens resident a certain number of years.

(1) The State ratifying convention of New York, not satisfied with the provision of the Constitution which rendered a foreign-born person who was a citizen of the United States at the time of the adoption of this Constitution eligible to the Presidency, proposed that this article be so amended, "That no person, except natural-born citizens, or such as were citizens on or before the 4th day of July, 1776, or such as held commissions under the United States during the war and have at any time since the 4th day of July, 1776, become citizens of one or other of the United States, and who shall be a freeholder, shall be eligible to the places of President, Vice-President, or member of either House of the Congress of the United States."[1] This resolution was not introduced in the First Congress, but in (July) 1798, when the country was excited by the foreign complication, and the alien and sedition acts had just been passed, somewhat similar amendments were proposed in both the Senate and House by members from Massachusetts in response to a resolution passed by the Massachusetts and Connecticut legislatures.[2] The resolution proposed to render ineligible for the Presidency and to disqualify from service in Congress all but native-born citizens, or those resident in the United States at and since the Declaration of Independence. This was a Federalist affront to Gallatin, who had strongly opposed the alien and sedition act.[3] The Massachusetts and Connecticut resolutions further suggested as an alternative amendment, in case the above proposition should not be agreeable, the exclusion from these offices of all persons not naturalized at the passing of the amendment and all such as have not resided fourteen years in the United States previous to their election.[4]

(2) In addition to the resolution making a Senator or Representative ineligible to any civil office or appointment, treated elsewhere,[5] there were resolutions introduced which stipulated in specific terms that no member of either House should be eligible to the office of President or Vice-President. The one presented in 1846 continued the restriction for four years there-

[1] App., No. 50.
[2] App., Nos. 331, 333, 333b.
[3] Schouler, Vol. 1, p. 401.
[4] App., No. 333. Resolution tabled.
[5] Ante, par. 11.

after,[1] and one of two suggested in 1872 for two years thereafter.[2] Another resolution, more general in its provisions, but doubtless including Senators and Representatives among the class of persons restricted, was proposed in 1822.[3] By its provision any person holding any Government office at any time within four years next preceding the Presidential election was ineligible to the Presidency. This same resolution proposed increasing the age qualification from 35 to 45. In 1826 an amendment suggesting this same age qualification was introduced.[4]

(3) The amendments proposing the disqualification of secessionists were the same as those considered under the head of the Legislative department.[5]

(4) In the last of the "sixties" and the early "seventies," a movement was set on foot to enable naturalized citizens who had been fourteen years resident in the United States and fulfilled the qualifications as to age to become eligible to the Presidency. Four amendments proposing such a change in the Constitution were introduced during this time.[6]

37. CHOICE OF PRESIDENT AND VICE-PRESIDENT.

No question gave the framers of the Constitution so much trouble as the question of the method of the choice of the Executive.[7] The Convention, after vacillating between several plans, finally fell back upon the system of an indirect election through an electoral college.[8] This method of choosing the

---

[1] App., No. 746.

[2] App., Nos. 1347, 1351.

[3] App., No. 507. By Mr. Woodson of Kentucky.

[4] App., No. 561. In 1882 an amendment was proposed making Cabinet officers ineligible to the Presidency. App. No. 1551.

[5] Post, par. 128; ante, par. 11.

[6] App., Nos. 1226, 1332, 1337, 1358. One was reported adversely. The motion by Mr. Morgan of Ohio, the framer, to suspend the rules and pass the resolution was rejected in the case of each of the last two of these propositions.

[7] Wilson's remark in the Pennsylvania convention, Elliot, II, p. 511; Madison's letter of 1823; ibid., III, p. 332.

[8] Eleven different methods for selecting the Chief Executive were suggested: (1) By the National Legislature, by Ed. Randolph, Elliot's Debates, I, 144; V, 128. (2) By the State executives, Elbridge Gerry; ibid., I, 167; V, 174. (3) By the Congress constituted as under the Articles of Confederation, William Patterson; ibid., I, 176; V, 192. (4) By electors to be chosen by the people, Alexander Hamilton; ibid., I, 179; V, 205. (5) By electors to be chosen by the people of the several States, Gouverneur Morris; ibid., I, 262; V, 473. (6) By electors to be chosen by the people in districts, James Wilson; ibid., I, 156; V, 143. (7) By electors to be appointed by the State legislatures, Oliver Ellsworth; ibid., I, 211; V, 338. (8) By electors to be taken by lot from the National Legislature, James Wilson; ibid., I, 217; V, 362. (9) By the National Legislature, each State having one vote, Mr. Dayton, ibid., I, 262; V, 473. (10) By direct vote of the people, Mr. Carroll; ibid., I, 283; V, 472; Gouverneur Morris (by citizens); ibid., I, 208; V, 323. (11) By electors to be chosen for each

President was without doubt suggested by the system of electing Senators under the constitution of Maryland.[1] In that State "the Senators were selected by a body of electors chosen every five years by the inhabitants of the State for this particular purpose and occasion."[2] The principal considerations which led the members of the convention to favor this system was, on the one hand, their profound distrust of the people and their desire to preserve the relative influence of the States; and, on the other, their fear that if the election should be given to Congress the Executive might become dependent upon the legislative department.[3] Therefore, they determined to place the election in the hands of a small body of men "to be elected on account of their wisdom and character," who, it was expected, being entirely independent in their action of the people and the Congress, would exercise "discretion and discernment" in the choice of men "preeminent for ability and virtue."[4] No feature of the new instrument seems to have been contemplated by the framers with so much satisfaction and to have aroused so little opposition in the ratifying conventions as the article providing for the election of President and Vice-President.[5]

The system has not worked well in actual use, and no part of the Constitution has caused so much dissatisfaction and hence given rise to so many amendments to effect a change.[6] Although the letter of the instrument remains only slightly amended, in practice its spirit has been completely perverted from what was intended by its framers. The electoral colleges instead of being deliberative bodies are pledged in advance to vote for certain men, and hence have become mere agents, automata.[7] No better idea of the way in which an amendment is practically obtained, when it proves impossible to secure a

State in such manner as the legislature thereof may direct. From Committee August 31, 1787. Adopted. Several of the above were adopted, only to be reconsidered and defeated. That for the election by the two Houses of Congress was three times adopted, once unanimously, and as often reconsidered and rejected. See Atlantic Monthly, vol. 42, 543; No. Am. Rev., vol. 140, February, 1885; McKnight, The Electoral System of the United States, pp. 221-224; O'Neil, The American Electoral System, chap. XI.

[1] Constitution of Maryland (1776), Articles XIV-XVIII.

[2] J. H. Robinson, Original Features in the United States Constitution. Annals of Am. Acad., Vol. I, p. 229. Stevens, Sources of the Constitution, pp. 153-154. note.

[3] McKnight, pp. 30-33.

[4] Senator Morton's speech, Forty-third Congress, second session, Cong. Record, p. 627.

[5] "The Federalist," No. 67; also remarks of James Wilson and Chief Justice McKean in the Pennsylvania convention. Elliot, II, pp. 511, 542.

[6] Story, II, pp. 298-301.

[7] Morton's speech as above. Bryce, I, pp. 40-44.

constitutional amendment, can be gained than by examining the way this system of election has worked in actual practice. As a recent writer remarks:[1] "The legal processes of constitutional change are so slow and cumbrous that we have been constrained to adopt a serviceable framework of fiction which enables us easily to preserve the forms without laboriously obeying the spirit of the Constitution, which will stretch as the nation grows."

38. CHOICE OF PRESIDENTIAL ELECTORS: THE TWELFTH AMENDMENT.

For the first two elections the system of electing President and Vice-President worked smoothly, but by the time of the third election all was changed. Political parties had come into existence,[2] and Washington, who insisted upon retiring, was the only man who could command the united support of the entire nation. It at once became evident that a change was desirable, for the election of 1796 proved that by the existing method the will of the party in majority might be defeated by the elevation to the first position of the candidate who had been selected for the second place through the refusal of one elector to carry out the intention of the party. It also might prevent, as it did in this election, the President and the Vice-President from being of the same political party, inasmuch as some of the electors, fearing the result of a tie vote between their party candidates, threw away their votes for the second position, while thereby insuring the election of their candidate for the Presidency they permitted the opposition's candidate to secure the Vice-Presidency.

As early as January 9, 1797, even before the electoral vote was counted, Mr. Smith of South Carolina proposed a resolution declaring that the Constitution ought to be so amended that the Presidential electors be obliged in giving their votes to designate the person for whom they vote for President and Vice-President, respectively.[3] A very similar resolution was introduced in each of the three following years by as many different persons,[4] and the legislatures of Massachusetts and

---

[1] Woodrow Wilson, Congressional Government, p. 242.

[2] Even in 1789 tickets bearing names of electors were placed in the field, but by 1796 pledged lists of electors were common, and in Pennsylvania the beginning of the convention system was in operation. In 1800 Congressional caucuses to nominate candidates and thus forestall the action of the electoral colleges were first held. O'Neil, pp. 35, 46, 70.

[3] App., No. 328.

[4] App., Nos. 329, 334, 336.

Vermont favored this change.[1] No decisive action was taken—
a further trial of the old system was needed to show more fully
its dangers. The election of the year 1800 revealed anew the
inadequacy of the existing system. The dissatisfaction already
felt was greatly intensified by the critical experience of the tie
vote in this year. The legislatures of three States, Vermont,
New York, and North Carolina, presented resolutions to Congress early in the year 1802, proposing an amendment to the
Constitution in this particular.[2] In response to the desire of
the great body of the people, resolutions providing for this
change were immediately presented in both Houses.[3] In the
closing days of the session the House passed the amendment
by a vote of 47 yeas to 14 nays. The resolution was immediately brought to a vote in the Senate, but lacked one vote of
the necessary two-thirds, the vote standing 15 to 8.[4]

At the opening of the next session resolutions to change the
method of election were reintroduced, but were postponed
until the next Congress.[5] In the fall of 1803 the Vermont
legislature renewed their proposal, and Ohio instructed their
Representatives to favor the change.[6] A resolution was presented in the House on the first day of the session of the new
Congress, to which several amendments were proposed.[7] After
taking into consideration the different propositions, the select
committee reported a resolution to amend the method of
electing the Executive by requiring that the electors should
designate which votes they cast for President and which for
Vice-President. No change was to be made in the manner of
choosing the President in the eventual election, but the chance
of its occurrence was lessened.[8] This resolution, after several
unsuccessful attempts had been made to amend, passed the
House by a vote of 88 to 31. The Senate postponed its consideration, as meanwhile they had under discussion a resolution of their own, which had been introduced by Mr. Clinton
of New York. After various amendments to it had been

---

[1] App., Nos. 334a, 334b. Maryland also, during the winter of 1800-1801, passed resolutions proposing an amendment for the establishment of a uniform mode for the choice of
electors. App., No. 341a.

[2] App., Nos. 342, 344, 348, 351.

[3] App., Nos. 345, 352. The House proposition in its original form made provision also
for the choice of electors in districts. See post, par. 30.

[4] App., No. 345.

[5] App., No. 354.

[6] App., Nos. 360, 361.

[7] App., No. 356.

[8] The number of candidates sent to the House reduced from five to three. App., No. 359.

accepted, the Clinton resolution passed the Senate by the vote
22 yeas to 10 nays.[1]

Although all sections of the country, Republican and Federalist alike, had in previous years sought this change,[2] the
amendment now met with the systematic opposition of the
Federalists, who seemed determined either to defeat or muti-
late it. As soon as the Senate resolution came before the
House the Federalists raised the cry of unconstitutionality, on
the ground that the resolution had not received the vote of
two-thirds of the Senate, but only two-thirds of the Senators
present. The Republicans met this objection by appealing to
precedent in the case of some of the first ten amendments,
showing that two-thirds of the members present fulfilled the
constitutional requirement.[3] All their attempts to postpone
or to amend were in vain,[4] and even their appeal to State
rights was disregarded, for the House, on December 9, 1803,
concurred with the Senate by the exact constitutional majority—84 yeas to 42 nays, the vote of the Speaker being required
to make the necessary two-thirds majority.[5]

The amendment was sent to the States at a favorable time.
The Republicans were in the ascendency and Jefferson, who
was a candidate for reelection, was at the height of his popularity. The next Presidential election was approaching, and
the legislatures which assembled shortly after the submission
of the amendment took prompt action. Ten States shortly
ratified, and a proclamation of the Secretary of State, dated
September 25, 1804, declared the amendment in force.[6] The
legislatures of Massachusetts, Connecticut, and Delaware alone
rejected it.[7] "Each of these declared it unwise, impolitic, and
unconstitutional."[8]

[1] App., No. 358.
[2] See speech of Gregg of Pennsylvania, who showed that the measure was not a partisan one. Annals, p. 701.
[3] Annals of Congress, Eighth Congress, first session, pp. 648-653; post, par. 183.
[4] To abolish the Vice-Presidency, ante, par. 34; to prevent the Vice-President acting as
President in case of a failure to elect by the House, when the election devolved upon it;
to prevent reducing the number of candidates to be sent to the House. They claimed the
proposed change violated the spirit and design of the Constitution. O'Neil, p. 252.
[5] Only three Representatives from New England voted for it.
[6] See list after App., No. 358. McMaster, III, pp. 186-187.
[7] The New Hampshire legislature passed it, but the governor vetoed it. Post, par. 185.
[8] McMaster, III, p. 187. See also O'Neil, p. 95, for sectional address issued to the people of
Connecticut, which was in part as follows: "The plan of this amendment is to bury
New England in oblivion and put the reins of Government into the hands of Virginia
forever. They, the Democrats, have seized on a moment of delirious enthusiasm to make
a dangerous inroad on the Constitution and to prostrate the only mound capable of resist-
ing the headlong influence of the great States and preserving the independence and safety
of the small ones."

The twelfth amendment was a virtual recognition of the existence of political parties, and stimulated the growth of the system of the nomination of candidates and the pledging of electors, which had already made its appearance.[1]

39. CHOICE OF ELECTORS BY DISTRICTS.

The lack of uniformity in the choice of electors[2] early led to various attempts to secure an amendment to the Constitution prescribing a method which would be binding upon all. The mode most frequently suggested during the first quarter of this century was for the choice of Presidential electors by districts.[3] Some forty-two amendments of this character have been proposed. They naturally fall into two classes; the one providing that the States should be divided into as many districts as it was entitled to Senators and Representatives in Congress; the other for the choice of the electors in Congressional districts in each State, and the two remaining to be selected in some other way.

The first of these objects has been sought by thirty resolutions, introduced for the most part between 1800 and 1826.[4] The first proposition of this character was presented by Mr. Nicholas of Virginia, in 1800,[5] together with a resolution for the choice of Representatives by districts.[6] In 1802 the resolutions of the legislatures of Vermont, New York, and North Carolina, calling for the election of Presidential electors by districts, as well as the designation of the person voted for as

---

[1] For centralizing effect of amendment, see Adams, History of the United States, II, 132-133; Story, II, 302-304.

[2] See post, par. 40.

[3] In the election of 1796 six States employed the district system, viz: Massachusetts, Virginia, Kentucky, North Carolina, Maryland, and Tennessee (divided into three districts). O'Neil, p. 63. Wilson had suggested the plan in the Federal Convention, ante, p. 75, note 8. Gallatin favored the district system, letter to Jefferson September 14, 1801. Writings of Albert Gallatin (ed. by Henry Adams), I, p. 49. Hamilton also favored it, letter to Morris, April 6, 1802, Works VI, p. 556. Madison in a letter to George Hay of August 23, 1823, writes: "The district mode was mostly, if not exclusively, in view when the Constitution was framed and adopted." He shows advantage of the system and gave a "sketch" of an amendment which he drew up "for this faulty part of the Constitution in question." Works, III, pp. 332, 335. Jefferson seems also to have approved of it. McKnight, p. 387. See App., No. 77.

[4] The following introduced between 1800-1826: App., Nos. 338, 340, 345, 346, 350, 353, 355, 357, 373, 407, 409, 414, 450, 453, 455, 460, 463, 491, 532, 534, 537, 540, 555, 556, 738.

[5] Virginia had employed the district system in the three previous Presidential elections, but in 1800 by advice of Madison and Jefferson, who feared that their party might not secure all the electors, the change to the general-ticket system was made. O'Neil, p. 75. The Federalists in Massachusetts also changed from the district system to joint ballot by the legislature for the same purpose.

[6] Ante, par. 24.

President and Vice-President were presented to Congress. Such an amendment was favored by the leading men in both political parties.[1] Amendments proposing the district system were introduced in both branches of Congress. The resolution which passed the House in this session making provision for the designation of the persons voted for as President and Vice-President in its original form, also contained an article providing for the choice of electors by districts.[2] The resolution was divided so that the article establishing the district plan was not brought to a vote.

Owing to the great excitement which prevailed in North Carolina in consequence of the act of the legislature of that State in 1812, depriving the people of their traditional right to choose the electors, the Senators and Representatives from North Carolina were particularly zealous in advocating this amendment.[3] The circumstances attendant upon the choice of electors in Massachusetts and New Jersey in this same year also showed the desirability of a uniform system being prescribed. In the former State a deadlock between the two branches of the legislature had almost deprived the State of its vote, which loss was averted only by the calling an extra session of the legislature.[4] In the latter State, on the very eve of the election, the legislature, for partisan purposes, took the direct choice of electors to itself, depriving the voters of their expected suffrage.[5]

These events so aroused the Senate that the amendment proposed in 1813 by Senator Turner of North Carolina, upon the instruction of the new legislature of his State, passed that body by the vote of 22 to 9, but was not advanced to a vote in the House.[6] A similar amendment was repeatedly urged by Representatives from all sections of the country during the next few years.[7] In 1816 the legislature of Massa-

---

[1] Hamilton had favored this method in the Convention of 1787, and the passage of the resolutions by the New York legislature at this time were due to his efforts, ably seconded by De Witt Clinton. For attitude of Gallatin and Jefferson, see note 3 above.

[2] Ante, par. 38.

[3] App., Nos. 407, 414, 450, 455, 460, 463, 540. The action of the legislature was defended on the ground that large numbers of voters favorable to Madison had enlisted in the Army; that their absence might have made the State doubtful. O'Neil, 106; Niles' Register, IX, 349.

[4] McMaster, IV, 195; O'Neil, 104-105; Niles' Register, III, 128; IX, 349.

[5] McMaster, IV, 193-194; Stanwood, Presidential Elections, 61; O'Neil, 105-106; Niles' Register, III, 160.

[6] App., No. 409. See Niles' Register, III, 174-175.

[7] App., Nos. 414, 450, 453, 455, 460, 463, 491, 507 b, 532, 534, 537, 540, 555, 556.

chusetts added her indorsement of the district system to that of the States already referred to.[1] This was significant in view of her recent experience. The hostility to the Congressional caucus system of nominating candidates favored in this same year the passage of such an amendment, which was urged with renewed vigor by its champion, Mr. Pickens of North Carolina, but the support of two-thirds of the members of either branch of Congress could not now be secured.[2]

Some of the later amendments presented some peculiarities, one or two of which are worthy of mention. The one proposed by Mr. Livingston, in 1824, was extremely novel.[3] It provided that the voters meeting in their respective districts shall vote for one person to be President, another to be Vice-President, and the third to be an elector. The person having the greatest number of votes as President, Vice-President, and elector, respectively, shall be considered as entitled to the vote of such district for the said office. The electors to be called upon to serve only in case two persons have a majority of the whole number of district votes for President, in which event they shall assemble in their respective States and choose one of the two persons to be President.

The need of uniformity in the filling of vacancies in the electoral colleges was shown in the election of 1824.[4] This doubtless suggested the provisions of the amendment introduced by Mr. Saunders of North Carolina, in the following year.[5] It provided that when the electors assembled in their respective States, in case of the nonattendance of any elector, the electors present should fill the vacancies.[6] It further stipulated that the person having the greatest number of votes for President shall be President, if such number be one-third of the whole number.

---

[1] App., No. 453. Again, in 1819, App., No. 488a b. The Virginia legislature also approved of the North Carolina proposition in 1816. App., No. 451a. But the legislatures of Rhode Island, Connecticut, and Ohio disapproved. Massachusetts Archives, Misc. 8173–8183.

[2] App., Nos. 453, 460. Pickens's speech is quoted in part by McMaster, IV, 369–371. An editorial in Niles' Register (IX, 349) refers to this amendment, after the failure of Congress to consider it favorably, and says: "And we jog on in the old way, swindling and to swindle." The legislature of Illinois, in 1821, passed resolutions favoring an amendment for a uniform mode of electing President and Vice-President. App., No. 507b.

[3] App., No. 537.

[4] In that election vacancies in the college of electors had been supplied in New York by the electors present, in New Jersey by the governor, and in Virginia by the legislature.

[5] App., No. 540.

[6] This was done in Texas in 1872. Cong. Record, Forty-third Congress, second session, p. 627. Also in 1876 in Michigan, Oregon, Pennsylvania, Rhode Island and Vermont. Stanwood, pp. 340–342.

A group of seventeen additional resolutions made a distinct provision in regard to the choice of the two electors at large from each State, in addition to the electors chosen by districts.[1] These, with three exceptions, were introduced between the years 1817 and 1826. Senator Dickerson of New Jersey, in December of 1817, after laying before the Senate the proceedings of the legislature of his State in relation to amending the Constitution in regard to the election of President and Vice-President, introduced a resolution providing for its amendment in this particular, the two additional electors to be chosen as the legislatures of each State should direct.[2]

The legislature of North Carolina which, up to the previous session of Congress, had continued to advocate the other method of the division of State into electoral districts, now instruct their Senators to use their best endeavor to secure an amendment similar to the one proposed by Senator Dickerson.[3] The New Jersey resolution was not brought to a vote until March, when, although it received a good majority, it failed for the lack of the two-thirds vote of the Senate. To the resolution of these two States, at the next session of Congress, the legislatures of New York, New Hampshire, and Connecticut added the weight of their indorsement.[4] Again Senator Dickerson presented his resolution. This time the resolution was debated at much length, and three times referred to committees, and finally passed (28 to 10) the Senate February 3, 1819, but failed to be considered favorably by the House.[5]

Senator Dickerson continued to introduce this resolution in every session of Congress, with one exception, down to 1826, presenting it in all eight different times.[6] As he had been the first so he was the last to advocate its adoption at this period. This resolution passed the Senate twice afterwards, but each

---

[1] App., Nos. 468, 472, 482, 484. 485, 488, 489, 497, 500, 506, 519, 525, 529, 577, 869b, 1247, 1324.

[2] App., No. 468. The electors, when convened for the purpose of giving their votes, should have the power to fill such vacancies as there should be in their number. By act of 1845, "Each State may provide for the filling of any vacancy or vacancies which may occur in its college of electors, when such college meets to give its electoral vote." Rev. Stat. U. S., sec. 133. J. Q. Adams, while he refused to recommend any amendments to Congress while he was President, nevertheless favored the choice of the electors by districts, the two at large by the legislature of each State. But he would not change the contingency of its devolving upon the House of Representatives in case of no choice by the electors. "The House of Representatives was, of all others, the body peculiarly fitted for making the election." Memoirs, VII, p. 301. See post, par. 50.

[3] App., No. 472.

[4] App., Nos. 482, 484, 488.

[5] App., No. 485.

[6] App., Nos. 489, 500. 506, 519, 527, 577.

time it failed to be brought to a vote in the House.[1] This identical proposition was introduced by a Representative of South Carolina in the House in 1820 and secured a vote of 92 yeas to 54 nays, but this was short of the necessary two-thirds. The amendment never again came so near to success, for if it could have been pushed through the House it would have speedily received the indorsement of the Senate.[2]

An amendment, the first part of which was similar to that proposed by Senator Dickerson, was reported by the select committee of the House in 1823.[3] It differed, however, in many other details. The electors, besides filling vacancies in their number, were to appoint the two electors at large.[4]

Over thirty-five years later Mr. Douglas revived the proposition for the choice of electors by districts.[5] Two isolated propositions, introduced in the later "sixties," called up this plan for the last time. The first of these departed in certain features from the early plan in that only the States which were entitled to more than two Representatives were to be divided into districts, and only in such States shall two additional electors be appointed.[6] The second resolution conferred the choice of the two electors at large upon the voters of the State.[7]

40. CHOICE OF ELECTORS BY GENERAL TICKET IN EACH STATE.

The States have by the Constitution the right to choose electors as they prefer, except that Congress may fix the time of the election. As a result, in the early years a great variety of methods were in use, as, in the election of 1824, the electors were chosen in six of the States by the legislature,[8] in others

---

[1] In 1820 and 1822. App., Nos. 489, 506.

[2] App., No. 497. Ever afterwards the House refused to consider this amendment.

[3] App., No. 524.

[4] This method of choosing the two additional electors was employed in Maine and New York in 1828. Stanwood, p. 100; post, par. 40. Other clauses of this amendment made provision for case of no election, and division of the States into districts by Congress, if necessary. Post, pars. 50, 53.

[5] App., No. 869(1). The two electors at large to be chosen by the legislature in joint convention.

[6] App., Nos. 1247, 1248. A second election provided for in case no one received a majority of all the votes. If after the third election there is a tie, then it shall be decided by lot.

[7] App., No. 1324.

[8] Delaware, South Carolina, Vermont, New York, Georgia, Louisiana. It has been claimed that the election by the legislature of a State was a usurpation and "a departure from the Constitution." Report of Committee on Election of President, Forty-fifth Congress, second session, H. Rep., Vol. IV, No. 819. McDuffie, in a speech in 1825. For reference, see App., No. 542; but in McPherson v. Blacke (146 U. S., 1.) it was held that the power of the legislature to fix the method was complete. See also In re Green, 134 U. S., 377.

by districts, but in the larger number by general ticket.[1] The method of election was frequently changed, "according as the needs of the ruling party were best served." As indication of the need of a uniform system to prevent this political jugglery, Mr. Pickens cited, in a speech in 1816, "the disgraceful struggles which cost New York her electoral vote in 1789, and almost deprived Pennsylvania of hers in 1800 and Massachusetts of hers in 1812, and the sudden change of New Jersey on the very eve of an election" as "so many cases in point."[2]

As the general-ticket system was by the "twenties" in use in the majority of the States, an amendment adopting this practice seemed to be the one most likely to be successful; accordingly, Mr. Hooper of New Hampshire, in order to secure uniformity in the Presidential election, introduced, in 1828, a resolution declaring that the Constitution ought to be so amended that in each State the electors shall be chosen by a general ticket.[3] In the election of that year there was a very general change on the part of those States which had previously chosen electors through their legislatures to the popular system. The old method of choice by the legislature still obtained only in Delaware and South Carolina. In Maine and New York one elector was chosen for each Representative district, and the persons so chosen selected the two additional electors. Special electoral districts existed in Maryland and in Tennessee. The States which had repeatedly tried in vain for several years to secure the adoption of an amendment establishing the district system, especially Massachusetts, New Jersey, and North Carolina, went with the majority and adopted the system of election by general ticket, making eighteen States in all that employed this method.[4] In 1832 all but two States adopted the general-ticket system. South Carolina alone adhered to her old system of legislative appointment, which she

---

[1] Stanwood, p. 84; O'Neil, p. 122. For table of methods used by the States, see The Nation, vol. LII, p. 422; also reprinted in Hinsdale's Am. Govt. (2d ed.), p. 259. Six by district and twelve by the general-ticket system in 1824.

[2] Ante, par. 39; MacMaster, IV, 369-371; Stanwood, 15, 38, 39, 49, 60. Other cases, Massachusetts (1804). MacMaster, III, 187; Niles' Register, IX, 349. Massachusetts changed its method of choosing electors in every election between 1796 and 1820. In 1796, by district system; 1800, by legislature on joint ballot; 1804, by general ticket; 1808, by the legislature; 1812, electors chosen in the old common pleas circuits (district system); 1816, by the legislature; 1820, by districts; 1824, by districts, the two electors at large chosen by the voters of the entire State; 1828, by general ticket.

[3] App., No. 584. This had been suggested in the Constitutional Convention of 1787. Ante, par. 37.

[4] Stanwood's Presidential Elections, p. 100.

retained down to the civil war.[1] Maryland used the system of
electoral districts for the last time in 1832.[2] Thus, after 1832,
the method of choosing electors had become nearly uniform
throughout the country without the resort to an amendment
to the Constitution.[3] With but few exceptions, this system
has not been departed from, although a State legislature is
competent to establish any method it may choose.[4]

41. ELECTION OF THE PRESIDENT BY THE PEOPLE AS THE LEGISLATURE
OF THE STATES SHALL DIRECT.

The action of the States also took away the reason for another
group of amendments providing that the vote for President
and Vice-President shall be given in such manner as the legislature of each State may direct.

---

[1] South Carolina retained this system because the lower division of the State contained twice as many slaves but less number of free population than the upper. "The lower division was intrenched in the legislature." O'Neil, p. 126, note. See letter of Calhoun defending the practice, November, 1846. Works, vi, p. 257.

[2] Stanwood, pp. 110, 118.

[3] It is claimed that "the practical effect of the electoral system has been to increase the relative importance of the large States, and the practice of voting by general ticket was introduced by the large States for that purpose, and when introduced all were compelled to follow it." House Report, Vol. iv, No. 819, Forty-fifth Congress, second session. The large States were not the first to adopt the general-ticket system; in 1789 three States adopted it, viz, Pennsylvania, New Hampshire, and Maryland; of these only Pennsylvania could be reckoned as a large State. The number varied in nearly every election, but by 1816 five States used it, viz, New Jersey, New Hampshire, North Carolina, Rhode Island, and Ohio; of these only North Carolina could be reckoned as a large State, being sixth in population. The great change came in 1824, when twelve States seem to have adopted the system, viz, Pennsylvania, New Jersey, Connecticut, New Hampshire, Virginia, North Carolina, Rhode Island, Ohio, Indiana, Mississippi, Alabama, Missouri—the second, third, fourth, and fifth States in population and eight small ones. In a letter of August 23, 1823, Mr. Madison wrote: "The district mode was mostly, if not exclusively, in view when the Constitution was framed and adopted, and was exchanged for the general ticket and the legislative election as the only expedient for baffling the policy of the particular States which had set the example." Works, Vol. iii, pp. 332-333. Governor Carroll, in his message to the legislature of Tennessee, September 19, 1831, recommends the establishment of the general-ticket system of choosing electors, in order that the State may have its "full weight in the election for President and Vice-President hereafter." Am. An. Reg., Vol. vii, p. 273 (1831-32). From the above it is clear why the system became general.

[4] The following are the only cases of departure from the general-ticket system: The reconstructed State of Florida in 1868 and the newly admitted State of Colorado in 1876—there being insufficient time to provide for a general election—chose their electors through their legislatures. Stanwood, pp. 268, 328, 372. In 1892 the legislature of Michigan departed from the prevailing system and adopted the district system, one elector being chosen in each Congressional district, and for the choice of the two remaining electors the State was divided into two districts, each of which chose one of the electors at large. The constitutionality of this latter provision was questioned, but sustained by the Supreme Court of the United States in McPherson v. Blacke, 146 U. S., 1. The danger of other States following the example of Michigan led President Harrison in his annual message (December 9, 1891) to recommend that the permanency of the prevailing method should be secured by a constitutional amendment. Cong. Record, pp. 18, 19. This recommendation was not productive of results, but the next legislature of Michigan, being of a different political complexion from the legislature which had enacted the obnoxious law, repealed the same. See Bryce, i, p. 43.

The first of these amendments was proposed by Mr. Boon of Indiana, in 1826, and it provided that the vote shall be a direct vote, given as the legislature may prescribe.[1] Two others were presented in the House shortly after. One of these, offered by Mr. Hemphill of Pennsylvania, while still retaining the electoral college, provided that the people of the State should appoint, in such manner as the legislature should direct, the electors to which it was entitled,[2] thus insuring an election of the electors either by general ticket or by districts, and not by the legislature, as was still the practice in some of the States.

The other proposition, that of Mr. Livingston of Louisiana, was more explicit.[3] It stipulated that there should be a direct election by the people, either by district or general ticket, as the legislature of each State should direct; such mode not to be changed for a period of eight years, and in no case to be changed within three years of any Presidential election.[4]

42. ELECTION OF PRESIDENT AND VICE-PRESIDENT BY A GENERAL DIRECT VOTE.

Several of the amendments just discussed provide at the same time for some different method of electing the President in case there is no choice in the first election.[5] The same object was sought by another group of amendments intended to do away altogether with the machinery of electors. Thirty-seven propositions for the election of President by a general direct vote have been introduced, twelve of which fall in the period embraced by the years 1826 to 1837.[6]

In the election of 1824, Andrew Jackson, although he had somewhat the largest popular vote,[7] lacked an electoral majority, and was then defeated in the House of Representatives by a combination of the Clay and Adams men for Adams. This result caused general dissatisfaction with the prevailing system of election among Jackson's adherents. The fact that he

---

[1] App., No. 558.

[2] App., No. 561.

[3] App., No. 572. Mr. Livingston showed himself ready to further any scheme for the alteration of the existing method of electing President, for in 1824 he introduced one resolution to choose electors by districts (App., No. 537), and in 1826, besides the above, he proposed a general direct vote. App., Nos. 39, 42.

[4] Post, par. 50. To prevent such cases as cited in par. 40.

[5] Post, par. 50.

[6] App., Nos. 550, 554, 562, 568, 570, 572, 578, 583, 592, 623, 654, 669.

[7] For estimate of popular vote, see Stanwood, pp. 87-88, who estimates Adams's vote as one-third of the popular vote. Niles' Register, Vol. XLI, p. 444, claims that "the electoral vote obtained by Adams in 1824 represented a larger number of the people than the higher electoral vote of Jackson.'

had polled the largest popular vote, togther with his increasing popularity, suggested a method, the adoption of which would prevent the people's choice from being overruled, namely, a direct vote of the people, State lines being disregarded alto gether. Mr. McManus of New York first proposed this change in Congress January 4, 1826.[1] Within the next four years a similar amendment was introduced eight times in the House, two of these proposals coming from the legislatures of Ohio and Missouri.[2] In 1833 Senator Bibb of Kentucky called up the subject again, but the committee to which his resolution was referred reported as a substitute a proposition for the direct election of President by districts.[3]

Not until 1865 did the proposition again make its appearance. It was the first of a series of twenty-five resolutions of this character. Mr. Ashley and Senators Poland and Sumner were the most active in urging the adoption of this amendment during the early years of the second period of its popularity in Congress. Mr. Sumner advocated this change because the existing system was "artificial, cumbrous, radically defective, and unrepublican," and because, in common with Mr. Ashley, he expected that the proposed method would supersede the caucus or convention system of nominations.[4] There is little reason, however, to suppose that the adoption of this system would do away with the nominating convention. The greater number of these propositions required a majority of the popular vote to secure the election. In case no person received a majority twelve proposed a second election by the people,[5] while four others provided for the final choice by one or both branches of Congress.[6] Several others provided that a plurality of votes only

---

[1] App., No. 550.

[2] App., Nos. 554, 558. 562, 568, 578. 592, 601a. For peculiar provision of the Ohio resolution for the choice of electors to act only in case of no person receiving a majority, see post, par. 50; App., Nos. 578, 592.

[3] App., Nos. 628–630; post, par. 43. For resolutions from the legislature of Indiana approving a change in the method of election presented in 1837, and also suggesting a uniform series of three days for the election in all the States. App., No. 669. see post, par. 52. Some, as No. 554, provided that a plurality of votes should elect.

[4] The preamble to the resolution, App., No. 1352, declared: "The caucus or convention, after being the engine for nomination of President, allowing the people little more than to record its will, becomes the personal instrument of the President when elected, giving him a dictatorial power, which he may employ in reducing the people to conformity with his purposes and promoting his reelection, all of which is hostile to good government and of evil example," etc. See also Ashley's speech, App., No. 1227b; Orations and Speeches by J. M. Ashley, pp. 774, and following pages.

[5] App., Nos. 1104. 1127b, 1283c, 1352, 1368, 1389, 1464, 1505. 1536, 1626, 1668. 1695; post, par. 50.

[6] By joint convention of both Houses of Congress, App., Nos. 1078, 1314; by the House of Representatives, App., Nos. 1354, 1361.

should be necessary to elect, but in case of a tie Congress should decide.[1] One of these proposed that the person having the highest number of votes should be President and the person having the next highest should be Vice-President, proba bly in the hope of restoring the original respect and regard for the latter office.[2] The greater number of these resolutions were introduced in the period from 1872 to 1878, and the majority were presented by members from Western States.[3]

43. ELECTION OF PRESIDENT AND VICE-PRESIDENT DIRECTLY BY DISTRICTS.

A group of thirty-two resolutions, which also proposed conferring the choice of President directly upon the people, were designed to establish the district system.[4] These were similar to the propositions which had been introduced in the first quarter of the century, already discussed,[5] save that they did away with the electors. The first of these was introduced in 1823 by Senator Benton. From this time to the election of General Jackson, in 1828, this proposition was urged in every Congress.[6] Among these were three sets of resolutions in favor of the proposed change, from Tennessee, the General's State, while counter resolutions were received from other States.[7] In 1826 a resolution proposing this change was reported favorably by a select committee of the Senate through their chairman, Mr. Benton.[8] It was given extended consideration, but was not brought to a vote.[9] The House spent six weeks of this session in debating McDuffie's resolution, which declared that the Constitution ought to be so amended that a uniform system of voting directly for President, by districts, should be established in all the States, and so altered as to prevent the election devolving upon Congress. The two parts of the

---

[1] App., No. 1058; see post. par. 50. Four provided for the decision of the tie for President by the House, for the Vice-President by the Senate, each member to have one vote, Nos. 1408, 1420, 1443, 1446; two that the tie for either office should be decided by the House, Nos. 1359, 1367.

[2] App., No. 1731.

[3] Mr. Towshend. of Illinois, has introduced this amendment in every Congress since 1880. During the same period only one other member has proposed its adoption.

[4] App., Nos. 526, 541. 541a. 542. 544a. 547, 548, 552, 581a, 582, 600a, 601, 602, 610. 626, 627, 630, 631, 632, 641, 646, 656, 659, 672, 739, 765, 770, 773, 813, 1228, 1240, 1519.

[5] Ante, par. 39.

[6] McDuffie of South Carolina proposed it three times. App., Nos. 541, 542, 582.

[7] App., Nos. 541a, 548, 581a. Counter resolutions from Ohio and Indiana. Niles' Register, XXIX, pp. 125. 369. Maine, Massachusetts Archives, Nos. *17*4, *1*1*.

[8] App., No. 552.

[9] Mr. Dickerson proposed his plan as an amendment thereto. Ante. par. 39.

resolution were voted upon separately, the House recording itself against the district system by a vote of 90 yeas to 102 nays, but agreed to the second portion of the resolution.[1]

President Jackson, in each of his annual messages, strongly recommended that the Constitution be so amended, first, that the people should vote for the President and Vice-President directly; "for", said he, "in proportion as agents to execute the will of the people are multiplied there is danger of their wishes being frustrated; some may be unfaithful, all are liable to err;"[2] and, second, as to prevent the election of President devolving upon the House of Representatives, arguing that if the different departments of the Government were to be kept distinct, that the choice of the Executive by either branch of the legislative department must be discontinued or the Executive would become the creature of the legislative department.[3]

Although the President did not designate the specific method by which the direct vote should be given, yet it is known that he favored the amendment championed by his friend and supporter, Senator Benton. Mr. Benton changed the terms of the amendment which he had earlier introduced, to harmonize with President Jackson's views.[4] The first resolution proposed by him retained the provision that in case of no choice the election should devolve upon the House of Representatives, but the amendments presented by him after the election of Jackson stipulated that in the event of no election there should be a second election by the people between the two persons having the highest number of votes.[5] Senator Benton remained true to the pledge he made in 1824,[6] and continued to present this same resolution at different times down to 1844.

In the Twenty-third and Twenty-fourth Congresses select committees reported resolutions containing this provision.[7] In the course of the debate during the Twenty-third Congress, Mr. Benton declared that "the district system would break

---

[1] App., No. 542. See post, par. 50. The speeches of Benton, Dickerson, and McDuffie are all valuable as throwing much light on the workings of the existing system.

[2] First Annual Message, App., No. 596.

[3] App., Nos. 598, 602, 606, 610, 626, 631, 656, 659. For Madison's opinion, see Works, III, p. 332. For opposite view, held by J. Q. Adams, see Memoirs, VII, p. 301. Post, par. 50.

[4] App., No. 526.

[5] See post, par. 50.

[6] He said: "He would pledge himself to the Senate and to the American people to continue the subject with all the energy he was master of till he brought it to a conclusion." Gales & Seaton's Debates, p. 693.

[7] App., Nos. 630, 656.

the force of the large States;" but the amendment was opposed by John Tyler and other strong State Rights men because, as Tyler said, "it obliterated all State boundaries and dictated a course of action as if we were a nation and not a compact of States." They desired "to preserve the federative principle in the Constitution."[1]   In spite of the efforts of President Jackson and Senator Benton, the amendment was never brought to a vote.

This proposition was not suggested again until the early "fifties," when Andrew Johnson, then a member of the House from Tennessee, introduced a resolution similar to that of Mr. Benton's, in two different Congresses.[2]   At the next succeeding Congress, Mr. Ewing of Kentucky proposed the same amendment.[3]   The resolution received considerable discussion in this Congress.   In support of the measure, Mr. Ewing said, that "it had been advocated for a period of thirty years by such men as Benton, Van Buren, Dickerson, McDuffie, Hayne, Macon, R. M. Johnson of Kentucky, and recommended time and again by General Jackson, and opposed chiefly by Rufus King of New York."[4]

In 1860, while a member of the Senate, Andrew Johnson again proposed this method of election, adding to the measure as a sop to the slave-holding States, in addition to the proposition to divide the judiciary equally between the slave and free States, the section that in the elections of 1864 the President should be chosen from one of the slave-holding States and the Vice-President from one of the free States, in 1868 vice versa, and so alternating the President and Vice-President every four years between the slave and free States during the continuance of the Government.[5]

Andrew Johnson evidently was convinced of the desirability of the election by the direct vote of the people, given in districts, for in 1868, when President, he sent a special message to Congress, proposing, together with other changes in regard to the Executive, such an amendment, and at the opening of the next session of the Congress, in his annual message he renewed his previous recommendation.[6]   This amendment was proposed the last time in 1881 by Mr. Wallace of Pennsylvania.

---

[1] Niles' Register, vol. XLVI, 421.   Van Buren favored the district system, O'Neil, p. 253.
[2] App., Nos. 705, 770.
[3] App., No. 773.
[4] Cong. Globe, Thirty-third Congress, first session, p. 283.
[5] App., No. 813.
[6] App., Nos. 1228, 1240.

One interesting provision of this resolution was that the vote should be by secret ballot, thus foreshadowing the desirability of methods now in use in the majority of the States.[1]

44. ELECTION OF PRESIDENT AND VICE-PRESIDENT DIRECTLY BY A COMBINATION OF DISTRICTS AND VOTES AT LARGE.

Corresponding to the amendments proposed in an earlier period by Senator Dickerson and others, for the choice of the electors in districts, there were introduced during the early "seventies," in both the House and Senate, propositions of a somewhat similar nature save that the electoral colleges were to disappear.[2] Senator Oliver P. Morton of Indiana, who was at this time the most earnest and zealous advocate of the necessity of a change, called up the question through a resolution which he offered in March, 1873. It directed the Committee on Privileges and Elections, of which he was chairman, "to examine and report at the next session upon the best and most practical mode of electing the President and Vice-President, and providing a tribunal to adjust and decide all contested questions connected therewith."[3] The committee, in May, 1874, reported, presenting a proposition, in seven articles, as an amendment to the Constitution.[4] It provided that the people should vote directly for the President, each State being divided into districts equal to the number of Representatives to which it should be entitled. The person having the highest number of votes in each district for President should receive the vote of that district, which should count as one Presidential vote. The person receiving the highest number of votes in the State should receive two Presidential votes from the State at large. The candidate receiving the highest number of Presidential votes in the United States should be President. In case two persons have the same number of votes in any State, it being the highest number, they should receive each one Presidential vote from the State at large.[5]

Additional sections of the same article made provision for applying the foregoing provisions to the election of Vice-

---

[1] App., No. 1519.

[2] Ante, par. 39.   (1817–1826.)

[3] Cong. Record, Forty-third Congress, special session, p. 30.

[4] App., No. 1393. The report of the committee which accompanied the amendment was one of great ability. It was the work of Mr. Morton. Senate Reports, Forty-third Congress, first session, Vol. II, No. 395.

[5] If more than two, then no Presidential vote shall be counted from the State at large. If more than one receive the same number of votes in a district, it being the highest, no Presidential vote shall be counted for the district.

President, for conferring upon Congress the power to conduct
such election, when it choose to do so, to alter the division of
the State into districts, and to establish tribunals for the
decision of such election as may be contested.[1]

The resolution was not brought up for consideration by the
Senate until the following January, when it called out an important debate, Senators Morton and Anthony delivering long
and valuable speeches. Senator Morton's address especially
was a clear exposition of the working of the electoral system
up to that date.[2] It is worthy of note that he accurately fore-
cast the contested election of 1876. In opening his remarks
he declared it as his conviction that " no more important question can be considered by the Senate at this session of Congress, for, in my opinion, great dangers impend, owing to the
imperfection of the present system of electing the President
and Vice-President[3]." In support of the district system, he
quoted the figures from the report of the committee, which
showed that in the eight Presidential elections between the
years 1844 and 1872 four of the Presidents had received less
than a majority of the popular vote,[4] while during the same time
the district system, as shown by the Congressional elections,
approached more nearly by one-third to the whole popular vote
than the election by the present method. Two votes by the
proposed system were to be given by the State at large, in
order that "the autonomy and power of the small States "
might be preserved.

In the meantime a very similar resolution was reported to
the House by the Committee on Elections, which awakened
considerable interest,[5] but neither in the House or the Senate
was the proposition brought to a vote, the general opinion being
that the greatest danger lay in the matter of the electoral
count. Senator Morton introduced the same amendment in the
next Congress, but no action was taken beyond its reference.[6]

---

[1] Post, pars, 53, 54.

[2] Cong. Record, Forty-third Congress, second session, pp. 627-634. Senator Anthony
declared " all the machinery of the existing system is absurd." Senators Thurman and
Conkling also spoke agreeing that some change was necessary

[3] See also report of the committee as given on previous page.

[4] Polk, 1844, 50 per cent; Taylor, 1848, 47 per cent; Buchanan 1856, 45 per cent; Lincoln,
1860, 40 per cent. Ibid., also report of committee. For a table showing the difference
between the popular and electoral vote in all elections from 1832 to 1876, see House Reports, Forty-sixth Congress, first session, Vol. II, No. 347.

[5] App., No 1386. In lieu of the section conferring upon Congress power to create tri-
bunals to decide contested elections, was one making it the duty of the Supreme Court.
Post, pars. 54, 70. It was recommitted and again reported with Mr. Smith's substitute.
No 1393, post, par. 45.

[6] App., No. 1431. For criticism of the district system, see post, par. 51.

45. ELECTION OF PRESIDENT BY A DIRECT VOTE BY STATES.

In the Continental Congress and its successor, the Congress of the Confederation, all officers had been chosen by a vote by States. A similar principle was recognized in the Constitution, which provided in the electoral system that each State should have two votes, corresponding to the number of Senators, besides one for each Representative in Congress; and in case of no choice by the electors, the election should devolve upon the House of Representatives, the vote being taken by States, "the representation from each State having one vote."[1] Thirty-five propositions retaining this federative principle of the Constitution proposed that the President and Vice-President should be elected by a direct vote of the qualified voters, given by States. While doing away with the electoral colleges, the electoral ratio or votes of the States were to be retained. Such propositions were brought forward at two different periods, the first between the years 1826 and 1848, the second since 1875. In their general characteristics they fall naturally into two groups, corresponding very nearly to the periods just mentioned; the one providing that the persons receiving the greatest number of votes in a State should be declared to have received the entire vote of the State;[2] the other that the Presidential vote of each State should be divided among the candidates in proportion to the popular vote received by them in the State.

The earliest of the resolutions of the first group was presented by Mr. Haynes of Georgia, in 1826.[3] Eleven similar resolutions were proposed at different times within the next twenty years, the greater number, indeed, within the next ten.[4] Three of these resolutions, from the general assembly of Georgia and the legislatures of Alabama and Missouri, are interesting as showing with what jealous care the sovereignty and equality of the State was guarded.[5] The general assembly of Georgia declared their concurrence with the legislature of Missouri[6] in the proposal to amend the Constitution so as to

---

[1] Constitution, art. 2, sec. 1, cls. 2 and 3, as originally adopted, retained in article XII of the amendments.

[2] A number of votes equal to the number of Senators and Representatives to which the State was entitled in Congress.

[3] App., No. 559.

[4] App., Nos. 560, 583, 594ª, 600, 609, 641, 661, 663, 683, 735, 741.

[5] App., Nos. 583, 600.

[6] Ante, par. 42, App., No. 601a.

provide a uniform mode of electing President and Vice-President by the direct vote of the people, "provided such alterations can be so made that the sovereignty of the States be not invaded and the weight of the States and the present basis of representation be retained according to existing conditions of the Constitution."[1]   The Alabama and Missouri resolutions were very similar.[2]

The only essential difference between the amendments of this group was the provision for the method to be employed for the choice of President in case no one received a majority of the vote of all the States.[3]

This amendment, so frequently urged at this time, was not again presented until 1878, when it was revived by Mr. Sampson of Iowa.[4]   The same proposition has been introduced once since, in 1886.[5]

The amendments of the second group, providing for the division of the electoral or Presidential vote of the State, were for the most part introduced since 1875.   They were preceded by two isolated propositions which foreshadowed the terms of the amendment of the later period.   The first of these was presented by Mr. Lawrence of New York, in 1848.[6]   His plan proposed that the number of votes given to each person shall be estimated as such a proportion of the vote of the State[7] as the said vote shall bear to the whole number of votes given within the State for President.   "Any person receiving a majority of all the votes so estimated, given in all the States for President, shall be President."   By this method it is seen that the relative weight of each State is retained, and yet provision is made that the minority vote given in each State shall be counted.   To Mr. Lawrence should be given the credit of having been the first to suggest in Congress a system of proportional voting.

---

[1] Similar resolutions were introduced in the legislature of Maryland, Niles' Register, XXXVII, 428.   The legislature of Vermont nonconcurred with the Georgia resolution, Am. An. Reg., VI, 322.   The Georgia resolutions further declared it desirable to amend so that in no case shall the election devolve upon the House of Representatives if provision is made for securing to the States an equal vote in such decisions in the last resort.   App., No. 600

[2] App., Nos. 583, 594a.   The legislatures of Connecticut and Vermont disapproved of the Missouri amendment.   Massachusetts Archives, Nos. 99, 99.

[3] Post, par. 50, especially Mr. McComas's amendment, No. 661.

[4] App., No. 1467, in case of a tie in a State the vote to be equally divided.

[5] App., No. 1672.

[6] App., No. 754.

[7] Which was to be equal to the number of Senators and Representatives of said State in Congress.

Over twenty years later Mr. Ashley of Ohio, who was very zealous in his attempts to secure a new method of electing the President,[1] renewed the suggestion of a proportional division of the vote of each State among the different parties, but, curiously enough, his plan retained the colleges of electors.[2] With the renewal of the discussion of the desirability of changing the method of electing the President in 1874–75, the first of twenty resolutions suggesting anew the adoption of a system of a proportional division of the electoral vote of a State among the various candidates was presented.[3] It was introduced by Mr. Smith of New York as substitute for the amendment reported by the House Committee on Elections, which proposed the district system.[4] Mr. Smith's substitute was designed to meet the objection urged against a popular vote regardless of State lines, for it still proposed to leave to the States their weight of influence by an ingenious but complicated system of computing the votes.[5] This plan, Mr. Smith said in proposing it, he framed "for the purpose of obviating the danger and difficulty of a large accumulation of contested-election cases in the electoral districts proposed by the plan of the Committee on Elections, and to prevent the gerrymandering of States by partisan majorities in the construction of election districts, and to dispense with the cumbersome machinery of electoral districts, while preserving the autonomy of the States in the election of President and Vice-President.[6]

The next resolutions were suggested by the contested election of 1876. They were presented by Messrs. Maish, Springer,

---

[1] For other methods proposed by him, see ante, par. 42. From the variety of propositions he introduced he was known as "the suggesting member."

[2] The voters were to vote by ballot for President and Vice-President. Then the legislature of each State was to divide the total number of votes cast by the number of Senators and Representatives to which such State was entitled in Congress, and the product shall be the ratio of one elector. The legislature was then to appoint the electors, "taking care to secure to each candidate voted for in the State an equitable representation in the electoral college, as indicated by the number of votes returned for each candidate.' The electors thus appointed were to vote for one of the candidates named for President and Vice-President, respectively, by the voters at the general election. App. No. 1283f.

[3] App., Nos. 1386, 1437, 1438, 1439, 1441, 1475, 1493, 1503, 1508, 1537, 1538, 1542, 1569, 1589, 1624, 1639, 1640, 1697, 1705, 1735. It was generally supposed to be an entirely new plan.

[4] Ante, par. 44. App., No. 1386.

[5] It required that the aggregate vote for President in each State shall be divided by the number of Representatives apportioned to such State in the House of Representatives and twice the result or quotient shall be added to the vote of the candidate having the highest number of the popular vote in such State for President as, and for the State vote for, such candidate. The person having the highest number of votes in all the States, including the popular vote and the State vote, shall be President.

[6] Cong. Record, Forty-third Congress, second session, pp. 748–749.

and Cravens, in 1877, and were based on the same general principle as the preceding proposition, but differed as to the method
employed in computing the vote. Mr. Maish's plan provided
that the electoral vote of each State should be distributed
among the candidates in the proportion the electoral ratio
shall bear to the popular vote of each candidate.[1] The electoral ratio was the quotient obtained by dividing the whole
number of votes returned by the whole number of the State's
electoral vote. Mr. Maish's resolution has been introduced
four times since, twice by himself and twice by Mr. Beltzhoover, also from Pennsylvania.[2]

Mr. Springer's resolution proposed a like distribution among
the candidates of the electoral vote of the State, the candidate
having the largest fraction should have the odd Presidential
votes, if any remain, each State should be entitled to as many
votes as it had Senators and Representatives in Congress,
except that States having but one member of the House of
Representatives should be entitled to but two votes, and States
having but two members of the House of Representatives
should be entitled to but three votes in the election of President
and Vice-President.[3] Mr. Springer has introduced a resolution
proposing this amendment in every Congress since 1882, the
text of the proposed amendment being similar to the one first
submitted by him, save the provision for reducing the number
of electoral votes of the small States does not appear.[4]

Mr. Cravens's device for ascertaining the Presidential vote to
which each person voted for in any State was entitled, was to
multiply the whole number of votes of the qualified electors in
the State for such person by the number of Presidential votes
to which the State was entitled and divide the sum so obtained
by the aggregate votes of the qualified electors of the State
for all persons for President, using for that purpose not exceeding three decimal fractions.[5] Resolutions proposing a similar
method of computing the votes have been introduced eight
times since.[6] Two of these were reported favorably by the

---

[1] App., No. 1437.
[2] App., Nos. 1438, 1503, 1542, 1705; also introduced in the Fifty-first Congress by Mr.
Maish.
[3] App., No. 1439.
[4] App., Nos. 1569, 1624, 1640, 1735.   No. 1569 contains this provision; the others do not.
[5] The fractional part of a Presidential vote remaining shall be added to the Presidential
vote of the person receiving the highest number of votes in the State.   App., No. 1441.
[6] App., Nos. 1475, 1493, 1508, 1537, 1538, 1589, 1639, 1697.   All applied the foregoing provisions to the election of Vice-President.

Select Committee of the House of Representatives on the Election of President and Vice-President in 1878, and again in 1880.[1] Since 1881 Mr. Browne of Indiana has proposed this amendment in each Congress. All of these amendments were presented in the House, but none were ever brought to a vote. Some provided that the person having the highest number of votes should be President;[2] others that if no person had a majority the joint convention of the Senate and House should choose the President from the two highest on the list.[3]

Doubtless there is too much mathematics in some of these plans to make them popular,[4] but the simpler method of computing the vote proposed by Messrs. Maish and Springer might easily be understood. Some such application of the system of proportional representation to the election of President and Vice-President seems not only practicable, but peculiarly just and equitable, inasmuch as it not only preserves the weight of each State, but also gives a proportional part of the electoral vote to the minority candidate in each State.[5]

46. ELECTION FROM CANDIDATES DESIGNATED BY THE STATES.

Previous to the campaign preparatory to the Presidential election of 1832, the candidates for President had been nominated either by a caucus composed of the members of one party in Congress, or by the legislatures of the States, or even by certain counties in a State. Such nominations were far from carrying the weight possessed by the modern convention—the voice of a powerful party organization.

The practice of nominating by party convention was first inaugurated in the campaign for the election of President in 1832. In 1830 the first political national convention of delegates representing the people was held by the Anti-Masonic party.[6] The following year the same party inaugurated the practice of holding a national nominating convention, which

---

[1] App., Nos. 1475, 1508. Able and interesting reports: 1878. H. Rep., Forty-fifth Congress, second session, Vol. IV. No. 819. It contains a table applying the proposed system to the vote given in 1876 for President. The minority report appealed to the spirit of State rights to defeat the measure, fearing interference by the Federal Government in the States on the ground of intimidation. 1880, H. Rep., Forty-sixth Congress, second session, Vol. II, No. 347.

[2] As App., Nos. 1475, 1493, 1508. These made provisions for a tie to be settled as at present.

[3] As App., Nos. 1441, 1538.

[4] The method proposed by the Cravens plan is doubtless the most accurate, but correspondingly complicated.

[5] For further discussion of proportional plan, see post. par. 51, and note.

[6] Stanwood, p. 104-109.

practice was immediately adopted by the National Republican and the Democratic parties.[1] Thus was established our present system of nominating by party conventions.

However, there was one member of Congress at least who did not look with favor upon this method of nomination. Mr. Underwood of Kentucky, in 1838, and again in 1842, in connection with other amendments introduced by him, proposed a new method for the nomination and election of President and Vice-President.[2] It provided that the State legislatures, by a joint vote of each house, should, in behalf of their respective States, nominate candidates for the Presidency and Vice-Presidency, respectively. The governors of the States having reported the nominations to the President, he should publish the same by proclamation. The citizens should vote directly for one person so nominated for each office. The results of the votes given in the respective States should be forwarded to the President. Congress should canvass the votes. The person receiving a majority of all the votes should be declared elected. If no person received a majority, then both Houses of Congress in joint session should choose a President or Vice-President from among those nominated for that office. The votes should be given viva voce, each member having one vote, and a majority of the votes given should decide.[3]

The only other resolution which proposed the nomination of candidates by the States was introduced by Senator Davis, also of Kentucky, in 1862, and on three subsequent occasions. These proposed amendments are perhaps as curious as any which have been presented during the century. By the terms of the original resolution any State might, within thirty days before the time for the election of President, in any mode adopted by the State, nominate to Congress one candidate; and from the candidates so nominated by the States the two Houses of Congress, meeting together as a convention, should choose one as President of the United States. The unanimous vote of all members elected to both Houses was necessary for the election of the President. This was to be secured by the dropping of the candidates having the least number of votes after a stated time had been spent in balloting. In the same manner the

---

[1] Ibid. The Democratic convention was called to decide upon a candidate for Vice-President, as the party was united for the reelection of Jackson.

[2] App., Nos. 679, 724.

[3] In case a State should fail to nominate in the required manner or report the nomination made or the votes given in the manner and time required, the election shall be made without regard to such failure, and shall be valid.

Vice-President was to be elected from the remaining candidates. In case of no choice by the convention, the decision was to be referred to the Supreme Court.[1] The same proposition was again made by Mr. Davis early in the following year.[2] In December of 1864 Mr. Davis presented a long series of amendments which he desired should be submitted to a convention which should be called for the purpose of revising the Constitution. One of these proposed the same method of choice, changed in several particulars.[3] The first section of the resolution contained in a modified form the suggestion he had made earlier in this same year for the consolidation of certain of the Eastern States into three States "for Federal and national purposes only."[4] Provision was made that the President and Vice-President were to be taken alternately from the free and the slave States; that each State was to select one of its own citizens for either the Presidency or the Vice-Presidency, according as it was free or slave and as the free or slave States were entitled to the office. From the candidates so nominated the Supreme Court was to choose the President and Vice-President. In 1867 Mr. Davis proposed this method of nomination by the States for the last time, in a resolution similar to the one originally introduced by him nearly five years before, save that only a majority of the votes of the whole number of members of both Houses was by this proposition necessary to elect.[5]

47. ELECTION OF PRESIDENT BY LOT.

Among the many curious amendments proposed for the election of President, perhaps the most unique are three suggestions for the choice of the Executive by lot.[6] The first of these was introduced by Mr. Hillhouse, a Federalist Senator from Connecticut, in 1808, as one of the remarkable series of amendments presented by him at this time, for the preservation of the country from the evils engendered by the growth of parties

---

[1] App., No. 978.

[2] App., No. 980.

[3] App., Nos. 1039b-d.

[4] See post, par. 122., App., Nos. 987, 989. The earlier proposition had dealt only with New England. This proposed that Maine, New Hampshire, and Vermont should form one State; Massachusetts, Connecticut, and Rhode Island another, and Maryland, Delaware, and the Eastern Shore of Virginia a third.

[5] App., No. 1207.

[6] The plan for selecting electors by lot from the National Legislature was suggested by Wilson in the Federal Convention. Elliot's Debates, v, 362. Ante, par. 37, p. 75, note 8.

and party spirit.[1] This amendment provided that the Senators should hold their office for three years, and one-third retire annually. From the retiring Senators, one should be chosen by lot as President for the ensuing year, in the following manner: Each of these Senators should, in alphabetical order, draw a ball out of the box, one of which was colored; the Senator drawing the colored ball should be President.[2] In his speech in support of these amendments, Senator Hillhouse declared that his experience in Congress for seventeen years had convinced him that some such change as he proposed was necessary for the perpetuity of the Government. "I should not have proposed this mode," said he, "if any other could have been devised which would not convulse the whole body politic, set wide open the door to intrigue and cabal, and bring upon the nation incalculable evils, evils already felt, and growing more and more serious."[3] No action was taken by Congress upon these propositions,[4] but some twenty years later Hillhouse revived an agitation in favor of his plan outside of Congress, receiving letters favoring it from Chief Justice Marshall and William H. Crawford, but John Quincy Adams probably reflected the prevailing opinion when he wrote in his diary "a serious discussion of his amendments would be ridiculous."[5]

The second, presented by Mr. Vinton of Ohio, in 1844 and again in 1846, arranged that each State should by popular vote elect from its citizens a candidate for the Presidency. From these candidates one was to be chosen by lot.[6] The amusing details of this suggestion were that as many balls as there were Senators and Representatives from each State, inscribed with the name of the State, should be placed in a box. One ball should be drawn from the box and the candidate elected by the State, the name of which should be upon the ball drawn out, should be President.

[1] For other propositions, see ante, pars. 26, 30; post, pars. 56, 57, 59, 60.

[2] App., No. 392.

[3] Speech in full in American Register for 1809, Chap. II (p. 15). He said that this method was suggested from the experience of "some of the republics of Switzerland," Berne in particular. Ibid., pp. 17-18. He cited twelve reasons in favor of its adoption.

[4] John Adams wrote a criticism on these amendments. See Works, Vol. VI., pp. 523 et seq. It would seem he was dissuaded by his son from publishing it. See Memoir of John Quincy Adams, Vol. VII, pp. 225-226. For connection of Hillhouse with the schemes of a Northern Confederacy, ibid., p. 141. See also post, par. 60.

[5] Marshall wrote: "We shall no longer be under the banners of particular men. Strife will no longer effect its object; neither the people at large nor the councils of the nation will be agitated by the all-disturbing question, Who shall be President?" Harper's Weekly, April 28, 1877; O'Neil, p. 258. Adams's diary, as above.

[6] App., Nos. 740, 744.

The last, the most novel and complicated of the three, was reserved for Senator Powell of Kentucky to bring forward in 1864.[1] This scheme, containing eleven sections, still retained the electoral college, but it reduced considerably its number by providing that Congress should apportion among the several States the electors according to the following ratio of population in Federal numbers: One elector to each State having less than a million, two to each State having one, but less than two million, and so on to seven to each State having a population of eight millions. Each State having but one elector should be an electoral district, and each of the other States should be divided by Congress into districts equal to the number of its electors, each district to elect one elector. The electors should convene at the seat of government and form an electoral college on the first Monday of February, over which the Chief Justice of the United States should preside. The electors should then be distributed alphabetically into six classes as nearly equal as possible. Each class should choose an elector from the class next succeeding it, except class six, which should choose from class one. From the six so chosen two should be designated by lot, and from these two the college should choose one to be President, the other to be Vice-President. If the college should fail, except from exterior violence or intimidation, to make an election within twenty-four hours from the time it was formed, it should be dissolved, and a new election ordered, and the college should convene and proceed as before directed. Should there be no election by an electoral college before the 1st day of June, the Senate of the United States should form itself into an electoral college, and proceed according as was directed for the electoral college, within twenty-four hours. If they should fail to elect the office should devolve upon such officer of the Government as Congress should have theretofore directed. Then followed four other sections relating to further details of the system, one of which stipulated that every elector before entering upon the duties of his office should take an oath to support the Constitution, and declare that he had not and would not pledge his vote as an elector in favor of any person, or toward aiding any political party.

---

[1] App., No. 1026. The plan of Judge Nicholson of Kentucky.

48. ELECTION OF PRESIDENT FROM PRESIDENTIAL SECTIONS.

The desire that a President should be selected only out of a previously designated group of men is akin to the design to compel the choice of a man resident in a designated section. Two amendments have been proposed which divide the country into Presidential sections.[1] The first was introduced in 1822 by Mr. Montgomery of Kentucky; it did not change the method of the election, but provided for the creation of Presidential sections. The President was to be elected from each of four sections in rotation.[2] The New England States and New York were to constitute one section. The remainder of the Middle States, with Maryland and Virginia, another; the Southern States another, and Kentucky, Ohio, Indiana, Illinois, and Missouri another. There being twenty-four States in the Union at this time, it was provided that upon the admission of new States they should be incorporated within the section upon which they bordered. The number of the sections were to be determined by a "lottery" conducted in the presence of Congress. Provision was made for the division of any section when its population was shown by the census to be double that of the section containing the lowest represented number. The reception of the resolution may be inferred from the remark of its author: "However laughable it might appear to some gentlemen, he considered it a very serious matter."

The cause of the amendment was doubtless the jealousy awakened in the Middle States and New England, and still more in the West, by the fact that, with the exception of John Adams, all the Presidents up to this time had come from Virginia.[3]

The other resolution was introduced nearly forty years later, in February, 1861, shortly before the outbreak of the civil war. Entirely different motives prompted its introduction. It was an attempt by a Northern Democrat to make such a change in the Constitution that the Southern States would refrain from going out of the Union. Calhoun, in his speech of 1850 on the compromise, had made a somewhat similar proposition.[4] It

---

[1] See ante, par. 34, for Mr. Southard's plan for an executive council.

[2] App., No. 509.

[3] The amendment proposed by Andrew Johnson in 1860 for the election of the President and Vice-President by district provided that the President and Vice-President should alternately be chosen from the North and South. Ante, p. 91.

[4] Works, I, 393–396.

was now put forward by a Northern man, Mr. Vallandigham of Ohio.[1] The four sections contemplated by the amendment were to be known, respectively, as the North, the West, the Pacific, and the South.

Unlike the proposition of 1822, this amendment proposed changing the method of electing the President. It provided that two of the electors for the State at large should be appointed by each State as the legislature thereof should direct. The others should be chosen in the respective Congressional districts of the State. A majority of all the electors in each of the four sections should be necessary for the choice of President and Vice-President; and the concurrence of a majority of the States of each section should be necessary for the choice of President by the House of Representatives, and of the Senators from each section for the choice of Vice-President, whenever the right of choice should devolve upon either of them.

Further articles provided for the term of the President and for a special election in the case of a failure by the House and Senate to elect when the choice devolved upon them.

The adoption of this amendment would have enabled the Southern States to have prevented the election of any man to the Presidency who was openly hostile to the system of slavery. In addition, this amendment in effect gave the South a negative on all legislation hostile to its interests, for it provided that on the demand of one-third of the Senators of any one section, on any bill, order, resolution, or vote to which the concurrence of the House was necessary the vote should be held by sections and a majority of the Senators from each section voting should be necessary to its passage. It shared the fate of the other compromise measures introduced in the session of 1860-61.

49. ELECTION OF PRESIDENT AND VICE-PRESIDENT BY THE VOTERS AS CONGRESS SHALL DIRECT.

In addition to the amendments proposing to extend the power of the Federal Government to control and regulate the election of President and Vice-President, which are discussed in another paragraph, there have been three proposed amendments presented, conferring upon Congress the power to prescribe the method of electing the President.[2] The first of these was introduced in 1869 by Mr. Buckalew of Pennsylvania. It

---

[1] App., Nos. 901-903. See post. 49. 56, 86, 107.   [2] See post, par. 53.

provided that "Congress shall have power to prescribe the manner in which the electors shall be chosen by the people." This amendment, as was said in the debate, would have enabled Congress to prescribe the single district system or any other improved method as seemed best at any given time. This resolution, after being presented several times, was finally passed by the Senate, in connection with the House suffrage amendment.[1] The House refused to concur in the amendment, and the Senate, after receding from this article, failed to give the suffrage amendment the necessary two-thirds. The fifteenth amendment passed later without this article being incorporated in it.[2]

Twice since, in 1872 and in 1888, a very similar proposition, save that the vote should be given directly, without the intervention of electors, has been presented to Congress, the first time by General Banks, the last by Senator Cockrell.[3]

50. ELECTION OF PRESIDENT AND VICE-PRESIDENT IN CASE OF NO CHOICE AT THE FIRST ELECTION.

The greater number of the proposed amendments relating to the method of the election of President and Vice-President made provision for the method to be followed in case of no choice at the first election. The variety of the expedients proposed to effect an ultimate choice is only exceeded by the methods suggested for the primary election of the chief executive officers. Previous to the early "twenties" no amendment appears proposing any change in the clause of the twelfth amendment,[4] which provides that in case of no choice for President or Vice-President by the electors the election of the former shall be made by the House of Representatives, and of the latter by the Senate.[5]

---

[1] App., Nos. 1287, 1308. See post, par. 131.

[2] This amendment was first proposed as an additional article to the Senate suffrage amendment, later withdrawn and presented as a separate amendment, finally passed by the Senate as an additional article of the House suffrage amendment, and reconsidered as recorded above.

[3] App., Nos. 1356, 1715. Mr. Banks's proposition provided that the President and Vice-President should be "chosen by the electors qualified to vote in the election of Representatives to Congress," "in such manner and under such regulations as Congress may by law direct;" Mr. Cockrell's, for a direct vote "in such manner as Congress shall provide by law."

[4] Except Hillhouse's proposition of the choice of President by lot. Ante, par. 47.

[5] The twelfth amendment reduced the number of names submitted to the House from five to three. Compare art. 2, sec. 1, cl. 3, with the twelfth amendment. The Federalists had opposed this change made by the twelfth amendment as reducing the influence of the small States. Ante, par. 38, p. 79, note 4.

In 1823, as if in expectation of trouble in the next election, several amendments to alter this provision were introduced. The failure of the electors to choose a President in 1824, and the subsequent choice of Adams by the House, called forth a large number of resolutions proposing a variety of methods to diminish the probability of the election devolving upon the House of Representatives, some even stipulating that in no case should the choice be left to the House.[1] Naturally the friends of Jackson were the most zealous in urging this proposition,[2] and with some success, for in 1825 the House, after a six weeks' debate, agreed to a resolution to take away from the two Houses the power of participating in eventual elections,[3] but their committee were unable to agree upon "any specific plan," and were discharged.[4]

Although Congress was unable to agree upon any substitute for this provision of the Constitution, various expedients have been devised by individual members. These for convenience of treatment are classified into eleven groups, beginning with those proposing the least change, and proceeding to the most radical.

(1) The majority of the amendments in regard to the election of President and Vice-President did not propose to deprive Congress of the contingent power to elect, but some have suggested changes in the method and procedure of the

---

[1] As the resolutions from the legislatures of the following States: Tennessee, App., No. 581a (1827); Alabama, No. 583 (1828); Georgia, No. 600 (1830); Maine, No. 658a (1836); legislature of Vermont nonconcurred. Am. An. Reg., p. 322. Ohio, No. 655a (1836).

[2] See Sumner's Andrew Jackson, p. 106, for description of their hostility to President Adams. For Adams's views as to the propriety of election devolving upon the House, see his Memoirs, Vol. VII, pp. 301–303. For Jackson's position, see ante, par. 43. Van Buren said, "There was no point on which the people of the United States were more perfectly united than upon the propriety, not to say indisputable necessity, of taking the election of President from the House of Representatives." Quoted by O'Neil, p. 253. Madison wrote, in 1823: "An amendment of the Constitution on this point is justly called for by all its considerate and best friends." Works, Vol. III, p. 333.

[3] By a vote of 138 to 52. (This amendment was called for by the legislature of Georgia in 1826. App., No. 577a. In 1836 the legislatures of Ohio and Maine recommended this restriction. App. Nos. 655a, 658a.) At the same time a declaratory resolution in favor of the district system of election of President directly was defeated. Ante, par. 43.

[4] This failure showed that however generally it was agreed that the election ought not to devolve upon Congress, it was impossible to secure a sufficient number to agree upon any other plan. An article in Niles' Register referring to the action of the House, as above, said that the Southern States were opposed to "a further extension of the popular principle," while the greater States would not allow "a further extension of the Federal principle." "The large States will not give up one jot or tittle of the power that they have as to first choice of a President; nor will the small States abate their influence when the vote is to be taken by States." "We despair of a change * * * because of the three parties to the question, to wit, the large States whether holding slaves or not, the nonslave-holding States and the slave-holding States, and the small States." Vol. XXX, p. 233.

respective Houses in the event of the election devolving upon
it. One such, introduced in 1825, provided in case no one
received one-third of the whole number of votes given by the
electors, the House should choose the President under such
rules as they might agree upon.[1] Another, like that advocated
by Mr. Phelps of Connecticut, in 1826, proposed raising the
number of candidates again to five, as originally provided in
the Constitution, when the election fell to the House. If no
person received a majority after the second ballot, from the
two having the highest number of votes the Speaker should
choose one by lot.[2] Several, like the amendment reported by
the Senate Select Committee on Elections in 1824, stipulated,
in place of the vote being taken by States, that each Representative should have one vote, and after the first ballot a
plurality should elect.[3]

· Mr. Vallandigham's proposition, by which the country was
divided into sections, provided in case the election devolved
upon the House, the concurrence of a majority of States of
each section should be necessary for a choice.[4]

(2) Another variation would have continued to give to Congress the duty of making a choice if there was no election, but
a choice by joint ballot. Senator Dickerson repeatedly introduced an amendment which provided that in case no person
received a majority of the votes of the electoral college, then
from the highest number not exceeding three on the list of
those voted for as President, the Senate and House in joint
meeting should immediately, by ballot, choose the President.
A majority of the votes of all members present should be necessary to a choice on the first ballot, after which a plurality of
votes should elect.[5] In the amendments introduced by Mr.
Underwood of Kentucky, in 1838 and 1842, proposing the nomination of candidates by the State legislatures, and the election
by a direct popular vote, provision was made, in case no person
received a majority, for a joint convention of both Houses of
Congress to elect the President or Vice-President by a viva
voce vote from among those nominated for the office, a majority
of votes present to decide.[6] A similar method of deciding

---

[1] App., No. 540.
[2] App., No. 551.
[3] App., No. 534.
[4] App., No. 903. See ante, par. 48.
[5] Ante, par. 39. Madison, in 1823, wrote that of "the different remedies proposed" he
liked the joint vote of the two Houses best. Works, III, 334.
[6] App., Nos. 679, 724. Ante, par. 40.

the election, in case no person received a majority of the votes given directly for President and Vice-President, has been frequently suggested, especially in recent years. In most instances a majority vote of the joint convention was to decide, but some required a two-thirds vote.[1]

(3) A favorite device for avoiding recourse to Congress was the suggestion of a second election by the original electors. January 10, 1823, Senator John Taylor of Virginia proposed such an amendment, but the electors should vote for one of the two as President who should have received the greatest number of electoral votes at the first election. In case of a tie at the second election, then it should be the duty of the House of Representatives to choose one of them as President.[2] This amendment was later modified in a new draft, which provided that instead of an election by the House, that both Houses of Congress in joint convention should select the President. In the amendments introduced at this same session of Congress by Mr. McDuffie of South Carolina and by Senators Hayne and Van Buren, a similar provision was made for a second meeting of the electors in case of no choice at the first elections.[3] In Mr. McDuffie's resolution there was a peculiar provision that made it possible for two Presidents to be elected. It provided that the Senate and House in joint meeting should canvass the vote cast by the electors at their second meeting, and if no one had received a majority the joint meeting, each member having one vote, should choose a President. "If there be two or more persons, each of whom have the highest number of electoral votes given at the second meeting, *each one of them* shall be chosen. If there be only one person having the highest number of electoral votes, less than a majority, one of the persons who has one of the two highest number of votes shall be chosen."[4] Mr. Dromgoole of Virginia in subsequent years (1838 and 1845) twice presented an amendment similar to that introduced by Senator Taylor.[5]

(4) Two amendments presented in the same session of Congress, in 1826, made provision for a second choice of electoral colleges, the persons so chosen should, from the persons having the two highest number of votes at the first election, choose

---

[1] As App., Nos. 743, 1078, 1314, 1439, 1441. 1589, 1624, 1640, 1735.

[2] App., No. 517.

[3] App., Nos. 524, 527, 532.

[4] App., No. 524. ante, par. 34.

[5] App., Nos. 682, 743.

one, but the vote should be taken by States, each State having one vote.[1]

(5) In 1824 Mr. Livingston of Lousiana proposed an amendment for the election of President by a direct vote given in districts. This amendment provided that the citizens, at the same time they gave their vote for President and Vice-President, should also vote for an elector. In case no person was the choice of a majority of the whole number of districts, then the electors should assemble in their respective States and cast their votes for one of the two persons receiving the greatest number of district votes. In case of a tie, the one of the two who had the greatest number of votes of the electoral districts should be President.[2]   In 1827, upon the instruction of the legislature of Ohio, and again in 1829, Mr. Wright of Ohio presented an amendment of a somewhat similar kind.   It differed in that his resolution contemplated an election by a majority of the popular vote of the country, but the voters at the same time they voted directly for President and Vice-President were also to cast their ballots for electors equal to the number of Senators and Representatives to which their State was entitled.   In case of no person receiving a majority, the electors having the greatest number of votes should choose the President and Vice-President from the two persons having the greatest number of the direct votes.   In case of no election the choice should devolve on Congress.[3]

(6) Another proposition was for a popular election to follow the meeting of the electoral colleges, if there was no choice. The citizens of each State were to vote directly for one of the two highest candidates at the first election.   The votes were to be taken by States, each State having one vote.   This was presented by Mr. Hemphill of Pennsylvania, in 1826,[4] and a somewhat similar plan was proposed in the following year.[5]

(7) Still another modification of the system of double election is included in an amendment introduced in 1826 by James Buchanan, then a member of the House.   It provided that in case no election should be made by the electors, the States should choose the President from the two highest on the list, in such

[1] App., Nos. 556, 574.

[2] App., No. 537.

[3] App., Nos. 598, 592.

[4] App., No. 561.   In case of a tie the choice to be made as the present provisions of the Constitution direct.

[5] App., No. 580.

manner as the legislature thereof should direct, each State having one vote.[1] The only proposition of the whole series which left the choice to the legislatures of the States was presented by Mr. Stevens of Virginia in this same year. In case of no election in the primary colleges, the legislatures of the respective States were to choose, by joint ballot, one from the three persons having the highest number of electoral votes.[2]

(8) A large number of the amendments proposing various ways in which a direct vote should be given for President and Vice-President contained provisions for a second election conducted in the same manner as the first, but the candidates were to be restricted to the two receiving the largest number of votes at the first election. These propositions were presented within a few years subsequent to the election of 1824,[3] but the same plan was revived with the renewal of the introduction of resolutions for the election of the President by popular vote.[4]

(9) A modification of the last-mentioned plan, which received extended consideration in 1835–36, provided in case of no choice by the people at the second election, then the choice should be made by the House of Representatives.[5] Still others, like the amendment urged by Senator Benton, and in later years by Andrew Johnson, stipulated that if the two candidates in the second election received an equal number of votes, then the person who had received the greatest number of votes in the greatest number of States should be President.[6]

Mr. Morton's proposition, which, like Benton's, proposed establishing the district system, made no provision for the case of two or more persons receiving an equal number of Presidential votes, as the committee which reported the measure were unable to agree upon any plan to cover this contingency. That provision of the Constitution which confers the choice of the President in case of no election by the electors upon the House voting by States has frequently been attacked and stigmatized as unjust, but the possibility of the choice of a

---

[1] App., No. 555. A similar provision in Mr. Tucker's amendment of 1828. App., No. 585.
[2] App., No. 573.
[3] As the one presented by Mr. Dayton of South Carolina, in 1826. App., No. 574.
[4] App., Nos. 1104, 1227b, 1283a, 1352, 1368, 1389, 1464, 1505. 1506, 1626, 1608, 1695. See ante, par. 42. A second election was to be held only in case no one received a majority of the votes.
[5] App., Nos. 641, 654.
[6] App., Nos. 552, 601, 632, 765, 770, 813, 1240. Ante, par. 43.

" minority President " has never been more forcibly presented
than by Mr. Morton, who showed that under the apportionment
in force at that time (1875) it was possible for forty-five members of the House of Representatives to elect a President
against the wishes of the remaining two hundred and forty-
seven members.[1]

(10) Another favorite plan, in order that the choice might in
no instance devolve upon Congress, made provision for successive elections until some one should be elected. This was
first proposed in the thirties, but has frequently been urged
since.[2]

(11) Several of the proposed plans did away with the necessity of a second election by providing that a plurality of the
electoral or popular vote, as the case might be, should elect,
and the election was only to devolve upon Congress in the very
remote case of a tie.[3]

51. DISCUSSION OF SCHEMES FOR PRESIDENTIAL ELECTION.

All the proposed amendments affecting the election of President and Vice-President have now been considered.[4] It may
be well, however, to review some of the more important of
them.

Although at the time of the adoption of the Constitution
the electoral system excited little opposition, yet at no considerable interval since has it failed to be the object of
attack. First it was early found necessary to perfect the
system in some of the minor details by the adoption of the
twelfth amendment. We have already shown how the system has utterly belied the expectation of its framers, for the
electoral college, instead of exercising its own unfettered

[1] App., No. 1393, ante, par. 44. Record, p. 631. At that time forty-five members would
control the votes of nineteen States. "Nevada with 42,000 population would have an
equal vote with New York, having a population one hundred and four times as great."
As at present constituted sixty-six members, representing twenty-three States, could
elect the President in opposition to the will of the remaining two hundred and ninety-one
members. Such a combination while possible is of course not probable.

[2] By Mr. McComas of Virginia, in 1836. App., No. 661. In the seventies by Messrs.
Wright and Riddle. App., Nos. 1391, 1420, 1464.

[3] As Nos. 554, 1058; and the following: Four provided for the decision of the tie for the
President by the House, for the Vice-President by the Senate, each member to have one
vote. App., Nos. 1408, 1420, 1443, 1447. Two that the tie for either office be decided by
the House. App., Nos. 1359, 1367, ante, par. 42.

[4] The following resolutions to amend the Constitution in regard to the election of
President were introduced, but it has been impossible to classify them, as the text has
not been found. App., Nos. 657, 658, 863. Since par. 42 was sent to press, resolutions from
the legislature of Vermont (1818) favoring the district system have been found. App.
No. 480b.

will, has become a mere registering machine.[1] In the early
years there were various amendments proposed to secure a
uniform system of elections throughout the States. After
many attempts to secure the choice of electors by districts
had failed, nearly all the States by a sort of common understanding adopted the general ticket system, and this method,
although voluntary, has been retained ever since, with the
recent exception of Michigan,[2] and it seems to have become
ingrafted upon the Constitution,[3] or, as Professor Dicey would
say, to have become one of the "conventions" of the Constitution. In the years immediately succeeding the election of 1824
there was a concerted effort to so amend the Constitution that
the election of President should never again devolve upon the
House. In the course of a few years the excitement incident
to this election was allayed, and as there has been no case of
an election by the House since, there has been no popular
alarm over this complication. The dispute of 1876, when the
decision was in doubt several months, turned rather on the
method of canvassing the vote.[4]

Many of the plans proposed have been obviously impracticable. To leave the choice of the Chief Magistrate to a direct
popular vote of the entire country seems as unwise to-day as
it did at the time the Constitution was framed. In addition
to the vast premium placed upon fraud and intimidation, the
excitement of the election under the present system would be
greatly intensified. Furthermore, it would seem undesirable
to entirely do away with the influence of the States in the
election, owing to the long-established custom and the appro-
priateness of some recognition of the federal character of our
Union.

The system of electing the President by districts, either by
the electoral system or without it, or with the two votes of each
State given at large or otherwise, would manifestly come nearer
to representing the popular vote than does the present system,
especially if there was some assurance of a just and permanent

---

[1] The electors, however, are only bound by moral obligation and custom to cast their
votes for the candidates previously designated. In the election of 1824 three of the Clay
electors deserted him, "but for this defection Mr. Clay's name would have gone to the
House of Representatives instead of Mr. Crawford's, and possibly Mr. John Quincy
Adams would never have been President." Stanwood, p. 86. Unsuccessful attempts were
made to bribe one or more electors in 1876. Ibid., p. 330.

[2] See ante, p. 86, note 4.

[3] See Tiedman, The Unwritten Constitution of the U. S., chap. III.

[4] See ante, par. 50, p. 110, section 9, Morton's proposition.

arrangement of district boundaries.[1] But without that assurance,[2] which it would seem impossible to provide, there would still be the same danger of gerrymandering that there is in our Congressional elections. Of all the plans proposed, the district system has received the most favorable consideration in Congress. Not only did an amendment for the choice of electors by districts pass the Senate at four different times between 1813 and 1824,[3] but in subsequent discussions some application of the district system to the choice of President has received the support of many of the leading statesmen of the country.[4]

The proposition for the distribution of the electoral vote of each State among the candidates in the proportion the electoral ratio shall bear to the popular vote of each candidate seems the fairest and most desirable of all the plans presented, as it retains the relative importance of each State, and at the same time secures to the minority its due proportion of the vote.[5]

The almost countless variety of the plans proposed is not only indicative of the dissatisfaction there is with the present anomalous system, but also shows that it would be next to an impossibility to secure the adoption of a new method of election, owing to the difficulty of uniting a sufficient number of the States in favor of any one plan. The fact that it was impossible to secure the indorsement of any one of the plans proposed in the years succeeding the contested election of 1876 by even one branch of Congress indicates that the adoption of a new system of electing the Chief Magistrate is improbable before the present method of amending the Constitution is itself changed. Since 1876 no proposition for a change of the method of electing the President has been

---

[1] The adoption of the district system in any of the proposed forms would undoubtedly insure the election of a President in political sympathy with the majority in the House of Representatives.

[2] See Madison's Works, III, p. 333.

[3] In 1813, 1819, 1820, and 1824, and the amendment passed by the Senate in 1869 would have permitted its use. See ante. par. 33, note 1 : pars. 39, 49.

[4] See ante, pars. 39, 43, 44.

[5] The following are some of the reasons which have been urged for the adoption of the proportional system: (1) It provides for a direct vote. (2) It retains the electoral votes, while dispensing with electors and electoral colleges. (3) It is a more perfect expression of popular will. (4) Reduces the chance of a disputed election. (5) Renders impossible the election of a minority candidate. (6) Tends to eliminate pivotal States, and insures a real contest in each State. (7) Discourages and prevents unfairness and fraud. In this respect its superiority to other plans of amendment is conspicuous and unquestionable. "The effect of any common fraud would be inappreciable, and the motive for committing fraud removed." Ante. par. 45.

brought to a vote in Congress, and since 1880 even the slight promise of success implied in a favorable report by a committee of either House of Congress. has been lacking.[1] Likewise in recent years the general public has exhibited little interest in the matter.[2]

Some of the amendments for changing the method of electing the President contained clauses extending the time for casting the votes to two or three days, making our system more like the English. Three of these are cited by way of example.

One amendment for the election of President by a direct vote by districts provided that the first Thursday and succeeding Friday of August of 1828 and every fourth year thereafter should be the election days. This was reported by the select committee of the Senate in 1826.[3]

A resolution proposing that the election of President should be held uniformly in the several States on the first Monday and succeeding Tuesday and Wednesday in the month of September was received in 1837 from the legislature of Indiana.[4]

The fourth Monday of October and the two succeeding days was fixed for the election days by the amendment introduced by Mr. Underwood of Kentucky, in 1842, for the nomination of Presidential candidates by the different State legislatures and election by the people.[5]

It is noticeable that these propositions came largely from the frontier States, where the facilities for traveling were poor and more time was needed to reach the voting places.

By the terms of the Constitution, "Congress may determine the time of choosing the electors, and the day on which they shall give their votes, which shall be the same throughout the United States."[6] The original act of Congress, passed March 1, 1792, simply provided that electors were to be appointed thirty-four days preceding the first Wednesday in December.

[1] Amendment reported in 1880, App., No. 1508; ante, par. 45. Since the close of the first century of the history of the Constitution there has been one report by the House Committee on Election of President and Vice-President, February 7, 1893, Fifty-second Congress, second session, H. Rep. 2439.

[2] The following articles contain valuable discussions of the merits of one or more of the different plans: Atlantic, vol. 42, 543; vol. 63, 428; Arena, vol. 5, 286; Forum, vol. 12, 702; vol. 18, 532; No. Am. Rev., vol. 117, 383; vol. 124, 1, 161, 341; vol. 125, 68; vol. 140 (February).

[3] App., No. 552.

[4] App., No. 668.

[5] App., No. 724.

[6] Art. II, sec. 1, cl. 3.

The demand for a uniform day for the choice of electors led
to the frequent petition from the legislatures of the States for
Congress to fix such a day by law,[1] and also for the insertion
of a clause to this effect in certain of the proposed amendments
in regard to the election of President, as the one presented by
Mr. Gilmer, in 1835.[2] Ten years later Congress passed a law,
which is still in force, fixing upon the Tuesday after the first
Monday in November as the day for the choice of electors.[3]

Some of the proposed amendments, especially those introduced in recent years, make provision for a uniform day for
holding the election throughout the States;[4] some retain the
present date,[5] others fix upon another, usually somewhat
earlier.[6] Three of these in addition prohibit the voting for any
other officers, save Representatives to Congress, on the day
appointed for the election of Presidential electors.[7] Two of
these were presented just after the Presidential election of
1888, and were evidently suggested by a desire to prevent the
trading of Presidential votes for votes for State officers
between the different political parties, as it was alleged had
been done in New York in the election just held.

Although Congress has never gone to the extent of its constitutional powers in regulating elections to Congress,[8] various
amendments have been proposed which, if they had been
adopted, would have greatly increased that power of Congress
over the election of President. One of the first of these,
repeatedly introduced by Mr. Dickerson of New Jersey for the
election of President by districts, while not directly increasing the power of Congress, yet it limited the power of the legislature to alter the division of the State into districts at any
other time than the decennial census.[9] In 1823 a resolution
was introduced to give Congress power to make or alter the

[1] Especially in the thirties and early forties.
[2] App., No. 641.
[3] Revised Statutes of the United States, sec. 131.
[4] As App. Nos. 1437, 1438, 1503, 1508, 1537, 1542, 1589. 1639, 1672, 1697, 1705. 1731.
[5] As App., Nos. 1439, 1514, 1569, 1624, 1640, 1735.
[6] As App., No. 813, the first Tuesday in August. App., No. 1078, the second Tuesday in October. App., No. 1652, the third Tuesday in October.
[7] App., Nos., 1652, 1731, 1733. No. 1514, however, proposed the same day for the election of President and Vice-President, members of Congress, and State and county officers. See post, par. 84.
[8] See ante, par. 24.
[9] Ante, par. 39.

regulation prescribed by the State legislatures for the election of President, and to redistrict any State which was not divided as was directed.[1]

Many of the resolutions for the choice of the Executive aimed to give to Congress the same power in Presidential elections as it already possessed over the Congressional. Since the civil war there has been a marked tendency in this direction. Several amendments have been proposed authorizing Congress to prescribe "the time, place, and manner," and other regulations for conducting Presidential elections.[2] The one reported by the Committee on Privileges and Elections in both Houses in 1874–75, as well as that introduced by Senator Morgan, in 1876, conferred upon Congress the power to provide for the holding and conducting of all elections of President and Vice-President, and while it permitted the States to be divided into districts by the legislatures thereof, such division was subject to the revision of Congress.[3] In 1880 a resolution was introduced proposing that the following section should be added to the twelfth amendment: "The Congress shall have power by legislation to establish rules and regulations for certifying, transmitting, receiving, opening the votes of the electors, etc.[4] Up to the present time the procedure has been regulated by an act of Congress passed in 1792, which, with certain modifications, is still in force, although there is no express provision in the Constitution authorizing such a law. It would seem desirable that the control of the conduct of Presidential elections should be vested in Congress, but it is hardly probable that this reform will be secured.

54. SETTLEMENT OF CONTESTED PRESIDENTIAL ELECTIONS.

Not only is the power given to Congress to elect the President and Vice-President in case there is no choice by the electors, and to fix the time for the election, but it has also assumed authority to canvass and count the vote. The only ground for this authority is the ambiguous provision of the Constitution

---

[1] Mr. McDuffie of South Carolina, App., No. 524.

[2] As App., Nos. 1058, 1078, 1309, 1317, 1408, 1420, 1464, 1672. No. 1058, introduced by Mr Jenckes of Rhode Island, was all inclusive, "Congress shall have power to pass laws providing for registration of voters, for ascertaining the qualifications, for the time and manner of conducting such elections and for preventing frauds therein, and for declaring the result." Propositions to confer upon Congress the power to prescribe the method of electing the President by the people have been discussed in ante, par. 49.

[3] App., Nos. 1386, 1393, 1400.

[4] By Mr. Morgan of Alabama, App., No. 1513.

that "the President of the Senate shall, in the presence of the Senate and House of Representatives, open all the certificates, and the votes shall then be counted."[1] Three theories or interpretations of this clause have been held by Congress at three different periods in our history. The first theory, which held sway to 1821, was that the President of the Senate should count—that is, enumerate the votes. The second theory, which prevailed from 1821 to 1861, held that there was a "casus omissus" in the Constitution in this regard, and no one was empowered to "count," counting being interpreted in the sense of "canvassing." The third theory, which appeared in 1861, maintains that the two Houses shall "count," which is interpreted to mean to determine the legality of the votes.[2]

Acting on this last theory, Congress has determined all questions in regard to the doubtful votes since 1861 to 1887. Such questions have always been decided by party considerations, but in the contested election of 1876 it was impossible for Congress to determine the results of the election, under their existing rules, owing to the deadlock existing between the two Houses in which different political parties were in the majority. To meet this crisis, the "Electoral Commission" was created.

A premonition of the dangers likely to result from this uncertainty seems to have suggested an amendment to the Constitution shortly before each of the bitterly contested elections of 1800, 1824, and 1876. In 1798, while the issue of the contest in Pennsylvania was still in doubt, and the "Ross bill" was being framed,[3] Senator Marshall of Kentucky included in his amendment to the Constitution, relative to the election of the President, a clause which provided that in case any contest should arise relative to any vote for President, the same should be determined by the Senate, and for Vice-President, it should be decided by the House of Representatives.[4]

[1] Twelfth amendment.

[2] Abridged from McKnight, chapter I. Since 1804 in nine of the Presidential elections controversies have arisen on either or both of the following questions: (1) By whom shall the electoral votes be counted? (2) In what manner shall be declared which are proper electoral votes? See reports of the following committees: Senate Report, Forty-third Congress, first session, Vol. II, No. 395 (written by Mr. Morton); House Report, Forty-fifth Congress, second session, Vol. IV, No. 819; House Report, Forty-sixth Congress, first session, Vol. II, No. 6.

[3] For Ross bill, see O'Neil, pp. 77–83; McKnight, pp. 262–269. The Ross bill was perhaps suggested by the English practice of deciding election petitions. Grenville act of 1770, May, Vol. I, p. 263.

[4] App., No. 329. Consideration of resolution was postponed to the next Congress.

No further attempt was made to remedy this defect by means of an amendment until 1823, when it would seem, in anticipation of the trouble in the coming election, several propositions were introduced. Mr. Holmes, a Senator from Maine, in this year presented a resolution in both the Seventeenth and Eighteenth Congresses, which directed that all questions of the validity of the election of President, or of the proceedings therein should be determined by the members of both Houses in joint ballot. The rules of the proceedings should be determined by law, but no alteration of the rules should have effect until two years after it should have been made. Questions concerning the validity of the election of the Vice-President should be determined by the Senate.[1]

In the amendment proposed by Mr. Benton, in the same year, for the election of President by the vote of the citizens given directly in districts, a clause provided that in case two or more persons should have an equal number of votes in any such district elections, for the same office, that the returning officers should decide between them and certify accordingly.[2] This provision was typical of that contained in several of the other proposed amendments for taking the votes by districts, both those involving a choice by a direct vote and those by electors.[3]

For more than forty years no amendment bearing directly upon this subject was presented.[4] Finally, in 1865, Congress adopted the "twenty-second joint rule," which was "the first actual assumption by Congress of the power to accept or reject an electoral vote."[5] It provided that "No vote objected to shall be counted, except by the concurrent vote of the two Houses." It was passed to prevent the counting of the vote from the "reconstructed" States before Congress was ready to do so. Before this year closed an amendment had been proposed to confer upon Congress this much disputed power.[6] Dissatisfaction with this rule, as well as the reappearance of the problem in connection with the question of the legality of

[1] App., Nos. 521. 530.

[2] App., No. 526.

[3] App., No. 537. During the time the Senate passed a bill which provided that no vote could be rejected without the concurrent consent of both Houses. Lost in the House. McKnight, pp. 269–271; O'Neil, pp. 117–119.

[4] Indirectly the question was touched upon in some of the schemes proposing to abolish the electoral system.

[5] McKnight, pp. 271–273; see also O'Neil, pp. 171–173, 177–180; Stanwood, pp. 249–252.

[6] App., No. 1058; ante, par. 53, note.

certain electoral votes in 1868 and in 1872, led to the renewed
introduction of proposed amendments dealing with the question of contested elections.

As early as 1869, Mr. Robertson of South Carolina twice
proposed an amendment to give Congress power to establish
tribunals for determining all questions as to the validity of
the electoral vote of any State.[1]
In 1873 Senator Frelinghuysen advocated leaving the decision of all such disputes to the Supreme Court of the United
States.[2] A similar provision was incorporated into the articles proposed in 1874-75 by the House Committee on Elections and in the amendment thereto submitted by Mr. Wright.[3]
The resolutions reported by the Senate Committee on Privileges and Elections in 1874-75, and introduced by Mr. Morton
in the following year, were similar to the House resolutions
above referred to, save that they empowered Congress to establish tribunals for the decision of such elections as might be
contested.[4] Mr. Morton pointed out the danger of the present
method of declaring the results of the election, inasmuch as it
failed to provide any adequate method for the determination
of contested elections, and in addition placed arbitrary power
in the hands of the Vice-President.[5] Early in 1876, before the
Presidential election, three other amendments on this subject
were presented. Two of these made provision in case the two
Houses should not agree, when acting as judge of the returns
and elections, that the matter of disagreement should be referred
to the Supreme Court for final decision.[6] The third, proposed
by Senator Edmunds, was reported by the Committee on the
Judiciary in an amended form.[7] This resolution contained a

[1] App., Nos. 1315, 1318. No. 1317, introduced by Mr. Bromwell of Illinois proposed to
give Congress the power to decide as to the validity of the electoral vote, etc. Ante,
par. 53.
[2] App., No. 1362.
[3] App., Nos. 1386, 1391. These all provided that the returns of the election should be
made to the Supreme Court, who should canvass, determine, and publish the results.
[4] App., Nos. 1393, 1400. Ante, par. 44.
[5] Record. Forty-third Congress, second session, p. 628. Besides party bias, personal
interest might prejudice his decision, for the Vice-President may be one of the candidates
for office, as has been the case already six times in our history, although in all these cases
the duties of the office have been honestly performed. Adams in 1797; Jefferson in 1801;
declared a tie; Tompkins in 1821, a candidate for Vice-President; Van Buren in 1837;
Johnson in 1841, a candidate for Vice-President; Breckinridge in 1861, a candidate for
President. The Senate twice passed the Morton bill in 1875-76 to prevent the rejection
of any electoral vote except by consent of both Houses. In case of double returns, those
only to count "which the two Houses acting separately shall decide to be the true and
valid return." McKnight, p. 275.
[6] App., Nos. 1408, 1420. Proposed again in 1877, App., No. 1413.
[7] App., No. 1423.

provision for the return of the electoral votes to the Federal Supreme Court, and further directed that the person having the greatest number of votes for President considered by the court to have been lawfully given and certified, should be President, if such should be a majority of all votes cast. The court should, in the discharge of these duties, disregard errors of form and be governed by the substantial right of the matter. Action upon this amendment was postponed until the next Congress.

The English system of employing the judges to investigate contested election claims to seats in the House of Commons, and to make recommendation relative to what action shall be taken, doubtless suggested the expedient of referring the matter to the Supreme Court. It is probable that to secure the action of the Supreme Court in such an extrajudicial capacity an amendment to the Constitution would be required, although certain of the judges, contrary to their custom of not rendering extrajudicial opinions,[1] served on the Electoral Commission for the settlement of the contested election of 1876.

The election of 1876 had taken place when Congress reassembled, and the necessity of devising some means for reaching a decision was now made evident. President Grant, in his annual message, declared that "the attention of Congress can not be too earnestly called to the necessity of throwing some greater safeguard over the method of choosing and declaring the election of President. "Under the present system there seems to be no provided remedy for contesting the election in any one State."[2] To meet the crisis, several resolutions were presented.[3] The Senate at once took the Edmunds amendment into consideration. After it had been amended so as to permit its operating upon the determining of the vote in the last election, if ratified before the 1st of February, 1877, by the necessary number of States, the resolution was brought to a vote December 14, and defeated by the vote of 14 yeas to 31 nays.[4]

The election of 1876, settled in 1877 by an extraordinary tribunal, suggested permanent tribunals of some kind. In

---

[1] See Marshall's Life of Washington, Vol. v., p. 441; United States v. Yale Tod, 13 Howard, 52, note; United States v. Ferrara, ibid., 40, note; Gordon v. United States, 2 Wallace, 561; United States v. Jones, 117 U. S., 697. For practice of the judiciary in the States, see Thayer, Cases on Const. Law, Part I, pp. 175-176.

[2] App., No. 1430.

[3] App., Nos. 1431, 1436.

[4] The electoral bill of 1877, establishing the Electoral Commission, was passed instead. McKnight, pp. 276 et seq.

the fall of 1877 Senator Eaton of Connecticut proposed a means for determining contested elections more in keeping with the views of the champions of State rights.[1] This provided that a tribunal for the decision of all contested issues arising in a Presidential election should be established in each State. The governor of each State, by and with the advice of the senate, at least a year previous to the election, should appoint not less than five persons learned in the law, to whom should be referred, in such manner as the legislature of the State should direct, all such cases of contested election, and it should be their duty to hear and determine every such case and certify the same thirty days before the electors should be called upon to give their votes.

The resolution, first presented by Mr. Springer in 1877 and introduced by him in every Congress since 1882, relating to the election of President, stipulates that the joint convention of the Senate and House shall be the judge of the election, returns, and qualifications.[2] Various other amendments continued to be introduced, some renewing the propositions to refer the decision to the Supreme Court in case the two Houses could not agree,[3] others empowering Congress to declare by law by what authority the returns should be canvassed and in contested elections determined,[4] and still others to leave the decision to Congress itself.[5] Resolutions proposing to leave the decision of any contested election to the highest judicial tribunal of the State, and for the counting of the votes in accordance with the decision, have been introduced in every Congress since 1881.[6] Two resolutions foreshadowed the provisions of the law of 1887, one of these being reported by the select committee in the House in 1878.[7] •

Nothing, however, was done, although action was urged by the successive Presidents until 1887, when Congress decided that an amendment was not necessary, and passed a statute embodying in some degree the provisions proposed in the amendment of Senator Eaton, already referred to. It provides that tribunals appointed in and by each State shall

[1] App., No. 1453.
[2] App., Nos. 1439, 1624, 1640, 1735. This was to be the incoming rather than the outgoing Congress. Ante, par. 15.
[3] App., Nos. 1443, 1447.
[4] App., Nos. 1464, 1672.
[5] As App., No. 1508, reported by select committee of the House. To be counted as certified unless rejected by both Houses.
[6] App., Nos. 1537, 1589, 1639, 1697.
[7] App., Nos. 1475, 1493.

determine what electoral votes from the State are legal votes; in case the State has not appointed such a tribunal, then the two Houses of Congress, by concurrent vote, shall determine, in case of double returns, which votes are legal.[1]

By this act a method of counting the electoral vote has finally been devised which promises a prompt and equitable decision of contested elections. Thus Congress, in harmony with its claim of the past quarter of a century, has asserted its right to supply the "casus omissus" of the Constitution without waiting for a formal amendment.

55. EXCLUSION OF ELECTORS FROM APPOINTMENT BY THE PRESIDENT.

In order to guard against the danger of the President's rewarding electors, especially in times of great party excitement, by giving them offices after he took his seat, several proposals have been made to add to the disqualification of Senators and Representatives, forbidding their appointment to office during the time for which they have been elected, or for a longer period. There have been at least nine other resolutions providing that the Constitution should be so amended that neither electors nor members of Congress, in the event of the election of President devolving upon the House, should be appointed to any office within the appointing power of the President during the continuance of that President in office.[2] The first of these was presented by Mr. Smyth of Virginia, in 1823, and was the only one that included Presidential electors within its prohibition.[3]

The appointment of Clay to a Cabinet position by President Adams lent color to the charge of a bargain, and was the occasion that led to the proposal during the period 1826 to 1836 of seven distinct propositions to amend the Constitution as above. General Jackson himself took occasion to recommend such an amendment in his first annual message, in 1829, and again in 1831 he renewed his recommendation.[4]

The resolution introduced by Mr. Weems in 1826 had this peculiarity that it only proposed to make such members of Congress ineligible to appointment "as shall stand recorded as having voted upon the election."[5]

[1] Statutes of the United States, Forty-ninth Congress, second session, chap. 90, p. 373.
[2] App., Nos. 516, 557, 567, 581, 595, 596, 606, 635, 655, 980.
[3] App., No. 516.
[4] App., Nos. 596, 606.
[5] App., No. 567.

Only one other amendment of this character has been presented. A clause of the amendment presented by Senator Davis of Kentucky, in 1863, proposing a very novel scheme for the choice of President by both Houses of Congress meeting in joint session, provided that no Senator or Representative who should have voted for the candidate elected should be appointed to any office by the President.[1]

A somewhat analogous proposition related to the judges of the United States who might be called upon to canvass the returns of the election. The Edmunds resolution for the decision of contested-election cases by the Supreme Court stipulated that the justices of the court should be ineligible for election as President or Vice-President. On motion of Mr. Merrimon of North Carolina an additional provision was added to the original amendment, which debarred a judge of the Supreme Court from receiving appointment to any office under the United States Government until "the expiration of four years next after he shall have ceased to be such justice."[2]

56. TERM OF PRESIDENT AND VICE-PRESIDENT.

Over one hundred and twenty-five amendments have been submitted to change the term of President and fix the period of eligibility.[3] These were brought out chiefly by the fear that the President would use the patronage of his office to secure his reelection.[4] More than fifty of these have been propositions to fix the term at six years.[5] Such an amendment was proposed for the first time by Mr. Hemphill of Pennsylvania, in 1826, as one of the provisions of his resolution for the election of President. This change has been advocated at different periods ever since, within recent years more frequently than

---

[1] App., No. 1423; ante, par. 54.

[2] The Committee on the Judiciary reported the main resolution, but it was lost. See post, par. 70.

[3] In the Federal Convention various proposals were made in regard to the tenure of the Executive, varying from a three years' term to one of "good behavior," Elliot's Deb., v, pp. 142, 143, 327. Twice a seven years' term with restriction upon eligibility for reelection was adopted. Ibid., pp. 149, 369. The report of the committee of eleven of September 4, 1787, fixed the term at four years. This was the first time a four years' term had been proposed. It was evidently a compromise between the party desiring a limited term and the one advocating a life tenure. Ibid., p. 507.

[4] See Senator Wade's speech; Globe, Thirty-ninth Congress, first session, pp. 931-932; Sumner's speech; Globe, Forty-second Congress, second session, p. 259.

[5] One term of six years. App., Nos. 588, 591, 595a, 609, 645, 653, 660, 664, 667, 745, 869k, 869m, 874g, 905, 1198, 1204, 1336, 1356, 1369, 1388, 1389, 1402, 1403, 1412, 1412a, 1422, 1446, 1449, 1456, 1465, 1492, 1630, 1633, 1638, 1663, 1670, 1722, 1724. Six-year term, no limit as to eligibility: App., Nos. 904, 1375, 1395, 1396, 1404, 1412, 1439, 1498, 1534, 1509, 1624, 1640, 1732, 1735.

ever before. All but fourteen of these stipulated that the President should be ineligible to reelection.[1]

One proposition only has been presented which contemplated reducing the length of the term as fixed by the Constitution. This was the amendment presented by Senator Hillhouse, in 1808, in connection with his plan for the choice of President by lot from the retiring Senators. The term was placed at one year.[2] Besides the amendments proposing to increase the term to six years, only two propositions have been made to extend the present period to any other term of years. The first of these, fixing the term at five years, was proposed by Mr. Tucker, in 1831; the other, prolonging the term to eight years, was introduced by Mr. Hudd of Wisconsin, in 1888.[3]

A large number of the amendments did not propose to change the term of the President as fixed by the Constitution, but to limit the number of times the same person could be chosen President. The amendments on this phase of the subject naturally fall into three groups: First, propositions limiting the same person to two terms; second, propositions restricting the President from being eligible to a reelection until after the expiration of a certain number of years; and third, propositions restricting the President to one term only.[4]

(1) The convention which ratified the Constitution in New York proposed an amendment with the first of these objects in view.[5] This same proposition, however, was not advocated in Congress itself until 1823, when Mr. Dickerson presented an amendment for the election of President, in which such a provision appeared.[6] A similar clause was incorporated in the resolution of the Senate Committee on Elections in the next year.[7] Another resolution from this same committee, which was limited to this subject, passed the Senate at this session by the unusually large majority of 36 yeas to 3 nays, but was not reported from the committee in the House.[8] A similar amendment, introduced by Mr. Dickerson, passed the Senate in 1826, but the vote in the House on its commitment showed

[1] As above. See following discussion.

[2] App., No. 392. See ante, par. 47.

[3] App., Nos. 605, 1717.

[4] The propositions to change the term to six years and render the President forever after inoligible are included in this classification.

[5] App., No. 65.

[6] App., No. 520.

[7] App., No. 534.

[8] App., No. 535.

that it could not secure the support of two-thirds of that body.[1]
In 1830 Senator Dickerson made another ineffectual attempt
to secure the adoption of this amendment, but it was not even
brought to a vote in the Senate.[2] Not until 1876 was this same
proposition revived. In that year the House, to forestall all
attempts on the part of the friends of General Grant to secure
for him a third term, passed by the decisive vote of 234 to 18
a resolution which declared, "That in the opinion of this House,
the precedent established by Washington and other Presidents
of the United States, in retiring from the Presidential office
after their second term, has become by universal concurrence
a part of our republican system of government, and that any
departure from this time honored custom would be unwise,
unpatriotic, and fraught with peril to our free institutions."[3]
A month later it was proposed that this unwritten amendment
should be incorporated into the Constitution, but the majority
of the House were in favor of an amendment limiting the
tenure to one term.[4] This amendment was proposed for the
last time in 1880, and was doubtless suggested by the attempt
of some of General Grant's friends to secure for him the
Republican nomination at the Chicago convention of that year.[5]
It was argued by some who had been opposed to a third term
in 1876, that the interval of four years that had intervened
would "not be a breach of the unwritten Constitution."

(2) Had the amendment suggested by two of the ratifying
conventions been adopted, the designs of the Grant men in
1880 would have been thwarted by the terms of the Constitution.[6] These amendments provided that no person should be
capable of being President for more than eight years in any
term of sixteen and fifteen years, respectively.[7]

In the First Congress Mr. Tucker of South Carolina moved
to add an amendment to the list to be recommended to the
States, making it impossible for any person to be President

---

[1] App., No. 545. Dickerson's speech gave a review of the plans before the Constitutional Convention. Interesting to note that Benton voted against it, later with Jackson
he favored one term only.

[2] App., No. 604.

[3] December 15, 1875. Introduced by Mr. Springer; House Journal, pp. 66–67. As early
as 1872 the New York Herald had raised the cry against "Cæsarism." See article by
McMaster in Forum, November, 1895. For Grant's letter in regard to a third term, see
McPherson's Hand Book of Politics for 1876, p. 154.

[4] App., No. 1411.

[5] App., Nos. 1511, 1515.

[6] Virginia, North Carolina. App., Nos. 38, 91.

[7] In the convention of 1787, Mr. Pinckney had proposed "that no person should be eligible for more than six years in any twelve." Rejected, five States to six. Elliot v, p. 368.

more than eight years in any term of twelve years. It was lost,[1] and in the Senate a motion to add an amendment similar to that proposed by Virginia was also lost.[2]

Possibly Washington may have been influenced somewhat by these propositions when, in 1796, he was urged to accept a reelection for a third term.

In 1803 a committee of the Senate reported a resolution that provided "that no person who had been twice successively elected President shall be eligible as President until four years elapse, when he may be eligible to the office for four years, and no longer." But the Senate rejected it by the emphatic vote of 4 to 25.[3]

From 1826 to 1850 there were seven resolutions presented, four of which were introduced by Mr. Underwood of Kentucky, to prevent any President from being eligible to office for the next ensuing term.[4] Since 1873 this same restriction has been proposed eleven times in connection with a proposition to fix the term at six years.[5]

(3) The simplest and most effective remedy would seem to be the restriction of all Presidents to a single term, a provision which the Federal Convention had first unanimously adopted.[6] Over ninety proposed amendments have affirmed that principle. It was presented to Congress first in 1815 as one of the amendments proposed by the Hartford convention, by the member from Massachusetts and Connecticut, upon the instruction of their legislatures.[7] In addition these resolutions provided that the President should not be elected from the same State two terms in succession, thus showing New England's jealousy of Virginia.[8]

This change was not again suggested until after the defeat of Jackson, in 1824. Then this proposition was presented

---

[1] App., No. 205.
[2] App., No. 279.
[3] App., No. 362. No amendment seems to have been called out in opposition to the invitation extended to Jefferson by the legislatures of several States to accept a third term. The legislatures of Georgia, Maryland, New Jersey, North Carolina, Pennsylvania, Vermont, the senate of New York, and the house of delegates of Virginia, requested him to accept a third term. Jefferson, however, declined. See "Reply to Vermont Address." Writings of Jefferson, VIII, 121; also ibid. IV, 565; V, 407. For his criticism of this feature of the Constitution at the time of its adoption, see ibid. II, 317, 330, 355, 586; III, 13. For his opinion in 1813, see ibid., VI, 213.
[4] App., Nos. 564, 609. 674, 690, 718, 755, 760.
[5] Five of these by Mr. Springer. App., Nos. 1375d, 1395, 1396, 1404, 1439, 1498. 1534, 1569, 1624, 1640, 1735.
[6] This provision fixed the term at seven years. Elliot, I, pp. 208–209.
[7] App., Nos. 431, 439, 447.
[8] See Adams, New Eng. Federalism for J. Q. Adams's comment on this, p. 322.

repeatedly, both as a direct amendment and as a provision of many of the amendments proposing a new method of electing the President. Between the years 1826 and 1846 this change was proposed some forty-five times.¹ Jackson, in each of his eight annual messages, recommended to Congress an amendment restricting the eligibility of any person to the Presidency to one term of four or six years.² In 1835 a resolution of this character was considered at length.³ Representatives from all sections advocated the change at different times. John Quincy Adams, in his "Jubilee Address," in 1839, when referring to the fact that the example of Washington and Jefferson had been held obligatory upon their successors, declared: "If this [practice] is not entirely satisfactory to the nation it is rather by its admitting one reelection than by its interdicting a second."⁴ That this reflected the public sentiment of the time is shown by the fact that within the decade embraced by the years 1832 to 1842 the legislatures of at least nine States proposed resolutions favoring the restriction to a single term.⁵ The Whig party committed itself to this principle, and its candidate in the election of 1840, General Harrison, both in his speeches during the campaign and in his inaugural, promised "to lay down at the end of the term faithfully that high trust at the feet of the people."⁶

After 1846 this amendment was not again proposed for several years.⁷ Mr. Vallandigham incorporated this restriction in his scheme for electing the President, presented by him in 1861.

---

¹ App., Nos. 561, 579, 588, 589, 590, 591, 595a, 596, 602, 606, 624, 626, 631, 634, 640, 645, 646, 653, 659, 660, 664, 667, 681, 684, 694, 702, 704a, 705, 706a, 706b, 707, 708, 709, 710, 711, 712, 713, 717a, 726, 732, 742, 745, 748.

² Consistency of Jackson called in question. Niles' Register, Vol. XL, pp. 387–389.

³ App., No. 640.

⁴ The Jubilee of the Constitution, New York, 1839. Quoted by O'Neil, p. 236.

⁵ Georgia (1833), although three years before she had opposed the change. Senate Journal, Twenty-first Congress, first session, p. 98. Indiana (1837), Maine (1841), Massachusetts (1841), Rhode Island (1841), Connecticut (1841), Indiana (1841), Delaware (1841), Vermont (1841), Vermont (1842), Kentucky (1842).

⁶ Statesman's Manual, II, pp. 1199, 1200. Preamble of Sumner's resolution containing the above quotation. Globe, Forty-second Congress, second session, p. 259. This was the watchword of the Harrisburg convention of 1839, and the Whig party in 1844 nominated Clay on the platform of "a single term for the Presidency." See Clay's speech of June 27, 1840, and letter of September 13, 1842. In the former, after asking for a "provision to render a person ineligible to the Presidency after a service of one term," he said: "Much observation and deliberate reflection has satisfied me that too much of the time, the thought, and the exertion of the incumbent are occupied during the first term in securing his reelection. The public business consequently suffers." Chief Justice Marshall had written in 1828 that he was "disposed to try the effect of confining the Chief Magistrate to a single term." Niles' Register, XXXV, p. 314.

⁷ An article in Niles' Register in 1847 opposes this change. Vol. LXXII, p. 166.

It might be set aside at the desire of two-thirds of all the electors of each section or of the States of each section when the election devolved upon Congress.[1]

During the reconstruction period an amendment to render the President ineligible to a second term was presented frequently. Senators Wade and Sumner, Representative Ashley, and President Johnson repeatedly advocated this restriction.[2] Since 1874 the same proposition has been urged some twenty-one times, and on two occasions has been brought to a vote in the House.[3] In 1875 the amendment reported by the Committee on the Judiciary, fixing the term of the President at six years and rendering the President ineligible to reelection,[4] failed for the lack of the necessary two-thirds vote.[5] In the first session of the next Congress the question was called up anew by a majority and minority report of the Committee on the Judiciary. Both the reports agreed that the President should not be eligible to reelection, but differed as to the tenure, the majority favoring the present term of four years, the minority one of six years. The highest vote obtained for any of the amendments proposed was 145 yeas to 108 nays.[6] Within the last few years amendments limiting the President to one term of six years has been a favorite proposition.[7] Of these, one proposed to make the retiring President a Senator for life,[8] and two others, to pension him for the same period.[9]

---

[1] App., No. 904.

[2] App., Nos. 995, 1039a, 1104, 1114, 1192, 1194, 1194a, 1198, 1204, 1207, 1210, 1225, 1227c, 1229, 1241, 1283d, 1343, 1352, 1356, 1368, 1369. Senator Wade declared the absence of this restriction from the Constitution as "among the most glaring defects" in the same. Globe, Thirty-ninth Congress, first session, p. 932. See preamble to Sumner's resolution, Globe, Forty-second Congress, second session, p. 259. He declared that civil service reform without this restriction would be the play of Hamlet with Hamlet left out. This the friends of Grant considered as an attack upon him. For Sumner's speech attacking Grant in 1872, see Globe for May 31. Ashley's speech, see ref. App., No. 1227c.

[3] App., Nos. 1389, 1396, 1402, 1403, 1404, 1406, 1412, 1412a, 1449, 1498, 1551, 1630, 1633, 1638, 1663, 1670, 1715, 1717, 1722, 1724, 1732.

[4] The Vice-President also when the office of President devolved upon him.

[5] App., No. 1396. Vote 134 to 104. Not to affect the person then President. The constitution of the Confederate States had a similar provision.

[6] App., No. 1412.

[7] Buchanan in 1856 gave his adhesion to the principle; promised by Hayes; advocated by Tilden in 1876; favored by Cleveland in his letter of acceptance of 1884; called for by the People's Party in 1892. In the Fifty-third Congress a resolution to make the President ineligible to succeed himself was reported favorably. House Report No. 1658.

[8] App., No. 1403.

[9] App., Nos. 1551, 1633. The first provided for an annual pension of $6,000, the second for $10,000 annually.

57. COMPENSATION OF PRESIDENT.

Congress, acting under the provision of the Constitution, fixed the salary of the President at $25,000. Only two amendments have been proposed to change his compensation.

The first of these was introduced by Senator Hillhouse of Connecticut, in 1808, in connection with his series of amendments, providing that the compensation of the President shall not exceed $15,000 per year.[1] The other, suggested by excitement over a recent bill passed by Congress changing the compensation of members, was presented by Mr. Fuller of Massachusetts, in 1822, to fix the compensation of the President, Vice-President, and members of Congress, decennially.[2] In 1876 an attempt was made to reduce the President's salary to the old figure, it having been raised in 1873 to $50,000. The effort, however, failed, as President Grant vetoed the bill, and no attempt was made to pass it over the veto.[3]

In 1882 and in 1884 amendments were introduced providing that the President should not be eligible to a second term, but should be given a pension for life.[4] This is probably but the beginning of a movement to pension civil officers, as is customary in European countries.

58. POWERS OF THE PRESIDENT—THE VETO.

Remarkably few attempts have been made to interfere with the President in the exercise of the independent duties of his office, but, on the other hand, special exception has been taken to those powers, which have brought him into collision with Congress.[5] Of these the veto power has been most frequently attacked.

The amendments contemplating some change in the exercise of the veto power naturally fall into three distinct classes: First, attempts to destroy the power, second, attempts to diminish the power, and third, attempts to enlarge the power.

---

[1] App., No. 393.
[2] App., No. 513. Ante par. 13.
[3] Mason's Veto Power, Harvard Hist. Mon. No. 1, p. 46, App. A, No. 99. Mr. Southard's amendment to create an executive council in 1878 provided a salary of $30,000 for each with no perquisites. No. 1465. Ante p. 70.
[4] App., No. 1551. By Mr. Berry, one term of four years, with an annual pension for life of $6,000. App., No. 1633. By Mr. Millard, one term of six years, with an annual pension for life of $10,000.
[5] A motion to associate the national judiciary with the President as a council of revision was three times rejected in the Convention of 1787. Elliot v, pp. 154, 349, 429. Suggested by a similar council in New York under the constitution of 1777.

(1) Two amendments have been presented to deprive the President altogether of his important prerogative of the veto. The first of these resolutions was proposed by Mr. Lewis of Virginia, in the House in 1818.[1] It provided that in the future "the President of the United States shall not have the power of approving or disapproving any bill or bills or joint resolution passed by the Senate and House of Representatives." This proposition was but one of a series of amendments introduced by Mr. Lewis at this time, to curtail the power of the President.[2] Some of the series stipulated that the judges and Cabinet officers should be chosen by Congress.[3]

The second proposition of this class was introduced in the House in 1839, by Mr. Taliaferro, also of Virginia, in connection with a similar series of amendments depriving the Executive of the power of appointment and removal.[4] The article relative to the veto was as follows: "The assent of the President to bills passed by the two branches of Congress shall be dispensed with." No important action was taken on either of these resolutions.

(2) There have been some sixteen propositions to enable a bill to be passed over the President's veto by a majority vote of all the members of each House instead of two-thirds of those present. All but six of these amendments were introduced between the years 1833 and 1842. The frequency with which Jackson and Tyler used this power, especially the unexpected attitude of Tyler toward the measures of the Whig party, was the occasion that gave rise to these attacks upon the President's prerogative. The first of these resolutions was presented by Senator Kent of Maryland, in 1833, but was laid on the table in the next session of Congress.[5] Mr. Kent again introduced the measure, and in a speech in support of the proposed change concisely stated the arguments in its favor.[6] First, "the fact that the veto power as then exercised tended to unite the legislative and executive branches, a union which was contrary to the fundamental principles of our Government;" second, "the veto had been granted to Executives only as a means

---

[1] App., No. 475.

[2] This may have been suggested by Madison's veto of an internal improvement bill in 1817. Mason's Veto Power, App. A, No. 8.

[3] Post, pars. 59, 60.

[4] App., No. 691. Post, pars. 59, 60.

[5] App., No. 629.

[6] App., No. 636. "Startled by ascertaining something of the extent to which this power is susceptible of being abused, able and patriotic statesmen have suggested various expedients for its limitation." Niles' Register, vol. LXXII, pp. 165, 166.

of defense, and that recent Presidents had exceeded their authority," and lastly, " as the Executive was exceedingly apt to encroach upon the other branches of Government, the power of that department should be curtailed."[1]

Mr. Underwood of Kentucky was especially zealous in championing such a change, introducing a similar proposition at six different times, in 1842 at the request of the general assembly of his State.[2]

Two attempts made during Tyler's Administration are especially noteworthy. The first of these was a joint resolution submitted by Henry Clay, in December of 1841.[3] Clay was so aroused by Tyler's vetoes that he was led to term this power of the President "that parent and fruitful source of all our ills."[4] In addition to the clause to permit the passage of a bill over the veto by a majority vote, his resolution contained a provision which was calculated to prevent a "pocket veto." It was as follows: " If any bill shall be presented to the President within a period less than ten days from the termination of the session of Congress during which it shall have passed and shall not be returned by him at that session it shall be his duty to return it within the three first days of the succeeding session. If he shall not so return it, with his objections, within the time therein required the two Houses shall proceed to consider it as if it had been returned during the session at which it was passed, and if upon such reconsideration it shall again pass each House by a majority of all members it shall become a law." There was a very similar provision for the prevention of a "pocket veto" by the New York council of revision in the constitution of that State as adopted in 1777.[5] Probably Clay's resolution was modeled after the New York article. This resolution was considered in the Committee of the Whole at various times throughout the session, but was not brought to a vote.

In August of the following year a select committee of the House reported through their chairman, John Quincy Adams. The report, after denouncing Tyler's wholesale use of the veto

[1] Mason's Veto Power, p. 137.
[2] App., Nos. 648, 673, 720, 729, 755, 759. See Niles' Register, XLV, p. 416.
[3] App., No. 716. One presented in 1841 by Mr. Owsley, App., No. 714.
[4] Schurz, Henry Clay, II, pp. 221-222. At time of Jackson's veto of bank bill he had suggested this same amendment, ibid., I, p. 377. Note Harrison's views upon the veto power in his inaugural. Statesman's Manual, pp. 1200-1202.
[5] New York constitution, 1777, Art. III, Poore, Charters and Constitution, part 2, p. 1332. This constitution remained in force until 1821.

power as tyrannical and meriting impeachment, closed with a
recommendation for a constitutional amendment similar to that
proposed by Mr. Kent several years before.[1] The amendment
was rejected, as a two-thirds vote in the affirmative was not
secured, the vote standing 99 to 90.[2] These events illustrate,
as Carl Schurz says in referring to Clay's proposition, "the dangerous tendency of that impulsive statesmanship which will
resort to permanent changes in the constitution of the State in
order to accomplish temporary objects."[3]

Six attempts to obtain the same amendment have been made
at infrequent intervals since.[4] One of these, proposed by Mr.
Ashley, in 1869, was suggested by the contest between President Johnson and Congress.[5] This proposition was introduced
for the last time by Senator Stewart, in 1888, and probably was
called out by President Cleveland's frequent use of the veto
power.[6]

(3) In late years several attempts have been made to enlarge the power, especially by adopting a provision which is
found in many of the State constitutions.[7]

The practice of attaching "riders" to appropriation bills,
which became common during the sixties,[8] had grown to such
an extent that President Grant, in his annual message of
1873, recommended an amendment "to authorize the Executive to approve of so much of any measure passing the two
Houses as his judgment may dictate, without approving the
whole, the disapproved portions or portion to be subject to the
same rules as now. I would add that there should be no legislation in Congress during the last twenty-four hours of its
sitting except upon vetoes, in order to give the Executive an

---

[1] App., No. 730. Globe, Twenty-seventh Congress, second session, p. 896.

[2] Mason's Veto Power, pp. 70–71.

[3] Schurz, Clay, II, p. 222. See Niles' Register, LXVII, pp. 165–166. "The remedy was
worse than the disease." The Whig attack upon the veto led the Democratic party to
insert a "plank" in their platforms from 1844 to 1856 approving the power.

[4] App., Nos. 759, 1027, 1315a, 1359, 1614, 1725.

[5] App., No. 1315a. Reference to speech see App. Mr. Ashley had presented the resolutions impeaching the President. For other amendments proposed at the same time to
limit the power of the President see post, pars. 59, 63.

[6] Mason's Veto Power, pp. 89, 90, 127, 128. Since 1889 it has again been introduced by
Mr. Butler of North Carolina, in Fifty-fourth Congress, April 7, 1896.

[7] The constitutions of twenty States permit the veto of items in appropriation bills:
New York, New Jersey, Pennsylvania, Minnesota, Nebraska, North Dakota, Montana,
Wyoming, Idaho, West Virginia, Missouri, Arkansas, Texas, California, Colorado, Georgia,
Alabama, Florida, Louisiana. Mason's Veto Power, App. E, p. 216.

[8] Judge Reagan said that in the period 1862–1875, 387 measures of general legislation had
passed as provisions of appropriation bills. Davis Am. Const. Johns Hopkins University
Studies, third series, p. 489.

opportunity to examine and approve or disapprove bills understandingly." Such an amendment, continued the President, " would protect the public against the many abuses and waste of public moneys which creep into appropriation bills and other important measures passed during the expiring hours of Congress, to which otherwise due consideration can not be given."[1]

Early in 1876 two resolutions, embodying the President's recommendation in the case of appropriation bills, were introduced, the first by Mr. Faulkner of West Virginia.[2] President Hayes, in consequence of his struggle with Congress over the attaching of riders to appropriation bills, renewed the recommendation of his predecessor.[3] This suggestion was not acted upon, but shortly after resolutions to permit the veto of items in the appropriation bills or river and harbor bills were introduced. There has been a constant agitation in favor of this change, besides the recommendation of President Arthur in 1882,[4] some thirty-one resolutions of this character having been presented in the ten years since 1878, but in no case has the resolution been brought to a vote.[5]

The advantages to be derived from such an increase of the veto power of the President are obvious. In the first place, it would make the President practically independent of the coercive power of the legislative department, and, in addition, as President Grant pointed out, would check extravagant legislation.

Four attempts to extend the power of the veto in another way have been made. It was to be effected by requiring a two-thirds majority of all the members of each branch of Congress to pass a bill over the veto instead of two-thirds of the members present, as is the present practice.[6] These resolutions were probably suggested by President Arthur to the movers of the amendment, who, it is noticeable, were from his own State, as a mark of his displeasure in consequence of the passage of the river and harbor bill over his veto on the 2d

[1] App., No. 1371.

[2] App., Nos. 1414. 1424.

[3] House Journal, Forty-sixth Congress, second session. p. 1174. Mason's Veto Power, p. 137. The list furnished Mr. Mason was slightly incomplete.

[4] App., No. 1565a. This was in his first (annual) message after the passage of the river and harbor bill over his veto. Mason's Veto Power, pp. 104–105.

[5] App., Nos. 1414, 1450, 1476, 1479, 1480. 1489, 1495, 1445a, 1502, 1462, 1564, 1565a, 1567, 1568, 1574, 1576, 1579, 1581, 1586, 1587, 1593, 1595, 1600, 1610, 1645, 1655, 1659, 1662, 1665, 1696, 1708, 1728. Similar propositions have been introduced in each of the Congresses since 1889.

[6] Mason's Veto Power, p. 120.

of August, 1882. The amendment was first presented two days later, and was reintroduced in each of the two succeeding Congresses.[1] A few of the resolutions in regard to the veto of items in appropriation bills, previously cited, also contained the provision that such items could only be passed over the veto by a similar majority of each House. Mr. Randall of Pennsylvania was the first and most zealous advocate of this reform.[2]

59. LIMITATIONS UPON THE APPOINTING POWER OF THE PRESIDENT.

The two allied powers of the President, namely, of appointment and removal, the first of which is constantly used, have naturally given rise to much dissatisfaction and friction between the legislative and executive departments, so that it is not surprising that several amendments have been proposed to place limitations upon his exercise of these powers.[3]

In 1808 Mr. Hillhouse proposed a radical change in the power of appointment. His amendment provided that all the more important officers should be appointed by the President, by and with the advice of the Senate and House of Representatives. Congress could, by law, vest the appointment of such officers as they may think proper, either in the President, by and with the advice of the Senate, or in the President alone, or heads of Departments or courts of law.[4]

In addition, there have been several resolutions presented to vest the appointment of certain executive officials in Congress. In 1818 Mr. Lewis of Virginia introduced an amendment depriving the President of the power of appointing his own Cabinet ministers, and vesting the appointment in the Senate and House by joint ballot.[5] In 1828 Mr. Barbour, also

---

[1] Ibid., p. 138. App., Nos. 1565, 1594, 1610, 1655. These provided for the submission of every order, resolution, or vote, to which the concurrence of the Senate and House may be necessary, except on questions of adjournment, to the President for his consideration, thus extending the veto power of the President to concurrent resolutions.

[2] App., Nos., 1659, 1665, 1708.

[3] The conclusion of the Federal Convention, reached at the last moment, to confer upon the Senate the power to confirm appointments (Art. II, sec. 11, cl. 2), has enabled that body to encroach upon this power of the President more successfully than upon any other. Wilson foresaw the result of this provision, for he declared: "The President will not be the man of the people, but the minion of the Senate. He can not even appoint a tide-waiter without it." On the other hand, for the influence the President is able to exert over legislation, see comments of Senator Benton, Thirty Years' View, I, 86; Story, II, 337-347.

[4] No law vesting the power of appointment shall be for a longer term than two years. App., No. 395; post, 60.

[5] App., No. 477.

of Virginia, presented an amendment to exclude the President from appointing or removing the principal Treasury officers.[1] In 1836, and again in 1838, Mr. Underwood of Kentucky, in connection with the amendments regulating the removal of officers, submitted an article which made provision for making the Treasury Department independent of the Executive, and vesting the appointment of the Secretary of the Treasury and other financial officers in Congress.[2] This change was without doubt suggested by President Jackson's manipulation of the Treasury Department in his controversy with the United States Bank. A somewhat similar amendment, introduced by Clay, in 1841, received extended consideration.[3] It was caused by the open hostility existing between Tyler and the Whigs.

The amendment presented by Mr. Taliaferro of Virginia, in 1839, which is again considered under the subject of removals, vested all the appointments, except such as are otherwise directed by law in the Senate, by a viva voce vote on nomination of some Senator, and required Congress to provide for and to regulate by law all that concerns the removal from office and the filling of vacancies.[4] Other amendments in regard to the appointment of officials were offered in this same year,[5] In 1842 Mr. Underwood again presented his amendment, but this time it included the Post-Office Department, against which charges had been made, as well as the Treasury Department.[6]

Mr. Ashley, who seemed deeply convinced of the necessity of subordinating the executive and judicial authority to the legislative, in connection with other amendments designed to accomplish this end,[7] proposed in 1869 the election of the Cabinet officers by Congress in joint convention, for the term of six years, one to retire each year. The other appointments should be made as follows: "Each member of the executive council, including the President, shall, by and with the advice of the Senate, appoint all officers for his department."[8]

[1] App., No. 586.
[2] App., Nos. 649–651.
[3] App., No. 717.
[4] App., No. 692.
[5] Mr. Tallmadge of New York, App., No. 695.
[6] App., No. 719.
[7] See ante, par. 58; post, pars. 63, 72, 73.
[8] App., No. 1315b. Each Cabinet officer could be removed by concurrent vote of the House and Senate. The executive council should keep a record of each meeting and all official transactions, which shall be subject to examination by a committee of the two Houses.

Numerous amendments presented in recent years, either conferring the election of certain of the civil officers upon the people or vesting the appointment in another power, are treated elsewhere.[1]

60. REGULATION OF THE POWER OF REMOVAL.

In addition to the amendments limiting or entirely depriving the President of the power of appointment, there have been presented a number of resolutions regulating the removal of officials. In the First Congress Mr. Tucker proposed an amendment giving the President the power " to suspend any person from office whom he shall have reason to think unfit."[2]

The amendment presented by Mr. Hillhouse, in 1808, besides making provision for new regulations to govern the appointing power, required the consent of both the Senate and the House before any removal should be made.[3]

The introduction of the "spoils system" into national politics with the accession of Jackson to the Presidency, led to the censure of the President by the National Republican members of the Senate in 1829, but did not result in the presentation of any amendments until 1835. In that year Mr. Vance of Ohio introduced an amendment, by the terms of which the President was prohibited from removing any person from office without the concurrence of the Senate.[4] Webster maintained that the Senate already had full right to regulate the removal of officers, for the decision of 1789 was not in harmony with the Constitution.[5]

---

[1] Post, pars. 61, 64.

[2] App., No. 207. The question of removal came up first in the First Congress in connection with the bill creating the office of Secretary of the Treasury. By the casting vote of the Vice-President the bill passed with a provision allowing the removal by the President alone. The majority were probably influenced by respect for the exalted character of Washington Story, II, pp. 351–354, notes; Davis, Am. Consts., p. 492.

[3] App., No. 396. In the criticism found among John Adams's papers upon Hillhouse's amendments was the following referring to this proposition and the one in regard to the appointing power: "It reduces the President's office to a mere Doge of Venice; a mere head of wood; a mere tool of the aristocratic branch—the Senate." Works, Vol. VI, p. 534. See ante, par. 47.

[4] App., No, 639.

[5] Speech of February 16, 1835. Works, IV, 179 et seq. Calhoun took a similar position. Works, I, 345, 369. The Federalist, No. 77, maintained the same as now asserted by Webster. Madison, however, favored giving the power to the President alone. Story, II. 353–354; Kent, I, 289–290; Rüttimann, Das Nordamerikanische Bundesstaatsrecht (Zürich, 1867), I, 280; L. Dupriez, Les Ministres dans Les Principaux Pays D'Europe et D'Amerique, II, 40 (Paris, 1893).

Another proposition offered by Mr. Taliaferro of Virginia, in 1839, declared that the power of the President to remove from office and to fill vacancies thus created is not a power conferred on him by the Constitution, either expressly or by necessary construction of any power delegated to him. The amendment, however, prescribed as one of the duties of the President the commissioning of all the officers to be appointed under the Government, expressing in each commission the term of service of the office.[1]

In 1836, and four times thereafter, Mr. Underwood of Kentucky presented an amendment which provided that the terms of all offices except those provided for in the Constitution, and the mode of removal from office, should be regulated by Congress.[2]

The general assembly of Kentucky, in 1842, proposed an amendment to confine removals from office by the President to heads of Departments and those employed in the foreign service.[3] In the sixties the Senators from Kentucky were very solicitous in regard to the power of removal. In 1863 Senator Davis offered an amendment limiting the President's power to remove from office, in the case of all those officers in whose nomination the advice and consent of the Senate is required, until the next session of the Senate only, unless it should approve of such removal.[4] In the next year Senator Powell proposed as an additional article to the thirteenth amendment a provision to permit the President to remove at pleasure the principal officers in the Executive Departments and all persons connected with the diplomatic service. All other officers of the Executive Departments might be removed at any time for cause, by the President or other appointing power, but when so removed the removal should be reported to the Senate with the reasons.[5]

It is noteworthy that the "tenure-of-office act" of 1867[6] accomplished the object aimed at by some of these amendments; but this act was partially repealed in 1869, and wholly repealed in 1877, so that at the present time the full power of removal has been restored to the President. In 1882 an

---

[1] App., No. 692.
[2] In 1838, 1842, 1849, 1850, App., Nos. 651, 677, 722, 755c, and 762.
[3] App., No. 728.
[4] App., No. 979.
[5] App., No. 996.
[6] Called out by the hostility of Congress to Johnson.

amendment was presented the object of which has practically been accomplished by the above-mentioned act of 1877.[1]

These propositions were but an episode in the history of the amending power, for upon the decline of the influence of Jackson the attempts to amend the Constitution in these particulars, with the exception of the instances noted, end.

For the sake of completeness, it is necessary to refer to a few additional propositions in regard to the tenure of office. An amendment introduced in the Senate of the First Congress reveals the fear of some of a revival of the hereditary system. This interesting amendment was as follows: "That no man or set of men are entitled to exclusive or separate public emoluments or privileges from the community but in consideration of public services, which not being descendible, neither ought the offices of magistrate, Senator, or judge or any other public offices to be hereditary."[2]

Within recent years seven amendments have been proposed relative to fixing the tenure of civil officers of the United States. Six of these provide for a four-year term for all such officers except judges and heads of Departments and those whose duties were temporary in their nature, unless a longer term was fixed by law.[3] The remaining one proposed a five-year term.[4]

61. CIVIL SERVICE REFORM.

In addition to the propositions restricting the appointment to office of members of Congress, electors and certain other persons,[5] one curious attempt was made, previous to the civil war, to prevent certain abuses incident to the patronage system by means of an amendment to the Constitution. This amendment was proposed by Mr. Quincy of Massachusetts, January 30, 1811. It provided that "no person standing to any Senator or Representative in the relation of father, brother, or son,

---

[1] App., No. 1541. It conferred upon the President power to remove heads of Departments and bureaus, and all persons connected with the diplomatic service. All other officers could be removed when their services were unnecessary, or for cause, but the reasons should be reported to the Senate. In 1886, owing to some friction between President Cleveland and the Senate, an amendment was proposed to give the election of Senators to the people, because "The Senate, a subordinate branch of the legislative department, * * * is now attempting to interfere with the power confided solely to the President of removing officials." Preamble to App., No. 1674. See ante, p. 61, note 7.

[2] App., No. 270.

[3] App., Nos. 1344, 1376, 1405, 1517, 1532, elected by the people; No. 1547 appointed by a commission. See post. par. 61.

[4] App., No. 1566, appointed by a house of electors. Post, par. 61.

[5] Ante, pars. 12, 21, 55.

by blood or marriage, shall be appointed to any civil office under the United States, or shall receive any place, agency, contract, or emolument from or under any Department or office thereof." [1]

Mr. Wright moved to amend the same by adding a clause requiring "that each member of the Senate or House of Representatives, when he takes his seat, file a list of his relations precluded by the said resolution." No further attempt, in addition to amendments referred to elsewhere, was made to counteract the system of rotation in office until 1864. In that year Senator Powell of Kentucky included in his article, to change the method of electing the President, a paragraph which declared that "it shall not be deemed compatible with the duty of a President habitually to use the patronage of his office for the special advantage of any particular political party, or suffer the patronage of any subordinate office so to be used." [2]

Not until the agitation for the inauguration of reform in the civil service was well under way was another amendment suggested. In 1876 Mr. Williams of Michigan proposed a civil service reform amendment. It prohibited Senators and Representatives "from soliciting appointments to or removals from office." It further made provision for the creation of a commission of not less than five or more than nine which should have absolute advisory and confirmatory power in regard to appointments to and removals from office. Congress, however, was allowed to provide for the election of certain civil officers by the people of their respective States, districts, or locality, subject to removal by the civil service commission. [3]

Three years later, Mr. Turner introduced a resolution proposing that the Committee on Civil Service Reform in both branches of Congress should "be authorized and directed to inquire into and report upon the propriety of curtailing by constitutional amendment and by law the vast, corrupting, and dangerous patronage of the executive department." [4]

In the Forty-seventh Congress there were two amendments proposed depriving the President of a large share of the power to make appointments, by vesting this power in the one case in a commission, in the other in a house of electors. The first of these provided for the nomination and appointment of all public officers, except the heads of the Executive Departments, by a commission of three, composed of two commissioners appointed by the President—with the confirmation of the Senate—and the head of the Executive Department to which the business of the appointees belonged. Such appointments were to be temporary until confirmed by the Senate.[1] The other resolution proposed the creation of a house of electors, to be composed of one member from each State, elected by the people of the respective States, for the term of six years. Congress was to designate "what officers shall be elected, examined, or confirmed by the house of electors, and who shall make appointments for minor officers."[2]

Others have proposed as a remedy for the evils of the "spoils system" the making of many of the civil offices elective, thus rendering them in a large measure independent of the coercion of the Administration in power at Washington.[3]

62. MILITARY POWERS OF THE PRESIDENT.

Among the amendments proposed by the ratifying convention of the State of New York was one forbidding the President to command an army in the field in person, without the previous desire of the Congress.[4] In the First Congress Mr. Tucker, doubtless influenced by this proposal, attempted to have the words "Commander in Chief" struck out of the Constitution,[5] and the phrase "have power to direct the operations" inserted in their place.[6] No similar proposition has been presented in either of the four wars of the United States.[7]

63. THE PARDONING POWER OF THE PRESIDENT.

The New York convention which ratified the Constitution also proposed an amendment prohibiting the President granting pardon for treason without the consent of Congress, but

---

[1] App., No. 1547. The commission also had power of removal, subject to approval of the Senate. Their term was to be four years, subject to removal by the President with consent of the Senate.

[2] App., No. 1566. This resolution also provided for the election of postmasters by the people of the respective postal districts, subject to the confirmation of the house of electors or Postmaster-General, as Congress shall designate. The President was still to have the power of removal of any officer in the civil service for any reason except political.

[3] See post, par. 64. The preamble of No. 1427 recites the evils and degradation of the system whereby one hundred thousand officers of the United States are subject to the coercion of the Administration in power, required to act, vote, and contribute money in accordance with the central will, by means of which caucuses and elections are controlled.

[4] App., No. 67.

[5] Art. II, Sect. 2.

[6] App., No. 206.

[7] See comment on the power of the President to force a war upon the country, written at the time of the Mexican war. Niles' Register, vol. LXXII, pp. 165, 166.

permitting him to grant reprieves until the case was laid before Congress.[1]

Only one other amendment has been proposed on this subject. This was suggested in 1869 by Mr. Ashley, who arraigned President Johnson for the wholesale use of the pardoning power. He suggested that the approval in writing of a majority of the Cabinet should be required before the President could grant reprieves or pardons, and that no general amnesty or pardon to persons who may have been engaged in rebellion against the Government should be declared until the Congress had given its consent.[2]

64. ELECTION OF EXECUTIVE OFFICIALS.

There have been twenty-eight propositions presented to Congress to amend the Constitution relative to permitting the election of postmasters and other local officers by the people.[3] All of these have been introduced since 1848, and fifteen since 1881. The first time such a practice was suggested was in 1848, when Mr. Wentworth of Illinois offered a resolution to require the Committee on the Judiciary to inquire whether any alteration of the Constitution was necessary in order to refer the election of either postmasters, or land officers, or revenue officers, or officers of any other kind, now appointed by the President, by and with the advice of the Senate, directly to the people. The resolution was agreed to, but the committee does not appear to have ever reported. Two other amendments were submitted previous to the civil war—one upon the election of deputy postmasters, the other upon the election of postmasters and collectors.

The first amendment on this subject after the war was introduced in 1866 by Mr. Broomall. It proposed that assessors and internal-revenue collectors should be elected by the people.[4] A proposition for a popular election of some one or more classes of Federal officials has been presented in every Congress since 1871 down to the Forty-ninth Congress. Many of these, in addition to postmasters and revenue collectors, even provided that marshals, district attorneys and all other United States officials whose duties require them to live in the State,

---

[1] App., No. 66.
[2] App., No. 1315c.
[3] App., Nos. 751, 768, 776, 1193, 1331, 1334, 1344, 1376, 1379, 1405, 1417, 1427, 1444, 1517, 1526, 1527, 1532, 1546, 1554, 1556, 1558, 1566, 1582, 1598, 1618, 1646, 1658, 1664.
[4] App., No. 1193.

except judges, should be elected by the people of the State, district, or locality where they perform their duties.[1]

In harmony with the expedient which has been made use of in recent years by some of the Representatives as a means of settling the vexed question of patronage, Mr. Grout of Vermont introduced, in 1886, an amendment requiring the recommendation of a majority of voters for the appointment of postmasters.[2]

The efficiency of the present postal system would probably be impaired by conferring the election of postmasters upon the people. Not only would popular elections be likely to destroy the uniformity of the system, but it would tend to cause the officials to feel more responsibility to the local electors than to the central office at Washington, even though they were subject to removal by the head of the Department.

65. PUNISHMENT OF OFFICIAL MISCONDUCT.

Two amendments only have been introduced on this subject. The first of these—presented in 1838 by Mr. Southgate of Kentucky—provided that any officer convicted of embezzling public money should be declared forever thereafter incapable of holding any office of honor, trust, or profit under the Government, or of exercising the right of suffrage.[3]

The second was submitted in 1876 by Mr. Lord of New York. It declared that "the Congress shall enact suitable laws for the prevention and punishment of official misconduct and to insure official accountability," and further stipulated that any person convicted of bribery or converting the public money should not be pardoned, and should be disqualified from holding any office under the United States.[4]

66. STATUS OF THE EXECUTIVE.

In concluding this very important subject, it may be well to see what effect these proposed amendments have had on the position of the Executive. It is remarkable that among the multiplicity of propositions there has been no important movement to change the form of the Executive. With one exception, the only ones remarked were the attempts made in the

---

[1] App., Nos. 1331, 1334, 1376, 1379, 1405, 1417, 1427, 1526, 1532, 1546, 1554, 1558, 1598, 1618. Some included even judges. Post, par. 69. Most made provision for removals for cause either by the President or as Congress may by law direct.
[2] App., No. 1664. See also No. 1566, ante, par. 61.
[3] App., No. 688.
[4] App., No. 1426.

critical days just before the civil war by Southern men who, for the purpose of retaining their influence in this department of the Government, proposed that a dual Executive or a council should be substituted for the single Executive.

The question of the method of electing the President has already been discussed. The plans have been so various as to preclude the probability of any change, although it has long been recognized that reform is desirable. There is a growing conviction that the present system should give way to one which should more readily express the will of the majority of the people. The difficulty has been to find a plan free from flaws and then to unite the country in its support. In recent years more attention has been given to attempts to secure an amendment fixing the term of President at six years and making him ineligible to reelection than to changing the method of election.

Although there have been several attempts to deprive the President of certain of the powers conferred upon him by the Constitution, they have all, fortunately, failed. On the other hand, the recent movement to give the Executive power to veto items in appropriation bills is deserving of success, inasmuch as it would tend to check extravagant legislation.

There seems to be no need of an amendment contemplating reform in the civil service. Already it is sufficiently within the power of Congress to protect the service, and no amendment is likely to add force.

Of the five hundred amendments relative to the executive department which have been submitted, eleven have passed one House and one both Houses of Congress, being immediately ratified by the States.

In a word, then, it may be said that the status of the Executive is at the present time stable and strong. The tendency to-day is to increase rather than to diminish his power, and to make the office more independent of Congress.[1]

---

[1] Foster Com. on the Const., 1, 305.

Chapter IV.

AMENDMENTS AFFECTING THE FORM OF THE JUDICIARY DEPARTMENT.

67. STATUS OF THE JUDICIARY.

Inasmuch as the Constitution contains less detail in regard to the judiciary department than upon either of the other departments of the Government, the opportunity for change has been slight, and hence comparatively few attempts have been made to alter the provisions of the Constitution. The judiciary has been also the most conservative branch of the Government, and has almost entirely refrained from encroaching upon the prerogatives of either of the other departments, hence it has been the object of attack only in exceptional cases.[1] Most of the attempts to change the judiciary, as in the case of the legislative department, were made in the earlier years of our history under the Constitution. First appeared the movement to limit the jurisdiction of the Federal courts, which finally culminated in the eleventh amendment, forbidding the United States courts entertaining a suit instituted by a citizen of a State against a State. Next came the only considerable attack on the judiciary, in the propositions for the removal and impeachment of judges. Various suggestions have been made to render judges ineligible to other offices and thus keep the court free from political entanglements. Attempts have been likewise made from time to time to secure the appointment of the judges for a term of years, and hence to enable the popular will more readily to control their action.[2] The friction caused by the disputes between the States and the General Government called out several propositions for the creation of some tribunal other than the Supreme Court to decide such cases. Each of these subjects will be considered more in detail in the present chapter.

68. COMPOSITION AND NUMBER OF JUDGES.

The Constitution made provision in broad terms for the establishment of the judicial power[3] and left Congress to create by

---

[1] Bryce, I, 267-271.
[2] These were doubtless suggested by the growing practice in the States.
[3] Art. III, sec. 1.

law the superior courts, and to fix the number of judges of both the Supreme and inferior courts. Accordingly, on September 24, 1789, Congress organized the judicial system of the United States. The Supreme Court was constituted with a Chief Justice and five associates. From time to time as it became necessary to extend the jurisdiction of the circuit courts, additional judgeships were created. In 1807 Congress added an associate judge; in 1837 two more, and one in 1863.[1] Inasmuch as it has been possible to change the composition of the court by simple legislation, there have been but three attempts to secure a constitutional amendment on this subject. Two of these were resolutions in regard to judges of the Supreme Court and other courts, introduced by Mr. Williams of Pennsylvania, at two different times during the year 1867.[2] They were doubtless suggested by the trouble existing between Congress and President Johnson over the reconstruction policy. There was a vacant judgeship in the Supreme Court in consequence of the death of Judge Catron in 1865. Congress was unwilling to have the President fill the vacancy, inasmuch as it was probable that the Supreme Court would be called upon to decide in regard to the constitutionality of the reconstruction acts within a few months after the introduction of the last of these amendments. Congress passed a law over the President's veto[3] forbidding the filling of any vacancy until the number of associate judges should be reduced to six. Only one other amendment has been proposed on this subject. This was introduced by Mr. Whyte of Maryland, and proposed that the following section be added to the third article: "The Supreme Court of the United States shall consist of a Chief Justice of the United States and —— associate justices, and —— of whom shall constitute a quorum."[4] The number of the judges was left in blank, to be filled in according to the wisdom of Congress, but Mr. Whyte desired to place the number at thirteen. This was intended to relieve the judges from the pressure of work resting upon them, the court, owing to the rapid accumulation of cases, being months behind in its work.[5]

[1] By act of 1869 the number of the Supreme Court is fixed at one Chief Justice and eight associates.

[2] App., Nos. 1208, 1214. Text not given.

[3] Mason's Veto Power, App. A, No. 67.

[4] App., No. 1516.

[5] The Fifty-first Congress passed a law establishing new courts and creating fifteen new judgeships, to remedy this matter

There is no apparent need of constitutional amendments to secure the control of Congress over the judiciary. The legislative department has power to organize or to disorganize courts at will but has only rarely made use of its power. The need, if any, is for an amendment to render the judiciary still more independent.[1]

69. CHOICE OF JUDGES.

In accordance with the provision of the Constitution, judges of the Supreme Court and the inferior courts are appointed by the President "by and with the advice and consent of the Senate."[2] During the first ninety years of our history under the Constitution only four amendments have been proposed contemplating any change in the choice of judges. The first of these was introduced by Senator Hillhouse in 1808.[3] It provided that the appointment of judges of the Supreme Court and certain other officials should require the ratification of the House of Representatives as well as the Senate. Ten years later Mr. Lewis of Virginia presented an amendment which proposed to reduce the power of the President materially, as by its terms all appointments to offices and vacancies "in the judiciary of the United States" were vested in the Senate and House of Representatives on joint ballot.[4] No further amendments on this subject were proposed for nearly fifty years, when, in 1867, and again in the following year, Mr. Cobb, of Wisconsin, introduced a similar proposition for the choice of the judges of the Supreme Court. In addition, Congress should prescribe by law by what mode judges of the inferior courts of the United States and Territories should be appointed or elected.[5]

Within the last decade, in harmony with the general tendency toward popular election of Senators, United States marshals, district attorneys, revenue collectors, and postmasters, as shown by various resolutions, there have been a few attempts to secure the election of the judges of the inferior courts of the United States by popular vote.[6] The first of these was introduced by Mr. Voorhees of Indiana. It made provision for

---

[1] Foster, Com. on Const., pp. 303–304.

[2] Art. II, sec. 11, cl. 2.

[3] App., No. 395, ante, par. 59

[4] App., No. 476.

[5] App., Nos. 1196, 1227; also limited term to eight years. See post, par. 72.

[6] Probably suggested by the system in use in a large number of the States—at present thirty-one—of electing the State judiciary by popular vote. Bryce, I, 505; Hitchcock, Am. State Consts., 47–60.

the popular election of judges of the United States district courts in such manner as the legislatures of the States should provide by law, as well as for postmasters, revenue collectors, marshals, and district attorneys.[1]

Two similar resolutions were introduced within the next two years.[2]

70. JUDGES TO BE INELIGIBLE TO OTHER OFFICES.

Two of the State conventions that ratified the Constitution[3] incorporated into the series of amendments which they recommended a proposition prohibiting a judge of the Supreme Court "holding any other office under the United States, or any of them." This restriction without doubt was intended to prevent Executive influence over the judiciary, and to keep the judges free from prejudice in regard to any political or diplomatic question upon which it might be necessary later for them as judges to render a decision. This amendment was not suggested in the First Congress; and in 1794 Chief Justice Jay was appointed as a special envoy to England. Some objection to his appointment seems to have been made on the ground of his being the Chief Justice, which found expression in the resolution of the legislature of Virginia[4] proposing an amendment to the Constitution restricting judges from holding any other office or appointment whatever." Five years later two similar amendments were presented. The first of these was submitted by Senator Pinckney of South Carolina, February 3, 1800. It provided that neither the Chief Justice nor any judge of the United States should hold any other appointment or office "during his continuance in office as a judge of the United States, and that the acceptance of such other office shall vacate the appointment of any judge accepting the same."[5] In ten days Mr. Livingston of New York introduced the other proposition. It forbade the appointment of a United States judge during his continuance in office or within six months after he may have resigned the same, to any other than a judiciary office under the United States.[6] These were without doubt called out by the appointment in the previous year by Presi-

---

[1] App., No. 1526.
[2] App., Nos. 1545, 1582. One by Senator George also provided for a fourteen-year term and removal for disability. See post, par. 72.
[3] New York and Rhode Island. App., Nos. 72, 119. The Rhode Island proposition also proposed that Federal officers should be incapable of holding State offices.
[4] App., No. 327d.
[5] App., No. 335. McMaster, II, 474.
[6] App., No. 337.

dent Adams of Chief Justice Ellsworth as one of the three commissioners to France. The business of the Supreme Court at this time was so small that the temporary absence of the Chief Justice would not have seriously interfered with its work.

Some of the resolutions introduced in more recent years, proposing amendments either in regard to the judiciary or the election of President and Vice-President, have placed restrictions upon the eligibility of the Chief Justice, and in some cases upon all of the judges of the Federal courts, to other offices. The one introduced by Mr. Ashley, in 1869, was the most comprehensive and restrictive. He proposed rendering a Federal judge ineligible to any office under the National Government.[1] Mr. Powell included in his unique amendment, for the election of President by the electors out of their own number, a provision that no office should be incompatible with that of an elector except the office of Chief Justice of the United States.[2] An amendment suggested by Senator Poland, in 1872, stipulated that no judge of any court of the United States should be chosen President or Vice-President within two years after the termination of his judicial office.[3]

The amendment reported from the House Committee on Elections in 1874, as well as Mr. Smith's substitute proposition, both of which made provision for the canvassing of the returns of the Presidential election by the Supreme Court, rendered a person who has been a justice of the Supreme Court ineligible to the office of President.[4] A similar prohibition has been proposed on three other occasions.[5]

The Edmunds resolution, as reported by the Committee on the Judiciary in 1876, which also provided for the canvassing of the returns and for the decision of contested-election cases by the Supreme Court, was less stringent. It stipulated that justices of the Supreme Court should be ineligible to the Presidency until two years after the expiration of the term of service.[6] It was subsequently amended so that a judge of the Supreme Court was debarred from receiving appointments to

---

[1] App., No. 1315d. In his speech Mr. Ashley said, "One-third or more (of the members of the Supreme Court) are crazed with the glitter of the Presidency." Globe, App., Fortieth Congress, third session, p. 210.

[2] App., No. 1026. Ante, par. 47.

[3] App., No. 1351. This amendment also made Senators and Representatives ineligible for the Presidency during their term.

[4] App., No. 1386.

[5] App., Nos. 1345, 1474, 1482.

[6] App., No. 1423.

any office under the United States until four years next after he had ceased to be such justice.

71. REMOVAL OF JUDGES—IMPEACHMENT.

The framers of the Constitution, in order to secure the independence of the judiciary, very wisely provided that the judges should hold their office during good behavior,[1] hence they could be removed only by impeachment. The ratifying convention of New York appears to have been dissatisfied with that provision of the Constitution which vested in the Senate the sole power to try impeachments,[2] for it included in the series of amendments which it recommended an elaborate article on this subject. It proposed that the court for the trial of impeachments should consist of the Senate, the judges of the Supreme Court of the United States, and the first or senior judge of the highest court of general and ordinary common law jurisdiction in each State, a majority of those present being necessary to convict.[3] In the series of amendments proposed by Mr. Benson of New York, in 1791, for the creation and conduct of general judicial courts, were articles providing that judges of this court might be impeached by the most numerous branch of the State legislature, as well as the House of Representatives, the impeachment to be tried by a court established by an act of Congress, to be held in each State, and to consist only of United States Senators, judges of the United States Supreme Court, and judges of the general judicial courts. A two-thirds vote was necessary for conviction.[4]

Immediately upon the failure of the Senate to convict Judge Chase in the celebrated impeachment trial in 1805,[5] John Randolph, who had been one of the House managers of the trial, in his discomfiture, proposed an amendment so as to make United States judges removable by the President on the joint address of both Houses of Congress.[6]

[1] Art. III, sec. 1.
[2] Art. I, sec. 3, cl. 6.
[3] App., No. 70. It further gave Congress power to pass the necessary laws for the establishment and regulation of this court. This was modeled after the provision in her constitution.
[4] App., Nos. 306, 307, 308.
[5] For Jefferson's connection with the attempt to impeach Chase, see Willoughby, The Supreme Court, pp. 90-92; Morse, Jefferson, pp. 262-263. His great disappointment is seen in his letters. "Impeachment is not even a scarecrow." Works, VII, pp. 256; see also ibid., pp. 134, 192, 216. For account of trial see Foster, Com. on Const. I, pp. 533-542; Adams, U. S., II, Chap. X.
[6] App., No. 306. Suggested probably by the English system. See Jefferson's Works, VII, p. 256. A similar provision in five of the State constitutions of the Revolutionary period. Davis, Am. Consts. pp. 506, 530. See ante, par. 29, for amendment introduced by Nicholson reflecting on the judicial fairness of the Senate. Also Bryce, I, p. 268.

The resolution was referred to the Committee of the Whole by a vote of 68 to 33. In the following year he reintroduced this amendment and it received considerable discussion.[1] Between the years 1807 and 1812 nine amendments were presented on the removal of judges.[2] Among these were the resolutions of the legislatures of the States of Vermont, Massachusetts, and Pennsylvania,[3] but in Massachusetts the next legislature revoked and annulled the instructions of the preceding year.[4] There was some difference in these propositions as to the majority required to pass such a joint address. Some, as that proposed by Mr. Wright of Maryland, simply required a majority of the members present,[5] others required a two-thirds[6] or a three-fifths vote of each House,[7] while the Massachusetts proposition called for a majority of the House of Representatives and two-thirds of the Senate.[8] The proposition submitted by Mr. Maclay also provided that on all trials of impeachment "a majority of the Senate shall be competent to conviction."[9] This was probably suggested by the fact that a majority vote had been secured on some of the articles in the trial of Judge Chase, but all fell short of the two-thirds essential to convict. Two additional amendments in regard to the removal of judges were presented, one in 1816 by Mr. Sanford of New York, the other in 1822 by Mr. Holmes of Maine. The former provided for the removal of any judge of the Federal courts whenever the President and two-thirds of both Houses of Congress should consider that such action would promote the public good.[10] The latter was similar to Randolph's proposition.[11]

With these amendments the only considerable attack on the personnel of the judiciary practically ends, although propositions have since been submitted at two widely separated periods

---

[1] App., No. 371.

[2] App., Nos. 380, 381, 382, 383, 385, 389, 398, 402, 405. The popular branch of the legislatures of Virginia and Tennessee approved of this amendment. History of this attack, see Adams, U. S., vol. IV, pp. 204–207. For reasons which induced presentation of No. 405 (presented by Adams), see Niles' Register, II, p. 109.

[3] The legislature of Rhode Island requested their Senators and Representatives to oppose such an amendment. Annals of Congress, Eleventh Congress, second session, p. 631.

[4] Resolves of Massachusetts, November 14, 1808, vol. XII, p. 12, 317.

[5] App., No. 402.

[6] Mr. Tiffin of Ohio, App., No. 380.

[7] Mr. Campbell of Tennessee, App., No. 382.

[8] App., No. 389.

[9] App., No. 383.

[10] App., No. 456.

[11] App., No. 508a.

by two different members of Congress. Over a quarter of a century later Mr. Underwood of Kentucky twice proposed an amendment which declared that whenever a majority of the members of each branch of Congress should concur in an address to the President for the removal of any judge, his office should be vacant from the day of the delivery of such address.[1] In 1867 Mr. Williams of Pennsylvania twice renewed the proposal for the removal of judges by the President on the address of two-thirds of each branch of Congress.[2]

72. TERM OF JUDGES—AGE LIMIT.

The life tenure of judges was agreed to by the unanimous vote of the Convention of 1787. From time to time attempts have been made to limit this tenure either by prescribing an age limit or by fixing upon a definite term of years. The first of these propositions was introduced by Senator Pope of Kentucky, in 1809, in connection with a provision for the removal of judges. It proposed that judges should not continue in office after attaining the age of 65.[3] A second, submitted by Mr. Eastman of New Hampshire, in 1826, fixed the age limit at 70.[4] Some ten years later a motion was made directing the Committee on the Judiciary " to inquire at what age judges shall be rendered incompetent to serve."[5] An age limit was proposed for the last time by Mr. Ashley, in 1869, in connection with his amendment for a twenty-year term for judges. It required the retirement of judges at 70 years with a pension for life.[6] These resolutions were evidently intended to guard against the chance of a judge remaining on the bench after he had lost his vigor and acumen. The object has been attained by the act of April 10, 1869, providing for a retiring allowance.[7]

The second group of amendments on this subject was probably suggested by a desire to bring the judges more directly

[1] App., Nos. 755b, 761.
[2] App., Nos. 1208, 1214. A judge may be removed on the address of the legislature in thirty-six of the States. Bryce, I, p. 506; Davis, J. H. U. Studies. 3d series, pp. 506, 530; Foster, Com. on the Const., I, sec. 96, pp. 605–606. An amendment, proposed by Mr. George, in 1882, for the term and election of judges of the inferior courts, provided that the President, with the consent of two-thirds of the Senate, may remove a judge for disability. App., No. 1545.
[3] App., No. 398.
[4] App., No. 575.
[5] App., No. 638.
[6] App., No. 1315d. Mr. Ashley said it was a sad sight to see " one-third of its members sleeping upon the bench and dying with age, and one-third or more crazed with the glitter of the Presidency." Globe, App., Fortieth Congress, third session, p. 210; ante, par. 70.
[7] Revised Statutes, 1878, sec. 714.

under popular influence. Three of these amendments introduced in 1807–08, calling for the removal of judges,[1] also
stipulated that the judges should hold office for a limited term
of years.[2] This same proposition was not again introduced
until the early thirties,[3] when three resolutions proposing
such a change were presented.[4] Between the years 1839 and
1844 Senator Tappan of Ohio offered at four different times
an amendment limiting the judges to a term of seven years.[5]

Andrew Johnson was particularly zealous in advocating an
amendment to limit the judges to a term of twelve years, one-
third retiring every four years. This amendment was first
presented by him in the early fifties, when a member of the
House.[6] In 1860, when Senator, he recommended the same
proposition in connection with his compromise amendment, and
in this draft he provided that all the vacancies should be filled
by persons one-half coming from slaveholding States and one-
half from nonslaveholding States, so that the court should be
equally divided between the two sections.[7] In 1868, as President, he again urged in a special message to Congress the
necessity of limiting the term of judges to twelve years.[8]

In the later sixties there were five additional propositions
to change the tenure of judges to a stated term of years. Two
of these resolutions proposed an eight-year term,[9] two a ten,
and the remaining one a twenty-year term.[10] In 1879 the amendment proposing a twelve-year term was again revived.[11] The
preamble of this last resolution characterized "the life tenure

---

[1] Ante, par. 71.

[2] App., Nos. 380, 383, 385.

[3] Jefferson's fear and jealousy of the power of the judiciary was so aroused that in 1822
we find him suggesting this means of controlling the court. In a letter to William T.
Barry, of July 2, 1822, he writes: "Before the canker is become inveterate, before its
venom has reached so much of the body politic as to get beyond control, remedy should
be applied. Let the future appointment of judges be for four or six years and renewable
by the President and Senate. This will bring their conduct at regular periods under
revision and probation and may keep them in equipoise between the general and special
governments. * * * That there should be public functionaries independent of the
nation, whatever may be their demerits, is a solecism in a republic of the first order of
absurdity and inconsistency." Works, VII, p. 256, see pars. 71, 77.

[4] App., Nos. 605, 608, 637, 638, 639. Another presented in 1848 by Mr. Thompson of Mississippi, No. 752.

[5] App., Nos. 700, 704, 731, 737.

[6] App., Nos. 767, 772.

[7] App., No. 815. Ante, p. 91.

[8] App., No. 1232.

[9] Both by Mr. Cobb of Wisconsin, App., Nos. 1196, 1227; also proposed choice by both
Houses of Congress; ante, par. 69.

[10] App., Nos. 1246, 1315d, 1320.

[11] By Mr. Finley of Ohio, twice; App., Nos. 1478, 1494.

of office" as "a relic of the Old World and incompatible with
the genius and spirit of our republican form of government,
placing public functionaries above a due sense of responsibility
to the people."[1]

73. COMPENSATION OF JUDGES.

The ratifying convention of Virginia proposed an amendment which provided that the salary of a judge should not be
increased or diminished during his continuance in office otherwise than by general regulations of salary, which should take
place in a revision of the subject at stated periods of not less
than seven years.[2] The North Carolina convention incorporated this same recommendation into their series of proposed
amendments,[3] and it was likewise moved in the Senate as an
additional article to the Bill of Rights, but it failed to pass.[4]
The only other change suggested to the provision of the Constitution on this subject was a verbal one, made in connection
with an amendment on the removal of judges in 1809, by Mr.
Pope.[5]

74. ESTABLISHMENT AND JURISDICTION OF INFERIOR COURTS.

Circuit and district courts were created by Congress in 1789
under the power in the Constitution to establish "inferior
courts." The ratifying convention of Virginia proposed an
amendment, which the North Carolina convention copied, the
aim of which was to take from Congress the power to create
Federal courts inferior to the Supreme Court, other than courts
of admiralty.[6] This same proposition was introduced in the
Senate during the first session of Congress.[7] Attempts were
likewise made in the House to substitute for the words "tribunals inferior to the Supreme Court" wherever they appear
in the Constitution, the words "courts of admiralty," thus
accomplishing the same end which the Virginia amendment
had in view.[8]

The New York convention also included in their series of
proposed amendments a proposition limiting the jurisdiction

[1] Life tenure for judges is only retained in four of the States. Bryce, 1, p. 506.
[2] App., No. 45.
[3] App., No. 98.
[4] App., No. 287.
[5] App., No. 398.
[6] App., Nos. 39, 92.
[7] App., No. 284.
[8] App., Nos. 201, 208, 237.

of the inferior courts of the United States to the trial of cases
of admiralty and maritime jurisdiction, and for the trial of
piracies, in all other cases the causes should be tried in the
State courts with the right of appeal to the Supreme Court.[1]
A resolution somewhat similar to this last provision was introduced in the Senate in 1793. It proposed to so amend Article
III, section 1, of the Constitution as to enable Congress to vest
the judicial power of the United States "in such of the State
courts as it shall deem fit."[2]

The above propositions were all intended to decrease the
number and power of the Federal inferior courts, but on the
last day of the third session of the First Congress (March 3,
1791), Mr. Benson of New York introduced a series of fourteen
amendments making provision for the establishment and regulation of new Federal courts to be known as general judicial
courts. Such courts were to be created in each State, and
minute provision was made for the composition and jurisdiction of the court, for the duties of the judges and other officials, as well as regulations governing their relation with other
courts, and the necessary procedure in regard to impeachments.[3] The consideration of the series was postponed to the
next Congress, but there is no record that it was again
introduced.[4]

75. JURISDICTION OF THE COURTS.

Exception was early taken to the extensive jurisdiction conferred on the United States courts by the Constitution. Among
the amendments proposed by Massachusetts and New Hampshire there was one intended to deny, in the case of suits
between citizens of different States, the right of an appeal to
the Supreme Court except the matter in dispute was of the
value of $3,000,[5] and the Massachusetts proposition further
stipulated that the Federal judicial power should not extend
at all to such cases unless the matter in dispute was of the
value of $1,500. A proposition similar to the Massachusetts

---

[1] App., No. 69.

[2] App., No. 319. In the German Empire the state courts perform the functions of the
federal courts. Hart's Federal Government, Harv. Hist. Mon., No. 2, sec. 249.

[3] App., Nos. 298-312.

[4] In 1801 the Federalists, just before passing out of power, in order to retain their control of the judiciary, passed the circuit court act, creating twenty-three new judges. In
1802 the Republicans repealed the act, thus throwing out of office the new judges appointed
by President Adams. McMaster, U. S., II, pp. 474, 606-611; Schouler, U. S., I, pp. 488-89;
II, pp. 23-24.

[5] App., Nos. 7, 20.

amendment was rejected in the First Congress by the Senate.[1] This was the first attempt to fix, by constitutional provision, a limit of value to the matter in controversy.

Jealousy of the power conferred upon the Supreme Court was early shown by other propositions to limit the extent of its jurisdiction. The amendment of the Virginia and North Carolina conventions, recently referred to, was presented as a substitute for the article in the Constitution relative to the Federal court.[2] This proposition omitted from the list of cases over which the United States courts should have jurisdiction several of those enumerated in the Constitution, thus curtailing the influence of the Federal court and the power of the General Government.[3] A similar amendment was introduced in the Senate during the First Congress.[4]

Another set of amendments attacked the clause which was later construed to admit suits against States. Mr. Tucker, in 1789, in the House proposed to so amend this clause that it should read as follows: "Cases between a State and foreign States, and between citizens of the United States. States claiming the same lands under grants of different States."[5]

The clause affecting suits as to lands gave rise to a proposition by the New York convention forbidding the extension of the Federal judicial power to such controversies unless they relate to claims of territory or jurisdiction between States and individuals under the grants of different States.[6]

Another cause of grievance was the retroactive jurisdiction given to the court. The Virginia and North Carolina conventions included a provision in their amendment prohibiting the judicial power of the United States from extending to cases where the cause of action originated before the ratification of the Constitution,[7] except in territorial disputes and suits for debts due to the United States.[8] This likewise failed in the First Congress, but the Rhode Island convention in 1790 renewed the proposition.[9]

---

[1] App., No. 256.

[2] App., Nos. 39, 92; ante par., 74.

[3] The following clauses were to be omitted: "Between a State and citizens of another State; between citizens of different States, and between a State, or the citizens thereof, and foreign States, citizens, or subjects."

[4] App., No. 284.

[5] App., No. 209.

[6] App., No. 73.

[7] This would have thrown out the Gideon Olmstead case. Post, p. 157, note 6; p. 160.

[8] App., Nos. 39, 92.

[9] App., No. 108.

76. JURISDICTION OF THE COURTS—SUITS AGAINST STATES.

Uneasiness was early felt over the question of the suability of a State,[1] as is shown by the action of the ratifying convention of Rhode Island in declaring, May, 1790, that the judicial power of the United States, in cases in which the State may be a party, does not extend to criminal prosecutions, or to authorize any suit by a person against a State; and in order to remove all doubt they proposed an amendment asserting that Congress did not have power to interfere with a State in the redemption of its paper money.[2]

When, a few years later, the Supreme Court in its first important constitutional decision[3] held that a State could be sued by an individual citizen of another State, State sovereignty was instantly aroused, especially in Georgia, Maryland,[4] New York,[5] and Massachusetts,[6] whose officers had been cited to appear before the bar of the Federal court as defendants in such suits. The legislature of Georgia expressed its indignation by passing a law subjecting to death " without benefit of clergy" any officer who should serve such a process against that State. Many of the other States, being heavily in debt, joined the movement to secure an amendment. The first effort in Congress to secure an amendment to the Constitution in regard to this question was made early in 1793, when a resolution containing the exact phraseology of the present eleventh amendment was introduced in the Senate, considered, and postponed.[7] Before the close of the year the legislatures of several States, following the example of Massachusetts, passed resolutions calling on their Representatives to take

---

[1] Madison and Marshall in the Virginia convention both denied that the Constitution would warrant the exercise by the Supreme Court of the power to summon an unwilling State as defendant against an individual. Elliot's Debates, III, 533, 555. Hamilton held in the Federalist (No. LXXXI) that the provision only applied to action to be brought by a State, and not against it. See also Hans v. Louisiana, 134 U. S., 1, for historical review.

[2] App., No. 108. The Rhode Island legislature had already (1786) had trouble with its State judiciary over a legal-tender law it had passed to force the acceptance of the State paper at its face value, in the case of Trevitt v. Weeden, 2 Chandler's Criminal Trials, 269. See also article by J. B. Thayer in Harvard Law Review, Vol. VII, No. 3; Adams in Atlantic Monthly, Vol. LIV, pp. 618–619; Coxe, Judicial Power and Unconstitutional Legislation, p. 234 et seq.; Willoughby, The Supreme Court, p. 31; Cooley, Const. Limitations, p. 160, note 3. McMaster, Vol. I, pp. 331–341; post, par. 137.

[3] Chisholm v. Georgia, 2 Dallas, 419. McMaster, Vol. II, pp. 182–186.

[4] Van Stophorst v. Maryland, 2 Dallas, 401.

[5] Oswald v. New York, 2 Dallas, 401, 415.

[6] Vassal v. Massachusetts, Hildreth, IV, 407, 446; Pitkin, Hist. of the United States, II 335, 341; Const. Hist. as Seen in Am. Law, 70–71.

[7] App., No. 313.

speedy and effectual measures to secure the adoption of this amendment to the Constitution.[1] In the next session of Congress the amendment was reintroduced in the Senate.[2] Two unsuccessful attempts were made to amend it—one by Gallatin,[3] to permit suits against States in the United States courts instituted by individuals only in cases arising under treaties;[4] the other to permit the jurisdiction of the United States to extend as provided in the Constitution, except when the cause of action shall have arisen before the ratification of the amendment.[5] This, if passed, would have retained the jurisdiction of the court over all future cases, but would have dismissed all the previous cases, such as those then agitating the country, which had arisen out of the Revolutionary war.[6]

The amendment passed the Senate by the large majority of 23 yeas to 2 nays. In the House an attempt to amend was made by adding to the article the following words: "When such States shall have previously made provision in their own courts whereby such suits may be prosecuted with effect." It received only 8 votes in its favor, and the Senate proposition passed by a vote of 81 yeas to 9 nays, and soon after received the necessary ratification and became incorporated into the Constitution as the eleventh amendment.[7]

But even this amendment did not go far enough in restricting the jurisdiction of the Federal courts to satisfy all. In 1805 Senator Breckenridge of Kentucky introduced an amendment from the legislature of his State, which read: "The judicial power of the United States shall not be construed to

---

[1] App., Nos. 319a, 319b, 319c, Massachusetts, Connecticut, and Virginia. The Massachusetts resolutions declared that the power claimed of compelling a State to be made a defendant in United States courts in such cases is "dangerous to the peace, safety, and independence of the several States and repugnant to the first principles of a Federal Government." The Virginia resolutions declared " the decision of the Supreme Federal Court incompatible with and dangerous to the Sovereignty and Independence of the Individual States, as the same tends to a general consolidation of these confederated Republicks."

[2] App., No. 321.

[3] App., No. 322.

[4] If such a provision had been adopted the recent trouble with Italy caused by the Louisiana episode might have been avoided by giving the relatives of the persons killed an opportunity to seek redress in the United States courts.

[5] App., No. 323.

[6] It would have prevented further action in the Gideon Olmstead case, which was not finally settled until 1809. The case grew out of the seizure of the sloop *Active* in 1778 and the difference in the decisions rendered by the Pennsylvania court of admiralty and the Committee of Appeal of the Congress of the Confederacy. Annals of Congress, Eleventh Congress, second session, pp. 2253–2270. Post, par. 77.

[7] App., No. 321, for list of States ratifying. In Hollingsworth v. Virginia, 3 Dall., 378, decided in 1798 it was declared that the amendment had been constitutionally adopted, not requiring the signature of the President.

extend to controversies between a State and the citizens of another State; between citizens of different States; between citizens of the same State claiming land under grants of different States, and between a State and the citizens thereof and foreign States, citizens, or subjects."[1] This same amendment was indorsed in the following year by the legislatures of Georgia, Pennsylvania, New Jersey, and Vermont.[2] In 1807 Henry Clay, shortly after his first appearance in Congress, while filling the unexpired term of Senator, submitted a resolution similar to that proposed by the Senator from his State two years before.[3]

In 1833 the legislature of Georgia, in her call for a constitutional convention, expressed a desire that the Constitution should be so amended "that the jurisdiction and process of the Supreme Court may be clearly and unequivocally settled."[4] This subject was without doubt suggested by the recent conflict of jurisdiction between the Supreme Court and the State of Georgia in the Cherokee cases.[5]

Some of the resolutions in regard to the establishment of the tribunals other than the Supreme Court for the settlement of disputes arising between the States and the General Government, which are discussed in the following section, would have conferred upon the Senate or some other body the duty of pronouncing upon the constitutionality of State laws, but an amendment introduced in 1846 proposed not only to absolutely prohibit the judicial department from declaring void "any act of Congress or of any State legislature, on the ground that it is contrary to the Constitution of the United States or contrary to the constitution of any particular State,"[6] but also failed to confer this power upon any other branch or department of the Federal Government.

But few propositions relative to the jurisdiction of the Supreme Court have since been presented, and these few within recent years. The only other attempt to restrict the jurisdiction of the Federal courts was made in 1882 by members from Mississippi in both branches of Congress.[7] On the other hand,

---

[1] App., No. 365. For other attacks on the Federalist judiciary at this same period, see ante, pp. 149–150, and notes.

[2] App., Nos. 365a, 370, 375a, 378. Rhode Island disagreed, H. J., Vol. v, reprint, p. 328.

[3] App., No. 379.

[4] App., No. 617.

[5] Cherokee Nation v. Georgia, 5 Peters 1; Tassels v. Georgia, Von Holst I, pp. 433–458; See post, par. 77, 5 Peters, 1; Worcester v. Georgia, 6 Peters, 515.

[6] App., No. 750. See post, par. 77.

[7] App., Nos. 1555, 1559.

there have been two propositions which show a tendency to extend rather than to curtail the jurisdiction of the courts. The first of these, introduced in 1872, was intended primarily to facilitate the decision of the constitutionality of any Federal law. It provided that the Supreme Court "shall have original jurisdiction in all cases involving or affecting the constitutionality of any Federal law, so far as to determine the question of the constitutionality of the same," and "upon the application of any State, corporation, or person, suggesting the unconstitutionality of any Federal law or any part thereof," should, within six months from the date of the application, determine the question.[1] It is worthy of note that the second of these, and also the last amendment presented relative to the judiciary, proposed to rescind the eleventh amendment, and give Congress power to provide "by appropriate legislation for the legal enforcement of the obligations of contracts entered into by any of the States of the Union."[2] This was introduced by Mr. Moore, in 1883, and is the only attempt that has been made to repeal the eleventh amendment since its adoption. This proposition was probably suggested by the impunity with which some of the States have repudiated their debts.[3]

77. OTHER TRIBUNALS FOR THE SETTLEMENT OF DISPUTES BETWEEN THE STATES AND THE GENERAL GOVERNMENT.

In consequence of the difficulty arising out of the relations between the States and the United States, there have been six amendments introduced at different periods providing for some other tribunals higher than the Supreme Court. These will be considered chronologically.

(1) The New York convention of 1788 proposed that a person aggrieved by any judgment of the Supreme Court, in any cause in which the court had original jurisdiction, should, upon application, have a commission review the case with power to correct the errors in the judgment, sentence, or decree. This commission was to consist of not less than seven men learned in the law, appointed by the President upon the confirmation of the Senate.[4]

---

[1] App., No. 1346. It further made provision for extending the appellate jurisdiction of the Supreme Court to all cases "where the writ of habeas corpus will lie in the several Federal courts inferior to the Supreme Court."

[2] App., No. 1573.

[3] Virginia had been particularly prominent in this movement. Attempt was made by creditors to collect from Louisiana by transferring their evidence of indebtedness to other States (New Hampshire v. Louisiana and New York v. Louisiana, 108 U. S., 76), but failed. See also Haus v. Louisiana, 134 U. S., 1.

[4] App., No. 71.

(2) The creation of a new tribunal to determine disputes between the States and the General Government has been thrice suggested. The legislature of Pennsylvania, in consequence of the State being obliged to yield in the famous Gideon Olmstead case [1] to the decision of the Supreme Court, passed a resolution in 1809 instructing their Senators and Representatives to use their influence to procure an amendment to the Constitution so that an impartial tribunal may be established to determine disputes between the General and State governments.[2] This amendment was not concurred in by a single State. On the contrary, the legislatures of several of the States formally disapproved of it,[3] among them Virginia, Ohio, Kentucky, and Georgia. This fact is of especial interest in view of their subsequent action.

In like manner, the legislature of Georgia in 1833 expressed its desire for an amendment authorizing the establishment of some tribunal of last resort for the settlement of all such disputes.[4]

---

[1] The Pennsylvania authorities had forcibly resisted the enforcement of the decision of the Supreme Court affirming the decision given by the Committee of Appeal of the Congress of the Confederacy. In this case, decided in 1809, the Supreme Court first found itself called upon to declare a State law void. United States v. Peters, 5 Cranch, 115; Constitutional History as Seen in American Law, pp. 82-85; Hildreth, III, pp. 155-164; Story, I, p. 282, note; ante, par. 76. For other references, see Foster, Com. on Const., p. 143, note 14.

[2] App., No. 397; Annals of Congress, Eleventh Congress, second session, pp. 2253-2270; Annual Register (1809), pp. 150-175; ibid. (1810), pp. 113-136; Jour. of Senate of Penn. (1808-09), pp. 268 et seq.

[3] The following States are known to have passed resolutions of "disapproval:" New Hampshire, Vermont, New Jersey, Maryland, Virginia, North Carolina, Georgia, Ohio, Kentucky, and Tennessee. No. Am. Rev., October, 1830, pp. 507-512; Niles' Register, vol. XLII, pp. 92-93, 318-319; vol. XLIII, pp. 84-85, 93, Suppl., p. 24; The Aurora, February 8, 1810; Jour. of Senate of Penn. (1808-09), p. 268; ibid. (1809-10), pp. 74, 166, 281; ibid. (1810-11), pp. 37, 41, 165; ibid. (1811-12), p. 95. The legislature of Virginia unanimously declared that "they are of the opinion that a tribunal is already provided by the Constitution of the United States, to wit, the Supreme Court, more eminently qualified * * * to decide the disputes aforesaid in an enlightened and impartial manner than any other which could be created." "The creation of a tribunal such as is proposed by Pennsylvania would, in our opinion, tend rather to invite than to prevent collisions between the Federal and State courts. It might also become in process of time a serious and dangerous embarrassment to the operation of the General Government." Compare with subsequent action of Virginia, pp. 161-162, note 5. On the other hand, in 1831 the legislature of Pennsylvania declared that the Supreme Court had jurisdiction on constitutional questions. Story, vol. I, p. 282, note 1; Am. An. Reg., vol. 6, pp. 336-337.

[4] App., No. 618. Counter replies from Massachusetts and Virginia. Am. An. Reg., vol. VI, pp. 356-357, 316-317, 336-337. Resolves of Massachusetts, vol. XIX, pp. 411-423. Governor Troup, in a letter to the Senators and Representatives of Georgia in Congress, under date of February 21, 1827, writes: "I consider all questions of mere sovereignty as matter for negotiation between the States and the United States until the competent tribunal shall be assigned by the Constitution itself for the adjustment of them." * * * "According to my limited conception, the Supreme Court is not made by the Constitution of the United States the arbiter in controversies involving rights of sovereignty between the States and the United States." Niles' Register, XXXII, 20. See reply of the legislature of Georgia to Marshall's issue of the writ of error in case of Tassels. Niles' Register, XXXIX, 338; Von Holst, History of the U. S., I, 455.

Their own controversies with the United States authorities[1] and the recent nullification movement in South Carolina[2] naturally suggested this amendment.

A third proposition was that such controversies should be referred to the Senate.

In the early twenties the Democracy was greatly excited over the recent decisions of the Supreme Court extending and strengthening the powers of the General Government.[3] At the opening of Congress in 1821 Senator Johnson of Kentucky, later Vice-President, introduced an amendment which provided that in all controversies to which the judicial power of the United States should be construed to extend to which a State should be a party, and in all cases in which a State should desire to become a party, "in consequence of having a constitution or law of such State questioned, the Senate of the United States shall have appellate jurisdiction."[4] This resolution led to an interesting debate, in which the right of the Federal court to declare a State law unconstitutional was called in question. Senator Johnson opened the discussion with the remark that his resolution was prompted by the decision which had declared unconstitutional an act of the Kentucky legislature called the "occupying claimant law." Later, in an elaborate speech attacking the recent decisions of the Supreme Court, he showed that the Federal judiciary had declared unconstitutional and void the laws of nine of the States.[5] "I know of no clause in the Federal Constitution,"

[1] Cherokee Nation v. Georgia, 5 Peters. 1; Tassels v. Georgia; copy of writ (1830), Niles Register, XXXIX, 338; Worcester v. Georgia, 6 Peters. 515; Von Holst, 1, 433–458; Bryce, 1 268 269; Reply of Massachusetts legislature (1831) against the action of Georgia Jour. of Senate of Penn. (1830–31), p. 541.

[2] See preamble of the resolutions passed by the legislature of South Carolina calling for a convention to amend the Constitution of the United States. Am. An. Reg., vol. VIII, 295. See post, paras. 83, 177.

[3] Even Jefferson from his retirement felt called upon to write in 1820: " The judiciary of the United States is the subtle corps of sappers and miners constantly working under ground to undermine the foundations of our confederate fabric. They are constantly constructing our Constitution from a coordination of a general and a special government to a general and supreme one alone." Works. VII, 192; see also ibid., 134, 216, 256.

[4] App. No. 501. Sumner, Andrew Jackson, p. 128. This would correspond with the practice of the present German Empire. Hart. Fed. Govt., sec. 260.

[5] New Hampshire, New York, New Jersey, Pennsylvania, Maryland, Virginia, Ohio, Kentucky, and Georgia, in the following cases: New Hampshire (1819), Dartmouth College v. Woodward, 4 Wheaton. 518. New York (1819). Sturges v. Crowninshield, 4 Wheaton. 122. New Jersey (1812). New Jersey v. Wilson, 7 Cranch. 164. Pennsylvania (1808). United States v. Peters, 5 Cranch, 115. Maryland (1819), McCulloch v. Maryland, 4 Wheaton, 316. Virginia (1821), Cohens v Virginia, 6 Wheaton. 264. Ohio (1819–1821). Ohio Bank Tax Case (Bank of United States v. Osborn et al), 9 Wheaton, 738; Niles Register XVII. 139 XIX,

he continued, "that gives the power to the judiciary of declaring the law and constitution of a State repugnant to the Constitution of the United States and therefore null and void. No express grant, no fair instruction, contains it, and the States never designed so to impair their sovereignty as to delegate this power to the Federal judiciary.[1] But they have

65, 85, 129, 147, 227, 294, 310, 337, 346, 361, 449. Kentucky (1819), Kentucky Bank Tax *v.* Bank of United States, Niles' Register, xv, 436; xvi, 56. Kentucky (1820-1824), Occupying Claimant Law Case, Niles' Register, xxi, 48. S. J., Eighteenth Congress, first session. p. 183. Georgia (1810), Fletcher *v.* Peck (Yazoo claims), 6 Cranch, 87. For discussion in Virginia legislature over the decision of McCulloch *v.* Maryland, and resolutions to create a tribunal to decide such cases, see Niles' Register, xvii, 289, 311-315, 447. As a result of the case of Cohens *v.* Virginia, the legislature of Virginia passed resolutions declaring "that there is no rightful power" "in the Federal judiciary to arraign the sovereignty of a Commonwealth before any tribunal but that which resides in the majesty of the people." Niles' Register, xix, 211, 340-341, 417-418; xxi, 404. The legislature of Ohio, in consequence of the decision of the United States circuit court in the above-cited bank case, passed a series of resolutions indorsing the "Virginia and Kentucky resolutions of 1798 and 1800," declaring their right to tax the bank, and protesting "against the doctrine that the political rights of the separate States, * * * and their powers as sovereign States may be settled and determined in the Supreme Court of the United States, so as to conclude and bind them in cases contrived between individuals and where there are no one of them parties direct." Niles' Register, xix, 339-341; ibid., xxi, 342-343. The legislatures of New Hampshire and Massachusetts replied maintaining a contrary view, and declaring the jurisdiction of the court and "that the preservation and due exercise of this power is essential to the peace and safety of the Union." Niles' Register, xx, 313; xxi, 404. The legislature of Kentucky passed in the early twenties, repeatedly, resolutions "remonstrating and protesting" against the decision of the United States courts concerning the "occupying claimant law." One of these declared the decision an "infringement of the sovereignty of the State" and requested their Senators and Representatives "to secure the passage of a law requiring the concurrence of two thirds of the court in all cases involving the validity of a law of any State or an increase in the number of judges." S. J., Eighteenth Congress, first session, p. 183; Niles' Register, xxi, 406. In 1829 the legislature of Virginia passed the following resolutions: "Resolved, That the Constitution of the United States being a federative compact between sovereign States, in construing which no common arbiter is known, each State has the right to construe the compact for itself." They declared the tariff acts unconstitutional. Am. An. Reg., Local Hist., p. 131. See also resolutions of South Carolina, Georgia, and Alabama of this same period; ibid., pp. 136-138, 140-142, 147. No. Am. Rev., xxxi, 487. Post, pars. 148. 156. See resolutions of the legislature of Delaware in 1833, in reply to those of South Carolina, declaring that the Constitution established the Supreme Court for the settlement of controversies between the United States and the respective States. S. J., Twenty-second Congress, second session, 157-158. Post, par. 177. In 1859 the legislature of Wisconsin, after the Supreme Court, in Ableman *v.* Booth, 21 Howard, 506, declared a law of the State unconstitutional, passed resolutions in which a "positive defiance is urged as the rightful remedy." Lalor, iii, 162; Landon, pp. 239-240. Other references, see Story, i, pp. 261, note 3; 272, 281, note 1; 282, note 1. Niles' Register, xliii, Supplement.

[1] Mercer of Maryland said in the Federal Convention of 1787: "I disapprove of the doctrine that the judges as expositors of the Constitution have authority to declare a law void. Laws ought to be well and cautiously made and then be uncontrollable." Elliot, v, 429. Upon the rejection of the motion to give to Congress the power of negativing such laws as were unconstitutional, Gouverneur Morris pointed out that this power would rest with the judiciary. Elliot, v, 321. See Bryce for comment on this remark, i, 257. See also Roger Sherman's remarks, Elliot, v, 321. Marshall in the Virginia convention asserted the same principle. Elliot, iii, 553. For origin of the practice of the judiciary declaring legislative act void, consult the following: Brinton Coxe, Judicial Power and Unconstitutional Legislation, Parts ii-iv in passim; James B. Thayer, Har-

assumed it, and to counteract the evils which must result from this assumption a responsible tribunal of appeal should be provided." "Is it not," he inquired, "equally the duty of Congress to declare the opinion of the Federal judiciary null and void in every case where a majority of Congress might deem it repugnant to the Constitution?"[1] The resolution was repeatedly considered, but was finally laid on the table.[2]

(3) Another method for the decision of all questions of constitutional power was suggested by Senator Davis of Kentucky, in 1867. It was "that the Constitution should be so amended as to create a tribunal with jurisdiction to decide all questions of constitutional power that shall arise in the Government of the United States and all conflict of jurisdiction between it and the State governments,"[3] the tribunal to consist of one member from each State, appointed by the State, to hold his office during good behavior, and a majority of the whole number of the tribunal to be necessary to make a decision. In 1871 Senator Davis introduced a similar amendment specifying more in particular over what questions the tribunal should have jurisdiction and providing for the details of the procedure and composition of the tribunal. Among other duties imposed upon this body, was that of opening and counting the votes of the electors of the President and Vice-President.[4] The decisions of the Supreme Court sustaining the constitutionality of most of the reconstruction acts probably called out this proposition.

78. SUMMARY OF THE PROPOSITIONS RELATIVE TO THE JUDICIARY.

As we review the various propositions that have been considered in the preceding pages, we see that since the eleventh

vard Law Review, VII, No. 3; Brooks Adams, Atlantic Monthly, November, 1884; C. B. Elliott, The Legislature and the Courts, Political Science Quarterly, V, 224; W. W. Willoughby, The Supreme Court of the United States, Chapter V; also Story, Chapter IV, with notes. For list of statutes declared void by Federal courts, see Davis, Appendix to the Report of the Decisions of the Supreme Court of the United States, 131 U. S., ccxxxv et seq. See Coxe's criticism of this list, chapter II.

[1] Annals of Congress, Seventeenth Congress, first session, pp. 80-81. Holmes offered, as an amendment to the proposition. one for the removal of judges on address of Congress. See ante, par. 71.

[2] A resolution was introduced in the legislature of Maryland in 1831 for the decision of the constitutionality of State laws by the Senate of the United States and for the concurrence of two-thirds of the Senate to declare any State law unconstitutional. Niles' Register, XXXIX, 357. For amendment introduced in 1846, taking away this power from the Federal Government, see ante, par. 76, p. 158.

[3] App., No. 1223.

[4] App., No. 1305.

amendment has been secured, there has been no considerable movement to alter the provisions of the Constitution relative to this department. The few attacks made in the early years of the present century were either the outgrowth of party hos tility to the political complexion of the judiciary, which was strongly Federalist, or the expression of the spirit of States rights, which viewed with alarm the nationalizing tendency of the decisions of the Supreme Court under the leadership of John Marshall.[1] No great dissatisfaction has been felt with the judiciary, and hence there has been a general tendency to retain the present system, with such changes as can be effected by law. In recent years there have been one or two attempts to increase the number of judges, in order to decrease the amount of work required of the judges of the Supreme Court, but inasmuch as the number of judges is fixed by law and not by the Constitution, there is no need of an amendment to effect this change, as is shown by the law recently passed by the Fifty-first Congress for the creation of new courts and judgeships. The last attempt to change the judiciary by means of an amendment indicates that there is at present a tendency to increase rather than to restrict the jurisdiction of the Federal courts.

[1] For estimate of the influence of Marshall, see article by Henry Hitchcock in Constitutional History as Seen in American Law, chapter II; Bryce, I, 267, 384-385.

CHAPTER V.

PROPOSED AMENDMENTS AFFECTING THE POWERS OF THE GOVERNMENT.

79. DIVISION OF POWERS BETWEEN THE STATES AND THE GENERAL GOVERNMENT.

In the formation of the Government, one of the most difficult things proved to be the setting aside the powers of the General Government from those of the States. Historically, there were many powers which had been exercised by the colonies, and later by the States, in which the English Government and the Continental Congress and the Congress of the Confederation had never shared. The principle tacitly adopted was that the States should retain all not expressly delegated to the Union. Then it was agreed that the grant of power to the Federal Government should be expressed in a few broad phrases. No attempt was made to enumerate minutely, but generally principles requiring later interpretation were admitted. Hence disputes quickly arose, and parties championing either broad or strict construction were formed. During the one hundred years there have been successive controversies. Considerable difficulty has been experienced in the attempts to discriminate between the powers granted by the Constitution to the States and General Government, respectively. Especially was this true in questions concerning taxation and commerce. Naturally, attempts have been made to secure amendments, either to remedy defects or to establish some favorite principle. It is noteworthy that of the propositions early brought before the States for ratification two were simply in conformation of the principles adopted by the Convention.[1] The change in the relative powers and importance of the States and the Union is due to the growth of custom, and especially to the effect of the civil war.

80. RESERVATION OF NONDELEGATED POWERS TO THE STATES.

The Massachusetts convention was the first to adopt the plan of proposing amendments to the Constitution at the time they

---

[1] The ninth and tenth amendments.

ratified it. One of the amendments which this convention most desired to have added to the Constitution was a clause distinctly reserving the nondelegated powers to the States, hence they placed first in the series which they recommended an article which stipulated " that it be explicitly declared that all powers not delegated by the aforesaid Constitution are reserved to the several States, to be by them exercised."[1] The plan thus suggested of proposing amendments was taken up by six of the other ratifying conventions. A favorite subject for their recommendation was a provision similar to one quoted above.[2] In accordance with the desire so generally expressed, Mr. Madison included in the series of amendments proposed by him in the First Congress a provision similar to that recommended by the States.[3] It was in these words: "The powers not delegated by this Constitution, nor prohibited by it to the States, are reserved to the States respectively."[4] Several unsuccessful attempts were made in both Houses to insert the word "expressly" before the word "delegated."[5] The amendment finally passed Congress at the same time as the others of the series, with the addition of the words " or to the people " at the end of the article.[6]

81. EFFECT OF EXPRESSED PROHIBITIONS ON CONGRESS.

Another phase of the same agitation grew out of the fear that the expressed inhibition on Congress against the exercise of certain powers might be construed into an assumption of powers not so prohibited. To meet this case the constitutional convention in Virginia also recommended an additional article as a guide in the interpretation of the Constitution and to prevent the extension of the power of Congress.[7] It was in these words: "That those clauses which declare that Congress shall not exercise certain power be not interpreted, in any manner whatsoever, to extend the power of Congress; but that they be construed either as making exception to the specified power when this shall be the case, or otherwise, as inserted

---

[1] App., No. 1.

[2] Convention in New Hampshire, South Carolina, Virginia, and North Carolina also proposed a similar amendment. App., Nos. 11, 14, 26, 78.

[3] App., Nos. 145, 190.

[4] A similar provision in the constitutions of New Hampshire, Massachusetts, Indiana, and West Virginia.

[5] App., Nos. 191, 192, 231, 232, 233, 265, 266.

[6] App., No. 266.

[7] The North Carolina convention incorporated this amendment in her series as well as several of the other propositions of the Virginia convention. App., No. 95.

merely for greater caution."[1] This might also have been considered an additional guaranty of the rights of the States, but Mr. Madison in his series had so changed this proposition that it had reference only to the rights reserved to the people. It read: "The exception here or elsewhere in the Constitution made in favor of particular rights shall not be so construed as to diminish the just importance of other rights retained by the people, or as to enlarge the powers delegated by the Constitution, but either as actual limitations of such powers, or as inserted merely for greater caution."[2] The committee reported this amendment in the form in which it was adopted[3] and as it now appears in the ninth amendment:[4] "The enumeration in the Constitution of certain rights shall not be construed to deny or disparage others retained by the people."[5]

82. SUITS AGAINST STATES.

In only one case has the Constitution been so construed as to arouse a sufficient number of the States to secure its emendation. This was occasioned by the decision of the Supreme Court that they would entertain suits instituted by individuals against States.[6]

After several preliminary attempts had been made, an amendment passed Congress September 5, 1794, forbidding the judicial power of the United States extending "to any suit in law or equity, commenced or prosecuted against one of the United States by citizens of another State, or by citizens or subjects of any foreign State," and was declared to have been ratified[7] in a message of the President to Congress, dated January 8, 1798. In general, the effect of this amendment has been salutary, and only one effort has been made to annul it.[8]

83. IMPLIED POWERS OF CONGRESS.

In view of the increasing tendency to rely upon the doctrine of implied powers, in 1806, Mr. Clopton of Virginia presented an amendment providing that the necessary and proper

[1] App., No. 42.
[2] App., No. 139.
[3] App., Nos. 177, 178.
[4] App., No. 229.
[5] In 1864 Mr. Davis proposed an amendment considerably expanding this article. App., No. 1039a.
[6] Considered more fully, ante, par. 76.
[7] App., No. 321.
[8] App., No. 1573. Proposed in 1882. See ante, par. 76.

clause of section 8, Article I, in regard to the powers granted to Congress, "shall be construed so as to comprehend only such laws as shall have a natural connection with and immediate relation to the powers enumerated in the said section, or to such other powers as are expressly vested by the Constitution in the Government of the United States, or in any department or office thereof."[1] No further attempt was made to amend the Constitution in regard to the division of powers until some twenty-three years later. In December, 1829, Mr. Hall of North Carolina introduced a resolution in the House calling for the appointment of a select committee to "inquire into the expediency of amending the Constitution so as to define more clearly the separation between the powers delegated to the Government of the United States and those retained by the people, or delegated to the State governments."[2] The House refused to agree to the resolution. This was just previous to the nullification by South Carolina, but the proposition may have been prompted by a desire to settle the question of a protective tariff. On January 9, 1833, Congress received an application from the State of Georgia for the call of a constitutional convention to amend the Constitution.[3] In the call some thirteen particulars were enumerated in which the resolutions declared the experiences of the past had clearly proved that the Constitution required amendment.

The first two of these were as follows: First, "That the powers delegated to the General Government, and the right reserved to the States or to the people may be more distinctly defined," and the second, "That the power of coercion by the General Government over the States, and the right of a State to resist an unconstitutional act of Congress may be determined."[4] There is no occasion to look far to discover the events which suggested these propositions. Obviously they were, first the nullification of South Carolina, which was still

---

[1] App., No. 377.

[2] App., No. 599.

[3] Alabama also made application, and South Carolina called for a convention of the States. See post, par. 177.

[4] App., Nos. 613,614. The preamble declared that "there exist many controversies growing out of the cases in which Congress claims to act under construction or implied powers, out of the disposition of Congress to act under assumed powers, and out of the right of jurisdiction either claimed or exercised by the Supreme Court, all of which tend to diminish the affection of the people for their own Government," etc., "to a dissolution of our happy Union, and a severance of the States into hostile communities, each regarding and acting toward each other with the bitterest enmity."

in its height, for the President's special message on the situation was not sent to Congress until a week later; and second, Georgia's own troubles with the Federal judiciary over the Indian land question.[1] Nothing, however, came of the application; it was simply received and tabled. In 1864 Mr. Davis proposed, as one of the series of amendments to be submitted to a convention of the States, an article which provided that "in giving construction to the Constitution," in regard to "all rights, liberties, or privileges assured by it to the people, or powers reserved to the States, and all denial, restriction, or limitation of powers to the United States, the Federal Government, or any of its officers," this rule shall be inflexibly adhered to, namely, "that its particular or express language shall not be abrogated, impaired, or in any way affected by any of its general language or provision, or by any implications resulting from it."[2]

84. PERFORMANCE OF NATIONAL FUNCTIONS BY THE STATES.

The extreme jealousy with which the rights of the States were guarded can be seen by the character of an amendment proposed by the ratifying convention of South Carolina. This amendment declared that "Whereas it is essential to the preservation of the rights reserved to the several States, and the freedom of the people under the operation of a general government, that the right of prescribing the manner, time, and place of holding the election to the Federal Legislature should be forever inseparably annexed to the sovereignty of the several States: This convention doth declare that the same ought to remain, to all posterity, a perpetual and fundamental right in the local government, exclusive of the interference of the General Government, except in cases where the legislature of the States shall refuse or neglect to perform and fulfill the same according to the terms of the said Constitution."[3]

It was not until 1860 that there was presented another amendment that can be properly classified under this head. Mr. Hindman of Arkansas included in the series of amendments introduced by him on the 12th of December, as a solution of the question of the hour, an article which stipulated that "all Federal officers exercising their functions within the

---

[1] See ante, par. 77.
[2] App., No. 1039p. For other articles of this series, see post. par. 103.
[3] App., No. 10.

limits of the States" shall be appointed by State authority.[1]
But this proposition came to naught; like all the others presented at this time it failed to meet the difficulty. In 1865
two resolutions were proposed to amend the ninth section of
the first article which has reference to the powers denied the
United States Government. In what particulars can not be
stated, for, unfortunately, the text is not given, but probably
they contemplated extending the power of the central Government.[2] A proposition the converse of that brought forward
by South Carolina was prepared by Mr. Hibbard of New
Hampshire, December 9, 1872. It authorized Congress to fix
a uniform day for holding State elections.[3] This amendment
was probably suggested by a sense of the desirableness of
such a change, and by the belief that it could not be secured
without a constitutional requirement. The States have, however, gradually come to adopt for their election the day set by
Congress for the national elections. There are still several
exceptions.[4]

85. GUARANTY OF THE STATE GOVERNMENT.

In addition to the guaranty contained in the Constitution,
the ratifying convention of Rhode Island recommended as an
amendment that "the United States shall guarantee to each
State its sovereignty, freedom, and independence, and every
power, jurisdiction, and right which is not by the Constitution
expressly delegated to the United States."[5] Rhode Island had
been led to ratify the Constitution in part by the apprehension
that the threat which had been made to divide her territory
among her neighbors might be carried into effect. Now that
she had joined the Union, she naturally desired a constitutional
guaranty that her integrity should be maintained, for she fully
realized that as the smallest of the States of the Union, she
was practically helpless against her larger and more powerful
sisters. No other amendment of a similar character appears
to have been presented until ninety years later. In 1880 Mr.
Acklen of Louisiana proposed an amendment guaranteeing not

---

[1] App., No. 811.
[2] Mr. Stevens of Pennsylvania, App., No. 1042, and Mr. Benjamin of Missouri, App., No. 1062.
[3] App., No. 1355. No. 1514 also provided that the first Tuesday after the first Monday in November in each year for the Presidential election should be fixed for the election for President and Vice-President, members of Congress, and State and county officers.
[4] Notably Vermont, Rhode Island, Oregon, Arkansas, Florida, and Georgia.
[5] App., No. 104.

only the integrity of the Union, but also the right of the States
to "enforce their own local laws for their individual government
by and through their own self chosen and elected representatives and officials," without interference by the Federal Government.[1] This was intended to check the growing tendency
toward centralization.[2]

There have been two resolutions—the one to explain, the
other to extend the power conferred upon the Federal Government by Article IV, section 4, of the Constitution, which provides that "The United States shall guarantee to every State
in this Union a republican form of government, and shall protect
each of them against invasion, and, on application of the legisa-
lature, or of the executive (when the legislature can not be convened), against domestic violence." The first of these was presented by Mr. Florence of Pennsylvania, in 1861.[3] One of
the series of articles introduced by him at this time declared
that the regulation of slavery within its limits was exclusively
the right of each State, and that the Constitution shall never
be altered or amended to impair this right of each State without its consent; it, however, stipulated that this article shall
not be construed to absolve the United States Government
from rendering assistance to suppress insurrection or domestic
violence, as provided in the Constitution. This proviso was
doubtless suggested to meet the case of a State calling upon
the officers of the General Government to assist in quelling a
slave insurrection; otherwise they might refuse to render
assistance on the ground that the regulation of slavery was
exclusively the right of each State.

The second resolution, proposed by Mr. Drake of Missouri,
in 1870, authorized the United States to protect "each State
against domestic violence whenever it shall be shown to the

[1] App., No. 1509.
[2] The preamble to this resolution declares that the "growing tendency to the centralization of power in the Federal Government has awakened throughout the country a just
fear that in the near future the perpetuity of this Union may again be imperiled by internal commotion," etc., "thereby wrecking the peace and prosperity of the Republic and
breaking down the doctrines of perpetual union of the States finally and fully settled by
the war, as well as infringing upon that home rule of the States guaranteed by the Constitution." The right of local self-government belonging to the people of each State is,
in eleven of the older States, declared a constitutional right which the National Government can never infringe, viz, New Hampshire, Massachusetts, Vermont, Maryland, Virginia, West Virginia, North Carolina, Missouri, Texas, Colorado, and Georgia. Stimson,
American Statute Law, par. 193.
[3] App., No. 878.

President, in such such manner as Congress may by law prescribe, that such violence exists in such State."[1] This amendment was prompted by a desire to give Congress constitutional
authority for using force in the Southern States to put down
the Kluklux Klan and other similar organizations which were
terrorizing the negro, knowing full well that the State governments, as provided in the Constitution, would not call on the
National Government for assistance, as the party in power in
the most of these was politically opposed to the negro.[2]

86. ACKNOWLEDGMENT OF SECESSION.

Remembering the frequently repeated argument of 1860-61,
that the case of the rebellion of a State had not been foreseen
by the framers of the Constitution, it is interesting to observe
an amendment proposed by the ratifying convention of North
Carolina; it provided that "Congress should not declare any
State to be in rebellion without the consent of at least two-
thirds of all the members present in both Houses."[3] Not until
the period just previous to the civil war were any further
amendments relative to the secession of a State introduced in
Congress, but among the numerous propositions presented
during the second session of the Thirty-sixth Congress were
several upon the subject which was then uppermost in the
public mind. December 17, 1860, three days before the ordinance of secession was passed by the South Carolina convention, Mr. Sickles of New York presented a resolution to
amend the Constitution, providing that "Whenever a convention of delegates, chosen in any State by the people thereof
under the recommendation of its legislature, shall rescind and
annul its ratification of the Constitution, the President shall
nominate and, by and with the advice of the Senate, shall
appoint commissioners, not exceeding three, to confer with the
duly appointed agents of such State, and to agree upon the
disposition of the public property of the United States lying
within such State, and upon the proportion of the public debt
to be assumed and paid by such State; and upon the approval
of the settlement agreed upon by the President and its ratifi-

---

[1] App., No. 1328.
[2] The resolution was referred to the Committee on the Judiciary, who subsequently
reported it adversely.
[3] App., No. 89. For sketch of secession movements, see Foster, Com. on the Const.,
secs. 31, 36.

cation by two-thirds of the Senate present, the President shall
forthwith issue his proclamation declaring the assent of the
United States to the withdrawal of such State from the
Union."[1] In the following February, Mr. Vallandigham of
Ohio, in connection with his well-known proposition for the
division of the Union into four sections, by which division the
slave States practically formed one section, proposed an
article forbidding the secession of a State without the consent
of the legislatures of all the States of the section to which the
State proposing to secede belongs, and empowering the President "to adjust with seceding States all questions arising
because of their secession; but the terms of adjustment shall
be submitted to the Congress for their approval before the
same shall be valid."[2]

87. LIMITATION ON SECESSION.

The above amendments were manifestly intended to facilitate the peaceful secession of the Southern States. In the
same session three other amendments were presented either to
restrict or to absolutely prohibit such action. The one introduced by Mr. Florence of Pennsylvania, January 28, 1861, as
one of his series of compromise amendments, provided that
" No State, or the people thereof, shall retire from the Union
·without the consent of three-fourths of the States."[3] This
was referred to the Select Committee on the Condition of the
Country. Two weeks later Mr. Ferry of Connecticut proposed
a resolution instructing the Committee on the Judiciary "to
inquire into the expediency of so amending the Constitution
as expressly to forbid the withdrawal of any State from the
Union without the consent of two-thirds of both Houses of
Congress, the approval of the President, and the consent of all
the States." Objection was made to the resolution, so it was
not received.[4]

In the closing days of this session, after seven States had
already withdrawn and several others were preparing to take
similar action, Senator Doolittle of Wisconsin, who subse-

---

[1] App., No. 824. Referred to the Select Committee on the Condition of the Country.

[2] App., No. 904. It would seem that the same proposition was reintroduced by him in
1862. Riddle, Recollection of War Times, pp. 165-166. See also App., No. 977; ante,
par. 48.

[3] App., No. 891.

[4] App., No. 910.

quently opposed the passage of the reconstruction amendments, submitted an amendment absolutely prohibiting the secession of a State.[1]

This was the last amendment of this character for the time being, but in 1864, Mr. Saulsbury of Delaware included in the series of compromise propositions, offered by him as a substitute for the thirteenth amendment, a provision prohibiting the withdrawal of a State "without the consent of three-fourths of all the States, expressed by an amendment proposed and ratified in the manner provided for in the Constitution."[2] In the three following years amendments were introduced, two of which declared the perpetuity of the Union under the Constitution, and prohibited any State from passing any ordinance of secession.[3] One proposed placing an article in the Constitution defining the status of a State in rebellion. This amendment was based upon the principles of the so-called "State suicide theory." By its provisions a State in rebellion was to be considered "as having forfeited all its rights and privileges as a State," and as having reverted to the condition of a Territory, "subject, like all other Territories, to the disposition of Congress."[4] These amendments were either tabled or indefinitely postponed, as Congress doubtless felt that the result of the war guaranteed better than any amendment could do the perpetuity of the Union unimpaired.[5]

---

[1] App., No. 952, to be added to the peace convention amendments. It was in these words: "No State, or any part thereof, heretofore admitted or hereafter to be admitted into the Union, shall have power to withdraw from the jurisdiction of the United States, and this Constitution and all the laws passed in pursuance of its delegated power shall be the supreme law of the land therein, anything contained in any constitution, act, or ordinance of any State legislature or convention to the contrary notwithstanding."

[2] App., No. 1016.

[3] App., Nos. 1063, 1199. No. 1065 declared that "Paramount sovereignty shall reside in the United States, and every citizen thereof, or of any State or Territory therein, shall owe faith, loyalty, and allegiance to the United States." In 1880 an amendment guaranteeing both the integrity of the Union and that of the States was presented. App., No. 1509; see ante, par. 85.

[4] App., No. 1106.

[5] The constitutions of several of the States, adopted in the years immediately succeeding the civil war, and most of them States which had been in rebellion, contain various declarations, as follows: (1) The constitutions of eight States declare the Constitution of the United States the supreme law of the land. (2) Five declare that the State shall always remain a member of the American Union. (3) Six, that no law shall be passed in derogation of the paramount allegiance of the citizens of the State to the United States Government. (4) Five, that there is no right on the part of the State to secede or dissolve its connection with the Union. (5) Six, that all attempts at secession ought to be resisted by the State (Virginia, North Carolina, Florida, and South Carolina); by the Federal Government (Nevada). Stimson, Am. Statute Law, I, p. 39, pars. 190-192.

88. LIMITATIONS ON THE STATES BY THE "RECONSTRUCTION AMENDMENTS."

The effort of the Southern States to throw off the authority of the General Government resulted in the only amendments which have ever passed limiting the powers of the States.[1] First, by the thirteenth amendment the establishment or perpetuation of slavery is forbidden. Second, by the fourteenth amendment any discrimination against citizens is forbidden, that article declaring that "No State shall make or enforce any law which shall abridge the privileges or immunities of citizens of the United States; nor shall any State deprive any person of life, liberty, or property without due process of law, nor deny to any person within its jurisdiction the equal protections of the laws." Third, by the fifteenth amendment the requirement of certain qualifications for the suffrage is forbidden.

Already the individual was amply protected from the tyranny of the central power, now the sphere of individual liberty was extended by the imposition of restrictions upon State aggression. Except for the power of enforcement, no additional power is given to the United States by the "reconstruction amendments." They are in terms a subtraction from the powers of the States and the United States, but in effect "the position of the United States is changed from that of a passive noninfringer of individual liberty to that of an active defender of the same against the State."[2]

89. TERRITORIAL POWERS.

Few subjects occupy so many pages of the statute books, the documents of Congress, and the reports of the Supreme Court as those relating to the territory of the United States, and the questions growing out of it. Few subjects have led to such passionate political debates as the disposition of public lands and the erection of Territories. Upon few important subjects have there been so small a number of amendments proposed. Notwithstanding the fact that the Constitution is silent as to the annexation of territory, and very vague as to the regulation and government of it, the only subject upon which numerous attempts have been made to secure modifications of the

---

[1] In the First Congress the House passed an amendment protecting the individual against a State infringing the right of trial by jury, the right of conscience, freedom of speech and the press. App., No. 228. See post, par. 97.

[2] Burgess, Political Science and Const. Law, i, p. 185.

Constitution, is the establishment of slavery in the Territories, and that phase of the subject will be taken up later.[1]

The one portion of the territory over which the United States has the clearest power of government—the District of Columbia—has given rise to more numerous propositions.

90. THE EXCLUSIVE POWERS OF CONGRESS OVER THE SEAT OF GOVERNMENT AND OTHER SITES.

The provision of the Constitution which vested in Congress the exclusive power of legislation over the Federal town and other Federal territory within the States seemed to some of the State conventions to be too broad, and calculated to cause conflict of jurisdiction. Hence, the conventions in Virginia and North Carolina proposed an amendment restricting the power of legislation, giving to Congress authority only over such regulations as respect the police and good government of such territory.[2] The proposal made in the Senate during the first session of Congress, to add such an amendment to the series to be submitted to the States, failed.[3]

The New York ratifying convention also recommended two amendments on this subject. The first of these provided that the inhabitants of the district in which the seat of government should be situated should not be exempt from paying the like taxes, etc., as shall be imposed on the other inhabitants of the State in which such district may be, neither should any person be privileged within the district from arrest for crimes committed or debts contracted without the district.[4] In this connection it is interesting to recall that the location of the seat of government had not yet been fixed, and that New York had strong reason to hope that it might be located within her boundaries.

The other proposal of the New York convention had reference to the same right of Congress to legislate over Federal territory situated within the States.[5] It provided, as did a similar amendment presented by Mr. Tucker[6] in the First Congress, that Congress should not make any law to prevent the laws of the States respectively, in which the places may be, from extending to such places in all civil and criminal matters, except to such persons as are in the service of the United States, nor to them with respect to crimes committed without such places.

---

[1] Post., pars. 109–112.   [3] App., No. 283.   [5] App., No. 57.
[2] App., Nos. 37, 90.   [4] App., No. 56.   [6] App., No. 202.

In subsequent years, after the seat of government had been located in the District of Columbia, and the population of the District had increased, the fact became more noticeable that its inhabitants—contrary to the general principles of our system of government—were deprived of the privilege of voting in Federal elections, and even had no voice in making their own local regulations. President Monroe, in 1818, in his annual message, called the attention of Congress to the anomaly existing in our system, and recommended to their consideration the problem whether an arrangement better adapted to the principles of our Government could not be devised, which will never infringe the Constitution nor affect the object which the provision in question was intended to secure.[1]

In 1844 a proposition was made to so amend the Constitution that Congress should retain the power of exclusive legislation over the Government buildings and grounds in the District of Columbia and in Federal territory situated in other States; but all rights of legislation over other parts of the District of Columbia should be retroceded to the States of Maryland and Virginia whenever the legislatures of these States should signify a willingness to accept the same.[2] This amendment was probably suggested by the slavery question, as were several other propositions which will be considered in connection with the slavery amendments.[3]

91. ABRIDGING TERRITORY.

The peace of 1783 left several perplexing boundary controversies affecting territory normally within the area of the United States. The British continued to occupy posts within the northwestern frontier; the Spaniards retained their hold in west Florida, above the parallel of 31°. In the southwest also, Georgia stubbornly laid claim to a large area of territory then occupied by Indians.

It is therefore easy to account for the presentation in 1794 of an amendment dealing with both these problems. This proposed amendment declared that the powers of the Government should not extend to curtail or abridge the limits of the United States as defined by the Treaty of Paris in 1783, nor should the

[1] App., No. 480. Const., Art. I, sec. 8, cl. 17.
[2] App., No. 736.
[3] Post, par. 112.

State rights of preemption to Indian hunting grounds within
its limits, after a fair treaty and sale, be questioned.[1]

The Jay treaty of 1794 and the Spanish treaty of 1795 put
an end to the exterior boundary disputes; and in 1802 a settlement of the Georgian land claims was reached. When, in 1826,
and again in 1842, the negotiations with England threatened
to deprive Maine of a part of the territory to which she asserted
title, no attempts to secure an amendment is recorded.

92. ANNEXATION OF TERRITORY.

The next year after the Georgia controversy was laid at
rest, the annexation of Louisiana brought on a new controversy with the New England States. No formal attempt was
made to introduce an amendment in Congress relative to the
annexation of Louisiana. It seems necessary, however, to
consider certain amendments drawn up by President Jefferson.[2]

In July, 1803, news arrived of the treaty concluded at Paris,
April 30, between the United States and the French Republic,
for the purchase of Louisiana. President Jefferson considered that there was no constitutional authority for the annexation of foreign territory by treaty, and prepared the following draft of an amendment which was to be submitted to the
States: "The province of Louisiana is incorporated with the
United States, and made part thereof, the rights of occupancy
in the soil and of self-government all confirmed to the Indian
inhabitants as they now exist." Then, after creating a special
constitution for the territory north of the thirty-second parallel, reserving it for the Indians until a new amendment to
the Constitution should give authority for white ownership,
the draft provided for erecting the portion south of latitude
32° into a territorial government, and vesting the inhabitants
with the rights of other territorial citizens.[3]

This draft he sent to his Cabinet, but none of them considered an amendment necessary. Jefferson was not ready to
yield his views at once, and in August he proposed a new and
briefer draft. "His first," Mr. Adams says, was "almost a

---

[1] App., No. 326.

[2] See Henry Adams's History of the U. S. for extended account, Vol. II, Chap. IV, V, VI.
Story, Vol. II, p. 168, note 1; Vol. I, p. 373, note 2; Jefferson's Works, Vol. IV, pp. 500, 504,
505. For Federal opposition, see Fisher Ames's Works, Vol. I, p. 323; Foster, Com. on
Const., I, sec. 31, pp. 116-118.

[3] Henry Adams, Hist. U. S., Vol. II, pp. 86, 87.

constitution in itself." It read as follows: "Article XIII. Louisiana, as ceded by France to the United States, is made a part of the United States; its white inhabitants shall be citizens and shall stand as to their rights and obligations on the same footing with other citizens of the United States in analogous situations, save only that as to the portion thereof lying north of an east and west line drawn through the mouth of Arkansas River, no new State shall be established nor any grant of land made, other than to Indians in exchange for equivalent portions of land occupied by them, until an amendment to the Constitution shall be made for these purposes. Florida, also, whensoever it may be rightfully obtained, shall become a part of the United States; its white inhabitants shall thereupon be citizens, and shall stand as to their rights and obligations on the same footing with other citizens of the United States in analogous situations."[1]

Jefferson's party friends and advisers considered that the introduction of an amendment would be inexpedient, and tried to dissuade him from urging such a change. Finally their efforts met with success. In a letter to Senator Nicholas of Virginia, Jefferson writes: "I confess I think it important in the present case to set an example against broad construction by appealing for new power to the people. If, however, our friends shall think differently, certainly I shall acquiesce with satisfaction, confiding that the good sense of our country will correct the evil of construction when it shall produce ill effects."[2]

Nothing further was heard of amendments from the President, but Senator John Quincy Adams of Massachusetts, adhering to the views first set forth by Jefferson, after waiting in vain for some move from the Executive, finally, on the 25th of November, 1803, moved "that a committee be appointed to inquire whether any, and if any, what further measures may be necessary for carrying into effect the treaty whereby Louisiana was ceded to the United States."[3] His motion failed to be recorded, and the Senate unanimously laid it on the table.

[1] Lalor, I, p. 609. Letter to Levi Lincoln of August 30, 1803. Works, Vol. IV, p. 504, 505.

[2] Adams, II, p. 91. See comments of Judge T. M. Cooley on Jefferson's attitude, in pamphlet entitled Louisiana, p. 16.

[3] Annals of Congress, Eighth Congress, first session, p. 106. Adams said the annexation was "an assumption of implied powers greater in its consequences than all the assumption of implied power in the twelve years of Washington's and Adams's administrations put together." Cooley, Louisiana.

93. ADMISSION OF NEW STATES.

Only two other amendments have been offered relative to the admission of new States, except those presented in connection with the slavery question, which are treated under that subject.[1] The first of these was drawn up by the Hartford convention, and brought to the attention of Congress at the same time as the other amendments proposed by this assembly in 1815. This amendment stipulated that no new State should be admitted without the concurrence of two-thirds of both Houses of Congress.[2]

The New England States doubtless believed that such an amendment was necessary for their protection, in view of the fact that by means of the votes of the members from the new States measures inimical to their interests could be pushed through Congress. This had been the case in 1812, when war had been declared contrary to the desire of a large majority of the people of New England.[3] This series of resolutions, as introduced by Massachusetts and Connecticut members in obedience to the instructions of their respective legislatures, called out resolutions of disapproval from the legislatures of several of the other States.[4]

The second proposition was not presented until over half a century later, in 1871, and was designed to prevent the too early admission of new States. It provided that hereafter no Territory or District should be admitted as a State that did not contain a population that would entitle it to at least one Representative according to the ratio of representation at the time of its application for admission.[5]

---

[1] Post, par. 110. Even in the Constitutional Convention hostility was shown by some of the members to new States, and an attempt was made to restrict their representation in the National Legislature. Mr. Gerry gave formal expression to this hostility in his motion of July 14: "That in order to secure the liberties of the States already confederated, the number of representatives in the first branch of the States, which shall hereafter be established shall never exceed in number the representation from such of the States as shall accede to this confederation." Elliot, v, p. 310. Four States favored it, five opposed it, and one, Pennsylvania, was divided.

[2] App., Nos. 426, 434, 442. Story, II, p. 169, note 2.

[3] For address of the Congressional minority, see Niles' Register, II, pp. 309–315.

[4] Ante, par. 22, p. 45. The house of representatives of Massachusetts, in 1844–1845, passed strong State rights resolutions against the admission of Texas. H. J., February 28, 1845, p. 509. Foster, Com. on Const., I, p. 118.

[5] App., No. 1341. In 1871, besides Delaware there were of the new States Nebraska, Nevada, and Oregon which did not have a population equal to the representative ratio. According to the census of 1890, the population of Delaware, Idaho, Montana, Nevada, and Wyoming, respectively, did not equal the ratio of representation now in force, which is one for every 173,901 inhabitants of a State.

94. REPRESENTATION OF THE TERRITORIES AND THE DISTRICT OF COLUMBIA IN CONGRESS.

Each Territory has long been entitled to send a Delegate to the House of Representatives, but he has no vote. In recent years, Delegates from the Territories have presented four distinct proposals in Congress to give them voting members in the House of Representatives. No important action has been taken relative to any one of them.[1]

The District of Columbia, although the seat of the Federal Government and more populous than some States, has under the Constitution no share in the Presidential and Congressional elections, and has not by law received even the privilege of sending a Delegate to Congress. One of the above-mentioned resolutions included the District of Columbia in its provisions.[2] As recently as 1888 Senator Blair introduced an amendment to give to the District representation in the two Houses of Congress and votes in the electoral college.[3] Since the admission of six new States, in 1889 and 1890, the question of changing the peculiar status of an inhabitant of the Territories is not now as urgent as formerly,[4] but the problem in regard to the District of Columbia still confronts the nation.

95. DISPOSITION OF THE PUBLIC LANDS.

It is somewhat remarkable that during the periods when the questions relating to the public lands were prominent in the deliberations of Congress, only one proposal was made to amend the Constitution relative to their disposal.

When the legislature of Georgia, in 1833, petitioned Congress to call a convention to amend the Constitution, they included as one of the questions they desired to have considered, an amendment which should settle the "right to and disposition of the public lands of the United States."[5]

It was not, however, until the early seventies, after large tracts of the Government land had come into the possession of

---

[1] App., Nos. 1348, 1394, 1454, 1510. No. 1394 also provided that each Territory should be entitled to choose one elector for President and Vice-President.

[2] App., No. 1454.

[3] App., No. 1726. The District should have as many electors for President and Vice-President as it has members in Congress, but their representatives in Congress were not to participate in joint convention of the two Houses, nor in proceedings touching the choice of President and Vice-President, nor in the organization of either House of Congress.

[4] Utah admitted in 1896.

[5] App., No. 622. See letter of Governor Troup of Georgia to the Secretary of War, of June 3, 1825. Niles' Register, Vol. XXVIII, p. 240; also, Von Holst, U. S. Hist., Vol. I, pp. 438–439. See post, par. 146.

railroads and speculators, that any further amendments upon this subject were suggested. In 1871 Mr. Coghlan of California proposed an amendment prohibiting the disposal of the public lands except to actual settlers.[1] The motion to suspend the rules and pass the resolution was lost. The following year Mr. Coghlan tendered the same resolution.[2] The only other proposition to amend the Constitution in this particular was offered in this same year.[3] The time is now passed when such an amendment would be productive of good, and it seems unlikely that the power of Congress " to dispose of the territory and other property of the United States " will be abridged.

96. RELATION OF THE UNITED STATES WITH INDIVIDUALS.

Under the head of personal relation, are without doubt the most important class of proposed constitutional amendments. As proof of this statement, it is only necessary to recall that all but two of the fifteen amendments that now form a part of the Constitution relate to the rights and duties of persons.

First in point of time came that series of amendments which were added to the Constitution so soon after the organization of the Government "as to justify the statement that they were practically contemporaneous with the adoption of the original."[1] These were dictated by the jealousy of the States, as " further express limitations upon possible powers of the Federal Government."

Down to 1860, a period of over sixty years, but few amendments were offered touching the relations of the General Government with individuals, although during the greater part of this period a contest was going on over the institution of African slavery, between those who desired its curtailment and ultimate extinction and those who desired additional safeguards for its security and perpetuation. It was only upon rare occasions and at infrequent intervals that either side tried to accomplish their end through an amendment. Doubtless all recognized the futility of such an attempt.

It was therefore not until 1860 that any general movement was made still further to define the relation of the General

---

[1] App., No. 1340.
[2] App., No. 1357.
[3] App., No. 1350. Similar to Mr. Coghlan's, save that grants of land might also be made for common school education of the people of the respective States and Territories.
[4] Slaughterhouse Cases, 16 Wall., 125.

Government with the individual. Then it was that an avalanche of propositions fell upon Congress, urged on by a desire of preserving the Union, and with some hope that the country might possibly in such a crisis ratify an amendment.

With the outbreak of the rebellion these proposals for the moment ceased, but the exigencies and results of the war soon gave rise to a new order of amendments. The provisions of some of these were incorporated in the thirteenth, fourteenth, and fifteenth amendments. "These reconstruction amendments," says Mr. Justice Swayne in his dissenting opinion in the Slaughterhouse cases, "are a new departure and mark an important epoch in the constitutional history of the country. They trench directly upon the power of the States and deeply affect those bodies besides. They are in this respect at the opposite pole from the first series."[1] In the years since, amendments have been frequently presented still further to increase the power of the General Government in this sphere, in order to secure the better protection of the individual in the exercise of his civil and political rights.

97. THE FIRST TEN AMENDMENTS.

In many of the States opposition to the ratification of the Constitution was based upon the absence of specific reservation of the rights of the people. The precedent of the great English declaratory statutes had been followed in the elaborate Bill of Rights which prefaced most of the State constitutions.[2] In vain did the friends of the Constitution urge that the General Government was in its nature limited, and that all rights not expressly granted must be retained. The people did not feel secure in the enjoyment of life, liberty, and property without a written guaranty to protect them from encroachments of the General Government. To this end one hundred and twenty-four articles of amendment were proposed by the seven conventions which suggested additions to the Constitution.[3] In this numerous series, in addition to the miscellaneous sug-

---

[1] Slaughterhouse Cases, 16 Wall, 125.

[2] Stevens. Sources of the Constitution of the United States, pp. 211-213.

[3] Massachusetts, 9 amendments; South Carolina, 4; New Hampshire, 12; Virginia, 20; New York, 32; North Carolina, 26; Rhode Island, 21. The Rhode Island series was not passed until 1790, and hence only the 103 propositions passed by the other six conventions were before Congress at the time they drew up the 12 they sent out to the States. For admirable treatment of the origin of our Bill of Rights see Stevens, Chap. VIII, also Story, I, pp. 211-213. App., Nos. 1-124.

gestions treated elsewhere,[1] were included many specific guaranties of individual rights.

In response to this general demand, Mr. Madison, early in June, introduced in the first session of the First Congress a series of amendments embracing the most important of the propositions recommended by the different State conventions.[2] The special committee of one from each State to whom the series was referred, reported them back in a modified form.[3] After a long debate in the Committee of the Whole, during which many changes were proposed,[4] and not a few effected, seventeen amendments finally passed the House of Representatives by the necessary two-thirds majority.[5] Two of these were rejected by the Senate, one affording protection to the individual against a State infringing the rights of trial by jury, the right of conscience, freedom of speech and of the press,[6] and the other in regard to the distribution of power among the departments.[7]

The fact that an amendment protecting the individual from State encroachment was included in the series of amendments passed by the House would seem to indicate that the members of the First Congress considered the first ten amendments as binding only against the General Government. The question as to the extent of their application has frequently come before the United States Supreme Court, and that body has repeatedly declared that the first ten amendments do not guarantee the individual against the State.[8]

The remaining fifteen were by compression and modification in the Senate reduced to twelve.[9] After a committee of conference had still further modified some of the articles,[10] the series of twelve received the approval of two-thirds of both Houses of Congress, and went out to the States for their ratification. Subsequently the series, except the two in regard to

---

[1] Ante, pars. 9, 12, 13, 16, 18, 22, 28, 29, 30, 31, 56, 62, 63, 70, 73, 75, 77, 80, 86, 90. Post, pars. 99, 101, 103, 116, 137, 138, 152, 157, 158, 161, 162, 163, 164, 181.

[2] App., Nos. 126-146. Story, 1, p. 211, note 3.

[3] App., Nos. 147, 148, 149, 154, 155, 158, 160, 165, 166, 169, 173, 177, 179, 181, 183, 188, 190, 193.

[4] App., Nos. 147-214, also 231, 232, 234-240.

[5] App., Nos. 215-230, 233.

[6] App., No. 228.

[7] App., No. 230; see ante, par. 7.

[8] As in the decision given in Barron v. Baltimore, 7 Peters, 243, and United States v. Cruckshank, 92 U. S., 542.

[9] App., Nos. 220, 221, 227, 229, 242, 243, 254, 266, 288, 291, 292, 293.

[10] App., Nos. 295, 296, 297.

the apportionment and compensation of members of Congress,[1] were ratified by a sufficient number of the States, and the first ten amendments, or, as they are sometimes termed, the American Bill of Rights, became part of the Constitution.[2]

98. DOCTRINAIRE PROPOSITIONS ON THE RIGHTS OF MAN.

Of the various amendments proposed during the consideration by Congress of this series of propositions, the greater part involved only slight change, and more often merely verbal. Several, however, are worthy of notice as showing the political philosophy of the day. Mr. Madison placed as the first amendment in the series presented by him an article defining the basis of power.[3] It provided "that there be prefixed to the Constitution a declaration that all power is originally vested in, and consequently derived from, the people. That government is instituted and ought to be exercised for the benefit of the people; which consists in the enjoyment of life and liberty, with the right of acquiring and using property, and generally of pursuing and obtaining happiness and safety. That the people have an indubitable, inalienable, and indefeasible right to reform or change their Government, whenever it may be found adverse or inadequate to the purposes of its institution."

The committee reported a much briefer preamble, declaring that the government was derived from the people.[4] After being adopted in Committee of the Whole it was stricken out by the House.

---

[1] App., Nos. 243, 295. See ante pars. 13, 22.

[2] App., No. 297, for list of States ratifying. All the States except Massachusetts, Connecticut, and Georgia acted favorably. In Massachusetts and Connecticut the influence of the Federalist leaders who had foolishly opposed the amendments in Congress predominated. The Massachusetts legislature on a concurrent resolution, rejected the first, second, and twelfth amendments, and agreed to the others, and ordered the appointment of a committee to bring in a bill or resolve declaring their adoption. The committee does not seem to have reported, and finally action was not taken. Senate Journal, Massachusetts, vol. 10, p. 192: Journals of the House of Representatives, Massachusetts, vol. 10, pp. 168, 169, 209, 217, 218. At the same time a concurrent resolution was passed appointing a joint committee " to consider what further amendments are necessary to be added to the Federal Constitution and report." The committee reported a series of twelve propositions, inasmuch as they were " convinced that the people of this State, when they adopted the Constitution of the United States, wished for and expected other and further amendments than those which have been recommended, and that they are now anxious to have their liberties more explicitly secured to them." For reprint of the report, see the American Historical Review, Vol. II, No. 1, pp. 99–105. "This group of ten amendments may, therefore, be regarded as a supplement or postscript to the original, and should not be regarded in the same category with the subsequent independent amendments." Report of New York State Bar Association, Vol. XIII, p. 139.

[3] App., No. 127.

[4] App., No. 147.

Subsequently there were three attempts, when the amendments were being considered in the Senate, to add an additional paragraph containing sentiments similar to the preamble quoted from Mr. Madison, all of which, however, proved unsuccessful. That the social-compact theory was popular in that day is shown by one of these resolutions,[1] which opens with the declaration that " there are certain natural rights, of which men, when they form a social compact, can not deprive or divest their posterity, among which are the enjoyment of life and liberty," etc. Another declares that magistrates are the trustees and agents of the people, and are therefore "at all times amenable to them."[2] The third asserts that the Government ought to be instituted for the common benefit and protection and security of the people, and that " the doctrine of nonresistance against arbitrary power and oppression is absurd, slavish, and destructive of the good and happiness of mankind."[3]

Two further attempts were made in the Senate to add a further guaranty of individual liberty.[4] One of these proposed amendments declared that " every freeman restrained of his liberty is entitled to a remedy, to inquire into the lawfulness thereof, and to remove the same, if unlawful, and that such remedy ought not to be denied or delayed." The other proposition was similar, only still more explicit. Both were rejected.

99. TITLES OF NOBILITY.

The provisions of the Constitution forbidding any person holding office under the United States Government, without the consent of Congress, from accepting any present or title from any king, prince, or foreign State did not seem sufficiently stringent to some of the State conventions.[5] The ratifying conventions of Massachusetts, New Hampshire, New York, and, later, Rhode Island,[6] proposed amendments either forbidding Congress from ever granting its consent, or for the accomplishment of the same end proposed eliminating the clause " without the consent of Congress." A similar change was proposed in the Senate and twice in the House of the First Congress, during the discussion of the subject of amending the Constitution, but failed to meet the approval of either

---

[1] App., No. 267.
[2] App., No. 268.
[3] App., No. 269.
[4] App., Nos. 272, 273.
[5] Const., Art. I, sec. 9, cl. 8.
[6] App., Nos. 9, 22, 75, 118.

branch.[1] No further amendments on this subject were presented until 1810. Early in that year Senator Reed of Maryland introduced an amendment relative to the acceptance of titles of nobility by American citizens.[2]

The resolutions were referred to a select committee of three, and twice afterwards recommended to a larger committee, who finally reported them in a modified form. Several amendments were presented during the debate, one of which was accepted. It was in these words: "If any citizen of the United States shall accept, claim, receive, or retain any title of nobility or honor, or shall, without the consent of Congress, accept and retain any present, pension, office, or emolument of any kind whatever from any emperor, king, prince, or foreign power, such person shall cease to be a citizen of the United States, and shall be incapable of holding any office of trust or profit under them or either of them."[3] Thus amended, the article passed the Senate by a vote of 19 yeas to 5 nays. The amendment was immediately considered in the House and passed by that body on the 1st day of May, only three votes being cast against it.

Unfortunately, the Annals of Congress and contemporary newspapers do not give any of the debate upon this interesting proposition. The only light thrown upon the subject by the Annals is the remark of Mr. Macon, who said " he considered the vote on this question as deciding whether or not we were to have members of the Legion of Honor in this country."[4] What event connected with our diplomatic or political history suggested the need of such an amendment is not now apparent.[5]

---

[1] App., Nos. 203, 240, 263.

[2] App., No. 299.

[3] App., No. 399.

[4] Annals of Congress, Eleventh Congress, second session, p. 2050. The files of four of the leading papers of the time have been examined without any additional light being thrown on the question.

[5] It is possible that the presence of Jerome Bonaparte in this country a few years previous, and his marriage to a Maryland lady, may have suggested this measure. An article in Niles' Register (vol. LXXII, p. 166), written many years after this event, refers to an amendment having been adopted to prevent any but a native-born citizen from being President of the United States. This is of course a mistake, as the Constitution in its original form contained such a provision; but it may be possible that the circumstances referred to by the writer in Niles relate to the passage of this amendment through Congress in regard to titles of nobility. The article referred to maintains that at the time Jerome Bonaparte was in this country the Federalist party, as a political trick, affecting to apprehend that Jerome might find his way to the Presidency through "French influence," proposed the amendment. They thought the Democratic party would oppose it as unnecessary, which would thus appear to the public as a further proof of their subserviency to French influence. "The Democrats, to avoid this imputation, concluded to carry the amendment. 'It can do no harm' was what reconciled it to all."

Possibly there was no particular event which suggested it, but it probably was only another means of expressing that animosity against foreigners and everything foreign, which manifested itself in various ways in the trying period just previous to the war of 1812.[1] That the amendment was in the line of popular sentiment may be inferred, otherwise we can not account for the nearly unanimous vote it received in Congress and the favorable reception it met with from the States.[2]

The amendment lacked only the vote of one State of being adopted.[3] It received the ratification of twelve States, and was passed by the Senate of South Carolina. It was generally supposed that the amendment had been concurred in by the requisite majority of the States. In the official edition of the Constitution of the United States, prepared for the use of the members of the House of Representatives of the Fifteenth Congress, the article appears as the thirteenth amendment to the Constitution.[4] This led to a resolution of inquiry,[5] as a result of which it was discovered that the house of representatives of South Carolina had not confirmed the action of the senate, and so the amendment had not been adopted.[6] However, the general public continued to think that this

---

[1] I am indebted to Professor McMaster for this suggestion. Good examples of the anti-foreign spirit may be seen in the laws enacted at this time by some of the States. In Kentucky a bill prohibiting the citation of the decision of any British court or any British treatise on law was proposed. With difficulty Henry Clay succeeded in obtaining an amendment limiting the restriction to such decisions as had been rendered, and to such works as had been written, since July 4, 1776. In this form it passed. In Pennsylvania a similar bill was introduced in 1809, and passed in 1810, and remained on the statute books for a generation. Schurz, Life of Henry Clay. I, pp. 49–50; McMaster, III, pp. 417–418. For other attacks on the system of English common law, see McMaster, III, p. 512. Another manifestation of the same spirit was the action of the House of Representatives of the Commonwealth of Pennsylvania. February 10, 1814, by a vote of 47 to 38 the House passed the following resolution: "Resolved, That this House dispense with the use of the Mace." Journal of the 24th House of Representatives of Pennsylvania. (1813–14) pp. 283, 292, 309.

[2] It passed both branches of the Legislature of Pennsylvania unanimously. Journal of Senate of Penn. (1810–11) p. 180; Journal of House of Representatives pp. 290, 294.

[3] See list given after App., No. 399.

[4] Also given in Vol. I, p. 71 of "The Laws of the United States of America." Phila. and Washington, 1815.

[5] Annals of Congress, Fifteenth Congress, first session, p. 530; Niles' Register, Vol. XIV, p. 150.

[6] App., No. 399. Certified copy of the proceedings of the State legislature of South Carolina in Bureau of Rolls and Library. Department of State. The minutes of the House of Representatives of South Carolina do not state the reasons for their opposition. Thus four States rejected it, viz. New York, Connecticut, Rhode Island, and South Carolina. Virginia does not appear from the records in the State Department to have taken any action.

amendment had been adopted,[1] and this misconception was perpetuated for over a third of a century in editions of the Constitution and school histories.[2]

100. DUELING.

Another attempt to regulate the behavior of American citizens by constitutional amendment arose out of the growth of public sentiment inimical to the practice of dueling; the first was presented in 1828, by Mr. Long of North Carolina, and was intended to prevent the practice of duelling.[3] Ten years later two other resolutions were introduced. The reason for their presentation at this time is apparent. On the 24th of February, 1838, Jonathan Cilley, a member of Congress from Maine, was killed in a duel with William J. Graves of Kentucky, also a member of Congress. On the 5th of March, Mr. Morgan of Virginia introduced the first of these resolutions, restricting all who should be connected with a duel, even including the seconds or the bearer of the challenge, from holding office.[4] The attempt to expel Graves from the House took place in the following December. Mr. Cushman of New Hampshire, a Northern man, offered a similar amendment.[5] This was the last attempt to amend the Constitution in this particular.

101. POOR RELIEF.

The disposition to make the Constitution a code of laws reached the fullest expression in an amendment to invest the central Government with the power and duty of legislating for the care of the poor. This suggested a radical departure from the system then in use and since followed. This amendment was proposed by the convention which ratified the Constitution in Rhode Island in 1790. It provided "that Congress should have power to establish a uniform rule of inhabitancy and settlement of the poor of the different States throughout the United States."[6]

---

[1] Illustration, see Niles' Register, Vol. xx. pp. 191, 255.

[2] Illustrative of this, the following : "A History of the United States," by B. J. Olney, A. M., New Haven, 1836. "Constitution of the United States of America." Printed by Francis Hart & Co., 63 Cortland street, New York. (No date.) "A History of the United States," by John Frost, Philadelphia, 1842. In "History of the United States," by Emma Willard, New York, 1829, it appears as the xv amendment. The first twelve sent out by the First Congress all being given as if ratified.

[3] App., No. 587.

[4] App., No. 685.

[5] App., No. 687.

[6] App., No. 192.

102. MARRIAGE AND DIVORCE.

Less sweeping is a proposition affecting personal rights and duties which arise out of the confusion caused by the different laws regulating marriage and divorce in the various States. At present a marriage in one State may be void in another; and serious complications arise as to inheritance and other questions. A national law for marriage and divorce is plainly unauthorized by the Constitution. In order to remove this difficulty, there have been five amendments proposed since 1884 to give Congress power to pass uniform laws on these subjects.[1] The proposition of Senator Dolph, in 1887, led to an interesting debate, but nothing was accomplished. In 1871 there was an amendment presented by Mr. King of Missouri, which prohibited the intermarriage of persons of the white and colored races.[2] From the preamble of this resolution it is evident that its author supposed that the States were deprived by the fourteenth amendment of the power to prohibit such marriages. The courts in general have not so held, and in several States mixed marriages are prohibited.[3]

103. HABEAS CORPUS, FREEDOM OF SPEECH AND OF THE PRESS.

The proposed amendments of the last half century have, however, been directed rather to the increase and protection of personal rights and privileges than to their abridgment. Since the adoption of the Bill of Rights there have been but two attempts to add to the Constitution further guarantee in regard to the rights of the press and of free speech and of the right of the people to assemble and to be protected against the military power.[4]

An effort to incorporate into the Constitution such a provision was made by Senator Saulsbury of Delaware, April 8, 1864, when he presented a long series of amendments as a substitute for the thirteenth amendment, then under discussion. The larger portion of the amendments of this series related to slavery, but the first few were more properly general guaranties

---

[1] App., Nos. 1605, 1609, 1656, 1688, 1736. Such an amendment reported adversely in Fifty-second Congress, first session. Strong minority report. H. Rep., vol. 4, No. 1290.

[2] App., No. 1339. See post, par. 172.

[3] Cooley, Const. Law, p. 240, note 1; Hitchcock, Am. State Const., pp. 26–27. Twelve States by statute, two in the constitution.

[4] The New York convention proposed an amendment prohibiting the suspension of the habeas corpus for a longer time than six months or until twenty days after the meeting of the Congress next following the passing of the act for such suspension. App., No. 55.

of the rights of the individual.[1] The first declared the right
of the people peaceably to assemble and worship God according
to the dictates of their conscience. In this connection it is
interesting to recall that this is the only amendment regularly
introduced which proposed to insert the word God into the
Constitution, although numerous petitions have been presented
from various religious societies for some acknowledgment of
God in the Constitution. The second of these amendments,
while declaring that the use of the public press shall not be
obstructed, provided that "criminal publication made in one
State against the lawful institution of another State shall not
be allowed." In reality, therefore, this amendment offered no
further guarantee of the freedom of the press, but, on the other
hand, proposed placing restrictions upon the utterances against
the institution of slavery. The remaining propositions declared
that the right of free speech should not be denied; that access
of citizens to the ballot box should not be obstructed either by
civil or military force; that the military shall always be subordinate to the existing judicial authority over citizens; that
the privilege of the writ of habeas corpus shall never be suspended in the presence of judicial authority, and that the
militia of a State or of the United States shall not be employed to invade the lawful rights of the people of any of the
several States.

A very similar but even longer series of amendments was
proposed by Senator Davis of Kentucky, an Old Line Whig,
in December of this same year. He submitted these as the
basis of all existing difficulties, and desired that they should
be considered by a convention of the States which he proposed
should be assembled "for the purpose of bringing about the
restoration of peace and union and the vindication of the
Constitution."[2] The resolution contained a series of detailed
guaranties to the people not only of all the rights mentioned
in the first ten amendments, but also of several other inherent
rights and liberties of the people which had been and were
being infringed by such acts as the suspension of the writ of
habeas corpus, by the proclamation of the President and its
subsequent approval by Congress, and the trial of citizens by
military tribunals even in States distant from the seat of war,
and certain other acts incidental to the exercise of the war

---

[1] App., Nos. 999–1002.
[2] See post, par. 177.

power.[1]   It forbade all such invasion of the rights of the people, and declared that "the infraction of any of these rights and privileges shall be held to be both a grievous private wrong and a public crime, and all persons who may commit it to become infamous and to be further punished by law without pardon or commutation."

These two series of amendments were evidently presented not with the expectation of their adoption, but rather as an arraignment of the President and the party in power and as a protest against the acts already mentioned.

104. PROTECTION OF PERSONAL LIBERTY.

Most of the propositions dealing with questions of personal relations up to the civil war were assertions of constitutional principles.   At the close of the war another very important group commands our attention.   These, for the most part, concerned the method by which the principle of individual liberty might be secured from assault.   The thirteenth amendment, conferring freedom upon all the slaves, will naturally be treated under the head of amendments affecting slavery.[2]   It was supplemented by the fourteenth amendment, although the provisions contained in the first section of this article, as interpreted by the courts, are not confined in their application to any one class of persons, yet inasmuch as it was simply intended to protect the freedmen, it will be considered under the same head as the thirteenth amendment.   It seems convenient to mention in this connection the only amendment which has been proposed dealing expressly with the Indian.   The legislature of Georgia included in the call issued by her in 1833 for a convention to amend the Constitution a clause calling for an amendment definitely settling the rights of the Indian.[3]   The need of such

---

[1] App., No. 1039b. See ante, par. 83. It guaranteed "the absolute right at all times and under all conditions of the people to the writ of habeas corpus and to trial by jury;" the exemption of all persons, except those in the Army and Navy, from arrest and immunity from trial and examination by military tribunals; that the military power was never to be brought into conflict with the civil authority, but should be employed to uphold the law and the courts. It guaranteed to the people at their elections the right to vote for those whom they prefer without constraint or intimidation; to freely discuss and pronounce their opinion on all public measures and the conduct of public officers; to their right to all sources of information by the purchase and transmission of books, newspapers, etc., without any obstruction, and to free trade and commerce with their fellow-citizens; to protection in their private property, which was not to be taken except to subserve some operation of the Federal Government, and then to receive full compensation or indemnity, as well as for all damages sustained by reason of the orders of the military officers of the United States. See Bryce, I, pp. 54, 55.

[2] Post, par. 123.

[3] App., No. 625.

an amendment had been suggested by Georgia's almost continuous struggle with the United States courts over the rights of the Creek and the Cherokee nation.

105. SLAVERY PROPOSITIONS BEFORE 1860.

Considering the long and violent legislative struggle over slavery, which lasted through a quarter of a century, it is remarkable that there were but few propositions to amend the Constitution in this respect before 1860. In addition to the amendment with regard to abolishing the representation for the slave population, introduced just previous to 1808 and again in 1815, and the resolution of Massachusetts, presented in 1844, all of which have been dealt with elsewhere,[1] there were a few others aimed either at the protection or abolition of slavery.

As early as 1818 Mr. Livermore of New Hampshire introduced a resolution prohibiting slavery, which failed to receive the consideration of the House.[2]

Again, in 1839, J. Q. Adams tried to introduce a series of amendments abolishing hereditary slavery after 1842, forbidding the admission of slave States after 1845, and prohibiting slavery or the slave trade at the seat of government.[3] Shortly after the compromise of 1850 an unsuccessful attempt was made still further to protect the interests of the slavocracy by the proposition of Mr. Daniel of North Carolina, that no amendment should be made abolishing or affecting slavery in any State without the concurrence of the slave States.[4] In the same year Mr. Disney of Ohio tried twice in vain to secure the consideration by the House of an amendment to the Constitution which asserted the rights of local government.[5] This was evidently prompted by a desire to insure the security of slavery, for it declared " that the people of every community have an inherent right to form their own domestic laws and to establish their own local government when they do not conflict with the Constitution," and, further, " that the will of the people of the District of Columbia ought at all times to govern the action of Congress in relation to the existence of slavery within its limits."[6]

---

[1] Ante, par. 22. Sketch of the History of Slavery, by Cooley: Story, II, Chap. XLVI.
[2] App., No. 474.
[3] App., Nos. 697, 698, 699.
[4] App., No. 764. Cadwalader of Pennsylvania, on December 15, 1856, gave notice of his intention to introduce a similar amendment. H. J., Thirty-fourth Congress, third session, p. 114.
[5] App., No. 758.
[6] For amendments before 1860 in regard to aiding the colonization of freedmen, see post, par. 115.

By the time of the opening of the second session of the
Thirty-sixth Congress, in December of 1860, the condition of
affairs was changed, and now amendments were freely offered,
upward of two hundred being presented to Congress during
this session. These multifarious propositions will be treated
according to their subject-matter; their chronological history
may be briefly disposed of.[1] At the opening of the session
President Buchanan recommended in his annual message three
explanatory amendments to the Constitution on the subject of
slavery.[2] The first of these was an express recognition of the
right of property in slaves; the second declared the duty of
protecting this right in the Territories, and the last, recognized
the validity of the fugitive slave law.

Nearly every prominent member of the Democratic party,
especially from the Northern and border States, suggested
amendments. No less than fifty-seven distinct resolutions
were presented during this session of 1860–61. Some of them,
in the effort to find some common ground for compromise and
conciliation, contained a long list of propositions dealing with
almost every conceivable phase of the slavery question.

The amendments introduced in the early part of the session
varied from the propositions advanced by Jefferson Davis, for
the express recognition and protection of property in slaves,[3]
to those advocated by Senators Crittenden and Douglas,
which, although conceding great rights to the slave States,
were more in the nature of a compromise.[4] Several propositions went to the length of insisting on a radical change in
the form of government, to the end that the slaveholders might
feel more security in the Union.[5] After the secession of South
Carolina and some of her sister States, propositions for the
amendment of the Constitution were even more numerous;
that advocated by Senator Crittenden seemed the most likely
to succeed, but it failed to receive the Republican vote and
the South preferred to secede rather than to consider anything

[1] An excellent résumé of the history of this Congress may be found in Rhodes, U. S.,
Vol. III, pp. 140–181; 253–271; 287–291; 305–308; 313–314. For a synopsis of various bills
and resolutions, see, also, McPherson's History of the Rebellion, pp. 48–90.

[2] App., Nos. 778, 780.

[3] App., No. 851.

[4] App., Nos. 827–833 and 836–850; 852a–h, 869a–m. See Foster, Com. on Const., I, pp. 169–
178.

[5] Ante, pars. 34, 48.

that was not adopted by nearly a unanimous vote.[1] In the last
days of February the amendments proposed by the peace congress, called at the request of Virginia, were presented to Congress.[2] Some of their main provisions were similar to those of
the Crittenden compromise, in that slavery should be prohibited
north of the parallels of 36° 30', and recognized and never interfered with by Congress south of that line, and that the Federal
Government was to pay for slaves rescued from officers; but
it made further concessions to Southern demands. Congress
was unable to agree on any of these measures, and the utmost
that could be obtained was the comparatively colorless Corwin
amendment.[3]

107. PROPOSITIONS OR LIMITATIONS ON ABOLITION.

A numerous class of amendments were intended to prevent
the abolition of slavery anywhere by national authority.[4] The
end was to be accomplished in one of the following ways: (1) By
an express recognition of the right of property in slaves, like
the amendment proposed by President Buchanan [5] in his annual
message at the opening of the Congress. Other amendments
of a similar nature were introduced by Senators Powell and
Jefferson Davis and Congressman Hindman of Arkansas.[6]
(2) By declaring either that Congress should have no jurisdiction over slavery, or that Congress should not interfere with
slavery within the States, or that the regulations of the right
to labor or service in any of the States was exclusively the right
of each State.[7] The Crittenden amendment and the peace convention resolutions contained such articles. In most cases
these propositions were simply one of a series of amendments,
and were usually accompanied by a provision that this article,
together with certain of those accompanying it, should be unamendable. For some time no agreement was reached. Finally
the House select committee of thirty-three reported, February
27, 1861, a resolution which read as follows: [8] "No amendment

---

[1] Rhodes, U. S., III, pp. 260–265. See Chittenden's Debates and Proceedings of the Peace
Convention. Foster, Com. on Const., I, p. 174 et seq.

[2] App., No. 917.

[3] App., No. 931; post, par. 107.

[4] App., Nos. 778–970.

[5] App., No. 778.

[6] App., Nos 782, 805, 851.

[7] App., Nos. 790, 801, 827, 833, 850, 852g, 853, 869, 869c, 874k, 876, 894, 897, 913, 917, 919, 928, 935,
950, 957, 969.

[8] As a part of their report. There were five propositions in all, but this was the only
one to amend the Constitution. See McPherson, pp. 57–62. Several had suggested this
amendment, December 24, in the Senate committee of thirteen and it was agreed to by
them. Journal of the committee, p. 11.

of this Constitution having for its object any interference within the States with the relation between their citizens and those described in section 2 of the first article of the Constitution as 'all other persons' shall originate with any State that does not recognize that relation within its own limits, or shall be valid without the assent of every one of the States composing the Union." [1] Mr. Corwin of Ohio immediately moved a substitute, which was accepted, but the resolution as amended was then rejected. The following day the vote was reconsidered, and the Corwin amendment passed by a vote of 133 to 65, in the following terms: "No amendment shall be made to the Constitution which will authorize or give to Congress the power to abolish or to interfere, within any State, with the domestic institutions thereof, including that of persons held to labor or service by the laws of said State." [2] When the Corwin resolution came up in the Senate, Senator Pugh of Ohio moved to substitute his resolution containing a series of seven articles and with a few exceptions covering nearly the same ground as the peace convention amendments. [3] Then Mr. Doolittle of Wisconsin presented as a substitute a resolution declaring that no State shall have power to secede, and asserting that the laws of the United States shall be supreme. [4] Three other resolutions were proposed, one of these being the series of the peace convention, and another authorizing the calling of a constitutional convention; but they all failed. [5] March 2 the amendment passed by a vote of 24 yeas to 12 nays, [6] the exact constitutional majority, and on the same day received the unnecessary approval of the President. [7] Only three States seem to have ratified it, Ohio and Maryland through their legislatures, and Illinois through a constitutional convention. [8] In the New England States it was rejected, and many others did not act upon it. [9] It was not regarded as a sufficient concession to hold the Southern States which had not as yet seceded, much less

---

[1] Proposed by Charles Francis Adams in committee. See Blaine, i, p. 260-268.

[2] App., No. 931.

[3] App., No. 942.

[4] App., Nos. 952, 953.

[5] App., Nos. 954, 955-965.

[6] In reality on the 3d of March, Sunday. Mr. Trumbull raised the point of order that two-thirds of all the Senators had not voted in the affirmative, but the Chair held, and was sustained, that only two-thirds of those present was necessary. See post, par. 183.

[7] See post, par. 184.

[8] App., No. 931. Ohio, May 13, 1861; Maryland, January 10, 1862; Illinois, February 14, 1862. The latter is the only case of a convention being held to ratify an amendment to the Federal Constitution. Was it valid? See post, par. 179.

[9] Stated upon the authority of Blaine, Twenty Years in Congress, i, pp. 266-267.

to win back those which had already taken that action. Other Northern States would have undoubtedly ratified it, if it had promised to stay secession, but the rapid approach of the civil war put it out of the public mind.[1] It is interesting to note, in this connection, that nearly three years later, February 8, 1864, Senator Anthony of Rhode Island introduced a resolution to repeal this joint resolution. The motion was referred to the Committee on the Judiciary, who were some months later discharged from its further consideration, and the entire matter was dropped.[2]

Just after the opening of the Thirty-seventh Congress, in July, 1861, Senator Saulsbury of Delaware presented a series of amendments "for the peaceable adjustment of national difficulties."[3] They were substantially the " Crittenden resolutions." Nearly a month later the Senate refused to consider them. Again, in 1864, Mr. Saulsbury included among the amendments offered by him as a substitute for the thirteenth amendment an article that the slave States south of 36° 30' should regulate for themselves the question of slavery.[4] In this same year Mr. Davis proposed in a somewhat similar series of amendments a proposition that each State should have the exclusive right over its local and domestic institutions.[5]

(3) In addition to a few amendments proposing radical changes in the form of government, an amendment was presented by Mr. Hindman of Arkansas, in 1860, which, in addition to other guaranties, called for such provisions as will secure to the slaveholding States, through their representatives in Congress, an absolute negative upon all action of Congress relating to the subject of slavery, and such amendments shall forever be unamendable.[6] Possibly this proposition suggested the amendment presented some two months later by Mr. Vallandigham, providing that a majority from each section shall be necessary for the passage of a bill.[7]

[1] Rhodes. United States. III, pp. 313-314. Rhodes thinks but for the outbreak of the war it would have been adopted.

[2] App., No. 1025. It would seem to be extremely doubtful whether Congress could recall an amendment when it has once been submitted. Jameson. Const. Conv., p. 634; post, par. 180, note.

[3] App., No. 971. Senate refused to consider it by a vote of 11 to 24.

[4] App., No. 1007.

[5] App., No. 1039f.

[6] App., Nos. 805-811.

[7] App., No. 902. The same seems to have been introduced by him in 1862. See ante, par. 86.

108. FUGITIVE SLAVES.

The amendments relative to abolition had little likelihood of passing, because the danger of interference by the General Government with slavery in the States seemed remote, but the propositions for the return of fugitive slaves deserve more careful attention. The experience of the country since 1850 showed that the Constitution as it stood did not secure the recovery of fugitives. The Southerners in the earlier days had maintained that there was no need of an amendment, since the Constitution already had a provision on the subject, but they bitterly complained that the law framed in 1793 to carry out this provision was not enforced.[1] As a part of the compromise of 1850 a more effectual law for the return of fugitive slaves was passed.[2] The act was so far out of sympathy with the usual methods of trial in the Northern States that its execution was resisted by able constitutional arguments, by forcible rescues,[3] and by a series of State enactments, the well-known "Personal liberty bills."[4] The Southern States felt and made much of these undeniable grievances.

(1) Among the numerous amendments presented in the session of 1860–61, some thirty-three amendments were proposed on the subject of fugitive slaves.[5] Subsequently others were introduced by Mr. Saulsbury later in 1861, and again, in the series offered by him as a substitute to the thirteenth amendment, in 1864.[6] Most of these amendments were intended to give a definite guaranty to the South that the right to the return of their slaves should not be infringed. The first method to secure this end was to declare the fugitive slave law superior to State constitutions or enactments. Such was the proposition embodied by President Buchanan in his annual message of December 4, 1860.[7] Congress was urged to submit to the States an amendment asserting the "right of the master to have his slave

---

[1] See resolutions of Georgia in 1840. Senate Journal, pp. 235–236. This was occasioned by the controversies between Georgia and Maine, New York and Virginia. For details see Niles' Register, LIII, 71–72; LV, 556; LVI, 215; LVII, 272; LIX, 374, 404; LX, 55, 60, 69, 70, 90, 150–152; LXI, 241, 372, 385; LXII, 86, 112, 117. Senate Journal (1842), 145, 146.

[2] A person claimed as a fugitive slave was to be returned without trial by jury or appearance before a judge, but simply on the certificate of a commissioner; and the fee was $10 if the slave was remanded and only $5 if he was declared a free man.

[3] McDougall, Fugitive Slaves, Chap. IV.

[4] Ibid., Chap. V; McPherson, pp. 44–47.

[5] App., Nos. 780, 787, 789, 794, 802, 803, 809, 817, 833, 849, 852g, 860, 868, 869g, 872, 874g, 874k, 881, 886, 888, 889, 894, 898, 914, 920, 927, 937, 939, 949, 950, 962, 964, 967, 971d, 971g, 971h.

[6] App., Nos. 1008, 1012, 1013.

[7] App., No. 780.

who has escaped from one State to another restored and delivered up to him, and of the validity of the fugitive slave law enacted for this purpose, together with a declaration that all State
laws in passing or defeating this right are violations of the Constitution, and are consequently null and void." In harmony
with this recommendation, various amendments were shortly
proposed. Some of these, as that introduced by Mr. Kellogg
of Illinois, expressly empowered Congress to pass laws necessary to secure the return of fugitives.[1]

The executives of Northern States had refused to comply
with a requisition for the extradition of men accused of assist-
ing slaves to escape, on the ground that the act alleged was
not considered a crime in a free State. To meet this difficulty,
some of these propositions, like that offered by Mr. Etheridge
and Mr. Pugh of Ohio, asserted that the laws of the State
from which persons flee shall be the test of criminality.[2] One,
introduced by Mr. Hindman,[3] proposed to enforce the return
of fugitives by providing that "any State whose legislature
has enacted, or may hereafter enact, laws defeating or impairing the right of the master to have his escaped slave delivered
up to him (according to the provisions of the fugitive slave
law of 1850) shall not be entitled to representation in either
House of Congress until the repeal of such nullifying statutes."

(2) Another class of amendments proposed to insure the
rights of the slaveowner by making compensation for fugitives that might be lost by reason of the legislation of any
State or the act of its constituted authorities, or by the rescue of
the fugitive, or by intimidation. Thus Crittenden and Douglas
proposed that Congress should have power to enact laws requiring the United States to pay to owners who should apply
for it, the full value of their fugitives in all cases when they are
unable to recover them by the marshal being unable to arrest by
reason of violence or intimidation.[4] The United States should
have a right in its own name to sue the county in which the
violence was committed, and the county in turn might sue and
recover from the wrongdoers. Another variation provided for
payment by the State.[5] Andrew Johnson of Tennessee insisted
on an "explicit declaration in the Constitution that it is the duty
of each State for itself to return fugitive slaves when demanded
by the proper authority or pay double their cash value out

---

[1] App., Nos. 898, 914.
[2] App., Nos. 860, 945.
[3] App., No. 809.
[4] App., Nos. 832, 849, 852f, 869j; also 874g, 971g.
[5] App., No. 794.

of the treasury of the State."[1]   Mr. English of Indiana also
offered an amendment requiring, that whenever a fugitive slave
was rescued, the city, county, or township in which such rescue was made should be liable to the master in double the value
of the slave.[2]   Still others, like that proposed by Mr. Clemens
of Virginia, gave the United States the right to impose a tax
on the county or city in which a fugitive slave was rescued by
violence as pay for the same, and the city or county had the
right to sue the wrongdoers.[3]

(3) On the other hand, a few amendments were offered looking to an amelioration of the act of 1850.   To meet the criticism directed against the fugitive slave law of 1850, that the
fugitive was not given the benefit of a trial by jury, Mr.
Florence of Pennsylvania introduced two articles,[4] one providing that "an alleged fugitive, on request, shall have a trial
by jury at the place to which he may be returned;" the
second provided "in case such person claimed to be a citizen
of another State, he should have the right of appeal, or of a
writ of error to the Supreme Court of the United States."

The series presented by Mr. Saulsbury of Delaware, April,
1864, as a substitute for the thirteenth amendment, in addition
to the sections prohibiting a State passing any law interfering
or obstructing the recovery of fugitives, contained a proposition similar to that of Mr. Florence, save that the article was
a little more favorable to the fugitive, inasmuch as it stipulated that the fugitive, on request, should have a trial by jury
before being returned.[5]

It is almost needless to add that there was not the slightest
hope that any of the three classes of amendments would be
adopted.   A compromise was no longer possible.   The question of slavery could be solved only by its destruction, which
was accomplished by the civil war.[6]

---

[1] App., No. 817.
[2] App., No. 802.
[3] App., No. 927.
[4] App., Nos. 888, 889.
[5] App., Nos. 1012, 1013.   Same in his proposition in 1861.   App., No. 971d.   In this same
year Mr. Sumner proposed an amendment to strike out the third paragraph of the second section of the fourth article.   App., No. 986b.
[6] There is reason, however, to think that the Northern States would have withdrawn
their objectionable acts if there had been reason to think that this action would have
kept the Southern States from secession.   Rhodes, History of the United States, III, pp.
147-148, 252-253, notes; McPherson, History of the Rebellion, pp. 44-47.   On December 17,
1860, Mr. Adrian's resolution recommending the repeal of all statutes, including personal
liberty bills, so called, enacted by State legislatures which were in violation of the Constitution, passed the House of Representatives by a vote of 154 to 14.   McPherson, p. 75.

109. SLAVERY IN THE TERRITORIES.

More promising at the beginning of the session of 1860–61, was the advocacy of amendments affecting the status of slavery in the Territories. All other slavery questions were by comparison insignificant. In the Territories appeared in its clearest form, the essential difficulty which divided the Union, the existence of a slaveholding section and a free section united under one government. Three attempts had been made to settle the question by law—in the compromises of 1820 and 1850, and the Kansas-Nebraska bill. One attempt had been made to settle it by judicial construction of the law in the Dred Scott decision.[1] If it could not be settled by constitutional amendment there was no hope of an agreement.

Among the amendments attempting to surmount the trouble and to preserve the Union, by far the largest group were those which had reference to slavery in the Territories and the District of Columbia.

(1) A considerable class made provision for a geographical division of the Territories, most of them by the parallel of 36° 30′ north latitude; slavery to be forbidden in all the Territories north of said division line, and to be permitted in the region south of said line; but a Territory of either section, when ready to enter the Union, was to be admitted with or without slavery, as its constitution should prescribe. Such amendments were introduced by Messrs. Crittenden, English, Johnson of Tennessee, Kellogg of Illinois, and Clemens of Virginia, and appeared also in the series framed by the peace convention.[2] They fairly represent the sentiment of the moderate men from the North and from the so-called border States. Some of the propositions stipulated that "persons held to service or labor" might be taken into any Territory south of 36° 30′, and the right to such service should not be impaired; but they should not be taken into any Territory of the United States while in a Territorial condition north of 36° 30′.[3]

As late as 1864, Senator Saulsbury introduced, in his series offered as a substitute for the thirteenth amendment, a provision in regard to slavery in the Territories south of 36° 30′.

(2) The doctrine of the "extension of the Constitution" to the Territories was set forth in another class, of which the

---

[1] Scott v. Sandford, 19 How., 393.

[2] App., Nos. 784, 796, 800, 816, 827, 852a, 858, 864, 874a, 875, 894, 896, 912, 917, 918, 923, 932, 942, 955, 971.

[3] App., No. 887.

recommendations of President Buchanan is typical. The Constitution was to be so amended that it should be the duty of Congress to protect the rights of slavery in all the Territories.[1] Others would have reached the same end by prohibiting Congress from making any regulation impairing the right of property in slaves in the Territories. Other amendments, like that introduced by Mr. Vallindigham, declared the equal right of any person from any section to migrate to the Territories, and forbade the impairment of the rights of either person or property in the Territories.[2]

(3) Senator Douglas brought forward his favorite principle of popular sovereignty in the proposition that Congress should make no law in respect to slavery in any Territory, but the status of each Territory in respect to servitude should remain unchanged until it reached a population of 50,000 whites.[3] Other sections of this same resolution made applicable to the Territories the clause of the Constitution in regard to fugitives from justice, and also extended the jurisdiction of the United States judicial power over the same.

(4) The principle of the Dred Scott decision was represented in a proposition forbidding the Territorial legislature, as well as Congress, from making any law respecting slavery.[4]

110. ADMISSION OF STATES.

Most of the articles to amend the Constitution contained a section which provided for the admission of the Territories into the Union, whether north or south of the dividing parallel, whenever they had fulfilled the conditions necessary for admission, with or without slavery, as their constitution should provide,[5] or limitations were sometimes added as in the series of amendments introduced by Mr. Florence of Pennsylvania, December 18, 1860. He provided that no new State should be admitted without the consent of two-thirds of all the members of both branches of Congress,[6] the yeas and nays being entered

---

[1] App., No. 1003.

[2] App., No. 906.

[3] App., No. 836. Also similar provision in other proposition submitted by him. App., Nos. 869a, 869m. The latter declared that "all Territorial governments shall be formed on the model and in the terms of the organic acts, approved September 9, 1850, called 'the compromise measures.'"

[4] App., Nos. 790, 792, 851, 871.

[5] App., Nos. 797, 800, 807, 823, 828, 852b, 858, 864, 869b, 874b, 877, 894b, 896, 912, 918, 923, 933, 942, 971. In 1864 Mr. Saulsbury presented the same in his substitute resolutions for the thirteenth amendment. App., No. 1005.

[6] Like the Hartford convention amendment, ante, par. 93.

on the journals. If such bill should be vetoed by the President it should require a three-fourths vote of all the members to pass it.[1]

Later, Mr. Florence introduced a proposition simply providing for the admission of a State when it had fulfilled the conditions, with or without slavery, as its constitution should direct, and it further provided that if the President refused to admit such Territory as a State this article should not deprive Congress of the power to admit such State.[2] As has been previously stated, the amendment introduced by Mr. Douglas provided that the status of each Territory in respect to servitude should remain unchanged until the Territory should have a population of 50,000 white inhabitants. When this number was secured, the white male citizens should proceed to form a constitutional government for themselves, and exercise all the rights of self government. And such new State should be entitled to one Delegate in the Senate, to be chosen by the legislature, and one Delegate in the House, to be chosen by the people. When such new State should contain the requisite population for a member of Congress, it should be admitted into the Union on an equal footing with the original States, with or without slavery, as its constitution should provide at the time of its admission.[3]

III. ACQUIREMENT OF NEW TERRITORY.

Other sections of the article just previously mentioned, as introduced by Mr. Douglas, prohibited the acquirement by the United States of any more territory, except by treaty or by the concurrent vote of two-thirds of each House of Congress. The occurrence of a case like that of New Mexico was to be guarded against by the provision that in the event of the annexation of new territory. "The status thereof in respect to servitude shall remain the same as at the time of its acquisition, until it shall be formed into a new State." But the annexation of Cuba was distinctly intimated in the clause: "The area of all new States are to be as nearly uniform in size as practicable, and shall not be less than 60,000 nor more than 80,000 square miles, *except in case of islands.*"[4]

---

[1] App., No. 826.
[2] App., No. 877.
[3] App., No. 837.   No. 869b, similar to the latter provision, introduced by Mr. Douglas.
[4] App., Nos. 839, 840.   An amendment similar to the first part of the foregoing was introduced by Mr. Etheridge of Tennessee shortly after this.   App., No. 859.

Messrs. Cochrane and Kellogg also suggested an amendment restricting the acquisition of any more territory except by treaty ratified by a vote of two-thirds of the Senate.[1] February 27, 1861, the peace convention amendments were submitted to Congress. One section in the series stipulated that no territory should be acquired by the United States, except by discovery and for naval and commercial stations, without the concurrence of a majority of all the Senators from the slave States and free States, respectively; nor should territory be acquired by treaty unless the vote of a majority of Senators for each class of States be cast as a part of the two-thirds necessary.[2] Subsequently the amendments proposed by the peace convention were reintroduced in the Senate at three different times.[3]

112. THE DISTRICT OF COLUMBIA AND PLACES UNDER FEDERAL JURISDICTION.

Another phase of the "irrepressible conflict" over territory was brought out in the numerous amendments introduced at this time relative to slavery in the District of Columbia and other places under Federal jurisdiction situated within the States.[4] The larger number of these amendments provided that Congress should have no power to abolish slavery in the District so long as it should exist in Virginia and Maryland, nor even then without the consent of the inhabitants, nor without making just compensation to the owners of slaves. It was usually further stipulated that Congress should not prohibit officers of the Federal Government or members of Congress whose duties required them to be in the District from bringing their slaves within said District, and holding them as such during the time these duties required them to remain there, and afterwards taking them from the District. Such amendments were proposed by Crittenden, Douglas, Florence, and Clemens. One of the amendments offered by Senator Saulsbury, in 1864, forbade slavery in the District of Columbia, but permitted persons to sojourn there with slaves. Others forbade Congress to interfere with slavery without the consent of Maryland.[5] Another proposed that the exclusive power to regulate or abolish the right to labor or service for life in the

---

[1] App., Nos. 874a, 916.

[2] App., No. 917.

[3] App., Nos. 934, 956, 969.

[4] App., Nos. 799, 806, 819, 830, 846, 852d, 855, 866, 869d, 874f. 880, 894, 917, 925, 935, 944, 957, 969, 971b.

[5] App., No. 917.

District of Columbia should be ceded to the State of Maryland, to be exercised in common with such rights in that State, subject, nevertheless, to the judicial jurisdiction of the District.[1]

The amendments of the peace convention further declared "that the bringing into the District of Columbia of such persons for sale, or placing them in depots to be afterwards transferred to other places for sale as merchandise, is prohibited."[2]

Another considerable class of amendments, besides prohibiting the abolition of slavery in the District of Columbia, further forbade Congress to prohibit slavery from existing in the arsenals, navy-yards, dockyards, forts, or other places under its exclusive jurisdiction within the limits of States that permit the holding of slaves.[3] Such a provision was included in the peace convention amendments, as well as in those of Crittenden, Johnson, Douglas, Florence, and others. Mr. Hindman of Arkansas would have changed the prohibition into a requirement that the Federal Government should protect property in slaves wherever the Federal jurisdiction extends.[4]

113. RIGHT OF TRANSIT WITH SLAVES.

Troublesome questions had arisen out of the fact that slaves brought by their masters into free States or in transit through free territory were often liberated. To meet the case, four amendments were introduced guaranteeing the rights of masters or owners to their slaves while sojourning in or in transit through any State or Territory of the United States.[5]

Three of these amendments were presented December 12, 1860. The remaining one was introduced by Mr. Florence, in January, 1861. At the same time he offered an amendment which declared that citizens of any State sojourning in another State should not be subject to violence or punishment, nor be injured in their persons or property without trial by jury and due process of law.[6] In the series of amendments offered by Mr. Saulsbury, in 1864, as a substitute for the thirteenth amendment, was a proposition to allow the right of transit with slaves south of 36° 30', but not north of said line.[7]

---

[1] Mr. Florence, January 28, 1861, App., No. 880.
[2] App., No. 917.
[3] App., Nos. 799, 806, 818, 829, 845, 852d, 865, 869d. 874f, 894, 917, 924, 936, 943, 958, 969, 971c.
[4] App., No. 806.
[5] App., Nos. 788, 793. 808, 882.
[6] App., No. 885.
[7] App., No. 1009.

114. SLAVE INSURRECTIONS AND CONSPIRACIES.

Another of the series which Mr. Florence proposed declared that all acts of any inhabitant of the United States tending to incite slaves to insurrection or action of domestic violence, or to abscond, should be considered contrary to law and as penal offenses.[1] Near the close of the session a somewhat different amendment was included in the series of propositions presented by Senator Pugh of Ohio and Senator Powell of Kentucky.[2] It declared that "Congress shall pass efficient laws for the punishment of all persons in any of the States who shall in any manner aid and abet invasion or insurrection in any other State." In 1864 Mr. Saulsbury included in the resolution offered as a substitute for the thirteenth amendment this identical proposition coupled with another which declared that all conspiracies in any State to interfere with lawful rights in any other State or against the United States should be suppressed.[3] These measures were naturally suggested by the insurrection at Harpers Ferry under John Brown, in October, 1859.

115. COLONIZATION OF FREE NEGROES.

The project of mitigating the evil of slavery and eventually of its abolition through the colonization of negroes had been a favorite scheme ever since the early years of the century, when "colonization societies" were established. This plan was especially urged by those philanthropists who were opposed to extreme measures. The Southern men likewise were not as a rule averse to the movement, for the presence of free negroes among them was undesirable.[4] It is not surprising, therefore, that during the discussion of the question of the constitutionality of Congress granting aid to the colonization movement, in the Twenty-second Congress, the proposal was twice made that the Constitution should be amended so as to give Congress the express power to assist the colonization of negroes.[5]

The first of these resolutions, introduced by Mr. Archer of Virginia, proposed the expediency of amending the Constitution so as to empower Congress "to appropriate the revenue

---

[1] App., No. 885.

[2] App., Nos. 948, 968.

[3] App., Nos. 1014, 1015.

[4] Von Holst, U. S. Hist., I, pp. 329-833; Rhodes, Hist. of U. S., I, pp. 381-382.

[5] Georgia and some of the Gulf States passed resolutions against Congress aiding colonization societies. See Niles' Register. XXXVII, p. 428. Between 1823-1825 Ohio and seven other States passed resolutions in favor of colonization or gradual emancipation. Jours. of house and senate of Penn. (1823-1826), in passim.

accruing from the proceeds of the sale of the public lands," in part,[1] "in the aid of the removal of such portion of the colored population of the States as they may respectively ask aid in removing, on such conditions and to such places as may be mutually agreed upon."[2] The remainder of the resolution authorized Congress to acquire suitable territory and to govern the same as Territories for such time as is necessary, after which the Territory should be established into a State or States independent of the United States and never should be admitted into the Union.[3]

The second resolution came from the legislature of Maryland, which State had been especially prominent in favoring the colonization movement. This resolution called for governmental aid "in the removal of the free people of color from the United States, if deemed in accordance with the Constitution;" and, if not, for such "an amendment to the Constitution as shall enable Congress to make such appropriation."[4] No important action was taken on either of these propositions.

Similar propositions do not appear again until the winter of 1860–61, when, Mr. Douglas revived this amendment,[5] which was later in the session advocated by Mr. Clemens of Virginia.[6] By the terms of this amendment the United States should be empowered to acquire districts of country in Africa and South America for the colonization, at the expense of the Federal Treasury, of such free negroes and mulattoes as the several States may wish to have removed from their limits, and from the District of Columbia and other places under the jurisdiction of Congress.

In 1862 President Lincoln in his annual message recommended to Congress the passage of three amendments in regard to slavery. One of these was to enable Congress to appropriate money and otherwise provide for colonizing free colored persons, with their own consent, at any place or places without the United States.[7]

Mr. Saulsbury also included in the articles submitted by him as a substitute for the thirteenth amendment a section which

---

[1] The resolution also covered internal improvements. See post, par. 156.
[2] See Webster's speech of March 7, 1850. Works, v, p. 364.
[3] App., No. 609b. Mr. Bailey, in 1825, had included in his amendment in regard to internal improvements provision for empowering Congress to promote also education, colonization, and the liberal and useful arts. App., No. 543; post, par. 171.
[4] App., No. 609c.
[5] App., No. 844.
[6] App., No. 930. See post, par. 120, note 1.
[7] App., No. 975.

permitted Congress to assist free persons of African descent to emigrate and colonize in Africa.[1]

As a result of the civil war, all the negroes were made free, and a general colonization scheme was thus rendered impossible. The present relations of the races seem to indicate that the negroes will remain a permanent element in the population of the United States.

116. THE FOREIGN SLAVE TRADE.

With the exception of the colonization schemes, the amendments upon slavery so far discussed were all attempts to settle the crisis of 1860–61. The slave trade was almost the only slavery question upon which there had been an earlier series of amendments.

By one of these compromises of the Constitution the importation of slaves prior to the year 1808 could not be forbidden by Congress. The ratifying convention of Rhode Island (May 29, 1790) was the only one of the State conventions proposing an amendment in regard to the slave trade.[2] This resolution declared: "As a traffic tending to establish and continue the slavery of any part of the human species is disgraceful to the cause of liberty and humanity, Congress shall, as soon as may be, promote and establish such laws as may effectually prevent the importation of slaves of every description." This protest denotes a marked change in the public sentiment, for many of the inhabitants of Rhode Island had engaged in the slave trade and a large number of unemancipated negroes still lived within her borders.

The approach of the year 1808, when the period of the compromise would terminate, was marked by the presentation of resolutions from seven States to prohibit the further importation of slaves.[3] The legislature of North Carolina appears to have been the first to propose this amendment, which it did in 1804.[4] The approval of the legislature of Massachusetts followed in 1804–05, and a member from that State immediately introduced in Congress an amendment embodying the sense of their resolutions. The next year similar resolutions were received from the legislatures of Vermont, New Hampshire,

[1] App., No. 1018.

[2] App., No. 120. The State had passed a gradual emancipation law in 1784.

[3] App., Nos. 361a, 362b, 368, 368a, 369, 372, 375, 384. See below.

[4] App., No. 361a, McMaster, Hist. of U. S., III. pp. 517–518. Du Bois, Suppression of the Slave Trade, p. 91. It is referred to in a resolution of the legislature of Georgia of non-concurrence. Massachusetts Archives, House Mis., 5927.

Maryland, and Tennessee, and early in 1808 from the legislature of Pennsylvania.

Early in 1807, however, Congress had passed an act forbidding the importation of foreign slaves after January 1, 1808, thus fixing upon the earliest date possible under the compromise clause of the Constitution.[1] The bill passed by very large majorities, the vote in the House being 113 to 5, but over some of the details there was an acrimonious discussion, in which John Randolph took a prominent part.[2] Notwithstanding this statute and various others, one of which made the slave trade piracy, the African slave trade continued to be a flourishing business.[3]

In 1860–61 numerous amendments were proposed among the compromise measures presented prohibiting the African or foreign slave trade.[4] That the South was ready to grant this concession is made evident by the fact that the foreign slave trade was prohibited by the constitution of the Confederate States.[5] In the series of amendments offered by Senator Saulsbury, in 1864, as a substitute for the thirteenth amendment, there was one prohibiting the African slave trade on pain of death and forfeiture of all the rights and property of persons engaged therein.[6]

117. INTERSTATE SLAVE TRADE AND INTRODUCTION OF FREE NEGROES.

Although the commerce clause of the Constitution gave Congress the right to prohibit the interstate slave trade, the States jealously asserted the privilege of prohibiting or permitting the

---

[1] Statutes at Large, II, p. 426.

[2] Principal opposition came from Brown of Rhode Island. See Niles' Register, VII, 49–53. Du Bois, pp. 94–108.

[3] The messages of the President, the reports of officials, and the debates in Congress all reveal the fact that the trade still went on. Numerous bills and resolutions have been presented on this subject. The following are the most important statutes passed by Congress down to the close of the Thirty-sixth Congress, 1860–61: (1) 1794, March 22, prohibiting outward slave trade. (2) 1798, April 7, prohibiting slave trade to the Mississippi territory. (3) 1800, May 10, forbidding American trading in slaves from one foreign country to another. (4) 1803, February 28, forbidding importation of slaves into States prohibiting it. (5) 1804, March 26, forbidding trade to Louisiana. (6) 1807, March 2, forbidding slave trade after January 1, 1808. (7) 1818, April 20, act in addition to act of 1807. (8) 1819, March 3, statute in addition to act of 1818. (9) 1820, May 15, statute making slave trade piracy. (10) 1823, January 30, continuing act of 1820 making slave trade piracy. Between 1828 and 1861, eleven appropriation bills for the suppression of the trade. 1860, June 16, amendment to act of 1819. 1862, July 17, act to amend slave-trade act. See Dr. W. E. B. Du Bois, The Suppression of the African Slave Trade to the United States of America. Appendix B in passim.

[4] App., Nos. 786, 848, 857, 869f, 872, 874i, 883, 899, 915, 917, 921, 938, 947, 963, 966, 971d, 969.

[5] Art. 1, sec. 9. Du Bois, Slave Trade, pp. 188–191.

[6] App., No. 1010.

traffic as they chose. They further claimed the right to prohibit the entrance of free negroes. The assertion of this right by South Carolina in the passage in 1820 and the subsequent enforcement of the "negro seamen act" led Attorney-General Wirt to pronounce this act unconstitutional.[1] This controversy doubtless suggested the amendment proposed by the legislature of Georgia in 1823, which declared that "no part of the Constitution ought to be construed, or shall be construed, to authorize the importation or ingress of any person of color into any one of the United States contrary to the laws of such State."[2] This resolution received the approval of at least three other of the slave States, and the disapproval of eight States.[3] Usually accompanying the amendments for the suppression of the foreign slave trade introduced in 1860–61, was another providing that Congress shall pass no law prohibiting or interfering with the interstate slave trade.[4]

118. THE QUESTION OF ABOLITION.

All the attempts to protect slavery by constitutional amendment came to an end with the breaking out of the civil war, in April, 1861. No sooner had the contest actually begun than the fugitives from the service of disloyal masters began to come within the Union lines. By the authorized action of commanding officers, seconded by later statutes, their return was forbidden.[5] Then by the act of July 17, 1862, all fugitives the property of persons engaged in rebellion were set free, and on June 28, 1864, the fugitive slave acts were totally repealed. April 16, 1862, slavery was abolished in the District of Columbia, and on the 19th of the following June in the Territories.

All the old questions had therefore been settled by the early action of Congress. Meanwhile the advance of public sentiment had urged upon the nation two new slavery problems— the abolition of slavery in the seceding States and its abolition in the slave States which had remained loyal. To accom-

---

[1] For account of complications resulting from this act, see Von Holst, III, 128–134.

[2] App., No. 538. Perhaps suggested also by the second Missouri compromise.

[3] Louisiana, Mississippi, and Missouri. App., Nos. 538a, 538b, 538c. Disapproved by Vermont, Maine, Connecticut, New Jersey, Delaware, Ohio, Indiana, and Kentucky. App., No. 538.

[4] App., Nos. 785, 798, 821, 831, 847, 852c, 856, 867, 869c, 874h, 894, 917, 926, 946, 959, 971c. The amendment agreed upon by the peace convention on this subject stipulated that Congress should not have "power to prevent the interstate slave trade the right of touching at ports, but not the right of transit in or through nonslave States, or sale or traffic against the laws thereof." App., No. 917. Ante, par. 112.

[5] McDougall, Fugitive Slaves, Chap. VI and Appendix C.

plish the first of these two great objects the war power of the
nation was employed, and to register that result and to extend
it over the whole country amendments were passed. The withdrawal of Southern members made it possible to secure a two-
thirds majority in both Houses of Congress, and the nonpar-
ticipation of the seceding States in the Government made it
possible to secure the necessary three-fourths majority of the
States.[1]

119. ABOLITION IN THE SECEDING STATES.

On the 22d of September, 1862, President Lincoln issued his
preliminary proclamation, providing that "all persons held as
slaves on the 1st of January, 1863, in any State or parts of
States then in rebellion should be thenceforward and forever
free." He further announced that at the next session of Congress he should recommend another proffer of national aid to
any States which should "voluntarily adopt immediate or
gradual abolishment of slavery within their respective limits,"
and further that all persons who had remained loyal should,
on the suppression of the rebellion, be "compensated for all
losses by acts of the United States, including the loss for
slaves."

In fulfillment of this promise, at the opening of the third
session of the Thirty-seventh Congress, December 1, 1862, the
President in his annual message recommended several amendments. One of these provided for the compensation of such
States as should abolish slavery before January 1, 1900.[2] The
other declared that "all slaves who shall have enjoyed actual
freedom by the chances of war at any time before the end of the
rebellion shall be forever free; but all owners of such who shall
not have been disloyal shall be compensated for them," etc.

In accordance with his proclamation, the Southern States
having refused to accept the proffered immunity and aid, the
President, on the 1st of January, 1863, issued the second and
final proclamation. It declared, "as a fit and necessary war
measure," that all the slaves of the rebel States and parts of
States "are, and henceforward shall be, free." Thenceforward,
as the Federal forces advanced. the emancipation proclamation
was applied, and no further proposition was made for an
amendment applying only to the seceding States.

---

[1] For discussion of the situation, see post, par. 186.
[2] Post, par. 120.

120. COMPENSATED EMANCIPATION.

To extend the principle of the proclamation of emancipation to the border States meant the alienation of loyal slaveholders, to permit slavery to continue in the North while it was prohibited in the South was contrary to the whole development of the struggle. A middle way was attempted by President Lincoln's favorite device of compensated emancipation, which had actually been applied in the District of Columbia. In his annual message of December 1, 1862, the President recommended the adoption of two amendments in regard to the compensation of slaves.[1] The first of these provided for the compensation by the General Government of such States as should abolish slavery before January 1, 1900; the second declared that all the slaves who should have enjoyed actual freedom by the chances of war at any time before its end should be forever free, but all the owners of such who should not have been disloyal should be compensated for them at the same rate as the State compensation, but no slave should be twice accounted for. A bill was presented in Congress proffering an indemnity; but the representatives from the border States defeated it. Later, after several of the border States had abolished slavery by their own act, amendments were introduced. The first of these was offered by Senator Powell of Kentucky, April 5, 1864, as an additional clause to the thirteenth amendment. It stipulated that no slave was to be emancipated unless the owner was first paid his full value.[2] Three days later, Senator Saulsbury submitted a resolution which provided that whenever any State should free its slaves, it might apply for pecuniary assistance, and Congress might grant such relief not exceeding $100 for each person liberated.[3] The last amendment on this subject was presented by Senator Davis of Kentucky, June 8, 1866, as an amendment to the resolution which later became the fourteenth amendment. The fourth section of this article among other things forbade the payment of any "claims for the loss or emancipation of any slaves." Mr. Davis proposed to insert in the sentence which guaranteed the validity of the public debt for the pay-

---

[1] App., Nos 973, 974. Blaine, Twenty Years in Congress, pp. 372-373, 445-448. Compensated emancipation and colonization had been suggested in 1861, when a resolution was proposed in the New York legislature to call upon their Representatives and Senators to urge the plan. See Rhodes III, pp. 270-271.

[2] App., No. 993.

[3] App., No. 1017.

ment of pensions and bounties, the following: "Including bounties promised to the owners of slaves enlisted into the military service of the United States by act of Congress of February 29, 1864."[1]

121. COMPENSATION FOR SLAVES PROHIBITED.

The implied pledge in Lincoln's message and the express act of Congress led, after the war, to fears that compensation might be secured later. It was early foreseen that naturally those who had lost their slaves by the result of the war, especially those whose investments had been largely in that class of property, would, in their peculiar distress, apply for remuneration for their losses. If the compensation was made it would, in connection with the already vast debt of the war, seriously impair the national credit. Accordingly, the statesmen of the Republican party deemed it wise, in order to preclude the possibility of such an event, to secure a constitutional prohibition. The first resolution proposing such an amendment was introduced by Mr. Williams of Oregon, in the Senate on the 5th of January, 1866.[2] Somewhat later in the year, Mr. Lawrence of Ohio presented a similar amendment in the House, which he renewed on two different occasions during this Congress.[3] Four similar amendments were presented in the Senate previous to the consideration of the fourteenth amendment.[4] May 10 the House passed a resolution in the form reported by the Committee on Reconstruction.[5] This resolution contained in its fourth section a clause forbidding the United States or any State paying "any claim for compensation for loss of involuntary service or labor." Seven amendments to this clause were proposed in the Senate, including the one previously referred to as presented by Senator Davis.[6] The resolution submitted by Senator Clark of New Hampshire[7] was substituted for the entire section, and the fourth section of the fourteenth amendment now stands in this form. In 1867, before the ratification of the fourteenth amendment had been assured, Mr. Ashley of Ohio introduced as one of a series of amendments an identical proposition.[8]

[1] App., No. 1187.
[2] App., No. 1067. Committee on the Judiciary reported it adversely.
[3] App., Nos. 1074, 1075, 1076.
[4] App., Nos. 1105, 1122, 1129, 1133.
[5] App., Nos. 1140; 1134d in Senate.
[6] App., Nos. 1146, 1151, 1163, 1175c, 1182, 1186, 1187. Ante, par. 120.
[7] App., No. 1182.
[8] App., No. 1221.

122. TOTAL ABOLITION URGED.

Long before the question of compensation was closed, the institution of slavery had ceased to exist in nearly all parts of the Union. Public sentiment demanded that freedom should be conferred not simply by proclamation, or by ordinary legislation, but guaranteed by the organic law of the land.

In response to this feeling, Mr. Ashley of Ohio, on the 14th of December, 1863, presented to the House a resolution providing for the submission to the States of a proposition to amend the Constitution "prohibiting slavery or involuntary servitude in all of the States and Territories now owned or which may be hereafter acquired by the United States." The phraseology of the amendment differed but slightly from the thirteenth amendment as adopted, following the language of the ordinance of 1787.[1] On the same day Mr. Wilson of Iowa also proposed an amendment to the effect that "slavery being incompatible with free government, is forever prohibited in the United States; and involuntary servitude should be permitted only as a punishment for crime," and that Congress should have power to enforce the same by "appropriate legislation."[2] Both propositions were referred to the Committee on the Judiciary, but were not brought up for debate until the last day of the succeeding May, five months after their introduction. Four other resolutions of a similar character were subsequently introduced in the House during the session.[3] One of these was a simple resolution declaring that the Constitution ought to be so amended as to abolish slavery, and was designed to test the spirit of the House. It was passed by a vote of 78 to 62.

In the meantime the subject had been brought up in the Senate. January 11, 1864, Mr. Henderson of Missouri introduced a resolution proposing two amendments to the Consti-

---

[1] App., No. 981. See letter of Mr. Ashley of December 22, 1892, in "Orations and Speeches" of James M. Ashley, pp. 330-331, and appendix. The only difference was that in Ashley's proposition section 1 contained "its jurisdiction" instead of "their jurisdiction," and in section 2, "by laws duly enacted" instead of "by appropriate legislation." Blaine, Twenty Years in Congress, I, pp. 504-505. Mr. Ashley had also introduced the bill for the abolition of slavery in the District of Columbia, which was also modeled after the language of the ordinance of 1787.

[2] App., No. 982.

[3] Mr. Windom of Minnesota, Mr. Arnold of Illinois, Mr. Norton of Illinois, and Mr. Stevens of Pennsylvania. The last also made provision for striking out the clause in the Constitution for the return of persons held to service or labor. App., Nos. 1031, 1032, 1034, 1035.

tution.[1] The first of these provided, in terms similar to those of Wilson's resolution, for the abolition of slavery; the second, for the reduction of the majorities required for the proposal and ratification of amendments. It was referred to the Committee on the Judiciary.[2] A few days later, Mr. Sumner submitted a joint resolution declaring that "all persons are equal before the law, so that no person can hold another as a slave." With some Democratic opposition, it was referred, like the preceding, to the Committee on the Judiciary. February 1 the committee reported adversely on Mr. Sumner's resolution,[3] and proposed as a substitute for Mr. Henderson's proposition the article that subsequently became the thirteenth amendment.[4] Naturally, this amendment met with determined and violent opposition by those Senators who still believed in slavery. All the attempts to amend the article, save those urged by Senator Sumner in favor of a different phraseology, or to add additional sections,[5] were made by the few members who came from the slave States. Senator Garrett Davis of Kentucky was particularly conspicuous by reason of his long and very fiery speeches against the amendment, and the numerous "singular and factious amendments" which he presented from time to time, eight in all.[6] Like Sieyès, who in the days of the French Revolution was ever ready with a new draft of a constitution, so Mr. Davis was ever ready with an amendment. On the 3d of March he introduced two amendments as a substitute for the committee's proposition.[7] One of these provided that no negro should be a citizen of the United States or eligible to any office under the United States, the other that New England should be divided into two States. The division proposed was very singular, inasmuch as Maine and Massachusetts were to form the State of East New England, the rest of the States, West New England. Thus the latter State would not be formed of contiguous territory, but of two sections separated by many miles. Later, he introduced a new amendment for the division of New England which showed more regard for the geography of that region, but he withdrew it before it could come to a vote.[8] This was doubtless introduced to show his antipathy to Massachusetts, for he previously remarked that "the most effective single cause of the

---

[1] App., Nos. 983, 984.
[2] Post. par. 181.
[3] App., No. 1024.
[4] App., No. 985.
[5] App., Nos. 986, 998.
[6] App., Nos. 987, 988, 989, 990, 991, 992, 994.
[7] App., Nos. 987, 988.
[8] App., No. 989. See Ante, par. 46.

pending war has been the intermeddling of Massachusetts with the institution of slavery." The other amendments were submitted by him sometimes as substitutes for, and sometimes as additional sections to, the committee's resolutions. One of these provided that the slaves should not be entitled to their freedom until removed from the slave States by the Government of the United States;[1] another that Congress should provide for the distribution and settlement of all the freedmen of African descent in the United States among the several States and Territories in proportion to their white population;[2] another still, made provision for the nomination of candidates for the Presidency by the States and for the election of President by a unanimous vote of Congress. This same amendment was subsequently introduced by him as an independent proposition and is treated elsewhere.[3]

Senator Powell of Kentucky was not far behind his colleague in offering amendments. Some of his propositions were unobjectionable in themselves, but were evidently prompted by a desire to embarrass the abolition amendment. The antislavery men desired the thirteenth article to go before the people as a distinct proposition and unencumbered, and consequently thwarted these attempts to amend. Mr. Powell presented four distinct amendments,[4] one providing that "no slave should be emancipated unless the owner shall be first paid the full value thereof;" another on the term and eligibility of the President; another limiting the power of the President to make removals, and still another to prohibit riders. It was reserved for Senator Saulsbury of Delaware, on the day of the final vote on the question in the Senate, to present a substitute amendment containing the unparalleled number of twenty sections. These he declared he presented in a spirit of compromise and conciliation. The character of these propositions can be seen by an examination of the Appendix.[5] Suffice it to say here that the first article asserted certain rights of the people, which Mr. Saulsbury evidently considered had been abused in the past. The remainder of the sections were, to a large degree, similar to some of the propositions presented in the Thirty-sixth Congress in 1860-61. The first section declared that all the provisions of this article relating to slavery should not be altered without the consent of all the States

[1] App., No. 992.
[2] App., No. 994.
[3] Ante, par. 46.
[4] App., Nos. 993, 995, 996, 997.
[5] App., Nos. 999-1021.

maintaining that institution. None of the amendments presented by these three Senators received substantial support, several failing to receive more than two votes.

The amendment finally passed the Senate April 8, 1864, in the form reported by the committee, by the vote of 36 to 6.[1] The resolution was immediately sent to the House, but it did not come up for consideration until the last day of May. An attempt to throw it out on the first reading failed. During the consideration of the resolution Mr. Pendleton, of Ohio, the leader on the Democratic side, strenuously maintained that "three-fourths of the States did not possess the constitutional power to pass this amendment," nor, indeed, "all the States save one," because the institution of slavery "lies within the dominion reserved entirely to each State for itself."[2] Two unsuccessful attempts were made to amend, the one by Mr. Wheeler of Wisconsin, providing that the article should not apply to Kentucky, Missouri, Delaware, and Maryland until ten years after its ratification;[3] the other by Mr. Pendleton, who proposed that the amendment should be submitted to conventions of the people in the several States.[4] On June 15 the vote upon the amendment was taken, the vote standing 95 yeas to 66 nays. So the joint resolution failed, not having received a two-thirds majority in its favor.[5] Mr. Ashley moved a reconsideration, and, pending the action upon the motion, Congress adjourned.

123. ABOLITION SECURED BY THE THIRTEENTH AMENDMENT.

During the interim between the sessions, the Union arms had made progress, a movement for freedom had begun in the border States,[6] and, most important of all, Lincoln had been triumphantly reelected, and the Republican party had made gains in the election for the next Congress.

In such a turn of affairs the Thirty-eighth Congress reassembled for its second session. The President in his message

---

[1] The six negative votes were cast by Messrs. Davis of Kentucky, Hendricks of Indiana, McDougall of California, Powell of Kentucky, Riddle and Saulsbury of Delaware.

[2] Inasmuch as "the power to amend did not carry with it the power to revolutionize and subvert the form and spirit of the Government." Blaine, I, pp. 507, 537. Cong. Globe, Thirty-eighth Congress, first session, pp. 2992-2993; also ibid., Thirty-eighth Congress, second session, pp. 221-225. Replies of Messrs. Ashley, Cox, Garfield, Boutwell, and Rollins, see ibid., pp. 139, 192, 222, 245, 258, 263.

[3] App., No. 1022.

[4] App., No. 1023. See post, par. 179.

[5] App., No. 985.

[6] Maryland by her own action abolished slavery. See Cong. Globe, Thirty-eighth Congress, second session, p. 144.

at the opening of the session, after recounting the events of
the past and reminding Congress that the recent election made
it practically certain that the next Congress would pass the
proposed amendment, recommended that the House should
reconsider its action.[1]

On the 6th of January Mr. Ashley called up his motion of
reconsideration. The debate on the question lasted until the
last day of the month, when the resolution was reconsidered
and passed amid intense excitement by a vote of 119 yeas to
56 nays.[2] The amendment having now been adopted by both
Houses, was signed by the President,[3] and submitted to the
legislatures of the States. On the 18th of December, 1865, the
Secretary of State declared by proclamation that the amendment had been ratified by three-fourths of the States and had
become a part of the Constitution.[4]

124. CITIZENSHIP OF NEGROES DENIED.

The conflict over the status of the negro was by no means
ended when he became free. There had been many thousands
of free negroes before the war; the question of their legal
status, of their right to be citizens, or to enjoy the privileges
of citizens had been discussed in the Dred Scott decision; so
far as it had force, no negro could be or become a citizen of
the United States. The first amendments which appeared on
this subject were intended to affirm this principle. Mr. Florence of Pennsylvania, January 28, 1861, proposed that the
descendants of Africans should not be made citizens.[5] Other
amendments were introduced at about the same time to prevent persons of the African race exercising the franchise or
the right of holding office.[6] Senators Saulsbury and Davis
included in the series offered by them this same prohibition
relative to the citizenship of Africans.[9]

---

[1] App., No. 1038. Blaine, Twenty Years in Congress, pp. 534-536.

[2] For an account of how the requisite two-thirds majority was secured in the House, see
Riddle, Recollections of War Times, pp. 324-325; Wilson, Rise and Fall of the Slave
Power, III, p. 452. During the discussion of the amendment resolutions were presented
from the legislature of the State of New York, April 28, 1864, and from the constitutional
convention of the State of Missouri, January, 1865. App., Nos. 1036, 1044. A few days after
its passage the Delegates from the Territories attempted to present a communication
approving the amendment, but objection was made. App. No. 1045.

[3] See post, par. 184.

[4] See post, par. 186.

[5] App., No. 884.

[6] App., Nos. 844, 929, 951.

[7] App., Nos. 1011, 10391.

125. THE FOURTEENTH AMENDMENT.

The question recurred in a very perplexing form at about
the time of the passage of the thirteenth amendment.[1] Several
of the Southern States, while admitting the freedom of the
former slaves, passed acts placing them on a legal inferiority,
and in some cases established a system of obligatory contracts
practically akin to slavery.[2] Hence, a large number of amendments were proposed giving a definition of American citizenship and guaranteeing to all citizens the equal protection of
the laws. At the same time attempts were made to introduce
into the Constitution clauses in regard to the new apportionment of Representatives—made imperative by the implied
abrogation of the three-fifths ratio—and others relative to the
disability of all those who had taken part in the rebellion.
Complicated with these questions of citizenship and suffrage,
were the questions of the validity of the national debt, the
compensation for slaves, or the payment of the rebel debt.
Two joint resolutions proposing amendments fixing the basis
of representation and repudiating the rebel debt passed the
House, but had failed to receive the indorsement of the Senate.[3]

On the 30th of April, 1866, Mr. Stevens of Pennsylvania,
after severely censuring the Senate for their failure to pass
the amendments just referred to, reported from the Committee
on Reconstruction a joint resolution proposing an amendment
to the Constitution.[4] The several propositions which had been
referred to the committee had now been consolidated into this
one article. After slight amendments of detail, it was adopted
by both Houses of Congress,[5] and later ratified by the requisite number of States, and was added to the Constitution as
the famous fourteenth amendment. The other subjects included in this amendment will each be considered in its proper
place.[6]

126. CIVIL RIGHTS CLAUSES OF THE FOURTEENTH AMENDMENT.

The origin of the first section demands particular attention
in this place. Several earlier attempts had already been made

---

[1] See ante, par. 123.
[2] Lalor's Cyclopedia of Political Science: Article on reconstruction.
[3] App., Nos. 1055, 1079.
[4] Nos. 1135–1140.
[5] Nos. 1158–1163, 1177, 1180–1182, 1183. Story, II, Chap. XLVII. For history of the Joint
Committee on Reconstruction, see Foster, I, pp. 227–230.
[6] See ante, par. 22, (4), 121. Post, pars. 126, 128, 143, 144, 145.

to secure an amendment to the Constitution relative to the equality of the citizens before the law.

The first of these propositions, introduced in the House by Mr. Stevens of Pennsylvania, December 5, 1865, provided that "all national and State laws shall be equally applicable to every citizen, and no discrimination shall be made on account of race or color."[1] The next day Mr. Bingham of Ohio offered a resolution to amend the Constitution so as "to empower Congress to pass all necessary and proper laws to secure to all persons in every State of the Union equal protection in their rights, life, liberty, and property."[2] Both of these resolutions were referred to the Committee on the Judiciary. Within a few days, two other amendments of similar purport were introduced.[3] Senator Brown of Missouri submitted, February 1, 1866, a motion, which was passed, directing the Committee on Reconstruction to inquire into the expediency of amending the Constitution so as to declare with greater certainty the power of Congress to enforce and determine by appropriate legislation all the guaranties contained in that instrument, especially as to that which assures the citizens of each State the privileges and immunities of other States.[4] Mr. Williams suggested an amendment empowering Congress to enforce "all obligations, prohibitions, or disabilities" imposed by the Constitution on the several States.[5] A few days later, the Committee on Reconstruction reported in each branch of Congress a proposed amendment declaring that "the Congress shall have power to make all laws which shall be necessary and proper to secure to the citizens of each State all the privileges and immunities of citizens in the several States; and to all persons in the several States equal protection in the rights of life, liberty, and property."[6]

No important action was taken in either House upon the resolution. There seemed to be a common desire to await the final report of the committee. March 9, 1866, during the discussion in the Senate on the amendment passed by the House relative to the apportionment of Representatives, Senator Yates of Illinois moved an amendment thereto, declaring that "all citizens, without distinction of race, color, or previous condition of slavery, shall be protected in the full and equal

[1] App. A, No. 1049.   [3] App., Nos. 1060, 1061.   [5] App., No. 1107.
[2] App. A, No. 1056.   [4] App., No. 1105.   [6] App., Nos. 1109, 1110.

enjoyment and exercise of all their civil and political rights."[1]
It secured, however, only seven votes in its favor.[2]

The resolution reported to the House April 30, 1866, which
became the basis of the fourteenth amendment, contained in
the first section the provision that "no State shall make or
enforce any law which shall abridge the privileges or immunities of citizens; nor deprive any person of life, liberty, or property without due process of law; nor deny to any person the
equal protection of the laws."[3] This amendment passed the
House without change. It soon became evident that the Senate would not adopt the amendment in the form in which it
passed the House. Several attempts were made to amend
this first section, some of which were successful. Mr. Wade
offered a substitute for the entire resolution, but in the first
section he simply proposed to substitute for "citizens" the
words "persons born in the United States or naturalized by
the laws thereof."[4]

On May 30 Mr. Howard of Michigan, in behalf of the Senate members of the Joint Committee on Reconstruction, presented a series of resolutions which had been adopted by the
Republican caucus as a substitute for the House amendment.
The substitute was accepted. The first change thus introduced
was to prefix these words to the first clause of the amendment:
"All persons born in the United States and subject to the
jurisdiction thereof are citizens of the United States and of
the States wherein they reside."[5] This supplied a serious
omission in the original Constitution, for in that instrument
there had been no definition of citizenship.

Mr. Doolittle of Wisconsin moved to insert in this clause the
words "including Indians not taxed,"[6] but to all but ten Senators such a provision seemed superfluous. A few days later,
Mr. Fessenden of Maine secured the insertion of the words

---

[1] App. No. 1097.
[2] Senator Stewart suggested a similar proposition (App., Nos. 1128, 1143a), while Senator
Fessenden proposed an amendment prohibiting a State from making any law which shall
abridge the privileges, etc. App., No. 1134.
[3] App., No. 1135.
[4] App., No. 1147.
[5] App., No. 1158. A similar amendment was presented by Mr. Doolittle. App., No. 1175.
The amendment of Mr. Stewart, which he intended to propose to H. Res. 127, also contained
a definition of citizenship: "All persons born within the limits or under the jurisdiction
of the United States, and all persons naturalized under its laws, are and shall be both
citizens of the United States and citizens of the several States within which they reside,"
App., No. 1143a.
[6] App., No. 1164.

"or naturalized" in this sentence.[1] Mr. Yates of Illinois
offered a resolution to add to the amendment the provision
that "nothing in the foregoing sections shall abridge or in
any wise affect the right, franchise, or privilege of any inhabitants of the United States," but it failed to be acted upon.[2]
Mr. Reverdy Johnson of Maryland made an unsuccessful
attempt to strike out an important guaranty of this article,
which declared that no State should "make or enforce any law
which shall abridge the privileges or immunities of citizens of
the United States."[3]

Mr. Buckalew of Pennsylvania moved to amend by adding
to the resolution a sixth section making provision that the
amendment shall be submitted to the legislatures in the States,
the most popular branch of which shall be chosen next after
the passage of the amendment.[4] Mr. Doolittle proposed that
the amendment should be submitted to the States as five
separate articles, to be acted upon separately; but this motion
secured but eleven votes in its favor[5]—the "Administration
strength." Finally the consolidated amendment passed the
Senate June 8 in the form in which it now appears in the Constitution by the vote of 33 yeas to 11 nays. On the 13th the
House, by a single vote of 120 to 32, concurred in all the changes
made in the Senate, and the fourteenth article was sent to the
States for ratification.[6]

127. FURTHER ENFORCEMENT OF CIVIL RIGHTS.

The fourteenth amendment was not declared in force until
July 28, 1868, but during the year 1867 several additional
amendments in regard to the enforcement of civil rights were
proposed,[7] but pending the action of the State legislatures
upon the fourteenth amendment no further steps were taken
by Congress. During the discussion of the fifteenth amendment, in 1869, several propositions were presented to prevent
the right of a citizen of the United States to hold office from
being denied or abridged "on account of race, color, or previous condition of servitude."[8] The general subject came up
again at the time of the Kuklux movement in the South,
from 1872 to 1875. Congress passed an act in 1875 which was

---

[1] App., No. 1183.
[2] App., No. 1179.
[3] App., No. 1188.
[4] App., No. 1154. Post, par. 180.
[5] App., No. 1184.
[6] App., Nos. 1135–1140.
[7] App., Nos. 1194b, 1197, 1202, 1209, 1213, 1215, 1216, 1218.
[8] App., Nos. 1285, 1289a, 1289c, 1311. See post, 131.

intended to afford protection to all in the enjoyment of the rights guaranteed by the fourteenth amendment.[1]

When the question was brought before the Supreme Court in the Civil Rights Cases the act was held unconstitutional,[2] and the court further announced that the power of Congress to enforce the fourteenth amendment by appropriate legislation, does not extend to legislation prescribing the rights of the parties themselves between each other, but only to the correction and prohibition of legislation and action on the part of the State. Owing to this decision, six resolutions to amend the Constitution, in order to protect the civil rights and secure the equality of citizens, were introduced in the first session of the Forty-eighth Congress, 1883–84.[3]

The first of these was presented by Senator Wilson of Iowa, December 4, 1883, the second day of the session. It proposed to add to the Constitution, as article sixteen, the following: "Congress shall have power, by appropriate legislation, to protect citizens of the United States in the exercise and enjoyment of their rights, privileges, and immunities, and to assure to them the equal protection of the laws."[4] Two of the other propositions were offered by Southern members, Mr. Mackey of South Carolina and Mr. O'Hara of North Carolina. No further attempt has since been made to amend the Constitution relative to this subject.

125. DISABILITY OF PARTICIPANTS IN THE REBELLION.

While Congress and the States were thus cooperating to secure civil and legal equality to the former slaves, they were also providing for a withdrawal of certain rights from those who had participated as leaders in the movement of secession. The failure of the trial of Jefferson Davis for treason[5] put an end to any plans of legal punishment, and the wide-reaching pardons and amnesties of President Johnson seemed to restore the former belligerents to their previous privileges; but there was a popular demand that these men

---

[1] Statutes of the United States, Forty-third Congress, second session, chapter 114, pp. 335–337.

[2] 109 U. S., 3.

[3] App., Nos. 1575, 1588, 1596, 1599, 1611, 1612.

[4] App., No. 1575. An amendment proposed in 1880, in regard to the election and the free public schools, prohibited separation or distinction "on account of race, color, or social condition." App., No. 1514. See post, par. 172.

[5] The investigation of Mr. H. F. Blake, a member in the Seminary of American History, Harvard University, 1890–91, on Treason Trials, throws much light on this subject.

should not be eligible to places of honor and trust under the United States Government, at least for some years to come.

Four amendments relative to this subject were proposed in the early months of the year 1866, previous to the consideration of the resolution which became incorporated into the Constitution as the fourteenth amendment. The first of these, presented by Mr. Cullom of Illinois, February 16, provided that no officer of the Southern Confederacy should ever be eligible to hold any office under the United States Government.[1] About a month later, the same gentleman introduced a somewhat different resolution, which declared that "no person, except a citizen of the United States who has at all times borne true allegiance thereto, shall ever hold office under the United States."[2] Another resolution was presented to the House by Mr. McKee of Kentucky, which provided that no person should hold the office of President or Vice-President, Senator or Representative in Congress, or any office under the appointment of the President or Senate who had been or should be engaged in any armed conspiracy or rebellion against the Government, etc.[3]

In the meantime Senator Poland of Vermont had submitted to the Senate an amendment which stipulated that "no person who has been or shall be willingly engaged in rebellion against the United States shall exercise the elective franchise or hold any office under the authority of the United States or of any State."[4]

The report of the Committee on Reconstruction,[5] April 30, 1866, included as section 3 of its proposition preliminary to the fourteenth amendment, a clause by which "all persons who voluntarily adhered to the late insurrection" were excluded, until July 4, 1870, from the right to vote for Representatives or for Presidential electors. This third section was the only part of the committee's proposition which the House attempted to amend. Mr. Garfield moved to strike it out altogether.[6] Mr. McKee of Kentucky offered a substitute which forever excluded secessionists from holding any office under the Government,[7] and Mr. Beaman of Michigan submitted a substitute, declaring ineligible to any office under the United States

---

[1] App., No. 1111.
[2] App., No. 1125.
[3] App., No. 1112. A similar amendment presented by Mr. Baker of Illinois, No. 1124.
[4] App., No. 1116. Similar amendment presented in House. App., No. 1125.
[5] H. R. 127, App. No. 1137. Similar resolution presented in the Senate. App. No. 1134b.
[6] App., No. 1141.
[7] App., No. 1142.

Government any person included in any of the classes of persons enumerated. In this was included the President and Vice-President, the heads of departments, and the foreign agents of the so-called Confederate States of America; also all persons who had held any office, either civil or military, under the Government at the time of secession, who had given aid and comfort to the late rebellion.[1]

When the resolution reached the Senate there were twelve attempts to alter the third section. A disposition was shown by some Senators to make this section more stringent by increasing the period of disability, and also by increasing the number of offices from which ex-Confederates should be excluded.[2]

On the 30th of May Senator Howard of Michigan, in behalf of the Senate members of the Joint Committee on Reconstruction, presented a new draft as a substitute for the entire resolution. It proposed to insert in place of the third section the precise provision which now appears in the fourteenth amendment.[3] The section was so much more stringent than that for which it was substituted that several unsuccessful attempts were made to mitigate the terms of the amendment. They were introduced by adherents of the Administration, Hendricks of Indiana, Johnson of Maryland, Saulsbury of Delaware, Doolittle of Wisconsin, and Davis of Kentucky.[4] For some reason which has never been adequately explained, the Democratic Senators preferred the third section of the substitute. presented by Mr. Howard, to that of the corresponding section of the House amendment, although the terms of the latter were decidedly more mild. The vote by which the Senate proposition was substituted was nearly unanimous, and the entire amendment finally passed the Senate by a vote of 33 yeas to 11 nays.[5]

In November, 1867, before the adoption of the fourteenth amendment had become assured, Mr. Ashley introduced, in

[1] App., No. 1143.
[2] Such amendments were submitted by Senator Clark of New Hampshire and Senator Wilson of Massachusetts. App., Nos. 1144, 1153. On the other hand, Mr. Johnson of Maryland moved to strike out this section altogether (No. 1155), and Mr. Wade of Ohio offered a substitute to the resolution, in which the provision excluding rebels from the suffrage until 1870 was left out (Nos. 1147-1151).
[3] No. 1160.
[4] App., Nos. 1165, 1166, 1167, 1168, 1169, 1170, 1185. Mr. Van Winkle of West Virginia moved to add to the amendment an article extending amnesty to all other persons not mentioned in section 3, who had been engaged in rebellion, on their taking oath to support the Constitution. App., No. 1171.
[5] App., No. 1137. (Mr. Howard's proposition. App., No. 1160.)

H. Doc. 353, pt 2——15

connection with a series of propositions, an amendment to disqualify from holding any office under the United States, or under
any State, any person who was a member of any legislature or
convention which passed the ordinance of secession and who
voted therefor.[1]

The effect of the amendment thus laboriously framed was
smaller than had been expected. Little difficulty was found
in securing from time to time the two-thirds vote in both Houses
necessary to relieve individuals and classes from their disabilities. By 1880 there remained but a few score persons excluded
from the suffrage or from office, and several ex-officers in the
Confederate army and ex-members of the Confederate government were found in Congress.

129. RESTRICTIONS ON SUFFRAGE.

The conditions of suffrage fixed by the Constitution, namely,
that "the electors in each State shall have the qualifications
requisite for electors of the most numerous branch of the State
legislature,"[2] had given rise to two difficulties before 1860—
naturalization by States, and the question of the suffrage of
free negroes. The first of the difficulties called out the amendment introduced by Mr. Marshall of Kentucky, January 18,
1858.[3] It provided that the second section of the first article
be so amended "that only natural-born citizens of the United
States or the citizens naturalized according to an act of Congress shall be deemed qualified electors under the Constitution, to exercise the right to vote for a member of the House
of Representatives."

The question of the suffrage of free negroes gave rise to five
amendments introduced in the days just previous to the civil
war; these were in each case but one of a series of amendments, presented by their authors in the hope of preventing
the impending disruption of the Union.[4] The first of these
was submitted by Senator Douglas, December 24, 1860. It was
in these words: "The elective franchise and the right to hold
office, whether Federal, State, Territorial, or municipal, shall
not be exercised by persons of the African race, in whole or in
part."[5]

[1] App., Nos. 1213d, 1220.
[2] Art. 1, sec. 2, cl. 1.
[3] App., No. 777. This was the only amendment introduced in the Thirty-fifth Congress.
[4] App., Nos. 843, 852h, 869h, 929, 951.
[5] App., No. 843. The same provision appeared in the other resolutions introduced by
Messrs. Crittenden, Clemens, and Pugh, as above.

130. EXTENSION OF THE SUFFRAGE TO NEGROES.

Soon after the close of the war, the Southern States had granted the suffrage to the negroes, but the grant was revocable, and the disposition to discriminate against the negro was so manifest that a series of amendments was proposed compelling the States to continue or to extend to the negro the suffrage. During the debate on the fourteenth amendment, some of the amendments introduced proposed the reduction of the representation of a State whenever the right of suffrage was denied or abridged, except for participation in rebellion or other crimes. The fourteenth amendment only negatively aided the negro in securing the right of suffrage by laying the penalty of a decreased representation upon any State that should deny or abridge his right to vote. As time went on, it was deemed expedient to guarantee to the freedman the franchise.

In the opening days of the thirty-ninth Congress six distinct propositions looking to this end were offered. Two of these proposed establishing an educational standard of voting for Federal officers.[1] Mr. Boutwell was the first to suggest an amendment to the Constitution, providing that "no State shall make any distinction in the exercise of the elective franchise on account of race or color."[2] Another proposed to give Congress the power to prescribe the qualifications of electors of the members of the House of Representatives and Presidential electors, and "provide for the election and return of such officers."[3]

Meanwhile Mr. Henderson of Missouri, who had introduced the resolution which led to the thirteenth amendment, was preparing an amendment, which he submitted January 23, 1866. It read: "No State, in prescribing the qualifications requisite for electors therein, shall discriminate against any person on account of color or race."[4]

Shortly after this the resolution passed by the House to amend the Constitution in regard to the apportionment of Representatives came before the Senate for consideration.[5] Among the various attempts to amend this resolution were five in regard

[1] App., Nos. 1058, 1059.
[2] App., No. 1064. Mr. Elliott proposed a similar amendment. App., No. 1088.
[3] App., No. 1070.
[4] App., Nos. 1099, 1104.
[5] App., No. 1079.

to the suffrage.[1] Mr. Sumner proposed as a substitute for the amendment a declaration that "there shall be no oligarchy, aristocracy, caste, or monopoly invested with peculiar privileges or powers, and there shall be no denial of rights, civil or political, on account of color or race anywhere within the limits of the United States or the jurisdiction thereof, but all persons therein shall be equal before the law whether in the court room or at the ballot box." This resolution was temporarily withdrawn, but afterwards presented in a modified form, and rejected by a vote of 8 to 39.[2]

Mr. Henderson offered his proposition anew as an amendment to Mr. Sumner's resolution.[3] In spite of his warning to his Republican associates, that though they might reject this amendment now it would be required of them within five years, it was lost, by a vote of 10 yeas to 37 nays.

Senator Howard of Michigan submitted as a substitute an amendment enumerating the different classes of persons of African descent upon whom the right of franchise should be conferred. Among the classes mentioned were all males over twenty-one who were members of the Army and Navy, all who were able to read and write the English, French, or Spanish language, and all males in possession of property to the value of $250.[4] This amendment was not acted upon. His previous resolution having been rejected, Mr. Sumner now attempted to amend the resolution by inserting the clause "The elective franchise shall not be denied or abridged in any State on account of race or color." It was rejected, 8 to 38.[5] Mr. Yates of Illinois likewise presented a similar proposition in a more elaborate form. It also was rejected by nearly the same vote.[6]

Three other propositions to amend the Constitution relative to the suffrage were introduced before the close of this Congress. On April 30, 1866, the same day that the Committee on Reconstruction in the House reported the resolution which became the fourteenth amendment, Mr. Fessenden in the Senate reported from the Joint Committee of fifteen on the Condition of the States which formed the so-called Confederate States, a resolution to amend the Constitution. It provided that political power should be possessed in all the States

[1] App., Nos. 1093, 1094, 1096, 1097, 1099.
[2] App., No. 1093.
[3] App., No. 1099.
[4] App., No. 1094.
[5] App., No. 1096.
[6] App., No. 1097.

exactly in proportion as the right of suffrage should be granted, without distinction of color or race.[1]

Early in 1867 two amendments presenting the following new features were introduced: One to prohibit a State from depriving any citizen of the United States from voting at any Federal or State election;[2] the other contained a provision prohibiting any State from requiring more than a $250 property qualification, or as an educational test more than the ability to read the Constitution in English and to write one's name.[3]

In the early part of the Fortieth Congress, Senator Henderson reintroduced his amendment in somewhat different words. It read: "No State shall deny or abridge the right of its citizens to vote and hold office on account of race, color, or previous condition."[4] The resolution was referred to the Committee on the Judiciary and was not reported until nearly two years later, January 15, 1869, when it was taken as the basis of the fifteenth amendment. In this same year four very similar resolutions were presented.[5]

During the second session of the Fortieth Congress, one further attempt was made to secure an amendment on this subject. Mr. Newcomb of Missouri, March 9, 1868, offered a resolution instructing the Committee on the Judiciary of the House to report an amendment which should settle the qualifications of electors impartially and uniformly in all the States.[6]

131. THE FIFTEENTH AMENDMENT.[7]

The experience of the four years following the close of the war showed that the right of suffrage was too important and essential to be left to ordinary legislation. It should be incorporated into the Constitution. The indorsement of the action

---

[1] App., No. 1134. Senator Stewart offered an amendment. which he had previously introduced (App., No. 1128) to the committee's proposition. App., No. 1190.

[2] App., No. 1197, provided the citizens were of sound mind. unconvicted of any infamous offense, and had attained the age of 21, and had resided in the State one year.

[3] App., No. 1203. The same had been presented before, to be printed. App., No. 1194f.

[4] App., No. 1209 (March 7, 1867).

[5] App., Nos. 1212, 1213, 1215, 1217. Mr. Ashley, who presented two of these, proposed that after July 4, 1876, ability to read and write English should be a requirement for the suffrage. App., No. 1227e. conferring the suffrage on all citizens of age, was also introduced by him.

[6] App., No. 1224.

[7] Brief history of its proposal and adoption: See Foster, Com. on Const., I, sec. 52, pp. 325–329; Story, II, Chap. XLVIII (by Judge Cooley). The writer has not deemed it necessary to trace the political history of the "reconstruction amendments," as it has already been done many times.

of the Republican party at the polls in 1868, convinced the
rank and file of the party that another amendment was necessary. Accordingly, at the opening of the third session of the
Fortieth Congress, in 1868, eight distinct amendments were
introduced, the effect of which, if adopted, would have been to
extend the right of suffrage to the freedmen.[1] In a short time
three more amendments on this same subject were offered.[2]
Of these eleven amendments, seven were presented in the
House and four in the Senate. With one exception, they
were all referred to the Committee on the Judiciary in their
respective Houses.

The Committee on the Judiciary reported to the House on
the 11th of June, 1869, through their chairman, Mr. Boutwell
of Massachusetts, a joint resolution proposing an amendment
which provided that " the right of any citizen of the United
States to vote shall not be abridged by the United States or
any State by reason of race, color, or previous condition of
slavery of any citizen or class of citizens of the United States."[3]

This resolution gave rise to extended discussion, as Mr.
Boutwell remarked, "This debate has demonstrated two facts,
one is, there is a very general agreement that it is desirable
to submit an amendment to the Constitution; and the other is,
that there is a very great difference of opinion as to the details
of the amendment." The truth of this last statement appears
throughout the entire discussion preparatory to the passage of
the fifteenth amendment in both branches of Congress. Some
eleven amendments were offered in the House to the resolution
reported by the committee.[4]

One offered by Mr. Brooks of New York was very peculiar.
It provided that the right of any citizen to vote should not be
abridged "by reason of his or her race, sex, nativity, or age
when over twelve years of age, color or previous condition of
slavery."[5]

Mr. Shellabarger of Ohio, objecting to the amendment proposed by the committee as not preventing the limitation of
the suffrage on other grounds such as intelligence and property,
presented an amendment extending the right of suffrage to all
male citizens of suitable age and "sound mind," except those

---

[1] App., Nos. 1233, 1234, 1235, 1236, 1237, 1238, 1239, 1245.
[2] App., Nos. 1249, 1307, 1312.
[3] App., No. 1250.
[4] App., Nos. 1251–1260.
[5] App., No. 1251.

"who have engaged or may hereafter engage" in rebellion.[1]
Mr. Ward of New York offered an amendment allowing all to
exercise the right of suffrage, except such as have been convicted of treason or other crimes, on complying with certain
regulations concerning registration and naturalization.[2] Mr.
Bingham of Ohio introduced an amendment the "same in
substance" as his colleague's, with "one exception;" it excepted
those who might "hereafter engage in rebellion."[3] Mr. Boutwell, in response to the desire of several to test the sense of
the House, proposed to add the words "nor shall educational
attainments or the possession or ownership of property ever
be made a test of the right of any citizen to vote."[4]

All these amendments were rejected by decisive votes, and
the resolution as proposed by the committee, with only one
minor change, was passed by the House by a vote of 150 to 42,
on January 30, 1869. Meanwhile a similar discussion was
taking place in the Senate. The Committee on the Judiciary
at last, on the 15th of January, reported a substitute for the
amendment introduced by Mr. Henderson of Missouri[5] nearly
two years before.[6] Within the next few days seven amendments to the joint resolution were presented. One, offered by
Mr. Williams of Oregon proposed that "Congress shall have
power to abolish or modify any restrictions upon the right to
vote or hold office prescribed by the constitution or laws of
any State."[7] Mr. Pomeroy of Kansas submitted an amendment which stipulated that the right to vote and hold office
should not be "denied or abridged by the United States or
any State for any reason not equally applicable to all citizens."[8]
Mr. Buckalew of Pennsylvania presented as an additional
article an amendment making provision for the choice of Presidential electors.[9] This proposition was later withdrawn, but
it was shortly afterwards again presented to Congress. Mr.
Dixon of Connecticut moved that the resolution be submitted
to conventions in the States for ratification.[10] Mr. Davis of

---

[1] App., No. 1255. Somewhat similar amendments to this were Nos. 1107, 1245, 1252a,
1289a, 1289b, 1311, 1312, limited, however, to male citizens in most instances.
[2] App., No. 1256.
[3] App., No. 1257.
[4] App., No. 1258. Rejected, 45 to 95.
[5] Ante par. 130.
[6] App., No. 1284.
[7] App., No. 1285.
[8] App., No. 1289.
[9] App., No. 1287.
[10] App., No. 1286. Post, par. 179.

Kentucky proposed a new method of ratification by the vote of the people in each State.[1]

January 30, upon reception of the House amendment, the Senate immediately took it into consideration, laying aside its own resolution. This was done for the purpose of expediting any agreement between the two branches. On the 3d of February Mr. Stewart offered the amendment originally reported by the Committee on the Judiciary.[2] It changed the phraseology of the House amendment, and in addition declared that the right of a person to hold office should not be abridged. At the same time eight other amendments were offered.

Some of these provided that the right to vote and hold office should not be denied or abridged for any reason not equally applicable to all citizens.[3] Others gave the State the right to fix the "conditions of residence and age and registration laws."[4] An amendment to prevent the Chinese and Indians not taxed from voting or holding office was also presented.[5] One proposed to insert before the word "citizens" the words "natural born."[6] Attempts were also made to secure the submission of the amendment either to conventions or legislatures hereafter elected.[7] Between the 4th and the 9th of the month some fifteen substitute propositions were rejected by decisive votes. Some of these made provision for excluding from the right of suffrage those who had or who may hereafter engage in rebellion.[8] Others prohibited any discrimination in the exercise of the franchise or the right to hold office,[9] but the majority of the propositions were intended to make the terms of the article less stringent. Of this character was the resolution proposed by Mr. Bayard of Delaware which restricted the amendment in the application to Federal offices.[10] Mr. Davis of Kentucky proposed as an additional clause an amendment declaring that this provision is not intended to apply to, or in any way affect,

[1] App., No. 1288. Post, par. 182. Two others, App.. Nos. 1289a and 1289b. were ordered printed. One declared that the privilege of suffrage is hereby declared to be a right incident to citizenship, subject to be forfeited only on conviction of felony.

[2] App., No. 1261.

[3] Mr. Howard, App., No. 1204. Mr. Pomeroy, App., No. 1260.

[4] Mr. Fowler, App., No. 1266. Mr. Sawyer, App., No. 1267.

[5] Mr. Corbett, App., No. 1265. See post, par. 133.

[6] Mr. Williams, App., No. 1262.

[7] Mr. Buckalew, App., No. 1264. Mr. Dixon, App., No. 1268. Post, pars. 179, 180.

[8] Mr. Warner, App., Nos. 1270, 1282.

[9] Mr. Wilson, App., Nos. 1274–1275. Two similar resolutions were proposed as independent propositions. App., Nos. 1311, 1312.

[10] App., No. 1279.

the principles and forms of the governments of the several States as organized by their respective constitutions.[1] Mr. Sumner, believing an amendment unnecessary, as the same result could be secured by legislation " and because of the reflection the adoption of such an amendment would cast upon the Constitution," opposed the amendment and offered a substitute in the form of a bill expressive of his views, but it received only nine votes.[2] The remaining amendments were to a large extent modifications of, or additions to, the article. Some fifteen of these substitute propositions were rejected by decisive votes.[3] Finally, Mr. Wilson of Massachusetts offered a more " comprehensive " amendment, which proposed to add to the specifications of race and color those of " nativity, property, education, and creed."[4] This proposition gave rise to considerable discussion by those who seriously objected to the prohibition of an educational test, and the amendment failed to secure a majority, the vote standing 19 to 24. Subsequently the substitute suggested by Mr. Wilson was agreed to by a vote of 31 to 27. It read: " No discrimination shall be made in any State among the citizens of the United States in the exercise of the elective franchise or in the right to hold office in any State on account of race, color, nativity, property, education, or religious creed."[5]

Even after the amendment was ordered to be engrossed, Mr. Morton of Indiana was allowed to introduce, for the Committee on Representative Reform, the amendment which Mr. Buckalew of Pennsylvania had previously proposed, as an additional article. The aim of the amendment was to secure the choice of the election by a popular vote in every State.

---

[1] App., 1272.

[2] Senate Journal, Fortieth Congress, third session, pp. 229, 230.

[3] App., Nos. 1262-1282.

[4] App., No. 1274.

[5] App., No. 1275. This " would have altered the constitutions of more than one-half of the States." Foster, Com. on Const., 1, p. 325. At that time the following States required an educational test for voters: Connecticut, by the constitution of 1858; Massachusetts, by an amendment of 1857. Florida, by constitution of 1868, provided for educational qualifications for new electors after 1880. Since that date the constitution of Colorado of 1876 authorized the legislature to provide by law such a qualification for new electors after 1890. The recent constitutions of Mississippi (1891) and of South Carolina (1895) make provision for an educational test of such a nature that the majority of the negroes can be easily deprived of the franchise. On the other hand, the constitution of Alabama of 1875 prohibits any educational or property qualification for the suffrage or office. Rhode Island and Pennsylvania in 1869 both required an elector to own property, and several other States required the payment of a poll tax. Hitchcock, Am. State Constitutions, pp. 27-32.

To insure this result Congress was empowered to prescribe the manner in which the election should be conducted.[1] After a short discussion the addition was accepted by a vote of 37 to 19, and the two proposed amendments, included under one resolution, were adopted by the Senate, the vote standing 40 yeas to 16 nays. In form, therefore, the Senate had agreed to the House proposition with amendments. When the resolution thus altered was received in the House that body unwilling to accept such a radical and sweeping amendment, refused, by the decisive vote of 37 to 133, to concur and asked for a conference.[2] To this customary request the Senate declined to accede. An attempt to secure an abandonment of the Senate additions received 36 votes to 24, but only 31 votes against 27 could be summoned in favor of the original House proposition thus restored. The measure, therefore, failed for lack of a two-thirds vote in the Senate.

The Senate immediately (February 17) resumed the consideration of its own resolution which had been set aside by the House proposition. A very spirited discussion ensued, during which eleven amendments were proposed and rejected.[3] Of these the proposition of Mr. Howard of Michigan, that "citizens of the United States of African descent shall have the same right to vote and to hold office in States and Territories as other citizens," came the nearest to being accepted.[4] Mr. Dixon again proposed that the amendment should be presented to conventions in the States,[5] and Mr. Davis that it should be submitted to the legislatures hereafter to be chosen,[6] and Mr. Hendricks that it should be submitted to the legislatures of the several States the most numerous branches of which should be chosen next after the passage of the resolution.[7] After various unsuccessful attempts to prevent the amendment coming to a vote, the resolution was passed that same day, 35 yeas to 11 nays. It was substantially in the form finally accepted, save that the words "to hold office" were added after "the right to vote."[8] February 20 it came up for consider-

---

[1] App., Nos. 1281, 1308. See ante, par. 53.

[2] App., No. 1250.

[3] App., Nos. 1291–1301.

[4] App., No. 1296.

[5] App., No. 1299. Ante, par. 179.

[6] App., No. 1297. Ante, par. 180.

[7] App., No. 1298.

[8] It will thus be seen that the Senate had given up its insistance upon an amendment which prohibited discrimination by the States by means of religious, educational, or property qualification.

ation in the House. Five attempts were made to amend,[1] one of which was successful; namely, that offered by Mr. Bingham of Ohio, adding the words which the Senate had originally proposed, "nativity, property, creed," to the other specifications. Thus amended, the House passed the resolution by a vote of 140 to 37.[2]

The Senate in its turn rejected the House amendment, although it was substantially like that it had first adopted, and asked for a committee of conference. The House insisted on its amendment, but agreed to appoint a committee of conference. "The rule, indeed, seemed to be for each branch to desert its own proposition as soon as there was a prospect that the other branch would agree to it."[3]

The controversy was finally adjusted by the committees which reported the fifteenth amendment in the precise form in which it was finally incorporated in the Constitution.[4] Both Houses accepted the resolution thus amended, the House by a vote of 145 yeas to 44 nays, the Senate 39 yeas to 13 nays. Thus the fifteenth amendment was recommended to the States, by Congress, on the 26th of February, 1869—six days before the expiration of the Fortieth Congress and the inauguration of General Grant as President.[5]

On the 30th of March, 1870, the Secretary of State issued a proclamation declaring that the amendment had been ratified by the legislatures of twenty-nine of the States, which constituted the necessary three-fourths, and thus it was incorporated in the Constitution.

132. MISCELLANEOUS PROPOSITIONS ON THE SUFFRAGE SINCE THE FIFTEENTH AMENDMENT.

A few amendments have been presented since the passage of the fifteenth amendment, proposing additional regulations in regard to the suffrage.

The first of these was presented by Senator Pomeroy of Kansas twice during the year 1870. It declared that "the basis of suffrage in the United States shall be that of citizenship," "but each State shall determine by law the age of the citizen and the time of residence required for the exercise of the right of suffrage, which shall apply equally to all citizens; and

---

[1] App., Nos. 1302–1306.
[2] App., No. 1305.
[3] Blaine's Twenty Years of Congress, Vol. II, p. 417.
[4] Conference committee struck out the words "to hold office." Reason for the peculiar language used, see Foster, Com. on the Const. I, p. 328.
[5] App., No. 1284.

shall also make all laws concerning the time, place, and manner of holding elections for all State and municipal officers."[1] In 1875 President Grant in his annual message recommended that education should be made compulsory "so far as to deprive all persons who can not read and write from becoming voters after the year 1890, disfranchising none, however, on grounds of illiteracy who may be voters at the time this amendment takes effect."[2] In his last annual message President Grant renewed his recommendation of the previous year.[3] It has already been noticed that in 1866, when the early attempts were being made to give the suffrage to the negro, Mr. Howard had proposed an amendment to enfranchise all negroes who could read either English, French, or Spanish.[4] In the following year an amendment was introduced providing that after July 4, 1876, ability to read and write the English language should be a necessary qualification for the franchise.[5] When the fifteenth amendment was under consideration, several attempts were made to include in its provisions a clause regulating or forbidding the requirement by any State of an educational or property qualification for the suffrage.[6]

One amendment has been proposed since to require an educational test for the franchise for all citizens of the United States born after the adoption of the amendment.[7]

Congressman Bunker of Missouri proposed, in 1877, an amendment to restrict the application of the fifteenth amendment "to persons who were citizens of the United States on the 30th of March, 1870, when the amendment was adopted, and their issue."[8] Three other resolutions proposed that the Constitution should be amended so that the right to vote should not be abridged on account of nativity. The first of these was presented by Senator Butler of South Carolina, in 1883;[9] the other two were championed by Mr. Collins of Massachusetts, in subsequent years.[10]

---

[1] App., Nos. 1325, 1330.
[2] App., No. 1397.
[3] App., No. 1430.
[4] App., No. 1094.
[5] App., No. 1217.
[6] App., Nos. 1059, 1194f, 1203, 1258.
[7] App., No. 1514. It required each State to support a system of free public schools. See post, par. 172.
[8] App., No. 1445.
[9] App., No. 1578.
[10] App., Nos. 1603, 1650. In the Fifty-third Congress, third session, two amendments were proposed to prohibit the States from granting the right of the franchise to aliens. H. Res., 278, 280; Record, pp. 2425, 2477. At present in seventeen States an alien who has declared his intention to become a citizen of the United States can vote.

133. SUFFRAGE OF THE CHINESE.

When the suffrage amendment passed by the House was under discussion by the Senate, February 3, 1869, Mr. Corbett of Oregon submitted the following addition: "But Chinamen not born in the United States and Indians not taxed should not be deemed or made citizens."[1] The amendment was, however, rejected by the Senate on the 9th of the month.

Within a month after the submission to the States of the suffrage amendments, Mr. Johnson, of California, moved in the House that the rules be suspended to enable him to submit the following resolution:[2] "Resolved, That in passing the resolution for the fifteenth amendment to the Constitution of the United States the House never intended that Chinese or Mongolians should become voters." The House, however, refused to suspend the rules by a vote of 42 yeas to 106 nays.

134. WOMAN'S SUFFRAGE.

The first attempts to amend the Constitution so that the right of suffrage should be extended to women were made when the reconstruction amendments were before Congress. Upon the 23d of January, 1866, Mr. Brooks of New York, after presenting a petition from several thousand woman suffragists, gave notice of his intention to introduce an amendment to the resolution then pending,[3] by inserting the word "sex" after the word "color," so that this portion of the amendment should read: "That whenever the elective franchise shall be denied or abridged in any State on account of race or color or sex, all persons therein of such race or color or sex shall be excluded from the basis of representation."[4] In each of the following years, until the early seventies, one or more amendments were proposed, the terms of which involved the extension of the franchise to women.[5] Two of these deserve further notice. Mr. Brooks again, in 1869, championed the cause of woman's suffrage, by offering as a substitute for the suffrage amendment a very singular proposition in these words: "The right of any person of the United States to vote shall not be denied or abridged by the United States or any State by reason of his or her race, sex, nativity, or age

---

[1] App., No. 1265.
[2] App., No. 1322. The constitution of California of 1879 expressly withholds the right of suffrage from natives of China. Art. XIX of the Constitution makes other discriminations against them.
[3] Amendment in regard to the apportionment of Representatives.
[4] App., No. 1085.
[5] App., Nos. 1197, 1239, 1245, 1251, 1269, 1289, 1319, 1327, 1348.

when over twelve years, color or previous condition of slavery of any citizen or class of citizens of the United States."[1] This resolution was not brought to a vote.

During the consideration of the suffrage amendments in the Senate, Senator Pomeroy of Kansas made an ineffectual attempt to substitute for the House amendment and the Senate amendment,[2] respectively, an article of such liberal terms that the enfranchisement of women must follow its adoption. It was as follows: "The right of citizens of the United States to vote and hold office shall not be denied or abridged by the United States or any State for any reason not equally applicable to all citizens."[3] The animus of the proposition is seen in a remark made by Mr. Pomeroy: "I have studied this form of government to no purpose if its logic does not lead me to universal and impartial suffrage."

The first of another series of amendments on the same subject made its appearance in 1878; twelve resolutions to extend the right of suffrage to women have since been introduced into Congress, six in the Senate and six in the House.[4] The first of these was presented by Senator Sargent of California, in 1878. Senators Lapham of New York and Blair of New Hampshire, and Congressman Reed of Maine, have each presented a woman's suffrage amendment twice. Usually these resolutions have been reported back by the committee to which they have been referred with extended reports both from the majority and minorty. Since 1882 these resolutions in the Senate have been referred to the Select Committee on Woman's Suffrage.[5] The amendment submitted by Senator Blair in the first session of the Forty-ninth Congress, was finally brought to a vote in the second session and rejected, 16 yeas to 34 nays.[6] The last amendment on this subject was presented in 1888 by Mr. Mason of Illinois, "by request." It contains the singular provision of extending the right of suffrage to "widows and spinsters," presumably on the ground that there is no voter to represent their interests.[7]

---

[1] App., No. 1251.

[2] To amend the House amendment February 3, 1869; to amend the Senate amendment January 29, 1869.

[3] App., Nos. 1269, 1289.

[4] App., Nos. 1458, 1504, 1506, 1560, 1561, 1580, 1590, 1636, 1671, 1689, 1700, 1723.

[5] Reported favorably in 1884. Senate Report No. 399, Forty-eighth Congress, first session.

[6] App., No. 1636.

[7] App., No. 1723. In Wyoming and the recently admitted State of Utah. women have full suffrage. In Colorado, in 1893, the people voted in favor of general woman suffrage. Women

135. PRESENT CONDITION OF THE SUFFRAGE.

The principle of leaving to the States the determination of the qualifications for the franchise has in general approved itself. The only deviation from this principle is in the case of the fifteenth amendment, which was the outcome of great politi cal causes.

The fifteenth amendment was framed not because of any feeling of dissatisfaction with the working of the old system, but to meet the exigencies of the time—the enfranchisement of the negro. At present there is no disposition to extend, or even to enforce the extension of the fifteenth amendment by additional amendments.[1] Since the adoption of the last amend ment the number of proposals has been small. The only con siderable movement to secure an additional amendment comes from the woman suffragists. There is no popular demand for a further extension of the franchise.

Although there is some uneasiness on account of the increase in the naturalization of foreigners, no amendment to restrict the rights of naturalized citizens has been proposed sine 1858. Possibly the propositions of recent years forbidding the denial or abridgment of the right to vote on account of nativity, were called out by the fear that at some future time the States might pass laws discriminating against citizens of foreign birth.

136. PRESENT STATUS OF PERSONAL RIGHTS.

The freedom of the individual is now completely assured, and the thirteenth, fourteenth, and fifteenth amendments stand as an unalterable statement of the fact. There has been no effort to secure a new amendment on this subject. Slavery and the questions arising out of its abolition have given rise to more than five hundred of the amendments proposed, but happily the subject has now passed out of politics.

The possession of the legal rights of suing and being sued, and kindred rights, leads to but little trouble, and has called out few amendments. Citizenship is still a troublesome ques tion. The complications of national and State citizenship have

---

formerly voted in the Territory of Washington, but do not possess general suffrage under the State constitution. In a limited way, mainly as to taxation or the selection of school officers, woman suffrage exists in twenty-four other States and two Territories. For woman's suffrage in New Jersey under the Constitution of 1776, see Foster, Com. on the Const., I, p. 320, note 4.

[1] There has been, however, a movement to enforce by law the provision of the amendment. The latest phase of this movement was the Federal election bill in the Fifty-first Congress.

not been sufficiently cleared up by the fourteenth amendment,
nor are the rights of citizens protected by national legislation,
except from the aggression of the States. Although the
decisions of the Supreme Court in regard to the scope of the
amendments have been a great disappointment to the framers
of the reconstruction amendments, it is probably better that
the States should be the repositories of these rights; at any
rate, it is certain that the temper of the country is such, that
at present, the States would not accept any further Constitutional amendment on this subject.

A great advance was made in the settlement of the question
of personal rights by the thirteenth, fourteenth, and fifteenth
amendments, and the subject is not likely to be reopened by
amendment either for their extension or restriction.

137. FINANCIAL POWERS—EARLY OBJECTIONS.

No influence so strongly contributed to the establishment of
the Constitution as the financial helplessness of the Confederation. In endowing the new Government with adequate
powers of taxation, the new instrument excited the jealousy
of the States and led to the suggestion of a large number of
amendments in the State ratifying conventions.

(1) The first series of demands looked to the publication
of an annual report of the national finances. The conventions
of Virginia, North Carolina, and Rhode Island desired that an
amendment should be added to the Constitution making more
definite the clause in that instrument. requiring the accounts
of the public money to be published from time to time, by providing that such accounts should be published at least once
a year.[1] The same proposition was advanced in the Senate
during the first session of Congress, but that body failed to
see that there was any more need of a constitutional provision
in this case than there was in regard to the annual publication
of the journals of Congress.[2] The fact that such documents
have been published throughout the one hundred years at
regular intervals proves that they were right in both cases.

(2) The very word "excise" was disagreeable to our fore-
fathers, bringing before them recollections of the most unpopular English tax; therefore it is not surprising to find that
the New York convention included in its series of proposed
amendments one declaring that Congress shall not impose any

---

[1] App., Nos. 31, 83, 114.   [2] App., No. 276. Ante, par. 18.

excise on any article the growth, production, or manufacture of the United States, ardent spirits excepted.[1] The early Congresses, so far from heeding the suggestion, under Hamilton's direction, laid an excise; in 1794 the tax brought about the well-known whisky insurrection.

(3) The New York and Rhode Island conventions desired the Constitution to be so amended that no money should be borrowed without the consent of two-thirds of the members present in each House of Congress.[2] The restriction had nothing to recommend it, and the proposition does not again appear.

(4) The same conventions likewise proposed an amendment prohibiting Congress from ever laying a capitation or poll tax.[3] No such tax has ever been laid and an amendment would therefore have been superfluous.

(5) The two States of North Carolina and Rhode Island, that delayed their ratification of the Constitution and entrance into the Union—conscious of their own sins in the emission of paper money[4]—proposed through their respective conventions an amendment expressly stipulating "that Congress shall not, directly or indirectly, either by themselves or through the judiciary, interfere with any one of the States in the redemption of paper money already emitted and now in circulation, or in liquidating or discharging the public securities of any one of the States, but each State shall have the exclusive right of making such laws and regulations for the above purpose as they think proper."[5] A short time after this, it will be remembered, the central Government assumed the States' debts in accordance with Hamilton's scheme. The general principle of this proposition has been approved as warranted by the Constitution in the decision of the Supreme Court in the Virginia coupon cases.[6]

(6) Among the radical changes proposed by Mr. Tucker of South Carolina, in the First Congress, was one by which the States, instead of being prevented from laying duties on imports or exports, except where absolutely necessary for executing its

---

[1] App., No. 47.
[2] App., Nos. 53, 116.
[3] App., Nos. 60, 111.
[4] See ante, p. 156, note 2. McMaster, I, pp. 285-286; 331-341.
[5] App., Nos. 102, 106.
[6] Virginia Coupon Cases, 114 U. S., 269.

inspection laws, should be allowed to lay such duties on imports and exports, or any duty of tonnage as should be uniform in their operation on the citizens of all the several States in the Union.[1] The members of the House, mindful of the defects of the Articles of the Confederation, were in no mood to consider such a proposition. The only later attempt to assert it was in the nullification movement of South Carolina, in 1833.

(7) It is interesting to note, in view of the subsequent discussion over "the general welfare clause" of the Constitution, that an attempt was made, March 2, 1793, to amend this clause so that the entire provision would read: "That Congress shall have power to lay and collect taxes, duties, imports, and excises, to pay their debts and provide for the common defense and general welfare of the United States in the cases hereinafter particularly enumerated."[2] If this change had been made it would have prevented the champions of broad construction from appealing to the general welfare clause to justify the constitutionality of their proposed action.[3]

138. TAXATION—REQUISITIONS.

Except in the group of amendments just discussed,[4] and an indefinite proposition in 1871,[5] the question of taxation has given rise to few amendments. One clause, however, was so connected with sectional interests that it has several times been discussed. It is the provision that no capitation or other direct tax shall be laid unless in proportion to the census.[6] The feeling was general throughout the States that the Federal Government should not lay direct taxes if it could be avoided. The prejudice is seen in the fact that all seven of the State conventions, that proposed any amendments to the Constitution, included in their series a proposition on this subject. The convention of five States[7] proposed almost identically the same amendment, providing that when the income arising from the impost and excise are insufficient, the Congress instead of laying direct taxes shall first make requisitions upon the States to pay their proportion as determined by the census, which

---

[1] App., No. 204. Cf. Constitution. Art. 1, sec. 10, cl. 2.
[2] App., No. 316. Cf. Constitution. Art. 1, sec. 8, cl. 1.
[3] Mason's Veto Powers, par. 95.
[4] Ante, par. 137.
[5] Introduced by Mr. McNeely of Illinois, in the House, December 11, 1871. App. No. 1338.
[6] Constitution, Art. 1, sec. 9, cl. 4.
[7] Massachusetts, New Hampshire, South Carolina, New York, and Rhode Island. App., Nos. 4, 12, 17, 48, 111.

shall assess and collect the same as the legislature shall direct. In case the State neglect and refuse to pay its proportion, Congress may then lay such State's proportion together with interest. Similar propositions were introduced in both the House and Senate during the first session of Congress, but were rejected by emphatic votes.[1] This failure to receive the recommendation of Congress is somewhat remarkable in view of the unanimity of the State conventions in proposing it.

The Virginia and North Carolina conventions proposed an amendment which would have had the same effect as that proposed by the other conventions.[2] By the terms of this amendment it was provided that when Congress should lay a direct tax or excise they should inform the executive of each State of the quota of such State, and if the State should raise its quota at the required time the tax or excise laid by Congress should not be collected in such State. It is evident that all these proposals were designed to preserve the dignity of the State, and to restrict as far as possible the entrance of Federal officers and machinery within the jurisdiction of the State.

Another form of restriction was proposed by the Rhode Island convention amendment. Congress was not to lay a direct tax without the consent of the legislatures of three-fourths of the States.[3]

139. DIRECT TAXES.

Although some question has been raised as to the nature of direct taxes, and the Supreme Court has been called upon to define them,[4] the only amendment on this point was introduced in 1793. It provided that every tax should be deemed direct, other than taxes on imports, excises, transfers of property, and law proceedings.[5] This appears to have been an attempt to secure a clear definition of the direct tax.

140. APPORTIONMENT OF DIRECT TAXES.

The question of the manner of apportioning direct taxes has been important chiefly because of its connection with the apportionment of Representatives. Nevertheless, out of the

---

[1] App., Nos. 200, 236, 259.
[2] App., Nos. 28, 80.
[3] App., No. 112.
[4] Cooley, Const'al Law, p. 61 and notes; Foster, Com. on Const., 1, pp. 415–423.
[5] App., No. 316. This may have been presented in anticipation of the act of Congress of 1794 levying a tax upon carriages, which was held by the Supreme Court not to be a direct tax within the meaning of the Constitution. Hylton v. U. S., 3 Dallas, 171. Foster, pp. 418, 419.

large number of proposed amendments on the apportionment
Representatives, but a comparatively small number applied to
taxes.

Eighteen amendments have been introduced touching this
provision. The first was presented in 1804 by Senator Pickering of Massachusetts, and provided that Representatives and
direct taxes should be apportioned among the several States
according to the number of their free inhabitants.[1] Similar
amendments were proposed by the Hartford convention and
presented to Congress in 1815 by members from Connecticut
and Massachusetts upon the instruction of their legislatures.[2]
The only other propositions to amend this clause previous to
1860 came from the legislature of Massachusetts, in 1843-1844,
and were presented by John Quincy Adams.[3] They called forth
a prolonged and heated discussion over their acceptance.[4] In
1865 Mr. Sloan introduced a resolution to amend the Constitution so that direct taxes should be apportioned among the
several States according to the appraised value of taxable
property therein.[5] A similar proposition was offered by Senators Doolittle, Stewart and Mr. Lawrence[6] to supply the defi-
ciency in the resolution passed by the House on the apportionment of Representatives.[7] The same change was proposed by
Senator Lane about a month later.[8] Within a few months
Senators Sherman and Doolittle tried without avail to incorporate into the resolution destined to become the fourteenth
amendment a similar provision, but it was silent in regard
to the apportionment of direct taxes.[9] The proposition of the
Hartford convention was substantially revived in the amendments suggested by Messrs. Broomall, Blaine, Fessenden, and
others in the winter of 1865-66. These provided that direct
taxes should be apportioned according to the number of the
inhabitants of each State.[10] Mr. Conkling proposed that the

[1] App., No. 364. Ante, pp. 45, 46.
[2] App., Nos. 425, 433, 441. See ante, p. 46. Direct taxes had been levied during the war
of 1812. Stat. at Large III, 22, 164.
[3] App., No. 734.
[4] See ante, pp. 46-49.
[5] App., No. 1041.
[6] App., Nos. 1082b, 1092, 1100.
[7] H. R. No. 51. See ante, par. 22.
[8] App., No. 1119.
[9] App., Nos. 1157, 1174, 1176.
[10] App., Nos. 1053, 1069, 1077, 1087. Mr. Blaine's proposition being in connection with the
apportionment of Representatives, provided that those whose political rights were denied
or abridged should not be enumerated. Messrs. Fessenden's and Eliot's propositions
would exclude Indians not taxed.

apportionment should be according to their respective number
of citizens of the United States.[1] But none of the propositions
were favorably considered.

In recent years, a few further resolutions to alter the Constitution on this subject have been presented. Between 1876 and
1883 Mr. Reagan of Texas has six times introduced an amendment renewing the proposal that direct taxes shall be apportioned between the several States and Territories and the
District of Columbia in proportion to the value of the property
in each. It further provided that each State, Territory, and the
District of Columbia should have the right to collect its portion
of the same, if it elect to do so, by its own officers, and from
subjects of taxation provided by its own laws; upon neglect to
do so the taxes should be collected as might be provided by the
laws of the United States.[2] This amendment is substantially
a return to the system proposed at the time of the ratification
of the Constitution.

In the early seventies two other resolutions proposing to
prohibit or greatly restrict the powers of Congress to impose
duties on imports and excises, provided that the necessary revenue should be raised by a direct tax, apportioned among the
several States and Territories in proportion to the value of the
property in each.[3]

The whole question has become entirely academic since the
General Government appears to have abandoned direct taxes.
The last tax laid in this manner has been refunded to the States
which paid it.[4]

141. TAXATION OF CORPORATIONS BY STATES.

When, in the Yazoo cases and the Dartmouth College case of
1819, the Supreme Court held that a charter granted by a State
was a contract,[5] no one expected the great growth of the wealth
and power of corporations. In 1884, 1886, and 1888 Mr. Mc-
Comas of Maryland and one of his colleagues introduced an
amendment to the Constitution enabling the State to tax corporations, although exempted from taxation by their charters;

[1] App., No. 1073.

[2] App., Nos. 1407, 1442, 1486, 1533, 1601, 1661. Mr. Landers of Indiana introduced an
amendment making "wealth" the basis of apportionment. App., No. 1419.

[3] App., Nos. 1338, 1363. No. 1338 proposed to exempt from taxation the property of agricultural societies, school, religious, cemetery, and charitable purposes, as well as property
of the United States, State and municipal corporations. See post. pars. 145, 148.

[4] By act of the Fifty-first Congress. Congress has imposed direct taxes five times. 1798,
1813, 1815, 1816, 1861. See Foster, Com. on Const., I, sec. 69, pp. 413-423.

[5] 6 Cranch, 87, 4 Wheaton, 518.

and at the same time that clause of the Constitution which prohibits a State from passing any law impairing the obligation of contracts was to be declared inoperative in the cases under this new amendment.[1] No action was taken; the amendments are an indication of the dissatisfaction with the doctrines laid down in the cases of Fletcher v. Peck and Dartmouth College v. Woodward.[2] The decisions of the Supreme Court in recent years indicate a similar tendency.

142. EXPORT DUTIES.

Only one other provision as to taxation has been the object of amendment. The prohibition on export duty was undoubtedly intended to prevent undue taxation and the burdening of the agricultural States. At two different periods amendments— nine in all—have been offered to this clause so as to permit Congress to lay taxes on exports.

The first group were submitted during the war of 1812. Mr. Mitchell of New York presented the first amendments proposing this change in March, 1812.[3] In each of the three sessions of the Thirteenth Congress (1813–14) Mr. Jackson of Virginia introduced a similar proposition.[4] In January, 1814, the Committee of the Whole reported to the House their agreement to the second of these resolutions, but the resolution itself failed to come to a vote. The return of peace brought to an end the movement in favor of this change.

Not until the fourth year of the civil war was this amendment again suggested. In March, 1864, a motion was made by Mr. Blaine directing the Committee on the Judiciary to inquire into the expediency of proposing such an amendment.[5] Within the next two years a similar amendment was proposed at four different times by as many authors.[6] Mr. Stevens of Pennsylvania had been one of those who in 1865 had advocated as an amendment a tax on exports; in the following year he introduced in the House a resolution to so amend the Constitution

---

[1] App., Nos. 1622, 1623, 1649, 1701.

[2] The preamble of these resolutions recited the fact that under "the principle of the construction approved by the Supreme Court no hindrance can be seen to rich corporations making contracts with legislatures as they best may for perpetual exemption from all the burdens of supporting the Government."

[3] App. No. 404.

[4] App., Nos. 410, 415, 420. This was proposed to enable us to raise money on foreign consumption and to place us in a position where we could retaliate upon the powers of western Europe for the restrictions placed upon our commerce. Niles' Register, ii, p. 42.

[5] App., No. 1033.

[6] App., Nos. 1037, 1043, 1051, 1054.

as to permit Congress to lay an export duty on cotton.[1] This proposition was brought to a vote and rejected, 59 voting in favor to 61 against.[2] A similar resolution was proposed in 1884.[3] Both groups of amendments had a temporary cause and were dropped when the cause had passed away. The Government in both cases was engaged in war and embarrassed in its finances. The prohibition is so plainly advantageous to a large number of the States that a three-fourths vote to take it away can not be expected.

143. PAYMENT OF THE CONFEDERATE DEBT.

It was hardly to be supposed that any part of the debt incurred in carrying on the war against the United States would ever be assumed by the General Government. There was, however, some danger that the Southern States might assume it. In order to prevent any doubt on the subject, sixteen amendments were proposed. The first were offered by Messrs. Stevens, Bingham, and Farnsworth, December 5 and 6, 1865, in the House.[4] The latter was reported favorably by the Committee on the Judiciary, and on December 19 passed the House by the pronounced vote of 150 yeas to 11 nays. In the Senate four amendments on this subject were introduced previous to the presentation of the resolution which became the fourteenth amendment. Two of these were advocated by Charles Sumner and Henry Wilson.[5] When the Farnsworth amendment was received from the House it was referred to a committee, but meanwhile the fourteenth amendment having been passed by that body,[6] the consideration of this measure on the debt was indefinitely postponed.

When the fourteenth amendment as passed by the House came before the Senate, it was found to contain a stipulation that neither the United States nor any State should assume or pay any debt already incurred or which may hereafter be incurred in aid of insurrection or of war against the United States. Six amendments to this clause were proposed in the Senate,[7] but that presented by Senator Clark of New Hamp-

---

[1] App., No. 1189.
[2] App., No. 1191.
[3] App., No. 1620. Mr. Robinson of New York, for the encouragement of the home manufacture of our domestic products.
[4] App., Nos. 1052, 1055, 1057.
[5] App., Nos. 1066, 1105, 1121, 1130.
[6] App., No. 1139.
[7] App., Nos. 1145, 1150, 1162, 1175c, 1181, 1186.

shire was adopted and incorporated as section 4 of the amendment.[1] Mr. Davis of Kentucky moved to add the following
clause to the fourth section: "But the obligation of the United
States to pay for private property taken for public use in all
cases shall remain inviolate."[2] In 1867, before the success of
the fourteenth amendment was assured, Senator Dixon of
Connecticut and Congressman Ashley of Ohio alike introduced an amendment on this subject in connection with the
series of propositions offered by them.[3]

The provisions on this subject, as well as those on the payment of the national debt, were suggested by the apprehension
of some that should the South, by some political overturn,
again obtain control of the National Government, it might
either impair the credit of the Government by refusing to pay
its debts and pensions, or even cripple its finances by assuming the Confederate debt.

144. CLAIMS FOR DAMAGES ARISING OUT OF THE CIVIL WAR.

Although any attempt to make up the public losses occasioned by participation in the Confederacy was thus precluded,
there was serious danger that the Government might be called
upon to pay for private property destroyed or taken during
military operations. The special machinery provided by the
acts of 1855, 1863, and 1872 for the establishment of a court of
claims seemed inadequate. Hence the introduction, between
the years 1876–1881, of sixteen amendments relative to the
payment of claims.[4] The first of these presented by Mr.
Baker of Indiana, December 8, 1876, may be taken as typical.
It prohibited the payment of any claims for loss or damage
growing out of the taking, use, or destruction of property
during the late war if the owner ever gave any aid, counte-
nance, or encouragement to the rebellion.[5] Some were very
comprehensive and forbade the payment of all claims for property taken, used, injured, or destroyed by the United States
during the rebellion.[6] Another, submitted by Mr. Keifer of
Ohio, made provision for the establishment of a court of claims
with competent jurisdiction to render judgment on cases

[1] App., No. 1181.
[2] App., No. 1186.
[3] App., Nos. 1201, 1213e, 1221.
[4] App., Nos. 1432, 1435, 1452, 1455, 1468, 1469, 1471, 1477, 1477a, 1481, 1484, 1485, 1487, 1491, 1525.
[5] App., No. 1432.
[6] App., Nos. 1477a, 1525.

involving claims against the Government.[1]   June 19, 1878,
upon a motion of Mr. Conger of Michigan, the House suspended the rules and passed by the vote of 145 to 61 a resolution so to amend the Constitution that the payment of claims
to disloyal persons for property taken, used, injured, or
destroyed during the war of the rebellion should be prohibited.[2]   This amendment the Committee on the Judiciary of
the Senate reported in an amended form, but although the
Senate devoted some time to its consideration, it failed to be
brought to a vote.

The large number of claims lodged against the Government,
besides calling forth the amendments referred to in the previous paragraph, suggested also the desirableness of fixing
some limitation in the time for the presentation of claims
against the United States.   Several propositions of this character have been presented in the form of amendments to the
Constitution.[3]   The first of these was introduced as early as
1874, by Senator Wright of Iowa, even before any amendment
in regard to the payment of Southern war claims had been
suggested.   This resolution stipulated that all claims must be
presented within ten years at least next after they accrue.
Later amendments reduced the time to six years.   The last
of these resolutions was presented in 1886.   In this connection it may be suitable to mention two other resolutions; one
proposed by Mr. Springer of Illinois, in 1881, which provided
that all claims against the United States shall be determined
by such tribunals as Congress may establish;[4] the other, presented by Mr. Seymour of Connecticut, in 1886, proposed to
empower Congress to make provision by a general law for
bringing suits against the Government,[5] and forbade all
special acts.

145 PAYMENT OF THE NATIONAL DEBT.

Several of the amendments just treated, prohibiting the payment of the Confederate debt, contained also a clause guaranteeing the payment of the national debt.   The first of these were
suggested by Charles Sumner (January 5, 1866) and Senator
Lane of Kansas (March 13).[6]   The original resolution, which
was the basis of the fourteenth amendment, as reported by the

[1] App., No. 1471.
[2] App., No. 1477.
[3] App., 1383, 1392, 1461, 1468, 1497, 1608, 1654.

[4] App., No. 1529.
[5] App., No. 1675.
[6] App., Nos. 1066, 1120.

House had, however, no clause guaranteeing the national debt. Propositions to insert such a clause were made by Messrs. Wade of Ohio, Howard of Michigan, and Clark of New Hampshire. The last gentleman's amendment was accepted and now appears as a part of section 4 of the amendment.[1]

In 1873 Mr. Myers of Pennsylvania presented an amendment providing for the payment of the principal and interest of the public debt by the imposition of duties on imports, but that the annual current expenses of the Government of the United States should be assessed upon the several States and Territories.[2] All questions as to the good faith of the nation have long since been set at rest.

146. DISTRIBUTION OF THE SURPLUS

An earlier set of amendments had been called out by the fact that there was likely to be no debt to pay. The legislature of Georgia, in 1833, suggested in their call for a constitutional convention the advisability of so amending the Constitution that it may prescribe what disposition shall be made of the surplus revenue, when such revenue is found to be on hand.[3] Two years later, when an actual surplus began to accumulate, Mr. Calhoun made a more definite proposition. Twice during the year 1835 he introduced an amendment for the distribution of the surplus revenue among the States until 1843.[4] This date was fixed upon as the limit; for by the compromise tariff of 1833 the duties would be reduced to the minimum rate of 20 per cent in that year, and this would cause a corresponding reduction of the revenue. Without waiting for the formality of a constitutional amendment, the acts of 1836 caused the deposit of $27,000,000 with the States, and the bad results of that action have prevented the presentation of any similar propositions.[5]

147. EXPENDITURES—APPROPRIATION BILLS.

Except in the case of the surplus, no amendments have been suggested to change the objects of expenditure. The increas-

---

[1] App., Nos. 1138, 1149, 1161. 1175b, 1180. The two amendments made by Senator Dixon and Mr. Ashley, as referred to in the previous paragraph, also contained the provision guaranteeing the United States debt. App., Nos. 1200, 1213c, 1221.

[2] App., No. 1363. It stipulated that the debt should be consolidated at a uniform rate of interest, or should be extinguished by the payment of $50,000,000 of the principal annually. See ante, par. 140.

[3] App., No. 621.

[4] App., Nos. 643, 647.

[5] Bourne's Surplus Revenue. See ante, par. 95.

ing extravagance of the appropriation bills, and the manner in which they are urged through in conference, suggested a reform. In 1876 Mr. Cook proposed an amendment to limit the power of Congress to make appropriations " over and above the estimates sent to Congress by the executive department."[1] In the early eighties Mr. Turner of Kentucky presented to the consideration of three successive Congresses an amendment requiring that the yeas and nays should be recorded on all appropriations exceeding $10,000.[2] The provision requiring the vote of each member to be recorded would tend to cause each member to become better informed and weigh the subject well before giving his vote.[3] Although the principle of the amendment is a good one, in practice it would probably be made a means of fillibustering.

Other amendments have been introduced either suggesting reforms in the method of administering the finances or in the manner of making appropriations.[4] To prevent the growing practice of inserting clauses appropriating money in bills of an entirely foreign nature, and of attaching "riders" upon general appropriation bills and other measures, it has twice been proposed, in recent years, to so amend the Constitution as to require that every act shall embrace but one subject-matter, and the matter properly connected therewith, which subject shall be embraced in the title.[5]

148. PROTECTIVE TARIFFS.

No one subject except slavery has caused so much debate in Congress as the tariff; yet although there have been frequent discussions over the constitutionality of a protective tariff, especially in the earlier years, only three attempts have been made to settle the controversy by means of a constitutional amendment.

The legislature of Georgia, in 1833, in its application to Congress to call a convention, declared that the experience of the past had clearly proved that the Constitution needed amend-

---

[1] App., No. 1422a. "This restriction shall not prevent Congress from diminishing the said estimates if they think proper."

[2] App., Nos. 1512, 1540, 1591.

[3] A similar provision is found in many of the constitutions of the States, and their experience seems to have demonstrated the wisdom of the provision.

[4] App., Nos. 1062, 1481a, 1567. The latter provided that all bills appropriating money should specify the exact amount of each appropriation, and the purpose for which it was made.

[5] App., Nos. 1375a, 1501. Suggested by the contest between President Hayes and Congress. Mason, Veto Power, p. 48; ante, p. 133.

ment; they asked that the principle involved in a tariff for the
direct protection of domestic industry might be settled, and
also "that a system of Federal taxation may be established
which shall be equal in its operation upon the whole people
and in all sections of the country."[1] The question of protection had recently forced itself upon the attention of the country
through the success of the protectionists in passing the tariff
of 1828. The States of Georgia, Alabama, South Carolina,
North Carolina, Mississippi, and Virginia protested against it
as unjust and unconstitutional; these protests proving to be of
no effect, South Carolina had attempted to put in force the
doctrine of nullification.[2]

It was over thirty years before the next proposition on this
subject was introduced. In 1864 Senator Saulsbury included
in the series of amendments proposed by him, as a substitute
for the thirteenth amendment, one which provided that duties
on imports might be imposed for revenue, but should not be
prohibitory or excessive in amount.[3] The last of these amendments, presented in 1871, proposed the abolition of duties on
imports and excises and the substitution of a direct tax
instead.[4]

149. PROHIBITION OF SPECIAL LEGISLATION.

The great increase in recent years in the amount of special
and private legislation has led to several attempts to counteract this evil by means of a constitutional provision. Some
thirteen resolutions of this character have been introduced
since 1876.[5] The first of these was presented in that year by
Mr. Springer of Illinois, prohibiting Congress passing any
special law in a long list of enumerated cases, among which
were included the granting of pensions, land or prize money,
or relief to any person, or authorizing the payment of any
claims against the United States, except to pay the judgments
of courts or commissions. It also forbade the granting to any
corporation any special or exclusive privileges, subsidy, immunity, or franchise,[6] and in all cases where a general law could

---

[1] App., Nos. 615, 616.

[2] For protests see post, par. 156, note; also, Journal of Senate of Pennsylvania (1829–30),
pp. 30, 31; Ibid. (1832–33), pp. 307, 308. Canning is said to have declared that "he would
make the people of America reduce their tariff or dissolve the Union." Bishop, Hist. of
Manufact., II, pp. 333–334.

[3] App., No. 1019.

[4] App., No. 1338. See ante, par. 140.

[5] App., Nos. 1415, 1462, 1472, 1473, 1483, 1488, 1528, 1583, 1606, 1642, 1653, 1673, 1693.

[6] App., No. 1415.

be made applicable no special law should be enacted. A similar resolution has been proposed by Mr. Springer at eight different times since.[1] the aim of which was to limit the legislative power "to enactment of laws general in their application and effect to all sections and persons within the jurisdiction of this Constitution."

Mr. Beach of New York, who was also very active in urging an amendment which should prevent Congress from passing private bills, in addition has presented two propositions to prohibit the giving or loaning of public property or credit in aid of private or corporate enterprises.[2] Two amendments of a similar nature had previously been proposed. One of these, presented in 1869, forbade Congress passing any "law granting subsidies to corporations or companies to aid in the construction of railroads, canals, or other public improvements," as long as the national debt shall exceed the sum of $500,000,000.[3] The other, introduced in 1873, prohibited Congress guaranteeing or paying the indebtedness of any State, Territory, District, or any municipal corporation.[4]

The prohibition proposed by these various amendments is analogous to the restrictions in many of the recent State constitutions,[5] and is prompted by the unwillingness of the people to trust their representatives. It is contrary to the long-accepted practice of the United States, and possibly would tend to reduce the feeling of Congressional responsibility. Perhaps a more effective remedy would be the severe application of the veto to doubtful cases.[6]

150. STATUS OF FINANCIAL LEGISLATION.

Since the early years there has been little disposition shown to restrict, by means of amendments, the power of the General Government over the collection of the revenue, except in regard to the imposition and collection of direct taxes, and in a slight degree the customs. Likewise there has been little effort to

---

[1] App., Nos. 1472, 1488, 1528, 1583, 1642, 1673, 1693.

[2] App., Nos. 1607, 1653.

[3] App., No. 1316. "Except to complete such as are already commenced in which the United States has a large interest." The Union Pacific Railroad doubtless suggested this.

[4] App., No. 1375.

[5] Bryce, I, pp. 491, 552–553; Hitchcock, Am. State Const., pp. 34–44.

[6] President Cleveland applied this remedy during his first term to nearly three hundred cases. See Mason's Veto Power, App. A, Nos. 133 to 433; also pp. 90–93, 128–129, 132–133. See ante, par. 58, for discussion of the proposition to give the President power to veto items in appropriation bills.

place any check upon the power of Congress to make expend-
itures, save in recent years there have been some indications
of a desire to fix limitations to special legislation, and to prevent extravagant appropriations.[1]

The debt of the United States and of the States are on an
entirely different basis; the United States debt being guaranteed by the Constitution, while the State's debts are assumed
by the laws of the State. At the close of the civil war, the
various propositions guaranteeing the national debt, prohibiting the payment of the Confederate debt, and the claims of
disloyal persons, resulted in the incorporation of a section in
the fourteenth amendment embodying the provisions of some
of these various resolutions.

In general, Congress has exercised the extensive power conferred upon it with good results.

151. COMMERCIAL POWER.

It will be remembered that the great cause for the failure of
the Government under the Articles of Confederation was that
the Congress had no power over the subject of commerce, and
the attempt to amend the Articles in order to give them control
over it, even to a limited degree, met with failure.[2] Owing to
the critical condition into which the whole country had been
brought by the system of permitting each State to make its
own navigation laws. the framers of the Constitution deemed
it wise to give to Congress express powers over all commerce
not confined to the limits of a State. In addition, the subjects
of the post-office, coinage, weights and measures, patents and
copyrights were also expressly committed to the General Government. Out of this large assemblage of powers flowed many
implied powers. It is not surprising, therefore, that in the
early years there was serious apprehension that the Federal
Government might abuse these powers, and that many attempts
have been made to limit or define the implied powers, and that
not a few efforts have been made to increase the catalogue of
express powers.

152. CHARTERING CORPORATIONS.

Almost the earliest evidence of jealousy toward the commercial powers of the Government is the action of the ratifying

---

[1] On the other hand, there has been one attempt, following the financial crisis of 1873,
to confer upon Congress full power "to pass necessary laws to protect the financial
affairs of the people of the United States." App., No. 1375o.
[2] The last amendment on commerce was proposed by the Congress April 12, 1783.

conventions of five of the States.[1] Mindful of the evils of the great commercial monopolies of the Old World, such as the British East India Company and the Dutch East India Company, they were desirous that no such monopolies should secure recognition from the United States Government, and to that end they proposed as an amendment to the Constitution an article declaring "that Congress erect no company of merchants with exclusive advantage of commerce." The attempt made in both the House and the Senate to include a similar amendment in the series recommended to the States by the First Congress failed.[2] The last effort to secure such an amendment was made in 1793, in the Senate of the Second Congress, but the resolution was tabled.[3]

153. NATIONAL BANKS.

Not only did Congress decline to tie its hands and take away any implied power of chartering corporations, but it proceeded in 1791 to create the United States Bank and grant it a monopoly of its privileges for twenty years. The act provoked the first and one of the most searching discussions of the powers of Congress, but led to no amendments. During the interim of 1811-1815, when the bank was not in existence, Mr. Jackson of Virginia thrice introduced, in connection with the amendment authorizing the appropriation of money for internal improvements, an amendment conferring power upon Congress to establish a national bank.[4] In January, 1814, the proposition was reported favorably by the Committee of the Whole House, but upon its consideration in the next session of Congress it was struck out of the series of amendments.

Upon the return of peace, a new national bank was established by the party that had formerly been opposed to it. In the financial crisis of 1818-19, the State banks becoming jealous and the people believing that the bank had done much to produce their ills, under the leadership of the Democratic-Republican party, a movement was begun in Maryland, which Pennsylvania, Ohio, and other States promised to follow, to attempt to tax the institution out of the State. The banks

---

[1] Namely: Massachusetts, New Hampshire, New York, North Carolina, and Rhode Island. App., Nos. 5, 18, 51, 99, 123.
[2] App., Nos. 239, 262.
[3] App., No. 315.
[4] App., Nos. 413, 418, 423.

resisted the Maryland law, and this gave rise to the celebrated case of McCulloch v. The State of Maryland.[1] In this opinion the Supreme Court, through Chief Justice Marshall, declared the State tax unconstitutional and asserted the power of Congress to establish such an institution. In the meantime, in deference to the popular clamor, the Fifteenth Congress ordered an investigation of the bank, in which certain abuses, misappropriation of funds, and defalcation in certain of the branches, especially those located in Philadelphia and Baltimore, were discovered. Upon the disclosure of the report, the legislature of Pennsylvania, within which State the central office of the bank was located, early in January, 1820, presented to Congress a resolution to amend the Constitution so as to prevent the establishment by Congress of any bank except within the District of Columbia, the branches of which were to be confined to the District.[2] Within a short time the legislatures of Tennessee, Ohio, Indiana, and Illinois passed resolutions concurring in the resolution proposed by the legislature of Pennsylvania.[3] No action, however, was taken by Congress beyond reforming the bank.

The legislatures of at least eight States passed resolutions of nonconcurrence.[4] The reply of the legislature of South Carolina is of especial interest, in view of the decidedly different position taken by the legislature of that State on a similar question within seven years. This resolution, passed in December of 1821, declared that they were "of the opinion that as Congress is constitutionally vested with the right to incorporate a bank, it would be unwise and impolitic to restrict its operations within such narrow limits as the District of Columbia. They apprehend no danger from the exercise of the power which the people of the United States have confided to Congress; but believe that in the exercise of these

[1] 4 Wheaton, 316.
[2] App., Nos. 492, 495. Passed by the legislature March 29, 1819; vote of House, 81 to 4.
[3] App., Nos. 492a, 494, 496, 506a.
[4] The legislatures of New Hampshire, Vermont, Massachusetts, Connecticut, New York, New Jersey, South Carolina, and Georgia. Journal of the House of Representatives of Pennsylvania (1819-20), pp. 538-539; ibid. (1820-21), pp. 65-67, 462; ibid. (1822-23), pp. 75-76, 420-421, 646-647; ibid. (1823-24), pp. 25-26. Resolves of Massachusetts, Vol. XVI, pp. 118-120. Massachusetts Archives, Nos. 6886, 8859. The resolution of the legislature of Georgia declared that it was "not expedient to deny absolutely" the power of Congress to establish a bank, "although impressed with the belief that the original grant of such power should be accompanied with a restriction requiring the assent of each and every State to the location of the said bank or any branch thereof within the limits of such State." Journal of the House of Representatives of Pennsylvania (1822-23), pp. 646-647.

powers that body will render them subservient to the great purpose of our national compact."[1]

President Jackson, soon after entering upon his Administration, attacked the bank, and in 1832 vetoed a bill to recharter it, on the ground that the bill was "unconstitutional because he disapproved of it."[2] The next proposition to determine the question of its constitutionality by an amendment arose out of this controversy. The legislature of Georgia, in its proposition for a constitutional convention in 1833, indicated as a subject for discussion, "The power of chartering a bank and of granting incorporation," that it may be "expressly given to or withheld from Congress."[3] The bank debates of 1841 and 1862 led to no amendments; few questions of constitutional law seem so well settled as the right to create national banks.

In the early seventies an amendment was twice proposed prohibiting Congress from hereafter chartering private corporations to carry on business within the States.[4] The same resolution suggested that the Constitution should be so amended as to prohibit Congress as well as the States from passing any law impairing the obligation of contracts.[5]

154. ISSUING OF BANK NOTES.

After the expiration of the charter of the second United States Bank, in 1836, the controversy was renewed in a new form. On one of the last days of 1836 a resolution, the text of which unfortunately is not given, was introduced to amend the Constitution by inserting provisions restricting the incorporation of banks by States, and limiting them when incorporated to the issue of bank notes.[6]

The panic of 1837, which was caused by the inflation of the currency due to the issuing of notes by the State banks, led to the presentation of additional amendments prohibiting any State from incorporating banks for the issue of paper notes. The first of these was reported by a select committee

---

[1] Journal of the House of Representatives of Pennsylvania (1822–23), pp. 75–76.
[2] Mason's Veto Power. App. A, No. 14; also pp. 75–76.
[3] App., No. 619. See reply of Massachusetts legislature. Resolves of Massachusetts, Vol. XIX, p. 418.
[4] App., Nos. 1333, 1350.
[5] Bryce, I, p. 315.
[6] App., No. 655.

in March, 1837, but no further action was taken.[1] The next year Mr. Garland of Louisiana presented an amendment prohibiting State incorporated banks from issuing and circulating notes of the same or of a lower denomination than the highest denomination of the coins of the United States.[2] Mr. Buchanan of Pennsylvania, in 1840, at that time a member of the Senate, proposed a resolution that a select committee be appointed to inquire into the expediency of an amendment to prohibit the circulation of bank paper under the authority of the several States.[3] The resolution was considered and the committee was appointed, but there is no further record of their action. These amendments were simply an incident connected with the crisis of 1837.[4] Owing to the favor in which State banks were held, especially in the West and South, it would have been impossible to have secured an amendment, even if Congress had recommended one.

155. LEGAL-TENDER NOTES.

When the bank question arose again, in 1862, the amendments proposed bore rather on an associated subject—the issue of legal-tender notes by the Government during the civil war. As early as 1866, Mr. Thomas had introduced a resolution into the House instructing the Committee on the Judiciary to inquire into the expediency of proposing an amendment to the Constitution restricting the power of Congress to issue a paper circulating medium.[5] The resolution was agreed to, but nothing further was heard of amending the Constitution in this respect until 1870. The previous year, in the first legal-tender case, the Supreme Court had held that the notes were not legal tender for debts contracted previous to the passage of the act.[6] Doubtless in consequence of this decision an amendment was proposed by Mr. Ingersoll of Illinois, February 14, 1870, empowering Congress to issue United States notes and make them legal tender in payment of debts.[7] Soon after this the Supreme Court in the second of the legal-tender cases reversed its decision,[8] and accordingly it is not surprising to

---

[1] App., No. 671.

[2] App., No. 686.

[3] App., No. 701.

[4] They may possibly have been suggested by the decision of the Supreme Court in the case of Briscoe v. Bank of Kentucky, 11 Peters, 257 (1837).

[5] App., No. 1127.

[6] Hepburn v. Griswold, 8 Wallace, 603.

[7] App., No. 1326. See also Nos. 1333, 1350. Ante, par. 153.

[8] Knox v. Lee, 12 Wallace, 457.

find an amendment introduced in 1873 forbidding Congress to make anything but gold and silver legal tender in payment of debts.[1] The year 1874 was marked by the passage of the "inflation bill," which was vetoed by President Grant,[2] and an amendment similar to the one introduced the previous year was shortly afterward presented.[3]

It is of interest to note that incidental to the short career of the Greenback party, which was opposed to the resumption of specie payments, an amendment was presented by Judge Ewing of Ohio, and Mr. Oliver of Iowa, in 1878, providing for the issue of legal-tender notes and regulating the amounts thereof.[4]

March 3, 1884, the Supreme Court in the third legal-tender case, that of Julliard v. Greenman, decided that Congress may make Government notes legal tender in time of peace as well as war.[5] Just one week later four resolutions proposing amendments to the Constitution, relative to the issue of legal-tender notes, were presented. That these were directly suggested by the recent decision of the Supreme Court is shown by the text of the amendment proposed by Mr. Potter of New York.[6] This provided that Congress should not have power to make anything but "gold or silver coin a tender in payment of debts, except after a declaration of war, when the public safety may require it."

Amendments similar to this, save as to the last clause, were presented by Mr. Hewitt of New York[7] and Senator Bayard of Delaware.[8] The remaining amendment proposed by Senator Garland, while not going so far as these, proposed to limit the public debt of the United States by stipulating that the issue of legal-tender notes should never exceed the sum of $350,000,000, unless the bills providing for such increase should receive the concurrence of two-thirds of each House of Congress, the vote being recorded by yeas and nays in the journals.[9]

---

[1] App., No. 1378. Although another amendment was proposed at the same time to empower Congress to pass necessary laws to protect the financial "affairs of the people of the United States." No. 1375 (e).

[2] Mason's Veto Power, App. A, No. 92; also pp. 80–81.

[3] App., No. 1387.

[4] App., Nos. 1463, 1466. They also prohibited the United States or any State from authorizing the issue of any other kind of notes, by any person, association, or corporation.

[5] 110 U. S., 421.

[6] App., No. 1626.

[7] App., No. 1627.

[8] App., No. 1628.

[9] App., No. 1628.

156. INTERNAL IMPROVEMENTS.

A much more hotly contested use of implied powers, especially those growing out of the commerce clause, has been the expenditure of public money for internal improvements. Such a practice seems not to have been contemplated by the Federalists up to 1801. The act authorizing the building of the Cumberland road, passed March 29, 1806, was the first measure making provision for internal improvements out of the general funds.[1] In December of this year, President Jefferson in his annual message, in calling the attention of Congress to an anticipated surplus, recommended its "application" to the great purposes of the public education, roads, rivers, canals, and such other objects of public improvement as it may be thought proper. Public men seemed to agree as to the desirableness of internal improvements, and Gallatin. the Secretary of the Treasury, in anticipation of the adoption of such a policy, had already drawn up a plan for a system of national turnpikes and canals. The President, however, suggested that amendments should be added to the Constitution distinctly conferring this power upon Congress.[2] No action was taken upon this recommendation and the discussion of the constitutionality of such an act was reserved to a later day. The President again referred to the subject in his messages of October 27, 1807, and March 8, 1808, but no further suggestion was made to amend the Constitution on this subject until 1813, when Mr. Jackson of Virginia introduced two amendments, one empowering Congress to make roads, the other authorizing it to construct canals in any State, with the consent of the State within which the same shall be made.[3] The same resolutions were reintroduced by him in the remaining session of the Thirteenth Congress and were debated, but they led to no action.[4] President Madison in his annual messages of 1815 and 1816 suggested that the Government should undertake internal improvements. He reminded Congress that "any defect of constitutional authority which may be encountered can be supplied in a mode which the Constitution itself has providently pointed out."[5] Shortly after the last message, Madison vetoed an act making internal improvements

---

[1] Statutes at Large, II, 357.
[2] App., No. 376.
[3] App., Nos. 411, 412.
[4] App., Nos. 416, 417, 421, 422.
[5] App., Nos. 448, 457.

on the ground that it was unconstitutional.[1] President Monroe in his first annual message in 1817 recommended the adoption of an amendment to the Constitution conferring upon Congress the right in question.[2]

A week later, Senator Barbour of Virginia introduced an amendment empowering Congress "to pass laws appropriating money for constructing roads and canals, and improving the navigation of water courses." No improvements were to be made in any State without the consent of such State.[3] Whenever such appropriations were made the amount was to be distributed among the several States in proportion to the number of Representatives from each State, but the portion of any State, with its own consent, may be applied to internal improvements in any other State.

May 4, 1822, President Monroe vetoed "An act for the preservation and repair of the Cumberland road." The President recommended, however, that an amendment should be adopted giving the Federal Government power to make improvements for great national purposes.[4]

In his annual message of this year.[5] the President again invited the attention of Congress to the subject.[6] In 1817 John Quincy Adams opposed the President's purpose to mention the matter in his message. He feared it would provoke contest between the executive and legal departments. Further, he doubted the propriety of the President recommending amendments, inasmuch as the Constitution gave him no share in framing them.[7]

In response to the President's message, three amendments were proposed in this session of Congress, authorizing the appropriation of money for "great national purposes."[8]

In 1824, and again in 1825, Martin Van Buren, then a member of the Senate, introduced an amendment giving Congress power to make roads and canals.[9]

[1] Mason's Veto Power, App. A, No. 8.
[2] App., No. 465.
[3] App., No. 467.
[4] Mason's Veto Power, App. A, No. 9; also pp. 95–96.
[5] Seventeenth Congress, second session.
[6] App., No. 514.
[7] Adams: Memoirs, IV, pp. 463–464; VII, pp. 302. Post, par., 184.
[8] App., Nos. 515, 522, 523.
[9] App., Nos. 536 and 546a. See Jefferson, annoyance at the victory of the liberal constructionists. Morse's Jefferson. p. 329. See Van Buren's remarks in 1825. Debates, Nineteenth Congress, first session, pp. 20–21. Between 1826 and 1830, the legislatures of Virginia, South Carolina, Georgia, and Alabama repeatedly passed resolutions declaring

In the early part of the Nineteenth Congress (December. 1825), Mr. Bailey of Massachusetts presented a very explicit amendment to the Constitution, which besides giving Congress power to appropriate money for constructing roads and canals, further provided that it might "construct roads and canals for urgent purposes, of military, commercial, or mail communication, etc."[1]

Nothing further is heard of a constitutional amendment until Jackson's Administration. May 27, 1830, President Jackson vetoed the Maysville road bill, the first of a series of vetoes of internal-improvement bills.[2] The new test of the constitutionality of such bills as laid down by him was: "The general principle that the works which might be thus aided should be of a general, not local; national, not State, character."[3] Jackson, like his predecessors, Madison and Monroe, in similar cases recommended the adoption of an amendment. In his annual message of two years later (1832), and, again in 1834, he urges Congress "to refrain from the exercise of internal improvements" except of a national character, unless they first procure from the States such an amendment of the Constitution as will define its character and prescribe its bounds." In his message of 1834 he still further defines what national improvements were, and desired that an amendment embodying the definition should be adopted.[4] But such an amendment was not only impossible, but undesirable.

About this time Mr. Archer of Virginia[5] suggested the expediency of amending the Constitution so as to give Congress the power to appropriate the revenue accruing from the sales of the public lands "in aid of the construction of such works of

---

the appropriation of money by Congress for internal improvement within the State to be unconstitutional. At the same time they pronounced the protective tariff laws unconstitutional. The legislature of Tennessee, in 1821, passed resolutions declaring that the power over internal improvements had been "exercised to an unwarrantable extent." See Niles' Register, vol. XXIX, p. 293; vol. XXX, p. 38; vol. XXXII, pp.135–139; vol. XXXIII. pp. 325–328; vol. XXXV, pp. 309–310. This led to counter replies from other States. See Niles' Register, vol. XXXII, p. 169; vol. XXXIII, pp. 275, 321, 347, 387, 391; vol. XXXIV, pp. 300–302; vol. XXXVI, p. 55.   3 Am. An. Reg., 131, 136, 136–137, 137–138, 147.   Jour. of Senate of Pennsylvania (1827–28), pp. 593–623, Ibid. (1828–29), pp. 372–381; Ibid. (1831–32), vol. II, pp. 454–455.

[1] App., No. 543.

[2] Mason's Veto Power, App. A, Nos. 10, 11, 12, 13, 18. The legislature of Tennessee expressed its approval of "the views and sentiments of President Jackson" as expressed in this veto. Jour. of Senate of Pennsylvania (1831–32) vol. II, pp. 454–455.

[3] Mason, pp. 96–97.

[4] App., Nos. 611. House Journal, Twenty-third Congress, second session, pp. 28–32.

[5] 1832.

internal improvements as may be authorized, commenced, or patronized by the States respectively within which the same are to be executed."[1]

The legislature of Georgia, in its series of proposed amendments to the Constitution, in 1833, suggested that the practice of appropriating money for works of internal improvement should be either sanctioned by an express delegation of power or restrained by express inhibition.[2]

No further proposal to amend the Constitution was made until 1847, when President Polk, in a special message containing his reasons for vetoing a river and harbor bill, suggested that the State be allowed to pay tonnage duties for internal improvements, but should it be impossible to secure such by this means, "it is safer and wiser to apply to the States, in the mode prescribed by the Constitution, for an amendment whereby the power of the General Government may be enlarged."[3]

Although several internal-improvement bills have since been vetoed, this is the last time an amendment to the Constitution has been advocated. The question of the constitutionality of such a bill is no longer considered by Congress, which now habitually exercises this once doubted power; but the President is left to decide each particular case as it comes before him, whether the expenditure is national or local in its character.

157. NAVIGATION LAWS AND EMBARGOES.

Another subject which pertains both to the financial and commercial powers of the Government is that of the passage of laws regulating or taxing navigation. The first suggestion of an amendment on the question is found in the proposition of the North Carolina convention, in 1788.[4] This provides for a slight alteration in the last part of the sixth paragraph of the ninth section of the first article, so that it should read: "Nor shall vessels bound to a particular State be obliged to enter, clear, or pay duties in another;" thus striking out the restriction in regard to vessels bound from a State.

---

[1] App., No. 609a. See also ante sec. 115.
[2] App., No. 620.
[3] Statesman's Manual, p. 1725. Mason's Veto Power, App. A, No. 33; also p. 101.
[4] App., No. 101.

Far more significant were the propositions made by the ratifying conventions of Virginia and North Carolina. The convention of 1787, by a well-understood compromise had inserted no clause prohibiting the slave trade prior to 1808 in consideration that the power to tax and regulate commerce should be left free from any limitation as to navigation laws. The two States returned to the subject by urging an article prohibiting the passage of any law "regulating commerce," without the consent of two-thirds of the members present in both Houses.[1] A motion made in the Senate during the First Congress to add a similar proposition to the series about to be submitted to the States was defeated.[2]

The embargo of 1808-09, led the legislature of Massachusetts[3] to present to Congress an amendment limiting the duration of an act laying an embargo within the United States. This proposition called out during the year 1809-10 resolutions of approval from Connecticut and disapproval from Vermont, New Hampshire, Pennsylvania, Maryland, New Jersey, Delaware, North Carolina, and Tennessee.[4] The New England Federalists in the Hartford convention suggested the next and last amendment to limit the power of Congress over commerce. The proposals were presented to Congress in February, 1815, together with the others of the same series, by members from Connecticut and Massachusetts, as the resolutions of their respective State legislatures. The first of these limited the powers of Congress to lay an embargo for more than sixty days; the second provided that the concurrence of two-thirds of both Houses should be required " to interdict the commercial intercourse between the United States and any foreign nation."[5]

---

[1] App., Nos. 33, 85. The States of Maryland, Virginia, and Georgia had supported a somewhat similar proviso, which should be in force to 1808, in the Federal Convention. Elliot, I, 317.

[2] App., No. 278.

[3] The act of 1807 was in its time unlimited in duration and could be removed only by a subsequent act of Congress. The constitutionality of this act was most seriously questioned, and its constitutionality denied in the New England States. See Story, II. pp. 170-171. Adams, U. S. IV, pp. 416, 417.

[4] App., Nos. 397a, 397b. House Journal, Eleventh Congress, second session, pp.580,626; Annals of Congress, pp. 666, 1679, 1944. House Journal, Eleventh Congress, third session, p. 17; Annals of Congress, p. 383. House Journal, Twelfth Congress, first session, p. 161. Am. Reg., 1809, p. 181. Massachusetts Archives, Misc., 6662, 6663, 6665, 6816, 6823. Text of the Massachusetts proposition: To "thirty days after the commencement of the session of Congress next succeeding that session in which said law shall have been enacted." Resolves of Massachusetts, Vol. XII, pp. 476-477. Journal of Senate of Pennsylvania (1809-10), pp. 88-89, 166-169; Ibid. (1810-11), pp. 37-41; Ibid. (1811-12), pp. 95-96.

[5] App., Nos. 427, 428, 435, 436, 443, 444.

This series of resolutions also called out counter resolutions from the legislatures of several of the other States.[1]

The proposition to submit the power over commerce to a special limitation by requiring the concurrence of two-thirds of both Houses has never since found an advocate in Congress. Any such unusual and partial restriction seems unwise.

158. BANKRUPTCY LAWS.

The express power given to Congress to regulate bankruptcy has been exercised only at two different periods during the first century of the Constitution's life,[2] and only two amendments have been proposed upon the subject. The first was proposed by the New York ratifying convention. It contemplated restricting the power given to Congress by the Constitution to the passage of bankruptcy laws which should extend only "to merchants and other traders," the States being allowed to pass laws for the relief of other insolvent debtors.[3] The amendment was not, however, considered by the First Congress. The other amendment emanated from a Representative from New York. Mr. Walworth, in 1832, presented an amendment providing that the States may enact bankrupt or insolvent laws until Congress shall establish uniform laws on the subject.[4] Although no similar amendment has been passed, the States, whenever the Federal Government has refrained from legislating upon the subject, have exercised this power themselves, and such State laws have been held constitutional until Congress shall see fit to supersede them by a general law.[5]

159. PROTECTION OF TRADE-MARKS.

At the time the Constitution was adopted no distinction seems to have existed in the minds of the framers between

---

[1] House Journal, Fourteenth Congress, first session, pp. 278, 297, 672. See ante, par. 22. The New York reply declared that "the effect of these, if adopted, would be to create dissensions among the different members of the Union, to enfeeble the National Government, and to tempt all nations to encroach upon our rights." Niles', VIII. p. 100. Pennsylvania and New Jersey replied in nearly similar words. See, also, Niles', Vol. VII, Sup., pp. 49-53. J. Q. Adams said that, if adopted, they "would not have left enough of that instrument remaining to call it a ruin." Adams, New England Federalism, pp. 315-317 Holmes of Massachusetts showed that one-third of the Senate might be less than one-fifth of the nation, and more than one-third of the House, being the Representatives of three States out of the eighteen." Niles' Register, Vol. VII, pp. 49-53.

[2] In 1841 and in 1867 laws were passed. The last law was repealed in 1878.

[3] App., No. 64.

[4] App., No. 508.

[5] Sturges v. Crowingshield, 4 Wheaton, 122. Ogden v. Saunders, 12 Wheaton, 213.

copyright or patents and trade-marks. Congress passed an act protecting trade-marks, but in 1879 the Supreme Court held that a trade-mark was not within the meaning of the clause[1] in the Constitution which was intended to protect authors and inventors, but could be referred only to the commerce clause. Legislation, therefore, must be limited to the use of trade-marks in commerce "with foreign nations, among the several States, and the Indian tribes." The law passed by Congress was not so limited, but it embraced all commerce, therefore it was declared void for want of constitutional authority.[2]

Upon the reassembling of Congress in December of this year, Mr. McCoid of Iowa, in consequence of this decision, proposed an amendment conferring upon Congress the power to grant, protect, and regulate the exclusive right to adopt and use trade-marks. This resolution was first referred to the Committee on Manufactures, reported, and recommitted to the same committee; later, referred to the Committee on the Judiciary, and twice recommitted to the same.[3] In the next Congress it was again introduced, but this time no important action was taken.[4]

Although no amendment has been secured, Congress has gone to the limit of its power as indicated by the court. On the 3d of March, 1881, a law was passed applying to trade-marks in connection with commerce between States, foreign nations, and the Indian tribes.[5]

160. THE STATUS OF COMMERCIAL POWERS.

On the whole, the Constitution confers upon Congress more sweeping power over commerce than over any other subject. The exercise of this power has in the past caused the most friction, and it is the most likely to lead to collisions with the States in the future. Hence it is remarkable that so few amendments have been offered on the essentials of this power. No proposition whatever has been made to amend the Constitution in regard to foreign or interstate commerce.

The great power of chartering corporations, banks, and kindred institutions, notwithstanding frequent remonstrance, has been successfully asserted. The legal-tender notes, although

---

[1] Const., Art. I, sec. 8, cl. 8.
[2] Trade-Mark Cases, 100 U. S., 82 (1879).
[3] App., No. 1496.
[4] App., No. 1539.
[5] 21 Stat. L., 502.

they are naturally a part of the coining power, yet practically
they can be placed on a commercial basis. The last decision
of the Supreme Court in regard to the legal-tender notes has
been acquiesced in, although not without protest.

The internal-improvement policy, which was so long considered a doubtful use of the powers of the Government, has
finally been established without amendment. In addition,
protective tariffs, navigation acts, and embargoes have been
carried out. In conclusion, therefore, it would seem that there
is little need of an amendment to secure powers already so
fully exercised, and that there is no hope of obtaining any
amendment restricting the powers of Congress in this sphere.

161. FOREIGN AFFAIRS—THE TREATY-MAKING POWER.

Difficulties had arisen, during the Confederation, out of the
obstinacy of the States in performing acts forbidden by treaties with foreign nations.[1] The treaty power in the new Constitution was therefore very simple and explicit.[2] The Virginia
and North Carolina ratifying conventions proposed an article
providing that no commercial treaty shall be ratified without
the concurrence of two-thirds of the Senate, "but no treaty
dealing with the territorial rights and claims of the United
States, or their rights of fishing in the American seas or navi-
gating the American rivers, shall be made except in case of
the most urgent and extreme necessity." In such cases no
treaty shall be ratified without the concurrence of three-fourths
of the whole number of members of both Houses.[3] A motion
to add this identical proposition to the series to be recommended to the States was negatived by the Senate in the First
Congress.[4]

The North Carolina convention also proposed another amendment with reference to the validity of treaties.[5] By its terms
no treaty which was opposed to the existing laws of the United
States should be valid until such laws were repealed, nor should

---

[1] Story, II, p. 580–582.

[2] "He (the President) shall have power, by and with the advice of the Senate, to make
treaties, provided two-thirds of the Senators present concur." Art. II, sec. 11, cl. 2.
Story, II, pp. 324–337; 580–585, notes. In the Federal Convention a proposition to require
the assent of two-thirds of all the members of the Senate was rejected by a vote of six
States against five. Journal of Congress, 343–344.

[3] App., Nos. 32, 84.

[4] App., No. 277.

[5] App., No. 100.

any treaty be valid which was contradictory to the Constitution.[1]

The question whether the House of Representatives has the right to practically annul a treaty made in accordance with the Constitution, by withholding the appropriations necessary to carry out its provisions, has frequently given rise to very sharp and interesting debates. Although the House has sometimes threatened to withhold its cooperation, especially in the case of the Jay Treaty, it has never yet done so. As a result of the opposition to the Jay Treaty, the legislature of Virginia, before the close of the year in which it was adopted, passed resolutions recommending an amendment which provided "that no treaty containing any stipulation upon the subject of the powers vested in Congress shall become the supreme law of the land until it shall have been approved in those particulars by a majority in the House of Representatives, and that the President before he shall ratify any treaty shall submit the same to the House of Representatives."[2] This amendment does not seem to have received further indorsement at this time; moreover, it is somewhat remarkable, in view of the facts previously mentioned, that no similar suggestion to amend the Constitution was made until 1884.[3] In that year there was before the Senate a series of commercial treaties of such a nature that the power of Congress to levy duties on certain merchandise would be restricted thereby. This fact undoubtedly suggested the two amendments proposed in December of this year. One of them, introduced by Mr. Townshend of Illinois, provided that treaties should be made by and with the advice of the House of Representatives as well as the Senate.[4] The other, presented by Mr. Blanchard of Louisiana, required that the prior consent of Congress should be necessary to make reciprocity treaties affecting the revenues.[5] Mr. Blanchard reintroduced the same amendment the following year.[6]

---

[1] The courts have held when the provision of a law and a treaty conflict, the last in point of time must control. Cooley, Const'al Law, pp. 30–31, note 3.

[2] App., No. 327a.

[3] The Hawaiian reciprocity treaty of 1876 seems to acknowledge the claims of the House to pass upon treaties affecting the revenue, for it provided that it should not go into effect until the passage of an act of Congress to carry it into effect. The act was passed and approved August 15, 1878.

[4] App., No 1632. The same proposition was made in the Convention of 1787, but rejected, ten States against one. Journal of Convention, 339–340.

[5] App., No 1634.

[6] App., No. 1648.

In the tariff act of 1890 a contrary tendency was visible. Congress authorized the President, by law, to reestablish certain duties as to particular nations, unless he could secure treaties by which these nations granted certain commercial privileges.

162. WAR POWERS—DECLARATION OF WAR.

Since the Government of the Confederation had been created with express reference to carrying on the war with Great Britain, the powers in that respect were more complete than in its powers over foreign affairs. There was no difficulty in securing a liberal clause in the Constitution as to the declaration of war, the maintenance and discipline of armies, and the raising and employment of militia. These powers have been little disputed except during the war of 1812 and the civil war, and few efforts were made in these crises to curtail them.

Two attempts have been made to place the power to declare war under a special restriction. The New York and Rhode Island ratifying conventions proposed that an amendment should be made to the Constitution, to the effect that Congress should not declare war without the concurrence of two-thirds of both Houses.[1] No similar amendment was suggested until the report of the Hartford convention was presented to Congress, in 1815. One of the amendments of this interesting series proposed a like restriction upon the powers of Congress, the only exception permitted was for the defense of the territories of the United States when actually invaded.[2]

Another of the propositions of the indefatigable convention of North Carolina was that Congress should not introduce foreign troops into the United States without the consent of two-thirds of the members of both Houses.[3] Still another, submitted by the Rhode Island convention in 1790, stipulated that no person should be compelled to do military duty otherwise than by voluntary enlistment, except in cases of general invasion.[4]

163. WAR POWERS—THE ARMY.

A curious evidence of the prevalent fear that the republican government might be destroyed is seen in the amendments

[1] App., Nos. 54, 117.

[2] App., Nos. 429, 437, 445. For replies of other States, see ante, pars. 22, 157. The report of the New York committee declares, if this amendment were adopted, "no nation would ever fear our power." Niles', Vol. VIII, p. 100.

[3] App., No. 103.

[4] App., No. 109.

proposed in 1788–89, relating to the war power. The ratifying conventions of five States[1] desired that no standing army should be kept up in time of peace without the consent of a very large majority of both Houses of Congress. Some of these placed the majority required at three-fourths of the members of each House, others at two-thirds.[2] Two amendments of a similar character were rejected by the Senate in 1789.[3]

The same effect was sought by other amendments urged by the Virginia and North Carolina conventions. They would have prohibited the enlistment of soldiers for any longer term than four years, except in time of war, and then for no longer term than the continuance of the war.[4] Two attempts in the First Congress to secure similar amendments were defeated.[5]

164. THE MILITIA.

Even the paragraph as to the militia[6] did not escape censure. The Virginia and North Carolina conventions proposed still another amendment on the war power, which conferred upon each State the power of organizing, arming, and disciplining its own militia, whenever Congress should omit to provide for the same, and in addition that the militia should not be subject to martial law except when in actual service.[7] This amendment, also, the Senate in 1789 declined to recommend to the States.[8]

The New York ratifying convention proposed an amendment providing that the militia of a State should not be compelled to serve without its limits for a longer term than six weeks without the consent of the legislature of its State.[9]

No further amendments in regard to the militia were proposed until after the war of 1812. In that war the militia, upon which great reliance had been placed, proved inefficient,

---

[1] New Hampshire, Virginia, New Jersey, North Carolina, and Rhode Island. Story, II. 88, note. Individual liberty was guarded from the military power by the second and third amendments.

[2] App., Nos. 23, 34, 52, 86, 115.

[3] App., Nos. 252, 280.

[4] App., Nos. 35, 87.

[5] App., Nos. 252, 281.

[6] "Congress shall have power to provide for organizing, arming, and disciplining the militia, and for governing such part of them as may be employed in the service of the United States." Const., Art. I, sec. 8, cl. 16.

[7] App., Nos. 36, 88.

[8] App., No. 282. See Story, II, 112–114.

[9] App., No. 74.

and the New England States had declined to send their militia outside of their own borders on the call of the Government. It is not surprising, therefore. that in 1817, and again in 1818,[1] General Harrison of Ohio introduced an amendment which should give Congress power, concurrently with the States, to provide for the training of the militia, and also "for teaching in the primary schools and other seminaries of learning in the several States the system of discipline prescribed for the militia," in order that the militia might become "a safe and effectual national defense."

165. MILITARY PENSIONS.

One consequence of the war and financial powers, taken together, seems to have escaped the attention of the Convention. The question of half pay to the Revolutionary officers had caused the Newburgh address of 1783. Under the new Constitution, Congress made many grants, and especially very liberal land grants to old soldiers. As the arable lands were not sufficient after the civil war, a very liberal and even wasteful scale of pensions was adopted. One amendment has been proposed to prevent the repeal of the general pension laws, or the decrease of the rate of pension granted under the same It was introduced in the Fiftieth Congress, by Mr. Peters of Kansas.[2] No such provision seems necessary; the payment once begun can hardly be withdrawn, except by the gradual dying off of the recipients.

166. POLICE POWER.

In the division of powers between the States and the General Government, it seems to have been intended that to the States should be left entire control over internal order, and the relations of man with man, except as the relations grew out of Federal law. Questions of morality, of the relation of employer and employed, of education, have wisely been committed to smaller communities. Four different questions, however, have suggested an extension of the nation's powers; they are polygamy, divorce. the traffic in intoxicating liquors, and the protection of labor.[3]

---

[1] App., Nos. 464, 470.

[2] App., No. 1714.

[3] The amendments on divorce are considered under Personal Relations, ante, par. 102.

167. PROHIBITION OF POLYGAMY.

From about 1850 the establishment of the Mormons in Utah has kept the question of polygamy before the public mind. Congress has by repeated measures attempted to stamp it out in the Territories, but no control could be exercised over State action on this subject.

President Grant in his annual message in 1875 suggested that an amendment prohibiting polygamy should be recommended to the States for their adoption.[1] No immediate action was taken on this suggestion. In 1879 the first proposed amendment dealing with the question was introduced by Mr. Burrows.[2] Since 1882 there have been seventeen amendments prohibiting polygamy, or polygamy and bigamy, within the United States, presented to Congress.[3] A few of these have been reported favorably from the committees. During the Fiftieth Congress eight such amendments were proposed, one of which was framed by the Committee on the Judiciary,[4] but Congress has not deemed it necessary to wait for an amendment to enable it to deal with polygamy.

168. THE MANUFACTURE AND SALE OF INTOXICATING LIQUORS PROHIBITED.

From the beginning of the Washingtonian movement the States have been urged to pass laws restraining or prohibiting the traffic in liquors. It is only in very recent years that like suggestions have been made as to national legislation. There have been fourteen resolutions presented in Congress to amend the Constitution so as to prohibit the manufacture and sale of intoxicating liquors.[5] The first of these was introduced by Mr. Blair of New Hampshire, at that time a member of the House,[6] in December, 1876. During the same session of Congress the legislature of Maine presented to Congress a resolution praying for the passage of this resolution. Mr. Blair has not failed to introduce a similar amendment in any subsequent Congress.[7] Since 1881 Senator Plumb of Kansas vied with

---

[1] App., No. 1399.
[2] App., No. 1500.
[3] App., Nos. 1544, 1557, 1584. 1597, 1644, 1677, 1678, 1679, 1680, 1688, 1692, 1709, 1710, 1712, 1713, 1718, 1734.
[4] App., No. 1718.
[5] App., Nos. 1433, 1460, 1521, 1522, 1523, 1524, 1549, 1552, 1577, 1616, 1635, 1637, 1690, 1699.
[6] App., No. 1433.
[7] App., Nos. 1460, 1521, 1522, 1577, 1636, 1690. His resolution provided that "the assent of any State to the article shall not be rescinded nor reversed."

him in presenting prohibitory amendments. Although several of these amendments have been reported from the committee, no important action has been secured.

To counteract the prohibitory movement, there was introduced, in 1884, by Mr. Deuster of Wisconsin, an amendment to prevent Congress or the legislature of any State or Territory enacting " any law prohibiting or abridging the manufacture or sale of any article or merchandise composed or prepared in whole or in part of any product of the soil."[1] Recent decisions of the Supreme Court deny to the States any power to interfere in the traffic in liquors imported from other States and sold in the original packages.[2] The whole subject is however so confused that a constitutional amendment affirming the power of the States to regulate the traffic seems desirable.

109. PROTECTION TO LABOR.

Within recent years, a number of amendments have been proposed which denote a tendency toward paternalism. Congress has passed an act fixing eight hours as the standard day's labor in the Government service,[3] and has also prohibited the immigration of persons under contract. Acts have also been passed against the use of convict labor on Government contracts. Repeated efforts have been made to ingraft provisions on all these subjects into the Constitution. In 1884 Mr. Davis of Massachusetts proposed an amendment, giving Congress power to regulate the hours of labor[4] "which persons may be employed in the manufacture of textile fabrics, and in other industries." This resolution was reported from the Committee on Labor, but was not reached on the Calendar. This same amendment has been reintroduced twice by Mr. Davis.[5] The first amendment prohibiting the contracting of convict labor was introduced by Mr. Fiedler of New Jersey, in 1883.[6] The amendment was reported unamended from the Committee

---

[1] App., No. 1613. Prohibition amendments to the State constitution were adopted in the following States: Kansas, in 1880; Iowa, in 1882; Maine, in 1884; Rhode Island, in 1886, since repealed.

[2] Leisy v. Hardin, 135 U. S., 100. Congress immediately passed an act extending to the States authority over this subject. 26 Stat. at Large, 313. See Cooley Constitutional Law, p. 70, note 5.

[3] The constitution of California of 1879 led the way by prescribing eight hours as a legal day's work on all public works. Seventeen other States, either by statute or constitutional provision, have regulations in regard to an eight-hour labor day.

[4] App., No. 1604.

[5] App., Nos. 1651, 1702.

[6] App., No. 1592.

on Labor. In 1886 two additional amendments on this same subject were presented, the one by Mr. Lovering of Massachusetts, the other by Mr. Willis of Kentucky.[1]

170. EDUCATION.

Among the subjects which were distinctly intended by the Constitution to be left to the States was the regulation of education.[2] The New England States, in 1789, had the best system of public schools, although poor and little developed, but entirely subject to State control. In the Northwest ordinance, provision was made for later free schools, and land was set apart for the purpose. As each Territory was formed a similar reservation of land was made. Later Congresses reserved land for future State universities. In 1862 a large grant of land scrip was made to all of the States for the establishment of agricultural colleges. Still later, Congress appropriated money for schools among the freedmen.[3] In 1888 and 1889 a large sum was appropriated for "experimental stations" in the States, and in 1891 new subsidies were given to State universities. Thus the readiness of Congress to cooperate with the States by gifts of land and money has been shown. In addition, a series of amendments have been offered looking either to the establishment of national institutions of learning or to enforce the establishment and support of schools by the States.

171. ESTABLISHMENT OF A NATIONAL UNIVERSITY.

In view of an anticipated surplus, President Jefferson in his annual message of 1806 recommended the adoption of an amendment permitting the application of such a surplus to the purpose of " the public education " and internal improvements. He suggested that a national university should be established.[4] No further amendment on this subject was presented for ten years. In 1816 Mr. Atherton of New Hampshire urged such a measure, but the House declined to consider it.[5] In the next year President Monroe in his first annual message suggested " that it be recommended to the States to

[1] App., Nos. 1666, 1069.

[2] In the convention of 1787 a motion to establish a National University was defeated, 4 to 6, one State divided. Elliot, v, 544.

[3] Hart's, Disposition of Our Public Lands, in Quarterly Journal of Economics, Vol. I, pp. 169, 251.

[4] Story, II, 165, 192. App., No. 376. Adams, Writings of Gallatin, Vol. I, pp. 313–319. For Washington's plans for a National University, see Dr. Goode's monograph, Am. Hist. Association, Papers, Vol. IV, part 2. B. A. Hinsdale, Views of the Presidents in relation to a National University.

[5] App., No. 461.

include in the amendment" proposed sanctioning internal improvement "a right in Congress to institute seminaries of learning."[1] Only one other amendment relative to the establishment of a national university has been proposed; this was presented by Mr. Bailey of Massachusetts, in 1825, in his resolution empowering Congress to make internal improvements, to promote education, colonization, and the liberal and useful arts.[2]

172. THE STATES TO PROVIDE FREE PUBLIC SCHOOLS.

No attempt to secure or control common school education by the National Government was made until the end of the civil war. Soon steps seemed necessary for the elevation of the recently emancipated slaves. The Southern States were at first hostile to any effort to educate the negro. It seemed to statesmen who had freed the slaves that they must not only guarantee to them civil and political rights, but also give them the opportunity of securing an education.

To that end, Mr. Delano of Ohio, in 1865, and Messrs. Kelso of Missouri and Ashley of Ohio, in 1867, introduced amendments providing that each State shall establish and maintain a thorough and efficient system of free public schools throughout the State, sufficiently numerous for the accommodation of all the children of the State.[3]

In 1871 Senator Stewart proposed an amendment stipulating that "there should be maintained in each State and Territory a system of free common schools."[4] In 1874 Senator Stewart presented a new amendment upon the subject, providing that in case any State fail to maintain a common school system under which all persons between the ages of five and eighteen years shall receive free of charge such elementary education as Congress may prescribe, "the Congress shall have power to establish therein such a system and cause the same to be maintained at the expense of such State."[5]

In 1875 President Grant in his annual message earnestly recommended an amendment "making it the duty of each of the several States to establish and forever maintain free public schools for all the children.[6] Several amendments were shortly

---

[1] App., No. 466.

[2] App., No. 543.

[3] App., Nos. 1060, 1197, 1222. In case a State shall neglect to carry this into effect, it fell to the duty of Congress to enforce the same.

[4] App., No. 1342. Reported favorably, but postponed.

[5] App., No. 1381.

[6] App., No. 1397.

submitted in regard to the appropriation of money to sectarian schools.[1] One of these provided that a system of free common schools should be maintained in each State and Territory.[2] Since that time only four amendments have been presented. One, introduced by Mr. McCoid of Iowa, in 1880,[3] made provision for the establishment and maintenance by each State of a system of free public schools,[4] and stipulated that "no citizen of the United States, born therein after the adoption of this amendment, who has not attended public or other schools for the period of five years, and who is unable to read and write, shall be entitled to vote," or be counted in the enumeration for Representatives. This resolution further provided that the failure of any State within two years after the adoption of this article to carry out its provisions should be deemed a failure to maintain a republican form of government, and Congress may deprive it of its representation in Congress or in the electoral college until it shall comply with the condition imposed by Congress. An amendment, introduced by Mr. Brown in 1884, for the protection of civil rights, aimed to secure the enjoyment of equal privileges and advantages in their attendance upon the common schools, to all persons within the United States.[5]

The remaining two were offered in the Fiftieth Congress; one empowering Congress to grant aid to the common school system of the several States,[6] the other, championed by Senator Blair, provided that each State should establish and maintain a system of free public schools, and the United States should guarantee the support and maintenance of such a system.[7] Most of the States now show a commendable zeal in taxing themselves for their own educational systems. The Blair bill, appropriating $77,000,000 of the national fund to State schools, finally failed, and it seems likely that no further attempts will be made to amend the Constitution in this particular.

---

[1] See post, par. 173.

[2] Mr. Sargent of California, App., No. 1401.

[3] App., No. 1514.

[4] "Schools must be kept during eight months of each year, for the attendance of all children between the ages of 5 and 21, without distinction or separation on account of race, color, or social condition." See ante, pars. 79, 132.

[5] App., No. 1612.

[6] App., No. 1711. Not to exceed $10,000,000 annually, to be distributed pro rata among the States.

[7] App., No. 1727.

An amendment of another character was presented in 1871. It provided that the fourteenth amendment should not be construed as prohibiting the States from making and enforcing laws for the separate education of the white and the colored races.[1] The fourteenth amendment has not been held by the courts as prohibiting the separate education of the two races, so long as equal provisions for their education are made.[2]

173. RELIGION.

Since the adoption of the first amendment, there has been no amendment suggested on the subject of religion until recent years.[3]

Included in several of the amendments on education, were clauses setting forth that no sectarian use should be made of public school funds,[4] and in several cases distinctly guaranteeing religious liberty. President Grant, in connection with his recommendation of public schools, in his message of 1875 further advised forbidding the teaching in such schools of any particular religious tenets and prohibiting the granting of any school funds and school taxes for the benefit of any religious sect.[5] He also suggested an amendment declaring "the church and state forever separate and distinct, but each free within their proper spheres, and that all church property shall bear its own proportion of taxation."[6] In the House immediate action was taken in accordance with the President's recommendation. Mr. Blaine introduced a resolution that embodied a part of the changes suggested by the President.[7] This amendment provided that "no State shall make any law respecting an establishment of religion or prohibiting the free exercise thereof," and it prohibited the appropriation of public school money by any State to sectarian schools. In Mr. Stewart's amendment of 1871 there had been a provision similar to this last clause.[8] The "Blaine amendment," after slight

---

[1] App., No. 1339. Also prohibited the intermarriage of the races. See ante, par. 102. No. 1514 forbade separation (see previous page).

[2] Cases cited in Cooley, Principles of Constitutional Law, p. 242, note 3. The constitutions of West Virginia, North Carolina, Tennessee, Missouri, Texas, Georgia, and Alabama provide that white and colored children shall be taught in separate schools. Hitchcock, American State Constitutions, p. 26.

[3] See Stevens, Sources of the Constitution of the United States, pp. 214, note 1. 218; Elliot's Deb., v, p. 131.

[4] First proposed by Mr. Burdett in 1870, App., No. 1329.

[5] App., No. 1397.

[6] App., No. 1398.

[7] App., No. 1401.

[8] App., No. 1342. Ante, par. 172.

modifications, passed the House August 4, 1876, by a vote of 180 to 7. When the amendment was presented to the Senate, Senators Frelinghuysen, Sargent, and Christiancy immediately proposed substitutes.[1] The Committee on the Judiciary reported the amendment in more explicit terms, and it received 28 votes. The negative votes were, however, 16, and it thus failed for the lack of a two-thirds vote.[2]

Five other amendments dealing with this subject have since been introduced, three in the House at this same session of Congress.[3] One of these, presented by Mr. O'Brien of Maryland, in addition to provisions similar to those in the Blaine amendment, contained a clause modeled after a provision in the Maryland constitution, excluding ministers and preachers of the gospel of any denomination from holding any office under the United States,[4] and in addition forbade the requirement of any religious test as a qualification for any office in any State or under the United States.[5] Mr. Edmunds, in 1878, attempted to revive the subject in the Senate.[6]

The amendment submitted by Senator Blair, in 1888, in addition to the provision previously considered, stipulated that no State should maintain an establishment of religion, and forbade appropriation for sectarian schools.[7]

The provisions of the State constitutions are in almost all instances adequate on this subject, and no amendment is likely to be secured.[8]

---

[1] App., No. 1401.

[2] The Republican platform of 1876 recommended an amendment "forbidding the application of any public funds or property for the benefit of any schools or institutions under sectarian control." In 1880 it recommended an amendment to prohibit the legislature of a State making any law respecting the establishment of religion and appropriating public funds to the support of sectarian schools.

[3] App., Nos. 1410, 1413, 1428, 1459, 1514.

[4] The following States in their constitutions also excluded clergymen from holding office: Maryland, constitution of 1867, art. 3, sec. 11; also in the constitution of New York of 1821, art. 7, sec. 4; North Carolina constitution of 1776, art. 31; constitution of South Carolina of 1790, art. 1, sec. 23, and constitution of 1865, sec. 30; Delaware, art. 7, sec. 8 (while he continues to exercise pastoral functions); Kentucky, art. 2, sec. 27; Tennessee, art. 9, sec. 1. Active clergy are also excluded from House of Commons. May, Parl. Practice, p. 30.

[5] App., No. 1410.

[6] App., No. 1459. The article was not to be construed to prohibit the reading of the Bible in any school or institution.

[7] App., No. 1727. Ante, par. 172.

[8] At least twenty-three States have constitutional barriers to sectarian appropriations. Many petitions to "put God in the Constitution" have been received, but no formal resolution to amend to that effect has been found during the first century. In the Fifty-fourth Congress such an amendment has been introduced.

174. SUMMARY OF AMENDMENTS ON THE POWERS OF THE GOVERNMENT.

With the exception of the subject of personal relations, the number of amendments proposing a change in the provisions of the Constitution affecting the powers of the Government has been comparatively small. Only about three hundred in all have been presented. With the exception of the early years, the larger number of the proposed amendments have contemplated an extension of the power conferred upon Congress rather than the placing of restrictions upon its actions. Of these, three have received the indorsement of the House of Representatives. The provisions of the one passed in 1865, prohibiting the payment of the Confederate debt,[1] were later incorporated into the fourteenth amendment.[2] Of the other two, passed respectively in 1876 and 1878, the one prohibited the appropriation of any money or property to any religious sect,[3] the other forbade the payment of claims to disloyal persons.[4] Both failed to receive the approval of the Senate.

The wisdom of the members of the Convention of 1787 in defining the powers of the Government in broad and general terms has become more and more evident as time has elapsed, for, owing to this fact, it has been possible to readily adapt the Constitution to the changed conditions and circumstances of advancing years. The doctrine of implied powers has been accepted to such an extent that in the most important cases where amendments have been sought, the same results have been secured without their adoption.[5]

To a much smaller degree has it been possible to secure any change by these unwritten amendments of the provisions of the Constitution prescribing the form of the government, for here the Constitution admits of less freedom of interpretation, being very much more explicit in its terms.

175. PROPOSITION TO CHANGE THE NAME OF THE COUNTRY.

One interesting proposition—which it has been impossible to classify elsewhere—to change the name of our country has been introduced. This singular amendment was presented by

---

[1] App. No. 1057.
[2] App. No. 1139.
[3] App. No. 1401.
[4] App. No. 1477.
[5] Post, par. 188. Tiedman, The Unwritten Constitution of the United States, pp. 42-44; Story, II, p. 165; McMaster, in Shaler's, United States, II, p. 500.

Mr. Anderson of Missouri, in 1866. He proposed, in case the Constitution was again to be opened for amendment, that our country should hereafter "be known and styled America," inasmuch as its present name was "not sufficiently comprehensive and significant to indicate the real unity and destiny of the American people as the eventual, paramount power of this hemisphere."[1]

---

[1] App., No. 1108.

CHAPTER VI.

PROCEDURE AS TO CONSTITUTIONAL AMENDMENTS.

176. METHOD OF AMENDMENT.

The Constitution of the United States, in Article v, provides for its own amendment whenever two thirds of the Houses of Congress, or a convention called upon the application of two-thirds of the State legislatures, shall propose amendments, which in either case shall be valid when ratified by the legislatures of or conventions in three-fourths of the several States, as Congress may direct.[1] Thus it appears that amendments may be proposed in one of two ways—either by Congress or a convention called by Congress in response to the request of the necessary number of the State legislatures. Also discretionary power is given to Congress to choose one of the two methods of ratification permissible, namely, either by the legislatures of States or by conventions in the several States. The amount of discretion allowed in this clause plainly indicates the expectation of the framers of the Constitution, that the amending machinery would be frequently put into operation.[2] It is therefore remarkable that only one of the methods of proposing amendments has been used, and that it has always been accompanied by one method of ratification.[3]

177. GENERAL CONVENTIONS.

In making provision for a Federal convention,[4] the framers of the Constitution doubtless had in mind the possibility of a future fundamental revision, and in addition wished to provide when necessary for a body having a direct mandate from the people to propose amendments.[5] The fact that nearly two

[1] Of the two exceptions enumerated in the article one is obsolete; the other, in regard to equal representation of a State in the Senate, has as much force to-day as ever.

[2] See Hamilton's remarks in the Federal Convention, Elliot, v, 530.

[3] With the exception of the proposed thirteenth amendment in 1861, which was ratified by a convention in Illinois in 1862. See post, par. 179.

[4] The first provision agreed to for securing amendments provided only for a convention, on application of the legislatures of two-thirds of the States, August 6, 1787. Elliot, v. 381.

[5] See advantages of a convention referred to by Nicholas in the Virginia convention, ibid., iii, 101–102.

hundred constitutional conventions have been called to frame
or revise the State constitutions,[1] renders it all the more
remarkable that this method of proposing amendments to the
Constitution of the United States has never been put in operation. This may be accounted for in part by the fact that
there has never been a time when a general revision of the
Constitution has been widely desired. Although conventions
for the proposal or ratification of amendments have never
been assembled, yet occasions have arisen when their trial
has been urged. Passing over the propositions for a second
convention, which were made in the Federal Convention itself,
and in the States at the time of their ratification of the Constitution,[2] we find that the Government had scarcely been
established when Virginia and New York made application for
a convention to draft amendments.[3] In the winter of 1832–33,
the legislature of South Carolina passed resolutions declaring
it "expedient that a convention of the States be called as
early as practicable to consider and determine such questions
of disputed powers as have arisen between the States of this
Confederacy and the General Government."[4] This seems to
have led to the legislatures of Georgia and Alabama passing
resolutions in conformity to Article V, petitioning Congress
to call a Federal convention to consider the proposal of amendments.[5] The legislature of Delaware, on the other hand, in
reply to the resolutions of South Carolina, declared that
the Constitution does not recognize any such tribunal or political assemblage as a convention of the States, but has provided for modes of amendment, if amendment be necessary, in
the fifth article; * * * "any other mode, therefore, must
be repugnant to its provisions;" that any such convention
"must be a convention of the people," "and not a convention of the States;"[6] and "that it is not expedient for Congress to call a convention for proposing amendments at this
time."[7]

---

[1] Jameson, Constitutional Convention, p. 550. Tiedman, Unwritten Constitution, p. 42.
[2] Article by E. P. Smith in Jameson's Essays, p. 46.
[3] App., Nos. 125, 126.
[4] Senate Journal, Twenty-second Congress, second session, p. 83.
[5] App., Nos. 612a, 613–625.
[6] "That such a convention of the States, if assembled, could have no such power as that
set forth by the resolutions of South Carolina."
[7] Senate Journal, Twenty-second Congress, second session, pp. 157–158. For Resolves of
Massachusetts in disapproval to Resolves of South Carolina, see Resolves of Massachusetts, Vol. XIX, pp. 401–402; for report and reply of Massachusetts legislature disapproving of the Georgia resolutions, see ibid., pp. 411–423.

Again, in the sessions of Congress just previous to the rebellion, when there was a general desire that every means should be tried before resorting to a civil war, petitions from the legislatures of six States,[1] besides nine propositions from members of Congress, were received calling for a drafting convention.[2] On the invitation of Virginia, a peace convention was also held, at which commissioners from twenty-one States were present.[3] As a result of its work, the convention recommended to Congress a series of amendments to the Constitution.[4] In this same session of Congress, Mr. Florence of Pennsylvania offered the following singular amendment: "The reserved power of the people in three-fourths of the States to call and form a national convention to alter, amend, or abolish this Constitution, according to its provisions, shall never be questioned, notwithstanding the direction in Article V of the Constitution."[5]

Propositions for a convention were also offered at three different times during the period of the civil war, and again in 1866.[6] Of those presented during the course of the war, the first was introduced by Mr. Vallandigham, in 1861, the other two by Senator Davis of Kentucky, who proposed such a convention of the States for the purpose of bringing about the restoration of peace and the Union.[7]

---

[1] Virginia, Kentucky, New Jersey, Ohio, Illinois, and Indiana. The convention in Missouri also approved of a similar course. Stephen, War between the States, II, p. 364.

[2] App., Nos. 812, 834, 835, 873, 895, 900, 908, 911. 931n, 941, 954, 970, 970a, 940a.

[3] App., No. 873. See ante, pars. 106, 107. Chittenden, Debates and Proceedings of the Peace Convention; McPherson, History of the Rebellion, pp. 67–70. Twenty-two States appointed commissioners, but several did not attend. Foster, Commentary on Constitution, I, p. 173.

[4] App., Nos. 917.

[5] App., No. 892.

[6] App., Nos. 972, 976, 1039a, 1115. The latter by Senator Lane of Kansas, for the Committee on the Judiciary to inquire into the expediency of calling a convention. The framers of the Confederate constitution, evidently profiting by the experience of the past, determined to make it easier to assemble a convention to amend. Provision was made that upon the demand of any three States legally assembled in their several conventions, the congress shall summon a convention of all the States to take into consideration such amendments as the said States shall concur in suggesting at the time when the said demand is made; the same to be submitted to the States for ratification, if agreed on by said convention, voting by States. Article V, of Confederate constitution. McPherson, History of the Rebellion, p. 99.

[7] App., No. 976, submitted in 1862, called for a convention to meet in Louisville, Ky., on the first Monday in April, 1863, to take into consideration the condition of the United States and the proper means for the restoration of the Union. Each State to send as many delegates as it is entitled to Senators and Representatives in Congress. App., No. 1039a (1864), called for a convention for a similar purpose, and for the vindication of the Constitution, and the construction of additional and adequate guaranties of the rights and liberties of the people. He presented a series of propositions as the basis of a lasting settlement of all difficulties. See ante, par. 103.

Senator Ingalls, in 1876, in consequence of the disputed Presidential election in that year, introduced a resolution recommending the legislatures of the States to apply to Congress to call a convention to revise and amend the Constitution.[1] This resolution made full provision for the holding of the convention, and for the submission of the revised draft of the Constitution to a convention in each State, chosen by the people thereof.[2] In 1884 an attempt was made to create a commission to call a convention,[3] and as recently as 1886 a minority report of the Committee on Election of President and Vice-President suggested the recommendation of such a convention, owing to "the imperative necessity of a substantial change in the organic law," and the failure of Congress to give due consideration thereto.[4]

178. PROPOSED AMENDMENTS IN CONGRESS—PROCEDURE.

A brief examination of the reception and procedure upon proposed amendments in Congress will suffice to show how very little chance there is of such a proposition being brought to a vote in the branch of Congress in which it is introduced. Almost invariably a proposition to amend is in the form of a joint resolution, although there have been a very few bills introduced providing for amendments to the Constitution.[5]

In general, upon the introduction of a resolution proposing an amendment, it is customary, after it has been read twice, to refer it to some committee, usually to the Committee on the

[1] App., No. 1429.

[2] This made provision for a convention composed of as many delegates from each State as it is entitled to Senators and Representatives in Congress. Two to be chosen by the legislature in each State, the others in the Congressional districts, but no person holding any office of profit or honor under any State or the United States to be eligible as a delegate. The convention should assemble at Columbus, Ohio, May 2, 1877, the Chief Justice of the Supreme Court of the United States to be the presiding officer. Said convention should revise the Constitution and report "such alterations and amendments in the nature of an entire instrument," which should be reported to the President of the United States, who should immediately submit the same to a convention of delegates chosen in each State by the people thereof, under recommendation of the legislature, for their assent and ratification.

[3] App., No. 1631. This resolution, after reciting the failure of Congress to recommend needed amendments, provided for the appointment of a commission of seventy-six persons by the President, composed of two persons from each State from different political parties, for the purpose of considering and proposing to the States the propriety of the legislatures of at least two-thirds of the States uniting in calling a convention on the 4th of July, 1887, for the purpose of proposing amendments to the Constitution.

[4] App., No. 1660. House Rep., No. 2493, Forty-ninth Congress, first session, p. 5. See ante, par. 35.

[5] Manual and Digest of the Rules and Practice of the House of Representatives, Fifty-third Congress, second session, pp. 404-405.

Judiciary, unless there is a committee on the subject to which the amendment refers; thus in recent years the amendments in regard to the election of President and Vice-President have been referred in the House to the Committee on Election of President and Vice-President. In case the proposition is favored by a considerable number of members, who are particularly zealous in urging it, sometimes it is possible to secure the appointment of a select committee to which it is referred. All the most important propositions, like those now a part of the Constitution, were so referred.

Of the more than eighteen hundred propositions to amend the Constitution, introduced in Congress during the first century of its legislative history, over one-half have received no further consideration beyond their reception and reference to a committee. The remainder have either been reported or received further discussion, but only a very small percentage of these have been brought to a vote.

Only two attempts have been found which proposed to change in any way the customary method of procedure. The first of these was introduced in 1826, by Mr. Herrick of Maine.[1] It proposed to regulate the time for introducing amendments, prohibiting their proposal save in every tenth year.[2] This was without doubt suggested by the flood of amendments which came pouring into Congress at about this time, to change the method of electing the President, owing to the defeat of Jackson in 1824. This regulation, however, failed to meet the approval of the House and it was never called up from the table.

The other attempt was made by Mr. Beach of New York at the opening of the Forty-ninth Congress, in 1885.[3] It was evidently called out by the marked increase, in recent years, of the number of constitutional amendments proposed, and the desirability of giving them more extended consideration. The resolution made provision for the appointment of a standing committee of fifteen members of the House, "to be known as the Committee on Constitutional Amendments, to which shall be referred all resolutions and bills proposing amendments to

---

[1] App., No. 571. See ante, par. 4.

[2] Some of the State constitutions have provisions of this character. In Pennsylvania, New Jersey, and Tennessee it is unconstitutional to submit more than one plan of amendment, in the case of the first two States during five years, the latter six years. Borgeaud, Adoption and Amendment of Constitutions, p. 189. By the constitution of Vermont, 1870, amendments could be proposed only at intervals of ten years.

[3] House Journal, Forty-ninth Congress, first session, p. 81.

the Constitution." This resolution was referred to the Committee on Rules, but was never reported.[1]

179. RATIFICATION BY CONVENTIONS.

Several notable attempts have been made to have certain amendments submitted to conventions in the several States, instead of to State legislatures, for their ratification or rejection.[2] Such propositions were made in connection with several of the amendments proposed in 1860 and 1861, notably in the case of the Crittenden amendments. The so-called "Corwin amendment" of 1861, although "proposed by Congress" to the legislatures of the several States for ratification, was "ratified" by a constitutional convention ordained by the people of the State of Illinois on February 14, 1862.[3] As the other mode of ratification had been prescribed by Congress, the question naturally arises whether this could be considered a valid ratification, although in connection with this amendment it has no practical significance, as only two other States ratified it,[4] and the progress of the war placed its adoption out of the realm of possibility. This is the only case where a constitutional convention in any State has acted upon an amendment submitted by Congress.

Since that time attempts have been made by the opponents of the proposed amendments, then under consideration by Congress, to make provision for this method of ratification. It was suggested by them as offering a better chance for the defeat of the amendment in the States. When the thirteenth amendment was about to be submitted to the States this method of ratification was proposed.[5] The true reason for the introduction of this resolution was soon shown to be an effort to accomplish its defeat, for the speech of its author, Mr. Pendleton of Ohio, instead of being an argument in favor of the ratification by conventions, consisted simply of a statement of his reasons for thinking the time inauspicious for changing the Constitution, the country being engaged in a civil war. The resolution was rejected by a decisive vote.

---

[1] Stated by W. A. Muller, a member of the Historical Seminary in American History. Harvard, 1891, from his work on the Committee System.

[2] Original form of amendment provided for ratification by conventions only. Elliot, v, pp. 123, 381.

[3] Certified copy in Bureau of Rolls and Library, State Department.

[4] Ohio and Maryland. See par. 107.

[5] App., No. 1023.

A similar attempt was made in vain by Senator Dixon of Connecticut, when the fifteenth amendment was under consideration.[1] His objections seemed directed against the unequal system of representation in the Connecticut legislature. He therefore urged his plan when the House suffrage amendment was before the Senate, and he also presented it as an amendment to the resolution which later became the fifteenth amendment. Congress had power, he said, if it ordered the ratification of the amendment to be by conventions, to declare that "the convention should be chosen in such a manner that it should represent the people." He further maintained that this was a question upon which the people had never had an opportunity to canvass or to express their opinion, therefore the body called upon to ratify it should be chosen subsequently to its submission. The previous amendments which were submitted to the State legislatures for ratification, especially the first twelve, did not relate to the States at all, but simply curtailed the powers of Congress. Now the proposition is to provide that a power which has always heretofore been held by the States as their own power and their own right shall be taken from them. It is therefore proper that the people should have an opportunity of making known their will in regard to the proposed change.[2] He was answered by his colleague, Senator Ferry, who declared that the question had been discussed before the people, and he further asserted that the same reason that prevented this mode of ratification from being adopted in the previous cases was pertinent now. Congress and the people have never used that power of submission to convention, because the machinery of conventions was dilatory, expensive, and unwise. The Constitution has provided for the speediest correction by the submission of an amendment to the legislatures. The delays incident to the assembling of a convention may be so many that it may be years before the evil can be removed which the amendment was proposed to remedy.[3]

180. REGULATION OF THE RATIFICATION BY LEGISLATURES.

Several attempts have been made in Congress to specify that a proposed amendment should be brought before legisla-

---

[1] App., Nos. 1268, 1286.
[2] Globe, Fortieth Congress, third session, pp. 828, 855, 1040. See post, par. 180.
[3] Ibid.

tures hereafter elected for ratification.[1] On May 23, 1866, when the fourteenth article was under consideration in the Senate, a resolution providing that this amendment should be submitted to legislatures which shall be chosen, or the members of the most popular branch which shall be chosen next after the submission of the amendment, and at its first session, was presented by Mr. Buckalew of Pennsylvania.[2]

The resolution further stipulated that no acceptance or rejection shall be reconsidered or again brought in question at any subsequent session; nor shall any acceptance of the amendment be valid if made three years from the passage of this resolution. This last clause was doubtless suggested by the recent action of New Jersey in regard to the thirteenth amendment. That amendment had been rejected by the legislature of that State, December 1, 1865, and notice of its action had been duly sent to the United States Secretary of State. When that officer proclaimed the adoption of the amendment by the ratification of twenty-seven States on the 18th of December, 1865, no mention was made of New Jersey. However, on January 23, 1866, the legislature of New Jersey reconsidered its previous action and approved the amendment.[3] When the fifteenth amendment was before Congress, the Democrats made a systematic attempt to render its success doubtful by endeavoring to secure its submission to the States for ratification by some untried method. Propositions similar to the one previously presented by Mr. Buckalew were now submitted by several of the Senators, and gave rise to an extended discussion.[4] The argument in favor of the measure, as presented by the various Democratic speakers,[5] was based on the ground that the question ought to come

---

[1] The form of proposal adopted in 1789 has usually been observed in the resolutions proposing amendments. It is as follows: " Resolved by the Senate and House of Representatives of the United States of America in Congress assembled, That the following articles be proposed as amendments to the Constitution of the United States, which, when ratified by three-fourths of the State legislatures, shall become valid to all intents and purposes as a part of the same." Sometimes, a little variation in the language, as in No. 931, the "Corwin amendment," or No. 1057, the latter as follows: " Resolved by the House of Representatives (the Senate concurring), that the following amendment to the Constitution of the United States, be, and the same hereby is, proposed to the legislatures of the several States for ratification. Another, devised during the reconstruction period as No. 1106 (1867), reads: "Be it resolved, etc., that upon the ratification of this amendment by three-fourths of the States represented in Congress," etc.

[2] App., No. 1154.

[3] Jameson's Constitutional Conventions, p. 624.

[4] App., Nos. 1263, 1297, 1298, 1302.

[5] Senators Davis, Hendricks, Saulsbury, Dixon, and Bayard. Globe, Fortieth Congress, third session, pp. 1309-1314.

directly before the people in the election of their representatives; that it was unfair to submit the amendment to the legislatures now in session, for they had not been chosen with a
view to the question or the principles involved in the amendment. In truth, the issue had not been raised in the late campaign, for the Republican party had declared in their platform
that "the question of suffrage in all the loyal States properly
belongs to the people of those States."[1] Indeed, in some of
the States, namely, Ohio, Kansas, Michigan, and Connecticut,
the question of universal suffrage had been submitted to a
popular vote and by large majorities had been condemned.
Mr. Buckalew made the best constitutional argument in support of the measure.[2] He claimed, first, that by necessary im-
plication Congress had the power to make such regulations;
secondly, that it is wise and expedient to adopt some general
rule by which there shall be equal, fair, uniform, and timely
action in the several States; thirdly, that the plan proposed
would give all the advantages of a convention system without
its disadvantages of inconvenience and expense, for it would
give the people of every State a full and complete opportunity
of passing upon the amendment; fourthly, that this plan, by
designating the legislature which shall act upon the amendment, removes all possibility of question as to what particular
legislature or legislatures are to act upon it, or as to the length
of the time the amendment is open for ratification.[3] The difficulty of having amendments ratified and then having the
ratification rescinded, or having an amendment rejected and
afterwards ratified by the legislature of the same State, both
of which events had occurred in the case of the recent amendments in several of the States, would be avoided.[4] The Republicans took up the defense of the customary method.
Mr. Morton led the discussion for his party.[5] He held that
such a proposition was in violation of the Constitution, for it
proposed to select a legislature in the future to which this
amendment is to be submitted. What legislature does the

---

[1] McPherson, History of the Reconstruction, p. 364.

[2] Globe, pp. 1311–1313.

[3] In 1873 the senate of Ohio passed a vote ratifying the amendment on the compensation
of members of Congress, proposed by Congress in 1789, which had failed. Jameson,
p. 635.

[4] Jameson, pp. 627, 628, 631; Manual and Digest, Fifty-first Congress, second session,
pp. 37–40, Story, vol. 2, pp. 649, note 1.

[5] Globe, pp. 1313.

provision in the Constitution refer to? Obviously those in existence at the time the amendment is submitted. If they fail to act upon it, it is possible that future legislatures may, but Congress has no right to withdraw the power from the existing legislature and say that the legislature in existence in 1869 shall not act upon it, but that those of 1870 or 1872 may act. Others based their argument upon precedent.[1] It was declared that the fourteen amendments then a part of the Constitution had been submitted in every instance to legislatures, and, without exception, an examination of the record shows that a majority of the legislatures had been chosen before the proposed amendment was sent out to the people. Naturally, these attempts all met with failure, receiving only Democratic support. Mr. Buckalew's resolution on division received 13 yeas to 43 nays.[2]

In the same year that the fifteenth amendment passed the new constitution of Tennessee was adopted. It contained a provision that no amendment to the Constitution of the United States may be ratified by any convention or assembly of the State which was not elected after such amendment was submitted.[3] It may be an open question whether any such restriction imposed by a State constitution is valid, but Tennessee is the only State which has made such a provision, and there has, of course, been no opportunity to test its constitutionality. Mr. Buckalew's proposition was revived in 1882 by Mr. Berry of California, who, to obviate the question of constitutionality raised by Mr. Morton, proposed it as a formal amendment to the Constitution.[4]

The other method of proposal by Congress and ratification by the State legislatures has been adopted in the case of all the amendments which now form a part of the Constitution. The preference for this form is doubtless due to its manifest advantage, inasmuch as the bodies called upon to act are always in existence, and if not in session can be quickly summoned.

It would seem desirable, owing to the complications that may arise, that Congress should adopt a series of regulations governing the procedure to be followed by the legislatures in acting upon an amendment submitted to them for ratification. Mr.

---

[1] Mr. Ferry of Connecticut.

[2] Mr. Blaine, although he voted for the amendment, admitted afterwards that the point raised by the opposition was well taken. Twenty years in Congress, Vol. II, pp. 413, 414.

[3] Constitution of 1870, art. 2, sec. 32.

[4] App., No. 1550.

Morton of Indiana, recognizing this, proposed, in the next Congress following the discussion already referred to, a resolution prescribing the rules to be followed on such occasions. This resolution was without doubt directly suggested by the recent struggle in the legislature of Indiana, where the Democrats by sharp parliamentary tactics attempted to prevent the ratification of the fifteenth amendment.[1] It provided that on the sixth legislative day of the session of any State legislature, each house should proceed, at noon, to the consideration of any amendment which may have been submitted by Congress to the legislatures of the States for ratification, "Provided, that such amendment may not have been acted upon at any preceding session of said legislature." If the amendment "shall receive the vote of a majority of the members elected to each house * * * it shall be held to be duly ratified by such legislature."[2] A similar resolution was introduced in the House a few days later by a Representative from the same State as Mr. Morton, but no important action was taken by either House upon this subject.[3]

The question how long an amendment is open to adoption or rejection by the States is raised by the action of the senate of Ohio, in 1873, which, "acting upon the theory that once proposed, an amendment to the Constitution is always open to ratification,"[4] passed, at the time of the popular disapproval with the passage by Congress of the so-called "salary-grab act,"[5] a resolution ratifying the amendment proposed by the First Congress, in 1789, in regard to the compensation of members of Congress.[6] This amendment had failed at the time to

---

[1] The Democratic Senators tried to break a quorum, but were prevented by locked doors. In the House of Representatives all the Democrats save ten resigned, thus reducing the membership to less than two-thirds of the members elected, in the hope of preventing or invalidating the action of that body. The Speaker, however, ruled that the House was competent to proceed, and two-thirds of the members present voted to ratify the amendment. The question as to its validity was raised in Congress. McPherson, History of Reconstruction, pp. 490–91, note; Foster, Com. on the Const., p. 329, note 24.

[2] App., No. 1321. The resolution further prescribed that in case final action was not taken on the first day, the houses should meet the next day at the same hour, and so continue to meet from day to day until final action was taken upon such amendment. "Nor was the action of the legislature to be hindered or prevented by resignation or withdrawal, or the refusal to qualify, of a minority of either or both houses." The second section made provision for the certified copies of the action of each house to be forwarded by the governor to the President. Two other resolutions were introduced by Mr. Bromwell of Illinois, "declaratory of the law and right of amending the Constitution." The text it has been impossible to find. App., Nos. 1113, 1211.

[3] App., No. 1323.

[4] Jameson, Constitutional Convention, p. 635.

[5] See ante, par. 13.

[6] App., No. 243. Ante, par. 13.

receive the necessary number of votes to secure its incorporation into the Constitution. In commenting upon this action of the Ohio senate, Judge Jameson urges the desirability of the passage of "a constitutional statute of limitation, prescribing the time within which proposed amendments shall be adopted or be treated," in order that "the danger of confusion or conflict" may be avoided.[1]

181. PROPOSITIONS TO CHANGE THE MAJORITIES REQUIRED BY ARTICLE V.

In view of the difficulty with which an amendment is secured, as has been shown in the previous pages, it is somewhat surprising that there has not been more effort to change the method of amendment. The first proposal of this character was made by the convention in Rhode Island at the time it ratified the Constitution, May 29, 1790.[2] Rhode Island had remained outside of the Union until practically forced to come in, owing to the jealousy of their State's rights, and she now proposed, as a further guaranty to the rights of the State, to make it more difficult to secure an amendment. The stipulation was that after the year 1793 no amendment to the Constitution should be made "without the consent of eleven of the States heretofore united under the Confederation." Possibly also the admission of new States was kept in mind, and this article was designed to insure the preponderance of the original thirteen, even after they should be outnumbered.

On the other hand, two propositions have been made looking to a reduction both in the majority of the vote required or proposed and in the number necessary to ratify. The first, introduced by Senator Henderson of Missouri, on the 11th of January, 1864, in connection with the resolution for the abolition of slavery, which, as amended ultimately, was incorporated into the Constitution as the thirteenth amendment, was an article proposing a reduction of the majorities required for the proposal and ratification of amendments.[3]

---

[1] Jameson, pp. 635-636. He raises the question, by what majority shall the resurrected amendment be adopted, by three-fourths of the States then in the Union, or what number? Another reason why a statute of limitation should be passed is suggested by the motion of Senator Anthony, in 1864, to repeal the joint resolution of the Thirty-sixth Congress (1861) submitting the so-called "Corwin amendment" to the States. (App., No. 102?). Jameson maintains that Congress does not possess the power to recall an amendment which has once been submitted. Constitutional Convention, p. 634. See ante, par. 107.

[2] App., No. 107.

[3] App., No. 984.

This article provided that whenever a majority of the members elected to each House, or a convention called on the application of the legislatures of a majority of the several States, should propose amendments,[1] these in either case should be valid when ratified by the legislatures of or conventions in two-thirds of the several States, as Congress should direct.[2] The committee reported a substitute for Mr. Henderson's abolition amendment, but made no mention of his proposition to change the method of amendment, and there is no record that Mr. Henderson advanced any argument in favor of the change. The other resolution, submitted by Mr. Porter of Virginia, in 1873, proposed a more radical change in the method of the amendment than the one just discussed, and suggested a system the characteristics of which were more national than federal. It provided that "Congress, whenever three-fifths of both Houses of Congress deem it necessary, may propose amendments to the Constitution, or may call a convention for proposing amendments and revising the Constitution," and shall be required to call such a convention "on the application of the legislatures of any number of States, embracing three-fifths of the enumerated population of the several States." Amendments proposed by either of these methods were to be valid "when approved and ratified by a majority of the electors in the several States voting thereon, and qualified to vote for Representatives in Congress."[3] It will be seen that this proposed a system analogous to that adopted by many of the States for amending their constitutions.

182. RATIFICATION BY POPULAR VOTE.

For seventy years after the propositions of the Rhode Island convention, no further suggestion was made for altering the method of amending the Constitution. In the session of 1860–61 there were five proposals to take the sense of the people on certain amendments.[4] This novel proposition was first made by Senator Crittenden, who admitted that the reason for suggesting this unusual method was because of his fear that

---

[1] As was the prevailing provision in the State constitutions.

[2] The method of ratification of amendment provided for by article V of the constitution of the Confederate States, also fixed upon "the legislatures of two-thirds of the several States, or by conventions in two-thirds thereof, as the one or the other mode of ratification may be proposed by the general convention." McPherson, History of the Rebellion, p. 99.

[3] App., No. 1364.

[4] App., Nos. 852, 861, 874, 894, 909. A method provided in most of the State constitutions. In Delaware alone the people have no direct voice.

a two-thirds majority of the two Houses of Congress could not be secured to recommend his constitutional amendments to the States.[1] This proposition was warmly seconded by Douglas.[2]

Even if the people had expressed their indorsement of a certain proposition by an overwhelming majority, this would not legally have secured the amendment, but would have been, so to speak, a plebiscite on the question, and simply made known to Congress the temper of the people at large.[3] This undoubtedly would have great weight in influencing the action of Congress and the other constitutional bodies to which an amendment might be submitted for ratification.

Another form of the same desire to consult the people is seen in a proposed amendment to the fifteenth amendment, suggested in 1869 by Mr. Davis of Kentucky.[4] It provided that this and all future amendments should be submitted to the vote of the people of each State; a majority of the people entitled to vote in three-fourths of the several States should be necessary for its ratification.

In support of his resolution, Senator Davis asserted that "it was unseemly, not in accord with the principles and analogies of our system of government, and unsafe in practice to submit amendments either to legislatures or conventions," but the safest method, the one most in accord with the principles of our Government, "is to submit a proposition which can not be changed, nor modified nor altered, to the sovereign people themselves."[5] As it would plainly be unconstitutional to apply this method of ratification to the fifteenth amendment before Article V of the Constitution had been changed, this resolution failed to receive the support of the members of Mr. Davis's own party.

---

[1] Globe, p. 264.

[2] Globe, App., p. 38, et seq. See Rhodes, vol. III, pp. 254, 260, 265, with notes, who maintains that if the measure had been adopted, the Crittenden compromise "would have carried the Northern States by a great majority," and its results would have been "to impel a majority of the Republican Senators and Representatives to give it their support." The preamble of a similar resolution, submitted by Mr. Cochrane in the House (No. 874a), recited the same facts and declared whereas it is a cardinal principle of our representative system that the representatives shall obey the will of the people, it is deemed proper and necessary to ask the opinion and judgment of the people of the several States in the proposed amendments to the Constitution, etc.

[3] For the Swiss Referendum, see Hart's Federal Government, par. 189, to some extent adopted in some of the States. The legislature of California, in November, 1892, called for a popular vote on the question of choosing United States Senators by popular vote. The people voting in favor, the legislature passed resolutions favoring the "plan to be presented to Congress." Influence of State action here seen. See Bryce, I, chap. 39. E. P. Oberholtzer, The Referendum in America. Also Bryce, I, p. 101, note 1.

[4] App., No. 1288.

[5] Globe, p. 674.

183. WHAT CONSTITUTES THE TWO-THIRDS MAJORITY REQUIRED BY ARTICLE V?

The question as to what constitutes the "two-thirds of both Houses," required by Article V for the recommendation of an amendment to the Constitution by Congress, was first raised at the time of the action of Congress submitting the twelfth amendment to the States. This amendment was passed by a two-thirds vote of the members of each House present, but not by a two-thirds majority of all the members of the Senate and House, respectively.[1] The Federalists therefore claimed that the constitutional majority had not been obtained. In reply to this the friends of the amendment appealed to precedent, showing that some of the most important of the first ten amendments had been passed by a two-thirds vote of the members of the House present.[2] This failed to silence the Federalists, and the legislatures of the three Federal States of Massachusetts, Connecticut, and Delaware, in their resolutions rejecting the amendment, reiterated the charge of unconstitutionality. The question does not seem to have been raised again until 1861, when it came up in connection with the vote of the Senate on the so-called "Corwin amendment."[3] It was held by the Chair that two-thirds of those present was the constitutional requirement, and in this opinion he was sustained by the Senate. This ruling does not seem to have been questioned since.[4]

184. IS THE SIGNATURE OF THE PRESIDENT ESSENTIAL TO CONSTITUTIONAL AMENDMENTS?

This question was first raised in the case of Hollingsworth v. The State of Virginia,[5] in which case the validity of the eleventh amendment was called in question, in that it appeared that the "amendment was never submitted to the President for his approbation." The court, however, unanimously held that the amendment had been constitutionally adopted, and Mr. Justice Chase, in his opinion, declared that the President "has nothing to do with the proposition or adoption of amendments to the Constitution." The question, however, has since been several times the subject of discussion in Congress. The

---

[1] See ante, par. 38.

[2] Randolph's speech. Annals of Congress, Eighth Congress, first session, pp. 632-633. See Journal of the House of Representatives for August 21, 1789, and Journal of Senate, September 9, 1789.

[3] App., No. 931. For similar ruling in connection with the passage of bills over the veto, see Mason's Veto Power, p. 119.

[4] See speech by Mr. Ashley, January 6, 1865, Globe, p. 136.

[5] 3 Dallas, 378.

first time, in 1803, when the amendment in regard to the election of President and Vice-President, which later became the twelfth amendment, was under consideration. A motion in the Senate to submit the amendment to the President for approval was rejected by the decisive vote of 7 to 23.[1] In 1861 President Buchanan signed the proposed amendment prohibiting Congress from interfering with slavery in the States. This act failed to call out any protest or objection.

When the thirteenth amendment had been passed by Congress, it was inadvertently submitted to the President and he signed it and notified Congress to that effect.[2] The Senate, on the motion of Senator Trumbull, immediately passed a resolution "that such approval was unnecessary to give effect to the action of Congress in proposing said amendment, * * * and shall not constitute a precedent for the future." This opinion of the Senate coincides with the decision of the court, and was in harmony with the practice in the case of all the amendments proposed—with the single exceptions noted—and is based on sound common sense.[3] President Johnson acted in accordance with this view in 1866 in the case of the fourteenth amendment. In a message to Congress, he informed that body that in submitting the amendment to the States for ratification, his action, and that of the Secretary of State, were "purely ministerial and in no sense whatever committing the Executive to an approval or a recommendation of the amendment to the State legislatures or to the people."[4]

John Quincy Adams even questioned the propriety of the President recommending amendments to Congress, inasmuch as the Constitution gives him no share in framing them. In 1817, when Secretary of State, he opposed President Monroe's intention to propose an amendment on internal improvements partially because of this reason.[5] Later, while President, he refused to recommend an amendment in regard to the election of President for similar reasons.[6] The majority of the Presidents, both before and since, have not shared his scruples.

[1] App., No. 358.

[2] Cong. Globe, Thirty-eighth Congress, second session, p. 588.

[3] See discussion of this in Jameson, Constitutional Convention, pars. 559-560; Mason, Veto Power, par. 106.

[4] Message of June 22, 1866. In this message he alluded to "the fact that the joint resolution was not submitted by the two Houses to the approval of the President, and that of the thirty-six States which constitute the Union, eleven are excluded from representation in either House of Congress." He waived the question of "its constitutional validity," as well as of "the merits of the article." Wilson, Slave Power, III, p. 659.

[5] Memoirs, IV, pp. 463-464.

[6] Ibid., VII, p. 302.

185. IS THE SIGNATURE OF THE GOVERNOR ESSENTIAL TO AN AMEND-
MENT TO THE FEDERAL CONSTITUTION APPROVED BY THE LEGISLA-
TURE OF THE STATE?

There has been a great lack of uniformity in the actual practice by the governors of the States in this respect. This lack
of uniformity can be observed in the action of the States upon
the various amendments submitted to them. In the case of
the thirteenth amendment, for example, the act of ratification
of the legislature of Massachusetts was approved by the governor, while the signature of the governor of Pennsylvania does
not appear upon the certified copy of the similar act of the
legislature of that State, although the executives of both States
possessed the veto power.[1]

That this question might become an important one, is shown
by the action of the governor of New Hampshire in vetoing the
resolutions of the legislature of that State ratifying the twelfth
amendment.[2] As the vote of the State was not needed to make
up the three-fourths vote required for the ratification of the
amendment, the question does not seem to have come up for judicial determination. It is believed that the framers of the Constitution did not anticipate that the chief executives of the States
would participate with the legislative bodies in the approval or
disapproval of amendments submitted, for at the time the Constitution was framed but one of the States conferred upon the
governor the veto power.[3] Moreover, the language of the Constitution is that the amendment shall be valid "when ratified
by the legislatures of three-fourths of the States." Although
at the present time in all but four of the States[4] the governor
possesses the veto power, and to that extent is a part of the
lawmaking power, is it not well to bear in mind that the language of the Federal Constitution is not that amendments shall
be valid "when ratified by the lawmaking power of three-
fourths of the States." Governor Bramlette of Kentucky
seems to have adopted the view that his duties were merely
ministerial, at the time the resolutions of the legislature of
that State rejecting the thirteenth amendment were presented
to him for approval. Although he regretted the action of the

---

[1] Bulletin of the Bureau of Rolls and Library of the Department of State, No. 7, pp. 538,
547. The same lack of uniformity appears also in the case of resolutions passed by the
legislatures of the States, proposing amendments to the Federal Constitution. In some
cases they are signed by the governor of the State; in others he simply transmits them
as requested by the legislature.

[2] McMaster, History of the United States, III, p. 787.

[3] Massachusetts. See Mason's Veto Power, par. 8.

[4] Rhode Island, Ohio, Delaware, and North Carolina.

legislature, he declined to return the resolutions with his dissent "on the ground that the action of the legislature was complete without his approval."[1]

Is not the legislature, when passing upon an amendment to the Federal Constitution, acting in the capacity of a convention rather than exercising its ordinary legislative powers? If this be true, why should the governor have anything more than a ministerial function to perform? The most reasonable view would seem to be that the signature of the chief executive of a State is no more essential to complete the action of the legislature upon an amendment to the Federal Constitution than is that of the President of the United States to complete the action of Congress in proposing such an amendment.

186. WHAT CONSTITUTES THREE-FOURTHS OF THE STATES?

This question first seriously arose at the time the proposition which afterwards was adopted as the thirteenth amendment was before Congress.[2] At that time several of the States being in rebellion against the Government they were without representation in Congress. It was held by some that such States should not be counted as included in the Union.[3] Thus we find amendments presented with the following enacting clause: "Be it resolved * * * that upon the ratification of this amendment by three-fourths of the States represented in Congress it shall become valid to all intents and purposes as part of the Constitution."[4]

The question was undecided when the thirteenth amendment was sent to the States. When the legislatures of twenty-seven States had ratified this amendment, which was exactly three-fourths of all the States in the Union, the Secretary of State issued a proclamation declaring it a part of the Constitution.[5] Of these States, however, several had been in rebellion

---

[1] Jameson, p. 630. For discussion of the question whether the signature of the governor is necessary in amending a State constitution, see ibid., pars. 552, 561, 562. In such cases, in general, the governor does not have any opportunity to pass upon the actual amendment, but in some States the resolution of the legislature proposing an amendment for popular approval comes before him for his approval. Black, Const. Law, p. 47.

[2] In the case of the eleventh amendment, it was for some time uncertain whether Tennessee should be counted, but it was finally found that twelve States had ratified before Tennessee had been admitted, and hence adopted by the action of twelve States. App., No. 321.

[3] See speech of Ashley, January 6, 1865, on the thirteenth amendment, Congressional Globe, p. 140; Scofield's speech, January 11, ibid., p. 141; Sumner's resolution of February 4, 1865, Congressional Globe, p. 588.

[4] App., No. 1196 (in 1867).

[5] December 18, 1865. See list of States ratifying, App., No. 985.

and had not been readmitted to representation in Congress; in fact, it was not until three years later that the majority of them were restored to the full enjoyment of this right. "The question as to whether they could give valid assent to an amendment to the Constitution was one which might possibly be raised." "If they could not participate in the enactment of statute law, how could they participate in the far weightier duty of framing the organic law of the Republic?"[1] In the case of the fourteenth and fifteenth amendments, the requisite majority was secured through the policy pursued by Congress of requiring from the States late in rebellion, as one of the conditions precedent to their recognition and the admission of their representatives in the Federal Legislature, the ratification of one, and in most instances of both, of these amendments. By this expedient the authoritative settlement of this question was rendered unnecessary.[2]   Bancroft Library

187. CAN A STATE RECONSIDER ITS ACTION UPON A CONSTITUTIONAL AMENDMENT?

Three States, after giving their consent to the fourteenth amendment,[3] and one after similar action upon the fifteenth amendment,[4] declared through resolutions passed by their legislatures that they withdrew their consent. In all but one of these instances this action was taken before the amendment had been ratified by three-fourths of the legislatures of the several States, and it was contended that such action could be taken previous to the incorporation of the amendment into the Constitution. The Secretary of State, in canvassing the votes upon the fourteenth amendment,[5] being in doubt how such cases should be regarded, issued a certificate reciting the facts and declaring the adoption of the amendment in case the ratification of the two States which had attempted to recall their consent was still to be considered valid.[6] Congress immediately passed a concurrent resolution declaring the ratification of the amendment valid and sufficient,[7] and on the

---

[1] Blaine, I, p. 540; II, pp. 112, 113.   Foster, Com. on Const., I, p. 227.   The thirteenth amendment "never obtained the requisite ratification," "unless the validity of this action by the governments of the former insurgent States, organized by Lincoln and Johnson, is recognized."

[2] Cooley, Constitutional Law, pp. 210-211.

[3] New Jersey, Ohio, and Oregon, but the latter withdrew her consent after the adoption of the amendment. See App., Nos. 1135-1140.

[4] New York. App., No. 1284.

[5] Acting under the law of April 20, 1818, U. S. Stat. L., III, p. 439.

[6] July 20, 1868. U. S. Stat. L., XV, p. 706.

[7] July 21, 1868. U. S. Stat. L., XV, p. 708.

28th of July, 1868, the Secretary of State issued a second proclamation declaring the amendment to be a part of the Constitution.[1]

On the other hand, in the case of the thirteenth amendment, one State, which had previously rejected the amendment, reconsidered its action.[2] Four similar cases occurred in connection with the fourteenth amendment,[3] and two with the fifteenth amendment,[4] some even subsequent to the proclamation declaring the adoption of the respective amendments. All these States, where the action had been taken previous to the issuing of such proclamation, were included by the Secretary of State in the list of States ratifying.

From the above it would seem that practice has decided that a State having once given its consent the question is closed and it can not recall its action, but, on the other hand, that a State that has rejected an amendment can reconsider its action at any time previous to the incorporation of the amendment into the Constitution.[5]

188. THE DIFFICULTIES OF AMENDMENT.

In summarizing the results of the attempts to amend the Constitution during the first century of its history, we find that besides the fifteen amendments now a part of the organic law,[6] only four have been proposed by Congress to the States for ratification.[7] Two of these, one on the apportionment of Representatives,[8] the other on titles of nobility,[9] failed of adoption by only one ratification. In addition, nine have passed the Senate[10] and nine the House of Representatives.[11]

The failure to secure amendments in the past does not seem to prevent the frequent introduction of new proposals to change the Constitution. In the Forty-ninth Congress there were no

---

[1] Ibid.

[2] New Jersey.

[3] North Carolina, South Carolina, Georgia, and Virginia.

[4] Ohio, New Jersey. Pennsylvania reconsidered its action refusing to ratify the amendment in regard to the apportionment of Representatives, the first of the twelve submitted by Congress in 1789. Her first action was taken March 10, 1790. Senate Journal, First Congress, second session, p. 39. Her action in ratification of this amendment October 26, 1791. Senate Journal, Second Congress, first session, p. 11. See App., No. 295.

[5] For full discussion, see Jameson, Constitutional Convention, paras. 576–584; also, Cooley, Constitutional Law, pp. 211, 212, with notes.

[6] These constitute but four groups in point of time and purpose.

[7] App., Nos. 243, 295, 399, 931.

[8] App., No. 295, ante, par. 22.

[9] App., No. 399, ante, par. 99.

[10] App., Nos. 409, 485–486, 489–490, 505–506, 535, 545, 1308, 1676, 1691.

[11] App., Nos. 228, 230, 345, 359, 1055, 1079, 1250, 1401, 1477.

less than fifty-four resolutions, and in the Fiftieth Congress forty-eight, to amend the Constitution.[1]

In the light of the history of the different movements to secure amendments, we cannot believe that the expectation of the framers of the Constitution has been fulfilled.[2] Nothing of strength has been added to the Constitution by amendment except in the case of the "reconstruction amendments," and these were carried only after a civil war.[3]

Why, it may be asked, have so few of the more than eighteen hundred propositions looking to the amendment of our fundamental law been successful? In part because some were suggested as cures for temporary evils, others were trivial or impracticable, still others found a place in that unwritten constitution which has grown up side by side with the written document, and whose provisions are often as effective as those contained in the organic law;[4] but the real reason for the failure of those other amendments which have been called for repeatedly by the general public has been due to the insurmountable constitutional obstacles in their way.[5] "It would

---

[1] In the Fifty-second Congress even more—64 in the first session and 9 in the second session; 73 in all.

[2] Speech of Iredell in North Carolina convention, July 29, 1788: "The constitution of any government which can not be regularly amended when its defects are experienced reduces the people to this dilemma: They must either submit to its oppression or bring about amendments more or less by a civil war. The Constitution before us can be altered with as much regularity and as little confusion as any act of assembly—not, indeed, quite so easy, which would be extremely impolitic, but it is a most happy circumstance that there is a remedy in the system itself for its own fallibility, so that alterations can without difficulty be made, agreeable to the general sense of the people." Elliot, iv, pp. 176, 177. The experience of the first few years confirmed this view. In an article in the American Register for 1809, p. 8, discussing the question of amendments, is the following: "There is little doubt that in the lapse of a few generations the Constitution of the United States will undergo a total but gradual change."

[3] "The sovereign of the United States has been roused to action but once during the course of ninety years. It needed the thunders of the civil war to break his repose, and it may be doubted whether anything short of impending revolution will ever again arouse him to activity. But a monarch who slumbers for years is like a monarch who does not exist. A federal constitution is capable of change, but for all that a federal constitution is apt to be unchangeable." Dicey, Law of the Constitution (4th ed.), p. 140.

[4] Such changes must be sought in the statutes, in the decision of the courts, and in the customs and practices of the several departments of the Government. See article by Prof. McMaster in Shaler's United States, ii, p. 500. "It is almost incorrect to say that throughout this period ' (1804-1865, during which the Constitution was not altered in either word or syllable) "the Constitution was unamended, for it was so expanded by the decisions of Marshall that they amounted to virtual amendments to its text." Report of a committee of the New York State Bar Association, 1890. Reports of the New York Bar Association, Vol. xiii, p. 140.

[5] "When we consider that these legislatures in turn act through two separate assemblies, each at all times suitably impressed with its own importance and independence, and generally jealous and suspicious of dictation from the Federal Government, we realize the difficulty of securing the coincidence of so many assemblies and so many minds on a

seem," as a well-known American writer has truly said, "that no impulse short of the impulse of self-preservation, no force less than the force of revolution, can nowadays be expected to move the cumberous machinery in Article v."[1]

When we contrast this paucity of amendments with the frequency of constitutional revision and change in the States, it is the more striking.[2] Only one of the original States lives under its first constitution, namely, Massachusetts, and that instrument has been amended far more than the Federal document. It is doubtless true that this tendency to change has been in some instances carried too far, and that the constitutions of some of our States enter so much into detail that their provisions partake more of the nature of the statutory than the fundamental law.[3] Still many salutary changes have been effected, and these constitutions are, in consequence, much better adapted to meet the needs of the present age. The fact that the modern State constitutions have entered so largely into technique and detail render them less likely to be permanent and increases the necessity of amendment. This being true, one of the demands of the time is for greater facility in procuring amendments.[4]

Fortunately, the Federal Constitution, owing to the fact that it deals only with the most general elements of government, has proved so elastic as to adapt itself to new contingencies and circumstances, and thus the necessity of amendment has been reduced to a minimum.[5] There still remain, however, certain desirable reforms, rendered apparent by more than a

---

single proposition in the exact form proposed." Ibid., p. 138. "Only five times in a century of constitutional government has the Constitution been changed, an immunity which must be attributed not only to its original completeness, but to the conservative spirit of the national and State legislatures and the intrinsic difficulties attending the process." Ibid., p. 141.

[1] Woodrow Wilson, Congressional Government, pp. 242-243.

[2] The total number of distinct constitutions, either newly adopted or completely revised in the one hundred and ten years subsequent to the Declaration of Independence was 104, and to these several constitutions 214 partial amendments have been adopted. The average life of a State constitution has been twenty-seven years. Hitchcock, American State Constitutions, pp. 13, 14. Davis, American Constitutions, pp. 475, 476. See also Bryce for later figures, 113 constitutions and 240 partial amendments. Vol. I, pp. 457, 458. See also ibid., chaps. 38, 39. Up to 1897 the number of partial amendments is 300.

[3] Reasons for this, see Bryce, I, pp. 458-462, 490-493. Hitchcock, pp. 34-47.

[4] Jameson, J. F. An Introduction to the Study of the Constitution and Political History of the States, p. 14.

[5] "If there is any one thing to which we owe the permanency of our government, it is this, that so little is settled dogmatically; that so much is left for experiment." McMaster in Shaler's, United States, II, p. 500.

century's experience and the changed conditions of our people and age. Although constructive statesmanship did not end with the adoption of the Constitution, as some would have us believe,[1] and although there exists to-day more wisdom and capacity in matters pertaining to the science of government than at the time the Constitution was formed, still it has proved to be impossible to secure these reforms because they can be effected only by a formal amendment.[2]

Nearly all Americans will agree that a rigid constitution has its excellencies,[3] but is there not a limit to the degree of rigidity desirable? Did not the framers of our Federal Constitution, while seeking "to avoid the dangers attending a too frequent change of their fundamental code," advert "to an opposite danger to be equally shunned—that of making amendments too difficult?"[4] Has not the mode provided proved to be of

---

[1] At no time in the century have there failed to be present in Congress members who, out of regard for the memory of the "fathers," "look at the Constitutions," as Jefferson said, "with sanctimonious reverence and deem them like the ark of the covenant, too sacred to be touched." Two examples will suffice: Speech of Mr. Purviance of North Carolina, December 7, 1803; Annals, pp. 692, 693. He opposed "any innovation on the sacred charter, because when we shall have once begun to make incursions on it, there is no knowing at what point of progress we shall stop. * * * As for myself, while one fragment of this sacred charter remains, I will hug it to my heart and cherish it as I would the vital juices of my existence. I believe that it is now absolutely perfect; if it be once invaded the work of destruction will not be arrested until the happiness and liberties of our country are destroyed." Mr. English of New Jersey, in a speech January 10, 1893, said: "I object to all and any of this tinkering with the Constitution; the horror that is in my nature at any profane touch upon the Constitution" etc. * * * "Let us pause before we further amend the Constitution and lay profane hands upon it, to reflect whether or not we are setting a precedent which may be evil or bring evils upon the Republic. Let the Constitution stand. * * * Go no further if you value that inheritance which your fathers gave you and which their sons are bound to defend and support." Record, Fifty-second Congress, second session, p. 491. Such persons should read Jefferson's comment, (Works, VII, pp. 14, 15), and also Jackson's message, where he says, "Evils which can be clearly traced to an organic defect in the Constitution ought not to be overlooked through a too scrupulous veneration of the work of our ancestors." Senate Journal, Twenty-first Congress, second session, pp. 21–22.

[2] Changes which could be effected by interpretation it has been possible to secure, but any change affecting any provision in regard to the form of the government it has been impossible to secure, as for example, the abolition of the Electoral College, the popular election of Senators, the lengthening the term of Representatives, conferring upon the President power to veto items in appropriation bills, etc.

[3] Cooley, Constitutional Law, pp. 21, 22.

[4] Jameson, Constitutional Convention, p. 549. "Provisions regulating the time and mode of effecting organic changes are in the nature of safety valves, they must not be so adjusted as to discharge their peculiar function with too great facility, lest they become the ordinary escape pipes of party passion; nor, on the other hand, must they discharge it with such difficulty that the force needed to induce action is sufficient to explode the machine. Hence the problem of the constitution maker is, in this particular, one of the most difficult in our whole system, to reconcile the requisites for progress with the requisites for safety." Ibid.

such a character that in some instances "discovered faults" have been perpetuated?[1] While continuing to follow the wise injunction of the "Father of the Country" "to resist with care the spirit of innovation upon the principles of the Constitution," may we not do well to make such constitutional modifications as "experience"—"the surest standard by which to test the real tendency of existing constitutions"—has shown desirable?[2] Certainly the facts plainly show that the cause of the difficulty is, to use the words of Chief Justice Marshall, that the machinery of procuring an amendment is "unwieldy and cumbrous."[3] The majorities required are too large.[4] Under the present system, according to the population given in the census of 1890, it was possible for eleven States with a population of less than 2,350,000 to defeat any constitutional amendment although it was desired by the more than 60,000,000 inhabitants of the other States.[5]

"When in a democratic political society," says Professor Burgess, "the well matured, long and deliberately formed will of the undoubted majority can be persistently and successfully thwarted, in the amendment of its organic law, by the will of the minority, there is just as much danger to the State from revolution and violence as there is from the caprice of the majority, where the sovereignty of the bare majority is acknowledged."[6]

---

[1] See the Federalist, No. 43, Hamilton's ed., p. 346; Story, Constitutional Law, II, par. 1828.

[2] Washington's Farewell Address, Sparks, Writings of Washington, XII, pp. 223, 224.

[3] Baron v. Baltimore, 7 Peters, 761.

[4] Patrick Henry anticipated this and advanced it in the Virginia convention as one of his reasons for opposing the ratification of the Constitution. Elliot's Deb., III, pp. 48-50.

[5] The eleven States of Delaware, Rhode Island, Vermont, Oregon, Nevada, North Dakota, South Dakota, Montana, Washington, Idaho, and Wyoming, with a total population of 2,344,115, or 3.7 per cent of the total population of the United States (1890). The figures are equally striking if the vote instead of the population is taken. The minority report of the House Committee on Election of President and Vice-President in 1878 showed that on the basis of the figures of the election of 1876 the legislatures elected by 282,230 voters could successfully resist a constitutional amendment desired by 8.123,559 voters, or more than 96 per cent. House Reports, Forty-fifth Congress, second session, IV, No. 819, p. 18. See also Burgess, Political Science and Constitutional Law, I, pp. 150-154.

[6] Burgess, I, p. 152.

ADDENDA.

Since the pages upon the legislative department were sent to press six additional resolutions of State legislatures proposing amendments to the Federal Constitution have been found.

Add to page 66, note 7: The legislatures of Georgia and Pennsylvania passed resolutions concurring with the resolutions of the legislature of Tennessee changing the term of Senators to four years. App. Nos. 419a, 419b. Ten States passed resolutions of nonconcurrence. See also App. No. 419.

Add to page 35, note 1: The legislatures of Kentucky and Georgia in 1817 also passed resolutions proposing an amendment to prohibit Congress from passing any bill changing the compensation of Members which should take effect during the life of the existing Congress. App. Nos. 461a, 467a. For resolutions of nonconcurrence from four States, see App. No. 461a.

Add to page 57, notes 2 and 3: The legislature of Vermont in 1818 and the general assembly of Illinois in 1821 passed resolutions recommending an amendment providing for the election of Representatives and Presidential electors by districts. App. Nos. 480a, 480b, 506b, 506c.

H. Doc. 353, pt. 2——20

The endeavor has been made to make this list of proposed amendments as complete as possible, and it is believed that all the most important resolutions have been included, but owing to the poor indexing of the early volumes of the journals and debates, it is probable that some propositions have been overlooked. Amendments recommended by State legislatures have been found in several cases not recorded in the journals. It is likely that there are other such cases. The system of numbering employed does not always indicate a separate resolution, for often one resolution relates to several different subjects, hence it has been found convenient to separate an amendment into its distinct subjects, and number accordingly. Since this calendar was first compiled several additional propositions, as well as the text of other proposed amendments, not given in the official records of Congress, have been found through the examination of the original printed resolutions on file in the Senate document room at Washington. Likewise various resolutions from the legislatures of different States have been found in the Massachusetts Archives in the Statehouse, Boston, and also recorded in the journals of the senate and house of representatives of the Commonwealth of Pennsylvania for the earlier years of the century. Without changing the original numbers, these have been inserted in their proper chronological order, by making use of alphabetical suffixes, as 319*a*, 971*b*, etc.

In cases where the text of the proposed amendment is not given in the journals or Record, the files of the original printed resolutions, covering the last thirty-five years of the period, may be consulted in the Senate document room.

EXPLANATION OF SIGNS.

A single star (*) placed before the number of an amendment indicates that the resolution passed one House of Congress.

A double star (**), both Houses of Congress, and a triple star (***), that the amendment was ratified by the States. A number in a bracket following the number of an amendment signifies that the resolution was proposed as an amendment or a substitute to the resolution the number of which is in the brackets. The sign (°) before a page number indicates that on that page will be found the text of the proposed amendment.

EXPLANATION OF ABBREVIATIONS.

The letters S. J. and H. J. refer to the Senate and House journals, respectively. Annals, to the Annals of Congress; Globe, to the Congressional Globe; Com. indicates committee; H. R. and S. R. indicate House resolutions and Senate resolutions.

In references to the journals and debates, etc., sess. stands for session, and Cong. for Congress.

CALENDAR OF AMENDMENTS.

1. 1. Division: Reservation of nondelegated powers.
2. 2. Legislative: Apportionment of Representatives.
3. 3. Legislative: Restriction on Federal control over election of Senators and Representatives.
4. 4. Finance: Restriction upon the levying of direct taxes.
5. 5. Commerce: Commercial monopolies prohibited.
6. 6. Personal Relations: Indictment by grand jury.
7. 7. Judiciary: Jurisdiction of Federal courts.
8. 8. Personal Relations: Trial by jury in civil action.
9. 9. Personal Relations: Titles of nobility.
   1788, Feb. 6. Proposed by the Massachusetts convention at the time of the ratification of the Constitution. Elliot's Debates, 1, pp. °322–324.
10. 1. Legislative: Restriction on Federal control over election of Senators and Representatives.
11. 2. Division: Reservation of nondelegated powers.
12. 3. Finance: Restriction upon the levying of direct taxes.
13. 4. Personal Relations: Oath.
    1788, May 23. Proposed by the South Carolina convention at the time of the ratification of the Constitution. Elliot's Debates, 1, p. °325.
14. 1. Division: Reservation of nondelegated powers.
15. 2. Legislative: Apportionment of Representatives.
16. 3. Legislative: Restriction on Federal control over election of Senators and Representatives.
17. 4. Finance: Restriction upon the levying of direct taxes.
18. 5. Commerce: Commercial monopolies prohibited.
19. 6. Personal Relations: Indictment by grand jury.
20. 7. Judiciary: Jurisdiction of Federal courts.
21. 8. Personal Relations: Trial by jury in civil cases.
22. 9. Personal Relations: Titles of nobility.

23. 10. War: Standing army in time of peace.
24. 11. Personal Relations: Religion.
25. 12. Personal Relations: Right to bear arms.

> 1788, June 21. Proposed by the New Hampshire convention at the time of the ratification of the Constitution. Elliot's Debates, 1, pp. °325-326.

26. 1. Division: Reservation of nondelegated powers.
27. 2. Legislative: Apportionment of Representatives.
28. 3. Finance: Restriction upon the levying of direct taxes.
29. 4. Legislative: Senators and Representatives ineligible to civil office during term.
30. 5. Legislative: Publication of journals annually.
31. 6. Finance: Publication of Treasury accounts.
32. 7. Foreign affairs: Ratification of treaties.
33. 8. Commercial: Restriction in passage of navigation laws.
34. 9. War: Standing army in time of peace.
35. 10. War: Period of enlistment of soldiers limited.
36. 11. War: Regulation of the militia.
37. 12. Territorial: Restriction on the powers of Congress over the Federal town.
38. 13. Executive: Limitation upon eligibility of President.
39. 14. Judiciary: Jurisdiction of Federal courts.
40. 15. Personal Relations: Rights of defendant in criminal trials.
41. 16. Legislative: Restriction on Federal control over the election of Senators and Representatives.
42. 17. Personal Relations: Rights reserved.
43. 18. Legislative: To regulate the alteration of the compensation of Senators and Representatives.
44. 19. Legislative: Court for the trial of impeachment of Senators.
45. 20. Judiciary: Regulate the alteration of the salary of judges.

> 1788, June 25. Proposed by the Virginia convention, together with a bill of rights, at the time of the ratification of the Constitution. Elliot's Debates, III, pp. 659-661.

46. 1. Legislative: Apportionment of Representatives.
47. 2. Financial: Excise tax prohibited.
48. 3. Financial: Restriction upon the levying of direct taxes.
49. 4. Legislative: Restriction upon the Federal control over the election of Senators and Representatives.
50. 5. Personal Relations: Restrictions upon naturalization of citizens.
51. 6. Commerce: Commercial monopolies prohibited.
52. 7. War: Standing army in time of peace.
53. 8. Financial: Regulate the borrowing of money on United States credit.
54. 9. War: Restriction on the declaration of war.
55. 10. Personal Relations: Restricting the suspension of habeas corpus.
56. 11. Territorial: Restricting the power of Congress over the Federal town.
57. 12. Territorial: Power of Congress over other Federal territory.
58. 13. Legislative: Regulate the alteration of the compensation of Senators and Representatives.
59. 14. Legislative: Publication of Journals: Open session: Yeas and nays.

60. 15. Financial: Capitation tax prohibited.
61. 16. Legislative: Term of eligibility of Senators: Recall of Senators.
62. 17. Legislative: Senators and Representatives ineligible to civil office during term.
63. 18. Legislative: Filling vacancies of Senators.
64. 19. Commerce: Application of Federal bankruptcy law restricted.
65. 20. Executive: No third term.
66. 21. Executive: Power to grant pardon for treason prohibited.
67. 22. Executive: Restricting the President from commanding the Army in the field in person.
68. 23. Judiciary: Writs, process, etc., in the name of, etc.
69. 24. Judiciary: Jurisdiction of the Federal courts.
70. 25. Judiciary: Courts for trial of impeachments.
71. 26. Judiciary: Commission to revise judgment of Supreme Court.
72. 27. Judiciary: Judges of Supreme Court ineligible to other offices.
73. 28. Judiciary: Restriction over cases involving land controversies.
74. 29. War: Restriction on period of service of militia without the State.
75. 30. Personal Relations: Titles of nobility.
76. 31. Legislative, Executive, Judiciary: Oath.
77. 32. Executive: Choice: To permit the choice of an elector in districts by inhabitant of the district for one year.

> 1788, July 26. Proposed by the New York convention, together with a bill of rights, at the time of the ratification of the Constitution. Elliot's Debates, 1. pp. 329-331.

78. 1. Division: Reservation of nondelegated powers.
79. 2. Legislative: Apportionment of Representatives.
80. 3. Financial: Restriction in the levying of direct taxes.
81. 4. Legislative: Senators and Representatives ineligible to civil office during term.
82. 5. Legislative: Publication of journals.
83. 6. Financial: Publication of Treasury accounts.
84. 7. Foreign Affairs: Ratification of treaties.
85. 8. Commercial: Restriction in passage of navigation laws.
86. 9. War: Standing army in time of peace.
87. 10. War: Term of enlistment of soldiers limited.
88. 11. War: Regulation of militia.
89. 12. War: Restriction on Congress declaring a State in rebellion.
90. 13. Legislative: Restriction on the powers of Congress over the Federal town.
91. 14. Executive: Limitation upon the eligibility of President.
92. 15. Judiciary: Jurisdiction of Federal courts.
93. 16. Personal Relations: Rights of defendant in criminal trial.
94. 17. Legislative: Restriction on Federal control of election of Senators and Representatives.
95. 18. Personal Relations: Rights reserved.
96. 19. Legislative: Regulate the alteration of the compensation of Senators and Representatives.
97. 20. Legislative: Tribunal for trial of impeachment of Senators.
98. 21. Judiciary: Regulate the alteration of salary of judges.

99. 22. Commercial: Commercial monopolies prohibited.

100. 23. Foreign Affairs: Treaties opposed to laws of the United States not valid.

101. 24. Commercial: Regulation of commerce and navigation laws.

102. 25. Financial: Congress restricted from interfering with the redemption of a State's paper money, etc.

103. 26. War: Restriction upon the introduction of foreign troops into the United States.

> 1788, Aug. 2. Proposed by the first constitutional convention of North Carolina as necessary for their ratification of the Constitution, together with a bill of rights. Elliot's Debates, IV, pp. °244-247.

104. 1. Division: Reservation of nondelegated powers.

105. 2. Legislative: Restriction on Federal control of election of Sentors and Representatives.

106. 3. Judiciary: Jurisdiction of Federal courts.

107. 4. Amendment: After 1793, 11 of the original 13 States required for the ratification of an amendment.

108. 5. Judiciary: Extent of jurisdiction.

109. 6. Personal Relations: Military duty.

110. 7. Financial: Capitation tax prohibited.

111. 8. Financial: Restriction in levying of direct taxes.

112. 9. Financial: Consent of three-fourths of State legislature necessary for a direct tax.

113. 10. Legislative: Publication of the journals.

114. 11. Financial: Publication of Treasury accounts.

115. 12. War: Standing army in time of peace.

116. 13. Financial: Regulation on the borrowing of money on United States credit.

117. 14. War: Restricting the declaration of war.

118. 15. Personal Relations: Titles of nobility.

119. 16. Judiciary: Judges of Supreme Court ineligible to office and Federal officers incapable of holding State offices.

120. 17. Commercial: Abolition of the slave trade.

121. 18. Legislative: Recall of Senators.

122. 19. Police Power: Authorizing Congress to establish a rule for the settlement of the poor throughout the United States.

123. 20. Commercial: Commercial monopolies prohibited.

124. 21. Legislative: Yeas and nays.

> 1790, May 29. Proposed by the Rhode Island convention at the time of their ratification of the Constitution. Elliot's Debates, I, pp. °336-337.

125. Amendment: Convention to amend the Constitution.

> 1789, May 6. 1st Cong., 1st sess. Mr. Bland of Virginia, in the House, presented an application from the legislature of Virginia, bearing the date of Nov. 14, 1788, for a convention to amend the Constitution. Ordered entered in the journals and carefully preserved. H. J., pp. °34-35 (reprint, pp. °28-29).

126. Amendment: Convention to amend the Constitution.

> 1789, May 6. 1st Cong., 1st sess. Mr. Lawrence of New York, in the House, presented an application from the legislature of New York, bearing the date of Feb. 5, 1789, for a convention to amend the Constitution. Ordered entered on the journals and carefully preserved. H. J., p. °36 (reprint, pp. 29-30).

127. Preamble: Basis of powers.
128. Legislative: Apportionment of Representatives.
129. Legislative: Compensation of members.
130. Personal Relations: Freedom of religion and right of conscience.
131. Personal Relations: Freedom of speech and of press.
132. Personal Relations: Right to assemble and of petition.
133. Personal Relations: Right to keep and bear arms.
134. Personal Relations: Quartering of soldiers in time of peace.
135. Personal Relations: Trials for crime: Rights of property.
136. Personal Relations: Bail, fines, and punishment.
137. Personal Relations: Search and seizure.
138. Personal Relations: Rights of defendant in criminal cases.
139. Personal Relations: Reserved rights of the people.
140. Personal Relations: No State shall violate the rights of conscience:
     Freedom of the press: Trial by jury.
141. Personal Relations: Restriction in cases open to appeal.
142. Personal Relations: Trial in criminal cases by jury.
143. Personal Relations: Suits at common law trial by jury.
144. Distribution of Powers: To the departments.
145. Division of Powers: Nondelegated powers reserved to the States.
146. Ratification of the Constitution: Change number of art. 7 to art. 8.

> 1789, June 8. 1st Cong., 1st sess. By Mr. Madison of Virginia. In the House: referred to Com. of the Whole. Annals, I, pp. °433–436, 450. July 21. Com. of the Whole discharged and referred to a special com. Annals, pp. 660–665. July 28, com. report. Annals, p. 672.

147 [127]. Preamble: Derivation of powers from the people.

> 1789, Aug. 13. 1st Cong., 1st sess. Art. 1 of the report of the special com. considered in the House. Annals, p. 707. Aug. 14: passed by Com. of the Whole. Ibid., 719. Aug. 19: rejected by House. Ibid., p. 766.

148. Preamble: Amendment: Submitted to the States.

> 1789, Aug. 13. 1st Cong., 1st sess. Art. 1 of the special com. report considered. Mr. Sherman moved an amendment. Annals, p. 708. Aug. 19, Mr. Sherman's motion renewed, and passed. Ibid., p. 766.

149 [128]. Legislative: Apportionment of Representatives.

> 1789, Aug. 14. 1st Cong., 1st sess. Art. 1, sec. 2, par. 3, of com. report; considered. Annals, p. °719. Amended by Mr. Sedgwick. Ibid., p. 728.

150 [149]. Legislative: Apportionment of Representatives.

> 1789, Aug. 14. 1st Cong., 1st sess. By Mr. Vining of Delaware. To amend art. 1, sec. 2, par. 3, of com. report; negatived. Annals, p. °719.

151 [149]. Legislative: Apportionment of Representatives.

> 1789, Aug. 14. 1st Cong., 1st sess. By Mr. Ames of Massachusetts. To amend art. 1, sec. 2, par. 3, of com. report; negatived. Annals, pp. 720–725.

152 [149]. Legislative: Apportionment of Representatives.

> 1798, Aug. 14. By Mr. Sedgwick of Massachusetts, to amend art. 1, sec. 2, par. 3, of com. report; passed. Annals, pp. 725–728.

153 [149]. Legislative: Apportionment of Representatives.

> 1789, Aug. 14. By Mr. Ames of Massachusetts, to amend art. 1, sec. 2, par. 3 of com report; suggested. Annals, p. 728; Aug. 19, made motion. Ibid., 766. Aug. 20, several amendments proposed and tabled. Ibid., 766. Aug. 21, resolution of Mr. Ames passed in an amended form. Ibid., 731.

154 [129]. Legislative: Compensation of members.

> 1789, Aug. 14. Art. 1, sec. 6, of com. report passed. Annals, pp. °728, 729.

155 [130]. Personal Relations: Freedom of religion.

1780, Aug. 15. Art. 1, sec. 9, of report of special com. considered and amended. Annals, p. 729. Mr. Sherman moved to strike out the entire amendment. Ibid., p. 730.

156 [155]. Personal Relations: Freedom of religion.

1780, Aug. 15. By Mr. Livermore of New Hampshire, to amend art. 1, sec. 6, of com. report: passed. Annals, p. 731.

157 [155]. Personal Relations: Freedom of religion.

1780, Aug. 15. By Mr. Madison of Virginia, to amend art. 1, sec. 9, of special com. report: motion withdrawn. Annals, p. 731.

158 [131]. Personal Relations: Freedom of speech and of the press, etc.

1780, Aug. 15. Report of com. Fourth proposition, second clause, considered: passed. Annals, pp. 731, 747.

159 [158]. Personal Relations: Freedom of speech and of the press.

1780, Aug. 15. By Mr. Sedgwick of Massachusetts, to amend article of com. report: negatived. Annals, pp. 730, 731-747.

160 [133]. Personal Relations: Right to keep and bear arms.

1780, Aug. 17. Report of com. Fourth proposition, fourth clause, considered: passed. Annals, pp. 749-752.

161 [160]. Personal Relations: Right to keep and bear arms.

1789, Aug. 17. By Mr. Gerry of Massachusetts, to amend article of com. report: not seconded. Annals, p. 750.

162 [160]. Personal Relations: Right to keep and bear arms.

1780, Aug. 17. By Mr. Jackson of Georgia, to amend article of com. report: not seconded. Annals, p. 750.

163 [160]. Personal Relations: Right to keep and bear arms.

1780, Aug. 17. By Mr. Benson of New York, to amend article of com. report: negatived. Annals, p. 751.

164 [160]. Personal Relations: Right to keep and bear arms.

1780, Aug. 17. By Mr. Gerry of Massachusetts, to amend article of com. report: not seconded. Annals, p. 751.

165 [160]. Personal Relations: Standing army in time of peace.

1780, Aug. 17. By Mr. Burke of South Carolina, to amend article of com. report by adding a clause as above: negatived. Annals, p. 751.

166 [134]. Personal Relations: Quartering of troops.

1780, Aug. 17. Report of com. Fourth proposition, fourth clause, considered: passed. Annals, p. 752.

167 [166]. Personal Relations: Quartering of troops.

1780, Aug. 17. By Mr. Sumter of South Carolina, to amend article of com. report: negatived. Annals, p. 752.

168 [166]. Personal Relations: Quartering of troops.

1789, Aug. 17. By Mr. Gerry of Massachusetts, to amend article of com. report: negatived. Annals, p. 752.

169 [135] [136]. Personal Relations: Trial: Rights of defendant.

1780, Aug. 17. Report of com. Fourth proposition, fifth clause, considered: passed as amended by Mr. Lawrence. Annals, p. 753.

170 [169]. Personal Relations: Trial: Rights of defendant.

1780, Aug. 17. By Mr. Benson of New York, to amend article of com. report: negatived. Annals, p. 753.

171 [169]. Personal Relations: Trial: Rights of defendant.

1780, Aug. 17. By Mr. Partridge of Massachusetts, to amend article of com. report: negatived. Annals, p. 753.

172 [169]. Personal Relations: Trial: Rights of defendant.
　　1789, Aug. 17. By Mr. Lawrence of New York, to amend article of com. report; passed. Annals, p. 753.

173 [137]. Personal Relations: Freedom from search and seizure.
　　1789, Aug. 17. Report of com. Fourth proposition, seventh clause, considered; passed as amended by Mr. Gerry. Annals, p. 754.

174 [173]. Personal Relations: Freedom from search and seizure.
　　1789, Aug. 17. By Mr. Gerry of Massachusetts, to amend article of com. report: passed by Com. of the Whole. Annals. p. 754.

175 [173]. Personal Relations: Freedom from search and seizure: Warrants.
　　1789, Aug. 17. By Mr. Benson of New York. to amend article of com. report; negatived. Annals. p. 754.

176 [173]. Personal Relations: Freedom from search and seizure: Warrants.
　　1789. Aug. 17. By Mr. Benson of New York. to amend article of com. report: negatived. Annals, p. 754.

177 [139]. Personal Relations: Reserved rights of the people not disparaged.
　　1789, Aug. 17. Com. report. Fourth proposition. eighth clause passed. Annals, p. 754.

178 [139]. Personal Relations: Reserved rights of the people.
　　1789. Aug. 17. By Mr. Gerry of Massachusetts. to amend article of com. report: not seconded. Annals, p. 754.

179 [140]. Personal Relations: No State shall infringe the equal rights of conscience. Freedom of speech and of press, etc.
　　1789, Aug. 17. Report of special com. Fifth proposition, art. 1, sec. 10, considered, passed as amended by Mr. Livermore. Annals, p. 755.

180 [179]. Personal Relations: No State shall infringe the equal rights of conscience, freedom of speech and of press, etc.
　　1789, Aug. 17. By Mr. Livermore of New Hampshire. to amend fifth proposition: passed Com. of the Whole. Annals, p. 755.

181 [141]. Personal Relations: Trials: Appeal to the Supreme Court.
　　1789. Aug. 17. Report of com. Sixth proposition, art. 3, sec. 2, passed. Annals, p. 755. Mr. Benson moved to strike out first part: not seconded. Ibid., 755.

182 [181]. Personal Relations: Trials: Appeal to the Supreme Court.
　　1789, Aug. 17. By Mr. Sedgwick of Massachusetts, to amend article of com. report; negatived. Annals, p. 756.

183 [142]. Personal Relations: Rights of defendant in criminal trial.
　　1789, Aug. 17. Report of com. Seventh proposition. art.3, sec.2, passed as amended by Mr. Livermore. Annals, p. 756.

184 [183]. Personal Relations: Rights of defendant in criminal trial.
　　1789, Aug. 17. By Mr. Burke of South Carolina. to amend article of com. report: negatived. Annals. p. 756.

185 [183]. Personal Relations: Rights of defendant in criminal trial.
　　1789. Aug. 17. By Mr. Livermore of New Hampshire, to amend article of com. report: passed. Annals, p. 756.

186 [183]. Personal Relations: Rights of defendant in criminal trial.
　　1789. Aug. 17. By Mr. Burke of South Carolina, to amend the article of com. report; negatived. Annals, p. 760.

187 [1-124]. Amendments: Proposed by the States.

> 1789, Aug. 18. By Mr Gerry of Massachusetts, that such of the amendments to the Constitution proposed by the several States as are not in substance comprised in report of com be referred to Com. of the Whole; negatived (16 to 34). H. J., p. 102. Annals, p. 757.

188 [183]. Personal Relations: Rights of defendant in criminal trial.

> 1789, Aug. 18. Com. report. Seventh proposition, second clause, passed. Annals, pp. 759 760.

189 [183]. Personal Relations: Rights of defendant in criminal trial.

> 1789, Aug. 18. By Mr. Burke of South Carolina, to amend article of com. report; negatived. Annals, p. 760.

190 [145]. Division of Powers: Non delegated powers reserved.

> 1789, Aug. 18. Com. report. Ninth proposition, considered and passed, as amended by Mr. Carroll. Annals, p. 761.

191 [190]. Division of Powers: Non delegated powers reserved.

> 1789, Aug. 18. By Mr. Tucker of South Carolina, to amend article of com. report: negatived. Annals, p. 761.

192 [190]. Division of Powers: Non delegated powers reserved.

> 1789, Aug. 18. By Mr. Carroll of Maryland, to amend article of com. report: passed Com. of the Whole. Annals, p. 761.

193 [146]. Power of Amendment: Ratification of the Constitution.

> 1789, Aug. 18. Report of com. Tenth proposition, to change art. 7 to art. 8, passed Com. of the Whole. Annals, p. 761.

194. Legislative: Term of Representatives.

> 1789, Aug. 18. By Mr. Tucker of South Carolina, to add to art. 1, sec. 2, clause 2; referred to Com. of the Whole; negatived. H. J., p. °103. Annals, p. °761.

195. Legislative: Election and term of Senators.

> 1789, Aug. 18. By Mr. Tucker of South Carolina, to add to art. 1, sec. 2, clause 3; referred to Com. of the Whole: negatived. H. J., p. °103. Annals, p. °761.

196. Legislative: Time, place, and manner of election.

> 1789, Aug. 18. By Mr. Tucker of South Carolina, to amend art. 1, sec. 4, clause 1; referred to Com. of the Whole: negatived. H. J., p. °103. Annals, p. °761.

197. Legislative: State to judge of election of Senators and Representatives.

> 1789, Aug. 18. By Mr. Tucker of South Carolina, to amend art. 1, sec. 5, clause 1; motion to refer to Com. of the Whole negatived. H. J., p. °103. Annals, p. °761.

198. Legislative: Rules of proceedings of Congress.

> 1789, Aug. 18. By Mr. Tucker of South Carolina, to amend art. 1, sec. 5, clause 2; motion to refer to Com. of the Whole negatived. H. J., p. °103. Annals, p. °762.

199. Legislative: Exclude members of Congress from office.

> 1789, Aug. 18. By Mr. Tucker of South Carolina, to amend art. 1, sec. 6, clause 2; motion to refer to Com. of the Whole negatived. H. J., p. °103; Annals, p. °762.

200. Finance: Direct taxes.

> 1789, Aug. 18. By Mr. Tucker of South Carolina, to add to art. 1, sec. 8, clause 1; referred to Com. of the Whole; negatived. H. J., p °103; Annals. p. °762.

201. Judiciary: Courts of admiralty.

> 1789, Aug. 18. By Mr. Tucker of South Carolina, to amend art. 1, sec. 8, clause 9; referred to Com. of the Whole; negatived. H J., p. °104; Annals, p. °762.

202. Territorial: Legislation of Federal districts.

> 1789, Aug. 18. By Mr. Tucker of South Carolina, to add to art. 1, sec. 8, clause 17; referred to Com. of the Whole; negatived. H. J., p. °104; Annals, p. °702.

203. Personal Relations: Titles of nobility, presents, etc., prohibited.

> 1789, Aug. 18. By Mr. Tucker of South Carolina, to amend art. 1, sec. 9, clause 7; referred to Com. of the Whole. H. J., p. °104; Annals, p. °702.

204. Finance: Duties on imports and exports.

> 1789, Aug. 18. By Mr. Tucker of South Carolina, to amend art. 1, sec. 10, clause 2; referred to Com. of the Whole. H. J., p. °104; Annals, p. °702.

205. Executive: Term of office of President.

> 1789, Aug. 18. By Mr. Tucker of South Carolina, to add to art. 2, sec. 1, clause 5; referred to Com. of the Whole; negatived. H. J., p. °104. Annals, p. °702.

206. Executive: Military power of the President.

> 1789, Aug. 18. By Mr. Tucker of South Carolina, to add to art. 2, sec. 2, clause 1; referred to Com. of the Whole; negatived. H. J., p. °104; Annals, p. °702.

207. Executive: Powers of the President, to suspend.

> 1789, Aug. 18. By Mr. Tucker of South Carolina, to add to art. 2, sec. 2, clause 3; referred to Com of the Whole; negatived. H. J., p. °104; Annals, p. °702.

208. Judiciary: Courts of admiralty.

> 1789, Aug. 18. By Mr. Tucker of South Carolina, to amend art. 3, sec. 1; motion to refer to Com. of the Whole negatived. H. J., p. °104; Annals, p. °702.

209. Judiciary: Jurisdiction of Supreme Court.

> 1789. Aug. 18. By Mr. Tucker of South Carolina, to amend art. 3, sec. 2, clause 1; referred to Com. of the Whole; negatived. H. J., p. °104; Annals, p. °702.

210. Legislative, Executive, Judiciary: Oath of office.

> 1789, Aug. 18. By Mr. Tucker of South Carolina, to amend art. 6, clause 3; referred to Com. of the Whole, negatived. H. J., p. °104; Annals, p. °702.

211 [156]. Personal Relations: Freedom of religion.

> 1789, Aug. 20. By Mr. Ames of Massachusetts, to amend fourth amendment of com. report; passed. Annals, p. °766.

212 [160]. Personal Relations: Right to bear arms.

> 1789, Aug. 20. Sixth amendment of report of com. amended; passed. Annals, p. 767.

213 [169]. Personal Relations: Trial by jury.

> 1789, Aug. 21. By Mr. Gerry of Massachusetts, to amend fourth proposition, second clause, of com. report; negatived. Annals, p. °767.

214 [169]. Personal Relations: Criminal trials.

> 1789, Aug. 21. By Mr. Gerry of Massachusetts, to amend fourth proposition, second clause, of com. report; passed. Annals, p. 767.

*215 [140]. Legislative: Apportionment of Representatives.

> 1789, Aug. 21. Art. 1 of the report to the House; passed by House. H. J., p °107; Annals, p. °773. See Nos. 242. 295 for amendment in Senate and amendment of conference com.

*216 [154]. Legislative: Compensation of members of Congress.

> 1789, Aug. 21. Art. 2 of the report to the House; passed by House H J., p. 107; Annals, pp. °728 729. See No. 243 for amendment in Senate.

*217 [156] [211]. Personal Relations: Freedom of religion and right of conscience.

> 1789, Aug. 21. Art. 3 of the report to the House; passsed by House. H. J., p. °107. See No. 217 for amendment in Senate and of conference com.

*218 [158]. Personal Relations: Freedom of speech and of the press, etc.

1789, Aug. 21. Art. 4 of the report to the House; passed by House. H. J., p. °107; Annals, pp. °731-747. See No. 251 for amendment in Senate and its incorporation in art. 3.

*219 [160]. Personal Relations: Right to keep and bear arms.

1789, Aug. 21. Art. 5 of the report to the House: passed by House. H. J., p. °107. See No. 253 for Senate amendments.

***220 [166]. Personal Relations: Quartering of troops.

1789, Aug. 21. Art. 6 of report to House; passed by House. H. J., p. °107. Sept. 4-24, passed by Senate. S. J., pp. 119, 131, 145, 148. See No. 297 for list of States ratifying.

***221 [174]. Personal Relations: Search and seizure: Warrants.

1789, Aug. 21. Art. 7 of report to House; passed by House. H. J., p. °108. Sept. 4-24, passed by Senate. S. J., pp. 119, 131, 145, 148. See No. 297 for list of States ratifying.

*222 [172]. Personal Relations: Trial for crimes. Rights of property.

1789, Aug. 21. Art. 8 of report to House; passed by House. H. J., p. °107. See No. 254 for amendment in Senate.

*223 [185] [188]. Personal Relations: Right of defendant in criminal cases.

1789, Aug. 21. Art. 9 of report to House; passed by House. H. J., p. °108; Annals p. °756. See No. 254 for amendment in Senate and conference com.

*224 [188]. Personal Relations: Right of trial by jury, etc.

1789, Aug. 21. Art. 10 of report to House: passed by House. H. J., p. °108. See No. 255 for amendment in Senate.

*225 [181]. Personal Relations: Appeal to Supreme Court limited.

1789, Aug. 21. Art. 11 of report to House: passed by House. H. J., p. °108. See No. 257 for amendment in Senate.

*226 [143]. Personal Relations: Trial by jury in suits at common law.

1789, Aug. 21. Art. 12 of report to House: passed by House. H. J., p. °108; Annals, p. °760. See No. 258 for amendment in Senate.

***227 [169]. Personal Relations: Bail, fines, etc.

1789, Aug. 21. Art. 13 of report to House; passed by House. H. J., p. °107. Sept. 7-24, passed by Senate as Art 10. S. J., pp. 121, 131, 145, 148. See No. 297 for list of States ratifying.

*228 [180]. Personal Relations: The States prohibited from infringing certain rights.

1789, Aug. 21. Art. 14 of report to House; passed by House. H. J., p. °108. Sept. 7, rejected by Senate. S. J., p. 121.

***229 [177]. Personal Relations: Reserved rights.

1789, Aug. 21. Art. 15 of report to House; passed by House. H. J., p. °108. Sept. 7-24, passed by Senate. S. J., pp. 122, 131, 145, 148. See No. 297 for list of States ratifying.

*230 [144]. Distribution: Powers among the three departments of Government.

1789, Aug. 21. Art. 16 of report to House; passed by House. H. J., p. °108. Annals pp. °760-761. Sept. 7, rejected by Senate. S. J., p. 122.

231 [192]. Division: Nondelegated powers reserved.

1789, Aug. 21. Art. 17 of report of House; passed by House as amended by Mr. Sherman. H. J., pp. °108-109.

232 [231]. Division: Nondelegated powers reserved.

1789, Aug. 21. By Mr. Gerry of Massachusetts, to amend art. 17; **negatived** (17 to 32). Annals, pp. °767-768.

*233 [231]. Division: Nondelegated powers reserved.

> 1789, Aug. 21. By Mr. Sherman of Connecticut, to amend art. 17; passed the House. Annals, p. °768. See No. 206.

234. Legislative: Election of Senators and Representatives.

> 1789, Aug. 21. By Mr. Burke of South Carolina, to add an amendment; negatived (23 to 28). H. J., p. °109; Annals, pp. 768–773.

235 [234]. Legislative: Election of Senators and Representatives.

> 1789, Aug. 21. By Mr. Sedgwick of Massachusetts, to amend Mr. Burke's amendment; negatived. Annals, pp. °770–772.

236. Finance: Requisitions.

> 1789, Aug. 22. By Mr. Tucker of South Carolina, to add an amendment; negatived (9 to 39). H. J., p. °110; Annals, pp. °773–777.

237. Judiciary: Inferior courts: Courts of admiralty.

> 1789, Aug. 22. By Mr. Tucker of South Carolina, in the House, to amend art. 1, sec. 8, clause 9; negatived. H. J., p. °111; Annals, p. °778.

238. Legislative. Executive, Judiciary: Oath of office.

> 1789, Aug. 22. By Mr. Tucker of South Carolina, in the House, to amend art. 6, sec. 3; negatived. H. J., p. °111; Annals, p. °778.

239. Commerce: Commercial monopolies.

> 1789, Aug. 22. By Mr. Gerry of Massachusetts, to amend; negatived. H. J., p. °111; Annals, p. °778.

240. Personal Relations: Titles of nobility.

> 1789, Aug. 22. By Mr. Gerry of Massachusetts, to amend; negatived. H. J., p. °111; Annals, p. °778.

241 [215]. Legislative: Apportionment of Representatives.

> 1789, Sept. 2. Motion to amend art. 1 in the Senate; negatived (12 to 6). S. J., p. °115; Annals, p. 74.

*242 [215]. Legislative: Apportionment of Representatives.

> 1789, Sept. 2. Motion to amend art. 1; passed. S. J., p. °115; Annals, pp. °74–75. See No. 205 for further amendment.

**243 [216]. Legislative: Compensation of members.

> 1789. Sept. 3. Motion to amend art. 2; passed. S. J., pp, °116, 131.
>
> Ratified by the legislatures of the following States: Maryland, Dec. 19, 1789. S. J., p. 106. 1st Cong., 2d sess. North Carolina. Dec. 22, 1789. S. J., p. 103. 1st Cong., 2d sess. South Carolina, Jan. 19, 1790. S. J., p. 50, 1st Cong., 2d sess. Delaware. Jan. 28, 1790. S. J., p. 35, 1st Cong., 2d sess. Vermont, Nov. 3, 1791. S. J., p. 98, 2d Cong., 1st sess. Virginia, Dec. 15, 1791. S. J., p. 69. 2d Cong., 1st sess.
>
> Rejected by New Jersey, Nov. 20, 1789. S. J., p. 190, 1st Cong., 2d sess. New Hampshire. Jan. 25, 1790. S. J., p. 105, 1st Cong., 2d sess. Pennsylvania, March 10, 1790. S. J., p. 30, 1st Cong., 2d sess. New York, March 27, 1790. S. J., p. 53. 1st Cong., 2d sess. Rhode Island, June 15, 1790. S. J., p. 110, 1st Cong., 2d sess.
>
> The journals give no record of the action of the legislatures of Massachusetts. Connecticut, and Georgia. For copies of the resolutions of ratification passed by the legislatures of the States, see Documentary History of the Constitution of the United States, Vol. 11, pp. 325–390, in Bulletin of the Bureau of Rolls and Library of the Department of State. No. 7.

244 [217]. Personal Relations: Freedom of religion and right of conscience.

> 1789. Sept. 3. Motion to amend art. 3; negatived: reconsidered and passed; motion to strike out art. 3; negatived. S. J., p. °116. See Nos. 247, 288.

245 [217]. Personal Relations: Freedom of religion, etc.

> 1789. Sept. 3. Motion to amend art. 3; negatived. S. J., p. °116.

246 [217]. **Personal Relations:** Freedom of religion, etc.
> 1789, Sept.3. Motion to amend art.3: negatived. S.J.,p. °117.

247 [217]. **Personal Relations:** Freedom of religion.
> 1789, Sept.3. Motion to amend art.3; passed. S.J.,p. °117. See No.288 for
> further amendment. Ibid., p.129.

248 [218]. **Personal Relations:** Freedom of speech and press, etc.
> 1789, Sept.3. Motion to amend art.4: negatived. 14 to 2. S.J.,p. °117.

249 [218]. **Personal Relations:** Freedom of speech and press, etc.
> 1789, Sept.3. Motion to amend art.4; negatived. S.J.,p. °117.

250 [218]. **Personal Relations:** Freedom of speech and press, etc.
> 1789, Sept.3. Motion to amend art.4: negatived. S.J.,p. °117.

251 [218]. **Personal Relations:** Freedom of speech and press, etc.
> 1789, Sept 4. Motion to amend art.4; passed. S.J.,p.118. Sept.9, stricken
> out. S.J.,p. °129.

252 [219]. **Personal Relations:** Standing army.
> 1789, Sept. 4. Motion to add to art. 5 an amendment as above; negatived,
> 9 to 6. S. J., p. °118.

253 [219]. **Personal Relations:** Right to keep and bear arms.
> 1789, Sept. 4. Motion to amend art. 5; passed. S. J., p. °119. See Nos.290,
> 291 for further amendment.

*254 [222]. **Personal Relations:** Trial for crime: Freedom from second
trial.
> 1789, Sept. 4. Motion to amend art. 8: passed. S. J., p. °119. See No.297 for
> further amendment.

255 [224]. **Personal Relations:** Indictment by grand jury.
> 1789, Sept 4 Motion to amend art. 10 as above: passed. S. J., p. °119. Sept.
> 9, art. 10 stricken out

256 [225]. **Judiciary:** Extent of jurisdiction.
> 1789, Sept. 4. Motion to insert in place of art. 11; negatived. S. J., p. °119.

257 [225]. **Personal Relations:** Appeal to higher court.
> 1789, Sept. 4. Motion to amend art. 11: passed. S. J., p. °119. Sept. 9,
> art. 11 stricken out. Ibid., p. 130.

258 [226]. **Personal Relations:** Trial by jury in suits at common law.
> 1789, Sept. 7. Motion to amend art. 12, passed. S. J., p. °121; Annals p.
> °76. See No.283 for further amendment.

259. **Finance:** Requisitions instead of direct taxes.
> 1789, Sept. 7. Motion to add an amendment as above; negatived. S. J., p.
> °121; Annals p. °76.

260. **Legislative:** Elections of Senators and Representatives.
> 1789, Sept.7. Motion to add an amendment as above; negatived. S. J., p.
> °122.

261. **Legislative, Executive, Judiciary:** Oath of office.
> 1789, Sept.7 Motion to add an amendment to amendment, art.6, sec.3:
> negatived. S.J., p. °122; Annals p. °76.

262. **Commerce:** Commercial monopolies.
> 1789, Sept.7. Motion to add an amendment as above; negatived. S. J., p.
> °122.

263. **Personal Relations:** Titles of nobility.
> 1789, Sept. 7. Motion to add an amendment as above; negatived. S. J., p.
> °122.

264. **Legislative:** A debtor of the United States excluded from Congress.
> 1789, Sept. 7. Motion to add an amendment as above; negatived. S. J., p.
> °122.

265 [233]. Division: Nondelegated powers reserved.
   1789. Sept. 7. Motion to amend art. 17: negatived. S. J., p. °122.

***266 [233]. Division: Nondelegated powers reserved.
   1789. Sept. 7. Motion to amend art. 17; passed. S. J.. pp. 122-123, 131, 145, 148.
   See No. 297 for list of States ratifying.

267. Personal Relations: Natural rights, life, liberty, etc.
   1789. Sept. 8. Motion to add an amendment as above; negatived. S. J., p. °123.

268. Personal Relations: Source of powers.
   1789. Sept. 8. Motion to add an amendment as above: negatived. S. J., p. °124.

269. Personal Relations: Government instituted for the people.
   1789. Sept. 8. Motion to add an amendment as above; negatived. S. J., p. °124.

270. Personal Relations: Tenure of office.
   1789. Sept. 8. Motion to add an amendment as above: negatived. S. J.. p. °124.

271. Distribution: Of powers among the legislative. executive. and judiciary.
   1789. Sept. 8. Motion to add an amendment as above: negatived. S. J., p. °124.

272. Personal Relations: Redress, when restrained of liberty.
   1789. Sept. 8. Motion to add an amendment as above; negatived. S. J.. p. °124.

273. Personal Relations: Right of remedy for injuries, etc.
   1789. Sept. 8. Motion to add an amendment as above: negatived. S J., p. °124.

274. Legislative: Publication of journals.
   1789. Sept. 8. Motion to add an amendment as above; negatived. S. J., p. °125.

275. Legislative: Members of Congress excluded from office.
   1789. Sept. 8. Motion to add an amendment as above; negatived. S. J.. p. °125.

276. Finance: Publication of accounts of public moneys.
   1789. Sept. 8. Motion to add an amendment as above; negatived. S. J., p. °125.

277. Foreign Affairs: Commercial and territorial treaties.
   1789. Sept. 8. Motion to add an amendment as above; negatived. S. J., p. °125.

278. Commerce: Navigation laws.
   1789. Sept. 8. Motion to add an amendment as above; negatived. S. J., p. °125.

279. Executive: Term limited.
   1789. Sept. 8. Motion to add an amendment as above; negatived. S. J., p. °126.

280. War: Standing army in time of peace.
   1789. Sept. 8. Motion to add an amendment as above; negatived. S. J.. p. °126.

281. War: Period of enlistment of soldiers.
   1789. Sept. 8. Motion to add an amendment as above; negatived. S J., p. °126.

282. War: State militia.
   1789. Sept. 8. Motion to add an amendment as above, negatived. S. J.. p. °126.

283. Territorial: Congress power over the "Federal town," etc.

　　1789, Sept. 8. Motion to add an amendment as above; negatived. S. J., p. °126.

284. Judiciary: Extent of jurisdiction.

　　1789, Sept. 8. Motion to add an amendment as above; negatived. S. J., p. °126.

285. Legislative: Election of Senators and Representatives.

　　1789, Sept. 8. Motion to add an amendment as above; negatived. S. J., p. °127.

286. Legislative: Tribunal for trying impeachment of Senators.

　　1789, Sept. 8. Motion to add an amendment as above; negatived. S. J., p. °127.

287. Judiciary: Salary of judges.

　　1789, Sept. 8. Motion to add an amendment as above; negatived. S. J., p. °127.

*288 [247]. Personal Relations: Freedom of religion, of speech, and of press.

　　1789, Sept. 9. Motion to amend art. 3; passed. S. J., p. °120.

289 [253]. Personal Relations: Right to keep and bear arms.

　　1789, Sept. 9. Motion to amend art. 5; negatived. S. J., p. °120.

290 [253]. Personal Relations: Right to keep and bear arms.

　　1789, Sept. 9. Motion to amend art. 5; passed. S. J., p. °120. See below for further amendment.

***291 [290]. Personal Relations: Right to keep and bear arms.

　　1789, Sept. 9. Motion to amend art. 5; passed. S. J., pp. °120, 131, 145, 148. See No. 297 for list of States ratifying.

***292 [254]. Personal Relations: Trial for crimes: Rights of property.

　　1789, Sept. 9. Motion to change art. 8 to art. 7 and amend; passed. S. J., pp. °129-130, 131, 145, 148. See No. 297 for full list of States ratifying.

***293 [258]. Personal Relations: Trial in civil cases.

　　1789, Sept. 9. Motion to change art. 12 to art. 9 and amend; passed. S. J., pp. °130, 131, 145, 148. See No. 297 for list of States ratifying.

294 [255]. Personal Relations: Trial by jury, etc.

　　1789, Sept. 9. Motion to reconsider art. 10 and restore certain words struck out lost on a tie vote (8 to 8). S. J., p. °130.

**295 [242]. Legislative: Apportionment of Representatives.

　　1789, Sept. 23. Amendment to art. 1 reported by the conference com. Sept. 25; passed House. H. J., p. °152; Annals, p. °913. Passed Senate. S. J., pp. °145, 148, 150.

　　Ratified by the legislatures of the following States: New Jersey, Nov. 20, 1789. S. J., p. 190, 1st Cong., 2d sess. Maryland, Dec. 19, 1789. S. J., p. 106, 1st Cong., 2d sess. North Carolina, Dec. 22, 1789. S. J., p. 103, 1st Cong., 2d sess. South Carolina, Jan. 19, 1790. S. J., p. 50, 1st Cong., 2d sess. New Hampshire, Jan. 25, 1790. S. J., p. 105, 1st Cong., 2d sess. New York, Mar. 27, 1790. S. J., p. 53, 1st Cong., 2d sess. Rhode Island, June 15, 1790. S. J., p. 110, 1st Cong., 2d sess. Virginia, Oct. 25, 1791. S. J., p. 30, 2d Cong., 1st sess. Pennsylvania, Sept. 21, 1791. President sends a message (Oct. 28, 1791) announcing that Pennsylvania reconsiders her action of Mar. 10, 1790, and now ratifies the first article. Sept. 21, 1791. S. J., p. 11. Vermont, Nov. 3, 1791. S. J., p. 98, 2d Cong., 1st. sess.

　　Rejected by Delaware, Jan. 28, 1790. S. J., p. 35, 1st Cong., 2d sess.

　　The journals give no record of the action of the legislatures of Massachusetts, Connecticut, and Georgia. See references to Documentary History of the Constitution of the United States under No. 243 for resolutions of the legislatures.

***296 [247]. Personal Relations: Freedom of religion, of speech, and of press.

> 1789, Sept. 23. Amendment to art. 3 reported by the conference com. Sept. 25; passed House. H. J., p. °152; Annals, p. °913. Passed Senate, S. J. pp. °145, 148, 150. See No. 297 for list of States ratifying.

***297 [254]. Personal Relations: Right of defendant in criminal cases.

> 1789, Sept. 23. Amendment to art. 8 reported by the conference com. Sept. 25; passed House. H. J., p. °152; Annals, p. °913. Passed Senate. S. J., pp. °145,148,150.
>
> The ten amendments were ratified by the legislatures of the following States: New Jersey, Nov. 20,1789. S. J., p. 199, 1st Cong., 2d sess. Maryland, Dec.19,1789. S. J., p.106,1st Cong.,2d sess. North Carolina, Dec.22.1789. S. J. p.103, 1st Cong., 2d sess. South Carolina, Jan. 19,1790. S. J., p. 50, 1st Cong., 2d sess. New Hampshire, Jan.25,1790. S. J., p.105, 1st Cong., 2d sess. Delaware, Jan. 28,1790. S. J., p.35, 1st Cong., 2d sess. Pennsylvania, Mar. 10, 1790. S. J., p. 30,1st Cong., 2d sess. New York, Mar. 27, 1790. S. J., p. 53, 1st Cong., 2d sess. Rhode Island, June 15,1790. S. J., p. 110. 1st Cong., 2d sess. Vermont, Nov. 3, 1791. S. J., p.98, 2d Cong., 1st sess. Virginia, Dec. 15,1791. S. J., p. 69, 2d Cong., 1st sess.
>
> The journals give no record of the action of the legislatures of Massachusetts, Connecticut, and Georgia. For copies of the resolutions of ratification passed by the legislatures of the States, see Documentary History of the Constitution of the United States, Vol. II, pp. 325-390 (in Bulletin of the Bureau of Rolls and Library of the Department of State, No. 7).

298. Judiciary: A "general judicial court" in each State.

299. Judiciary: Composition.

300. Judiciary: Jurisdiction.

301. Judiciary: Relation of circuit and judicial courts.

302. Judiciary: Number necessary for a quorum.

303. Judiciary: Fees: Proceedings.

304. Judiciary: Appointment of officers of the court.

305. Judiciary: Writs in the courts.

306. Judiciary: Impeachment.

307. Judiciary: Trial of impeachment.

308. Judiciary: Extent of judgment.

309. Judiciary: Judges.

310. Judiciary: Judges.

311. Judiciary: Number of judges.

312. Judiciary: Duties of officers.

> 1791, Mar.3. 1st Cong.,3d sess. By Mr. Benson of New York. Introduced; consideration deferred to next Congress. H.J., pp. °98-100; Annals, p. °1976-1977.

313. Judiciary: Jurisdiction, States, parties.

> 1793, Feb. 20. 2d Cong., 2d sess. Motion in the Senate by Mr. Sedgwick; considered and postponed. S.J., pp. °65,71; Annals, pp. °651,652,656.

314. Finance: Limitation on taxation.

315. Commerce: Commercial monopolies prohibited.

> 1793, Mar. 2. 2d Cong., 2d sess. Motion in the Senate; tabled. S.J., p. °84; Annals, p. °663.

316. Finance: Direct taxes defined.

317. Executive Offices: Members of Congress excluded.

318. Legislative: Officials and bankers ineligible to Congress.

> 1793, Mar. 2. 2d Cong., 2d sess. Motion in the Senate; tabled. S.J., p. °84; Annals, p. °663.

319. **Judiciary: Courts in which the power is vested.**

    1793, Mar. 2. 2d Cong., 2d sess. Motion in Senate, tabled. S. J., p. °84; Annals, p. °663.

319a. **Judiciary: Suability of a State.**

    1793, Sept. 27. Resolutions of the legislature of Massachusetts. Resolves of Massasachusetts, Vol. IX, A., p. 108.

319b. **Judiciary; Suability of a State.**

    1793, Oct. 2, Thursday. Resolution of the general assembly of Connecticut. Copy of resolution in Massachusetts Archives, Senate Mis., $\frac{1667}{00}$; Cat. of Doc. and Papers of Senate of Mass., Vol. I, p. $\frac{142}{90}$.

319c. **Judiciary: Suability of a State.**

    1793, Dec. 3. Resolution of the legislature of Virginia. Copy of resolution in Massachusetts Archives. Senate Mis., $\frac{1667}{00}$.

320. **Legislative: Bank officers and stockholders ineligible to Congress.**

    1793, Dec. 24. 3d Cong., 1st sess. Motion in Senate; considered; amendments made and agreed to; rejected (12 to 13). S. J., pp. °20, 31, 32, 33; Annals, pp. °23, 31, 32.

***321. **Judiciary: Extent of jurisdiction.** (The XI Amendment.)

    1794, Jan. 2-14. 3d Cong., 1st sess. Motion in Senate considered. Mr. Gallatin attempts to amend. Passed (23 to 2). S. J., pp. °23, 29, 30, 31, 74; Annals, pp. °25, 30.

    Jan. 15-Mar. 12. Reported to the House. Read twice; to Com. on the Whole. Attempt to amend. Negatived (8 to 77); passed (81 to 9). H. J. pp. °80, 81, 164, 165, 166, 185, 186; Annals, pp. 225, 476, 477, 478.

    The journals show that the President reported the action of the legislatures of the States as follows: Message of the President. Jan. 8, 1795, announced the ratification of the legislatures of New York, Massachusetts, and Vermont. 3d Cong., 2d sess., S. J., p. 41. Message of the President, Feb. 17, 1795, announced the ratification of New Hampshire. 3d Cong. 2d sess., S. J., p. 69. Message of the President, Feb. 25, 1795, announced the ratification of Georgia. 3d Cong., 2d sess. S. J., p. 84. Message of the President, Mar. 2, 1795, announced the ratification of Delaware. 3d Cong. 2d sess., S. J., p. 103. Message of the President, Jan. 29, 1796, announced the ratification of Rhode Island and North Carolina (Feb. 7, 1795). S. J., 4th Cong. 1st sess., p. 61. See Documentary History of the Constitution of the United States, Vol. II, pp. 402-404. Message of the President, Jan. 8, 1798, announced the ratification of Kentucky (Dec. 7, 1794) and the ratification of the amendment by the legislatures of three-fourths of the States. 5th Cong., 2d sess., S. J., p. 51; Annals, p. 483. See Documentary History of the Constitution, Vol. II, pp. 394-396. Message of the governor of Virginia, Feb. 12, 1798, giving notification of the ratification of Virginia (Nov. 18, 1794). 5th Cong., 2d sess., S. J., p. 113. See Documentary History of the Constitution Vol. II, pp. 392-393.

    Certified copies of the action of the legislatures, in the Bureau of Rolls and Library, State Department, show that in addition the following States ratified the amendment: Maryland. Dec. 26, 1794. Documentary History of the Constitution, Vol. II, pp. 397-400. Connecticut, May session, 1794. Ibid., p. 401. South Carolina, Dec. 4, 1797. Ibid., pp. 405-407.

    There is no record in the journals or at the Department of State, of the action of New Jersey, Pennsylvania, and Tennessee. It is probable that they did not ratify. The Secretary of State was in doubt for some time as to whether the amendment had received the necessary number for ratification or not, owing to the admission of Tennessee, June 1, 1796, some two years after the submission of the amendment. It was finally shown to have received the ratification of three-fourths (12) of the States prior to the admission of Tennessee, and hence all doubt as to its adoption was removed. See letters of Timothy Pickering, Secretary of State. Domestic Letters, Vol. X, pp. 104, 212-214, 310-311, 328, 336-337, in the Bureau of Rolls and Library, Department of State.

322 [321]. Judiciary: Extent of jurisdiction.

> 1794, Jan. 14. 3d Cong., 1st sess. By Mr. Gallatin of Pennsylvania. Motion to amend; rejected. S. J., p. °30; Annals, p. °30.

323 [321]. Judiciary: extent of jurisdiction.

> 1794, Jan. 14. 3d Cong., 1st sess. Motion in the Senate to amend the original motion; rejected. S. J., p. °30; Annals, p. °30.

324 [321]. Legislative: Bank officials ineligible to Congress.

> 1794, Jan. 16. 3d Cong., 1st sess. Motion in the Senate to amend the original motion; rejected (12 to 13). S. J., p. °33; Annals, p. °32.

325 [321]. Judiciary: Extent of jurisdiction.

> 1794, Mar. 4. 3d Cong., 1st sess. Motion in the House to amend original motion of the Senate on judicial power; rejected (8 to 77). H. J., pp. °164, 165; Annals, p. °476.

326. Territorial powers: Not to curtail or abridge the limits.

> 1794, Jan. 9. 3d Cong., 1st sess. Motion in the Senate; tabled. S. J., p. °27; Annals, p. °28.

327. Legislative: Expiration of term (June 1).

> 1795, Mar. 3. 3d Cong., 2d sess. By Mr. Burr of New York; tabled. S. J. pp. °112, 113; Annals, p. °853.

327a. Foreign Affairs: Treaties to be submitted to House of Representatives in certain cases.

327b. Judiciary: Trial of impeachments by some tribunal other than the Senate.

327c. Legislative: Term of Senators, three years.

327d. Judiciary: United States Judges ineligible to other offices.

> 1795, Dec. 15. Resolutions of the legislature of Virginia. Copy in Massachusetts Archives. Senate Mis., 2075; Cat. of Doc. and Papers of the Senate of Massachusetts, p. ¹⁄₂°.

328. Executive: Choice of: Electors to designate in their ballots person voted for as President, etc.

> 1797, Jan. 9. 4th Cong., 2d sess. By Mr. W. Smith of South Carolina; to Com. of the Whole. H. J., p. °85; Annals, p. °1824.

329. Executive: Choice of: Electors to designate; contested elections determined.

> 1798, Jan. 24. 5th Cong., 2d sess. By Mr. Marshall of Kentucky, in the Senate; considered and postponed. Annals, p. °493.

330. Legislative: Qualifications necessary for eligibility.

331. Executive: Qualifications necessary for eligibility.

> 1798, July 7. 5th Cong., 2d sess. By Mr. Goodhue of Massachusetts; tabled. S. J., p. °436; Annals, p. °602.

332. Legislative: Qualifications necessary for eligibility.

333. Executive: Qualifications necessary for eligibility.

> 1798, July 9. 5th Cong., 2d sess. By Mr. Foster of Massachusetts, in the House, from the legislature of Massachusetts; tabled. Annals, pp. °2132–2133; Resolves of Massachusetts, Vol. x, pp. 31.

333a. Executive: Qualifications necessary for eligibility.

333b. Legislative: Qualifications necessary for eligibility.

> 1798, Oct., 2d Thursday. Resolutions of the general assembly of Connecticut approving Massachusetts resolves. Copy in Archives of Massachusetts. Senate Misc. ²¹⁄₂°. (Cat. of Doc. and Papers in Archives of Senate, Vol. I, p. ²¹⁄₄.)

334. Executive: Choice of: Electors to designate person voted for as President.

> 1790, Feb. 16. 5th Cong., 3d sess. By Mr. Foster of New Hampshire, in the House; tabled. Motion to refer to Com. of the Whole; lost (56 to 28). Annals, p. 2919.

334a. Executive: Choice of: Electors to designate persons voted for as President.

> 1790, Feb. 28. Resolution of the legislature of Massachusetts. Resolves of Massachusetts, Vol. x, p. 60.

334b. Executive: Choice of: Electors to designate persons voted for as President.

> 1790. Resolutions of the legislature of Vermont. Referred to in Resolves of Massachusetts, Vol. x. p. 153.

335. Judiciary: Judges restricted from holding other offices.

> 1800, Feb. 3. 6th Cong., 1st sess. By Mr. Pinckney of South Carolina; Read; tabled; considered. S. J., pp. °78, 122; Annals, pp. °41, 42, 63.

336. Executive: Choice of: Electors to designate persons voted for.

> 1800, Feb. 4. 6th Cong., 1st sess. Motion in the House; to Com. of the Whole. H. J., pp. °136, 137; Annals. p. °510.

337. Judiciary: Judges ineligible to other offices.

> 1800, Feb. 13. 6th Cong., 1st sess. By Mr. Livingston of New York, in the House; tabled. Annals, p. °523.

338. Executive: Choice of: Electors to be chosen by districts.

> 1800, Mar. 14. 6th Cong., 1st sess. By Mr. Nicholas of Virginia, in the House; tabled. Annals, p. °627.

339. Legislative: Representatives to be chosen by districts.

> 1800, Mar. 14. 6th Cong., 1st sess. By Mr. Nicholas of Virginia. in the House; tabled. Annals, p. °628.

340. Executive: Choice of: Electors to be chosen by districts.

> 1800, Nov. 21. 6th Cong., 2d sess. By Mr. Nicholas of Virginia; referred to a select com.; com. report adversely. H. J., pp. °8, 110; Annals, pp. °785, 941-946.

341. Legislative: Representatives to be chosen by districts.

> 1800, Nov. 21. 6th Cong., 2d sess. By Mr. Nicholas of Virginia: referred to a select com; com. report adversely. H. J., pp. °9, 110; Annals, pp. °785, 941-946.

341a. Executive: Uniform mode for the choice of President.

> 1801, Feb. 17. Resolution of the legislature of Maryland. Resolves of Massachusetts, Vol. x, p. 213.

342. Executive: Choice of: Election of President and Vice-President.

343. Legislative: Election of Representatives.

> 1802, Feb. 1. 7th Cong., 1st sess. By Mr. Morris of Vermont, from the general assembly of Vermont. H. J., pp. 187, 188; Annals, p. 472.

344. Choice of Executive:

> 1802, Feb. 15. 7th Cong., 1st sess. By Mr. Walker of New York, from the legislature of New York; read; to Com. of the Whole. H. J., pp. 239, 254; Annals, p. 500.

*345 Executive: Choice of: Electors to designate persons voted for as President and Vice-President: Electors to be chosen by districts.

> 1802, Feb. 19-May 1. 7th Cong., 1st sess. Motion in House; referred to Com. of the Whole; considered; section in regard to the choice of electors by districts rejected; as amended, read third time; passed (47 to 14).
>
> May 3. Received in Senate; rejected (15 to 8). H. J., pp. °254, 255, 545, 546, 551, 552, 553, 561; S. J., pp. °267, 273; Annals, pp. °303, 304, °602, 603, 1255, 1288, 1293, 1296.

346. Executive: Choice of: Electors to be chosen by districts.
347. Legislative: Representatives to be chosen by districts.

> 1802, Feb. 19. 7th Cong., 1st sess. By Mr. Bradley of Vermont. from the legislature of Vermont. S. J., pp. °101, 102; Annals, p. °190.

348. Executive: Choice of.
349. Legislative: Election of Representatives.

> 1802, Feb. 20. 7th Cong., 1st sess. By Mr. Stanley of North Carolina, from the legislature of North Carolina: read and referred to Com. of the Whole. H. J., pp. 256-7; Annals, p. 629.

350. Executive: Choice of: Electors to be chosen by districts.
351. Executive: Choice of: Designation of person voted for as President.

> 1802, Feb. 24. 7th Cong., 1st sess. By Mr. Morris of New York, from the legislature of New York; read. S. J., pp. °105-106; Annals, p. °191.

352. Executive: Choice of: Designation of person voted for as President.

> 1802, Apr. 12. 7th Cong., 1st sess. By Mr. Clinton of New York; tabled; considered; postponed to next session. S. J., p. °188; Annals, p. °259.

353. Executive: Choice of: Electors to be chosen by districts.

> 1802, Apr. 16. 7th Cong., 1st sess. By Mr. Bradley of Vermont, in the Senate; postponed to next session. Annals, pp. °253, 264, 293.

354. Executive: Choice of: Designation of person voted for as President.

> 1803, Jan. 3. 7th Cong., 2d sess. By Mr. Leib of Pennsylvania; referred to Com. of the Whole; postponed. H. J.. pp. °57-58, 220; Annals, p. 304.

355. Executive: Choice of: Electors to be chosen by districts.

> 1803, Feb. 1. 7th Cong., 2d sess. By Mr. Huger of South Carolina; debated; to Com. of the Whole; postponed. H. J., pp. °185, 220, 221; Annals, pp. °449, 481-486, 492, 493.

356. Executive: Choice of: Designation of person voted for as President.

> 1803, Oct. 17. 8th Cong., 1st sess. By Mr. Dawson of Virginia; referred to Com. of Whole; to a select com.; amendment moved by Mr. Nicholson and by Mr. Clopton. H. J., pp. °11; Annals, pp. °272, °375, °377.

357. Executive: Choice of: Electors to be chosen by districts.

> 1803, Oct. 20. 8th Cong., 1st sess. By Mr. Huger of South Carolina; referred to select com. H. J., p. °28; Annals, pp. °380-381.

***358. Executive: Choice of.

> 1803, Oct. 21-Dec. 2. 8th Cong., 1st sess. By Mr. Clinton of New York; read; to select com.; report of com. considered; amended; report further amendments; passed Senate (22 to 10).
>
> Dec. 5-9. Received in the House; considered; Mr. Elliot's amendment rejected; Mr. Dana's motion to strike out all in regard to Vice-Presidents rejected; other amendments rejected; read third time, and passed (83 to 42). S. J., pp. °21-24, 26, 27, 51, 57, 64, 65, 66, 67, 74, 75, 76, 77, 79, 81, 89, 91, 93, 95, 99; H. J., pp. 164, 170, 172, 173-185, 190, 191, 195; Annals, pp. °16, 19, 20, 21, 81, 91, 106, 107, 108-210, 642, 646-663, 663-775.
>
> The amendment was declared in force by a proclamation of the Secretary of State, dated September 25, 1804. See circular letter of James Madison, Secretary of State, Domestic Letters, Vol. XIV, pp. 381-382, Bureau of Rolls and Library, Department of State. Ratified by the legislatures of the following States: Georgia, May 19, 1804; Kentucky; Maryland, November session; New Jersey, Feb. 23, 1804; New York; North Carolina; Ohio, December session, 1803; Pennsylvania, Jan. 7, 1804; Rhode Island, February session, 1804; South Carolina; Tennessee, July 27, 1804; Vermont, Jan. 30, 1804; Virginia, December session, 1803. Rejected by Connecticut May session, 1804; Delaware; Massachusetts; New Hampshire (vetoed by the governor).
>
> Poor's Charters and Constitutions, Vol. I, p. 22. For copies of the ratification of several of the States, see Documentary History of the Constitution of the United States, Vol. II, pp. 408-451 (in Bulletin of the Bureau of Rolls and Library of the Department of State, No. 7).

*359. Executive: Choice of: Designation of person voted for as President.

> 1803, Oct. 26-28. 8th Cong., 1st sess. By Mr. Varnum, from com.; considered in Com. of the Whole; attempts to amend by Messrs. Clay and Nicholson; recommended to Com. of the Whole; reported and amended; read third time, and passed (88 to 31).
> Oct. 28. Received by the Senate; postponed. H. J., pp. °48, 49, 51, 54; S. J., pp. 31, 104; Annals, pp. 27, 218, °383, 420–431, 490–497, 516–545.

360. Executive: Choice of.

> 1803, Nov. 10. 8th Cong., 1st sess. By Mr. Bradley of Vermont, from the legislature of Vermont; read. S. J., p. 50; Annals, p. 75.

361. Executive: Choice of: Designation of person voted for as President.

> 1803; Nov. 11. 8th Cong., 1st sess. By Mr. Worthington of Ohio, from the legislature of Ohio; read. S. J., p. 51; Annals, p. 76.

361a. Commerce: Importation of slaves prohibited.

> 1804, Dec. 14. Resolutions of the general assembly of North Carolina. Journal of the Senate of the Commonwealth of Pennsylvania (1804–05), pp. °112–113.

362. Executive: After two terms ineligible for four years.

> 1803, Dec. 12. 8th Cong., 1st sess. Report of Senate select com.; rejected (4 to 25). S. J., pp. °90–91; Annals, pp. °213–215.

362a. Legislative: Recall of Senators by State.

> 1804 (?). Resolution of the legislature of Virginia; referred to in Senate Journal, Massachusetts Legislature (1803–04), Vol. xxix, p. 231.

362b. Commerce: Importation of slaves prohibited.

> 1804, June 20. Resolution of the legislature of Massachusetts. Resolves of Massachusetts, Vol. xi, pp. °204–205. Connecticut and Maryland answer that it is inexpedient. Resolves, June, 1805; p. 18.

363. Legislative: Apportionment of Representatives to free inhabitants.

364. Finance: Apportionment of direct taxes to free inhabitants.

> 1804, Dec. 7. 8th Cong., 2d sess. By Mr. Pickering of Massachusetts; tabled. S. J., p. °39; Annals, p. °21. From legislature of Massachusetts. For reply of legislature of Georgia disapproving, see Archives of Massachusetts, House Misc. 5927. Report and resolution of the legislature of Pennsylvania, Journal of Senate of Pennsylvania (1804–05), pp. °50–55, °79–84. Reply of legislature of Kentucky, ibid, pp. 160–162. Other replies, see ante, p. 46, note 1.

365. Judiciary: Extent of jurisdiction.

> 1805, Feb. 8. 8th Cong., 2d sess. By Mr. Breckenridge of Kentucky; (legislature of Kentucky) read and tabled. S. J., pp. °131–132; Annals, p. °53. Pennsylvania concurred; Massachusetts nonconcurred. Resolves of Massachusetts, Vol. xi, p. 304–306. New Jersey nonconcurred. Jour. of Senate of Penn. (1806–07), pp. °196–197.

365a. Judiciary: Extent of jurisdiction.

> 1805, Dec. 7. Resolution of the legislature of Georgia approving the above resolution of Kentucky. Copy in Massachusetts Archives, House Misc. 5927.

366. Judiciary: Removal of judges on joint address of both Houses.

> 1805, Mar. 1. 8th Cong., 2d sess. By Mr. J. Randolph of Virginia; referred to Com. of the Whole. H. J., p. °159; Annals, p. °1213.

367. Legislative: Recall of Senators.

> 1805, Mar. 1. 8th Cong., 2d sess. Motion by Mr. Nicholson; referred to Com. of the Whole. H. J., p. °160; Annals, p. °1214. For resolution of legislature of Massachusetts disapproving, see Massachusetts Senate Journal (1803–04), Vol. xxix, p. 231.

368. Commerce: Importation of slaves prohibited.

> 1805, Mar. 3. 8th Cong., 2d sess. By Mr. Varnum of Massachusetts, from the legislature of Massachusetts; read and tabled. H. J., p. °171; Annals, pp. °1221-22. Resolves of Massachusetts, Vol. XI, p. 239.

368a. Commerce: Importation of slaves prohibited.

> 1805, Nov. 4. Resolution of the general assembly of Tennessee. Journal of Senate of Pennsylvania (1805), p. 265. Copy in Massachusetts archives, House Misc., 5926. Legislature of Georgia disapproved of a similar amendment. See Ibid. House Misc., 5927.

369. Commerce: Importation of slaves prohibited.

> 1806, Jan. 20. 9th Cong., 1st sess. By Mr. Oliver of Vermont, from the legislature of Vermont; read and tabled. H. J. (reprint), Vol. V, p. 238. Annals, pp.343-344.

370. Judiciary: Extent of jurisdiction.

> 1806, Jan. 22. 9th Cong., 1st sess. By Mr. Maclay of Pennsylvania, from the legislature of Pennsylvania; read; considered; postponed. S. J., pp. °84. 222 253; Annals, pp., °68, 198, 210. Disapproved by general assembly of New Jersey. See copy of minutes of Nov. 6, 1806, in Massachusetts Archives. Senate Misc., 3520.

371. Judiciary: Removal of judges.

> 1806, Feb. 7. 9th Cong., 1st sess. By Mr. J. Randolph of Virginia; referred to Com. of the Whole; considered in Com. of the Whole; report disagreement; motion to postpone: lost. H. J., pp. °204, 206, 267; Annals, pp. °446, 499-507.

372. Commerce: Importation of slaves prohibited.

> 1806, Feb. 10. 9th Cong., 1st sess. By Mr. Tenney of New Hampshire, from the legislature of New Hampshire; read and tabled. H. J. pp. 206, 207; Annals, p. 448.

373. Executive: Choice of: Elector to be chosen by districts.

> 1806, Mar. 29. 9th Cong., 1st sess. By Mr. Thomas of New York; tabled. H. J., pp. °389-390; Annals, pp. °804-895.

374. Legislative: Government contractors excluded from House of Representatives.

> 1806, Mar. 29. 9th Cong., 1st sess. By Mr. Newton of Virginia; tabled; referred to Com. of the Whole. H. J., pp. °389, 405, 406; Annals, pp. °804, 933.

375. Commerce: Importation of slaves prohibited.

> 1806, Apr. 7. 9th Cong., 1st sess. By Mr. Wright of Maryland, from the legislature of Maryland. S. J., pp. °271, 282; Annals, p. °229, 232. Similar resolutions seem to have been proposed by the legislature of Maryland in the next year. See letter of governor of Maryland. Massachusetts Archives, Misc., °549.

376. Commerce: Internal improvements.

> 1806, Dec. 2. 9th Cong., 2d sess. By President Jefferson. Statesman's Manual, p. 191.

377. Division of Powers: Necessary and proper laws.

> 1806, Dec. 11. 9th Cong., 2d sess. By Mr. Clopton of Virginia; referred to Com. of the Whole. H. J., p. °42; Annals, pp. °131-148.

378. Judiciary: Extent of jurisdiction.

> 1806, Dec. 26. 9th Cong., 2d sess. By Mr. Elliot of Vermont in the House, from the legislature of Vermont, concurring with the resolution of the legislature of Kentucky; read. Annals, p. 216; H. J., reprint, vol. 5, pp. 496, 499.

379. Judiciary: Extent of jurisdiction.

> 1807, Feb. 20. 9th Cong., 2d sess. By Mr. Clay of Kentucky; considered and postponed. S. J., pp. °178, 200; Annals, pp. °76, 90.

380. Judiciary: Composition, term of office, and removal.

>1807, Nov. 5. 10th Cong., 1st sess. By Mr. Tiffin of Ohio; referred to a select com. S. J., pp. °26, °27, 131, 132; Annals, pp. °21, °22, 99.

381. Judiciary: Removal of judges.

>1808, Jan. 25. 10th Cong., 1st sess. By Mr. Robinson of Vermont, in the Senate, referred to select com. Annals, pp. 99. (From legislature of Vermont.) Jour. of Senate of Pennsylvania (1807–08) pp. °105–107. The legislatures of Rhode Island and Delaware disapproved. Annals, 11th Cong., 1st sess., p. 631. Jour. of Senate of Pennsylvania (1807–08) pp. °258–260.

382. Judiciary: Removal of judges.

>1808, Jan. 30. 10th Cong., 1st sess. By Mr. Campbell of Tennessee; referred to Com. of the Whole. H. J., p. °318; Annals, p. °1525.

383. Judiciary: Term of office: Removal: Impeachment.

>1808, Feb. 22. 10th Cong., 1st sess. By Mr. Maclay of Pennsylvania, in Senate; by Mr. Whitehill in House, from the legislature of Pennsylvania; read; to select com. S. J., pp. °169, 170; Annals, p. °133, 1680. Jour. of Senate of Pennsylvania (1807–08) pp. °163–170.

384. Commerce: Importation of slaves punishable.

>1808, Feb. 23. 10th Cong., 1st sess. By Mr. Maclay of Pennsylvania, from the legislature of Pennsylvania; read. S. J., pp. °172, 173; Annals, p. °134. Journal of Senate of Pennsylvania (1807–08) pp. °174, 203. Amer. State Papers, Misc. I, p. 716.

385. Judiciary: Term and removal.

>1808, Feb. 24. 10th Cong., 1st sess. By Mr. Whitehill of Pennsylvania, from the legislature of Pennsylvania; read; to Com. of Whole. H. J., pp. 402–403; Annals, pp. 1680–1682. See No. 383.

386. Legislative: Recall of Senators.

>1808, Feb. 29. 10th Cong., 1st sess. By Mr. Clopton of Virginia, from the legislature of Virginia; passed by the legislature Feb. 9, 1808; read twice; to Com. of the Whole. H. J., pp. °422, 423; Annals, p. °1696. Disapproved of by the legislatures of Maryland, Massachusetts, Vermont, New Jersey, Tennessee, Georgia. Jour. of Senate of Pennsylvania (1807–08) pp. °321, 118, 312; Ibid, (1809–10) p. 88; Ibid. (1810–11) p. 37; Ibid. (1811–12) p. 95; also ante p. 65, note 1.

387. Legislative and Executive Officers: Government contractors excluded from office: Members of Congress excluded from office.

>1808, Mar. 1. 10th Cong., 1st sess. By Mr. Van Horn of Maryland; tabled; to Com. of the Whole. H. J., p. °429; Annals, p. °1714.

388. Legislative: Removal of Senators.

>1808, Apr. 11. 10th Cong., 1st sess. By Mr. Giles of Virginia, in the Senate, from the legislature of Virginia. Annals, p. 325. See No. 386.

389. Judiciary: Removal of judges.

>1808, Apr. 12. 10th Cong., 1st sess. By Mr. Adams of Massachusetts, from the legislature of Massachusetts; referred to select com. S. J., p. 271; Annals. p. 331; Resolves of Massachusetts, Vol. XII, A (pp. 212–213), pp. 118–119. Resolution repealed by the next session of the legislature and instructions revoked. Ibid. (p. 317), p. 211.

390. Legislative: Article 1: Term one year, and election of Representatives.

391. Legislative: Article 2: Term of Senators three years.

392. Executive: Choice of, Article 3: By lot from the retiring Senators.

393. Executive: Article 4: Compensation.

394. Executive: Legislative: Article 5: Vice-Presidency abolished: Speaker of Senate.

395. Executive: Article 6: Appointing power limited.

396. Executive: Article 7: Power to fill vacancies and make removals.

> 1808, April 12. 10th Cong., 1st sess. By Mr. Hillhouse of Connecticut; read. S. J., p. 273; Annals, pp. °356-358; speech in full in American Register (1809), Chap. ii.

397. Judiciary: Impartial tribunal to determine disputes between the General and State governments.

> 1809, June 4. 11th Cong., 1st sess. American State Papers, Vol. ii, No. 265, pp. °2-7. Niles' Reg. xliii, Suppl. p. 24. Passed by the legislature of Pennsylvania Apr. 3. Jour. of House of Representatives of Pennsylvania (1808-09) pp. °615-620, °692-697, 786-798, 843, 910. Jour. of Senate of Pennsylvania (1808-09) pp. 268 et seq.
>
> 1809, Annals, pp. 2253-2270; °2266. American Register (1809), pp. 150-175, Disapproved by the legislature of Massachusetts. Resolves of Massachusetts. Vol. xii, p. 365. For resolutions of disapproval from the legislatures of eight other States, see ante p. 160, note 3.

397a. Commerce: Limit duration of embargo.

> 1809, June 19. Resolution of the legislature of Massachusetts. Resolves of Massachusetts, Vol. xii (p. 356), pp. °476-477; Massachusetts Senate Journal, Vol. xxx. p. 88; House Journal, Vol. xxx, p. 123. Disapproved by the legislature of Delaware (December, 1809) and the legislature of Maryland (January-February, 1810). Massachusetts Archives, Legislative Doc., 6816, 6823. Disapproved of also by the legislatures of Vermont, New Hampshire, New Jersey, Pennsylvania, North Carolina, and Tennessee. Journal of Senate of Pennsylvania (1809-10) pp. 88-89, 166-169; Ibid. (1810-11) pp. 37-41; Ibid. (1811-12) pp. 95-96. Ante p. 264, note 4.

397b. Commerce: Limit duration of embargo.

> 1809. Resolution of the general assembly of Connecticut approving the resolution of the legislature of Massachusetts. American Register, 1809, p. 181.

398. Judiciary: Composition, term, removal.

> 1809, Dec. 4. 11th Cong., 2d sess. By Mr. Pope of Kentucky; read twice; to com. S. J., pp. °22, 26, 28, 29; Annals. pp. °480, 483.

**399. Personal Relations: Titles of nobility.

> 1810, Jan. 18-Apr. 27. 11th Cong., 2d sess. By Mr. Reed of Maryland; read twice; to select com. of three; reported with amendment; considered; recommitted to a select com. of five: reported with amendment; recommitted; reported further amended; considered; amendment by Mr. Reed and Mr. Lloyd; considered; amendment to last report passed (26 to 1). Mr. Pope's amendment rejected (12 to 14). Further amended; read third time, and passed (19 to 5).
>
> Apr. 27-May 1. Received in the House; read; to Com. of the Whole; considered in Com. of the Whole; reported; read third time; passed (87 to 3). S. J., pp. °83, 86, 92, 95, 96, 117, 124, 127, 140, 248, 295, 290, 335, 360, °361, 362, 363, 372, 390, 395, 396: H. J., pp. 609, 611, 645, 646; Annals, pp. °530, 547, 549, 571, 572, 576, 635, 671, 672, 1997, 2006, 2050.
>
> Ratified by the legislatures of the following States: Maryland, Dec. 25, 1810; Kentucky, Jan. 31, 1811; Ohio. Jan. 31, 1811; Delaware, Feb. 2, 1811; Pennsylvania, Feb. 6, 1811; New Jersey, Feb. 13, 1811; Vermont, Oct. 24, 1811; Tennessee, Nov. 21, 1811; Georgia, Dec 13, 1811; North Carolina, Dec. 23, 1811, Massachusetts, Feb. 27, 1812; New Hampshire, Dec. 10, 1812; total 12. Rejected by New York, March 12, 1811 (by the Senate); Connecticut, May session, 1813; South Carolina, approved by the Senate, Nov. 28, 1811; postponed by the House, Dec. 21, 1811; reconsidered; committee reported unfavorably; not considered, Dec. 7, 1813; Rhode Island, Sept. 15, 1814; total 4.
>
> Virginia, action is not recorded in journals or Department of State. Annals of Congress, 15th Cong. 1st sess. pp. 530, °855, 1074; H. J., 95, 221, 282. Letter of

****399. Personal Relations: Titiles of nobility—Continued.

> John Q. Adams, Secretary of State, Report Book (Dec. 1817, July 1821), pp. 14–15;
> Bureau of Rolls and Library, Department of State. For reprints of the cer-
> tified copies of the action of the various State legislatures, in Bureau of Rolls
> and Library, Department of State, see Documentary History of the Consti-
> tution of the United States, Vol. ii, pp. 452–515. (Bulletin of the Bureau of
> Rolls and Library of the Department of State, No. 7.)

**400. Executive offices: Senators and Representatives excluded from civil
office.**

> 1810, May 1. 11th Cong., 2d sess. By Mr. Macon of North Carolina; read;
> tabled. H. J., pp. °639,640; Annals, p. 2028.

**401. Executive offices: Senators and Representatives excluded from civil
office.**

> 1810, Dec. 10. 11th Cong., 3d sess. By Mr. Macon of North Carolina; read;
> to Com. of the Whole; considered; to select com.; reported; considered in
> Com. of the Whole; attempt to amend; reported to House in an amended
> form. Mr. Hubbard's amendment failed; House concur with Com. of the
> Whole (71 to 40); Speaker declared question lost; appeal taken, but Chair
> sustained and amendment failed. H. J., pp. °25, 26, 61, 96, 181–185, 210, 211, 212,
> 213, 214, 215, 217, 218, 219; Annals, pp. °380, 458, 841, 867, 905.

402. Judiciary: Removal of judges.

> 1811, Jan. 29. 11th Cong., 3d sess. By Mr. Wright of Maryland; motion to
> consider lost. H. J., pp. °189, 190; Annals, pp. °836, 857.

**403. Executive: Appointments to civil office of relatives of Senators or
Representatives prohibited.**

> 1811, Jan. 30. 11th Cong., 3d sess. By Mr. Quincy of Massachusetts;
> referred to Com. of the Whole; attempt to amend in Com. of the Whole by
> Mr. Wright. H. J., pp. °181–185.

404. Finance: Duties on exports.

> 1812, Mar. 12. 12th Cong., 1st sess. By Mr. Mitchell of New York; read.
> H. J., p. °483; Annals, p. °1291.

405. Judiciary: Removal of judges.

> 1812, Apr. 13. 12th Cong., 1st sess. By Mr. McKim of Maryland; read and
> tabled. H. J., p. °587; Annals, p. °1317.

405a. Legislative: Term of Senator four years.

> 1812. Resolution of the legislature of Tennessee. Niles' Register (Dec. 5,
> 1812), Vol. iii, p. 224; Vol. vi, p. 16.

406. Legislative: Election of Representatives by districts.

407. Executive: Choice of: Election of electors by districts.

> 1813, Jan. 18. 12th Cong., 2d sess. By Mr. Pickens of North Carolina; com-
> mitted to Com. of the Whole. H. J., pp. °183, 184; Annals, p. °848.

408. Legislative: Election of Representatives by districts.

> 1813, Jan. 20. 12th Cong., 2d sess. By Mr. Turner of North Carolina, from
> the legislature of North Carolina; read twice; to select com. S. J., pp. °176–
> 178, 190; Annals, pp. °57, 58.

*409. Executive: Choice of: Election of electors by districts.

> 1813, Jan. 20–Feb. 17. 12th Cong., 2d sess. By Mr. Turner of North Carolina,
> from the legislature of North Carolina; read twice; to select com.; report;
> amendments made; considered in Com. of the Whole, and agreed to as
> amended by com.; Mr. German's amendment lost; read third time; passed
> Senate (22 to 9).
>
> Feb. 18. Received in the House; read twice; to Com. of the Whole. S. J.,
> pp. °125–128, 130, 180, 202, 212, 213, 217, 219, 220, 221, 226, 227, 228, 229; H. J., pp. 319,
> 327; Annals, pp. °57–58, 77, 89, 91, 1080, 1082.

410. Finance: Tax on exports.

411. Commerce: Internal improvements, roads.

412. Commerce: Internal improvements, canals.

413. Finance: National Bank.

> 1813, July 10. 13th Cong., 1st sess. By Mr. Jackson of Virginia: read; tabled. H. J., pp. °190–191; Annals, p. 431.

413a. Legislative and Executive: Uniform mode of electing Senators, Representatives, and electors.

> 1813, Dec. 14. 13th Cong., 2d sess. By Mr. Wright, in House, for a com. to devise uniform mode; com. appointed. Niles' Register, Vol. v, p. 272.

414. Executive: Choice of: Election of electors by districts.

> 1813, Dec. 20. 13th Cong., 2d sess. By Mr. Pickens of North Carolina; read; to Com. of the Whole; considered; House concur with Com. of the Whole in disagreement (83 to 64). H. J., pp. °50–51, 90, 96, 107, 257; Annals, pp. °797, 798, 849.

415. Finance: Tax on exports.

416. Commerce: Internal improvements, roads.

417. Commerce: Internal improvement, canals.

418. Finance: National Bank.

> 1814, Jan. 5. 13th Cong., 2d sess. By Mr. Jackson of Virginia; read; tabled; considered by Com. of the Whole; report their agreement to the House. H. J., pp. °102, 251, 257; Annals, p. °849.

419. Legislative: Term of Senators four years.

> 1814, Feb. 9. 13th Cong., 2d sess. By Mr. Grundy of Tennessee, in the House, from the legislature of Tennessee; passed Oct. 17, 1813; to Com. of the Whole. Annals, p. 1264; Niles' Register, Vol. v, p. 207. Resolutions of non-concurrence from the legislature of Massachusetts, New Hampshire, Vermont, Rhode Island, Maryland, and North Carolina. Jour. of Senate of Penn. (1813–14) pp. °188; Ibid (1814–15) p. 18; app. pp. 9–12, 32.

419a. Legislative: Term of Senators four years.

> 1814 Nov. 9. Resolution of the legislature of Georgia. Jour. of Senate of Pennsylvania (1814–15) p. 17. Niles' Register, Vol. x, p. 177. Resolutions of the legislatures of North Carolina (Dec. 19, 1815) and Ohio (Feb. 27, 1816) of nonconcurrence. Archives of Massachusetts. House Misc. 8105, 8183; Annals 14th Cong., 1st sess., p. 365. Resolutions of Rhode Island, Louisiana, and New Hampshire of non-concurrence. Jour. of Senate of Penn. (1814–15) p. 38; Ibid, (1816–17); app. pp. 20, 25; Ibid, (1817–18) p. 156.

419b. Legislative: Term of Senators four years.

> 1814, Feb. 21. Resolutions of the legislature of Pennsylvania. Journal of the Senate of Pennsylvania (1813–14) pp. 182, 205, 229, °238, °273; Journal of House of Reps. (1813–14) °70–71; 260, 320, 357. For resolutions of non-concurrence, see No. 419.

420. Finance: Tax on exports.

421. Commerce: Internal improvements, roads.

422. Internal improvements, canals.

> 1814, Sept. 27. 13th Cong., 3d sess. By Mr. Jackson of Virginia: referred to Com. of the Whole; considered; recommitted; postponed indefinitely. H. J., pp. °31, 39, 41, 62, 556; Annals, pp. °324, 326, 1101.

423. Finance: National Bank: Congress: Power to establish.

> 1814, Sept. 27. 13th Cong., 3d sess. By Mr. Jackson of Virginia; referred to Com. of the Whole; considered by com. and struck out. H. J., pp. °31, 39; Annals, 324–326, 339.

424. Legislative: 1. Apportionment of Representatives to free persons.

425. Finance: Apportionment of direct taxes to free persons.

426. Territorial: 2. Admission of new States on two-thirds vote only.

427. Commerce: 3. Congress: Power to lay embargo limited.

428. Commerce: 4. Congress: Power to interdict commercial intercourse limited.

429. War: 5. Congress: Power to declare war.

430. Personal Rights: Executive Officers: 6. No person hereafter naturalized eligible to office.

431. Executive: 7. One term only: Not from same State twice in succession.

> 1815, Feb. 28. 13th Cong., 3d sess. By Mr. Dana of Connecticut, from the legislature of Connecticut; read. S. J., p. °485; Annals, p. 281. For replies of States non-concurring see ante p. 46, note 5. In addition North Carolina non-concurred. Jour. of Senate of Pennsylvania (1815-16); app. pp. 32-34.

432. Legislative: 1. Apportionment of Representatives to free persons.

433. Finance: Apportionment of direct taxes to free persons.

434. Territorial: 2. Admission of new States on two-thirds vote only.

435. Commerce: 3. Congress: Power to lay embargo limited.

436. Commerce: 4. Congress: Power to interdict commercial intercourse limited.

437. War: 5. Congress: Power to declare war.

438. Executive Officers: 6. No persons hereafter naturalized eligible to office.

439. Executive Officers: 7. One term only: Not from same State twice in succession.

> 1815, Mar. 2. 13th Cong., 3d sess. By Mr. Varnum of Massachusetts, from the legislature of Massachusetts; read. S. J., 494; Annals, p. 284.

440. Legislative: 1. Apportionment of Representatives to free persons.

441. Finance: Apportionment of direct taxes to free persons.

442. Territorial: 2. Admission of new States only by two-thirds vote.

443. Commerce: 3. Congress: Power to lay embargo limited.

444. Commerce: 4. Congress: Power to interdict commercial intercourse limited.

445. War: 5. Congress: Power to declare war.

446. Executive Officers: 6. No person hereafter naturalized eligible to office.

447. Executive: 7. One term only: Not from same State twice in succession.

> 1815, Mar.3. 13th Cong., 3d sess. By Mr. Pickering of Massachusetts: tabled. H. J., p. °765-6; Annals, p. °1269, 1270.

448. Commerce: Internal improvements.

> 1815, Dec. 5. 14th Cong., 1st sess. By President Madison in his seventh annual message. Statesman's Manual, p. 382.

449. Legislative: Election of Representatives by districts.

450. Executive: Choice of: Election of electors by districts.

> 1816, Jan. 5. 14th Cong., 1st sess. By Mr. Pickens of North Carolina (from the legislature of North Carolina); to Com. of the Whole. H. J., p. °129-30; Annals, p. °461. Jour. of Senate of Pennsylvania (1815-16); app. pp. °29-30.

451. Legislative: Term of Senators three years.

> 1816, Jan. 25. 14th Cong., 1st sess. By Mr. Bibb of Georgia; read twice; considered in Com. of the Whole; failed to be read third time (7 to 24). S. J., pp. °112, 120, 147, 178, 222, 242; Annals, pp. °44, 161, 163.

451a. Executive: Choice of: Electors by districts.
451b. Legislative: Election of Representatives by districts.

1816, Feb. 20. Resolution of the general assembly of Virginia, approving the resolutions of North Corolina. Massachusetts Archives. House Misc., 8178. Journal of Senate of Pennsylvania (1816–17); app. pp. °17–18.

452. Legislative: Election of Representatives by districts.
453. Executive: Choice of: Electors by districts.

1816, Feb. 27. 14th Cong., 1st sess. By Mr. Varnum of Massachusetts. from the legislature of Massachusetts; read; to a select com. of five; considered in Com. of the Whole; reported to Senate; considered; attempt to refer to a select com. to consider a direct vote for President defeated (12 to 21); motion to strike out second clause defeated (12 to 20); postponed (18 to 14). S. J., pp. °224–226, 246, 247, 282, 317–320; Annals, pp. 158, 164, 177, 227; Resolves of Massachusetts, Vol. xv, pp. °155–157. Vermont non-concurred. Jour. of Senate of Pennsylvania (1817–18), pp. °341–343.

453a. Legislative: Election of Representatives by districts.

1816. Resolutions of the legislature of New Jersey. Niles' Register, Vol. xiii, p. 272.

454. Legislative: Election of Representatives by districts.
455. Executive: Choice of: Electors by districts.

1816, Mar. 6. 14th Cong., 1st sess. By Mr. Pickering of Massachusetts; to Com. of the Whole. H. J., p. °446; Annals, pp. °1150, 1151.

456. Judiciary: Removal of judges.

1816, Mar. 7. 14th Cong., 1st sess. By Mr. Sanford of New York; read; considered. S. J., pp. °268, 282; Annals, pp. 170, 177.

456a. Executive: Choice of: Electors by districts.

1816, Apr. 22. 14th Cong., 1st sess. By Mr. Barbour, in Senate; by Mr. Pleasants, in House; resolution from the legislature of Virginia, agreeing with resolutions of North Carolina. Annals, pp. 336–337, °1404.

457. Commerce: Internal improvements.

1816, Dec. 3. 14th Cong., 2d sess. By President Madison in his eighth annual message. Statesman's Manual, p. 335.

458. Legislative: Compensation of Senators and Representatives.

1816, Dec. 10. 14th Cong., 2d. sess. By Mr. Barbour of Virginia; read twice; to a select com. S. J., p. °30; Annals, pp. °30, 40.

458a. Legislative: Compensation of Senators and Representatives.

1816. Resolution of the legislature of Massachusetts. Niles' Register (Dec. 14, 1816), Vol. ix. pp. °239, 259.

459. Legislative: Election of Representatives by districts.
460. Executive: Choice of: Electors by districts.

1816, Dec. 11. By Mr. Pickens of North Carolina; to Com. of the Whole; considered by com.; reported to the House. Mr. Pickering moved an amendment; tabled; attempt to consider defeated. H. J., pp. °54, 55, 78, 84, 89, 94, 341; Annals, pp. °257, 329, 341.

461. Personal Relations: Establishment of a national university.

1816, Dec. 12. 14th Cong., 2d sess. By Mr. Atherton of New Hampshire; read; refused to consider. H. J., p. °63; Annals, p. °268.

461a. Legislative: Compensation of members of Congress.

1817, Jan. 17. Resolutions of the legislature of Kentucky. Jour. of Senate of Pennsylvania (1817–18), pp. °61–62. Resolutions of nonconcurrence from the legislatures of Vermont, Ohio, Illinois, and New Hampshire. Ibid., pp. 343–344; Ibid. (1818–19), pp. 146, 715; Jour. of House of Rep. of Pennsylvania (1818–19), p. 38.

462. Legislative: Election of Representatives by districts.

463. Executive: Choice of: Election of electors by districts.

> 1817, Jan. 21. 14th Cong., 2d sess. By Mr. Pickens of North Carolina, from the legislature of North Carolina, resolution indorsing resolution of the legislature of Massachusetts. H. J., p. °243; Annals, p. °694.

464. War: Power of the General Government to train militia.

> 1817, Feb. 3. 14th Cong., 2d sess. By Mr. Harrison of Ohio; that a com. be appointed to inquire if an amendment is necessary; tabled.
> Feb. 28. Mr. Harrison introduced an amendment; read; tabled. H. J., pp. 328, °488; Annals p. °1041.

465. Commerce: Internal improvements

466. Personal Relations: Power of Congress to establish seminaries of learning.

> 1817, Dec. 2. 15th Cong., 1st sess. By President Monroe in his first annual message. Statesman's Manual, p. 402.

467. Commerce: Internal improvements.

> 1817, Dec. 9. 15th Cong., 1st sess. By Mr. Barbour of Virginia; read twice; to a select com.; reported; considered; postponed (22 to 9). S. J., pp. 23, 24, 176, 190, 247, 283; Annals, pp. 21, 22.

467a. Legislative: Compensation of members of Congress.

> 1817, Dec. 16. Resolutions of the legislature of Georgia concurring with the resolutions of Kentucky. Jour. of Senate of Pennsylvania (1817-18), p. °467.

468. Legislative: Election of Representatives.

469. Executive: Choice of: Election of electors.

> 1817, Dec. 23. 15th Cong., 1st sess. By Mr Dickerson of New Jersey, from the legislature of New Jersey; read twice; to a select com.; reported with amendments; considered in Com. of the Whole; reported to House; failed to pass (20 to 13). S. J., pp. 48, 49, 51, 119, 138, 149, 152, 157, 192, 203, 210, 212, 214, 220, 214, 220; Annals, pp. 65, 67, 176, 229, 242; nonconcurred in by the legislatures of Mississippi and Ohio. Jour. of House of Rep. of Pennsylvania (1818-19), pp. 35, 145.

470. War: Power of the General Government to train militia.

> 1818, Jan. 9. 15th Cong., 1st sess. By Mr. Harrison of Ohio. To Com. of the Whole. H. J., p. °128; Annals, p. 611.

471. Legislative: Election of Representatives.

472. Executive: Choice of: Election of electors.

> 1818, Jan. 19. 15th Cong., 1st sess. By Mr. Macon of North Carolina, in the Senate, from the legislature of North Carolina, concurring in resolution proposed by New Jersey, to select a com. on same subject; reported with amendments. Annals, pp. 114, 136; Jour. of Senate of Pennsylvania (1817-18), pp. °224-225. Resolutions of Georgia and Ohio nonconcurring. Ibid., pp. °466-467; Ibid. (1818-19), pp. °91-92.

473. Legislative: Compensation of members of Congress.

> 1818, Feb. 5. 15th Cong., 1st sess. By Mr. Campbell of Tennessee; in Senate, from the legislature of Tennessee; received and entered by vote of 19 to 14. Annals, p. 170; Jour. of Senate of Pennsylvania (1817-18), p. °279.

474. Personal Relations: Slavery prohibited.

> 1818, Apr. 4. 15th Cong., 1st sess. By Mr. Livermore of New Hampshire; read; motion to consider failed. H. J., pp. °420-421; Annals, pp. °1675-1676.

475. Executive: 1. Veto abolished.

476. Judiciary: 2. Appointed by Congress.

477. Executive Officers: 3. Choice of Cabinet officers by Congress.

478. Judiciary and Executive Officers: 4. Vacancies, etc.

479. Executive Officers: 6. Exclusion of members of Congress.

> 1818, Apr. 16. 15th Cong., 1st sess. By Mr. Lewis of Virginia; read; tabled. H. J., pp. °478–479; Annals, pp. °1744–1745.

480. Territorial: District of Columbia.

> 1818. Nov. 17. 15th Cong., 2d sess. By President Monroe in his third annual message. A somewhat blind clause that might mean an amendment. States-man's Manual, p. 411.

480a. Legislative: Election of Representatives by districts.

480b. Executive: Choice of: Election of electors by districts.

> 1818, Nov. 11. Resolutions of the legislature of Vermont. Jour. of Senate of Pennsylvania (1818–19), pp. °219–220.

481. Legislative: Election of Representatives by districts.

482. Executive: Choice of: Election of electors by districts.

> 1818, Nov. 25. 15th Cong., 2d sess. By Mr. Sanford of New York, in the Senate, from the legislature of New York, a resolution indorsing the resolution of North Carolina; read. Annals, pp. °23, 24.

483. Legislative: Election of Representatives by districts.

484. Executive: Choice of: Election of electors by districts.

> 1818, Nov. 25. 15th Cong., 2d sess. By Mr. Storer of New Hampshire, in the Senate, from the legislature of New Hampshire, resolution indorsing resolutions of the general assembly of New Jersey; read. Annals, pp. °24–25.

*485. Choice of Executive: Election of electors.

486. Legislative: Election of Representatives by districts.

> 1818, Dec. 2; 1819, Feb. 3. 15th Cong., 2d sess. By Mr. Dickerson of New Jersey; read twice; to a select com.; reported with amendments; considered in Com. of the Whole, and was amended; passed to third reading; vote reconsidered; to a select com.; reported with amendments; considered in Com. of the Whole; recommitted; considered; passed to third reading, and passed (28 to 10).
> 1819, Feb. 5–26. Received by the House; read twice; to Com. of the Whole; Com. of the Whole discharged from further consideration by vote of 79 to 73. S. J., pp. 45, 54, 77, 82, 118, 126, 144, 149, 153, 156, 162, 180, 193, 200, 206, 212, 215, 221; H. J., pp. 232, 233, 320; Annals, pp. 33, 39, 139, 174, 190, 197, 203, 207, 1038, 1420.

487. Legislative: Election of Representatives by districts.

488. Executive: Choice of: Election of electors by districts.

> 1818, Dec. 7. 15th Cong., 2d sess. By Mr. Doggett of Connecticut, in the Senate, from the legislature of Connecticut; read. Annals, p. °42.

488a. Legislative: Election of Representatives by districts.

488b. Executive: Choice of: Electors by districts.

> 1819, Feb. 18. Resolution of the legislature of Massachusetts. Resolves of Massachusetts. Vol. xv, pp. °706–707.

*489. Executive: Choice of: Election of electors.

490. Legislative: Election of Representatives by districts.

> 1819, Dec. 4; 1820, Jan. 27. 16th Cong., 1st sess. By Mr. Dickerson of New Jersey; read twice; to select com ; reported; ordered to a third reading; passed.
> 1820, Jan. 28–April 20. Received by the House. Read twice; to Com. of the Whole; considered in Com. of the Whole; reported; House refuse to consider. S. J., pp. 25, 28, 125, 127; H. J., pp. 179, 345, 380, 436; Annals, pp. 22, 24, 40, 233, 278, 992, 1691.

491 [489] [490]. Executive and legislative: Election of.

> Attempt to amend by Mr. Lloyd in the Senate; lost, 12 to 30. S. J , p, °125.

492. Finance: Congress prohibited from establishing a national bank except in District of Columbia.

> 1820, Jan. 5. 16th Cong., 1st sess. By Mr. Lowrie of Pennsylvania, in the Senate, from the legislature of Pennsylvania (passed March 27, 1819); read Annals, p. °70. Jour. of the House of Representatives of Pennsylvania (1818-19), pp. °200, 341, 601, 757, 765, 767; Senate Jour. of Pennsylvania (1818-19), p. 525. For replies of other States, ante, p. 256, note 4.

492a. Finance: Congress prohibited from establishing a national bank except in District of Columbia.

> 1819, Nov. 29. Resolutions of the general assembly of Tennessee concurring with resolutions of the legislature of Pennsylvania. Jour. of House of Rep. of Pennsylvania (1820-21), p. °67.

493. Executive officers: Members of Congress excluded.

> 1820, Jan. 24. 16th Cong., 1st sess. By Mr. Cobb of Georgia; read twice; to Com. of the Whole; considered in com.; amended; reported; considered; on motion to pass third reading, failed (72 to 87). H. J., pp. °166, 171, 345, 384, 414; Annals, pp. 1691, 1859. (See article in Niles' Register, Vol. XVIII, pp. 137-138.)

494. Finance: Congress prohibited from establishing national banks except in District of Columbia.

> 1820, Jan. 26. 16th Cong., 1st sess. By Mr. Noble of Indiana, from the legislature of Indiana, a resolution concurring in resolution of legislature of Pennsylvania; read. Annals, p. °258.

495. Finance: Congress prohibited from establishing banks except in District of Columbia.

> 1820, Jan. 31. 16th Cong., 1st sess. By Mr. Baldwin of Pennsylvania: read; to Com. of the Whole. S. J., p. °184; Annals, p. °1022. See No. 492.

496. Finance: Congress prohibited from establishing banks except in District of Columbia.

> 1820, Feb. 16. 16th Cong., 1st sess. By Mr. Trimble of Ohio, in the Senate, from the legislature of Ohio, a resolution concurring with the resolution of the legislature of Pennsylvania: read. Annals, p. 417. Jour. of Senate of Pennsylvania (1819-20), pp. °283-284.

497. Executive: Choice of: Election of electors.

498. Legislative: Election of Representatives.

> 1820, Nov. 20. 16th Cong., 2d sess. By Mr. Smith of North Carolina; read twice; to Com. of the Whole; considered in Com. of the Whole; reported; passed to third reading; postponed; failed to pass (92 to 54). H. J., pp. 23, 24, 36, 52, 56, 172; Annals, pp. 459, 504, 967. (See article in Niles' Register, Vol. XIX. p. 195.) Resolution of North Carolina nonconcurred in by legislature of South Carolina. See Resolves of Massachusetts, Vol. XVI, p. 118.

499. Legislative: Election of Representatives by districts.

500. Executive: Choice of: Election of electors.

> 1820, Nov. 22. 16th Cong., 2d sess. By Mr. Dickerson of New Jersey; read twice; to a select com.; reported with amendments; reported inexpedient to amend; considered in Com. of the Whole; tabled. S. J., pp. 25, 27, 145, 230; Annals, pp. 22, 23, 256, 257.

501. Judiciary: Appeal to Senate when a State is a party.

> 1821, Dec. 12. 17th Cong., 1st sess. By Mr. Johnson of Kentucky; read twice; considered in Com. of the Whole; tabled. S. J., pp. 25, 68, 66, 72, 86, 117, 131, 184, 199; Annals, pp. °23-25, 68-92, 96-114.

502. Legislative: Choice of Representatives by districts.

503. Executive: Choice of.

> 1821, Dec. 15. 17th Cong., 1st sess. By Mr. Whitman of Maine: read twice; to Com. of the Whole. H. J., pp. °59, 63; Annals, pp. °551-552, 553.

504. Legislative: Apportionment: Limit number of Representatives to two hundred.

> 1821, Dec. 18. 17th Cong., 1st sess. By Mr. Barbour of Virginia; read twice; considered in Com. of the Whole: postponed indefinitely. S.J., pp. 30, 32, 80, 133, 183; Annals, p. 28–29. 33, 286. Niles' Register, Vol. XXI, p. °268.

*505. Legislative: Choice of Representatives.

506. Executive: Choice of: Election by districts, etc.

> 1821, Dec. 19; 1822, Mar. 11. 17th Cong., 1st sess. By Mr. Dickerson of New Jersey; read twice; considered in Com. of the Whole; referred to select com. of five; report of com. with amendment; considered in Com. of the Whole, and com. amendments disagreed to and others made. Reported to the Senate; amended; read third time, and passed (29 to 11).
>
> 1822, Mar. 11–12. Received in the House; read twice; to Com. of the Whole. S. J., pp. 32, 34, 36, 72, 73, 89, 125, 158, 173, 179. H. J., pp. 338, 341. Annals, pp. 33, 34, 38, 116–125, 155, 197, 281, 283, 1249, 1250, 1260.

506a. Finance: National banks prohibited, save in District of Columbia.

506b. Executive: Choice of: Uniform mode of election by districts.

506c. Legislative: Choice of Representatives by districts.

> 1821, Dec. 20. 17th Cong., 1st sess. By Mr. Thomas of Illinois. in the Senate, from the legislature of Illinois, resolution concurring in resolution of the legislatures of Pennsylvania and Vermont: read. Annals, p. 35. Jour. of Senate of Pennsylvania (1820–21), p. °715.

507. Executive: Choice of: Officeholders ineligible, age qualification.

> 1822, Jan. 10. 17th Cong., 1st sess. By Mr. Woodson of Kentucky; read; tabled. H.J., p. °136; Annals, p. 692.

508. Commerce: Bankruptcy, effect of State acts.

> 1822, Mar. 12. 17th Cong., 1st sess. By Mr. Walworth of New York: read twice; to Com. of the Whole. H.J., pp., °340–341, 355; Annals, pp., °1268, 1303.

508a. Judiciary: Removal of judges by joint address of Congress.

> 1822, Jan. 15. By Mr. Holmes of Maine, as amendment to No. 501; read. Annals, p. °114.

509. Executive: Choice of: Division of United States into "Presidential sections."

> 1822, Apr. 27. 17th Cong. 1st sess. By Mr. Montgomery of Kentucky. H.J., pp., °502–503; Annals. pp., °1700–1701.

510. Legislative: Compensation of Representatives.

511. Executive Officers: Members of Congress excluded.

> 1822, Apr. 30. 17th Cong., 1st sess. By Mr. Blair of South Carolina; read twice; tabled. H.J., p. °519; Annals, p. °1752.

512. Legislative: Compensation of members of Congress.

> 1822, May 1. 17th Cong., 1st sess. By Mr. Conkling of New York; read; tabled. H.J., p. °533; Annals. p. °1708.

513. Legislative and Executive: Compensation fixed decennially.

> 1822, May 2. 17th Cong., 1st sess. By Mr. Fuller of Massachusetts; read; tabled. H.J., pp. °542–543; Annals, p. °1777.

514. Commerce: Internal improvements.

> 1822, Dec. 3. 17th Cong., 2d sess. By President Monroe in his sixth annual message; also May 4, 1822, in a special message. Statesman's Manual, p. 447.

515. Commerce: Internal improvements.

> 1822, Dec. 11. 17th Cong., 2d sess. By Mr. Talbot, a motion to refer that part of President's message to a select com. S. J., p. 26; Annals, pp. °27, 29.

516. Executive Offices: Ineligibility of Presidential electors.

    1823, Jan. 6. 17th Cong., 2d sess. By Mr. Smyth of Virginia; read twice; to Com. of the Whole. H. J., p. °102, 105; Annals, pp. °489, 508, 510.

517. Executive: Choice: By electors, case of no majority.

    1823, Jan. 10. 17th Cong., 2d sess. By Mr. Taylor of Virginia; read twice; to a select com.; a new draft. Substitute presented by Messrs. Dickerson and Holmes; considered. S. J., pp. 78, 85, 111, 117, 146, 151, 163, 171, 178; Annals, pp. °101, 105, 107; °158, °176, 194, 200, °223, 228, 266.

518. Legislative: Choice of Representatives by districts.

519. Executive: Choice.

520. Executive: Choice: No third term.

    1823, Jan. 30. 17th Cong., 2d sess. By Mr. Dickerson of New Jersey, as a substitute to Mr. Taylor's; read. S. J., p. 117; Annals, pp. °176, 194, 200.

521. Executive: Choice: Decision of contests.

    1823, Feb. 11. 17th Cong., 2d sess. By Mr. Holmes of Maine, as an amendment to Mr. Taylor's; read. S. J., p. 146; Annals, pp. °223, 228, 254, 266.

522. Commercial Powers: Internal improvements.

    1823, Jan. 15. 17th Cong., 2d sess. By Mr. Reid of Georgia; read; refused to consider. H. J., pp. °132, °147; Annals, p. °627.

523. Commercial Powers: Internal improvements.

    1823, Feb. 11. 17th Cong., 2d sess. By Mr. Smith of Maryland; read twice; considered in Com. of the Whole. S. J., pp. 144, 150, 208; Annals, pp. °200, 227, 290.

524. Executive: Choice: By districts.

525. Legislative: Choice of Representatives by districts.

    1823, Dec. 5. 18th Cong., 1st sess. By Mr. McDuffie of South Carolina, that a select com. be appointed to inquire; appointed. Mr. McDuffie reports for com. a resolution to amend; read twice; to Com. of the Whole. H. J., p. 83; Annals, p. °866.

526. Executive: Choice: Direct vote by districts.

    1823, Dec. 11. 18th Cong., 1st sess. By Mr. Benton of Missouri; read twice; considered in Com. of the Whole; referred to com. and reported. S. J., pp. 34, 37, 41, 42, 46, 86; Annals, pp. °32, 36, 44, °100-102.

527. Executive: Choice: Case of no majority.

    1823, Dec. 15. 18th Cong., 1st sess. By Mr. Hayne of South Carolina; read twice; to select com.; report of com. S. J., pp. 40, 46, 86; Annals, pp. °41, 44. 100, 102.

528. Legislative: Choice of Representatives.

529. Executive: Choice: By districts, etc.

    1823, Dec. 16. 18th Cong., 1st sess. By Mr. Dickerson of New Jersey; read twice; to a select com.; report of com. considered in Com. of the Whole; indefinitely postponed. S. J., pp. 44, 86, 95, 104, 121, 124, 142, 145, 148, 150, 168, 177, 196, 222, 241, 243, 244; Annals, pp. °43, 103, 116, 130, 133, 100, 165, 167.

530. Executive: Choice: Decision of contests.

    1823, Dec. 16. 18th Cong., 1st sess. By Mr. Holmes of Maine; read twice; to a select com.; report of com. S. J., pp. 44, 86; Annals, p. °44.

531. Executive: Choice: Case of no majority.

    1823, Dec. 20. 18th Cong., 1st sess. By Mr. Mills of Massachusetts; read twice; to select a com.; report of com. S. J., pp. 61, 86; Annals, pp. °64, 74.

532. Executive: Choice: Election of electors by districts.

    1823, Dec. 20. 18th Cong., 1st sess. By Mr. Van Buren of New York; read twice; to a select com.; report of com. S. J., pp. 61, 86, 89, 95; Annals, pp. °73, 74.

533. Legislative: Choice of Representatives by districts.

534. Executive: Choice of electors by districts; no third term.

1824, Jan. 8. 18th Cong., 1st sess. By Mr. Benton of Missouri, from the select com. to which the several propositions were referred; read and considered. S. J., pp. 86, 95, 104, 121, 124, 142, 145, 148, 150), 168, 177, 196, 222, 241, 243, 244; Annals, pp. °99-100, 103, 116, 130, 133, 160, 165, 167.

*535. Executive: Choice; no third term.

1824, Jan. 9–30. 18th Cong., 1st sess. By Mr. Benton of Missouri, from the select com.; read twice; considered; read third time, and passed Senate (36 to 3.)
Jan. 30. Received in the House; read twice; to Com. of the Whole. S. J., pp. 89, 95, 104, 105, 124, 142, 143; H. J., pp. 187, 191; Annals, pp. 103, 110, 154, 159, 160.

536. Commercial Powers: Internal improvements.

1824, Jan. 22. 18th Cong., 1st sess. By Mr. Van Buren of New York; read twice; considered in Com. of the Whole. S. J., pp. 124, 128 137; Annals, pp. °136, 138, 151.

537. Executive: Choice of, by districts.

1824, Jan. 24. 18th Cong., 1st sess. By Mr. Livingston of Louisiana; received and tabled. H. J., p. 171; Annals, p. °1179.

538. Commerce: Importation or ingress of persons of color.

1824, Feb. 6. 18th Cong., 1st sess. By Mr. Abbott of Georgia, from the legislature of Georgia (Dec. 22, 1823); read twice; to Com. of the Whole. H. J., p. °208; Annals, p. °1399. Disapproved by the legislature of Vermont (1825). Massachusetts Archives. Senate Misc., °½°°; also by the legislatures of Maine, Ohio, New Jersey, Indiana, Connecticut, Delaware, and Kentucky, Jour. of House of Rep. of Penn. (1823-24), pp. 820, 947; Ibid. (1824-25), pp. 326, 408; Jour. of Senate of Penn. (1825-26). pp. 41. 42, 145, 204.

538a. Commerce: Importation or ingress of persons of color.

1826, Jan. 30. Resolution passed by the legislature of Louisiana, approving the amendment proposed by the legislature of Georgia. Massachusetts Archives. Senate Misc., °½°⁴. Journal of Senate of Pennsylvania (1825-26), p. °478.

538b. Commerce: Importation or ingress of persons of color.

1825, Jan. 22. Resolutions of the legislature of Missouri concurring with the resolutions of the legislature of Georgia. Jour. of Senate of Pennsylvania (1824-25), p. °736.

538c. Commerce: Importation or ingress of persons of color.

1825, Jan. 28. Resolutions of the legislature of Mississippi concurring with the resolutions of the legislature of Georgia. Jour. of Senate of Pennsylvania (1824-25), p. °557.

539. Executive: Choice of.

1824, Dec. 30. 18th Cong., 2d sess. By Mr. Strong of New York, in the House. Debates, p. °101.

540. Executive: Choice of: Electors by districts.

1825, Jan. 4. 18th Cong., 2d sess. By Mr. Saunders of North Carolina; read twice; to Com. of the Whole. H. J., pp. °103, 104; Debates, pp. °128-129.

541. Executive: Choice of, directly by districts.

1825, Mar. 1. 18th Cong., 2d sess. By Mr. McDuffie of South Carolina; read; tabled. H. J., pp. °287-288.

541a. Executive: Choice of, directly by districts.

541b. Executive Offices: Members of Congress excluded.

1825, Nov. 25. Resolutions of the general assembly of Tennessee. Niles' Register, Vol. XXIX, pp. 369, 429; Massachusetts Archives. Senate, °½°. Jour. of Senate of Pennsylvania (1825-26), pp. °159-160. Disapproved of by the legislatures of Indiana (Jan. 20, 1826) and Maine (Feb. 17, 1826). Massachusetts Archives. Senate, °½¹, °½⁴. Jour. of Senate of Pennsylvania (1825-26), pp. 364, 399; Vermont nonconcurred, ibid. (1826-27), p. 109.

542. Executive: Choice of, directly by districts, not to devolve upon
Congress.

> 1825, Dec. 9. 19th Cong., 1st sess. By Mr. McDuffie of South Carolina; read;
> to Com. of the Whole; com. report at various times that they have not
> agreed; com. ordered to report a resolution; com., unable to agree "on a
> specific plan," is discharged. H. J., pp. °32, 262, 264, 267, 275, 283, 290, 306, 318, 322,
> 324, 326, 340, 342, 371, 375, 387, 389, 392, 395, 400, 410.

543. Commercial Powers: Internal improvements: National university.

> 1825, Dec. 13. 19th Cong., 1st sess. By Mr. Bailey of Massachusetts; read.
> H. J., pp. °47–48; Debates, pp. °801–802.

544. Executive Officers: Members of Congress excluded.

> 1825, Dec. 13. 19th Cong., 1st sess. By Mr. Mitchell of Tennessee. H. J.,
> pp., °50, 309.

544a. Executive: Choice of, directly, not to devolve upon Congress.

> 1825, Dec. 14. By Mr. Benton of Missouri; motion to appoint select com.;
> Mr. Hayne proposed amendment; Mr. Macon's amendment agreed to. S. J.,
> pp. °40, 45; Debates, pp. °16, °19.

*545. Executive: Choice: No third term.

> 1825, Dec. 19-1826, Apr. 3. 19th Cong., 1st sess. By Mr. Dickerson of New
> Jersey; read twice; to a select com.; report of com. with amendment con-
> sidered; amendment of com. concurred in; read third time; passed Senate
> (32 to 7).
>
> 1826, Apr. 4-5. Received in the House; read twice; to Com. of the Whole.
> S. J., pp. 46, 54, 102, 110, 199, 213, 216, 220, 221, 222; H. J., 412, 414; Debates, pp.
> °19, 374, 375, 376, 377, 405, 406, 407, 412, 414.

546. Executive Offices: Members of Congress excluded.

> 1825, Dec. 19. 19th Cong., 1st sess. By Mr. Cobb of Georgia; read twice;
> considered; tabled. S. J., pp. 47, 54, 165, 200, 227, 318; Debates, pp, °19, °114, 704.

546a. Commercial Powers: Internal improvements.

> 1825, Dec. 20. 19th Cong., 1st sess. By Mr. Van Buren of New York; for a
> select com. to prepare and report an amendment. S. J., p. 50; Debates, pp.
> °20-21.

547. Executive: Choice: Election directly by district.

> 1825, Dec. 29. 19th Cong., 1st sess. By Mr. Cook of Illinois; read twice; to
> select com. H. J., pp. °103, 309, 410; Debates, p. °845.

548. Executive: Choice, by direct vote by districts.

549. Executive offices: Members of Congress excluded.

> 1826, Jan. 3. 19th Cong., 1st sess. By Mr. White, in Senate; by Mr. Cocke
> of Tennessee in House, from the legislature of Tennessee. S. J., pp. 74, 152;
> H. J., pp. 109, 309. See Niles' Register. Vol. XXIX, pp. 315-316.

550. Executive: Choice of, by direct vote.

> 1826, Jan. 4. 19th Cong., 1st sess. By Mr. McManus of New York; referred
> to a select com. with other resolution. H. J., pp. °115, 309, 410.

551. Executive: Choice of.

> 1826, Jan. 11. 19th Cong., 1st sess. By Mr. Phelps of Connecticut; read.
> H. J., pp. °141, 309, 410; Debates, p. °940.

552. Executive: Choice of, by direct vote by districts.

> 1826, Jan. 19. 19th Cong., 1st sess. By Mr. Benton of Missouri, from the
> select com.; read twice; considered in Com. of the Whole; amendment pro-
> posed by Mr. Dickerson. S. J., pp. 102, 120, 195, 309; Debates, pp. °52-53, °692,
> 693. Report of com. printed in Niles' Register, Vol. XXIX, pp. 337-347.

553. Legislative: Election of Senators by the electors.

> 1826, Feb. 14. 19th Cong., 1st sess. By Mr. Storrs of New York; read; tabled.
> H. J., pp. °258, 309; Debates, p. °1348.

554. Executive: Choice of, by direct popular vote; plurality only shall be necessary.

> 1826, Feb. 16. 19th Cong., 1st sess. By Mr. Garnsey of New York; read: to Com. of the Whole; to a select com. H. J., pp. °263, 309, 410; Debates, pp. °1377-1378.

555. Executive: Choice of, in no case by House of Representatives.

> 1826, Feb. 20. 19th Cong., 1st sess. By Mr. Buchanan of Pennsylvania; referred to Com. of the Whole. H. J., pp. °273, 309, 410; Debates, p. °1418.

556. Executive: Choice of: Choice of electors by districts.

> 1826, Feb. 20. 19th Cong., 1st sess. By Mr. Dorsey of Maryland; referred to Com. of the Whole. H. J., pp. °274, 309, 410; Debates, p. °1418.

557. Executive Offices: Exclusion of Representatives when election of President devolves upon the House, etc.

> 1826, Feb. 21. 19th Cong., 1st sess. By Mr. Powell of Virginia; read; to Com. of the Whole. H. J., pp. °277, 309, 410; Debates, p. °1419.

558. Executive: Choice, by direct vote.

> 1826, Feb. 22. 19th Cong., 1st sess. By Mr. Boon of Indiana; to Com. of the Whole. H. J., pp. °281, 309, 410; Debates, pp. °1428-1429.

559. Executive: Choice: Vote directly: State ratio retained; case of second election.

> 1826, Feb. 22. 19th Cong., 1st sess. By Mr. Haynes of Georgia; read; to Com. of the Whole. H. J., pp. °281, 309, 410; Debates, p. °1429.

560. Executive: Choice: Vote directly: State ratio retained.

> 1826, Feb. 24. 19th Cong., 1st sess. By Mr. Thomson of Pennsylvania: read; to Com. of the Whole. H. J., pp. °285, 309, 410; Debates, p. °1402.

561. Executive: Choice: States to prescribe method of choice of electors: qualification of age; one term of six years.

> 1826, Feb. 24. 19th Cong., 1st sess. By Mr. Hemphill of Pennsylvania: read: to Com. of the Whole. H. J., pp. °286, 309, 410; Debates, p. °1402.

562. Executive: Choice; by a general per capita vote.

> 1826, Feb. 24. 19th Cong., 1st sess. By Mr. Sloane of Ohio; referred to Com. of the Whole. H. J., pp. °287, 309, 410; Debates, p. °1403.

563. Executive: Choice.

> 1826, Feb. 24. 19th Cong., 1st sess. By Mr. Ward of New York, for a joint com. to consider whether an amendment ought to be made; if so, to report; read; tabled. H. J., pp. °287, 309, 410; Debates, p. °1403.

564. Executive: Choice of: President ineligible for six years.

565. Executive: Choice of: Uniform system of voting by districts for electors.

566. Executive: Choice of: Plurality vote of electoral college shall elect; viva voce vote when election devolves upon Congress.

567. Executive offices: Members voting excluded.

> 1826, Feb. 24. 19th Cong., 1st sess. By Mr. Weems of Maryland; to Com. of the Whole. H. J., pp. °287-288, 309, 410; Debates, pp. °1463-1464.

568. Executive: Choice by direct vote of the people.

> 1826, Feb. 24. 19th Cong., 1st sess. By Mr. Livingston of Louisiana; to Com. of the Whole. H. J., pp. °288, 309, 410; Debates, p. °1464.

569. Executive offices: Exclusion of members of Congress.

> 1826, Mar. 1. 19th Cong., 1st sess. By Mr. Benton of Missouri, from the select com.; read and considered. S. J., pp. 165, 200, 227, 318; Debates, p. °114.

570. Executive: Choice by direct vote of the people.

> 1826, Mar. 7. 19th Cong., 1st sess. By Mr. Kellogg of New York; to Com. of the Whole. H. J., pp. °310-320, 410; Debates, p. °1541.

571. Amendment: Amendments only to be proposed decennially.

> 1826, Mar. 8. 19th Cong., 1st sess. By Mr. Herrick of Maine; read twice; tabled. H. J., pp. °323,325; Debates, p. 1554.

572. Executive: Choice by popular vote directly.

> 1826, Apr. 3. 19th Cong., 1st sess. By Mr. Livingston of Louisiana; referred to select com. H. J., p. °409; Debates, p. °2007.

573. Executive: Choice: Case of no election.

> 1826, Apr. 3. 19th Cong., 1st sess. By Mr. Stevenson of Virginia; referred to select com. H. J.. p. °410; Debates, p. °2007-2008.

574. Executive: Choice: Case of no election.

> 1826, Apr. 4. 19th Cong., 1st sess. By Mr. Drayton of South Carolina; referred to select com. H. J., p. °414; Debates, p. °2010.

575. Judiciary: Limiting the age of judges.

> 1826, Apr. 7. 19th Cong., 1st sess. By Mr. Eastman of New Hampshire. H. J., p. °420; Debates, p. °2008.

576. Legislative: Choice of Representatives by districts.

577 [552]. Executive: Choice, by districts, etc.

> 1826, May 8. 19th Cong., 1st sess. By Mr. Dickerson of New Jersey, as an amendment to resolution of the select com. of Jan. 19. S. J., p. 309; Debates, p. °692.

577a. Executive: Election not to devolve upon House of Representatives.

> 1826, Dec. 22. Resolution of the legislature of Georgia. Copy in Massachusetts Archives. Senate, °347. Jour. of Senate of Pennsylvania (1826–27), pp. °333–334; nonconcurred in by Vermont. Jour. of House of Rep. of Penn. (1827–28), p. °730.

578. Executive: Choice, by direct vote, in case of no election by electors.

> 1827, Feb. 20. 19th Cong., 2d sess. By Mr. Wright of Ohio, from the general assembly of Ohio; tabled; to Com. of the Whole. H. J., p. 317; 20th Cong., 2d sess., H. J., p. 75.

579. Executive: Choice: One term only.

580. Executive: Choice: Provision in case of no majority.

581. Executive Offices: Members of Congress excluded.

> 1827, Dec. 19. 20th Cong., 1st sess. By Mr. Smyth of Virginia. H. J., pp. °70-71.

581a. Executive: Election directly and conclusively by the people.

> 1827, Oct. 20. Resolution of the legislature of Tennessee. Niles' Register, Vol. XXXIII, pp. 161, °183-185, 186, 198. Am. An. Reg., Vol. III: (Local Hist.) p. 152.

582. Executive: Choice: Not to devolve on Congress in any case; by a direct popular vote by districts; the electoral ratio of States retained.

> 1827, Dec. 19. 20th Cong., 1st sess. By Mr. McDuffie of South Carolina; referred to Com. of the Whole. H. J., p. °71-72.

583. Executive: Choice, by a direct popular vote by States; not to devolve on Congress.

> 1828, Feb. 4-5. 20th Cong., 1st sess. By Mr. Moore of Alabama, in the House, and by Mr. King of Alabama, in the Senate, from the legislature of Alabama; tabled. H. J., p. °246; S. J., p. 134.

584. Executive: Choice, by general ticket.

> 1828, Feb. 15. 20th Cong., 1st sess. By Mr. Whipple of New Hampshire; to Com. of the Whole. H. J., p. °300.

585. Executive: Choice: Election of President as the legislatures of States shall direct; case of no choice.

> 1828, Feb. 15. 20th Cong., 1st sess. By Mr. Tucker of South Carolina; to Com. of the Whole. H. J., pp. °304-305.

586. Finance: Treasury officers not to be appointed by the President.

> 1828, Mar. 22. 20th Cong., 1st sess. By Mr. Barbour of Virginia; considered; to Com. of the Whole. H. J., p. °436, 442, 446, 447; Debates, p. 1954, 1955.

587. Personal Relations: Prevention of duelling.

> 1828, May 26. 20th Cong., 1st sess. By Mr. Long of North Carolina; read and tabled. H. J., p. °880.

588. Executive: Choice: One term only.

> 1828, Dec. 18. 20th Cong., 2d sess. By Mr. Smyth of Virginia; report of com. considered. Mr. Smyth moved an amendment; considered; tabled. H. J., pp. 78, 154, 250, 251, 252, 255, 259, 267, 270, 272, 286. 296, 308, 311; Debates, p. °119.

589 [588]. Executive: Choice: One term only.

> 1829, Feb. 6. 20th Cong., 2d sess. By Mr. Weems of Maryland, an amendment to Mr. Smyth's resolution. H. J., p. °259; Debates, p. 322.

590 [588]. Executive: One term, six years.

> 1829, Feb. 7. 20th Cong., 2d sess. By Mr. Condict of New Jersey, as an amendment to No. 588. H. J., p. °259; Debates, p. 322.

591 [588]. Executive: Choice: One term, six years.

592. Executive: Choice, by direct vote: also for electors in case a second election is required.

593. Executive Offices: Exclusion of members of Congress.

594. Legislative: Term of Senators, four years, to be chosen as the legislature shall direct.

595. Executive Offices: Exclusion of Representatives, when the election of President devolves upon House.

> 1829, Feb. 13. 20th Cong., 2d sess. By Mr. Wright of Ohio, as an amendment to No. 588; tabled. H. J., pp. °280-281, 256, 296, 308, 311; Debates, pp. °362, 371.

595a. Executive: Choice of : without electors, retaining the relative weight of each State: In no case by House of Representatives.

> 1829, Jan. 23. Resolution of the legislature of Missouri. Copy in Massachusetts Archives. Senate, °⁰⁹⁰. Jour. of House of Rep. of Penn. (1829-30), pp. °124-125. Nonconcurred in by the legislatures of Vermont (Oct. 29, 1829) and Connecticut (May, 1830), Massachusetts Archives. Senate, °⁰¹⁰, °⁰²¹⁰.

595b. Executive: One term only, six years.

> 1829, Feb. 4. Resolution of the legislature of Louisiana. Copy in Massachusetts Archives. Senate, ⁸⁷⁰⁴. Replies of the legislatures of Georgia, concurring, Jour. of House of Rep. of Pennsylvania (1829-30), p. °644; Maryland and Vermont, nonconcurring. S. J., 21st Cong., 1st sess., pp. °98-99; Niles' Register, Vol. xxvii, p. 428; Am. An. Reg., Vol. vi, p. 322. Jour. of Senate of Penn. (1830-31), p. °100.

596. Executive: Choice: One term, six years.

597. Executive Offices: Members of Congress ineligible to.

> 1829, Dec. 8. 21st Cong., 1st sess. By President Jackson in his first annual message. Referred to a select com. in House; report of Com.; read twice; to Com. of the Whole. S. J., p. 9; H. J., pp. 15, 31, 242.

598. Finance: Apportionment of the surplus.

> 1829, Dec. 8. 21st Cong., 1st sess. By President Jackson in his first annual message, proposing an amendment if the measure is not warranted by the constitution. Statesman's Manual, p. 705; H. J., p. 19; S. J., p. 13.

599. Division of Powers: Defining power of the General and State govments.

> 1829, Dec. 21. 21st Cong., 1st sess. By Mr. Hall of North Carolina, that a select com. be appointed to consider the expediency of an amendment: read; not agreed to (62 to 84). H. J., p. °65.

600. Executive: Choice of, by direct vote of the people, the ratio of the States retained: In no case shall election fall to the House of Representatives.

> 1830, Jan. 25-Feb. 1. 21st Cong., 1st sess. By Mr. Forsyth of Georgia, in Senate; by Mr. Wilde of Georgia in the House. Resolution of the legislature of Georgia; read. H. J., p. °237; S. J., p. °(98-99). Nonconcurred in by legislature of Vermont. Am. An. Reg., Vol. VII, p. 322. Jour. of Senate of Pennsylvania (1830-31), p. °100.

600a. Executive: Choice of President and Vice-President.

> 1830, Feb. 1. 21st Cong., 1st sess. By Mr. McDuffie, from Select Com. on the President's Message. Read twice; to Com. of the Whole. H. J., p. 242.

601. Executive: Choice of President and Vice-President.

> 1830, Mar. 12. 21st Cong., 1st sess. By Mr. Benton of Missouri, in harmony with President's recommendation. Read twice: to a select com.; reported; considered. S. J., pp. 183, 186, 190, 321,

601a. Executive: Election of President by direct vote of the people.

> 1830, Mar. 16. 21st Cong., 1st sess. By Mr. Benton of Missouri, from the legislature of Missouri. S. J., p. 187.

602. Executive: Choice: One term only.

> 1830, Dec. 7. 21st Cong., 2d sess. By President Jackson in his second annual message. H. J., p. 23; S. J., 21; Statesman's Manual, p. 744.

603. Executive: Choice: One term only.

> 1830, Dec. 9. 21st Cong., 2d sess. Report of the com. to whom this action of the President's message was referred; Mr. Tucker's amendment considered. H. J., pp. 36, 38. °89-90, 145, 371; Debates, pp. °379, °408.

604. Executive: Choice: No third term.

> 1830, Dec. 29. 21st Cong., 2d sess. By Mr. Dickerson of New Jersey; read twice; to select com.; report: considered: tabled. S. J., pp. 50, 63-76, 88; Debates, pp. °23-24.

605 [604]. Executive: Choice: One term of five years.

> 1831, Jan. 5. 21st Cong., 2d sess. By Mr. Tucker, as an amendment to report of select com.; read; tabled. H. J., p. °145; Debates, p. 408.

605a. Judiciary: Term of judges.

> 1831, Jan. 28. 21st Cong., 2d sess. By Mr. Lecompte of Kentucky; motion to suspend the rules and consider the same. H. J., p. °234; Debates, p. °540, 717.

606. Executive: Choice: Exclusion of Congressmen: One term only.

607. Legislative: Apportionment of Representatives.

> 1831, Dec. 6. 22d Cong., 1st sess. By President Jackson in his third annual message. H. J., p. °20; Statesman's Manual, p. 764. Com. appointed to consider the same. H. J., p. 40; Debates, p. 1432.

608. Judiciary: Term of judges.

> 1832, Jan. 30. 22d Cong., 1st sess. By Mr. Lecompte of Kentucky. House refuses to consider (127 to 41). H. J., pp. °253, 406; Debates, p. °1856.

609. Executive: Choice, by direct popular vote: State ratio retained: President ineligible for next term.

> 1832, Mar. 2. 22d Cong., 1st sess. By Mr. Root of New York; to a select com. May 26, 1832, report an amendment—one term only of six years; to Com. of the Whole. H. J., pp. °429, 501, 663, 803; Debates, pp. °1903, 2164, 2595, 3102.

609a. Commercial: Internal improvements.

609b. Personal Relations: Aid colonization of certain number of the colored population.

> 1832, Jan. 31. 22d Cong., 1st sess. By Mr. Archer of Virginia; ordered printed; referred to Com. on Rahway Colonization Society Memorial. H. J., p. °272; Debates, °1663, °1675.

609c. Personal Relations: Colonization of "Free people of Color."

> 1832, Mar. 15. 22d Cong., 1st sess. By Mr. Smith of Maryland, from the legislature of Maryland. S. J., p. 186; Am. An. Reg., Vol. VII, pp. 234–5.

610. Executive: Choice: Term of office.

611. Commerce: Internal improvement.

> 1832, Dec. 4. 22d Cong., 2d sess. By President Jackson in his fourth annual message. S. J., pp. 15, 17; H. J., pp. 18, 20.

612. Executive Offices: Members of Congress excluded.

> 1832, Dec. 17. 22d Cong., 2d sess. By Mr. Wickliffe of Kentucky; considered. H. J., pp. °70, 83, 91; Debates, p. 883–894.

613. Division of Powers: Call of a convention: Defining power of General and State governments.

614. Division of Powers: Defining power of coercion and right of resistance by the State.

615. Finance: Protective tariff, principles to be defined.

616. Finance: Federal taxation.

617. Judiciary: Jurisdiction.

618. Judiciary: Tribunal to settle disputes between General and State governments.

619. Finance: Chartering of bank.

620. Commerce: Internal improvements.

621. Finance: Distribution of surplus.

622. Territorial Power: Distribution of public lands.

623. Executive: Choice of, by the people.

624. Executive: Choice of: One term only.

625. Personal Relations: Rights of Indians.

> 1833, Jan. 9. 22d Cong., 2d sess. Mr. Forsyth of Georgia presented resolution from the legislature of Georgia, adopted Dec. 12, 1832, making application for a convention to amend the Constitution as designated. S. J., pp. °65–66; Am. An. Register, Vol. VIII. p. °295.

625a. Division of Powers: Call of a convention of States.

> 1833, Jan. 15. Resolution of the legislature of South Carolina, calling for a convention of the States to consider and determine the disputed power of the General and State governments. S. J., p. °83.

625b. Amendment: Call of a Federal convention.

> 1832. Resolutions of the legislature of Alabama, recommending the call of a Federal convention to propose amendments. Am. An. Register, Vol. VIII, p. 297.

626. Executive: Choice, by the people: One term only.

> 1833, Dec. 3. 23d Cong., 1st sess. By President Jackson in his fifth annual message. S. J., p. 19; H. J., p. 24.

627. Executive: Choice of.

> 1833, Dec. 9. 23d Cong., 1st sess. By Mr. Benton of Missouri; read twice; to a select com; com. report a substitute. S. J., pp. 36, 296, 302; Debates, pp. 20, 1879; Globe, pp. 17, 424.

628. Executive: Choice, by the people: In no case to devolve upon the House of Representatives.

> 1833, Dec. 11. 23d Cong., 1st sess. By Mr. Bibb of Kentucky; read twice; to a select com.; reported a substitute; tabled. S. J., pp. 39, 262, 278, 285, 291, 302, 311: Debates, pp. 1724.1813, 1843, 1954; Globe, pp. 20, 379, 307, 405, 418, 428, 439. (Text of substitute, Niles' Register, Vol. xlvi, p. °421.)

629. Executive: Revoke veto by a majority vote of all Members.

> 1833, Dec. 24. 23d Cong., 1st sess. By Mr. Kent; read; tabled. S. J., pp. 65, 74; Globe, pp. °52, 73.

630 [628]. Executive: Choice, by direct popular vote: In no case to devolve upon the House of Representatives: Uniform system by districts: In case of no majority, a second election by the people.

> 1834, June 5. 23d Cong., 1st sess. From the select com. as a substitute for Mr. Bibb's resolution. S. J., p. 302; Globe, pp. 418, 428, 439. Niles' Register, Vol. xlvi, p. °421.

631. Executive: Choice: One term only.

> 1834, Dec. 2. 23d Cong., 2d sess. By President Jackson in his sixth annual message. Com. appointed to consider; report unable to agree. H. J., pp. 27, 55, 294: Debates, pp. 1126-1127; Globe, p. 36.

632. Executive: Choice. by direct popular vote, by districts.

> 1834, Dec. 15. S. R. 3, 23d Cong., 2d sess. By Mr. Benton of Missouri; read twice; tabled. S. J., pp. 42, 48, 71, 97; Debates, pp. 216, 217; Globe, pp. 36, 120.

633. Executive: Choice, by direct popular vote by districts: Election in no case to devolve on Congress.

634. Executive: Choice: One term only.

635. Executive Offices: Members of Congress excluded.

> 1834, Dec. 19. 23d Cong., 2d sess. By Mr. Hamer of Ohio; referred to select com.: report unable to agree. H. J., pp. °110-111, 294; Globe, p. °52.

636. Executive: Reverse veto by a majority vote.

> 1835, Jan. 6. S. R. 6, 23d Cong., 2d sess. By Mr. Kent; read twice; tabled. S. J., pp. 77, 83, 105, 177; Debates, pp. °540-551; Globe, pp. 96, 108, 269, 270.

637. Judiciary: Term of judges.

> 1835, Jan. 7. 23d Cong., 2d sess. By Mr. Hamer of Ohio; to Com. on Judiciary for inquiry; amendments proposed; postponed. H. J., pp. °178, °185, °186, 207; Debates, pp. °942, 943, 965, 966; Globe, pp. °103, 111.

638 [637]. Judiciary: Term of judges; age limit.

> 1835, Jan. 8. 23d Cong., 2d sess. By Mr. Hardin, as an amendment to Mr. Hamer's resolution. H. J., pp. °185-186.

639 [637]. Judiciary: Removal of judges, etc.

> 1835, Jan. 8. 23d Cong., 2d sess. By Mr. Vance of Ohio, as an amendment to Mr. Hamer's resolution; considered. H. J., pp. °185-186; Globe, pp. 157, 304.

640. Executive: Choice: One term only.

641. Executive: Choice, by direct popular vote by States.

642. Executive Offices: Members of Congress excluded.

> 1835, Jan. 31. 23d Cong., 2d sess. By Mr. Gilmer of Georgia; considered; attempt to amend; lost; considered. H. J., pp. °297-299, 377, 378, 450, 453-456, 471, 477; Debates, pp. °1126-1128, 1351, 1497, 1500-1504, 1525-1531; Globe, 181, 292, 303.

643. Finance: Distribution of surplus revenue.

> 1835, Feb. 9. S. R. 11, 23d Cong., 2d sess. By Mr. Calhoun of South Carolina; read twice; tabled; to select com.; report considered; tabled. S. J., pp. 148, 150, 200; Globe, pp. 220, 224.

644 [640-642]. Legislative: Election of Senators by the people.

> 1835, Feb. 13. 23d Cong.; 2d sess. By Mr. Hannegan of Indiana, to be added to Mr. Gilman's resolution; tabled. H. J., p. °378; Debates, p. 1351.

645 [640]. Executive: Choice: One term, six years.

    1835, Feb. 25. 23d Cong., 2d sess. By Mr. Speight of North Carolina, as an amendment to Mr. Gilmer's resolution; rejected. H. J., p. 454; Globe, p. 292.

646. Executive: Choice.

    1835, Dec. 2. 24th Cong., 1st sess. By President Jackson in his seventh annual message. S. J., pp. 31, 32; H. J., p. 35; Globe, p. 10.

647. Finance: Distribution of surplus revenue.

    1835, Dec. 29. 24th Cong., 1st sess. By Mr. Calhoun of South Carolina, in the the Senate. Debates, p. 52.

648. Executive: Article 1. Reverse veto by a majority vote.

649. Executive: Article 2. Independent Treasury Department.

650. Executive: Article 3. Secretary of Treasury elected by Congress.

651. Executive Officers: Article 14. Tenure and removal.

652. Executive Offices: Article 15. Members of Congress excluded.

    1836, Feb. 13, 24th Cong. 1st sess. S. R. 6. By Mr. Underwood of Kentucky; read. H, J., pp. °345-346; Globe, p. °184.

653. Executive: Choice: One term of six years.

654. Executive: Choice, by direct vote: Case of no election.

655. Executive Offices: Members of Congress excluded.

    1836, Feb. 13. S. R. 7, 24th Cong., 1st sess. By Mr. Peyton of Tennessee. H. J., pp. °347-349; Globe, p. 184.

655a. Executive: Prevent election devolving on Congress.

    1836, Feb. 29. Resolutions of the General Assembly of Ohio. Journal of the Senate of Pennsylvania (1835-536), Vol. II, p. °374.

656. Executive: Choice.

    1836, Mar. 30. H. R. 9, 24th Cong., 1st sess. Report of select com. to whom President's message was referred; to Com. of the Whole; amendments proposed. H. J., pp. 72, 601. Globe, pp. 27, 306, 307.

657 [656]. Executive: Choice.

    1836, Mar. 30. 24th Cong., 1st sess. By Mr. Dromgoole of Virginia, intended as a substitute to H. R. 9; to Com. of the Whole. H. J., p. 601; Globe, p. 306; Debates, p. 3015.

658 [656]. Executive: Choice.

    1836, Apr. 1. 24th Cong., 1st sess. By Mr. Taliaferro of Virginia, as an amendment to H. R. 9. H. J., p. 614; Globe, p. 313.

658a. Executive: Prevent election devolving on Congress.

    1836, Apr. 22. 24th Cong., 1st sess. By Mr. Shepley, resolutions of the legislature of Maine. S. J., p. 302; Globe, p. 383; Jour. of Senate of Pennsylvania (1835-36), pp. °421-422.

659. Executive: Choice.

    1836, Dec. 6. 24th Cong., 2d sess. By President Jackson in his eighth annual message. S. J., p. 27; H. J., p. 29.

660. Executive: Choice: One term only of six years.

661. Executive: Choice, by direct popular vote " viva voce:" State ratio retained.

662. Executive Offices: Members of Congress excluded.

    1836, Dec. 12. H. R. 18, 24th Cong., 2d sess. By Mr. McComas of Virginia; consideration postponed. H. J., pp. °50-52; Globe, p. °20.

663. Executive: Choice, by direct popular vote: State ratio retained.

664. Executive: Choice: One term of six years.

    1836, Dec. 29. 24th Cong., 2d sess. By Mr. Galbraith of Pennsylvania: read; to a select com. H. J., pp. °137-139; Globe, pp. 61, 62.

665. Finance: Issuing of bank notes.

   1836, Dec. 29. H. R. 27, 24th Cong., 2d sess. Resolution to amend referred
   to a select com. on amending Constitution. H. J., pp. 137, 140.

666. Executive: Choice.

   1837, Jan. 28. 24th Cong., 2d sess. Select com., to whom President's message
   was referred, report the H. R. 9 made at last session. H. J., pp. 58, 60. 203, 545;
   Globe, pp. 28, 136; Debates, pp. 1510, 1511.

667. Executive: Choice: One term only, six years.

668. Executive: Choice: Change time of election and have it uniform.

669. Executive: Choice, by direct vote: Provision for a second election in
   case of no choice.

670. Executive Offices: Members of Congress excluded.

   1837, Feb. 24. 24th Cong., 2d sess. By Mr. Boon of Indiana, from the general
   assembly of Indiana; tabled. H. J., p. °520; Globe, p. 252.

671. Finance: State bank paper.

   1837, Mar. 3. H. R. 28, 24th Cong., 2d sess. From the select com. H. J., p.
   °587; Globe, p. 279.

672. Executive; Choice, by districts.

   1837, Dec. 18. S. R. 1, 25th Cong., 2d sess. By Mr. Allen of Ohio; read and
   referred to a select com. S. J., p. 50; Globe, p. 17. °25, 26, 63.

673. Executive: Reverse veto by a majority.

674. Choice of Executive: President ineligible for the succeeding four
   years.

675. Executive: Independent Treasury Department.

676. Executive: Secretary of Treasury elected by Congress.

677. Executive Officers: Tenure and removal.

678. Executive Offices: Members of Congress excluded.

679. Choice of Executive: Nomination by State legislatures, election by
   direct vote from the list nominated.

   1838, Jan. 2. H. R. 1, 25th Cong., 2d sess. By Mr. Underwood of Kentucky;
   read; tabled; to Com. of the Whole. H. J., pp. °189-192, 483; Globe, pp. 190.

680. Executive Offices: Members of Congress excluded.

   1838, Jan. 2. H. R. 3, 25th Cong., 2d sess. By Mr. Wise of Virginia, that a
   com. to inquire be appointed; referred to a select com.; com. report, H. R. 3;
   read; to Com. of the Whole. H. J., pp. 195, 255, 256, 313; Globe, pp. °70, 92, 134.

681. Executive: Choice of: One term only.

   1838, Feb. 19. 25th Cong., 2d sess. By Mr. Rhett of South Carolina, in the
   House; read twice. Globe, p. °180.

682. Executive: Choice: Case of no election.

   1838, Feb. 19. H. R. 6, 25th Cong., 2d sess. By Mr. Dromgoole of Virginia;
   read; to Com. of the Whole. H. J., pp. °471-473; Globe, p. °190.

683. Executive: Choice, by direct vote by States: State ratio retained.

   1838, Feb. 19. H. R. 7, 25th Cong., 2d sess. By Mr. Williams of Tennessee;
   read; to Com. of the Whole. H. J., pp. °475-477.

684. Executive: Choice: One term only.

   1838, Feb. 19. 25th Cong., 2d sess. By Mr. Bell of Tennessee; tabled. H. J.,
   p. °478; Globe, p. 190.

685. Personal Relations: Persons connected with a duel excluded from
   office.

   1838, Mar. 5. H. R. 8, 25th Cong., 2d sess. By Mr. Morgan of Virginia; read
   twice. H. J., pp. °520-527; Globe, p. °210. Report of Com. on Duelling, Niles',
   Vol. LIV, pp. 139, 188.

686. Finance: State bank notes.
>   1838, Apr. 16. 25th Cong., 2d sess. By Mr. Garland of Louisiana; tabled. H. J., p. °764; Globe, pp. °250, °311.

687. Personal Relations: Persons connected with a duel excluded from office.
>   1838, Dec. 31. 25th Cong., 3d sess. H. R. 32. By Mr. Cushman of New Hampshire; read twice. H. J., p. °156; Globe, p. °85.

688. Finance: Any officer embezzling public money excluded from office.
>   1838, Dec. 31. 25th Cong., 3d sess. By Mr. Southgate of Kentucky; tabled, H. J., p. °170; Globe, p. °91.

689. Legislative: Term of Senators four years. One-half Senators retire every two years.

690. Executive: Choice: Term four years: Ineligible to two terms in succession.

691. Executive: Veto power dispensed with.

692. Executive: Power of removal from office.

692a. Executive Offices: Removals from office to be regulated by law.

692b. Executive Offices: Appointment made by the Senate.

693. Executive: President shall issue commissions.
>   1839, Jan. 14. H. R. 38, 25th Cong., 3d sess. By Mr. Taliaferro of Virginia; referred to Com. of the Whole. H. J., pp °282-283; Globe, p. °124.

694. Executive: One term, four years.

695. Executive Offices: Appointment of certain officers by Congress.

696. Executive Offices: Members of Congress excluded.
>   1839, Jan. 21. S. R. 10, 25th Cong., 3d sess. By Mr. Tallmadge of New York; read. S. J., p. 144; Globe, p. 185; Niles' Register, LV, 347.

697. Personal Relations: Hereditary slavery abolished after 1842.

698. Territorial: No slave State to be admitted.

699. Personal Relations: Slavery and slave trade abolished after 1845 in District of Columbia.
>   1839, Feb. 25. 25th Cong., 3d sess. By Mr. Adams of Massachusetts; in the House. Objection made to their reception. Globe, p. °218.

700. Judiciary: Limitation of term to seven years.
>   1839, Dec. 30-1840, July 17. S. R. 2, 26th Cong., 1st sess. By Mr. Tappan of Ohio; considered; tabled. S. J., pp. 50, 73, 400, 482, 485, 522; Globe, pp. 82, °86, 441, 516.

701. Finance: Prohibition of State bank notes.
>   1840, Feb. 24-27. 26th Cong. 1st sess. By Mr. Buchanan of Pennsylvania; referred to select com. S. J., pp. °198, 200; Globe, pp. °220, 224.

702. Executive: Choice: Ineligibility to a second term.
>   1840, Feb. 24. H. R. 1., 26th Cong. 1st sess. By Mr. Brown of Tennessee; read. H. J., pp. °443, 767; Globe, pp. °102. °223, 307.

703. Legislative: Regulations for contested elections.
>   1840, Mar. 9. 26th Cong. 1st sess. By Mr. Habersham of Georgia; laid over. H. J., p. °547; Globe, p. °253.

704. Judiciary: Limitation of term of judges.
>   1840, Dec. 15-21. S R. 2, 26th Cong., 2d sess. By Mr. Tappan of Ohio; read twice; considered. S. J., pp. 34, 50; Globe, pp. 18, 41.

704a. Executive: One term only, four years.
>   1840, Dec. 16-21. S. R. 3, 26th Cong., 2d sess. By Mr. Tallmadge of New York; read twice; tabled. S. J., pp. 40, 50; Globe, p. 25; Niles' Register, Vol. LIX., p. °252.

705. Executive: Choice: One term of four years.

> 1840, Dec. 17. H. R. 17, 26th Cong., 2d sess. By Mr. Hunt of New York: committed to Com. of the Whole. H. J., p. °65; Globe, p. °38.

70 Legislative: Term to begin December 1.

> 1840, Dec. 21. H. R. 18, 26th Cong., 2d sess. By Mr. Fillmore of New York; read twice; committed to Com. of the Whole. H. J., p. °87; Globe, p. °44.

706a. Executive: One term only.

> 1841, Jan. 6. 26th Cong., 2d sess. By Mr. Phelps of Vermont, from the legislature of Vermont; read. S. J., p. 84. Jour. of Senate of Penn. (1841), Vol. II, p. °44.

706b. Executive: One term only: Uniform day for choice of Presidential Electors.

> 1841, Jan. 23. 26th Cong., 2d sess. By Mr. White, from the general assembly of Indiana. S. J., p. 128; Massachusetts Archives. Senate, 10819. Jo. of Senate of Penn. (1841), Vol. II, p. °339.

706c. Executive: One term only.

> 1841, Feb. 26. Resolution of the State of Delaware. Copy in Massachusetts Archives. Senate Misc., 10814.

707. Executive: Choice: One term only.

> 1841, June 12. 27th Cong., 1st sess. By Mr. Randall of Maine, from the legislature of Maine; to Com. on Judiciary. H. J., p. °102.

708. Executive: Choice: One term only.

> 1841, June 18. 27th Cong., 1st sess. By Mr. Williams, of Maine, from the legislature of Maine; tabled. S. J., p. °49; Globe, p. 70.

709. Executive: Choice: One term only.

> 1841, June 18. 27th Cong., 1st sess. By Mr. Bates, of Massachusetts, from the legislature of Massachusetts; tabled. S. J., p. 49; Globe, p. 70.

710. Executive: Choice: One term only.

> 1841, June 22. 27th Cong., 1st sess. By Mr. Huntington of Connecticut, from the legislature of Connecticut; tabled. S. J., p. °53; Globe, p. 86.

711. Executive: Choice: One term only.

> 1841, June 23–Sept. 10. 27th Cong., 1st sess. By Mr. Brown of Tennessee; read; considered. H. J., pp. °186, 495; Globe, pp. °98, 447.

712. Executive: Choice: One term only.

> 1841, Aug. 3. 27th Cong., 1st sess. By Mr. Cranston of Rhode Island, from the general assembly of Rhode Island; received. H. J., p. °308.

713. Executive: Choice: One term only.

714. Executive: To pass bills vetoed by a majority.

> 1841, Sept. 10. 27th Cong., 1st sess. By Mr. Owsley of Kentucky. H. J., p. °494; Globe, p. °447.

715. Executive Offices: Exclusion of members of Congress.

> 1841-42, Dec. 29–Mar. 4. S. R. 2. 27th Cong., 2d sess. By Mr. Clay of Kentucky; read twice; considered. S. J., p. 58; Globe, pp. °69, 164-167, 200, 221, 237, 259, 260, 266, 282, 283.

716. Executive: Veto reversed by a majority: No "pocket veto."

> 1841-'42, Dec. 29–Mar. 4. S. R., 3, 27th Cong., 2d sess. By Mr. Clay of Kentucky; read twice; considered. S. J., pp. 58, 119, 136, 153, 166, 187, 191, 203; Globe, pp. °69, 164, 165, 167, 200, 221, 237, 259, 260, 266, 282.

717. Executive Officers: Secretary of the Treasury and Treasurer appointed and removable by Congress.

> 1841-42, Dec. 29–Mar. 4. S. R. 4, 27th Cong., 2d sess. By Mr. Clay of Kentucky; read twice; considered. S. J., p. 58; Globe, pp. °69, 164-167, 200, 221, 237, 259, 260, 266, 282.

717a. Executive: One term only.

1842, Jan. 6. 27th Cong., 2d sess. By Mr. Phelps, from the legislature of Vermont; ordered printed. S. J., p. °70.

718. Executive: Choice: New qualifications.

718a. Executive: Term, no two consecutive.

1842, Mar. 21–Aug. 30. H. R. 7, 27th Cong., 2d sess. By Mr. Underwood of Kentucky; to select com.; com. report; tabled. H. J., pp. 565, 1456; Globe, pp. °350, 973.

719. Executive: Deprived of appointing certain Cabinet officers.

1842, Mar. 21–Aug. 30. H. R. 7, 27th Cong., 2d sess. By Mr. Underwood of Kentucky; to select com.; com. report; tabled. H. J., pp. 565, 1456; Globe, pp. °350, 973.

720. Executive: Veto reversed by a majority.

1842, Mar. 21–Aug. 30. H. R. 7, 27th Cong., 2d sess. By Mr. Underwood of Kentucky; to select com.; com. report; tabled. H. J., pp. 565, 1456; Globe. pp.°350, 973.

721. Executive: Independent Treasury and Post-Office Departments.

1842, Mar. 21–Aug. 30. H. R. 7, 27th Cong., 2d sess. By Mr. Underwood of Kentucky; to select com.; com. report; tabled. H. J., pp. 565, 1456; Globe, pp. °350, 973.

722. Executive Officers: Terms and removal from office regulated by law.

1842, Mar. 21–Aug 30. H. R. 7, 27th Cong., 2d sess. By Mr. Underwood of Kentucky; to select com.; com. report; tabled. H. J., pp. 565, 1456; Globe, pp. °350, 973.

723. Executive Offices: Exclusion of members of Congress.

1842, Mar. 21–Aug. 30. H. R. 7, 27th Cong., 2d sess. By Mr. Underwood of Kentucky; to select com.; com. report; tabled. H. J., pp. 565, 1456; Globe, pp. °350, 973.

724. Executive: Choice: Nominations by State legislature: Direct vote.

1842. Mar. 21–Aug. 30. H. R. 7, 27th Cong., 2d sess. By Mr. Underwood of Kentucky; to select com.; com. report; tabled. H. J., pp. 565, 1456; Globe, pp. °350, 973.

725. Legislative: Limit number of Representatives.

1842, Mar. 21–Aug. 30. H. R. 7, 27th Cong., 2d sess. By Mr. Underwood of Kentuky; to select com.; com. report; tabled. H. J., pp. 565, 1456; Globe, pp.°350, 973.

726. 1. Executive: Choice: One term only.

727. 2. Executive: Exclusion of members of Congress.

728. 3. Executive: Power of removal limited.

729. 4. Executive: Veto diminished.

1842, Apr. 6–15. 27th Cong., 2d sess. By Mr. Underwood of Kentucky, from general assembly of Kentucky; referred to select com. H. J., pp. °677, 712; Globe, p. 426. By Mr. Crittenden, in Senate. S. J., pp. °272–273.

730: Executive: To pass bills vetoed by a majority.

1842, Aug. 16–17. 27th Cong., 2d sess. By Mr. J. Q. Adams of Massachusetts, from the select com; read; considered; failed (90 to 90). H. J., pp. 1296, °1352, 1355; Globe, pp. 877, 890, 906.

731. Judiciary: Limiting term of judges to seven years.

1842–43, Dec. 12–Jan. 16. S. R. 1, 27th Cong., 3d sess. By Mr. Tappan of Ohio; read twice; failed to be passed to third reading (11 to 24). S. J., pp. 24, 107; Globe, pp. 39, 41, 162.

732. Executive: Choice: One term only.

 1843-44, Dec. 18-Jan. 3. H. R. 1, 28th Cong., 1st sess. By Mr. Hunt of New York; read. H. J., pp. °63, 146.

733. Legislative: Apportionment of Representatives to free persons.

734. Finance: Apportionment of taxes to free persons.

 1843-44, Dec. 21-Apr. 4. 28th Cong., 1st sess. By J. Q. Adams of Massachusetts, from the legislature of Massachusetts (March, 1843); to select com.: consideration refused three times; report of com. adverse; report accepted (156 to 13). H. J , pp. °93-97, 281, 347, 409, 530, 531, 638, 642, 656, 608, 726, 727, 728. 733; Globe, pp. 62, °64, 65, 66, 73, 179, 180, 205, 229, 476, 481. Laws and Resolves of Massachusetts, Vol. xvi, chap. 60, p. 79.

734a. Legislative: Apportionment of Representatives to free persons.

734b. Finance: Apportionment of direct taxes to free persons.

 1844, Jan. 16. Resolutions of the legislature of Massachusetts. Laws and Resolves of Massachusetts, Vol. xvi. chap. 1. p. 293.

735. Executive: Choice: Vote directly by States.

 1844, Jan. 15. 28th Cong., 1st sess. By Mr. Dana of New York; laid over. H. J., p. °226; Globe, p. °144.

736. Territorial Power: To retrocede certain jurisdiction of Congress over District of Columbia to Virginia and Maryland.

 1844, Jan. 29. 28th Cong., 1st sess. By Mr. Campbell of South Carolina; read. H. J., pp. °307, 308; Globe, p. °203.

737. Judiciary: Limit term of judges to seven years.

 1844, Feb. 20. S. R. 4, 28th Cong., 1st sess. By Mr. Tappan of Ohio: read twice. S. J., pp. 128, 132; Globe. pp. 35, 297, 300.

738. Executive: Choice of electors by districts.

 1844, Mar. 11. 28th Cong., 1st sess. By Mr. Garrett Davis of Kentucky; laid over. H. J., pp. °555-556; Globe, p. °367.

739. Executive: Choice by districts.

 1844, June 15. S. R. 27, 28th Cong., 1st sess. By Mr. Benton of Missouri: read. S. J., p. 369; Globe, pp. 668, °686, 687.

740. Executive: From candidates of all the States, chosen by lot.

 1844, Dec. 17. H. R. 49, 28th Cong., 2d sess. By Mr. Vinton of Ohio; read twice; to Com. on Judiciary. H. J., p. °95; Globe, p. 40.

741. Executive: Choice: Vote directly by States.

 1844, Dec. 17. H. R. 50, 28th Cong., 2d sess. By Mr. Slidell of Louisiana; read twice; to Com. on Judiciary. H. J., p. °97; Globe, p. °41.

742. Executive: Ineligible to reelection.

 1844, Dec. 23. H. R. 52, 28th Cong., 2d sess. By Mr. W. Hunt of New York; read twice; to Com. on Judiciary. H. J., p. 125; Globe, 64.

743. Executive: Choice: Second election by joint convention of Congress.

 1845, Jan. 28. H. R. 69, 28th Cong., 2d sess. By Mr. Dromgoole of Virginia: read twice; to Com. on Judiciary. H. J., p. 290; Globe, p. 210.

744. Executive: From candidates of all the States, chosen by lot.

 1846, Jan. 13-Feb. 16. H. R. 8, 29th Cong., 1st sess. By Mr. Vinton of Ohio: read twice; to Com. of the Whole; considered. H. J., pp. 249, 411: Globe, pp. °194, 376.

745. Executive: Term six years, ineligible thereafter.

 1846, Jan. 21-Feb. 2. S. R. 8, 29th Cong., 1st sess. By Mr. Bagley of Alabama; read twice; tabled. S. J., pp., 113, 124; Globe, p. °226.

746. Executive: Members of Congress ineligible.

 1846, Jan. 21-Feb. 2. S. R. 8, 29th Cong., 1st sess. By Mr. Bagley of Alabama; read twice; tabled. S. J., pp. 113, 124; Globe, p. °226.

747. Executive Offices: Members of Congress excluded from Cabinet.
>1846, Jan. 21-Feb. 2. S. R. 8, 29th Cong., 1st sess. By Mr. Bagley of Alabama; read twice: tabled. S. J., pp. 113, 124; Globe, p. °226.

748. Executive: No second term.

749. Executive Offices: Members of Congress excluded from office.
>1846, Feb. 16-Aug. 3. 29th Cong., 1st sess. By Mr. W. Hunt of New York; read; not received. H. J., p. 463; Globe, pp. 377, °1180, 1181.

750. Judiciary: Judicial power not to declare a State act or act of Congress unconstitutional.
>1846-47, Dec. 22-Jan. 20. S. R. 2, 29th Cong., 2d sess. By Mr. Semple of Illinois; read twice; to Com. on Judiciary; discharged from consideration. S. J., pp. 64, 70, 116; Globe, pp. 61, 82, 213; Niles' Register, Vol. LXXI, p. °200.

751. Executive: Election of postmasters and other officers.
>1848, Jan. 17. 30th Cong., 1st sess. By Mr. Wentworth of Illinois; to Com. on Judiciary. H. J., p. °258; Globe p. °181.

752. Judiciary: Term of judges.
>1848, Mar. 13. 30th Cong., 1st sess. By Mr. J. Thompson of Mississippi; read; to Com. on Judiciary to report. H. J., p. °554; Globe, p. °458.

753. Amendment to the Constitution.
>1848, May 13. 30th Cong., 1st sess. By Mr. Brodhead of Pennsylvania, in the House; asked permission to introduce. Globe, p. 764.

754. Executive: Choice, direct vote by States.
>1848, Dec. 11-28. 30th Cong., 2d sess. By Mr. Lawrence of New York; to Com. on Judiciary; com. discharged; tabled. H. J., pp. °66, 67, 160; Globe, p. 25.

755. Executive: Reverse veto by majority vote.

755a. Executive: Ineligible to reelection for four years.

755b. Judiciary: Removal of judges by Congress.

755c. Executive Offices: Tenure of office.

755d. Executive Offices: Exclusion of members of Congress.
>1849, Feb. 23. S. R. 64, 30th Cong., 2d sess. By Mr. Underwood of Kentucky; read. H. J., p. 252; Globe, p. 585.

756. Legislative: Election of Senators by the people.
>1850, Jan. 14. S. R. 2, 31st Cong., 1st sess. By Mr. Clemens of Alabama; read twice; to Com. on Judiciary; report. S. J., pp. 77, 103; Globe, pp. °88, 150.

757. Division of Powers: Rights of local legislation.

758. Division of Powers: Right of establishing local government.
>1850, Jan. 28-Feb. 4. 31st Cong., 1st sess. By Mr. Disney of Ohio. First attempt not received; second time presented, tabled. Globe, pp. °228, °276; H. J., pp. °453-454.

759. Executive: Pass bills vetoed, by a majority.
>1850, Apr. 3. S. R. 17, 31st Cong., 1st sess. By Mr. Underwood of Kentucky; read twice; tabled. S. J., p. 248; Globe, p. °631.

760. Executive: Qualifications: Ineligibility to reelection for four years.
>1850, Apr. 3. S. R. 17, 31st Cong., 1st sess. By Mr. Underwood of Kentucky; read twice; tabled. S. J., p. 248; Globe, p. °631.

761. Judiciary: Removal of judges by Congress.
>1850, Apr. 3. S. R. 17, 31st Cong., 1st sess. By Mr. Underwood of Kentucky; read twice; tabled. S. J., p. 248; Globe, p. °631.

762. Executive Offices: Tenure of office.
>1850, Apr. 3. S. R. 17, 31st Cong., 1st sess. By Mr. Underwood of Kentucky; read twice; tabled. S. J., p. 248; Globe, p. °631.

763. **Executive Offices: Exclusion of members of Congress.**
1850, Apr. 3. S. R. 17, 31st Cong., 1st sess. By Mr. Underwood of Kentucky; read twice; tabled. S. J., p. 248; Globe, p. °631.

764. **Personal Relations: To prevent the abolition of slavery.**
1850, July 6. 31st Cong., 1st sess. By Mr. Daniel of North Carolina, in the House; not received. Globe, p. °1349.

765. **Executive: Choice directly by districts.**
1851, Feb. 21. H. R. 37, 31st Cong., 2d sess. By Mr. A. Johnson of Tennessee; read twice; to Com. of the Whole. H. J., p. 322; Globe, p. °627.

766. **Legislative: Senators elected by the people.**
1851, Feb. 21. H. R. 37, 31st Cong., 2d sess. By Mr. A. Johnson of Tennessee; read twice; to Com. of the Whole. H. J., p. 322; Globe, p. °627.

767. **Judiciary: Term of judges twelve years.**
1851, Feb. 21. H. R. 37, 31st Cong., 2d sess. By Mr. A. Johnson of Tennessee; read twice; to Com. of the Whole. H. J., p. 322; Globe, p. °627.

768. **Executive: Election of deputy postmasters.**
1851, Dec. 17. 32d Cong., 1st sess. By Mr. Allen of Massachusetts; to Com. on Judiciary to report. H. J., p. °112; Globe, p. °121.

769. **Legislative: Election of Senators by the people.**
1852, Jan. 15. H. R. 9, 32d Cong., 1st sess. By Mr. Mace of Indiana; read twice; to Com. on Judiciary. H. J., pp. 64, 215; Globe, p. 284.

770. **Executive: Choice directly by districts.**
1852, Feb. 2. H. R. 14, 32d Cong., 1st sess. By Mr. A. Johnson of Tennessee; read twice; to Com. on Judiciary. H. J., p. 306; Globe, p. °443.

771. **Legislative: Senators elected by the people.**
1852, Feb. 2. H. R. 14, 32d Cong., 1st sess. By Mr. A. Johnson of Tennessee; read twice; to Com. on Judiciary. H. J., p. 306; Globe, p. °443.

772. **Judiciary: Term of judges twelve years.**
1852, Feb. 2. H. R. 14, 32d Cong., 1st sess. By Mr. A. Johnson of Tennessee; read twice; to Com. on Judiciary. H. J., p. 306; Globe, p. °443.

773. **Executive: Choice directly by districts.**
1853, Dec. 12. H. R. 2, 33d Cong., 1st sess. By Mr. Ewing of Kentucky; to Com. on Judiciary; com. appointed to confer with Senate com. H. J., pp. 41, 64, 232, 238, 295; Globe, pp. 202, 238, 283, 204, 475, 1372.
1855, Feb. 2. H. R. 2, 33d Cong., 2d sess.; tabled. H. J., 203.

774 [773]. **Executive: Choice: One term only.**
1854, Feb. 24. H. R. 2, 33d Cong., 1st sess. By Mr. Taylor of Ohio; ask for com. on Mr. Ewing's resolution to inquire as above; objected to. Globe, p. 475.

775. **Legislative: Election of Senators by the people.**
1853-54, Dec. 12-June 10. H. R. 3, 33d Cong., 1st sess. By Mr. Mace of Indiana; read twice; to Com. on Judiciary; to select com. H. J., pp. 69, 980; Globe, pp. 38, 1372.

776. **Executive: Election of postmasters and collectors.**
1854, Jan. 30. 33d Cong., 1st sess. By Mr. Walbridge of New York, that a select com. inquire into expediency; failed. H. J., p. °292; Globe, p. 292.

777. **Legislative: Qualification necessary to vote for Representative.**
1858, Jan. 18. 35th Cong., 1st sess. By Mr. Marshall of Kentucky; read. H. J., p. 186; Globe, p. °327.

778. **Personal Relations: Recognition of the right of property in slaves.**

779. **Personal and Territorial Relations: Protection of this right in the Territories.**

780. Personal and Territorial Relations: Return of fugitive slaves.
 1860, Dec. 4. 36th Cong., 2d sess. By President Buchanan in his annual message. S. J., p. °18.

781. Amendment.
 1860, Dec. 4. 36th Cong., 2d sess. By Mr. Nelson of Tennessee; notice given. H. J., p. 10.

782. Personal Rights: Full protection to the rights of property.

783. Interstate Relations: Insuring the equality of the States.
 1860, Dec. 6. 36th Cong., 2d sess. By Mr. Powell of Kentucky, that this portion of the President's message be referred to select com. to inquire into condition of the country; considered; referred to com.: com. report; unable to agree. S. J., pp. 33, 35, 38, 40, 43, 46, 49, 66, 72, 76; Globe, pp. °19, 28, 47, 71, 85, 90, 116, 158, 172, 182, 211, 243.

784. Personal and Territorial Relations: Slavery in the Territories divided by the line of 36° 30'.

785. Commerce: Interstate slave trade permitted.

786. Commerce: Foreign slave trade prohibited.

787. Personal Relations: Return of fugitive slaves.

788. Personal Relations: Right to travel with slaves.

789. Personal Relations: Laws of Congress on return of fugitive slaves supreme.
 1860, Dec. 12. 36th Cong., 2d sess. By Mr. Cochrane of New York; received; referred. H. J., pp. °61-62: Globe, p. °77.

790. Personal Relations: Congress to have no jurisdiction over slavery.

791. Personal and Territorial Relations: Duty of Congress to protect slavery in the Territories.

792. Personal and Territorial Relations: Territorial legislatures to have no jurisdiction over slavery.

793. Personal Relations: Right to travel with slaves.

794. Personal Relations: Fugitive slaves.
 1860, Dec. 12. 36th Cong., 2d sess. By Mr. Leake of Virginia. H. J., p. °65; Globe, p. °77.

795. Amendment: Changes in form of Government required for the self-preservation of the slave-holding States.
 1860, Dec. 12. 36th Cong., 2d sess. By Mr. Jenkins of Virginia, that a com. be appointed to inquire what changes are necessary, suggesting several for consideration, as dual Executive; division of Senate into two bodies; making a majority of Senators from the two sections necessary for all action, and the creation of another advisory body or council. H. J., pp. °65-66; Globe, p. 77.

796. Personal and Territorial Relations: Slavery to be prohibited north of 36° 30' and protected south.

797. Territorial Powers: Admission of Territories.

798. Commerce: Interstate slave trade permitted.

799. Territorial Powers: Congress shall not abolish slavery in District of Columbia, etc.
 1860, Dec. 12. 36th Cong., 2d sess. By Mr. Mallory of Kentucky, that special com. be instructed to report as above. H. J., p. °67; Globe, p. °78.

800. Personal and Territorial Relations: Slavery in Territories: Admission of Territories.

801. Personal Relations: Slave property shall not be impaired.

802. Personal Relations: Remuneration for fugitives.
>1860, Dec. 12. 36th Cong., 2d sess. By Mr. English of Indiana, that the Com of Thirty-three be instructed to inquire. H. J., p °67; Globe, p. °78.

803. Personal Relations: Remuneration for fugitives.
>1860, Dec. 12. 36th Cong., 2d sess. By McClernand; com. to consider if an amendment is necessary. H. J., p. °68; Globe, p. °78.

804. Executive: Presidency abolished: Executive Council.
>1860, Dec. 12. 36th Cong., 2d sess. By Mr. Noell of Missouri, that Com. of Thirty-three inquire into expediency. H. J., pp. °69-70; Globe, p. °70.

805. Personal Rights: Express recognition of right of property in slaves.

806. Personal and Territorial Relations: Federal Government shall protect slavery in District of Columbia and Territories.

807. Territorial: Admission of Territories.

808. Personal Relations: Right to travel with slaves.

809. Personal Relations: Enforcement of return of fugitive slaves: Slave States a negative on all acts of Congress on slavery.

810. Power of Amendment: The above and three-fifths representation for slaves to be unamendable.

811. Division: Federal officers within States to be appointed by States.
>1860, Dec. 12. 36th Cong., 2d sess. By Mr. Hindman of Arkansas; referred to Select Com. on Condition of Country. H. J., p. °70; Globe, pp. °78-79.

812. Amendment: Call of a convention to amend.
>1860, Dec. 12. 36th Cong., 2d sess. By Mr. Larrabee of Wisconsin. H. J., p. °70; Globe, p. 79.

813. Executive: Choice, by districts: Case of no majority.

814. Legislative: Election of Senators by the people.

815. Judiciary: Term of judges: One-half from slave-holding States and one-half from nonslave-holding States.
>1860, Dec. 13. S. R. 48, 36th Cong., 2d sess. By Mr. Johnson of Tennessee; read twice; considered; postponed. S. J., p. 41; Globe, pp. °82-83.

816. Personal and Territorial Relations: Division of the Territories.

817. Personal Relations: Fugitive slaves.

818. Personal and Territorial Relations: Slavery may exist in United States forts, etc.

819. Personal and Territorial Relations: Slavery in the District of Columbia.

820. Power of Amendment: The three-fifths representation of slaves not to be changed.

821. Commerce: Interstate slave trade permitted.

822. Power of Amendment: These provisions to be unamendable.
>1860, Dec. 13. 36th Cong., 2d sess. By Mr. Johnson of Tennessee; read twice; considered; postponed. S. J., p. 41; Globe, pp. °82-83.

823. Territorial Powers: Admission of Territories: Right of property.
>1860, Dec. 17. 36th Cong., 2d sess. By Mr. Cochrane of New York. H. J., p. °81; Globe, p. 107.

824. Relation of State and Federal Governments: Provision for the assent of United States to a State's secession.
>1860, Dec. 17. 36th Cong., 2d sess. By Mr. Sickles of New York. Referred to Select Com. on State of the Country. H. J., p. °82; Globe, p. 107.

825. Personal and Territorial Relations: Right of property in slaves in the Territories.

826. Territorial Powers: Admission of new States.

> 1860, Dec. 18. 36th Cong., 2d sess. By Mr. Florence of Pennsylvania; referred to Select Com. on President's Message H. J., pp. °92-93; (Globe, pp. °105, 106, 121.

827. Territorial and Personal Relations: Slavery prohibited in territory north of and recognized south of 36° 30'.

828. Territorial Powers: Admission of Territories as States.

829. Territorial Powers: Slavery in territory of United States within slave States.

830. Territorial Powers: Slavery in the District of Columbia: Federal officers shall be permitted to bring their slaves into District of Columbia.

831. Commerce: Interstate slave trade permitted.

832. Personal Relations: United States responsible for rescued fugitive slaves.

833. Power of Amendment: The above provision, also the three-fifths slave representation and fugitive-slave clauses shall be unamendable, and no amendment shall be made giving Congress power to abolish slavery.

> 1860, Dec. 18. S. R. 50, 36th Cong., 2d sess. By Mr. Crittenden of Kentucky; read twice; postponed. S. J., pp. 49, 68; (Globe, p. °114.

834. Amendment: Call of a convention to amend.

> 1860, Dec. 18. 36th Cong., 2d sess. By Mr. Lane of Ohio; read. S. J., pp. °47-48; (Globe, p. °112.

835. Amendment: Convention to amend.

> 1860, Dec. 24. S. R. 51, 36th Cong., 2d sess. By Mr. Pugh of Ohio; read twice; to a select com.; reported; unable to agree. S. J., pp. 61, 66, 67; (Globe, p. °183.

836. Territorial and Personal Powers: Congress shall make no law as to slavery in the Territories.

837. Territorial and Personal Powers: Admission of Territories.

838. Territorial and Personal Relations: A representative without vote in the Senate and in the House given to the Territories.

839. Territorial and Personal Relations: Acquirement of new territory.

840. Territorial and Personal Relations: Area of all new States to be equal.

841. Personal Relations: Fugitive-slave clause to extend to Territories.

842. Judiciary: Jurisdiction extends to Territories.

843. Personal Relations: Franchise shall not be given to persons of the African race.

844. Personal Relations: Colonization of free negroes.

845. Territorial and Personal Relations: Slavery in United States territory.

846. Territorial and Personal Relations: Slavery in the District of Columbia: Right of Federal officers to hold slaves in the District of Columbia.

847. Commerce: Interstate slave trade permitted.

848. Commerce: African slave trade prohibited.

849. Personal Relations: United States required to pay for fugitive slaves released.

850. Power of Amendment: The above provision, also the three-fifths slave representation and fugitive slave clauses, shall be unamendable, and no amendment shall be made giving to Congress power to abolish slavery.

> 1860, Dec. 24. S. R. 52, 36th Cong., 2d sess. By Mr. Douglass of Illinois: read twice; to select com.; report; unable to agree. S. J., pp. 61, 66, 67; Globe, p. 183; Senate Reports, pp. °8-10.

851. Personal rights: Property in slaves recognized and protected.

> 1860, Dec. 24. 36th Cong., 2d sess. By Mr. Davis of Mississippi; considered; referred to a select com.; report; unable to agree. S. J., pp. °63, 66, 67: Globe, p. °190.

852. Amendment: To take the sense of the people on the following:

852a. Territorial and Personal Relations: Slavery prohibited in Territories north of and recognized south of 36 30'.

852b. Territorial Powers: Admission of Territories as States.

852c. Territorial Powers: Slavery in Federal territory within slave States.

852d. Territorial Powers: Slavery in the District of Columbia. Federal officers permitted to bring their slaves into the District.

852e. Commerce: Interstate slave trade permitted.

852f. Personal Relations: United States responsible for rescued fugitive slaves.

852g. Power of Amendment: The above provisions, also the three-fifths representation of slaves, and fugitive-slave clauses shall be unamend. able, and no amendment shall be made giving Congress power to abolish slavery.

852h. Personal Relations: Persons of the African race disqualified from holding office or exercising the franchise.

> 1861, Jan. 3-Mar. 2. S. R. 54, 36th Cong., 2d sess. By Mr. Crittenden of Kentucky; read twice; considered in Com. of the Whole; postponed; rejected and reconsidered; amended by Mr. Powell: attempt to substitute Peace Commission amendments; lost (7 to 28). Read third time; rejected (19 to 20). S. J., pp. 71, 76, 85, 87, 88, 89, 96, 97. 99, 105, 106, 107, 129, 133, 136, 137, °384, 385. 386, 387; Globe, pp. °114, 211, 237, 289, 300, 379, 402, 410, 443, 489, 506, 1088, 1185, 1403.

853. Personal Relations: Congress prohibited from interfering with slavery in the States.

854. Personal and Territorial Relations: Congress prohibited from interfering with slavery in Federal territory within slave States.

855. Territorial and Personal Relations: Slavery in District of Columbia.

856. Commerce: Interstate slave trade permitted.

857. Commerce: Slave trade prohibited.

858. Territorial and Personal Relations: Right of property in slaves in the Territories: Division line.

859. Territorial and Personal Relations: Annexation of territory.

860. Personal Relations: Return of fugitive slaves.

> 1861, Jan. 7. 36th Con., 2d sess. By Mr. Etheridge of Tennessee, in the House; read; motion to suspend rules and consider lost. Globe, p. °279.

861. Amendment: To take the sense of the people on certain amendments on February 15.

> 1861, Jan. 12. S. bill 537, 36th Cong., 2d sess By Mr. Bigler of Pennsylvania, in the Senate; read. Globe, p. 351.

862. Amendment: Protection of slavery.

> 1861, Jan. 14. 36th Cong., 2d sess., by Mr. English of Indiana, in the House, resolution providing for the adoption of the Crittenden resolution. Globe, pp. 362, 365, 498. See Nos. 827-833, 852-852h.

863. Executive: Choice.

> 1861, Jan. 14. H. R. bill 932. By Mr. Whitely of Delaware; read twice; to Com. on Judiciary. H. J., p. 185; Globe, p. 363.

864. Personal and Territorial Relations: Division line between free and slave Territories 36° 40'.

865. Personal and Territorial Relations: Congress shall not abolish slavery in its territory within slave States.

866. Personal and Territorial Relations: Congress shall not abolish slavery in the District of Columbia.

867. Commerce: Interstate-slave trade permitted.

868. Personal Relations: Congress required to pay for fugitive slaves escaped.

869. Power of Amendment: The preceding articles shall be unamendable.

> 1861, Jan. 15. 36th Cong., 2d sess. By Mr. Florence of Pennsylvania, in the House, to suspend the rules; entered. Globe, p. 378.

869a. Personal and Territorial Relations: Division line between free and slave Territories, 36 40'.

869b. Territorial Powers: Admission of Territories as States.

869c. Personal Relations: Congress prohibited from abolishing slavery in the States.

869d. Personal Relations: Congress prohibited from abolishing slavery in Federal territory within slave States, District of Columbia, or in Territories south of said line.

869e. Commerce: Congress prohibited from abolishing the interstate slave trade.

869f. Commerce: African slave trade prohibited.

869g. Personal Relations: Return of fugitive slaves.

869h. Personal Relations: Persons of the African race disqualified from holding office or exercising the franchise.

869i. Personal Relations: Colonization of free negroes.

869j. Personal Relations: United States required to pay for fugitive slaves rescued.

869k. Executive: Term, six years: Ineligible to reelection for six years.

869l. Executive: Electors chosen by the people in Congressional districts; two at large by the legislature.

> 1861, Jan. 18. 36th Cong., 2d sess. By Mr. Douglas of Illinois, as an amendment to S. R. 54. Globe, p. 443.

869m. Territorial and Personal Relations: Congress shall make no law as to slavery in the Territories.

> 1861, Jan. 18. 36th Cong., 2d sess. By Mr. Douglas; same as the preceding, save section 1. Intended as an amendment to S. R. 54. Globe, p. 443.

870. Amendment: Protection of slavery.

> 1861, Jan. 22. 36th Cong., 2d sess. Resolution from the legislature of Delaware, approving of the "Crittenden amendments;" read. S. J., p. 129.

871. Personal Relations: Legislation on slavery prohibited.

872. Commerce: African slave trade prohibited; fugitive slaves.

1861, Jan. 23. 36th Cong., 2d sess. By Mr. Morris of Pennsylvania, in the House. Globe, p. *527.

873. Amendment: Call of a peace convention to propose amendments.

1861, Jan. 28. 36th Cong., 2d sess. Resolution from the legislature of Virginia, extending an invitation to all the States to appoint commissioners to meet for the consideration of some adjustment. S. J., p. 149; Globe, p. 590.

874. Amendment: To take the sense of the people on the following amendments:

874ab. Territorial Relations: Division of the Territories by a line on parallel 36° 30'.

874c. Territorial Relations: Two-thirds vote of Senate necessary for acquiring new territory.

874d. Territorial and Personal Relations: Slavery prohibited north of said line; recognized and protected south of said line.

874e. Territorial Powers: Admission of Territories as States.

874f. Personal Relations: Congress prohibited from abolishing slavery in Federal territory within slave State and in District of Columbia.

874g. Personal Relations: Compensation for fugitive slaves rescued required.

874h. Commerce: Interstate slave trade permitted.

874i. Commerce: African slave trade prohibited.

874j. Executive: Term six years: Ineligible to reelection.

874k. Power of Amendment: The provision in regard to three-fifths representation for slaves, and the fugitive-slave clause shall be unamendable, and no amendment shall be made giving Congress power to interfere or destroy the domestic institutions of the States.

1861, Jan. 28. 36th Cong., 2d sess. H. bill 957. By Mr Cochrane of New York; read twice; to select com. H. J., p. 281; Globe, p. 597.

875. Territorial and Personal Relations: Slavery permitted in territory south of 36° 30'.

876. Personal Relations: Legislation abolishing slavery prohibited.

877. Territorial Powers: Admission of new States.

878. Power of Amendment: Legislative: Present right of Representatives shall not be altered.

879. Division of Power: Regulation of the right to labor to belong exclusively to the States.

880. Division of Power: Exclusive power of regulating labor in District of Columbia is ceded to Maryland.

881. Personal Relations: No State shall pass any law contrary to fugitive-slave law.

882. Personal Relations: Right of transit with slaves.

883. Commerce: African slave trade prohibited.

884. Personal Relations: Descendants of Africans excluded from citizenship.

885. Personal Relations: Acts tending to excite an insurrection by slaves are penal offenses.

886. Personal Relations: County of any State in which fugitive slave is rescued shall be liable for payment of full value.

887. Territorial and Personal Relations: Slaves shall not be taken into any territory north of 36° 30'.

888. Personal Relations: Fugitive slaves shall have trial by jury at the place to which they may be returned.

889. Personal Relations: Criminal trial of fugitive slaves.

890. Personal Relations: Citizens of any State sojourning in any other State shall have the right of trial by jury and due process of law.

891. Interstate Relations: No State shall secede without the consent of three-fourths of the States.

892. Power of Amendment: The right of the people in three-fourths of the States to call and form a convention to alter, amend, or abolish the Constitution shall never be questioned.

893. Power of Amendment: Articles 8, 9, 10 of these amendments shall not be altered without the consent of the slave States.

> 1861, Jan. 28. H. R. 67, 36th Cong., 2d sess. By Mr. Florence of Pennsylvania; read twice; to select com. H. J., p. 231; Globe, pp. °598; 479.

894. Amendment: Provision for a popular vote on propositions to amend, proposed by Mr. Crittenden.

> 1861, Jan. 28. H. R. 68, 36th Cong., 2d sess. By Mr. Vallandigham of Ohio; read twice; to select com. H. J., p. 232; Globe, p. 599. Same as S. R. 50. See Nos. 827-833.

895. Amendment: Protection of slavery.

> 1861, Feb. 1. 36th Cong., 2d sess. By Mr. Ten Eyck of New Jersey, from the legislature of New Jersey, indorsing the Crittenden amendments and appointing commissioners for the conference. S. J., p. 173.

896. Territorial and Personal Relations: Slavery prohibited in the Territories north of 36 , 30'; permitted south, etc.

897. Personal Relations: United States Government not to interfere with slavery in States where it exists, nor sustain slavery in any State where it is prohibited.

898. Personal Relations: Fugitive slaves.

899. Commerce: Foreign slave trade prohibited.

> 1861. Feb. 1. 36th Cong., 2d sess. By Mr. Kellogg of Illinois. H. J., p. 255; Globe, p. °690.

900. Amendments: Convention to propose amendments.

> 1861, Feb. 5. 36th Cong., 2d sess. President sends the resolution of the legislature of Kentucky; read; to Com. on Judiciary. S. J., pp. 189, 190; Globe, pp. 751, 762.

901. Territorial: Division of the country into four sections.

902. Legislative: On demand of one-third of Senators votes shall be taken by sections, and a majority from each section shall be necessary for the passage of a bill.

903. Executive: Choice: A majority of all the electors in each of the sections shall be necessary.

904. Executive: Term, six years.

905. Interstate Relations: No State shall secede without the consent of the legislatures of all the States of its section.

906. Personal Relations: Right of citizens from any section to migrate upon equal terms to the Territories.

907. Territorial Relations: Admission of new States.

> 1861, Feb. 7. 36th Cong., 2d sess. By Mr. Vallandigham of Ohio; received. H. J., p. 283; Globe, pp. °794-795.

908. Amendment: Convention to propose amendments.

> 1861, Feb. 9. 36th Cong., 2d sess. The Vice-President laid before the Senate resolutions from the Democratic convention of the State of Ohio; received (3 to 14); read; referred to a select com. S. J., p. 205.

909. Amendments: To ascertain the sense of the people on the Crittenden amendment.

> 1861, Feb. 11. H. R. 73, 36th Cong., 2d sess. By Mr. Martin of Virginia; read twice; to Com. on Judiciary. H. J., p. 205; Globe, p. 853.

910. Relation of State and Federal Governments: Preventing the withdrawal of States from the Union.

> 1861, Feb. 11. 36th Cong., 2d sess. By Mr. Ferry of Connecticut, in the House, that the Com. on Judiciary consider the expediency of an amendment; objection made. Globe, p. 854.

911. Amendment: Calling a national convention.

> 1861, Feb. 19. 36th Cong., 2d sess. By Mr. Fenton of New York, in the House; tabled. Globe, p. 1030.

912. Territorial and Personal Relations: Slavery prohibited in the Territories north of 36° 30'; permitted south.

912a. Territorial Powers: Admission of new States.

913. Personal Relations: United States Government not to interfere with slavery in States where it exists, nor sanction slavery in any State where it is prohibited.

914. Personal Relations: Return of fugitive slaves.

915. Commerce: Foreign slave trade prohibited.

916. Territorial Relations: Increase of territory restricted.

> 1861, Feb. 26. 36th Cong., 2d sess. By Mr. Kellogg of Illinois, as an amendment to the Crittenden amendments (Nos. 827-833); considered; rejected. Globe, pp. 1243, 1250.

917. Peace convention amendments.

> 1861, Feb. 27. 36th Cong., 2d sess. The Vice-President laid before the Senate a communication from the peace conventions of twenty-one States; read and referred to a select com.; reported as S. R. 70. S. J., pp. 322, 337; Globe, pp. 1254-1255. Same as given in Nos. 955-965.

918. Territorial and Personal Relations: Slavery prohibited in territory north of and permitted south of 36° 30'.

918a. Territorial Powers: Admission of new States.

919. Personal Relations: United States Government not to interfere with slavery in States where it exists nor sanction it where it is prohibited.

920. Personal Relations: Return of fugitive slaves.

921. Commerce: Foreign slave trade prohibited.

922. Territorial Relations: Increase of territory restricted.

> 1861, Feb. 27. 36th Cong., 2d sess. By Mr. Kellogg of Illinois, as an amendment to H. R. 64; rejected (33 to 158). H. J., pp. 410, 411; Globe, p. 1259.

923. Territorial and Personal Relations: Slave and nonslave-holding Territories divided: Admission of new States.

924. Territorial and Personal Relations: Congress shall not abolish slavery in its territory situated within slave-holding States.

925. Territorial and Personal: Congress shall not abolish slavery in District of Columbia.

926. Commerce: Interstate slave trade permitted.

927. Personal Relations: Pay for rescued fugitive slaves required.

928. Power of Amendment: The above articles shall be unamendable, also the three-fifths representation clause, and the fugitive-slave clause: No amendment shall be made abolishing slavery in States where it is permitted by law.

929. Personal Relations: Persons of the African race excluded from the franchise and office.

930. Personal Relations: Colonization of free negroes.

> 1861, Feb. 27. 36th Cong., 2d sess. By Mr. Clemens of Virginia, as an amendment to H. R. 64; rejected (80 to 113). H. J., pp. °407–410; Globe, pp. °1260–1261.

**931. Personal Relations: Amendment abolishing slavery prohibited.

> 1861, Feb. 27. H. R. 80; 36th Cong., 2d sess. From the Select Com. of Thirty-three. By Mr. Corwin of Ohio, as a substitute; accepted; rejected; reconsidered, and passed (133 to 65).
>
> Feb. 28–Mar. 2. Resolution received in the Senate; read twice; considered in Com. of the Whole; various amendments offered by Messrs. Pugh, Doolittle, Bingham, Grimes, Johnson; all rejected; passed (24 to 12). H. J., pp. 416, 418, 420, 426, 480, 486; S. J., pp. 339, 350, 360, 374, 375–379, 380–383, 390, 392, 396; Globe, pp. °1263, 1264, 1274, 1285, 1318, 1340, 1364, 1374, 1379, 1408.
>
> Ratified by the following States: Ohio, general assembly of, May 13, 1861. "Laws of Ohio," Vol. LVIII, p. °160. Maryland, general assembly of, Jan. 10, 1862. "Laws of the State of Maryland," 1861–62, Chapter XXI, pp. °21–22. Illinois, constitutional convention of the State of, Feb. 14, 1862. Documentary History of the Constitution of the United States, Vol. II, pp. °518–519. (Bulletin of the Bureau of Rolls and Library of the Department of State, No. 7.) See No. 1025.

931a. Amendment: Calling a national convention.

> 1861, Feb. 27. 36th Cong., 2d sess. By Mr. Burch, in the House, to be added to H. R. 80, for the several States through their legislatures to request Congress to call a convention; rejected (74 to 109). See No. 931.

932. Territorial and Personal Relations: Slavery prohibited in Territories north of and permitted south of 36° 30′.

933. Territorial and Personal Relations: No legislation to prevent the taking of slaves into said Territories: Admission of new States.

934. Territorial Powers: Annexation or acquirement of new territory.

935. Personal Relations: To prevent the abolition of slavery in slave States; to prevent the abolition of slavery in District of Columbia; to permit members of Congress to bring slaves with them.

936. Personal Relations: Congress not to interfere with slavery in territory of United States within States.

937. Personal Relations: Fugitive-slave clause.

938. Commercial: Foreign slave trade prohibited.

939. Power of Amendment: The first, third, and fifth sections, together with this section, and the three-fifths representation and the fugitive-slave clause, shall not be amended without the consent of all the States.

940. Personal Relations: Payment for fugitive slaves released.

> 1861, Feb. 28. S. R. 70, 36th Cong., 2d sess. By Mr. Crittenden of Kentucky, from the select com. to whom was referred the peace convention amendments; to be submitted to conventions in the several States; read twice; considered in Com. of the Whole; amendments proposed by Mr. Seward and Mr. Hunter rejected. S. J., pp. 337, 340, 353, 354, 374; Globe, pp. °1269–1270, 1271, 1305–1318, 1342, 1353.

940a. Amendment: Convention to amend the Constitution.

> 1861. Resolution of the legislature of Illinois, if application be made by any of the States declaring themselves aggrieved. Public Laws of Illinois. 1861. p. 281.

941. Amendment: That the legislatures of the States consider the calling of a convention.

> 1861, Feb. 28. S. R. 71, 36th Cong., 2d sess. By Mr. Seward of New York; read. S. J., p. 337; Globe, p. °1270.

942 [931]. Territorial and Personal Relations: Line for division of slave and nonslave territory.

943. Territorial Powers: Slavery in United States territory within slave States.

944. Personal Relations: Members of Congress permitted to bring slaves into the District of Columbia.

945. Personal Relations: Return of fugitives.

946. Commerce: Interstate slave trade permitted.

947. Commerce: African slave trade prohibited.

948. Personal Relations: Punishment of persons who incite insurrection.

949. Personal Relations: Payment for fugitive slaves released.

950. Power of Amendment: These propositions shall not be amendable; also the three-fifths representation clause and the fugitive-slave clause: Congress shall not abolish slavery in slave States.

951. Personal Relations: Persons of the African race excluded from the franchise and from office.

> 1861, Mar. 2. 36th Cong., 2d sess. By Mr. Pugh of Ohio, as an amendment to H. R. 80; rejected (14 to 25). S. J., pp. °377–379; Globe, p. °1368.

952 [931]. Relation of States with Federal Government: No State shall have power to secede.

953. Relation of States with Federal Government: All laws of the United States shall be the supreme law.

> 1861, Mar. 2. 36th Cong., 2d sess. By Mr. Doolittle of Wisconsin, as an amendment to H. R. 80; rejected (18 to 28). S. J., p. °379; Globe, p. °1270, °1370.

954 [931]. Amendment: That the States be invited to consider the call of a convention.

> 1861, Mar. 2. 36th Cong., 2d sess. By Mr. Grimes of Iowa, as an amendment to H. R. 80; rejected (14 to 25). S. J., p. °380; Globe, p. °1401.

955 [931]. Territorial and Personal Relations: Division line of 36° 30′ between slave and nonslave territory: No legislation to prevent taking slaves from any of the States into the said Territories.

956. Territorial Relations: Acquirement of new territory restricted.

957. Personal and Territorial Relations: Congress shall not have power to abolish slavery in any State: Congress shall not have power to abolish slavery in District of Columbia, nor prohibit Representatives from bringing their slaves into the District.

958. Personal and Territorial Relations: Congress shall not abolish slavery in United States: Property within slave States.

959. Commerce: Interstate slave trade within slave States.

960. Personal Relations and Finance: No higher rate of taxation on slaves than on land.

961. Commerce: Slave trade in District of Columbia prohibited.

962. Personal Relations: Enforcing the delivery of fugitive slaves.

963. Commerce: Foreign slave trade prohibited.

964. Power of Amendment: The first, third, and fifth sections, together with this section, and the three-fifths representation and fugitive-slave clauses of the Constitution shall not be amended without the consent of all the States.

965. Personal Relations: Payment for fugitive slaves rescued.

> 1861, Mar. 2. 36th Cong., 2d sess. By Mr. Johnson of Arkansas, as an amerdment to H. R. 80; presented the resolutions of the peace convention. S. J., pp. °380–382; Globe, pp. 1401–1402.

966. Commerce: African slave trade prohibited.

967. Personal Relations: Persons committing crimes against slaveholders shall be delivered up by States to which they flee.

968. Personal Relations: Punishment of persons aiding in insurrection.

> 1861, Mar. 2. 36th Cong., 2d sess. By Mr. Powell of Kentucky, as an amendment to S. R. 54. (See No. 852.) S. J., p. °384; Globe, pp. 305, °1404.

969. Amendment: Peace Convention Resolutions.

> 1861, Mar. 2. 36th Cong., 2d sess. By Mr. Crittenden of Kentucky, as an amendment to S. R. 54. The peace convention amendments rejected. S. J., pp. °384–386; Globe, pp. °1404–1405. Same as Nos. 955–965.

970. Amendment: Convention for proposing amendments.

> 1861, Mar. 18. 36th Cong., 2d sess. The Vice-President laid before the Senate the resolutions of the legislature of Indiana; read. S. J., pp. 420–421.

970a. Amendment: Convention for proposing amendments.

> 1861, Mar. 20. Resolutions of the general assembly of Ohio, making application for a convention to propose amendments. Laws of Ohio, Vol. LVIII, p. °181.

971. Territorial and Personal Relations: Slavery prohibited in Territories north of 36° 30 . but recognized south of 36° 30'.

971a. Territorial Relations: Admission of new States.

971b. Territorial and Personal Relations: Limitation upon the abolition of slavery in the District of Columbia: Federal officers permitted to bring their slaves into the District.

971c. Commerce: Interstate slave trade permitted.

971d. Commerce: African slave trade prohibited.

971e. Personal Relations: Return of fugitive slaves.

971f. Personal Relations: Congress to punish persons aiding invasions or insurrections in any State.

971g. Personal Relations: Compensation for fugitive slaves rescued.

971h. Amending Power: The above articles to be unamendable; also the three-fifths representation for slaves and fugitive-slave clauses: No amendment to abolish slavery in any State.

> 1861, July 12. 37th Cong., 1st sess. By Mr. Saulsbury of Delaware; read twice; motion to consider; lost (11 to 24). S. J., pp. 32, 177; Globe, pp. 78, 433.

972. Amendment: Convention to amend the Constitution.

> 1861, Aug. 5. H. R. 8, 37th Cong., 1st sess. By Mr. Vallandigham of Ohio; read twice; to Com. of the Whole. H. J., p. 239; Globe, p. 444.

973. Personal Relations: Compensation to States that abolish slavery before January 1, 1900.

974. Personal Relations: Slaves who have enjoyed freedom by the chances of war shall be forever free: All owners of such, if loyal, to be compensated.

975. Personal Relations: Colonization of free colored persons.

1862, Dec. 1. 37th Cong., 3d sess. By President Lincoln in his annual message. S. J., pp. °16–17.

976. Amendment: Convention of the States for reconstruction of the Union.

1862, Dec. 2. H. R. 104, 37th Cong., 3d sess. By Mr. Davis of Kentucky; read. S. J., p. 24.

977. Amendment.

1862, Dec. 2. 37th Cong., 3d sess. By Mr. Vallandigham; gave notice. H. J., p. 29. [Text not given.]

978. Executive: Choice.

979. Executive: Presidential power of removal from office.

980. Executive: Choice.

1862, Dec. 8. S. R., 106. 37th Cong., 3d sess. By Mr. Davis of Kentucky; read twice.

1863, Mar. 3. Nos. 2 and 3 presented by Mr. Davis as amendments to S. R. 106; considered; tabled. S. J., pp. 33, 405; Globe, pp. 16, 1501.

981. Personal Relations: Slavery prohibited.

1863, Dec. 14. H. bill 14, 38th Cong., 1st sess. By Mr. Ashley of Ohio; read twice; to Com. on Judiciary. H. J., p. 44; Globe, p. 19. For text see Orations and Speeches of J. M. Ashley, pp. 330–331.

982. Personal Relations: Slavery prohibited.

1863, Dec. 14. H. R. 9, 38th Cong., 1st sess. By Mr. Wilson of Iowa; read twice; to Com. on Judiciary. H. J., p. 45; Globe, p. °21.

983. Personal Relations: Prohibition of slavery.

984. Amendment: Reducing the majorities required.

1864, Jan. 11. S, 16, 38th Cong., 1st sess. By Mr. Henderson of Missouri; read twice; to Com. on Judiciary; com. report a substitute. (See No. 985.) S. J., pp. 67, 142; Globe, pp. 145, 553, °1313.

***985 [983]. Personal Relations: Prohibition of slavery. (The XIII Amendment.)

1864, Feb. 10–Apr. 8. S. 16, 38th Cong., 1st sess. By Mr. Trumbull, from the Com. on Judiciary, as a substitute for Mr. Henderson's amendment; considered; various attempts to amend. (See below.) Agreed to by Com. of the Whole. Further amendments proposed. Passed by vote of 38 to 6. S. J., pp. 67, 142, 694, °291–92, °300–301, °303, 304, °311, 313. 38th Cong., 2d sess. S. J., pp., 120, 122; Globe, pp. 145, 553, 604, °921, 1130, 1283, °1313, 1346, °1364, °1370, °1424, 1425, °1444, °1447, 1456, °1483, 1487–1490, 38th Cong., 2d sess; Globe, pp. 532.

1864, Apr. 9–June 16 (1865, Jan. 6–31). Received in the House; read; motion to reject; lost (55 to 76); read second time; considered; amendments proposed by Mr. Wheeler and Mr. Pendleton; read third time; failed to pass (95 to 66); motion to reconsider entered.

1865, Jan. 6–31. 38th Cong., 2d sess. Motion to reconsider called up; considered; reconsidered (112 to 57); amendment passed (119 to 56). 38th Cong., 1st sess. H. J., pp. 505, 728, 744, 810, 811, 812, 818; Globe, pp. °2612, 2723, 2939–2948, 2992, 2995, 3000, 3357, 38th Cong., 2d sess. H. J., 83, 86, 88, 90, 95, 97, 169, 171, 172, 203; Globe, pp. 138, 478, 530, 531, 537.

According to a proclamation of the Secretary of State, dated Dec. 18, 1865, the amendment was ratified by the following States: Illinois, Feb. 1, 1865; Rhode Island, Feb. 2, 1865; Michigan, Feb. 2, 1865; Maryland, Feb. 3, 1865; New York, Feb. 3, 1865; West Virginia; Feb. 3, 1865; Maine, Feb. 7, 1865; Kansas, Feb. 7, 1865; Massachusetts, Feb. 8, 1865; Pennsylvania, Feb. 8, 1865; Virginia. Feb. 9, 1865; Ohio, Feb. 10, 1865; Missouri, Feb. 10, 1865; Indiana, Feb. 16, 1865; Nevada, Feb. 16, 1865; Louisiana, Feb. 17, 1865; Minnesota, Feb. 23, 1865; Wisconsin, Mar. 1, 1865; Vermont, Mar. 9, 1865; Tennessee, Apr. 7, 1865; Arkansas, Apr. 20, 1865; Connecticut, May 5, 1865; New Hampshire, July 1, 1865; South

***985 [983]. Personal Relations: Prohibition of slavery. (The XIII Amendment.)—Continued.

Carolina, Nov. 13, 1865; Alabama, Dec. 2, 1865; North Carolina, Dec. 4, 1865; Georgia, Dec. 9, 1865. The following States not enumerated in the proclamation of Secretary of State also ratified this amendment: Oregon, Dec. 11, 1865; California, Dec. 20, 1865; Florida, Dec. 28, 1865; New Jersey, Jan. 23, 1866; Iowa, Jan. 24, 1866; Texas, Feb. 18, 1870. Manual and Digest of the House of Representatives, 53d Cong., 2d sess., pp. 36–37. Documentary History of the Constitution of the United States of America. Vol. II, pp. 520–637. (Bulletin of the Bureau of Rolls and Library, Department of State, No. 7.) Rejected by Delaware and Kentucky. Lalor, I, p. 608.

986 [985]. Personal Relations: Prohibition of slavery.

986a. Legislative: Apportionment of Representatives.

986b. Personal Relations: Repeal of the fugitive slave clause.

1864, Feb. 17. S. 16, 38th Cong., 1st sess. By Mr. Sumner of Massachusetts, as an amendment to com. resolution; received and ordered printed. Globe. p. 694.

987 [985]. Personal Relations: Negroes excluded from citizenship and office.

988 [985]. Territorial: Division of New England.

1864, Mar. 3. S. 16, 38th Cong., 1st session. Mr. Davis of Kentucky; a substitute for com. resolution; received. Globe, p. 921.

989 [985]. Territorial: New division of New England.

1864, Mar. 30. S. 16, 38th Cong., 1st sess. By Mr. Davis of Kentucky; a substitute for com. resolution; received; withdrawn. S. J., p. 291–92; Globe, p. 1346, °1364, °1370.

990 [985]. Personal Relations: Negroes excluded from citizenship and office.

1864, Mar. 31. S. 16, 38th Cong., 1st sess. By Mr. Davis of Kentucky. Reintroduces amendment of Mar. 3 as a substitute to com. resolution; rejected (6 to 28); (not a quorum); considered and rejected (5 to 32). S. J., pp. °291–92, 300–301; Globe, pp. °1370, °1424.

991 [985]. Personal Relations: Negroes excluded from citizenship and office.

1864, Apr. 5. S. 16, 38th Cong., 1st sess. By Mr. Davis of Kentucky. Reintroduces same amendment to be added to com. resolution; rejected. S. J., pp. 300–301; Globe, p. °1424.

992 [985]. Personal Relations: Slaves to be removed by the Government from slave States before being entitled to their freedom.

1864, Apr. 5. S. 16, 38th Cong., 1st sess. By Mr. Davis of Kentucky: to add to first section of com. amendment; rejected. Globe, p. °1424.

993 [985]. Personal Relations: Compensation of slaves emancipated required.

1864, Apr. 5. S. 16, 38th Cong., 1st sess. By Mr. Powell of Kentucky; to add to com. amendment; rejected (2 to 34). Globe, p. °1425.

994 [985]. Personal Relations: Distribution of freedmen through the States and Territories according to the white population.

1864, Apr. 5. S. 16, 38th Cong., 1st sess. By Mr. Davis of Kentucky; to add to com. amendment; rejected. Globe, p. °1425.

995 [985]. Executive: One term only, six years.

1864, Apr. 6. S. 16, 38th Cong., 1st sess. By Mr. Powell of Kentucky: to add at end of com. amendment as an independent proposition; rejected (12 to 32). S. J., p. °303; Globe, pp. °1444–1446.

996 [985]. Executive: President's power of removal from office.

> 1864, Apr. 6. S. 16, 38th Cong., 1st sess. By Mr. Powell of Kentucky, to add to com. amendment as an additional article; rejected (6 to 38). S. J., p. °303; Globe, pp. °1446-47.

997 [985]. Legislative: "Riders" prohibited.

> 1864, Apr. 6. S. 16, 38th Cong., 1st sess. By Mr. Powell of Kentucky, to add a separate article to com. amendment; rejected (6 to 37). S. J., p. °304; Globe, p. °1447.

998 [985]. Personal Relations: Prohibition of slavery.

> 1864, Apr. 8. S. 16, 38th Cong., 1st sess. By Mr. Sumner of Massachusetts, as a substitute to com. amendment; withdrawn. Globe, pp. °1483, °1487-1489.

999 [985]. Personal Relations: Religious freedom guaranteed.

1000. Personal Relations: Rights of the press: Restrictions.

1001. Personal Relations: Right of free speech, etc.

1002. Personal Relations: Rights of the people against the militia.

1003. Personal and Territorial: Slavery in territories south of 36° 30'.

1004. Personal and Territorial: Slavery in the District of Columbia.

1005. Territorial: Admission of Territories as States.

1006. Power of Amendment: Three-fifths representation of slaves not to be abolished without consent of slave States.

1007. Personal Relations: Slavery in States south of 36° 30' regulated by each State.

1008. Personal Relations: Return of fugitive slaves not to be obstructed.

1009. Personal Relations; Right of transit with slaves in slave States.

1010. Commerce: African slave trade prohibited.

1011. Personal Relations: Descendants of Africans excluded from citizenship.

1012. Personal Relations: Fugitive slaves may have trial by jury.

1013. Personal Relations: Fugitives charged with crime may have trial by jury.

1014. Personal Relations: Inciting slaves to insurrection a penal offense.

1015. Personal Relations: Conspiracies shall be suppressed.

1016. Interstate Relations: Consent of three-fourths of the States necessary for withdrawal from the Union.

1017. Personal Relations: Compensation of States by the National Government for freeing slaves.

1018. Personal Relations: Congress allowed to aid colonization of free negroes.

1019. Finance: Duties on imports for revenue permitted.

1020. Personal Relations: When slavery shall be abolished by all the States it shall be forever prohibited.

1021. Personal Relations: Power of Amendment: Provisions of this article in regard to slavery unamendable without consent of slave States.

> 1864, Apr. 8. S. 16, 38th Cong., 1st sess. By Mr. Saulsbury of Delaware, as a substitute for com. amendment; rejected (ayes 2, noes not counted). S. J., p. 311; Globe, pp. °1489-90.

1022 [985]. Personal Relations: Amendment not to apply to Kentucky, Missouri, Delaware, and Maryland for ten years after ratification.

> 1864, June 14. S. 16, 38th Cong., 1st sess. By Mr. Wheeler of Wisconsin, to amend S. R. 16; rejected. H. J., pp. 810, 812; Globe, pp. °2940, 2905.

1023 [985], Personal Relations: To submit the amendment to conventions within the States instead of legislatures.

> 1864, June 15. S. 16, 38th Cong., 1st sess. By Mr. Pendleton of Ohio, as a substitute for the first part of S. R. 16; rejected. H. J., pp. 811, 812; Globe, pp. 2992, 2995,

1024. Personal Relations: Slavery prohibited: Equality before the law.

> 1864, Feb. 8. S. R. 24. By Mr. Sumner of Massachusetts: read twice; to Com. on Judiciary; com. report adversely. S. J., pp. 134, 142; Globe, pp. °521, 522, 553.

1025. Personal Relations: To repeal Corwin amendment.

> 1864, Feb. 8. S. R. 25. By Mr. Anthony of Rhode Island; to Com. on Judiciary; com. discharged from further consideration. S. J., pp. 135, 428; Globe, pp. 522, 2218. See No. 931.

1026. Executive: Choice: Electors distributed according to population of States; nominations by lot from six names chosen; final choice by electors from the two so selected.

1027. Executive: Reversal of veto by majority.

1028. Executive: Not to use the patronage of office for advantage of any party.

1029. Executive: Choice: In case of vacancy in office of President and Vice-President.

1030. Executive: Choice: Oath of electors.

> 1864, Feb. 9. S. R. 26, 38th Cong., 1st sess. By Mr. Powell of Kentucky: read twice; to Com. on Judiciary; reported by com.; postponed. S. J., pp. 140, 667, 668; Globe, pp. °538, 3339.

1031. Personal Relations: Slavery prohibited.

> 1864, Feb. 15. H. R. 33, 38th Cong., 1st sess. By Mr. Windom of Wisconsin; read twice; to Com. on Judiciary. H. J., p. 263; Globe, p. °659.

1032. Personal Relations: Slavery prohibited.

> 1864, Feb. 15. 38th Cong., 1st sess. By Mr. Arnold of Illinois; read; tabled; motion to consider tabled. H. J., pp. 264, 265.

1033. Finance: Tax on exports.

> 1864, Mar. 24. 38th Cong., 1st sess. By Mr. Blaine of Maine: read; considered; to Com. on Judiciary. H. J., p. 424.

1034. Personal Relations: Slavery prohibited.

> 1864, Mar. 28. H. R. 52. By Mr. Norton of Illinois; read: to Com. on Judiciary. H. J., p. 436; Globe, p. 1324.

1035. Personal Relations: Slavery prohibited, fugitive-slave clause struck out.

> 1864, Mar. 28. H. R. 53. By Mr. Stevens of Pennsylvania: read twice; second article struck out; considered; postponed. H. J., pp. 536, 537; Globe, pp. 1336, 1680.

1036. Personal Relations: Abolition of slavery.

> 1864, Apr. 28. 38th Cong., 1st sess. By Mr. Morgan of New York. from the legislature of New York. S. J., p. 377.

1037. Finance: Export duty.

> 1864, Dec. 5. 38th Cong., 2d sess. By Mr. Davis of Maryland; read; to Com. on Ways and Means. H. J., p. 7.

1038. Personal Relations: Abolition of slavery.

> 1864, Dec. 6. 38th Cong., 2d sess. By President Lincoln in his annual message. S. J., p. 13.

1039. Legislative: Apportionment of Representatives.

1864. Dec. 7. 38th Cong., 2d sess. By Mr. Sloan of Wisconsin, that Com. on Judiciary inquire into expediency of amending; read; agreed to (60 to 56); motion to reconsider; tabled. H. J., p. 26.

1039a. Amendment: A convention of the States to consider the following propositions.

1039b. Territorial: Consolidation of certain States into three, for Federal purposes.

1039c. Executive: President to be chosen alternately from free and slave States.

1039d. Executive: One term only.

1039e. Executive: Choice by the Supreme Court from candidates nominated by the States: Senate to fill vacancy.

1039f. Judiciary: Justices of Supreme Court ineligible to any other office.

1039g. Executive: Limitation on President's power of removal.

1039h. Personal Relations: Protection of the individual in the enjoyment of various rights, exemption from military arrest, and trial by martial law: Relation of military to civil power.

1039i. Division of powers: The Constitution as the supreme law of the United States is superior to all acts of Congress, President, or other officers: Limitation on the power to suspend the Constitution.

1039j. Commerce: Freedom of commerce guaranteed.

1039k. Division of powers: Infraction of the above rights punishable as a private wrong and public crime.

1039l. Division of powers: Each State to regulate its domestic institutions.

1039m. Personal relations: Limitation upon the taking of private property by civil or military power: Indemnity and official liability.

1039n. Personal relations: Negroes debarred from citizenship.

1039o. Division of powers: Reserved rights.

1039p. Division of powers: Literal construction of the Constitution guaranteed.

1864, Dec. 12. S. R. 81, 38th Cong., 2d sess. By Mr. Davis of Kentucky; read; passed to second reading. S. J., p. 21: (Globe, p. 14.

1040. Legislative: Apportionment of Representatives.

1041. Finance: Apportionment of direct taxes to value of taxable property.

1865, Jan. 16. H. bill 673. By Mr. Sloan of Wisconsin: read twice; to Com. on Judiciary. H. J., p. 99; (Globe, p. °275.

1042. Division: Powers denied the United States.

1865. Jan. 28. 38th Cong., 2d sess. By Mr. Stevens of Pennsylvania: notice given. H. J., p. 100.

1043. Finance: Export duty.

1865, Jan. 23. S. R. 101, 38th Cong., 2d sess. By Mr. Dixon of Connecticut: read twice: to Com. on Judiciary: reported adversely. S. J., pp. 88, 213: (Globe, pp. °361, 980.

1044. Personal Relations: Abolition of slavery.

1865. Jan. 23. 38th Cong., 2d sess. By Mr. Brown of Missouri, from the constitutional convention of Missouri; read; tabled. S. J., p. 87.

1045. Personal Relations: Abolition of slavery.

> 1865, Feb. 4. 38th Cong., 2d sess. By Mr. Bennett of Colorado, in the House, a joint communication from the Delegates in Congress from the Territories of Colorado, Dakota, Idaho, Utah, Nebraska, Arizona, and New Mexico; objected to. Globe, p. °596.

1046. Legislative: Apportionment of Representatives.

> 1865, Feb. 6. S. R. 108, 38th Cong., 2d sess. By Mr. Sumner of Massachusetts; read twice; to Com. on Judiciary; reported adversely. S. J., pp. 138, 213; Globe, pp. °604, 980.

1047. Legislative: Apportionment of Representatives.

> 1865, Dec. 4. S. R. 1, 39th Cong., 1st sess. By Mr. Sumner of Massachusetts: referred to Com. on Judiciary; reported adversely; indefinitely postponed. S. J., pp. 6, 38, 549; Globe, pp. 2, 38, 3276.

1048. Legislative: Apportionment of Representatives.

> 1865, Dec. 5. H. R. 1, 39th Cong., 1st sess. By Mr. Schenck of Ohio; referred to Com. on Judiciary. H. J., p. 16, Globe, p. 9.

1049. Personal Relations: Civil rights.

> 1865, Dec. 5. H. R. 2, 39th Cong., 1st sess. By Mr. Stevens of Pennsylvania: referred to Com. on Judiciary. H. J., p. 18; Globe. p. °10.

1050. Legislative: Apportionment of Representatives.

> 1865, Dec. 5. H. R. 3, 39th Cong., 1st sess. By Mr. Stevens of Pennsylvania: referred to Com. on Judiciary. H. J., p. 18; Globe, p. °10.

1051. Finance: Provision prohibiting export duties repealed.

> 1865, Dec. 5. H. R. 4. 39th Cong., 1st sess. By Mr. Stevens of Pennsylvania: read twice; to Com. on Judiciary. H. J.. p. 18; Globe, p. °10.

1052. Finance: Rebel debt not to be paid.

> 1865, Dec. 5. H. R. 5, 39th Cong., 1st sess. By Mr. Stevens of Pennsylvania; read twice; to Com. on Judiciary. H. J., p. 18; Globe. p. °10.

1053. Legislative: Apportionment of Representatives and direct taxes.

> 1865, Dec. 5. H. R. 6, 39th Cong., 1st sess. By Mr. Broomall of Pennsylvania; read twice; to Com. on Judiciary. H. J., p. 32; Globe, p. 10.

1054. Finance: Provision prohibiting export duties repealed.

1055. Finance: Prohibit payment of rebel debt.

> 1865, Dec. 6. H. R. 8, 39th Cong., 1st sess. By Mr. Bingham of Ohio; read twice: to Com. on Judiciary. H. J.. p. 34; Globe, p. °14.

1056. Personal Relations: Civil rights.

> 1865, Dec. 6. 39th Cong., 1st sess. By Mr. Bingham of Ohio: read twice; to Com. on Judiciary. Globe, p. 14.

*1057. Finance: Prohibit payment of rebel debt.

> 1865, Dec. 6-19. H. R. 9, 39th Cong., 1st sess. By Mr. Farnsworth of Illinois; read twice; to Com. on Judiciary: reported with amendment; passed House (150 to 11).
>
> 1865, Dec. 20; 1866, June 20; received in the Senate; read twice; to Com. on Judiciary; reported; consideration indefinitely postponed. H. J., pp. 36, 92, 93, 879; S. J., pp. 50, 549; Globe, pp. 15, °87, 88, 3277, 3327.

1058. Executive: Choice by direct popular vote: Plurality vote to elect.

1058a. Suffrage: Congress given power to regulate elections.

> 1865, Dec. 11. H. R. 11, 39th Cong., 1st sess. By Mr. Jenkins of Rhode Island; read twice; to Com. on Judiciary. H. J., p. 38; Globe, p. 18.

1059. Personal Relations: Suffrage: Standard of voting for Federal offices.

1059a. Legislative: Apportionment of Representatives.

> 1865, Dec. 11. H. R. 12, 39th Cong., 1st sess. By Mr. Hubbard of Connecticut; read twice; to Com. on Judiciary. H. J., p. 38; Globe, p. 18.

1060. Personal Relations: Protection of civil rights: A system of common schools for all.

> 1865, Dec. 11. H. R. 13, 39th Cong., 1st sess. By Mr. Delano of Ohio; read twice; to Com. on Judiciary. H. J., p. 38; Globe, p. 18.

1061. Personal Relations: Equality before the law.

> 1865, Dec. 11. H. R. 14, 39th Cong., 1st sess. By Mr. Stevens of Pennsylvania: read twice; to Com. on Judiciary. H. J., p. 39; Globe, p. 18.

1062. Division of Powers: Powers denied the United States.

> 1865, Dec. 11. H. R. 16. 39th Cong., 1st sess. By Mr. Benjamin of Missouri: read twice; to Com. on Judiciary. H. J., p. 39.

1063. Division of Powers: Permanence of the Union guaranteed: Punishment for attempts to subvert or overthrow it.

> 1865, Dec. 13. S. R. 5, 39th Cong., 1st sess. By Mr. Stewart of Nevada: read twice; to Com. on Judiciary; reported adversely; indefinitely postponed. S. J., pp. 35, 549; Globe, pp. 35, 3276.

1064. Personal Rights: Franchise.

> 1865, Dec. 13. 39th Cong., 1st sess. By Mr. Boutwell of Massachusetts, that the Com. on Judiciary be instructed to inquire as to expediency of amending; read; to Com. on Judiciary. H. J., p. 63; Globe, p. 49.

1065. Division of Powers: Paramount sovereignty of the United States asserted: The Union indissoluble.

> 1865, Dec. 21. S. R. 8, 39th Cong., 1st sess. By Mr. Cragin of New Hampshire; read twice; to Com. on Judiciary: reported adversely; postponed indefinitely. S. J., pp. 59, 549; Globe, pp. 108, 3276.

1066. Finance: Protection of national debt: Prohibiting the payment of rebel debt.

> 1866, Jan. 5. S. R. 9, 39th Cong., 1st sess. By Mr. Sumner of Massachusetts; read twice; to Com. on Judiciary; reported adversely; postponed indefinitely. S. J., pp. 62 549; Globe, pp. 129, 3276.

1067. Personal Relations: Prohibition of compensation for slaves emancipated.

> 1866, Jan. 5. S. R. 10, 39th Cong., 1st sess. By Mr. Williams of Oregon; read twice; to Com. on Judiciary; reported adversely; postponed indefinitely. S. J., pp. 62, 549; Globe, pp. 120, 3276.

1068. Legislative: Apportionment of Representatives.

> 1866, Jan. 8. H. R. 30, 39th Cong., 1st sess. By Mr. Pike of Maine; read twice; to Com. on Judiciary. H. J., p. 113; Globe, p. 135.

1069. Legislative: Apportionment of Representatives and direct taxes.

> 1866, Jan. 8. H. R. 31, 39th Cong., 1st sess. By Mr. Blaine of Maine; read twice; to Com. on Judiciary. H. J., p. 116; Globe, pp. 136.

1070. Personal Relations: Qualification of electors.

> 1866, Jan. 10. H. R. 34, 39th Cong., 1st sess. By Mr. Rollins of New Hampshire; read twice; to Com. on Judiciary. H. J., p. 140; Globe, p. 171.

1071. Legislative: Apportionment of Representatives.

> 1866. Jan. 15. H. R. 39, 39th Cong., 1st sess. By Mr. Orth of Indiana; read twice; to Com. on Judiciary. H. J., p. 150; Globe, p. 235.

1072. Legislative: Apportionment of Representatives.

1073. Finance: Apportionment of direct taxes.

> 1866, Jan. 15. 39th Cong., 1st sess. By Mr. Conkling of New York; read twice; to Select Com. on Reconstruction; motion to reconsider; tabled. H. J., p. °146.

1074. Personal Relations: Remuneration for slaves forbidden.

> 1866, Jan. 16. H. R. 43, 39th Cong., 1st sess. By Mr. Lawrence of Ohio; read twice; to Com. on Judiciary. H. J., p. 158; Globe, p. 286.

1075. **Personal Relations: Remuneration for slaves forbidden.**
1866, Mar. 13. H. R. 43, 39th Cong., 1st sess. By Mr. Lawrence of Ohio; reintroduced in an amended form; recommitted. H. J., p. 397; Globe, p °1367, 1605.

1076. **Personal Relations: Remuneration for slaves forbidden.**
1866, Mar. 23. H. R. 43, 39th Cong., 1st sess. By Mr. Lawrence of Ohio; reintroduced with further alterations; recommitted; not acted upon. H. J., p. 454; Globe, p. °1605.

1077. **Legislative: Apportionment of Representatives and direct taxes.**
1866, Jan. 20. S. R. 22, 39th Cong., 1st sess. By Mr. Fessenden of Maine, from Com. on Reconstruction; not voted upon. S. J., p. 96; Globe, p. °337.

1078. **Executive: Choice: Direct popular vote: Case of second election.**
1866, Jan. 22. H. R. 47, 39th Cong., 1st sess. By Mr. Ashley of Ohio; read twice; to Com. on Judiciary. H. J., p. 174; Globe, p. 349.

*1079. **Legislative: Apportionment of Representatives and abridgment of representation.**
1866, Jan. 22-31. H. R. 51, 39th Cong., 1st sess. By Mr. Stevens of Pennsylvania, from Com. on Reconstruction; various amendments introduced. Jan. 24, Mr. Lawrence of Ohio; motion to recommit. Jan. 29, recommitted to com. Jan. 31, com. report. Mr. Schenck's substitute rejected; passed (yeas 120, nays 46). H. J., pp. 179, 213; Globe, p. °51, 535-538.

1080 [1079]. **Legislative: Apportionment of Representatives.**

1081. **Finance: Apportionment of direct taxes.**
1866, Jan. 22. H. R. 51, 39th Cong., 1st sess. By Mr. Sloan, as a substitute for com. resolution; read. Globe, p. °352.

1082 [1079]. **Legislative: Congress to regulate qualifications for electors for Representatives.**
1866, Jan. 23. H. R. 51, 39th Cong., 1st sess. By Mr. Kelley of Pennsylvania, as an additional article; read. Globe, p. °377.

1082a. **Legislative: Apportionment of Representatives.**
1866, Jan. 23. H. R. 51. By Mr. Baker, as an amendment to Mr. Kelley's proposition. Globe, p. °386.

1082b. **Legislative: Apportionment of Representatives.**

1082c. **Finance: Apportionment of direct taxes.**
1866, Jan. 23. H. R. 51. By Mr. Lawrence, as an amendment to H. R. 51. Amendments to this resolution proposed by Messrs. Eliot and Schenck. Globe, p. °385.

1083 [1079]. **Legislative: Apportionment of Representatives.**
1866, Jan. 23. H. R. 51, 39th Cong., 1st sess. By Mr. Orth of Indiana; read; but objection made to its introduction. Globe, p. °381.

1084 [1079]. **Legislative: Apportionment of Representatives: States prohibited from abridging the franchise.**
1866, Jan. 23. H. R. 51, 39th Cong., 1st sess. By Mr. Ingersoll of Illinois, as a substitute; read. Globe, pp. °385-°386.

1085 [1079]. **Personal Relations: Abridgment of representation.**
1866, Jan. 23. H. R. 51, 39th Cong., 1st sess. By Mr. Brooks of New York: notice of an amendment to insert word " sex;" read. Globe, p. °380.

1086 [1079]. **Legislative: Apportionment of Representatives.**

1087. **Finance: Apportionment of direct taxes.**

1088. **Personal Relations: Suffrage.**
1866, Jan. 24. H. R. 51, 39th Cong., 1st sess. By Mr. Eliot of Massachusetts. Globe, p. °406.

1089 [1079]. Legislative Apportionment of Representatives.

> 1866, Jan. 24. H. R. 51, 39th Cong., 1st sess. By Mr. Schenck of Ohio; moved as a substitute Jan. 31; rejected (29 to 131). H. J., 211; Globe, pp. °404, °407, 535-538.

1090 [1079]. Personal Relations: Abridgment of representation.

> 1866, Jan. 25. H. R. 51, 39th Cong., 1st sess. By Mr. Broomall of Pennsylvania, as a substitute. Globe, p. °433.

1091 [1079]. Legislative: Apportionment of Representatives.

1092. Finance: Apportionment of direct taxes.

> 1866, Feb. 6. H. R. 51, 39th Cong., 1st sess. By Mr. Doolittle of Wisconsin, as a substitute for H. R. 51. Mar. 9, reintroduced; withdrawn; reintroduced. Globe, pp. °673, 1287, 1289.

1093 [1079]. Personal Relations: Equal Rights.

> 1866, Feb. 13. H. R. 51, 39th Cong., 1st sess. By Mr. Sumner of Massachusetts; to amend H. R. 51; withdrawn. Globe, p. 852. Mar. 9, reintroduced; lost. Globe, p. 1288.

1094 [1079]. Personal Relations: Suffrage extended to certain classes of persons of African descent.

> 1866, Feb. 19. H. R. 51, 39th Cong., 1st sess. By Mr. Howard of Michigan; to amend H. R. 51. Globe, p. 915.

1095 [1079]. Legislative: Abridgment of representation.

> 1866, Mar. 9. H. R. 51, 39th Cong., 1st sess. By Mr. Clark of New Hampshire; to amend H. R. 51; passed (26 to 20). Globe, p. 1287. Reported by Com. of the Whole, and withdrawn by unanimous consent of the Senate. Globe, p. 1288.

1096 [1079]. Personal Relations: Suffrage.

> 1866, Mar. 9. H. R. 51, 39th Cong., 1st sess. By Mr. Sumner of Massachusetts; to amend H. R. 51; rejected (8 to 38). Globe, p. 1288.

1097 [1079]. Personal Relations: Equality of civil and political rights.

> 1866, Mar. 9. H. R. 51, 39th Cong., 1st sess. By Mr. Yates of Illinois, as a substitute for H. R. 51; rejected (7 to 38). Globe, p. °1287.

1098 [1096]. Legislative: Apportionment of Representatives.

> 1866, Mar. 9. H. R. 51, 39th Cong., 1st sess. By Mr. Clark of New Hampshire, as a substitute for Mr. Sumner's amendment; withdrawn. Globe, pp. 1284-1287.

1099 [1096]. Personal Relations: Equality of suffrage.

> 1866, Jan. 23. S, R. 23, 39th Cong., 1st sess. By Mr. Henderson of Missouri; referred to Com. on Reconstruction. Feb. 7, offered as an amendment to Mr. Sumner's amendment to H. R. 51; lost (yeas 10, nays 51). Globe, pp. 362, 702, 1284.

1100 [1091]. Legislative: Apportionment of Representatives and direct taxes.

> 1866, Mar. 9. H. R. 51, 39th Cong., 1st sess. By Mr. Stewart of Nevada, as an amendment to Mr. Doolittle's amendment. Globe, p. 1289.

1101 [1091]. Legislative: Apportionment of Representatives.

> 1866, Mar. 9. H. R. 51, 39th Cong., 1st sess. By Mr. Sherman of Ohio, to amend Mr. Doolittle's amendment. Globe, p. 1289.

1102 [1091]. Legislative: Apportionment of Representatives.

> 1866, Mar. 12. H. R. 51, 39th Cong. 1st sess. By Mr. Wilson of Massachusetts, as an amendment to Mr. Doolittle's amendment. Globe, p. 1321.

1103 [1079]. Legislative: Apportionment of Representatives.

> 1866, Mar. 12. H. R. 51, 39th Cong., 1st sess. By Mr. Sumner of Massachusetts, as a substitute. Globe, p. °1321.

1104. **Personal Relations: Franchise.**
  1866, Jan. 23. S. R. 23, 39th Cong., 1st sess. By Mr. Henderson of Missouri; read twice; to Com. on Reconstruction. S. J., p. 99. (Globe, p. °362.

1104a. **Executive: Choice: Direct popular vote: Second election by the people.**
  1866, Jan. 30. H. R. 54, 39th Cong., 1st sess. By Mr. Ashley of Ohio; read twice; to Com. on Reconstruction. H. J., pp. 207, 213; (Globe, p. 512.

1105. **Finance: Remuneration for slaves and payment of rebel debt forbidden.**
  1866, Jan. 24. S. R. 24, 39th Cong., 1st sess. By Mr. Wilson of Massachusetts; read twice; to Com. on Reconstruction. S. J., pp. 103, 140; Globe, pp. °391, 701.

1105a. **Personal Relations: Civil rights, etc.**
  1866, Feb. 1. 39th Cong., 1st sess. By Mr. Brown of Missouri, that Com. on Reconstruction be directed to inquire into expediency of amending: passed. S. J., p. 146; Globe, p. 566.

1106. **States in rebellion reduced to Territories.**
  1866, Feb. 5. H. R. 58, 39th Cong., 1st sess. By Mr. Kelso of Missouri: read twice; to Com. on Judiciary. H. J., p. 220; Globe. p. 645.

1107. **Division of Powers: To empower Congress to enforce on the States all obligations, prohibitions, or disabilities imposed by the Constitution.**
  1866, Feb. 5. H. R. 60, 39th Cong., 1st sess. By Mr. Williams of Pennsylvania; read twice; to Com. on Judiciary. H. J., p. 230; Globe, p. 645.

1108. **Changing name of the United States of America to America.**
  1866, Feb. 5. H. R. 61, 39th Cong., 1st sess. By Mr. Anderson of Missouri; read twice: to Com. on Judiciary. H. J., p. 231; Globe, p. 646.

1109. **Personal Relations: Civil rights.**
  1866, Feb. 13. H. R. 63, 39th Cong., 1st sess. By Mr. Bingham of Ohio, from Com. on Reconstruction: reintroduced; indefinitely postponed. H. J., pp. 207, 333, 796; Globe, p. °813, 1033, 2979.

1110. **Personal Relations: Equal civil rights.**
  1866, Feb. 13. S. R. 30, 39th Cong., 1st sess. By Mr. Fessenden of Maine, from Com. on Reconstruction: tabled. S. J., p. 152; Globe, p. °806.

1111. **Personal Relations: No officer of the Confederacy to be eligible.**
  1866, Feb. 16. 39th Cong., 1st sess. By Mr. Cullom of Illinois. H. J., p. °284.

1112. **Personal Relations: Civil disabilities.**
  1866, Feb. 19. H. R. 70, 39th Cong., 1st sess. By Mr. McKee of Kentucky; read twice; to Com. on Judiciary. H. J., p. 288; Globe, p. 919.

1113. **Amendment: Declaring the right of amending the Federal Constitution.**
  1866, Feb. 19. H. R. 72, 39th Cong., 1st sess. By Mr. Bromwell of Illinois; referred to Com. on Judiciary. H. J., p. 288; Globe, p. 919.

1114. **Executive: One term only.**
  1866, Feb. 20. S. R. 33, 39th Cong., 1st sess. By Mr. Wade of Ohio; read twice; ordered to lie on table; referred to Com. on Judiciary. Jan. 26, 1867, reported by Mr. Trumbull with an amendment. (See No. 1194.) S. J., pp. 178, 181; Globe, p. °831.

1115. **Amendment: Constitutional convention.**
  1866, Mar. 2. 39th Cong., 1st sess. By Mr. Lane of Kansas, for the Com. on Judiciary to inquire into expediency of recommending a convention. S. J., p. 197.

1116. Personal Relations: Civil disabilities.

> 1866, Mar. 8. S. R. 40, 39th Cong., 1st sess. By Mr. Poland of Vermont; read twice; to Com. on Reconstruction. S. J., p. 214; Globe, p. °1252.

1117. Legislative: Apportionment of Representatives.

> 1866, Mar. 12. S. R. 42, 39th Cong., 1st sess. By Mr. Grimes of Iowa; tabled. S. J., p. 242: Globe, p. °1320.

1118. Legislative: Apportionment of Representatives.

1119. Finance: Apportionment of direct taxes.

1120. Finance: Redemption of the national debt.

1121. Finance: Payment of rebel debt prohibited.

1122. Finance: Compensation for slaves prohibited.

> 1866, Mar. 13. 39th Cong., 1st sess. By Mr. Lane of Kansas; a motion for the Com. on Judiciary to report a resolution embracing the above provisions. Globe, p. °1350; S. J., p. °228.

1123. Legislative: Basis of representation.

> 1866, Mar. 14. H. R. 89, 39th Cong., 1st sess. By Mr. Ashley of Ohio; read twice; to Com. on Reconstruction. H. J., p. 400; Globe, p. 1375.

1124. Personal Relations: Confederates ineligible to office.

> 1866, Mar. 19. H. R. 91, 39th Cong., 1st sess. By Mr. Baker of Illinois; read twice; to Com. on Judiciary. H. J., p. 422; Globe, p. 1494.

1125. Personal Relations: Civil disabilities.

> 1866, Mar. 19. H. R. 94, 39th Cong., 1st sess. By Mr. Cullom of Illinois; com. amendment; read twice; to Com. on Judiciary. H. J., p. 422; Globe, p. 1495.

1126 Legislative: Apportionment of Representatives.

> 1866, Apr. 3. 39th Cong., 1st sess. By Mr. Hill of Indiana; gave notice. H. J., p. 489.

1127. Finance: Restricting issue of a paper circulating medium.

> 1866, Apr. 9. 39th Cong., 1 sess. By Mr. Thomas, that Com. on Judiciary inquire into expediency of amendment: read, considered, and agreed to. H. J., p. 524.

1128. Personal Relations: Civil rights or franchise guaranteed.

1129. Personal Relations: Compensation for slaves prohibited.

1130. Finance: Payment of rebel debt prohibited.

✓ 1131. Reconstruction.

> 1866, Apr. 12. S. R. 62, 39th Cong., 1st sess. By Mr. Stewart of Nevada, as a substitute for S. R. 48; read twice; to Com. on Reconstruction. S. J., p. 333; Globe, p. °1664, 1906.

1132. Legislative: Apportionment of Representatives.

> 1866, Apr. 16. H. R. 100, 39th Cong., 1st sess. By Mr. Hill of Indiana; read twice; to Com. on Reconstruction. H. J., p. 560; Globe, p. 1968.

1133. Personal Relations: Payment for slaves emancipated prohibited.

1133a. Legislative: Apportionment of Representatives.

1133b. Legislative: Readmission of Representatives and Senators from States in insurrection.

> 1866, Apr. 27. S. R. 76, 39th Cong., 1st sess. By Mr. Wilson of Massachusetts: read twice; to Com. on Reconstruction. S. J., p. 382; Globe, p. 2233.

1134. Personal Rights: Suffrage and civil rights.

1134a. Legislative: Apportionment of Representatives.

1134b. Personal Relations: Secessionists excluded from the franchise.

1134c. Finance: Payment of rebel debt forbidden.

1134d. Finance: Compensation for slaves forbidden.

> 1866, Apr. 30. S. R. 78, 39th Cong., 1st sess. By Mr. Fessenden of Maine, from Joint Com. on Condition of States which formed the Confederation; read; passed to second reading. S. J., p. 384; Globe, pp. 2265, 2560.

***1135. Personal Relations: Civil rights: Citizenship. (The XIV Amendment.)

***1136. Legislative: Apportionment of Representatives.

***1137. Personal Relations: Civil disabilities of secessionists.

***1138. Finance: National debt guaranteed.

***1139. Finance: Payment of rebel debt forbidden.

***1140. Finance: Compensation for slaves forbidden.

> 1866, Apr. 30–June 13. H. R. 127. By Mr. Stevens of Pennsylvania, from the Joint Com. on Reconstruction in the House; several amendments proposed. May 10, passed House (yeas 128, nays 37).
>
> May 27–June 8. In the Senate; received; various amendments proposed. Mr. Howard's substitute from the Com. on Reconstruction (Nos. 1158–1163) accepted. Mr. Fessenden's amendment to sec. 1 (No. 1189) agreed to. Mr. Williams's amendment to sec. 2 (No. 1177) agreed to. Mr. Clark's amendments to secs. 4 and 5 (Nos. 1180–1182) agreed to. Passed the Senate as amended, June 8 (yeas 33, nays 11). June 13. House concurred in Senate amendments (yeas 120, nays 32). H. J., pp. 630, 681, 686, 834; Globe, pp. °2286, 2545, °2463, 2504, °2537, °2768, °2769, °2771, 2803, 2804, °2869, °2890, °2897–99, °2900, °2918, °2921, °2941–42, 2942–86, 2986–91, °3029–40, °3041, 3148–49.
>
> According to a proclamation of the Secretary of State, dated July 28, 1868, this amendment was ratified by the legislatures of the following States: Connecticut, June 30, 1866; New Hampshire, July 7, 1866; Tennessee, July 19, 1866; New Jersey, Sept. 11, 1866; Oregon, Sept. 19, 1866; Vermont, Nov. 9, 1866; New York, Jan. 10, 1867; Ohio, Jan. 11, 1867; Illinois, Jan. 15, 1867; West Virginia, Jan. 16, 1867; Kansas, Jan. 18, 1867; Maine, Jan. 19, 1867; Nevada, Jan. 22, 1867; Missouri, Jan. 26, 1867; Indiana, Jan. 29, 1867; Minnesota, Feb. 1, 1867; Rhode Island, Feb. 7, 1867; Wisconsin, Feb. 13, 1867; Pennsylvania, Feb. 13, 1867; Michigan, Feb. 15, 1867; Massachusetts, Mar. 20, 1867; Nebraska, June 15, 1867; Iowa, Apr. 3, 1868; Arkansas, Apr. 6, 1868; Florida, June 9, 1868; North Carolina, July 4, 1868; Louisiana, July 9, 1868; South Carolina, July 9, 1868; Alabama, July 13, 1868; Georgia, July 21, 1868. Documentary History of the United States of America, Vol. II, pp. 641–771, 788–794. (Bulletin of Rolls and Library of the Department of State, No. 7.)
>
> Subsequent to the date of the proclamation of the Secretary of State, the following States also ratified: Virginia, Oct. 8, 1869; Mississippi, Jan. 15, 1870; Texas, Feb. 18, 1870. Ibid, pp. 772–782.
>
> Rejected by the following States: Delaware, Maryland, and Kentucky.
>
> New Jersey (Apr. 1868) Oregon (Oct. 15, 1868), and Ohio (Jan. 1868), passed resolutions to withdraw consent to ratification. North Carolina, South Carolina, Georgia, Virginia. and Texas, had first rejected this amendment. Digest and Manual of the House of Representatives, 53d Cong., 2d sess., pp. 37–39.

1141 [1137]. Personal Relations: Civil disabilities of secessionists.

> 1866, May 8. H. R. 127, 39th Cong., 1st sess By Mr. Garfield of Ohio, to strike out sec. 3; not acted upon. H. J., p. 681; Globe, p. °2463.

1142 [1137]. Personal Relations: Civil disabilities of secessionists.

> 1866, May 9. H. R. 127, 39th Cong., 1st sess. By Mr. McKee of Kentucky; to amend Mr. Garfield's motion by inserting a substitute for sec. 3; not acted upon. Globe, p. °2504.

1143 [1137]. Personal Relations: Civil disabilities of secessionists.

> 1866, May 10. H. R. 127, 39th Cong., 1st sess. By Mr. Beaman of Michigan, to amend original amendment by a substitute for sec. 3; not acted upon. Globe, p. °2537.

1143a. Personal Relations: Citizenship: Civil rights.

1143b. Legislative: Apportionment of Representatives.

1143c. Finance: Payment of rebel debt forbidden.

✓ 1143d. Finance: Compensation for slaves forbidden.

> 1866, May 14. H. R. 127. By Mr. Stewart; intended to be proposed as an amendment for H. R. 127; ordered printed. Globe, p. 2560.

1144 [1137]. Personal Relations: Civil disabilities.

1145 [1139]. Finance: Payment of rebel debt forbidden.

1146 [1140]. Finance: Compensation for slaves forbidden.

> 1866, May 23. H. R. 127, 39th Cong., 1st sess. By Mr. Clark of New Hampshire as a substitute for secs. 3 and 4 of H. R. 127. Globe, p. °2768.

1147 [1135]. Personal Relations: Civil rights.

1148 [1136]. Legislative: Apportionment of Representatives.

1149 [1138]. Finance: Public debt of the United States guaranteed.

1150 [1139]. Finance: Payment of rebel debt forbidden.

1151 [1140]. Finance: Compensation of slaves forbidden.

> 1866, May 23. H. R. 127, 39th Cong., 1st sess. By Mr. Wade of Ohio, as a substitute for H. R. 127. Globe, p. °2768.

1152 [1136]. Legislative: Apportionment of Representatives.

1153 [1137]. Personal Relations: Disability of secessionists.

> 1866, May 23. H. R. 127, 39th Cong., 1st sess. By Mr. Wilson of Massachusetts, as a substitute for secs. 2 and 3 of H. R. 127. Globe, p. °2769.

1154 [1135–40]. Amendment: Ratification.

> 1866, May 23. H. R. 127, 39th Cong., 1st sess. By Mr. Buckalew of Pennsylvania, as an additional section to H. R. 127. Globe. p. °2771.

1155 [1137]. Personal Relations: Civil disability of secessionists.

> 1866, May 24. H. R. 127, 39th Cong., 1st sess. By Mr. Johnson of Maryland, to strike out sec. 3 of H. R. 127. Globe, p. 2803.

1156 [1136]. Legislative: Apportionment of Representatives.

1157. Finance: Apportionment of direct taxes.

> 1866, May 24. H. R. 127, 39th Cong., 1st sess. By Mr. Sherman of Ohio, as substitute for secs. 2 and 3 of H. R. 127. Globe, p. 2804.

1158 [1135]. Personal Relations: Civil rights.

1159 [1136]. Legislative: Apportionment of Representatives.

1160 [1137]. Personal Relations: Civil disability of secessionists.

1161 [1138]. Finance: National debt guaranteed.

1162 [1139]. Finance: Payment of rebel debt forbidden.

1163 [1140]. Finance: Compensation for slaves forbidden.

> 1866, May 30. H. R. 127, 39th Cong., 1st sess. By Mr. Howard of Michigan, from the Com. on Reconstruction; accepted. Globe, pp. °2869, 2897, 2940.

1164 [1161]. Personal Relations: Citizenship of Indians.

> 1866, May 30. H. R. 127, 39th Cong., 1st sess. By Mr. Doolittle of Wisconsin. to amend sec. 3 of Mr. Howard's substitute; rejected (10 to 30). Globe, p. °2890.

1165 [1160]. Personal Relations: Civil disability of secessionists.

> 1866, May 30. H. R. 127, 39th Cong., 1st sess. By Mr. Hendricks of Indiana. to amend sec. 3 of Mr. Howard's substitute; rejected (8 to 34). Globe, pp. °2897–2899.

1166 [1160]. Personal Relations: Civil disability of secessionists.

> 1866, May 30. H. R. 127, 39th Cong., 1st sess. By Mr. Johnson of Maryland, to amend sec. 3 of Mr. Howard's substitute; rejected (10 to 32). Globe, p. °2899.

1167 [1160]. Personal Relations: Civil disability of secessionists.
1866, May 30. H. R. 127, 39th Cong., 1st sess. By Mr. Johnson of Maryland, to amend sec. 3 of Mr. Howard's substitute: rejected (10 to 32). Globe, p. 2900.

1168 [1160]. Personal Relations: Civil disability of secessionists.
1866, May 30. H. R. 127, 39th Cong., 1st sess. By Mr. Saulsbury of Delaware, to amend sec. 3 of Mr. Howard's substitute: rejected (10 to 32). Globe, p. 2900.

1169 [1160]. Personal Relations: Civil disability of secessionists.
1866, May 31. H. R. 127, 39th Cong., 1st sess. By Mr. Doolittle of Wisconsin. to amend sec. 3 of Mr. Howard's substitute; rejected (10 to 30). Globe, p. 2918.

1170 [1160]. Personal Relations: Civil disability of secessionists.
1866, May 31. H. R. 127, 39th Cong., 1st sess. By Mr. Doolittle of Wisconsin, to amend sec. 3 of Mr. Howard's substitute: rejected (10 to 32). Globe, p. 2921.

1171 [1158–1163]. Personal Relations: Amnesty for certain classes of secessionists.
1866, June 4. H. R. 127, 39th Cong., 1st sess. By Mr. Van Winkle of West Virginia, to add a section to H. R. 127; rejected (8 to 26). Globe, pp. 2941-2942.

1172 [1159]. Legislative: Apportionment of Representatives.
1866, June 4. H. R. 127, 39th Cong., 1st sess. By Mr. Hendricks of Indiana, to amend sec. 2 of H. R. 127; rejected. Globe, p. 2942.

1173 [1159]. Legislative: Apportionment of Representatives.

1174. Finance: Apportionment of direct taxes.
1866, June 4. H. R. 127, 39th Cong., 1st sess. By Mr. Doolittle of Wisconsin as a substitute for sec. 2; rejected (7 to 31). Globe, pp. 2942-2986.

1175 [1159]. Legislative: Apportionment of Representatives.

1175a. Finance: Compensation for slaves forbidden.

1175b. Finance: National debt guaranteed.

1175c. Finance: Payment of rebel debt forbidden.

1176. Finance: Apportionment of direct taxes.
1866, June 6. H. R. 127, 39th Cong., 1st sess. By Mr. Doolittle of Wisconsin; a substitute for sec. 2: rejected (7 to 31). Globe, pp. 2986-91.

1177 [1159]. Legislative: Apportionment of Representatives.
1866, June 6-8. H. R. 127, 39th Cong., 1st sess. By Mr. Williams of Oregon; a substitute for sec. 2; agreed to. Globe, pp. 2991, 3029-40.

1178 [1177]. Legislative: Apportionment of Representatives.
1866, June 6. H. R. 127, 39th Cong., 1st sess. By Mr. Howard of Michigan, to amend Mr. Williams's substitute; rejected. Globe, pp. 3039-3040.

1179 [1158]. Personal Relations: Civil rights.
1866, June 8. H. R. 127, 39th Cong., 1st sess. By Mr. Yates of Illinois, to add a section; not acted upon. Globe, p. 3037..

1180 [1161]. Finance: National debt guaranteed.

1181 [1162]. Finance: Payment of rebel debt prohibited.

1182 [1163]. Finance: Compensation for slaves prohibited.
1866, June 8. H. R. 127, 39th Cong., 1st sess. By Mr. Clark of New Hampshire, to substitute for secs. 4 and 5; agreed to. Globe, p. 3040.

1183 [1158]. Personal Relations: Citizenship.
1866, June 8. H. R. 127, 39th Cong., 1st sess. By Mr. Fessenden of Maine, to insert "or naturalized" in sec. 1; agreed to. Globe, p. 3040.

1184 [1135–1140]. Amendment: Division of amendment into five separate articles.

> 1866, June 8. H. R. 127, 39th Cong., 1st sess. By Mr. Doolittle of Wisconsin, to submit the amendment to the States as five separate articles; rejected (11 to 33). Globe, p. 3040.

1185 [1160]. Personal Relations: Civil disability of secessionists.

> 1866, June 8. H. R. 127, 39th Cong., 1st sess. By Mr. Davis of Kentucky, to amend sec. 3; rejected. Globe, p. 3041.

1186 [1180]. Personal Relations: Payment for private property.

> 1866, June 8. H. R. 127, 39th Cong., 1st sess. By Mr. Davis of Kentucky, to amend sec. 4; rejected. Globe, p. 3041.

1187 [1180]. Personal Relations: Remuneration to certain owners for slaves.

> 1866, June 8. H. R. 127, 39th Cong., 1st sess. By Mr. Davis of Kentucky, to amend sec. 4; rejected. Globe, p. 3041.

1188 [1183]. Personal Relations: Civil rights.

> 1866, June 8. H. R. 127, 39th Cong., 1st sess. By Mr. Johnson of Maryland, to amend sec. 1; rejected. Globe p. 3041.

1189. Finance: Export tax on cotton.

> 1866, May 7. H. R. 136, 39th Cong., 1st sess. By Mr. Stevens of Pennsylvania; read twice; to Com. on Judiciary; motion to reconsider; tabled. H. J., p. 676; Globe, p. 2431.

1190. Personal Relation: Suffrage.

> 1866, May 14. S. R. 78, 39th Cong., 1st sess. By Mr. Stewart of Nevada; as a substitute. Globe, p. 2560.

1191. Finance: Export duty on cotton.

> 1866, June 18. 39th Cong., 1st sess. By Mr. Stevens of Pennsylvania; rejected (50 to 61). H. J., p. 857; Globe, p. 3240.

1192. Executive: Choice: One term only: Mode and manner of election.

> 1866, July 23. 39th Cong., 1st sess. By Mr. Ashley of Ohio, that a select com. be appointed to consider all bills and resolutions on above subject; tabled (71 to 42). H. J., p. 1084; Globe, p. 4048.

1193. Executive Officers: Election of assessors and collectors of internal revenue by the people.

> 1866, July 27. 39th Cong., 1st sess. By Mr. Broomall of Pennsylvania, that the Com. on Judiciary inquire into expediency of amending Constitution; motion to suspend rules and introduce; lost. H. J., p. 1176.

1194. Executive: Choice: One term only.

> 1866, Dec. 5. S. R. 33, 39th Cong., 2d sess. By Mr. Wade of Ohio; referred to Com. on Judiciary; reported with an amendment; debated; amendments proposed by Mr. Poland. S. J., pp. 22, 147, 342; Globe, pp. 16, 775, 1140, 1143. [See No. 1114.]

1194a [1194.] Executive: One term only.

> 1867, Jan. 26. S. R. 33, by Mr. Trumbull, from Com. on Judiciary, as an amendment to S. R. 33. Globe, p. 775.

1194b. [1194]. Division of Powers: No State shall withdraw from the Union.

1194c. Finance: Payment of public debt.

1194d. Finance: Payment of rebel debt prohibited.

1194e. Personal Relations: Citizenship defined.

1194f. Legislative: Apportionment of Representatives: Property and educational qualifications.

> 1867, Feb. 6. S. R. 33, by Mr. Dixon of Connecticut, as an amendment to S. R. 33. Globe, p. 1045.

1195. Amendment: Power of amending the Constitution declared.

> 1867, Jan. 21. H. R. 239, 39th Cong., 2d sess. By Mr. Bromwell of Illinois; read twice; to Com. on Reconstruction. H. J., pp. 190, 200; Globe, pp. 615–616.

1196. Judiciary: Term, and choice of judges by Congress.

> 1867, Jan. 21. H. R. 242, 39th Cong., 2d sess. By Mr. Cobb of Wisconsin; read twice; to Com. on Judiciary. H. J., p. 202; Globe, p. 616.

1197. Personal Relations: Suffrage and civil rights.

1197a. Education: Common school system for all: Congress to enforce the same.

> 1867, Jan. 28. H. R. 248, 39th Cong., 2d sess. By Mr. Kelso of Missouri: read twice: to Com. on Judiciary. H. J., p. 276; Globe. p. 806.

1198 [1194]. Executive: One term of six years.

> 1867, Feb. 11. 39th Cong., 2d sess. By Mr. Poland of Vermont, as a substitute for S. R. 33. S. J., p. 242; Globe, p. 1143.

1199. Division of Powers: No State shall withdraw from the Union.

1200. Finance: Payment of public debt.

1201. Finance: Payment of rebel debt prohibited.

1202. Personal Relations: Citizenship defined.

1203. Legislative: Apportionment of Representatives: Property and educational qualifications.

> 1867, Feb. 11. S. R. 169, 39th Cong., 2d sess. By Mr. Dixon of Connecticut; read twice; tabled. S. J., p. 242; Globe, p. 1149.

1204. Executive: One term of six years.

1205. Executive: Abolish the Vice-Presidency.

1206. Executive: Choice by direct popular vote.

> 1867, Feb. 12. 39th Cong., 2d sess. By Mr. Poland of Vermont; for the Com. on Judiciary to consider the expediency of amending the Constitution. S. J., p. 246; Globe, p. 1185.

1207. Executive: Choice by Congress from candidates nominated by the States.

1207a. Executive: Term: Ineligible to reelection.

> 1867, Feb. 15. 39th Cong., 2d sess. By Mr. Davis of Kentucky, in Senate, as an amendment to S. R. 33. Globe, p. 1360.

1208. Judiciary: Removal of judges of Supreme Court on address of two-thirds of both Houses of Congress.

> 1867, Feb. 18. H. R. 286, 39th Cong., 2d sess. By Mr. Williams of Pennsylvania: read twice; to Com. on Judiciary. H. J., p. 414; Globe, p. 1313.

1209 [1284]. Personal Relations: Suffrage and right to hold office.

> 1867, Mar. 7. S. 8, 40th Cong., 2d sess. By Mr. Henderson of Missouri: read twice; to Com. on Judiciary. S. J., pp. 12, 27; Globe, p. 13.
>
> Jan. 15, 1869. Com. report an amendment, which in an amended form passes both Houses and is adopted by the States as the fifteenth amendment. [See No. 1284.]

1210. Executive: One term only.

> 1867, Mar. 7. S. R. 10, 40th Cong., 1st sess. By Mr. Cragin of New Hampshire; read twice; to Com. on Judiciary. S. J., pp. 13, 63; Globe, pp. 13, 198. 40th Cong., 2d sess. Reported. S. J., p. 666; Globe, p. 4093.

1211. Amendment: Declaratory as to procedure of amending the Constitution.

> 1867, Mar. 11. H. R. 5, 40th Cong., 1st sess. By Mr. Bromwell of Illinois. H. J., p. 30; Globe, p. 58.

1212. Personal Relations: Franchise not to be abridged on account of race or color.

> 1867, Mar. 28. H. R. 49, 40th Cong., 1st sess. By Mr. Ingersoll of Illinois; read twice; to Com. on Judiciary. H. J., p. 133; (Globe, p. 420.

1213. Personal Relations: Citizenship defined.

1213a. Personal Relations: Qualifications for the franchise.

1213b. Personal Relations: Civil rights not to be abridged by States.

1213c. Legislative: Apportionment of Representatives.

1213d. Personal Relations: Disability of secessionists.

1213e. Finance: Validity of United States debt guaranteed: Payment of rebel debt prohibited: No compensation for slaves.

> 1867, July 8. H. R. 62, 40th Cong., 1st sess. By Mr. Ashley of Ohio; read twice; to Com. on Judiciary. H. J., p. 169; Globe, p. 511.

1214. Judiciary: Removal of judges on address of two-thirds of both Houses.

> 1867, July 15. H. R. 75, 40th Cong., 1st sess. By Mr. Williams of Pennsylvania; read twice; to Com. on Judiciary. H. J., p. 210; Globe, p. 655.

1215. Personal Relations: Equal civil and political rights.

> 1867, July 17. S. R. 59, 40th Cong., 1st sess. By Mr. Wilson of Massachusetts; read; tabled. S. J., p. 163; Globe, p. 675. 40th Cong., 2d sess. Read twice; to Com. on Judiciary; reported adversely. S. J., pp. 19, 105; Globe, pp. 43, 378.

1216. Personal Relations: Citizenship defined.

1217. Personal Relations: Qualifications for the franchise.

1218. Personal Relations: Civil rights not to be abridged by States.

1219. Legislative: Apportionment of Representatives.

1220. Personal Relations: Disability of secessionists.

1221. Finance: Validity of United States debt guaranteed: Payment of rebel debt prohibited: No compensation for slaves.

> 1867, Nov. 30. H. R. 98, 40th Cong., 1st sess. By Mr. Ashley of Ohio; read twice; to Com. on Judiciary. H. J., p. 283; Globe, p. 814. 40th Cong., 2d sess. Motion to reconsider; discussed; withdrawn. Globe, pp. 18, °117, 119.

1222. Personal Relations: States to provide a system of free public schools.

> 1867, Dec. 10. H. R. 98, 40th Cong., 2d sess. By Mr. Ashley of Ohio; an amendment to sec. 2 of the original resolution. Globe, pp. 18, °117, 119.

1223. Judiciary: Tribunal to decide questions of constitutional power and conflict of jurisdiction between National and State governments.

> 1867, Dec. 16. 40th Cong., 2d sess. By Mr. Davis of Kentucky; read; considered. S. J., pp. °50–57, 95, 99; Globe. pp. °196, 470, 472, 492–498.

1224. Personal Rights: Qualifications of electors.

> 1868, Mar. 9. 40th Cong., 2d sess. By Mr. Newcomb of Missouri; that Com. on Judiciary report an amendment as above; read; to Com. on Judiciary. H. J., p. 491; Globe, p. 1790.

1225. Executive: One term only.

> 1868, Apr. 8. S. R. 133, 40th Cong., 2d sess. By Mr. Sumner of Massachusetts; read twice; to Com. on Judiciary. S. J., p. 379; Globe, p. °2275. 40th Cong., 3d sess. Com. reported adversely. S. J., p. 105; Globe, p. 578.

1226. Executive: Qualification for eligibility.

> 1868, May 18. H. R. 209, 40th Cong., 2d sess. By Mr. Robinson of New York; read twice; to Com. on Foreign Affairs. H. J., p. 703; Globe, p. °2526.

1227. Judiciary: Term of Judges, eight years: Choice by joint convention of Congress.

> 1868, May 18. H. R. 271, 40th Cong., 2d sess. By Mr. Cobb of Wisconsin: read twice; to Com. on Judiciary. H. J., p. 703; Globe, p. 2527.

1227a. Executive: Vice-Presidency abolished.

1227b. Executive: Choice by direct popular vote.

1227c. Executive: One term only, four years.

1227d. Executive: Vacancy in Presidential office to be filled by joint convention of Congress.

1227e. Personal Relations: Franchise.

1227f. Legislative: Apportionment of Representatives.

> 1868, May 30. 40th Cong., 2d sess. By Mr. Ashley of Ohio: in Com. of the Whole Globe, pp. °2713–2722.

1228. Executive: Choice by direct popular vote by districts.

1229. Executive: One term only.

1230. Executive. Succession in case of removal of both President and Vice-President.

1231. Legislative: Election of Senators by popular vote.

1232. Judiciary: Term of judges.

> 1868, July 18. 40th Cong., 2d sess. By President Johnson in a special message. S. J., pp. °692–693; Globe, p. °4210.

1233. Personal Relations: Suffrage.

> 1868, Dec. 7. S. R. 179, 40th Cong., 3d sess. By Mr. Cragin of New Hampshire; read twice; to Com. on Judiciary; reported adversely. S. J., pp. 7, 15, 105; Globe, pp. °6, 388, 378.

1234. Personal Relations: Suffrage.

> 1868, Dec. 7. S. R. 180, 40th Cong., 3d sess. By Mr. Pomeroy of Kansas; read twice: tabled. S. J., p. 7; Globe, pp. °6, 38.

1235. Personal Relations: Suffrage.

> 1868, Dec. 7. H. R. 363, 40th Cong., 3d sess. By Mr. Kelley of Pennsylvania: read twice; to Com. on Judiciary. H. J., p. 10; Globe. p. °9.

1236. Personal Relations: Suffrage.

> 1868, Dec. 7. H. R. 364, 40th Cong., 3d sess. By Mr. Broomall of Pennsylvania; read twice; to Com. on Judiciary. H. J., p. 10; Globe. p. °9.

1237. Personal Relations: Suffrage.

> 1868, Dec. 7. H. R. 366, 40th Cong., 3d sess. By Mr. Stokes of Tennessee: read twice; to Com. on Judiciary. H. J., p. 14; Globe. p. °11.

1238. Personal Relations: Suffrage.

> 1868, Dec. 7. H. R. 367, 40th Cong., 3d sess. By Mr. Maynard of Tennessee; read twice; to Com. on Judiciary. H. J., p. 14; Globe. p. 11.

1239. Personal Relations: Suffrage.

> 1868, Dec. 8. H. R. 371. 40th Cong., 3d sess. By Mr. Julian of Indiana; read twice; to Com. on Judiciary. H. J., p. 23; Globe, p. 21.

1240. Executive: Choice by direct popular vote by districts.

1241. Executive: One term only.

1242. Executive: Succession in case of removal of President and Vice-President.

1243. Legislative: Election of Senators by popular vote.

1244. Judiciary: Term of judges.

> 1868, Dec. 10. 40th Cong., 3d sess. By President Johnson in his annual message. S. J., p. °35.

1245. Personal Relations: Suffrage.

1245a. Legislative: Apportionment of Representatives.

> 1868, Dec. 14. H. R. 381. 40th Cong., 3d sess. By Mr. Ashley of Ohio: read twice; to Com. on Judiciary. H J., p. 55; Globe, p. 69.

1246. Judiciary: Term of judges, ten years.

> 1868, Dec. 14. H. R. 383, 40th Cong., 3d sess. By Mr. Loughridge of Iowa: read twice; to Com. on Judiciary. H. J., p. 56; Globe, p. 70.

1247. Executive and Legislative: Division of State into electoral districts.

1248. Executive: Choice: In case of no choice, a second election by electoral college.

> 1868, Dec. 17. S. R 189, 40th Cong., 3d sess. By Mr. McCreery of Kentucky; read twice; to Com. on Judiciary; reported and postponed. S. J., p. 56; Globe, pp. 121, 622.

1249. Personal Relations: Suffrage.

> 1869, Jan. 11. H. R. 399, 40th Cong., 3d sess. By Mr. Bromwell of Illinois; read twice; to Com. on Judiciary. H. J., p. 133; Globe, p. 282.

*1250 [1235]. Personal Relations: Suffrage.

> 1869, Jan. 11–30. H. R. 402. 40th Cong., 3d sess. By Mr. Boutwell of Massachusetts, from the Com. on Judiciary (as a substitute for H. R. 363), but at suggestion of Speaker made a distinct proposition: read twice; recommitted to Com. on Judiciary; motion to reconsider; various amendments proposed and a slight change agreed to; passed House (yeas 150, nays 42). H. J., pp. 130, 219, 232, 234, 235, 237; Globe, pp. °280, 555, 561, 641, °686, 692, °694, 722, °726, 744, 745.
>
> Jan. 30–Feb. 9. Received in Senate; read twice; to Com. on Judiciary; reconsidered and tabled; considered; various amendments offered, and Mr. Wilson's amendment agreed to; article on election of President added as an additional article, see Nos. 1281, 1287, 1308; passed Senate as amended (yeas 40, nays 16). S. J., pp. 170, 175, 191, 204, 206, 212, 220, °221–23, °225–231; Globe, pp. 740–741, 754, °827, °828, 834, °861, °864, 899, 911, 912, 978, °982, 999, 1008, °1012–14, °1029–30, °1035, °1040–42.
>
> Feb. 10–17. In the House, Mr. Ashley moves to amend as to election of President; amendments of Senate not concurred in by vote of 37 to 133; House asks for conference; Senate recede from their amendments by vote of 33 to 24 and reject, two-thirds not voting in favor (yeas 31, nays 27). H. J., pp. 312, 353; S. J., pp. 271, 285, 287; Globe, pp. 1055, °1107–1108, 1212, °1224, 1226, 1295, 1300.

1251 [1250]. Personal Relations: Woman suffrage.

> 1869, Jan. 23. H. R. 402, 40th Cong., 3d sess. By Mr. Brooks of New York, as an amendment to resolution; ordered printed. Globe, p. °501.

1252 [1250]. Personal Relations: Suffrage.

> 1869, Jan. 23. H. R. 402, 40th Cong., 3d sess. By Mr. Robinson of New York, as an amendment to resolution; ordered printed. Globe, p. °561.

1252a [1250]. Personal Relations: Suffrage.

> 1869, Jan. 27. H. R. 402, 40th Cong., 3d sess. By Mr. Bingham, as an amendment to resolution; ordered printed. Globe, p. °638.

1253 [1250]. Personal Relations: Suffrage.

> 1869, Jan. 28. H. R. 402, 40th Cong., 3d sess. By Mr. Shanks; gave notice of intention to amend by adding "property." Globe, pp. 686, 692.

1254 [1250]. Personal Relations: Suffrage: Those engaged in rebellion excluded.

> 1869, Jan. 28. H. R. 402, 40th Cong., 3d sess. By Mr. McKee, as a substitute for resolution (putting Mr. Shellabarger's amendment in affirmative form). Globe, p. 694.

1255 [1250]. Personal Relations: Suffrage: Those engaged in rebellion excluded.

    1869, Jan. 29. H. R. 402, 40th Cong., 3d sess. By Mr. Shellabarger of Ohio, as a substitute for resolution. H. J., p. 232; Globe, pp. °639, 722, and Appendix, p. 97.

1256 [1250]. Personal Relations: Suffrage.

    1869, Jan. 27. H. R. 402, 40th Cong., 3d sess. By Mr. Ward of New York, as a substitute for resolution; ordered printed. Globe, p. °638.

1257 [1250]. Personal Relations: States prohibited placing restriction on the elective franchise, except such as shall hereafter engage in rebellion.

    1869, Jan. 29, 30. H. R. 402, 40th Cong., 3d sess. By Mr. Bingham of Ohio, as a substitue for resolution; rejected (24 to 160). H. J., pp. 232, 235; Globe. pp. °722, 745.

1258 [1250]. Personal Relations: Suffrage: Educational test prohibited.

    1869, Jan. 29. H. R. 402, 40th Cong., 3d sess. By Mr. Boutwell of Massachusetts, to amend resolution; rejected (45 to 95). H. J., p. 231; Globe, pp. 726-728.

1259 [1250]. Personal Relations: Suffrage.

    1869, Jan. 29. H. R. 402, 40th Cong., 3d sess. By Mr. Boutwell of Massachusetts, to amend resolution by striking out "the" before "case;" agreed to. Globe, p. 726.

1260 [1257]. Personal Relations: Suffrage: Those engaged in rebellion excluded.

    1869, Jan. 29. H. R. 402, 40th Cong., 3d sess. By Mr. Shellabarger of Ohio, as an amendment to Mr. Bingham's amendment; rejected (62 to 125). H. J., p. 234; Globe, pp. °729, 744.

✓ 1261 [1250]. Personal Relations: Right to vote and hold office shall not be abridged.

    1869, Feb. 3. H. R., 402, 40th Cong., 3d sess. By Mr. Stewart of Nevada, in the Senate, upon the instruction of the Com. on Judiciary as a substitute; various attempts to amend, some of which were successful (Nos. 1275, 1277); amndement agreed to; amendment passed with an additional article. See Nos. 1281, 1308. Globe, pp. °828, 978.

1262 [1261]. Personal Relations: Suffrage.

    1869, Feb. 3. H. R. 402, 40th Cong., 3d sess. By Mr. Williams of Oregon, to amend resolution by inserting words "natural born" before "citizens;" considered; withdrawn Feb. 6. Globe, pp. °828, 809-906, 938-939; S. J., pp. 204, 206, 212.

1263 [1261]. Amendment: Ratification by legislature chosen next after passage of resolution.

    1869, Feb 3-9. H. R. 402, 40th Cong., 3d sess. By Mr. Buckalew of Pennsylvania; gave notice; Feb. 9 amendment introduced as an amendment to resolution; rejected (13 to 43). Globe, p. °828, 913. °1040; S. J., p. 228.

1264 [1261]. Personal Relations: Citizens of African descent, right to vote and hold office affirmed.

    1869, Feb. 3-8. H. R. 402, 40th Cong., 3d sess. By Mr. Howard of Michigan; gave notice; Feb. 8, introduced as an amendment to Mr. Stewart's; rejected (16 to 35). Globe, pp. °828, 985, °1008-1011; S. J., p. °227.

1265 [1261]. Personal Relations: Chinamen and Indians not taxed excluded from the terms of this amendment.

    1869, Feb. 3-9. H. R. 402. 40th Cong., 3d sess. By Mr. Corbett of Oregon; gave notice; Feb. 9, introduced as an additional amendment; rejected. S. J., p. °228; Globe. pp. 825, 939, 1035.

1266 [1261]. Personal Relations: Suffrage: Persons engaged in rebellion excluded.

> 1869, Feb. 3–9. H. R. 402, 40th Cong., 3d sess. By Mr. Fowler of Tennessee; gave notice; Feb. 9, introduced as a substitute to com. resolution; rejected (9 to 35). Globe, p. °878, °1020; S. J., 226.

1267 [1261]. Personal Relations: Suffrage.

> 1869, Feb. 3–9. H. R. 402, 40th Cong., 3d sess. By Mr. Sawyer of South Carolina; gave notice; Feb. 9, introduced as a substitute for com. resolution; rejected. Globe, p. 828, °1029; S. J., p. °226.

1268 [1261]. Amendment: To be ratified by conventions.

> 1869, Feb. 3–9. H. R. 402, 40th Cong., 3d sess. By Mr. Dixon of Connecticut; gave notice; Feb. 9, introduced as an amendment to com. resolution; rejected (11 to 45). Globe, p. 828, 855, °1040; S. J., p. °228.

1269 [1261]. Personal Relations: Suffrage and right to hold office.

> 1869, Feb. 3. H. R. 402, 40th Cong., 3d sess. By Mr. Pomeroy of Kansas; gave notice; ordered printed. Globe, p. °828.

1270 [1261]. Personal Relations: Suffrage: Persons who may engage in rebellion excluded.

> 1869, Feb. 4. H. R. 402, 40th Cong., 3d sess. By Mr. Warner of Alabama, as a substitute for com. resolution; Feb. 8, rejected. Globe, p. °861, 101–102; S. J., p. °222.

1271 [1250]. Personal Relations: Suffrage.

> 1869, Feb. 4. H. R. 402, 40th Cong., 3d sess. By Mr. Pool, which he intended to propose as an amendment to H. R. 402; ordered printed. Globe, p. 864.

1272 [1261]. Personal Relations: Suffrage: Not to apply to or affect principle of State government.

> 1869, Feb. 8. H. R. 402, 40th Cong., 3d sess. By Mr. Davis of Kentucky; to be added to com. resolution; rejected. Globe, p. °982.

1273 [1261]. Personal Relations: Suffrage: No person excluded from his right to vote and hold office.

> 1869, Feb. 8. H. R. 402, 40th Cong., 3d sess. By Mr. Drake of Missouri, as a substitute for com. amendment; rejected. S. J., pp. °221–222; Globe, pp. °990, °1008.

1274 [1261]. Personal Relations: Equality of right to suffrage and office.

> 1869, Feb. 9. H. R. 402, 40th Cong., 3d sess. By Mr. Wilson of Massachusetts; as a substitute for com. amendment; rejected (19 to 24). S. J., pp. °222–223; Globe, pp. °1014–1015.

1275 [1261]. Personal Relations: No discrimination in the exercise of the franchise and the right to hold office in a State.

> 1869, Feb. 9. H. R. 402, 40th Cong., 3d sess. By Mr. Wilson of Massachusetts. as a substitute for com. amendment; similar to above; passed (31 to 27). S. J., p. 227; Globe, p. °1035, 1037–40.

1276 [1261]. Personal Relations: Suffrage: Not to be abridged for offense now committed.

> 1869, Feb. 9. H. R. 402, 40th Cong., 3d sess. By Mr. Henderson of Missouri; to be added to com. amendment; rejected. S. J., p. °226; Globe, p. °1020.

1277 [1261]. Personal Relations: Suffrage, etc.

> 1869, Feb. 9. H. R. 402, 40th Cong., 3d sess. By Mr. Conness of California; amendment to com. amendment; slight verbal change; accepted. S. J., p. 226; Globe, p. °1020.

1278 [1261]. Personal Relations: The right to vote not to be abridged for participation in rebellion.

> 1869, Feb. 9. H. R. 402, 40th Cong., 3d sess. By Mr. Vickers of Maryland; to be added to com. amendments; rejected (21 to 32). S. J., p. 226; Globe, pp. °1029–1032.

1279 [1261]. Personal Relations: Right to vote for Federal officers and hold Federal offices not to be abridged by any State.

> 1869, Feb. 9. H. R. 402, 40th Cong., 3d sess. By Mr. Bayard of Delaware; to amend the com. amendment; rejected (12 to 42). S. J., p. °227; Globe, pp. °1029-1030.

1280 [1261]. Personal Relations: Suffrage, etc.

> 1869, Feb. 9. H. R. 402, 40th Cong., 3d sess. By Mr. Sumner of Massachusetts, as an amendment for com. amendment; withdrawn. S. J., p. 227; Globe, pp. 897, 1030.

1281 [1250. 1261]. Executive: Choice: Electors chosen by the people: Congress may prescribe the manner.

> 1869. Feb. 9. H. R. 402, 40th Cong., 3d sess. By Mr. Morton of Indiana, from the Com. on Representative Reform, as an additional article; agreed to (37 to 19). No. 1250. Same as amendment offered to S. 8 and same as S. 200. S. J., p. °229; Globe, pp. °1041-1042. (See Nos. 1287 and 1308.)

1282 [1261]. Personal Relations: Suffrage: Only those who have engaged in rebellion excluded.

> 1869, Feb. 9. H. R. 402, 40th Cong., 3d sess. By Mr. Warner of Alabama, as an amendment to com. resolutions; rejected (5 to 47). S. J., p. 230; Globe, p. 1041.

1283 [1261]. Amendment: Preamble amended.

> 1869, Feb. 9. H. R. 402, 40th Cong., 3d sess. By Mr. Walton of Indiana, to amend preamble; agreed to. Globe, p. 1042.

1283a. Executive: Abolish Vice-Presidency.

1283b. Legislative: Senate elect its presiding officer.

1283c. Executive: By direct popular vote: Second election by people in case of no choice.

1283d. Executive: President ineligible to reelection.

1283e. Executive: Filling vacancy in Presidential office.

> 1869, Feb. 11. H. R. 402. By Mr. Ashley of Ohio, as amendment to Constitution, art. 1, sec. 2., clauses 4 and 5: art. 2, secs. 1, 2, 3, 4, and 6, and art. 12. Globe, p. °1107.

1283f. Executive: Choice: Vote by State: Divided proportionately among electors.

> 1869, Feb. 11. H. R. 402. By Mr. Ashley of Ohio, to strike out art. 16 of proposed amendment and substitute. Globe, p. °1108.

***1284 [1209]. Personal Relations: Suffrage.   (The XV Amendment.)

> 1867, Mar. 7. S. 8, 40th Cong., 2d sess. By Mr. Henderson of Missouri; read twice: to Com. on Judiciary. S. J., pp. 12, 27; Globe, p. 13.
>
> 1869, Jan. 15. 40th Cong., 3d sess. Com. on Judiciary report an amendment: various amendments (as below) proposed; com. amendment agreed to; amendments agreed to in Com. of the Whole; further amendments proposed.
>
> Feb. 17. Senate pass amendment (yeas 35, nays 11).
>
> Feb. 18-20. Amendment received in House: amendments proposed, and Mr. Bingham's amendment agreed to; passed (yeas 140, nays 37).
>
> Feb. 23-26. Senate disagree to House amendment; com. on conference; Senate agree to conference report (39 to 13). House agree (145 to 44). [Speaker voting yea]. S. J., pp. 105, 137, 158, 163, 288, °289, °290, °291, °292, 293, 318, 324, 329, 347, °351, °361, 362; H. J., p. 374, 406, 408, 409, 411, 424, 430, 449, 466; Globe, pp, 378, 491, °541-543, 668, °669, °670, °671-674, °708, °711, °1300, °1302-1306, °1308-1311, 1315, 1318, 1329, 1336, 1426-1428, 1466-1470, 1481, 1563-1564, 1593-1594, 1615, 1641-1644.
>
> According to a proclamation of the Secretary of State, dated Mar. 30, 1870, this amendment was ratified by the following States: Nevada, Mar. 1, 1869; West Virginia, Mar. 3, 1869; North Carolina, Mar. 5, 1869; Louisiana, Mar. 5, 1869;

***1284 [1209]. Personal Relations: Suffrage. (The XV Amendment)—Continued.

Illinois, Mar. 5, 1869; Michigan, Mar. 8, 1869; Wisconsin. Mar. 9, 1869; Massachusetts. Mar. 12, 1869; Maine, Mar. 12, 1869; South Carolina, Mar. 16, 1869; Pennsylvania. Mar. 26, 1869; Arkansas. Mar. 30, 1869; New York, Apr. 14, 1869; Indiana, May 14, 1869; Connecticut, May 19, 1869; Florida, June 15, 1869; New Hampshire, July 7, 1869; Virginia, Oct. 8, 1869; Vermont, Oct. 21, 1869; Alabama, Nov. 24, 1869; Missouri, Jan. 10, 1870; Mississippi, Jan. 17, 1870; Rhode Island, Jan. 18, 1870; Kansas, Jan. 19, 1870; Ohio, Jan. 27, 1870; Georgia, Feb. 2, 1870; Iowa, Feb. 3, 1870; Nebraska, Feb. 17, 1870; Texas, Feb. 18, 1870; Minnesota, Feb. 19, 1870. Documentary History of the Constitution of the United States of America. Vol. II. pp. 795–897. (Bulletin of Rolls and Library of the Department of State, No. 7.)

Subsequent to the date of the proclamation of the Secretary of State the legislature of New Jersey, having previously rejected the amendment, ratified it on Feb. 21, 1871. Ohio, previous to its ratification, had rejected this amendment (May 4, 1869). The legislature of New York passed resolutions withdrawing its consent to the ratification (Jan. 5, 1870). The States of California, Delaware, Kentucky, Maryland, Oregon, and Tennessee rejected this amendment. Digest and Manual of the House of Representatives, 53d Cong., 2d sess., pp. 39, 40.

1285 [1284]. Personal Relations: Suffrage and right to hold office.

1866, Jan. 21. S. 8, 40th Cong., 3d sess. By Mr. Williams, of Oregon, as a substitute for com. amendment; ordered printed. Globe, p. 401.

1286 [1284]. Amendment: Ratification by conventions.

1869, Jan. 25. S. 8, 40th Cong., 3d sess. By Mr. Dixon of Connecticut; gave notice; in an amendment to preamble. Globe, pp. 542–543. Jan. 25, introduced, Globe, p. 580; Jan. 29, called up. S. J., p. °163; Globe, p. °711.

1287 [1284]. Executive: Choice: Electors to be chosen by the people in the manner Congress may prescribe.

1869, Jan. 28. S. 8, 40th Cong., 3d sess. By Mr. Buckalew of Pennsylvania: to be added to the resolution; withdrawn and presented as a new proposition. S. 209; Globe, pp. °668–670. (See No. 1308.)

1287a. Personal Relations: Suffrage.

1869, Jan. 28. S. 8, 40th Cong., 3d sess. By Mr. Henderson of Missouri; to be printed. Globe, p. 674.

1288 [1284]. Amendment: New method of ratification, by vote of the people in each State, etc.

1869, Jan. 28. S. 8, 40th Cong., 3d sess. By Mr. Davis of Kentucky; to be added to the resolution; withdrawn. Globe, pp. °671–674.

1289 [1284]. Personal Relations: Suffrage.

1869, Jan. 29. S. 8, 40th Cong., 3d sess. By Mr. Pomeroy of Kansas; to amend resolutions. Globe, p. °708.

1289a [1284]. Personal Relations: Suffrage.

1869, Feb. 3. S. 8, 40th Cong., 3d sess. By Mr. Warner, to substitute for S. R. 8; ordered printed. Globe, p. °861.

1289b [1284]. Personal Relations: Suffrage.

1869, Feb. 4. S. R. 8, 40th Cong., 3d sess. By Mr. Pool, to add to S. R. 8; ordered printed. Globe, p. 864.

1289c [1250]. Personal Relations: Civil and political.

1869, Feb. 5. 40th Cong., 3d sess. By Mr. Sumner of Massachusetts, as an amendment to H. R. 402; ordered printed. S. J., p. °227; Globe, p. 1030.

1290 [1284]. Personal Relations: Suffrage.

1869, Feb. 17. S. 8, 40th Cong., 3d sess. By Mr. Stewart of Nevada; to amend the resolution; slight verbal change agreed to in Com. of the Whole. Globe, p. 1300.

1291 [1284]. Personal Relations: Right of suffrage and holding office.
1869, Feb. 17. S. 8, 40th Cong., 3d sess. By Mr. Drake of Missouri, as a substitute for resolution; rejected. S. J., p. °289; Globe, pp. °1302-1304.

1292 [1284]. Personal Relations: Suffrage.
1869, Feb. 17. S. 8, 40th Cong., 3d sess. By Mr. Bayard of Delaware; to strike out the words " vote and" in amendment; rejected (6 to 29). S. J., p. °290; Globe, p. 1304.

1293 [1284]. Personal Relations: Suffrage.
1869, Feb. 17. S. 8, 40th Cong., 3d sess. By Mr. Howard of Michigan: to strike out "by the United States or;" rejected (18 to 22). S. J., °290: Globe, p. °1304.

1294 [1284]. Personal Relations: Suffrage not denied for alleged crime.
1869, Feb. 17. S. 8, 40th Cong., 3d sess. By Mr. Doolittle; to add to the article: rejected (13 to 30). S. J., p. °290; Globe, p. °1305.

1295 [1284]. Personal Relations: Suffrage.
1869, Feb. 17. S. 8, 40th Cong., 3d sess. By Mr. Fowler; to amend the article; rejected (5 to 30). S. J., p. °291; Globe, p. 1306.

1296 [1284]. Personal Relations: Declaratory of the rights of citizens of African descent to vote and hold office.
1869, Feb. 17. S. 8, 40th Cong., 3d sess. By Mr. Howard of Michigan; as a substitute for resolution; rejected (22 to 27). S. J., p. 291; Globe, pp. 1308-11. Motion of Mr. Yates to reconsider lost (16 to 29). Globe, p. 1318. S. J., p. 292.

1297 [1284]. Amendment: To be submitted to the legislatures of the States hereafter to be chosen.
1869, Feb. 17. S. 8, 40th Cong., 3d sess. By Mr. Davis of Kentucky, as an amendment to resolution; rejected. S. J., p. 291: Globe, p. 1309.

1298 [1284] Amendment: To be submitted to the legislatures of the States chosen next after the passage of this resolution.
1869, Feb. 17. S. 8, 40th Cong., 3d sess. By Mr. Hendricks of Indiana; to be added to the resolution; rejected (12 to 40). S. J., p. °292; Globe, p. 543, °1311.

1299 [1284]. Amendment: To submit these amendments to conventions.
1869, Feb. 17. S. 8, 40th Cong., 3d sess. By Mr. Dixon of Connecticut; as an amendment to the resolution; rejected (10 to 39). S. J., p. °292; Globe, p. °1315.

1300 [1284]. Personal Relations: Suffrage and right to hold office.
1869, Feb. 17. S. 8, 40th Cong., 3d sess. By Mr. Drake, as a substitute for resolution; ruled out of order. Globe, p. °1318.

1301 [1284]. Personal Relations: No person to be deprived of suffrage by any State for participating in the late rebellion.
1869, Feb. 17. S. 8, 40th Cong., 3d sess. By Mr. Vickers of Maryland, as an amendment to resolution; rejected. Globe, p. °1318.

1302 [1284]. Amendment: To be ratified by legislatures hereafter elected.
1869, Feb. 20. S. 8, 40th Cong., 3d sess. By Mr. Woodward of Pennsylvania, in the House, as an amendment to resolution. Mr. Boutwell would not yield the floor for it. Globe, p. °1426.

1303 [1284]. Personal Relations: Suffrage.
1869, Feb. 20. S. 8, 40th Cong., 3d sess. By Mr. Shellabarger of Ohio, as a substitute for resolution; withdrawn. H. J., p. 406; Globe, pp. 1426, 1428.

1304 [1284]. Personal Relations: Suffrage.
1869, Feb. 20. S. 8, 40th Cong., 3d sess. By Mr. Logan, to strike out "and hold office;" rejected (70 to 95). H. J., pp. 406, 408; Globe, pp. 1426, 1428.

1305 [1284]. Personal Relations: Suffrage.
1869, Feb. 20. S. 8, 40th Cong., 3d sess. By Mr. Bingham of Ohio; to amend resolution; agreed to (92 to 71). H. J., pp. 406, 409; Globe, pp. 1426, 1428.

1306 [1284]. Personal Relations: Suffrage.

> 1869, Feb. 20. S. 8, 40th Cong., 3d sess. By Mr. Lawrence of Ohio, as a substitute for resolution; read, but Mr. Boutwell would not yield the floor. Globe, p. °1427.

1307. Personal Relations: Suffrage.

> 1869, Jan. 19. S. R. 190, 40th Cong., 3d sess. By Mr. Thayer of Nebraska: read twice; tabled. S. J., p. 118; Globe, p. °440.

*1308 [1287, 1281, 1250]. Executive: Choice: Electors chosen in the manner Congress may prescribe.

> 1869, Jan. 28. S. R. 209, 40th Cong., 3d sess. By Mr. Buckalew of Pennsylvania. Same as proposed to S. R. 8 and withdrawn: read twice; to Com. on Representative Reform; reported back. S. J., p. 157; Globe, pp. 668, 674, 704, 708. Passed the Senate Feb. 9 as an additional article to H. R. 402. (No. 1250.) House disagree and Senate recedes from amendment, and the entire resolution failed. Globe, pp. °1042-1044, 1295-1300. Report of com. on bill. S. R., 772. Globe, p. 1769; Globe Appendix, pp. 268-279.

1309. Executive: Choice: By districts.

1310. Legislative: Representatives chosen in districts apportioned by Congress.

> 1869, Feb. 1. H. R. 428, 40th Cong., 3d sess. By Mr. Spalding of Ohio; read twice; to Com. on Revision of the Laws. H. J., p. 240; Globe, p. °768.

1311. Personal Relations: Suffrage and right to hold office guaranteed.

> 1869, Feb. 2. S. R. 215, 40th Cong., 3d sess. By Mr. Wilson of Massachusetts: read twice; tabled. S. J., p. 189; Globe, p. 781.

1312. Personal Relations: Suffrage.

> 1869, Feb. 5. H. R. 441, 40th Cong., 3d sess. By Mr. Lawrence of Ohio: read twice; to Com. on Judiciary. H. J., p. 286; Globe, p. 919.

1313. Legislative: Popular election of Senators; term of Representatives, four years.

> 1869, Feb. 8. H. R. 443, 40th Cong., 3d sess. By Mr. Selye of New York; read twice; to Com. on Judiciary. H. J., p. 295; Globe, p. 957.

1314. Executive: Choice by direct popular vote; in case of tie, by joint convention of Congress.

> 1869, Feb. 8. H. R. 444, 40th Cong., 3d sess. By Mr. Miller of Pennsylvania; read twice; to Com. on Judiciary. H. J., p. 296; Globe, p. 957.

1315. Executive: Tribunal for deciding the validity of electoral vote.

> 1869, Feb. 13. S. R. 224, 40th Cong., 3d sess. By Mr. Robertson of South Carolina; read twice; to Com. on Judiciary. S. J., pp. 256, 295; Globe, pp. 1159, 1341.

1315a. Executive: To pass bill over veto by a majority vote of all.

1315b. Executive Officers: Appointment of Cabinet officers and their subordinates.

1315c. Executive: Pardoning power.

1315d. Judiciary: Term, age limit, etc.

1315e. Legislative: Proportional representation or minority representation.

> 1869, Feb. 13. 40th Cong., 3d sess. By Mr. Ashley of Ohio; in Com. of the Whole House. Globe, p. 1190; App., pp. 207-215.

1316. Finance: Limitations on power of Congress to grant subsidies.

> 1869, Feb. 15. H. R. 453, 40th Cong., 3d sess. By Mr. Miller of Pennsylvania; read twice; to Com. on Judiciary. H. J., p. 345; Globe, p. 1219.

1317. Executive: Choice: To empower Congress to make rules to govern the time and mode of making returns of the electoral colleges and time and manner of counting electoral vote, and the work of deciding the validity thereof.

> 1869, Feb. 15. H. R. 456, 40th Cong., 3d sess. By Mr. Bromwell of Illinois; read twice; to Com. on Judiciary. H. J., p. 346; (Globe, p. 1220.

1318. Executive: Tribunal for deciding validity of electoral vote.

> 1869, Mar. 8. S. R. 7, 41st Cong., 1st sess. By Mr. Robertson of South Carolina; read twice; to Com. on Judiciary; reported adversely: indefinitely postponed. S. J., pp. 24, 40; Globe, pp. 29–61, 62.

1319. Personal Relations: Suffrage based on citizenship, without distinction of sex.

> 1869, Mar. 15. H. R. 15, 41st Cong., 1st sess. By Mr. Julian of Indiana; read twice; to Com. on Judiciary. H. J., p. 41; (Globe, p. 72.

1320. Judiciary: Term, ten years; provisions for retiring existing judges.

> 1869, Mar. 15. H. R. 22, 41st Cong., 1st sess. By Mr. Loughridge of Iowa; read twice; to Com. on Judiciary. H. J., p. 43; Globe, p. 74.

1321. Amendment: Prescribing the manner of procedure by State legislature.

> 1869, Mar. 17. S. R. 32, 41st Cong., 1st sess. By Mr. Morton of Indiana; read twice. S. J., p. 54; Globe, p. 102.

1322. Personal Relations: Chinese shall not be given the franchise.

> 1869, Mar. 22. 41st Cong., 1st sess. By Mr. Johnson of California; moved to suspend rules; lost. H. J., p. 96.

1323. Amendment: Manner of ratifying amendments by States prescribed.

> 1869, Mar. 29. H. R. 57, 41st Cong., 1st sess. By Mr. Shanks of Indiana; read twice; to Com. on Judiciary. H. J., p. 129; Globe, p. 334.

1324. Executive: Choice of electors: Two at large; the others by districts.

> 1869, Dec. 22. H. R. 101, 41st Cong., 2d sess. By Mr. Lawrence of Ohio; referred to Com. on Revision of the Laws. H. J., p. 103; Globe, p. 306.

1325. Personal Rights: Suffrage.

> 1870, Jan. 21. S. R. 103, 41st Cong., 2d sess. By Mr. Pomeroy of Kansas; read twice; to Com. on Judiciary; com. discharged from further consideration. S. J., pp. 129, 985; Globe, pp. 653, 634, 5314.

1326. Finance: Power of Congress to issue legal-tender notes.

> 1870, Feb. 14. H. R. 159, 41st Cong., 2d sess. By Mr. Ingersoll of Illinois; referred to Com. on Judiciary. S. J., p. 317; Globe, p. 1262.

1327. Personal Relations: Suffrage.

> 1870, Apr. 4. H. R. 230, 41st Cong., 2d sess. By Mr. Julian of Indiana; referred to Com. on Judiciary. H. J., p. 569; Globe, p. 2401.

1328. War: The United States shall protect each State against domestic violence.

> 1870, Apr. 18. S. R. 176, 41st Cong., 2d sess. By Mr. Drake of Missouri; read twice; to Com. on Judiciary; reported adversely. S. J., pp. 507, 985; (Globe, pp. 2739, 5314.

1329. Religion and Education: Prohibition of appropriations to sectarian schools.

> 1870, Apr. 18. H. R. 254, 41st Cong., 2d session. By Mr. Burdett of Missouri; referred to Com. on Judiciary. H. J., p. 633; Globe, p. 2754.

1330. Personal Relations: Suffrage.

> 1870, Dec. 8. S. R. 260, 41st Cong., 3d sess. By Mr. Pomeroy of Kansas; read twice; tabled. S. J., p. 30; Globe, p. 38.

1331. Executive: Election of certain Federal officers by the people.

> 1871, Jan. 4. H. R. 438, 41st Cong., 3d sess. By Mr. Coburn of Indiana: read twice; to Com. on Judiciary. H. J., p. 102; Globe, p. 308.

1332. Executive: Age and residence necessary for eligibility.

> 1871, Jan. 17. S. R. 284, 41st Cong., 3d sess. By Mr. Yates of Illinois; read twice; to Com. on Judiciary; reported adversely and postponed indefinitely. S. J., pp. 129, 164; Globe, pp. °538, 1263.

1333. Legislative Powers: Congress prohibited from chartering corporations, etc., or imparing obligations of contract.

> 1871, Mar. 7. H. R. 1, 42d Cong., 1st sess. By Mr. Potter of New York; read twice; to Com. on Judiciary. H. J., p. 14; Globe, p. 12.

1334. Executive Officers: Election and appointment of officers.

> 1871, Mar. 13. H. R. 26, 42d Cong., 1st sess. By Mr. Coburn of Indiana: referred to Com. on Judiciary. H. J., p. 44; Globe, p. 80.

1335. Judiciary: Provision for a constitutional tribunal.

> 1871, Mar. 16. S. R. 2, 42d Cong., 1st sess. By Mr. Davis of Kentucky; read twice; to Com. on Judiciary. S. J., pp. 50, 157; Globe, pp. °120, 882.

1336. Executive: Term, six years; ineligible to reelection.

> 1871, Dec. 6. H. R. 49, 42d Cong., 2d sess. By Mr. Potter of New York; read twice; to Com. on Judiciary. H. J., p. 35; Globe, p. 23.

1337. Executive: Naturalized citizens eligible to the offices of President and Vice-President.

> 1871, Dec. 11. H. R. 52, 42d Cong., 2d sess. By Mr. Morgan of Ohio; read twice; to Com. on Judiciary; motion to suspend rules and pass rejected (90 to 75). H. J., p. 50; Globe, p. 57.

1338. Finance: Taxation; direct tax.

> 1871, Dec. 11. H. R. 53, 42d Cong., 2d sess. By Mr. McNeely of Illinois; read twice; to Com. on Judiciary. H. J., p. 52; Globe, p. 58.

1339. Personal Relations: Marriage and education of white and colored inhabitants of the United States.

> 1871, Dec. 11. H. R. 54, 42d Cong., 2d sess. By Mr. King of Missouri; read twice; to Com. on Judiciary. H. J., p. 53; Globe, p. 58.

1340. Territorial: Admission of Territories as States.

> 1871, Dec. 11. H. R. 55, 42d Cong., 2d sess. By Mr. Coghlan of California; read twice; to Com. on Judiciary; motion to suspend rules and pass rejected (86 to 87). H. J., pp. 54, 649; Globe, p. 59.

1341. Territorial: Requiring a certain population in a Territory prior to its admission as a State.

> 1871, Dec. 18. H. R. 62, 42d Cong., 2d sess. By Mr. Comingo of Missouri: read twice; to Com. on Judiciary. H. J., p. 85; Globe, p. 197.

1342. Education: Common school system.

> 1871, Dec. 19. S. R. 3, 42d Cong., 2d sess. By Mr. Stewart of Nevada: read twice; to Com. on Judiciary; reported; postponed indefinitely. S. J., pp. 63, 846; Globe, pp. °206, 3892.

1343. Executive: One term only.

> 1871, Dec. 21–1873, Jan. 11. S. R. 4, 42d Cong., 2d sess. By Mr. Sumner of Massachusetts; read twice; considered; postponed. S. J., pp. 77, 103; Globe, pp. 206, °259, 354. Considered in Com. of the Whole; to Com. on Judiciary: considered; 42d Cong., 3d sess. Globe, p. 74; S. J., p. 42.

1344. Executive Officers: Tenure of office in general, four years.
    1872, Jan. 8. H. R. 70, 42d Cong., 2d sess. By Mr. McCrary of Iowa; referred to select Com. on Reorganization of the Civil Service. H. J., p. 116; Globe, p. 303.

1345. Judiciary: Judges of the Supreme Court ineligible to Presidency.
    1872, Jan. 8. H. R. 72, 42d Cong., 2d sess. By Mr. Snapp of Illinois; read twice; to Com. on Judiciary. H. J., p. 119; Globe, p. 305.

1346. Judiciary: To give the Supreme Court appelate jurisdiction in certain cases.
    1872, Jan. 15. H. R. 73, 42d Cong., 2d sess. By Mr. McIntyre of Georgia; referred to Com. on Judiciary. H. J., p. 154; Globe, p. 388.

1347. Executive Offices: Exclusion of members of Congress from Presidency, Vice-Presidency, etc.
    1872, Jan. 22. H. R. 81, 42d Cong., 2d sess. By Mr. Parker of Missouri; referred to Com. on Judiciary. H. J., p. 196; Globe, p. 499.

1348. Legislative: To give the Territories members in full standing in the House of Representatives.

1348a. Personal Relations: Suffrage extended to women.
    1872, Mar. 4. H. R. 107, 42d Cong., 2d sess. By Mr. Jones of Wyoming; referred to Com. on Judiciary. H. J., p. 449; Globe, p. 1400.

1349. Legislative. Election of Senators by the people.
    1872, Apr. 8. H. R. 128, 42d Cong., 2d sess. By Mr. Hawley of Illinois; referred to Com. on Judiciary. H. J., p. 646; Globe, p. 2270.

1350. Territorial Powers: Public lands.

1350a. Legislative and Commercial: Congress prohibited from impairing obligations, contracts, etc.
    1872, Apr. 29. H. R. 142, 42d Cong., 2d sess. By Mr. Golladay of Tennessee; referred to Com. on Judiciary. H. J., p. 765; Globe, p. 2884.

1351. Executive: Exclusion of members of Congress and judges from the office of President and Vice-President.
    1872, May 6. H. R. 149, 42d Cong., 2d sess. By Mr. Poland of Vermont; referred to Com. on Judiciary. H. J., p. 149; Globe, p. °3083.

1352. Executive: Choice: Election by direct vote of the people.

1352a. Executive: One term: President ineligible for reelection.

1352b. Executive: Vice-Presidency abolished: Filling vacancy in Presidential office.
    1872, May 30-1873, Jan. 16. S. R. 7, 42d Cong., 2d sess. By Mr. Sumner of Massachusetts; read twice. S. J., p. 886; Globe, p. 4036. Passed over, 42d Cong., 3d sess. Globe, p. 632.

1353. Executive: Veto power modified: A majority of all members elected to pass.
    1872, May 31. S. R. 8, 42d Cong., 2d sess. By Mr. Tipton of Nebraska; read twice; to Com. on Judiciary. S. J., p. 906; Globe, p. 4106.

1354. Executive: Choice: Election by direct vote of the people.
    1872, Dec. 9. H. R. 161, 42d Cong., 3d sess. By Mr. Lynch of Maine; read twice; to Com. on Judiciary. H. J., p. 45; Globe, p. 82.

1355. Amendment: Authorizing Congress to pass a law for holding State elections in all the States on the same day.
    1872, Dec. 9. H. R. 162, 42d Cong., 3d sess. By Mr. Hibbard of New Hampshire; read twice; to Com. on Judiciary. H. J., pp. 45, 46; Globe, p. 82.

1356. Executive: Choice: Term of office, six years; one term only; by direct vote of people.
    1872, Dec. 9. H. R. 163, 42d Cong., 3d sess. By Mr. Banks of Massachusetts; read twice; to Com. on Judiciary; considered. H. J. p. 46; Globe, pp. 82, °1601.

1357. Territorial : Disposal of the public lands to actual settlers only.

> 1872, Dec. 9. H. R. 165, 42d Cong., 3d sess. By Mr. Coghlan of California; read twice ; to Com. on Judiciary. H. J. p. 49 ; Globe, p. 84.

1358. Executive : Naturalized citizens eligible to the office of President and Vice-President.

> 1872, Dec. 16. 42d Cong., 3d sess. By Mr. Morgan of Ohio, in the House. Motion to suspend rules and pass resolution rejected (82 to 71). H. J. p. 87 ; Globe, p. °226.

1359. Executive : Choice : Election by direct vote of the people.

1359a. Legislative : Election of Senators by direct vote of the people.

> 1872, Dec. 20. H. R. 171–172, 42d Cong., 3d sess. By Mr. Porter of Virginia ; read twice ; to Com. on Judiciary. H. J. p. 109 ; Globe, p. 334.

1360. Legislative : Official term of Representatives, four years.

> 1873, Jan. 6. H. R. 174. 42d Cong., 3d sess. By Mr. Porter of Virginia ; read twice ; to Com. on Judiciary. H. J. p. 119 ; Globe, p. 351.

1361. Executive : Choice : Election by direct vote of the people.

> 1873, Jan. 6. H. R. 177. 42d Cong., 3d sess. By Mr. Lynch of Maine ; read twice ; laid over. H. J., p. 122 ; Globe, p. °353.

1362. Executive : Choice : Supreme Court to decide disputes in elections.

> 1873, Jan. 7. S. R. 10, 42d Cong., 3d sess. By Mr. Frelinghuysen of New Jersey. S. J., p. 111 : Globe, p. °368.

1363. Finance : Payment of the public debt.

> 1873, Jan. 13. H. R. 178, 42d Cong., 3d sess. By Mr. Meyers of Pennsylvania ; read twice ; to Com. on Judiciary. H. J., p. 158 ; Globe, p. 537.

1364. Amendments : Prescribing the mode of amending the Constitution.

> 1873, Jan. 13. H. R., 180, 42d Cong., 3d sess. By Mr. Porter, of Virginia ; read twice ; to Com. on Revision of the Laws. H. J., p. 159 : Globe, p. 538.

1365. Executive : Choice : Election by the direct vote of the people.

> 1873, Feb. 17. H. R. 197. 42d Cong., 3d sess. By Mr. Porter, of Virginia ; read twice ; to Com. on Judiciary. H. J., p. 416 ; Globe, p. °1425.

1366. Legislative : Election of Senators by the people.

> 1873, Jan. 31. S. R. 11, 42d Cong. 3d sess. By Mr. Harlan of Iowa ; read twice ; passed over. S. J., p. 254 ; Globe, p. °992, 1419.

1367. Executive : Choice : Election by direct vote of the people.

> 1873, Feb. 17. 42d Cong., 3d sess. By Mr. Porter of Virginia, that the Com. on Judiciary consider and report an amendment: agreed to. H. J., p. 416; Globe, p. 1425.

1368. Executive : Choice : Election by direct vote of the people.

1368a. Executive : One term only.

1368b. Executive : Vice-Presidency abolished.

> 1873, Dec. 1. S. R. 1, 43d Cong., 1st sess. By Mr. Sumner of Massachusetts; read twice; considered in Com. of Whole; referred to Com. on Privileges and Elections. S. J., pp. 7, 188; Record, pp. 2, 951.

1369. Executive : One term of six years.

> 1873, Dec. 1. S. R. 2, 43d Cong., 1st sess. By Mr. Sumner of Massachusetts; read twice; referred to Com. on Privileges and Elections. S. J., pp. 8, 38; Record, pp. 2, 58.

1370. Legislative : Election of Senators by the people.

> 1873, Dec. 1. S. R. 3, 43d Cong., 1st sess. By Mr. Windom of Minnesota; read twice; to Com. on Privileges and Elections. S. J., pp. 8, 38; Record, pp. 3, 58.

1371. Executive : To allow the veto of portions of bills.

1371a. Legislative: Restriction of legislation at extra sessions.
> 1873, Dec. 2. 43d Cong., 1st sess. By President Grant in his annual message. S. J., p. 18.

1372. Legislative: Compensation.
> 1873, Dec. 4. H. R. 1, 43d Cong., 1st sess. By Mr. De Witt of New York; read twice; referred to Com. on Salaries. H. J., pp. 18, 44: Record, p. 59.

1373. Legislative: Compensation.
> 1873, Dec. 4. H. R. 2, 43d Cong., 1st sess. By Mr. Roberts of New York; read twice; to Com. on Salaries. H. J., p. 44; Record, p. 59.

1374. Legislative: Compensation.
> 1873, Dec. 4. H. R. 4, 43d Cong., 1st sess. By Mr. Arthur of Kentucky; read twice; to Com. on Judiciary. H. J., p. 50; Record, p. 65.

1375. Finance: Congress to enact no law guaranteeing the debts of any State, Territory, etc.

1375a. Legislative: Each act of Congress to embrace but one subject-matter.

1375b. Legislative: Compensation of Congress.

1375c. Executive: Term of President, six years; no successive terms.

1375d. Legislative: Election of Senators by the people.

1375e. Finance: Congress to pass laws to protect financial affairs.
> 1873, Dec. 4. H. R. 5, 43d Cong., 1st sess. By Mr. Wilson of Indiana; read twice; to Com. on Judiciary. H. J., p. 50; Record, p. 65.

1376. Executive Officers: Tenure of office.
> 1873, Dec. 4. H. R. 13, 43d Cong., 1st sess. By Mr. McCrary of Iowa; read twice; to Com. on Civil Service Reform. H. J., p. 54; Record, p. 67.

1377. Legislative: Compensation.
> 1873, Dec. 8. H. R. 15, 43d Cong., 1st sess. By Mr. Hale of Maine; from the Com. on Salaries; read twice; recommitted to same com. H. J., p. 83; Record, p. 92.

1378. Finance: Silver and gold only shall be legal tender.
> 1873, Dec. 11. S. R. 4, 43d Cong., 1st sess. By Mr. Hamilton of Maryland; read twice; tabled. S. J., p. 59; Record, p. 122.

1379. Amendment: Election and appointment of officers.
> 1874, Jan. 5. H. R. 27, 43d Cong., 1st sess. By Mr. Coburn of Indiana; read twice; to Com. on Judiciary. H. J., p. 178; Record, p. 371.

1380. Legislative: Election of Senators by the people.
> 1874, Jan. 5. H. R. 28, 43d Cong., 1st sess. By Mr. Hawley of Illinois; read twice; to Com. on Judiciary. H. J., p. 179; Record, p. 371.

1381. Legislative: Election of Senators by the people.
> 1874, Feb. 18. 43d Cong., 1st sess. By Mr. Hager; resolutions from the legislature of California, in favor of an amendment as above; referred to Com. on Privileges and Elections. S. J., p. 264; Record, p. 1580.

1382. Legislative: Election of Senators by the people.
> 1874, Apr. 14. H. R. 86, 43d Cong., 1st sess. By Mr. Creamer of New York; read twice; to Com. on Judiciary; com. discharged from further consideration. H. J., p. 1041; Record, p. 4299.

1383. Finance: Limiting time for presentation of claims against the United States.
> 1874, May 19-1875, Jan. 22. S. R. 9, 43d Cong., 1st sess. By Mr. Wright of Iowa; read twice. S. J., p. 588; Record, p. 94001. 43d Cong., 2d sess. Considered; to Com. on Privileges and Elections. S. J., p. 147; Record, p. 624.

1384. Personal Relations: Common school system.

1874, May 25. S. R. 10, 43d Cong., 1st sess. By Mr. Stewart of Nevada; read twice; to Com. on Judiciary. S. J., p. 613; Record, p. °4215-4216.

1385. Legislative: Election of Senators by the people: Congress shall have power to conduct the same.

1874, June 1. H. R. 100, 43d Cong., 1st sess. By Mr. Parker of Missouri: read twice; to Com. on Judiciary. H. J., p. 1072; Record, p. 4428.

1386. Executive: Choice: Election by the people in districts (eight sections): Supreme Court to canvass the returns: Justices of the Supreme Court excluded.

1874, June 22-1875, Feb. 16. H. R. 116, 43d Cong., 1st sess. By Mr. Smith of New York, from the Com. on Elections; read twice; recommitted to said com. H. J., p. 1286; Record, p. °5378. Report of com. Mr. Smith's substitute. (four sections), 43d Cong., 2d sess. Record, pp. °748, °1321-1322; H. J., pp. 258, 479.

1387. Finance: Gold and silver only shall be legal tender: Obligation of contracts shall not be impaired.

1874, Dec. 8. H. R. 122, 43d Cong., 2d sess. By Mr. Roberts of New York; read twice; to Com. on Judiciary; com. discharged from further consideration; tabled. H. J., pp. 32, 200; Record, pp. 19, °754.

1388. Executive: Official term, six years; ineligible to reelection.

1874, Dec. 14. H. R. 124, 43d Cong., 2d sess. By Mr. Storm of Pennsylvania; read twice; to Com. on Judiciary. H. J., p. 58; Record, p. 70.

1394. Territorial: Territories: To be given a Representative in House of Representatives and one elector in electoral college.

1875, Jan. 25. H. R. 146, 43d Cong., 2d sess. By Mr. Maginnis of Montana: read twice; to Com. on Territories. H. J., p. 245; Record, p. 698.

1395. Executive: Term of office, six years: President ineligible to two successive terms.

1874, May 11. H. R. 98, 43d Cong., 1st sess. By Mr. Morrison of Illinois; Record, p. 3769.

1875, Jan. 26. Reported by Com. on Judiciary with H. R. 147 as substitute.

1396. Executive: Term of office, six years; ineligible to two successive terms.

1875, Jan. 26. H. R. 147, 43d Cong., 2d sess. By Mr. Potter of New York, from Com. on Judiciary; read twice: motion to read a third time rejected, (yeas 134, nays 104). H. J., pp. 261-264; Record, pp. °757-761.

1397. Education: Public schools.

1398. Religion: Separation of church and state.

1399. Police Power: Prohibition of polygamy.

1875, Dec. 7. 44th Cong., 1st sess. By President Grant in his annual message. S. J., p. 9.

1400. Executive: Choice: Election by direct popular vote by districts.

1875, Dec. 9. S. R. 1, 44th Cong., 1st sess. By Mr. Morton of Indiana: read twice; to Com. on Privileges and Elections. Record, p. 187.

* 1401. Religion: Prohibiting the appropriation of any money or property to any religious body or sect.

1875, Dec. 14-1876, Aug. 4. H. R. 1, 44th Cong., 1st sess. By Mr. Blaine of Maine; read twice; to Com. on Judiciary. Mr. Loud from Com. on Judiciary reported an amendment as a substitute; agreed to; resolution passed (180 to 71).

1876, Aug. 5-14. Received by the Senate; read twice: to Com. on Judiciary with several substitute amendments; com. report an amendment; considered and com. amendment agreed to; read a third time; motion to pass lost (28 to 16). H. J., pp. 38, 69; °1383-84, 1389; S. J., pp. 797, 804, 812, 825, °827-828, 834, 861, 870; Record, pp. °205, 5189-5192 °5245, 5357, °5453-5461, 5561, 5502, 5580-5595.

1401a [1401]. Religion: Prohibiting the appropriation of any money or property to any religious body or sect.

    1876, Aug. 7. By Mr. Frelinghuysen of New Jersey, in the Senate, as a substitute for H. R. 1: referred to Com. on Judiciary. Record, p. °5245.

1401b [1401]. Religion: Prohibiting the appropriation of any money or property to any religious body or sect.

    1876, Aug. 7. By Mr. Sargent of California, in the Senate, as a substitute for H. R. 1; referred to Com. on Judiciary. S. J., p. 805; Record, p. °5245.

1401c [1401]. Religion: Prohibiting the appropriation of any money or property to any religious body or sect.

    1876, Aug. 7. By Mr. Christiancy of Michigan, in the Senate, as a substitute for H. R. 1; referred to Com. on Judiciary. Record, p. °5246.

1402. Executive. One term of six years.

    1875, Dec. 14. H. R. 2, 44th Cong., 1st sess. By Mr. Randall of Pennsylvania; read twice; to Com. on Judiciary; com. report H. R. 41 as a substitute (No. 1412). H. J., p. 30; Record, pp. °205, °470.

1403. Executive: One term of six years, thereafter Senator for life.

    1875, Dec. 14. H. R. 6, 44th Cong., 1st sess. By Mr. Harrison of Illinois; read twice; to Com. on Judiciary. H. J., p. 44; Record, p. 208.

1404. Executive: Term of six years; no successive terms.

    1875, Dec. 14. H. R. 7, 44th Cong., 1st sess. By Mr. Morrison of Illinois; read twice; to Com. on Judiciary. H. J., pp. 44, 45; Record, p. 209.

1405. Executive officers: Tenure of office.

    1875, Dec. 14. H. R. 9, 44th Cong., 1st sess. By Mr. McCrary of Iowa; read twice; to Com. on Judiciary. H. J., p. 47; Record, p. 211.

1406. Executive: One term only.

    1875, Dec. 15. H. R. 13, 44th Cong., 1st sess. By Mr. Caulfield of Illinois; read twice; to Com. on Judiciary. H. J., p. 68; Record, p. 228.

1407. Finance: Apportionment of direct taxes.

    1876, Jan. 6. H. R. 26. 44th Cong., 1st sess. By Mr. Reagan of Texas; read twice; to Com. on Judiciary. H. J., p. 127; Record, p. °296.

1408. Executive: Choice: Election by direct vote of the people.

    1876, Jan. 6. H. R. 27, 44th Cong., 1st sess. By Mr. Oliver of Iowa; read twice; to Com. on Judiciary. H. J., p. 129; Record, p. °299.

1409. Legislative: Election of Senators by the people.

    1876, Jan. 6. H. R. 28, 44th Cong., 1st sess. By Mr. Oliver of Iowa; read twice; to Com. on Judiciary. H. J. 129; Record, p. °299.

1410. Personal Relations: No state religion: Ministers excluded from office: No appropriation to religious sects.

    1876, Jan. 17. H. R. 36, 44th Cong., 1st sess. By Mr. O'Brien of Maryland; read twice; to Com. on Judiciary. H. J., p. 196; Record, p. °440.

1411. Executive: No third term.

    1876, Jan. 18. H. R. 40. 44th Cong., 1st sess. By Mr. New of Indiana; read twice; to Com. on Judiciary. H. J., p. 206; Record, p. °449.

1412. Executive: No second term.

    1876, Jan. 18. H. R. 41. 44th Cong., 1st sess. By Mr. Knott from Com. on Judiciary, as a substitute for H. R. 2 (No. 1402); read twice; read third time; motion to pass failed (145 to 108). H. J., pp. 212, 260, 275, 315, 320, °321, 322, °323, 324, 325; Record, pp. °470, °804-813, °839-846.

1412a [1412]. Executive: No second term.

    1876, Jan. 18. H. R. 41, 44th Cong., 1st sess. Mr. Frye presented minority report with an amendment for six-year term; rejected (72 to 184); H. J., pp. 212, 275, 315, °323, 324; Record, pp. 470, 807, 808, 846.

1413. **Personal Relations: Unsectarian distribution of public money.**

1876, Jan 18. H. R. 44, 44th Cong., 1st sess. By Mr. Williams of Wisconsin, read twice; to Com. on Judiciary. H. J.. p. 218; Record, p.. 476.

1414. **Executive: Veto items in appropriation bills.**

1876, Jan. 18. H. R. 45, 44th Cong., 1st sess. By Mr. Faulkner of West Virginia; read twice; to Com. on Judiciary. H. J., p. 220; Record. p. 477.

1415. **Legislative Powers: Prohibiting local or special laws in certain cases.**

1876, Jan. 19. H. R. 46, 44th Cong., 1st sess. By Mr. Springer of Illinois; read twice; to Com. on Judiciary. H. J., p. 224; Record, p. °500.

1416. **Executive: Term to begin May 1.**

1876, Jan. 24. H. R. 47, 44th Cong., 1st sess. By Mr. Lapham of New York; read twice; to Com. on Judiciary. H. J., p. 247; Record, p. °586.

1417. **Amendment: Civil service reform.**

1876, Jan. 24. H. R. 50, 44th Cong., 1st sess. By Mr. A. S. Williams of Michigan; read twice; to Com. on Judiciary. H. J., p. 253; Record, p. °591.

1418. **Legislative: Changing date of the meeting of Congress, and commencement of term of Senators and Representatives.**

1876, Jan. 24. H. R. 51, 44th Cong., 1st sess. By Mr. Wilson of Iowa; read twice; to Com. on Judiciary. H. J., p. 253; Record, p. °591.

1419. **Finance: Direct taxes shall be levied according to the wealth of each State.**

1876, Jan. 31. H. R. 57, 44th Cong., 1st sess. By Mr. Landers of Indiana; read twice; to Com. on Judiciary. H. J., p. 307; Record, p. 776.

1420. **Executive: Choice: By direct popular vote.**

1876, Jan. 31. S. R. 6, 44th Cong., 1st sess. By Mr. Wright of Iowa; read twice; to Com. on Privileges and Elections. S. J., p. 146; Record, p. 756.

1421. **Legislative: Election of Senators by the people.**

1876, Jan. 31. S. R. 7, 44th Cong., 1st sess. By Mr. Wright of Iowa; read twice; to Com. on Privileges and Elections. S. J., p. 157; Record, p. 756.

1422. **Executive: Term of President, six years: No person shall be eligible who has held office for four years.**

1876, Feb. 7. H. R. 62, 44th Cong., 1st sess. By Mr. Oliver of Iowa; read twice; to Com. on Judiciary. H. J., p. 350; Record, p. 918.

1422a. **Finance: To limit power of Congress in making appropriations to the amount of the estimate of the Executive Department.**

1876, Feb. 21. H. R. (Bill) 2191, 44th Cong., 1st sess. By Mr. Cook; to Com. on Judiciary. H. J., p. 431.

1423. **Executive: Choice: Supreme Court to canvass returns and decide contests: Justices of Supreme Court excluded from Presidency and Vice-Presidency.**

1876, Mar. 22-Dec. 12. S. R. 10, 44th Cong., 1st sess. By Mr. Edmunds of Vermont; read twice; to Com. on Judiciary; com. report with amendment. S. J., pp. 335, 496; Record, pp. 1873, 3042. Considered Dec. 12. By Mr. Edmunds as an additional article, making the amendment if ratified applicable to the 1876 contested election; accepted. By Mr. Merrimon of North Carolina; an amendment, making the justices of the Supreme Court ineligible for four years after retirement; accepted; read third time; rejected (14 to 31). 44th Cong., 2d sess. S. J., pp. 36, 39, 42, 45; Record, pp. °117-120, °140-144. 157-162.

1424. **Executive: Veto of items in appropriation bills.**

1876, Apr. 12. H. R. 107, 44th Cong., 1st sess. By Mr. Lapham of New York; read twice; to Com. on Judiciary. H. J., p. 872; Record, p. °2791.

1425. Legislative: Term of Representatives, three years; one-third retire annually.

> 1876, Mar. 6. H. R. 80, 44th Cong., 1st sess. By Mr. Williams of Wisconsin; read twice; to Com. on Judiciary. H. J., p. 518; Record, p. °1486.

1426. Executive Officers: Provision for punishment of official misconduct.

> 1876, June 12. H. R. 121, 44th Cong., 1st sess. By Mr. Lord of New York; read twice; to Com. on Judiciary. H. J., p. 1094; Record, p. °3761.

1427. Executive Officers: Election of certain local officers by the people: Removal of officers and punishment of the same.

> 1876, June 12. H. R. 121, 44th Cong., 1st sess. By Mr. Lord of New York; read twice; to Com. on Judiciary. H. J., p. 1094;* Record, p. 3761.

1428. Personal Relations: No established religion: No appropriation to religious sects.

> 1876, Aug. 8. H. R. 163, 44th Cong., 1st sess. By Mr. Lawrence of Ohio; read twice; to Com. on Judiciary. H. J., p. 1463; Record, p. °5318–5319.

1429. Amendment: Calling a convention to revise and amend the Constitution.

> 1876, Dec. 4. S. R. 27, 44th Cong., 2d sess. By Mr. Ingalls of Kansas; read; passed to second reading. S. J., p. 7; Record, p. °2.

1430. Executive: Choice: Choice and declaration of the election of President.

> 1876, Dec. 5. 44th Cong., 2d sess. By President Grant in his annual message. S. J., p. 20.

1431. Executive: Choice: By vote of the people by districts and States.

> 1876, Dec. 5. S. R. 28, 44th Cong., 2d sess. By Mr. Morton of Indiana; read twice; to Com. on Privileges and Elections. S. J., pp. 9, 29; Record, p. °17.

1432. Financial Powers: Forbidding payment of war claims.

> 1876, Dec. 8. H. R. 108, 44th Cong., 2d sess. By Mr. Baker of Indiana; read twice; to Com. on Judiciary. H. J., p. 48; Record, p. 110.

1433. Personal Relations: Prohibition of liquor traffic.

> 1876, Dec. 12. H. R. 170, 44th Cong., 2d sess. By Mr. Blair of New Hampshire; read twice; to Com. on Judiciary. H. J., p. 65; Record, p. 145.

1434 [1433]. Personal Relations: Prohibition of liquor traffic.

> 1877, Feb. 8. 44th Cong., 2d sess. By Mr. Frye of Maine; resolution from the legislature of Maine, praying for the passage of H. R. 170, Jan. 26, 1877; referred to Com. on Ways and Means. H. J., p. 400. Acts and Resolves of the State of Maine, 1877, Chap. 207, pp. 191–193.

1435. Financial Powers: Forbidding payment of war claims.

> 1876, Dec. 18. 44th Cong., 2d sess. By Mr. Hunter of Indiana; introduced; to Com. on Judiciary to report in twenty days; motion to suspend rules defeated twice. H. J., pp. °99-101, °179, 280; Record. p. °275. °489.

1436. Executive: Choice: Provision for decision as to the regularity of the return of the electoral votes.

> 1877, Jan. 30. 44th Cong., 2d sess. By Mr. Cox of New York: that Com. on Judiciary consider the advisability of an amendment as above; read; to Com. on Judiciary. H. J., p. °341; Record. p. °1118.

1437. Executive: Choice: By direct vote of the people by States, each candidate being given a proportional part of the electoral vote.

> 1877, Feb. 7. H. R. 189, 44th Cong., 2d sess. By Mr. Maish of Pennsylvania; read twice; to Com. on Judiciary. H. J., p. 393; Record, p. °1316.

1438. Executive: Election of President: Proportional vote.

1877, Oct. 29. H. R. 2. 45th Cong., 1st sess. By Mr. Maish of Pennsylvania; read twice; to Select Com. to Examine into Electoral Vote. H. J.. p. 55; Record, p. 173.

1439. Executive: Choice: Term: Election of President and Vice-President.

1440. Legislative: Election of members of Congress.

1877, Oct. 29. H. R. 11, 45th Cong., 1st sess. By Mr. Springer of Illinois; read twice; to Select Com. on Revision of Laws Regulating the Counting of the Electoral Vote. H. J., p. 75; Record, p. 186.

1441. Executive: Choice: By direct vote of the people.

1877, Oct. 29. H. R. 13, 45th Cong.. 1st sess. By Mr. Cravens of Arkansas; read twice; to Select Com. on Revision of Laws Regulating the Counting of the Electoral Vote. H. J., p. 82; Record, p. 191.

1442. Finance: Direct taxes.

1877, Oct. 29. H. R. 19, 45th Cong., 1st sess. By Mr. Reagan of Texas; read twice; to Com. on Judiciary. H. J., p. 86; Record, p. 193.

1443. Executive: Choice: By direct vote of the people.

1877, Nov. 3. H. R. 23, 45th Cong., 1st. sess. By Mr. Finley of Ohio; read twice; to Select Com. on the Ascertainment and Declaration of Result of Election of President and Vice-President. H. J., p. 128; Record, p. 233.

1444. Executive Officers: Election of postmasters by the local voters.

1877, Nov. 5. H. R. 27, 45th Cong., 1st sess. By Mr. Riddle of Tennessee; read twice; to Com. on Judiciary. H. J., p. 140; Record, p. 239.

1445. Personal Relations: Restricting the application of the fifteenth amendment.

1877, Nov. 5. H. R. 29, 45th Cong., 1st sess. By Mr. Buckner of Missouri; read twice; to Com. on Judiciary. H. J., p. 142; Record. p. 240.

1446. Executive: Choice: Term and eligibility.

1877, Nov. 6. H. R. 32, 45th Cong., 1st sess. By Mr. Oliver of Iowa; read twice; to Select Com. on Revision of Laws Regulating the Counting of the Electoral Vote. H. J., p. 152; Record, p. 250.

1447. Executive: Choice: By direct vote of the people.

1877, Nov. 6. H. R. 33, 45th Cong., 1st sess. By Mr. Oliver of Iowa; read twice; to Select Com. on Revision of Laws on Counting Electoral Vote. H. J., p. 152; Record, p. 250.

1448. Legislative: Election of Senators by the people.

1877, Nov. 6. H. R. 34. 45th Cong., 1st sess. By Mr. Oliver of Iowa; read twice; to Com. on Judiciary. H. J., p. 152; Record p. 250.

1449. Executive: One term of six years.

1877, Nov. 6. H. R. 36, 45th Cong., 1st sess. By Mr. House of Tennessee; read twice; to Select Com. on Revision of Laws Regulating the Counting of the Electoral Vote. H. J., p. 156; Record, p. 253.

1450. Executive: Veto of items in appropriation bills.

1877, Nov. 12. H. R. 41, 45th Cong., 1st sess. By Mr. Lapham of New York; read twice; to Com. on Judiciary. H. J., p. 191; Record, p. 353.

1451. Executive: Changing date of Inauguration Day to May 1.

1877, Nov. 12. H. R. 42, 45th Cong., 1st sess. By Mr. Lapham of New York; read twice; to Com. on Judiciary. H. J., p. 191; Record, p. 353.

1452. Finance: Prohibiting the payment of war claims.

1877, Nov. 12. H. R. 46, 45th Cong., 1st sess. By Mr. Hunter of Indiana; read twice; to Com. on Judiciary. H. J., p. 146; Record, p. 357. Mr. Hale demands previous question, 45th Cong., 3d sess. H. J., pp. °457-459.

1453. Executive: Choice: State tribunals to decide contested elections.
1877, Nov. 15. S. R. 7, 45th Cong., 1st sess. By Mr. Eaton of Connecticut; read twice; to Select Com. on Election of President and Vice-President. S. J., p. 66; Record, p. °415.

1454. Territorial: Granting to the Territories and the District of Columbia one member each in the House of Representatives.
1877, Nov. 27. H. R. 57, 45th Cong., 1st sess. By Mr. Corlett of Wyoming; read twice; to Com. on Territories. H. J., p. 276; Record. p. 726.

1455. Financial Powers: Prohibiting the payment of war claims to disloyal persons.
1877, Dec. 4. H. R. 61, 45th Cong., 2d sess. By Mr. Baker of Indiana; read twice: to Com. on Judiciary. H. J., p. 36; Record, p 13.

1456. Executive: Term of President and Vice-President, six years.
1877, Dec. 10. H. R. 65, 45th Cong., 2d sess. By Mr. Joyce of Vermont; read twice; to Com. on Judiciary. H. J., p. 72; Record, p. 94.

1457. Legislative: Election of Senators by the people.
1877, Dec. 10. H. R. 70, 45th Cong., 2d sess. By Mr. Rea of Missouri: read twice; to Com. on Judiciary. H. J., p. 76; Record, p. 97.

1458. Personal Relations: Granting the right of suffrage to women.
1878, Jan. 10. S. R. 12, 45th Cong., 2d sess. By Mr. Sargent of California; read twice: to Com. on Privileges and Elections; com. report adversely. S. J., pp. 75, 688; Record, p. 252, 1581. Minority report, 45th Cong., 3d sess. S. J., pp. 198, 292: Record, p. 1432.

1459. Religion and Education: States prohibited from making any law respecting an establishment of religion or appropriating public funds to sectarian schools.
1878, Jan. 10. S. R. 13, 45th Cong., 2d sess. By Mr. Edmunds of Vermont: read twice; to Com. on Judiciary. S. J., p. 75; Record, p. 252.

1460. Personal Relations: Prohibition of the liquor traffic.
1878, Jan. 14. H. R. 73, 45th Cong., 2d sess. By Mr. Blair of New Hampshire; read twice; to Com. on Judiciary. H. J., p. 176; Record, p. 310.

1461. Finance: Limitation of time for the presentation of claims.
1878, Jan. 21. H. R. 88, 45th Cong., 2d sess. By Mr. Dwight of New York; read twice; to Com. on Judiciary. H. J., p. 241; Record, p. 442.

1462. Legislative: Prohibition of special legislation in certain cases.
1878, Jan. 21. H. R. 91, 45th Cong., 2d sess. By Mr. Tipton of Illinois; read twice; to Com. on Judiciary. H. J., p. 245; Record, p. 444.

1463. Finance: Providing for the issue of legal-tender notes and regulating the amount.
1878, Jan. 21. H. R. 92, 45th Cong., 2d sess. By Mr. Oliver of Iowa: read twice; to Com. on Banking and Currency. H. J., p. 247; Record, p. 445.

1464. Executive: Choice: By direct vote of the people.
1878, Feb. 4. H. R. 102, 45th Cong., 2d sess. By Mr. Riddle of Tennessee: read twice; to Com. on Election of President and Vice-President. H. J., p. 348; Record, p. 737.

1465. Executive: Creating an executive council of three, in the place of the Presidency: Election of the council.
1878, Feb. 25. H. R. 119, 45th Cong., 2d sess. By Mr. Southard of Ohio: read twice; to Com. on Election of President and Vice-President. H. J., p. 507; Record, p. 130.

H. Doc. 353, pt. 2——26

1466. Finance: Providing for and regulating the issue of legal-tender notes.

> 1878, Mar. 11. H. R. 130, 45th Cong., 2d sess. By Mr. Ewing of Ohio; read twice; to Com. on Banking and Currency. H. J., p. 611: Record. p. 1644.

1467. Executive: Choice: By direct vote of the people, preserving the present relative power of the States.

> 1878, Mar. 18. H. R. 140, 45th Cong.. 2d sess. By Mr. Sampson of Iowa; read twice; to Com. on Election of President and Vice-President. H. J., p. 677; Record, p. 1837.

1468. Financial Powers: Payment of claims against the United States.

> 1878, Apr. 1. H. R. 149. 45th Cong.. 2d sess. By Mr. White of Pennsylvania: read twice; to Com. on Judiciary. H. J.. p. 709; Record, p. 2152.

1469. Financial Powers: Forbidding the payment of war claims.

> 1878, Apr. 1. H. R. 150, 45th Cong., 2d sess. By Mr. Hartzell of Illinois; read twice; to Com. on Judiciary. H. J., p. 771; Record, p. 2153.

1470. Legislative: Sessions of Congress.

> 1878. Apr. 10. H. R. 156, 45th Cong.. 2d sess. By Mr. Potter of New York; road twice; to Com. on Reform in the Civil Service. H. J.. p. 827; Record. p. 2422.

1471. Financial Powers: Payment of war claims: Establishment of a court of claims.

> 1878, Apr. 16. H. R 159, 45th Cong., 2d sess. By Mr. Keifer of Ohio: read twice; to Com. on War Claims. H. J., p. 852; Record, p. 2576.

1472. Powers of Congress: Special legislation prohibited.

> 1878, Apr. 22. H. R. 166, 45th Cong., 2d sess. By Mr. Springer of Illinois: read twice; to Com. on Reform in the Civil Service. H. J., p 918; Record, p. 2712.

1473. Finance: Prohibiting special or private pension or claim acts.

> 1878, Apr. 29. H. R. 170, 45th Cong.. 2d sess. By Mr. Turner of Kentucky; read twice; to Com. on Judiciary. H J.. p. 1000, Record, p. 2926.

1474. Legislative: Members ineligible to appointment to certain offices.

1474a. Judiciary: Judges of Supreme Court ineligible to the Presidency or Vice-Presidency.

> 1878, Apr. 29. H. R. 171. 45th Cong., 2d sess. By Mr. Turner of Kentucky; read twice; to Com. on Judiciary. H. J., p. 1000; Record, p. 2926.

1475. Executive: Choice: Proportional division of the vote by States.

> 1878, May 22. H. R. 183, 45th Cong.. 1st sess. By Mr. Southard of Ohio, from the Select Com. on the State of the Law Respecting Ascertainment and Declaration of the Results of Election of President and Vice-President. Mr. Sampson submits minority report; read twice; recommitted. Mr. Herbert submits minority views; recommitted. H. J., pp. 1128, 1129, 1135; Record, pp. 3685, 3714; House reports 4, No. 819.

1476. Executive: Veto of items in appropriation bills.

> 1878, June 15. S. R. 40, 45th Cong., 2d sess. By Mr. Morgan of Alabama; read twice; to Com. on Judiciary. S. J.. p. 704; Record, p. 4832.

*1477. Financial Powers: Payment of war claims to disloyal persons prohibited.

> 1878, June 19. H. R. 201, 45th Cong., 2d sess. By Mr. Conger of Michigan: motion to suspend rules and introduce and pass resolutions; passed House (145 to 61). H. J., pp. 1437. 1438; Record, p. 4883. Dec. 4. Resolutions received in the Senate; read twice; to Com. on Judiciary; com. report with an amendment; considered. 45th Cong., 3d sess. S. J.. pp. 30, 167, 223, 229, 230, 236; Record, pp. 30, 32, 753, 1030, 1047.

1477a. Financial Powers: Payment of war claims forbidden.

> 1878, June 20. H. R. 202, 45th Cong.. 2d sess. By Mr. Turner. A copy of the printed resolution in the Senate Document Room, not found recorded in the Journal.

1478. Judiciary: Term of judges, twelve years.

1879, Jan. 27. H. R. 223, 45th Cong., 3d sess. By Mr. Finley of Ohio; read twice; to Com. on Judiciary. H. J., p. 289; Record, p. 767.

1479. Executive: Veto of items in appropriation bills.

1879, Mar. 21-1880, Feb. 9. S. R. 4, 46th Cong., 1st sess. By Mr. McMillan of Minnesota; read twice; to Com. on Judiciary. S. J., p. 21; Record, p. °35. Reported adversely, 46th Cong., 2d sess. S. J., p. 204; Record, p. 751.

1480. Executive: Veto of items in appropriation bills.

1879, Apr. 14-1880, Feb. 9. S. R. 21, 46th Cong., 1st sess. By Mr. Morgan of Alabama; read twice; to Com. on Judiciary. S. J., p. 79; Record, p. 412. Reported adversely, 46th Cong., 2d sess. S. J., p. 204; Record, p. 751.

1481. Financial Powers: Payment of war claims to disloyal persons prohibited.

1879, Apr. 21. H. R. 2, 42d Cong., 1st sess. By Mr. Joyce of Vermont; read twice; to Com. on Judiciary. H. J., p. 113; Record, p. 605.

1481a. Civil Service and Finance: Reform in administration.

1879, Apr. 21. H. R. 12, 46th Cong., 1st sess. By Mr. Turner of Kentucky; read twice; to Com. on Judiciary. H. J., p. 143; Record, p. 624.

1482. Legislative: Members ineligible to appointment to certain offices.

1482a. Judiciary: Judges of the Supreme Court ineligible to the Presidency or Vice-Presidency.

1879, Apr. 21. H. R. 13, 46th Cong., 1st sess. By Mr. Turner of Kentucky; read twice; to Com. on Judiciary. H. J., p. 143; Record, p. 624.

1483. Legislative Powers: Special or private acts.

1879, Apr. 21. H. R. 14, 46th Cong., 1st sess. By Mr. Turner of Kentucky; read twice; to Com. on Judiciary. H. J., p. 143; Record, p. 624.

1484. Financial Powers: Prohibiting the payment of Southern war claims.

1879, Apr. 21. H. R. 17, 46th Cong., 1st sess. By Mr. Stevenson of Illinois; read twice; to Com. on Judiciary. H. J., p. 149; Record, p. 629.

1485. Financial Powers: Payment of war claims prohibited to any of the States in rebellion.

1879, Apr. 21. H. R. 18, 46th Cong., 1st sess. By Mr. Townshend of Illinois; read twice; to Com. on Revision of the Laws. H. J., p. 151; Record, p. 630.

1486. Finance: Apportionment of direct taxes and collection of same.

1879, Apr. 21. H. R. 24, 46th Cong., 1st sess. By Mr. Reagan of Texas; read twice; to Com. on Judiciary. H. J., p. 160; Record, pp. 636, 637.

1487. Financial Powers: Prohibiting the payment of war claims.

1879, Apr. 21. H. R. 26, 46th Cong., 1st sess. By Mr. Bragg of Wisconsin; read twice; to Com. on War Claims. H. J., p. 165; Record, p. 639.

1488. Legislative Powers: Special legislation prohibited.

1879, May 5. H. R. 51, 46th Cong., 1st sess. By Mr. Springer of Illinois; read twice; to Com. on Judiciary. H. J., p. 247; Record, p. 1060.

1489. Executive: Veto of items in appropriation bills.

1879, May 6. H. R. 57, 46th Cong., 1st sess. By Mr. Lapham of New York; read twice; to Com. on Judiciary. H. J., p. 257; Record, p. 1091.

1490. Executive: Change of date of Inauguration Day.

1879, May 6. H. R. 58, 46th Cong., 1st sess. By Mr. Lapham of New York; read twice; to Com. on Judiciary. H. J., p. 258; Record, p. 1091.

1491. Financial Powers: Claims against the United States.

1879, May 6. H. R. 59, 46th Cong., 1st sess. By Mr. White of Pennsylvania; read twice; to Com. on Judiciary. H. J., p. 258; Record, p. 1091.

1492. Executive: Term of office, six years: Inelegible to reelection.

1879, May 12. H. R. 67, 46th Cong., 1st sess. By Mr. Buckner of Missouri; read twice; to Com. on Judiciary. H. J., p. 288; Record p. 1285.

1493. Executive: Choice: Election of President and Vice-President.

1879, May 24. H. R. 75, 46th Cong., 1st sess. By Mr. Bicknell of Indiana; read twice; to Com. on Law Respecting Election of President. H. J., p. 380; Record, p. 1596.

1494. Judiciary: Term of judges, twelve years.

1879, June 16. H. R. 101, 46th Cong., 1st sess. By Mr. Finley of Ohio; read twice; to Com. on Judiciary. H. J., p. 507; Record, p. 2046.

1495. Executive: Veto of items in appropriation bills.

1879, Dec. 2. H. R. 124, 46th Cong., 2d sess. By Mr. White of Pennsylvania; read twice; to Com. on Judiciary. H. J., p. 33; Record, p. °16.

1496. Personal Relations: Provision for the granting and protection of trade-marks.

1879, Dec. 2. H. R. 125, 46th Cong., 2d sess. By Mr. McCoid of Iowa: read twice; to Com. on Manufactures; com. report; recommitted; considered and referred to Com. on Judiciary. Com. report a bill; resolution recommitted to Com. on Judiciary. H. J., pp. 34,82,125,126,760,1126,1137; Record, pp. 17, °78, °145-148, 1514.

1497. Financial Powers: Limiting time for presenting claims against United States.

1879, Dec. 4. 46th Cong., 2d sess. By Mr. Townshend of Illinois: that the Com. on Judiciary inquire into the expediency of amending as above: referred to Com. on Judiciary. H. J., p. 45.

1498. Executive: Term of six years. Ineligible to successive terms.

1499. Legislative: Term of Representatives, three years.

1879, Dec. 9. H. R. 131, 46th Cong., 2d sess. By Mr. Pound of Wisconsin; read twice; to Com. on Judiciary. H. J., p. 56; Record, p. °36.

1500. Personal Relations: Prohibiting polygamy.

1879, Dec. 10. H. R. Bill 2779. 46th Cong., 2d sess. By Mr. Burrows of Michigan; read twice; to Com. on Judiciary. H. J., p. 76; Record, p. °59.

1501. Legislative: Bills limited to one subject.

1879, Dec. 9. H. R. 134, 46th Cong., 2d sess. By Mr. Kelley of Pennsylvania; read twice; to Com. on Judiciary. H. J., p. 58; Record, p. 38.

1502. Executive: Veto of items in appropriation bills.

1879, Dec. 9. H. R. 135, 46th Cong., 2d sess. By Mr. Kelley of Pennsylvania; read twice; to Com. on Judiciary. H. J., p. 58; Record, p. 38.

1503. Executive: Election of President and Vice-President directly, proportional vote.

1879, Dec. 9. H. R. 136, 46th Cong., 2d sess. By Mr. Beltzhoover of Pennsylvania; read twice; to Com. on Judiciary. H. J., p. 59; Record, p. 38.

1504. Personal Relations: Extension of the suffrage to women.

1880, Jan. 19. S. R. 65, 46th Cong., 2d sess. By Mr. Ferry of Michigan; read twice; to Com. on Judiciary. S. J., p. 129; Record, p. °380.

1505. Executive: Choice: By direct vote of the people.

1880, Jan. 19. H. R. 172, 46th Cong., 2d sess. By Mr. Townshend of Illinois; read twice; to Com. on State of Law on Election of President. H. J., p. 250; Record, p. 391.

1506. Personal Relations: Suffrage based on citizenship.

1880, Jan. 20. H. R. 175, 46th Cong., 2d sess. By Mr. Loring of Massachusetts; read twice; to Com. on Judiciary. H. J., p. 274; Record, p. 418.

1507. Legislative: House of Representatives limited to three hundred.
> 1880, Feb. 2. H. R. 196, 46th Cong., 2d sess. By Mr. Browne of Indiana; read twice; to Com. on Judiciary. H. J., p. 379; Record, p. 653.

1508 [1493]. Executive: Choice: By direct vote in each State.
> 1880, Feb. 25. H. R., 223, 46th Cong., 2d sess. By Mr. Bicknell from Com. on State of Law Respecting Ascertainment and Declaration of the Result of the Election of President and Vice-President as a substitute for H. R. 75; read twice; recommitted; com. report; referred to Calendar. H. J., pp. 582, 888; Record, pp. 1124, 1903; House Reports, Vol. II, No. 347.

1509. Division of Powers: Guaranteeing the Union, the States, and certain rights of the States.
> 1880, Mar. 15. H. R. 241, 46th Cong., 2d sess. By Mr. Acklen of Louisiana: read twice; to Com. on Judiciary. H. J., p. 784; Record. p. 1559.

1510. Territorial: Granting the Territories one member each in the House of Representatives.
> 1880, Mar. 29. H. R. 267, 46th Cong., 2d sess. By Mr. Downey of Wyoming; read twice; to Com. on Judiciary. H. J., p. 904; Record, p. 1941.

1511. Executive: Ineligible after two terms.
> 1880, Apr. 12. H. R. 276, 46th Cong., 2d sess. By Mr. Geddes of Ohio; read twice; to Com. on Judiciary. H. J., p. 1005; Record, p. 2323.

1512. Legislative: Yeas and nays on large appropriation bills.
> 1880, May 17. H. R. 302, 46th Cong., 2d sess. By Mr. Turner of Kentucky; read twice; to Com. on Judiciary. H. J., p. 1759; Record, p. 3431.

1513. Executive: Choice.
> 1880, Dec. 8. S. R. 131, 46th Cong., 3d sess. By Mr. Morgan of Alabama; read twice; to Com. on State of Law on Election of President. S. J., p. 37; Record, p. °34.

1514. Elections: State and national elections on a uniform day.

1514a. Education: Free public schools.
> 1880, Dec. 13. H. R. 344, 46th Cong., 3d sess. By Mr. McCoid of Iowa; read twice; to Com. on Judiciary. H. J., p. 59; Record, p. 107.

1515. Executive: Term: No more than two terms.
> 1880, Dec. 20. H. R. 354, 46th Cong., 3d sess. By Mr. Frost of Missouri; read twice; to Com. on Judiciary. H. J., p. 100; Record, p. 271.

1516. Judiciary: Increasing the number of judges.
> 1880, Dec. 21. S. R. 138, 46th Cong, 3d sess. By Mr. Whyte of Maryland; read twice; to Com. on Judiciary. S. J., p. 77; Record, p. °286, 287.

1517. Executive Officers: Tenure of office: Certain civil offices limited to four years: Election of postmasters, etc.
> 1881, Jan. 10. H. R. 360, 46th Cong., 3d sess. By Mr. Carpenter of Iowa; read twice; to Com. on Reform in the Civil Service. H. J., p. 147; Record, p. 491.

1518. Legislative: Election of Senators by the people.
> 1881, Jan. 17. H. R. 368, 46th Cong., 3d sess. By Mr. White of Pennsylvania; read twice; to Com. on Judiciary. H. J., p. 188; Record, p. 685.

1519. Executive: Choice of: By direct vote of the people, by districts.
> 1881, Jan. 28. S. R. 148, 46th Cong., 3d sess. By Mr. Wallace of Pennsylvania; read twice; tabled; considered; to Select Com. on State of the Law Respecting the Ascertaining and Declaration of the Results of the Election of President and Vice-President. S. J., pp. 174. 242; Record, pp. 988, 1309, °1450-1459.

1520. Legislative: Election of Senators by the people.
> 1881, Jan. 31. H. R. 385, 46th Cong., 3d sess. By Mr. Weaver of Iowa, read twice; to Com. on Judiciary. H. J., p. 294; Record, p. 1072.

1521. Personal Relations: Prohibition of liquor traffic.
>   1881, Feb. 8. S. R. 153, 46th Cong., 3d sess. By Mr. Blair of New Hampshire;
>   read twice; to Com. on Judiciary. S. J., p. 221; Record, p. °1335.

1522. Personal Relations: Prohibition of liquor traffic.
>   1881, Feb. 15. S. R. 160, 46th Cong., 3d sess. By Mr. Plumb of Kansas; read
>   twice; to Com. on Judiciary. S. J., p. 259; Record, p. 1583.

1523. Personal Relations: Manufacture and sale of intoxicating liquors
prohibited.
>   1881, Feb. 21. H. R. 408, 46th Cong., 3d sess. By Mr. Ballou of Rhode Island;
>   read twice; to Select Com. on Alcoholic Liquor Traffic. H. J., p. 458; Record, p. 1893.

1524. Personal Relations: Manufacture, importation, and sale of liquor
prohibited.
>   1881, Feb. 21. H. R. 409, 46th Cong., 3d sess. By Mr. Joyce of Vermont; read
>   twice; to Select Com. on Alcoholic Liquor Traffic. H. J., p. 458; Record,
>   p. 1893.

1525. Financial Powers: Prohibiting the payment of war claims of disloyal persons.
>   1881, Feb. 28. H. R. 418, 46th Cong., 3d sess. By Mr. White of Pennsylvania;
>   read twice; to Com. on Judiciary. H. J., p. 529; Record, p. 2229.

1526. Executive Officers: Certain United States officers elected by the
people (of their States).
>   1881, Dec. 10. S. R 14, 47th Cong., 1st sess. By Mr. Voorhees of Indiana;
>   read twice; to Com. on Judiciary. S. J., p. 113; Record, p. °85.

1527. Executive Officers: Postmasters elected by the people.
>   1881, Dec. 13. H. R. 5, 47th Cong., 1st sess. By Mr. Sherwin of Illinois; read
>   twice; to Com. on Judiciary. H. J., p. 69; Record, p. 94.

1528. Legislative Powers: Special legislation prohibited.

1529. Finance: Claims against the United States determined by tribunals
appointed by Congress.
>   1881, Dec. 13. H. R. 6, 47th Cong., 1st sess. By Mr. Springer of Illinois; read
>   twice; to Com. on Judiciary; motion to suspend rules not seconded. H. J., p.
>   71; Record, pp. 96, °1057.

1530. Legislative: Limiting House of Representatives to 350 members.
>   1881, Dec. 13. H. R. 7, 47th Cong., 1st sess. By Mr. Browne of Indiana; read
>   twice; to Com. on Judiciary. H. J., p. 72; Record, p. 97.

1531. Personal Relations: Power of Congress to regulate trade-marks.
>   1881, Dec. 13. H. R. 9, 47th Cong., 1st sess. By Mr. McCoid of Iowa; read
>   twice; to Com. on Judiciary. H. J., p. 75; Record, p. 99.

1532. Executive Officers: Tenure of office: Election of postmasters.
>   1881, Dec. 13. H. R. 11, 47th Cong., 1st sess. By Mr. Carpenter of Iowa; read
>   twice; to Com. on Judiciary. H. J., p. 76; Record. p. 100.

1533. Finance: Direct taxes to be apportioned according to property
valuation.
>   1881, Dec. 19. H. R. 42, 47th Cong., 1st sess. By Mr. Reagan of Texas; read
>   twice; to Com. on Judiciary. H. J., p. 154; Record. p. 198.

1534. Executive: Term, six years: Ineligible to consecutive terms.

1534a. Legislative: Term of Representatives, three years.
>   1881, Dec. 19. H. R. 55, 47th Cong., 1st sess. By Mr. Pound of Wisconsin; read
>   twice; to Com. on Election of President and Vice-President. H. J., p. 164;
>   Record, p. 205.

1535. Executive: Offices and duties of the President and three Vice-Presidents.

> 1881, Dec. 21. H. R. (Bill) 2119, 47th Cong., 1st sess. By Mr. Hammond of Georgia; read twice; to Select Com. on State of the Law Relating to the Election of President and Vice-President. H. J., p. 189; Record, p. 239.

1536. Executive: Choice: By a majority of the votes of the people.

> 1881, Dec. 21. H. R. 63, 47th Cong., 1st sess. By Mr. Townshend of Illinois; read twice; to Select Com. on State of the Law Relating to the Election of President and Vice-President. H. J., p. 190; Record, p. 241.

1537. Executive: Choice: By direct vote in each State.

> 1881, Dec. 21. H. R. 64, 47th Cong., 1st sess. By Mr. Browne of Indiana; read twice; to Select Com. on State of the Law Relating to the Election of President and Vice-President. H. J., p. 190; Record, p. 241.

1538. Executive: Choice: Direct vote of the people.

> 1882, Jan. 9. H. R. 67, 47th Cong., 1st sess. By Mr. Cravens of Arkansas; read twice; to Select Com. on Election of President and Vice-President. H J., p. 215; Record, p. 275.

1539. Executive: Choice: Electors and their successors.

> 1882, Jan. 9. H. R. 72, 47th Cong., 1st sess. By Mr. McCoid of Iowa; read twice; to Select Com. on Election of President and Vice-President. H. J., p. 221; Record, p. 279.

1540. Legislative: Yeas and nays on large appropriation bills.

> 1882, Jan. 9. H. R. 75, 47th Cong., 1st sess. By Mr. Turner of Kentucky; read twice; to Com. on Rules. H. J., p. 224; Record, p. 282.

1541. Executive Officers: Regulating the removal of officers in the civil service.

> 1882, Jan. 9. H. R. 78, 47th Cong., 1st sess. By Mr. Buckner of Missouri; read twice; to Com. on Judiciary. H. J., p. 229; Record, p. 286.

1542. Executive: Choice: Directly: Vote divided proportionally.

> 1882, Jan. 9. H. R. 84, 47th Cong., 1st sess. By Mr. Beltzhoover of Pennsylvania; read twice; to Select Com. on Election of President and Vice-President. H. J., p. 236; Record, p. 291.

1543. Legislative: Election of Senators by the people: Additional Senator for every million population over 2,000,000.

> 1882, Jan. 9. H. R. 85, 47th Cong., 1st sess. By Mr. Bayne of Pennsylvania; read twice; to Com. on Judiciary. H. J., p. 237; Record. p. 292.

1544. Personal Relations: Prohibition of polygamy and bigamy.

> 1882, Jan. 9. H. R. 87, 47th Cong., 1st session. By Mr. Thomas of Illinois; read twice; to Com. on Judiciary. H. J., p. 237; Record, p. 293.

1545. Judiciary: Election of judges of the United States inferior courts by the people, and their removal for disability: Term, fourteen years.

> 1882, Jan. 18. S. R. 25, 47th Cong., 1st sess. By Mr. George of Mississippi; read and passed to second reading. S. J., p. 198; Record, p. 471.

1546. Executive Officers: Election of certain officers by the people.

> 1882, Jan. 18. S. R. 26, 47th Cong., 1st sess. By Mr. George of Mississippi; read and passed to second reading. S. J., pp. 198, 199; Record, p. 471.

1547. Executive: Power of appointment vested in a commission.

> 1882, Jan. 23. H. R. 108, 47th Cong., 1st sess. By Mr. Geddes of Ohio; read twice; to Com. on Judiciary. H. J., p. 366; Record, p. 565.

1548. Legislative: Election of members of Congress: Term, six years.

> 1882, Jan. 23. H. R. 110, 47th Cong., 1st sess. By Mr. Beltzhoover of Pennsylvania; read twice; to Com. on Judiciary. H. J., pp. 367–368; Record, p. 566.

1549. Personal Relations: Prohibition of liquor traffic.

> 1882, Jan. 24. S. R. 29, 47th Cong., 1st sess. By Mr. Plumb of Kansas; read twice. S. J., pp. 216, 380; Record, p. 580.

1550. Amendment: Regulation of ratification of amendments.

> 1882, Jan. 30. H. R. 116, 47th Cong., 1st sess. By Mr. Berry of California: read twice; to Com. on Judiciary. H. J., p. 423; Record, p. 724.

1551. Executive: One term only: Pension for life: No cabinet officers eligible.

> 1882, Jan. 30. H. R. 117, 47th Cong., 1st sess. By Mr. Berry of California; read twice; to Select Com. on Election of President and Vice-President. H. J., p. 423; Record, p. 724.

1552. Personal Relations: Prohibition of the liquor traffic.

> 1882, Feb. 8. S. R. 32, 47th Cong., 1st sess. By Mr. Blair of New Hampshire; read; tabled. S. J., p. 79; Record, p. °976.

1553. Legislative: Limiting number of members in the House of Representatives to 325.

> 1882, Feb. 13. H. R. 129, 47th Cong., 1st sess. By Mr. Herbert of Alabama; read twice; to Com. on Judiciary. H. J., p. 552; Record, p. 1089.

1554. Executive Officers: Election of certain United States officers by the people.

> 1882, Feb. 13. H. R. 133, 47th Cong., 1st sess. By Mr. Bayne of Pennsylvania; read twice; to Com. on Judiciary. H. J., p. 559; Record, p. 1003.

1555. Judiciary: Powers over cases "between citizens of different States," rescinded.

> 1882, Mar. 6. H. R. 153, 47th Cong., 1st sess. By Mr. Manning of Mississippi; read twice; to Com. on Judiciary. H. J., p. 740; Record. p. 1650.

1556. Executive Officers: Election of certain United States officers by the people.

> 1882, Mar. 8. S. R. 46, 47th Cong., 1st sess. By Mr. Saunders of Nebraska; read twice; to Com. on Judiciary. S. J., pp. 388, 651; Record, pp. °1697, °3467-3470.

1557. Personal Relations: Prohibiting polygamy and bigamy.

> 1882, Mar. 13. H. R. 166, 47th Cong., 1st sess. By Mr. Cox of North Carolina; read twice; to Com. on Judiciary. H. J., p. 801; Record, p. 1841.

1558. Executive Officers: Election of certain officers by the people.

> 1882, Mar. 21. S. R. 54, 47th Cong., 1st sess. By Mr. Pendleton of Ohio; read twice; to Com. on Civil Service Reform and Retrenchment. S. J., pp. 450, 758; Record, p. 2099.

1559. Judiciary: Power over cases "between citizens of different States," rescinded.

> 1882, Apr. 25. S. R. 59, 47th Cong., 1st sess. By Mr. George of Mississippi; read twice; to Com. on Judiciary. S. J., p. 625; Record, p. 3249.

1560. Personal Relations: Woman suffrage.

> 1882, May 2. S. R. 60, 47th Cong., 1st sess. By Mr. Lapham of New York; read twice; to Select Com. on Woman Suffrage; report of Com. S. J., pp. 655, 781; Record, pp. 3495, 4508.

1561. Personal Relations: Woman suffrage.

> 1882, July 10-1883, Mar. 2. H. R. 255, 47th Cong., 1st sess. By Mr. White of Kentucky; read twice; to Select Com. on Woman Suffrage. H. J., p. 1616; Record, p. 5859. Report of com.; referred to Calendar, 47th Cong., 2d sess. H. J., p. 537; Record, p. 3551.

1562. Executive: Veto of items in appropriation bills.

> 1882, July 24-1883, Feb. 6. H. R. 267, 47th Cong., 1st sess.   By Mr. Flower of New York; read twice; to Com. on Judiciary. H. J., p. 1721; Record, p. 6431. Proceedings, H. J., pp. 364, 546; Record, pp. 2137, °3611.

1563. Legislative: Election of Senators by the people.

> 1882, July 31. H. R. 276, 47th Cong., 1st sess.   By Mr. Townshend of Illinois; read twice; to Com. on Judiciary. H. J., p. 1765; Record, p. 6690.

1564. Executive: Veto of items in appropriation bills.

> 1882, Aug. 3. H. R. 287, 47th Cong., 1st sess.   By Mr. George R. Davis; read twice; to Com. on Judiciary. H. J., p. 1806; Record, p. °6884.

1565. Executive: Veto reversed only by two-thirds of all the members elected to the House: Concurrent resolutions of the Senate and House of Representatives shall be presented to the President for his consideration.

> 1882, Aug. 4. H. R. 289, 47th Cong., 1st sess.   By Mr. Hutchins of New York; read twice; to Com. on Judiciary. H. J., p. 1810; Record, p. 6885.

1565a. Executive: Veto of items in appropriation bills.

> 1882, Dec. 4.   47th Cong., 2d sess.   By President Arthur in annual message. S. J., p. 19.

1566. Executive Officers: Creating a house of electors to elect or confirm appointments in the civil service.

> 1882, Dec. 4. H. R. 294, 47th Cong., 2d sess.   By Mr. Norcross of Massachusetts; read twice; to Com. on Judiciary. H. J., p. 10; Record, p. 16.

1567. Legislative: Relative to appropriation bills: Specific appropriation bills.

1567a. Executive: Veto of items in appropriation bills.

> 1882, Dec. 5.   S. R. 110, 47th Cong., 2d sess.   By Mr. George of Mississippi; read twice; to Com. on Judiciary. S. J., p. 29; Record, p. 23.

1568. Executive: Veto of items in river and harbor bills.

> 1882, Dec. 5. S. R. 112, 47th Cong., 2d sess.   By Mr. Morgan of Alabama; read twice; to Com. on Judiciary. S. J., p. 29; Record, p. 23.

1569. Executive: Term, six years.

1570. Executive: Choice by the people: Vote divided proportionally.

1571. Legislative: Election of Representatives: Term, three years.

1572. Legislative: Congress to assemble annually on the first Wednesday in January.

> 1882, Dec. 11. H. R. 299, 47th Cong., 2d sess.   By Mr. Springer of Illinois; read twice; to Com. on Election of President and Vice-President. H. J., p. 62; Record, pp. 180, °190.

1573. Judiciary: Suits against States: Enforcement of contracts.

> 1883, Jan. 19. H. R. 321, 47th Cong., 2d sess.   By Mr. Moore; read twice; to Com. on Judiciary. H. J., p. 272; Record, p. °1356.

1574. Executive: Veto of items in appropriation bills.

> 1883, Feb. 1. S. R. 130, 47th Cong., 2d sess.   By Mr. McPherson of New Jersey; read twice; to Com. on Judiciary. S. J., p. 271; Record, p. 1875.

1575. Personal Relations: Congress to protect citizens.

> 1883, Dec. 4.   S. R. 5, 48th Cong., 1st sess.   By Mr. Wilson of Iowa; read twice; considered; to Com. on Judiciary. S. J., pp. 20, 78; Record, pp. 18, °133-137.

1576. Executive: Veto of items in appropriation bills.

> 1883, Dec. 5.   S. R. 8, 48th Cong., 1st sess.   By Mr. George of Mississippi; read twice; to Com. on Judiciary: reported adversely; postponed. S. J., pp. 48, 657; Record, pp. 37, 4267.

1577. **Personal Relations: Prohibition of liquor traffic.**

> 1883, Dec. 5. S. R. 16. 48th Cong., 1st sess. By Mr. Blair of New Hampshire; read twice; tabled. S. J., p. 48; Record, p. 37.

1578. **Personal Relations: Suffrage not be abridged on account of nativity.**

> 1883, Dec. 6. S. R. 17, 48th Cong., 1st sess. By Mr. Butler of South Carolina; read twice; to Com. on Judiciary; reported adversely; postponed. S. J., pp. 54, 455; Record, pp. 48, 2198.

1579. **Executive: Veto of items in appropriation bills.**

> 1883, Dec. 6. S. R. 18, 48th Cong., 1st sess. By Mr. Lapham of New York; read twice; to Com. on Judiciary; reported with amendment; considered. S. J., pp. 54, 555; Record, pp. 48, 3164. 48th Cong., 2d sess. S. J., pp. 42, 330; Record, pp. 104, 304, 1492, 1876.

1580. **Personal Relations: Woman suffrage.**

> 1883, Dec. 6–1885, Feb. 6. S. R. 19, 48th Cong., 1st sess. By Mr. Lapham of New York; read twice; to Com. on Woman Suffrage; reported. S. J., pp. 54, 476, 572; Record, pp. 48, 2361. 48th Cong., 2d sess.; considered. S. J., p. 240; Record, pp. 850, °1322–1325.

1581. **Executive: Veto of items in appropriation bills.**

> 1883, Dec. 6. S. R. 22, 48th Cong., 1st sess. By Mr. Morgan of Alabama; read twice; to Com. on Judiciary; reported adversely; postponed. S. J., pp. 54, 657; Record, pp. 48, 4267.

1582. **Executive: Election of certain officers by the people.**

> 1883, Dec. 10. S. R. 24, 48th Cong., 1st sess. By Mr. Voorhees of Indiana; read twice; to Com. on Judiciary. S. J., p. 64; Record, p. 54.

1583. **Legislative Powers: Prohibition of special legislation.**

> 1883, Dec. 10. H. R. 10, 48th Cong., 1st sess. By Mr. Springer of Illinois; read twice; to Com. on Judiciary. H. J., p. 56; Record, p. 64.

1584. **Personal Relations: Prohibition of polygamy.**

> 1883, Dec. 10. H. R. 12, 48th Cong., 1st sess. By Mr. Thomas of Illinois; read twice; to Com. on Judiciary. H. J., p. 50; Record, p. 66.

1585. **Legislative: Limitation of number of Representatives to 351.**

> 1883, Dec. 10. H. R. 2, 48th Cong., 1st sess. By Mr. Herbert of Alabama; read twice; to Com. on Judiciary. H. J., p. 47; Record, p. 58.

1586. **Executive: Veto of items in appropriation bills.**

> 1883, Dec. 10. H. R. 9, 48th Cong., 1st sess. By Mr. Payson of Illinois; read twice; to Com. on Judiciary. H. J., p. 55; Record, p. 64.

1587. **Executive: Veto of items in appropriation bills.**

> 1883, Dec. 10. H. R. 14, 48th Cong., 1st sess. By Mr. G. R. Davis of Illinois; read twice; to Com. on Judiciary. H. J., p. 59; Record, p. 67.

1588. **Personal Relations: Securing civil rights.**

> 1883, Dec. 10. H. R. 16, 48th Cong. 1st sess. By Mr. Calkins of Indiana; read twice; to Com. on Judiciary. H. J., p. 62; Record, p. 68,

1589. **Executive: Choice by direct vote in each State: Proportional.**

> 1883, Dec. 10. H. R. 18, 48th Cong., 1st sess. By Mr. Browne of Indiana; read twice; to Com. on Judiciary. H. J., p. 62; Record, p. 69.

1590. **Personal Relations: Enforcement of woman suffrage.**

> 1883, Dec. 10. H. R. 25, 48th Cong., 1st sess. By Mr. J. D. White of Kentucky; read twice; to Com. on Judiciary; report of com. H. J., pp. 74, 1121; Record, pp. 78, 3351.

1591. **Legislative: Yeas and nays on large appropriation bills.**

> 1883, Dec. 10. H. R. 26, 48th Cong., 1st sess. By Mr. Turner of Kentucky; read twice; to Com. on Rules. H. J., p. 75; Record, p. 79.

1592. Personal Relations: States not to hire out convict labor.
> 1883, Dec. 10. H. R. 34, 48th Cong., 1st sess. By Mr. Fiedler of New Jersey; read twice; to Com. on Labor; reported. H. J., pp. 96, 386. 1621; Record, pp. 97, 572, 5920.

1593. Executive: Veto of items in appropriation bills.
> 1883, Dec. 11. H. R. 35, 48th Cong., 1st sess. By Mr. Wemple of New York; read twice; to Com. on Judiciary. H. J., p. 96; Record, p. 97.

1594. Executive: Veto reversed only by two-thirds vote of all members elected to each House. Concurrent resolutions of the House of Representatives shall be presented to the President for approval.
> 1883, Dec. 11. H. R. 41, 48th Cong., 1st sess. By Mr. Hutchins of New York; read twice; to Com. on Judiciary. H. J., p. 102; Record, p. 101.

1595. Executive: Veto of items in appropriation bills.
> 1883, Dec. 11. H. R. 43; 48th Cong., 1st sess. By Mr. W. R. Cox of North Carolina; read twice; to Com. on Judiciary. H. J., p. 104; Record. p. 103.

1596. Personal Relations: Securing equality of citizenship.
> 1883, Dec. 11. H. R. 47, 48th Cong., 1st sess. By Mr. Keifer of Ohio; read twice, to Com. on Judiciary. H. J., p. 110; Record, p. 107.

1597. Personal Relations: Prohibiting polygamy.
> 1883, Dec. 11. H. R. 50, 48th Cong., 1st sess. By Mr. Rosecrans of California; read twice; to Com. on Judiciary. H. J., p. 114; Record, p. 110.

1598. Executive Officers: Choice of certain officers by the people.
> 1883, Dec. 11. H. R. 51, 48th Cong., 1st sess. By Mr. Bayne of Pennsylvania; read twice; to Com. on Judiciary; reported adversely. H. J., p. 115; Record, pp. 111. 896.

1599. Personal Relations: Protection of civil rights.
> 1883, Dec. 11. H. R. 53, 48th Cong., 1st sess. By Mr. Mackey of South Carolina; read twice; to Com. on Judiciary. H. J., p. 117; Record. p. 113.

1600. Executive: Veto of items in appropriation bills.
> 1883, Dec. 11. H. R. 56, 48th Cong., 1st sess. By Mr. Throckmorton of Texas; read twice; to Com. on Judiciary. H. J., p. 122; Record, p. 116.

1601. Finance: Apportionment and collection of direct taxes.
> 1883, Dec. 11. H. R. 57, 48th Cong., 1st sess. By Mr. Reagan of Texas; read twice; to Com. on Judiciary. H. J., p. 122; Record, p. 117.

1602. Legislative: Choice of Senators by the people.
> 1884, Jan. 7. H. R. 69, 48th Cong., 1st sess. By Mr. Townshend of Illinois; read twice; to Com. on Judiciary. H. J., p. 185; Record, p. 242.

1603. Personal Relations: Suffrage not to be abridged on account of nativity.
> 1884, Jan. 7. H. R. 73, 48th Cong., 1st sess. By Mr. Collins of Massachusetts; read twice; to Com. on Judiciary; reported with an amendment. H. J., p. 1315; Record, p. 4677.

1604. Personal Relations: Power of Congress to regulate hours of labor.
> 1884, Jan. 7. H. R. 74, 48th Cong., 1st sess. By Mr. Davis of Massachusetts; read twice; to Com. on Labor; reported. H. J., pp. 203, 1621; Record, pp. 250, 5920.

1605. Personal Relations: Power of Congress to regulate marriage and divorce.
> 1884, Jan. 8. H. R. 80, 48th Cong., 1st sess. By Mr. Ray of New York; read twice; to Com. on Judiciary. H. J., p. 218; Record, p. 279.

1606. Legislative Powers: Restrictions upon the passage of private bills.
> 1884, Jan. 8. H. R. 81, 48th Cong., 1st sess. By Mr. Beach of New York; read twice; to Com. on Judiciary. H. J., p. 218; Record, p. 279.

1607. Legislative Powers: Prohibition of grants or loan of aid to corporations or private undertakings.

    1884, Jan. 8. H. R. 82, 48th Cong., 1st sess. By Mr. Beach of New York; read twice; to Com. on Judiciary. H. J., p. 218; Record, p. 279.

1608. Finance: Limitation on time of presenting claims.

    1884, Jan. 8. H. R. 83, 48th Cong., 1st sess. By Mr. Beach of New York; read twice; to Com. on Judiciary. H. J., p. 218; Record, p. 279.

1609. Personal Relations: Power of Congress to regulate laws on marriage and divorce.

    1884, Jan. 8. H. R. 84, 48th Cong., 1st sess. By Mr. Beach of New York; read twice; to Com. on Judiciary. H. J., p. 218; Record, p. 279.

1610. Executive: Veto reversed only by two-thirds vote of members elected to that House.

1610a. Executive: Veto of items in appropriation bills.

1610b. Executive: Concurrent resolutions of Senate and House of Representatives shall be submitted to President for approval.

    1884, Jan. 8. H. R. 85, 48th Cong., 1st sess. By Mr. Beach of New York; read twice; to Com. on Judiciary. H. J., p. 218; Record, p. 279.

1611. Personal Relations: Protection of civil rights.

    1884, Jan. 8. H. R. 92, 48th Cong., 1st sess. By Mr. O'Hara of North Carolina; read twice; to Com. on Judiciary. H. J., p. 222; Record, p. 282.

1612. Personal Relations: Protection of civil rights.

    1884, Jan. 8. H. R. 94, 48th Cong., 1st sess. By Mr. Brown of Pennsylvania; read twice; to Com. on Judiciary. H. J., p. 230; Record, p. 288.

1613. Personal Relations: The sale and manufacture of articles from products of the soil shall not be prohibited or abridged.

    1884, Jan. 8. H. R. 96, 48th Cong., 1st sess. By Mr. Deuster of Wisconsin; read twice; to Com. on Judiciary. H. J., p. 238; Record, p. 294.

1614. Executive: Veto reversed by a majority of all members elected.

    1884, Jan. 8. H. R. 97, 48th Cong., 1st sess. By Mr. Sumner of Wisconsin; read twice; to Com. on Judiciary. H. J., p. 240; Record, p. 295.

1615. Legislative: Choice of Senators by popular vote.

    1884, Jan. 14. H. R. 105, 48th Cong., 1st sess. By Mr. Eldredge of Michigan; read twice; to Com. on Judiciary. H. J., p. 290; Record, p. 388.

1616. Personal Relations: Prohibition of liquor traffic.

    1884, Jan. 16. S. R. 41, 48th Cong., 1st sess. By Mr. Plumb of Kansas; read twice; to Com. on Education and Labor. S. J., p. 176; Record, p. 428.

1617. Legislative: Choice of Senators by popular vote.

    1884, Jan. 29. H. R. 141, 48th Cong., 1st sess. By Mr. Cox of North Carolina; read twice; to Com. on Judiciary. H. J., p. 435; Record, p. 735.

1618. Executive Officers: Election of certain officers by the people.

    1884, Jan. 31. S. R. 49, 48th Cong., 1st sess. By Mr. Pendleton of Ohio; read twice; to Com. on Civil Service and Retrenchment. S. J., p. 240; Record, p. 759.

1619. Executive: Offices and duties of President and three Vice-Presidents.

    1884, Feb. 4. H. R. 4408 (bill), 48th Cong., 1st sess. By Mr. Hammond of Georgia; read twice; to Com. on Judiciary. H. J., p. 481; Record, p. 858.

1620. Finance: Export tax on cotton.

    1884, Feb. 4. H. R. 147, 48th Cong., 1st sess. By Mr. Robinson of New York, in the House; read twice; to Com. on Ways and Means. Record, p. 862.

1621. Executive: Choice: Direct vote of the people.

1884, Feb. 11. H. R. 156, 48th Cong., 1st. sess. By Mr. Townshend of Illinois:
read twice; to Com. on Law Respecting the Election of President and Vice-
President. H. J., p. 548; Record, p. 1024.

1622. Finance: Taxation of corporations by States.

1884, Feb. 25. H. R. 177, 48th Cong., 1st sess. By Mr. McComas of Maryland;
read twice; to Com. on Judiciary. H. J., pp. 664. 672; Record, p. °1353.

1623. Finance: Taxation of corporations by States.

1884. Feb. 25. H. R. 178, 48th Cong., 1st sess. By Mr. McComas of Maryland;
read twice; to Com. on Judiciary. H. J., pp. 664, 672: Record, pp. °1353-1354.

1624. Executive: Choice: Election of President and Vice-President.

1625. Legislative: Election of members of Congress.

1884, Feb. 25. H. R. 185, 48th Cong., 1st sess. By Mr. Springer of Illinois;
read twice; to Com. on Election of President and Vice-President. H. J., p.
673; Record, p. 1359.

1626. Legislative Powers: Limitation of Congress relative to issue of
legal tender.

1884, Mar. 10. H. R. 198. 48th Cong., 1st sess. By Mr. Potter of New York;
read twice; to Com. on Judiciary. H. J., p. 786; Record, p. °1756.

1627. Legislative Powers: Limitation of Congress relative to issue of
legal tender.

1884, Mar 10. H. R. 199, 48th Cong., 1st sess. By Mr. A. S. Hewitt of New
York: read twice; to Com. on Judiciary. H. J., pp. 786, 1085; Record, p. °1756.

1628. Finance: Limitation upon the public debt.

1884, Mar. 10. S. R. 72, 48th Cong., 1st sess. By Mr. Garland of Arkansas;
read twice; tabled. S. J., p. 407; Record, p. °1745.

1629. Legislative Powers: Prohibiting Congress from making anything
except gold and silver legal tender.

1884, Mar. 10. 48th Cong., 1st sess. By Mr. Bayard of Delaware; read
twice; tabled. S. J., p. 407; Record, p. °1745.

1630. Executive: Choice: Term, six years: No second term.

1884, Mar. 12. S. R. 74. 48th Cong., 1st sess. By Mr. Jackson of Tennessee.
Read twice; to Com. on Judiciary; reported with an amendment. S. J., pp.
419, 687; Record, pp. °1790, 4496.

1631. Amendment: Provision for a commission to call a convention to
propose amendments to the Constitution.

1884, Apr. 14. H. R. 230, 48th Cong., 1st sess. By Mr. McCoid of Iowa: read
twice; to Com. on Judiciary. H. J., p. 1002; Record, p. 2939.

1632. Foreign Affairs: Ratification of treaties by the House of Representatives, as well as the Senate.

1884, Dec. 8. H. R. 291, 48th Cong., 2d sess. By Mr. Townshend of Illinois;
read twice; to Com. on Judiciary. H. J., p. 47; Record, p. 80.

1633. Executive: One term only, six years: Pension for life.

1884, Dec. 12. H. R. 299, 48th Cong., 2d sess. By Mr. Millard of New York;
read twice; to Com. on Judiciary. H. J., p. 78; Record, p. 218.

1634. Foreign Affairs: Previous consent of Congress required for making reciprocity treaties affecting the revenue.

1884, Dec. 19. H. R. 303, 48th Cong., 2d sess. By Mr. Blanchard of Louisiana: read twice; to Com. on Judiciary. H. J., p. 144; Record, p. 376.

1635. Personal Relations: Manufacture and sale of intoxicating liquors
prohibited.

1885, Dec. 8. S. R. 4, 49th Cong., 1st sess. By Mr. Plumb of Kansas; read twice;
to Com. on Education and Labor. S. J., p. 56; Record, p. 131.

1636. **Personal Relations: Extension of right of suffrage to women.**

1885, Dec. 9-1887, Jan. 25. S. R. 5, 49th Cong., 1st sess. By Mr. Blair of New Hampshire; read twice; to select Com. on Woman Suffrage; reported, S. J., p. 68; Record, pp. °137, 1049, 1690, 1720, 3057, 6047, 8014. 49th Cong., 2d sess. Considered; rejected (16 to 34). S. J., pp. 44, 205.

1637. **Personal Relations: Prohibition of the liquor traffic.**

1885, Dec. 9. S. R. 6, 49th Cong., 1st sess. By Mr. Blair of New Hampshire; read twice; tabled; considered; to Com. on Education and Labor; reported. S. J., pp. 68, 636, 1174; Record, pp. °137, 3817-3823, 7515.

1638. **Executive: One term of six years.**

1885, Dec. 15. S. R. 11, 49th Cong., 1st sess. By Mr. Jackson of Tennessee; read twice; to Com. on Judiciary. S. J., p. 91; Record, p. 180.

1639. **Executive: Choice: By direct vote in each State.**

1885, Dec. 15. H. R. 3, 49th Cong., 1st sess. By Mr. Browne of Indiana; read twice; to Com. on Election of President and Vice President. H. J., p. 131; Record, p. 341.

1640. **Executive: Choice: Term, six years: Election of President and Vice-President.**

1641. **Legislative: Election of members of Congress.**

1885, Dec. 21. H. R. 11, 49th Cong., 1st sess. By Mr. Springer of Illinois; read twice; to Com. on Election of President and Vice President. H. J., p. 151; Record, p. 375.

1642. **Legislative Powers: Prohibition of special legislation.**

1885, Dec. 21. H. R. 12, 49th Cong., 1st sess. By Mr. Springer of Illinois; read twice; to Com. on Judiciary. H. J., p. 151; Record, p. 375.

1643. **Legislative: Election of Senators by the people.**

1885, Dec. 21. H. R. 13, 49th Cong., 1st sess. By Mr. Townsend of Illinois; read twice; to Com. on Judiciary. H. J., p. 153; Record, p. 376.

1644. **Personal Relations: Prohibition of polygamy.**

1885, Dec. 21. H. R. 16, 49th Cong., 1st sess. By Mr. Thomas of Illinois; read twice; to Com. on Judiciary; reported an amendment (H. R. 176). H. J., pp. 154, 1698; Record, pp. 377, 4862. See No. 1679.

1645. **Executive: Veto of items in appropriation bills.**

1885, Dec. 21. H. R. 17, 49th Cong., 1st sess. By Mr. Payson of Illinois; read twice; to Com. on Judiciary; discharged from further consideration. H. J., pp. 156, 1332; Record, pp. 378, 3735.

1646. **Executive Offices: Election of postmasters by the people.**

1885, Dec. 21. H. R. 23, 49th Cong., 1st sess. By Mr. Matson of Indiana; read twice; to Com. on Judiciary. H. J., p. 163; Record, p. 383.

1647. **Legislative: Election of Senators by the people.**

1885, Dec. 21. H. R. 25, 49th Cong., 1st sess. By Mr. Weaver of Iowa; read twice; to Com. on Judiciary. H. J., p. 165; Record, p. 384.

1648. **Foreign Affairs: Previous consent of Congress required for making reciprocity treaties affecting the revenue.**

1885, Dec. 21. H. R. 27, 49th Cong., 1st sess. By Mr. Blanchard of Louisiana; read twice; to Com. on Judiciary. H. J., p. 180; Record, p. 396.

1649. **Finance: Taxation of corporations by States.**

1886, Jan. 5. H. R. 32, 49th Cong., 1st sess. By Mr. McComas of Maryland; read twice; to Com. on Judiciary. H. J., p. 197; Record, p. 416.

1650. **Personal Relations: Suffrage not to be abridged on account of nativity.**

1886, Jan. 6. H. R. 35, 49th Cong., 1st sess. By Mr. Collins of Massachusetts; read twice; to Com. on Judiciary. H. J., p. 200; Record, p. 418.

1651. Personal Relations: Power of Congress to regulate hours of labor.

    1886, Jan. 5. H. R. 37, 49th Cong., 1st sess. By Mr. Davis of Massachusetts; read twice; to Com. on Judiciary. H J., p. 201; Record, p. 418.

1652. Executive: Choice: Provision for uniformity of day for choosing electors and prohibit voting for any other officers on that day.

    1886, Jan. 5. H. R. 44, 49th Cong., 1st sess. By Mr. McAdoo of New Jersey; read twice; to Com. on Election of President and Vice-Presdent. H. J., p. 216; Record, p. 430.

1653. Legislative Powers: Prohibition of special legislation.

    1886, Jan. 5. H. R. 47, 49th Cong., 1st sess. By Mr. Beach of New York; read twice; to Com. on Judiciary. H. J., p. 230; Record, p. 431.

1654. Finance: Provision for a statute of limitation upon claims against the Government.

    1886, Jan. 5. H. R. 48, 49th Cong., 1st sess. By Mr. Beach of New York; read twice; to Com. on Judiciary. H. J., p. 220; Record, p. 433.

1655. Executive: Veto reversed only by two-thirds vote of the members elected: Veto of items in appropriation bills.

    1886, Jan. 5. H. R. 49, 49th Cong., 1st sess. By Mr. Beach of New York; read twice; to Com. on Judiciary; discharged from further consideration. H. J., pp. 220, 1322; Record, pp. 433, 3735.

1656. Personal Relations: Uniform laws on marriage and divorce.

    1886, Jan. 5. H. R. 50, 49th Cong., 1st sess. By Mr. Beach of New York; read twice; to Com. on Judiciary; report of com. tabled. H. J., pp. 220, 1698; Record, pp. 433, 4802.

1657. Legislative Powers: Prohibition of grants or loan of aid to corporations.

    1886, Jan. 5. H. R. 51, 49th Cong., 1st sess. By Mr. Beach of New York: read twice; to Com. on Judiciary. H. J., p. 230; Record, p. 433.

1658. Executive Officials: Election of certain officials by the people.

    1886, Jan. 6. H. R. 55, 49th Cong., 1st sess. By Mr. Bayne of Pennsylvania, in the House; read twice; to Com. on Judiciary. Record, p. 472.

1659. Executive: Veto of items in appropriation bills: Such items to pass veto require two-thirds vote of members elected in each House.

    1886, Jan. 6. H. R. 56, 49th Cong., 1st sess. By Mr. Randall of Pennsylvania; read twice; to Com. on Judiciary; discharged from further consideration. H. J., pp. 251, 1332; Record, pp. 476, 3735.

1660. Executive: Creating the office of Second Vice-President.

    1886, Jan. 6. H. R. 61, 49th Cong., 1st sess. By Mr. Dibble of South Carolina: read twice; to Com. on Election of President and Vice-President; reported with amendment. H. J., p. 258; House Reports, °Vol. 8, No. 2493; Record, pp. 481, 4680, 7833.

1661. Finance: Direct taxes.

    1886, Jan. 6. H. R. 65, 49th Cong., 1st sess. By Mr. Reagan of Texas; read twice; to Com. on Judiciary. H. J., p. 266; Record, p. 487.

1662. Executive: Veto of items in river and harbor bill.

    1886, Jan. 6. H. R. 66, 49th Cong., 1st sess. By Mr. Throckmorton of Texas; read twice; to Com. on Judiciary; discharged from further consideration; tabled. H. J., pp. 289, 1332; Record, pp. 488, 3735.

1663. Executive: One term, six years.

    1886, Jan. 7. H. R. 69, 49th Cong., 1st sess. By Mr. Millard of New York; read twice; to Com. on Election of President and Vice-President. H. J., p. 296; Record, p. 533.

1664. **Executive Officers: Recommendation of majority of voters necessary for appointment of postmasters.**
> 1886, Jan. 7. H. R. 70, 49th Cong., 1st sess. By Mr. Grout of Vermont; read twice; to Com. on Judiciary. H. J., p. 301; Record, p. 536.

1665. **Executive: Veto of items in appropriation bills: Such items to pass veto require two-thirds vote of members elected in each House.**
> 1886, Jan. 11. H. R. 77, 49th Cong., 1st sess. By Mr. Payne of New York; read twice; to Com. on Judiciary; discharged from further consideration. H. J., pp. 334, 1332; Record, pp. 590, 3735.

1666. **Personal Relations: Contracting of convict labor within the territorial limits of the United States prohibited.**
> 1886, Jan. 18. H. R. 84, 49th Cong., 1st sess. By Mr. Lovering of Massachusetts; read twice; to Com. on Labor. H. J., p. 396; Record, p. 724.

1667. **Executive: Creating the office of First, Second, and Third Vice-President.**
> 1886, Jan. 18. H. R. 90, 49th Cong., 1st sess. By Mr. Crain of Texas; read twice; to Com. on Judiciary. H. J., p. 407; Record, p. 733.

1668. **Executive: Choice: By a majority of the votes of the people.**
> 1886, Jan. 26. H. R. 93, 49th Cong., 1st sess. By Mr. Townshend of Illinois; read twice; to Com. on Election of President and Vice-President. H. J., p. 460; Record, p. 884.

1669. **Personal Relations: Contracting of convict labor prohibited.**
> 1886, Jan. 26. H. R. 102, 49th Cong., 1st sess. By Mr. Willis of Kentucky; read twice; to Com. on Labor. H. J., p. 476; Record, p. 896.

1670. **Executive: One term, six years.**
> 1886, Feb. 1. H. R. 107, 49th Cong., 1st sess. By Mr. McCreary of Kentucky; read twice; to Com. on Judiciary. H. J., p. 519; Record, p. 1033.

1671. **Personal Relations: Enforcement of woman suffrage.**
> 1886, Feb. 1. H. R. 109, 49th Cong., 1st sess. By Mr. Reed of Maine; read twice; to Com. on Judiciary; report adversely. H. J., pp. 520, 1521; Record, pp. 1034, 4241.

1672. **Executive: Choice: Election of President and Vice-President: Direct vote by States.**
> 1886, Feb. 8. H. R. 116, 49th Cong., 1st sess. By Mr. Little of Ohio; read twice; to Com. on Judiciary. H. J., p. 585; Record, p. 1216.

1673. **Legislative Powers: Prohibition of private or special laws in certain cases.**
> 1886, Feb. 8. H. R. 117, 49th Cong., 1st sess. By Mr. Springer of Illinois; read twice; to Com. on Judiciary. H. J., p. 591; Record, p. 1220.

1674. **Legislative: Election of Senators by the people.**
> 1886, Mar. 1. H. R. 131, 49th Cong., 1st sess. By Mr. Hill of Ohio; read twice; to Com. on Judiciary. H. J., p. 705; Record, p. 1917.

1675. **Finance: Provision made by general law for bringing suits against the Government.**
> 1886, Mar. 8. H. R. 135, 49th Cong., 1st sess. By Mr. Seymour of Connecticut; read twice; to Com. on Judiciary. H. J., p. 802; Record, p. 2187.

1676. **Executive and Legislative: New date for Inauguration Day (April 30).**
> 1886, Mar. 15–June 18. S. R. 55, 49th Cong., 1st sess. By Mr. Ingalls of Kansas; read twice; to Com. on Privileges and Elections; reported. Mr. Hoar of Massachusetts proposed an amendment, No. 1081; agreed to; passed. S. J., pp. 426, 668, 920, °940; Record, p. °2973, 4074, 4075, 5183, 5801, °5803.
> 1886, June 21. Received in the House; read twice; to Com. on Judiciary. H. J., pp. 1938, 1959; Record, p. 6015.

1677. Personal Relations: Prohibition of polygamy.

1886, Mar. 16. H. R. 140, 49th Cong., 1st sess. By Mr. Voorhees of Indiana: read twice; to Com. on Judiciary; reported; tabled. H. J., pp. 946, 1098; Record, pp. 2414, 4862. (See H. R. 176, No. 1679.)

1678. Personal Relations: Prohibition of polygamy.

1886, Mar. 22. H. R. 143, 49th Cong., 1st sess. By Mr. Van Eaton of Mississippi; read twice; to Com. on Judiciary; report of com. H. J., pp. 1013, 1698; Record, pp. 2636, 4862. (See H. R. 176, No. 1679.)

1679. Personal Relations: Prohibition of polygamy and polygamous associations.

1886, May 24. H. R. 176, 49th Cong., 1st sess. By Mr. Tucker, from the Com. on Judiciary: read twice; referred to Calendar. H. J., p. 1698; Record, p. 4863.

1680. Personal Relations: Bigamy and polygamy prohibited.

1886, June 2. S. R. 68, 49th Cong., 1st sess. By Mr. Cullom of Illinois; read twice; to Com. on Judiciary. S. J., p. 841; Record. p. °5132.

1681 [1676]. Executive and Legislative: New date for Inauguration Day (April 30).

1886, June 14. S. R. 70, 49th Cong., 1st sess. By Mr. Hoar of Massachusetts, as substitute of S. R. 55; read twice; tabled. S. J., p. 903; Record, p. 5643.

1682. Legislative: Changing the time of meeting of Congress.

1886, Dec. 7. H. R. 218, 49th Cong., 2d sess. By Mr. Crain of Texas; read twice; to Com. on Judiciary. H. J., p. 43; Record, p. 25.

1683. Legislative: Election of Senators by the people.

1886, Dec. 16. S. R. 89, 49th Cong., 2d sess. By Mr. Van Wyck of Nebraska: read twice; to Com. on Judiciary. S. J., p. 75; Record. p. 202.

1684. Legislative: Election of Senators by the people.

1887, Jan. 17. H. R. 239, 49th Cong., 2d sess. By Mr. Hermann of Oregon; read twice; to Com. on Judiciary; com. reported adversely. H. J., pp. 286, 395; Record, p. 735, 1086.

1685. Legislative: Sessions of Congress.

1887, Jan. 24. H. R. 242, 49th Cong., 2d sess. By Mr. Springer of Illinois; read twice: to Com. on Judiciary. H. J., p. 358; Record, p 955.

1686. Executive and Legislative: Time for commencement of terms changed.

1887, Jan. 31. H. R. 249, 49th Cong., 2d sess. By Mr. Crain of Texas; read twice: to Com. on Judiciary. H. J., p. 430; Record, p. 1303.

1687. Legislative: Election of Senators by the people.

1887, Feb. 14. H. R. 259, 49th Cong., 2d sess. By Mr. Little of Ohio; read twice; to Com. on Judiciary. H. J., p. 597; Record, p. 1735.

1688. Personal Relations: Power of Congress to legislate on marriage and divorce.

1887, Dec. 12. S. R. 2, 50th Cong., 1st sess. By Mr. Dolph of Oregon: read twice: tabled: considered; to Com. on Judiciary. S. J., pp. 50, 107, 255; Record, pp. 33, 128, 143. °165, 800).

1689. Personal Relations: Extension of the right of suffrage to women.

1887, Dec. 12 1889, Feb. 7. S. R. 11. 50th Cong., 1st sess. By Mr. Blair of New Hampshire; read twice; to Com. on Woman Suffrage. S. J., p. 49; Record, p. 34. Reported with amendment. 50th Cong., 2d sess. S. J., pp. 270, 388; Record, pp. 1591, 2240.

1690. Personal Relations: Prohibition of the liquor traffic.

1887, Dec. 12-1889, Mar. 2. S. R. 12, 50th Cong., 1st sess. By Mr. Blair of New Hampshire: read twice; to Com. on Education and Labor; report of com. S. J., pp. 50, 1070; Record, pp. 34, 5905. Refuse to consider (13 to 33). 50th Cong., 2d sess. S. J., p. 514: Record, pp. 2047, 2287, 2511. °2616.

*1691. Executive and Legislative: New date for Inauguration Day.

1887, Dec. 13. S. R. 13, 50th Cong., 1st sess. By Mr. Hoar of Massachusetts. read twice; to Com. on Privileges and Elections; reported with amendment; amended and passed.

1888, Feb. 2. Received in the House; read twice; to Com. on Judiciary; reported; motion to suspend rules and pass lost (yeas 129, nays 128). S. J., pp. 64, 229, 247; Record, pp. 49, 785, °835, 909, 1192, 1345–1353.

1692. Personal Relations: Bigamy and polygamy.

1887, Dec. 12. S. R. 3, 50th Cong., 1st sess. By Mr. Cullom of Illinois; read twice; to Com. on Judiciary. S. J., p. 49; Record, p. 34.

1693. Legislative Powers: Prohibition of private or special laws in certain cases.

1888, Jan. 4. H. R. 6, 50th Cong., 1st sess. By Mr. Springer of Illinois; read twice; to Com. on Judiciary. H. J., p. 187; Record, p 200.

1694. Executive: Choice: Election by a majority of the popular vote.

1888, Jan. 4. H. R. 7, 50th Cong., 1st sess. By Mr. Townshend of Illinois; read twice; to Com. on Election of President and Vice-President. H. J., p. 188; Record, p. 200.

1695. Legislative: Election of Senators by the people.

1888, Jan. 4. H. R. 8, 50th Cong., 1st sess. By Mr. Townshend of Illinois; read twice; to Com. on Judiciary. H. J., p. 188; Record, p. 200.

1696. Executive: Veto of items in general appropriation bills.

1888, Jan. 4. H. R. 9, 50th Cong., 1st sess. By Mr. Payson of Illinois; read twice; to Com. on Judiciary. H. J., p. 189; Record, p. 210.

1697. Executive: Choice: By direct vote in each State.

1888, Jan. 4. H. R. 11, 50th Cong., 1st sess. By Mr. Browne of Indiana; read twice; to Com. on Judiciary. H. J., p. 190; Record, p. 210.

1698. Legislative: Election of Senators by the people.

1888, Jan. 4. H. R. 12, 50th Cong., 1st sess. By Mr. Weaver of Iowa; read twice; to Com. on Judiciary. H. J., p. 192; Record, p. 212.

1699. Personal Relations: Prohibition of the liquor traffic.

1888, Jan. 4. H. R. 15, 50th Cong., 1st sess. By Mr. Dingley of Maine; read twice; to Com. on Judiciary; report of com. H. J., pp. 199, 695; Record. pp. 217, 1024.

1700. Personal Relations: Extension of the right of suffrage to women.

1888, Jan. 4. H. R. 16, 50th Cong., 1st sess. By Mr. Reed of Maine; read twice; to Com. on Judiciary. H. J., p. 200; Record, p. 218.

1701. Finance: Taxation of corporations by States.

1888, Jan. 4. H. R. 17, 50th Cong., 1st sess. By Mr. McComas of Maryland; read twice; to Com. on Judiciary; com. discharged from further consideration. H. J., pp. 201, 1008; Record. pp. 218, 1829.

1702. Personal Relations: Power of Congress to limit hours of labor.

1888, Jan. 4. H. R. 20, 50th Cong., 1st sess. By Mr. Davis of Massachusetts; read twice; to Com. on Judiciary; com. discharged from further consideration. H. J., pp. 201, 695; Record, pp. 218, 1024.

1703. Legislative and Executive: New date for Inauguration Day: Last Tuesday in April.

1888, Jan. 4. H. R. 21, 50th Cong., 1st sess. By Mr. Lodge of Massachusetts; read twice; to Com. on Judiciary. H. J., p. 202; Record, p. 219.

1704. Legislative: Election of Senators by the people.

1888, Jan. 4. H. R. 27, 50th Cong., 1st sess. By Mr. Hermann of Oregon; read twice; to Com. on Judiciary. H. J., p. 215; Record, p. 227.

1705. Executive: Choice: By direct vote, the electoral vote divided among the candidates proportionately.

> 1888, Jan 4. H. R. 28, 50th Cong., 1st sess. By Mr. Maish of Pennsylvania: read twice; to Select Com. on Election of President. Vice-President and Representatives in Congress. H. J., p. 215; Record, p. °228.

1706. Executive: Creating and defining the office of Second Vice-President.

> 1888, Jan. 4. H. R. 30, 50th Cong., 1st sess. By Mr. Dibble of South Carolina; read twice; to Select Com. on Election of President, Vice-President, and Representatives in Congress. H. J., p. 218; Record, p. °230.

1707. Legislative: Changing time of meeting of Congress and commencement of the term of Representatives.

> 1888, Jan. 4. H. R. 33, 50th Cong., 1st sess. By Mr. Crain of Texas; read twice: to Select Com. on Election of President, Vice-President, and Representatives in Congress; com. discharged from further consideration and referred to the Calendar. H. J., pp. 221, 650; Record, pp. °232, 924, 929. House Report No. 219.

1708. Executive: Veto of items in appropriation bills: Such items to pass veto require two-thirds vote of members elected to each House.

> 1888, Jan. 4. H. R. 35, 50th Cong., 1st sess. By Mr. Randall of Pennsylvania; read twice; to Com. on Judiciary. H. J., p. 227; Record, p. 236.

1709. Personal Relations: Prohibition of polygamy and polygamous association.

> 1888, Jan. 5. H. R. 45, 50th Cong., 1st sess. By Mr. Taylor of Ohio; read twice; to Com. on Judiciary; com. report H. R. 116 as a substitute. No. 1718 H. J., pp. 254, 878; Record, pp. 279, 1378.

1710. Personal Relations: Prohibition of polygamy.

> 1888, Jan. 9. H. R. 49, 50th Cong., 1st sess. By Mr. Springer of Illinois; read twice; to Com. on Judiciary; com. report H. R. 116 as a substitute. No. 1718 H. J., pp. 313, 878; Record, pp. 318, 1378.

1711. Legislative Powers: Power of Congress to grant aid to the common school system of the several States.

> 1888, Jan. 10. H. R. 63, 50th Cong., 1st sess. By Mr. Phelan of Tennessee; read twice; to Com. on Judiciary; com. discharged from further consideration. H. J., pp. 342, 651; Record, pp. 559, 929.

1712. Personal Relations: Prohibition of polygamy.

> 1888, Jan. 10. H. R. 64, 50th Cong., 1st sess. By Mr. Stewart of Vermont; read twice; to Com. on Judiciary. H. J., p. 343; Record, p. 360.

1713. Personal Relations: Prohibition of polygamy.

> 1888, Jan. 10. H. R. 67, 50th Cong., 1st sess. By Mr. Voorhees of Indiana; read twice; to Com. on Judiciary. H. J., p. 347; Record, p. 362.

1714. Legislative: Prohibition of the repeal of general pension laws.

> 1888, Jan. 23. H. R. 86, 50th Cong., 1st sess. By Mr. Peters of Kansas; read twice; to Com. on Judiciary. H. J., p. 508; Record, p. 633.

1715. Executive: Choice: One term: By direct vote of the voters: In case of no majority by joint convention.

> 1888, Jan. 31. S. R. 45, 50th Cong., 1st sess. By Mr. Cockrell of Missouri: read twice; to Com. on Judiciary. S. J., p. 244; Record, p. 820.

1716. Legislature: Limiting the number of Representatives to 250.

> 1888, Feb. 13. H. R. 108, 50th Cong., 1st sess. By Mr. Johnston of North Carolina; read twice; to Com. on Judiciary. H. J., p. 766; Record, p. °1151.

1717. Executive: One term. eight years.

> 1888, Feb. 20. H. R. 115, 50th Cong., 1st sess. By Mr. Hudd of Wisconsin; read twice; to Com. on Judiciary; reported adversely. H. J., p.859; Record, pp. 1343, 2501.

1718 [1700,1710,1712,1713]. Personal Relations: Prohibition of polygamy.

> 1888, Feb. 21. H. R. 116. 50th Cong., 1st sess. By Mr. Culberson of Texas from Com. on Judiciary, as a substitute for resolutions referred to them. H. J., p. 878; Record, p. 1378.

1719. Executive: Changing commencement of term of President and Vice-President.

1720. Legislative: Changing the date for the opening of Congressional term.

> 1888, Feb. 27. H. R. 120, 50th Cong., 1st sess. By Mr. Crain of Texas: read twice; to Com. on Election of President, Vice-President and Representatives in Congress; reported; motion to suspend rules and pass rejected (80 to 154) H. J., p. 947; Record, pp. 1515, 1703, °2619-24.

1721. Legislative: Election of Senators by the people.

> 1888 Mar. 27. H. R. 141, 50th Cong., 1st sess. By Mr. Oates from the Com. on Revision of the Laws, to which was referred memorial of the legislature of Iowa; read twice; tabled. H. J., p. 1345; Record, p. 2450.

1722. Executive: Term, six years: Ineligible to reelection.

> 1888, Apr. 16. H. R. 149, 50th Cong., 1st sess. By Mr. McComas of Maryland: read twice; to Com. on Judiciary. H. J., p. 1643; Record, p. 3009.

1723. Personal Relations: Extension of the right of suffrage to widows and spinsters.

> 1888, Apr. 30. H. R. 159, 50th Cong., 1st sess. By Mr. Mason of Illinois (by request); read twice; to Com. on Judiciary. H. J. p. 1784; Record, p. 3545.

1724. Executive: One term, six years.

> 1888, May 14. H. R. 167, 50th Cong., 1st sess. By Mr. Neal of Tennessee: read twice; to Com. on Judiciary. H. J. p. 1892; Record, p. 4089.

1725. Legislative and Executive; Veto reversed by a majority.

> 1888, May 14. S. R. 80, 50th Cong., 1st sess. By Mr. Stewart of Nevada: read twice; tabled; considered. S. J. pp. 814, 870, 885; Record, pp. 4081, 4500, 4572, 4664.

1726. Legislative: Granting representation to the District of Columbia in the two Houses of Congress.

1726a. Executive: Granting representation in electoral college to District of Columbia.

> 1888, May 15. S. R. 82, 50th Cong., 1st sess. By Mr. Blair of New Hampshire; read twice; to Com. on Privileges and Elections. S. J., p. 822; Record. p. 4144.

1727. Personal Relations: Respecting the establishment of religion and free public schools.

> 1888, May 25–Dec. 21. S. R. 86, 50th Cong., 1st sess. By Mr. Blair of New Hampshire; read twice; tabled. S. J., pp. 877, 1419; Record, p. °4615. Referred to Com. on Education and Labor, 50th Cong., 2d sess. S. J., p. 98; Record, p. 421, °433.

1728. Executive: Veto of items in appropriation bills.

> 1888, Aug. 23. H. R. 216, 50th Cong., 1st sess. By Mr. Crain of Texas: read twice; to Com. on Judiciary. H. J., p. 2646; Record, p. 7886.

1729. Legislative: To change requirement as to quorum.

> 1888, Oct. 1. H. R. 225. 50th Cong., 1st sess. By Mr. Wheeler of Alabama; read twice; to Com. on Judiciary. H. J., p. 2858; Record; p. 9073.

1730. Legislative: Election of Senators by the people.

> 1888, Oct. 20. S. R. 117, 50th Cong., 1st sess. By Mr. Mitchell of Oregon; read twice; to Com. on Privileges and Elections. S. J., p. 1509; Record, p. °9613.

1731. Executive: Choice by popular vote. Person having greatest number of votes to be President, next highest, Vice-President.

1731a. Executive: No local or State election, except for Representatives, to be held on same day.

> 1888, Dec. 4. H. R. 234, 50th Cong., 2d sess. By Mr. Stone of Kentucky; read twice; to Com. on Judiciary. H. J., p. 34; Record, p. 16.

1732. Executive: Term, six years.

> 1888, Dec. 6. S. R. 119, 50th Cong., 2d sess. By Mr. Butler of South Corolina; read twice; tabled. S. J., p. 42; Record, p. 59.

1733. Executive: Fixing a uniform day for the choice of Presidential electors, and prohibiting the election of other officers, except Representatives on the same day.

> 1888, Dec. 10. H. R. 238, 50th Cong., 2d sess. By Mr. McAdoo of New Jersey; read twice; to Com. on Judiciary. H. J., p. 64; Record, p. 121.

1734. Personal Relations: Prohibition of polygamy.

> 1888, Dec. 17. H. R. 242, 50th Cong., 2d sess. By Mr. Breckenridge of Kentucky; read twice; to Com. on Judiciary. H. J., p. 97; Record, p. °296.

1735. Executive: Term, six years.

1735a. Executive: Choice by the people: Vote divided proportionally.

1735b. Legislative: Election of Representatives: Term, three years.

1735c. Legislative: Congress to assemble annually on the first Wednesday in January.

> 1887, Jan. 2. H. R. 244, 50th Cong., 2d sess. By Mr. Springer of Illinois; read twice; to Com. on Election of President, Vice-President, and Representatives in Congress. H. J., p. 134; Record, p. 481.

1736. Personal Relations: Power of Congress to make uniform laws for marriage and divorce.

> 1889, Jan. 5. H. R. 247, 50th Cong., 2d sess. By Springer of Illinois; read twice; to Com. on Judiciary. H. J., p. 163; Record, p. 566.

Appendix B.

BIBLIOGRAPHY.

The following bibliography includes the full titles of the chief works used in the preparation of the study of this subject. This list is intended as a bibliography of the general subject of amendments to the Constitution of the United States, and not of any one or more of the fifteen amendments now a part of the Constitution. It does not appear that any formal treatise on this subject has been published. A short report of a committee of the New York Bar Association, which reviews the proposed amendments presented in the House of Representatives during a limited term of years, and two excellent brief articles by Prof. James Bach McMaster, cited below, are the only discussions known to the writer. With the exception of the Commentaries on the Constitution, there are no secondary authorities. Even in the Commentaries there is little, apart from the discussion of the method of amendment and the interpretation of the amendments which are now a part of the Constitution. For the necessary material the writer has been almost entirely dependent upon the journals and other official publications of Congress. Most of the works included in this list were mainly useful in connecting particular propositions with the political history of the time.

ADAMS, C. F. Memoirs of John Quincy Adams. IX. Philadelphia, 1876.

ADAMS, HENRY. New England Federalism. 1800-1815. Boston, 1877.

ADAMS, HENRY. History of the United States. 1801-1817. 9 vols. New York, 1889-1891.

ADAMS, JOHN. Work with Life of the Author. VI. Edited by Charles Francis Adams. 10 vols. Boston, 1850-1856.

ADAMS, JOHN QUINCY. Memoirs. VII. 12 vols. Philadelphia, 1874-1877.

AMERICAN ANNUAL REGISTER. Amendments to the United States Constitution. I, 57. New York, 1827.

AMERICAN ANNUAL REGISTER. VI, 336-337; VII, 273; VIII, 295. New York and Boston, 1827-1833.

AMERICAN REGISTER, for 1809. Chap. II.

AMES, FISHER. Works, with a selection of his Speeches and Correspondence. (Edited by Seth Ames.) 2 vols. Boston, 1854.

ASHLEY, J. M. Orations and Speeches. Philadelphia, 1893.

ATLANTIC MONTHLY. Presidential Elections. XVII, 543. (November, 1870.)

ATLANTIC MONTHLY. How to Elect a President. XVIII, 428. (March, 1889.)

BAKER, JOHN F. The Federal Constitution. New York, 1882.

BANCROFT, GEORGE. History of the Constitution. 2 vols. New York, 1882.

BATEMAN, WILLIAM O. Political and Constitutional Law of the United States of America. St. Louis, 1876.

BARNARD ET AL. How shall the President be Elected? Symposium by F. A. P. Barnard, William Purcell, H. L. Dawes, Roger A. Pryor, Z. B. Vance. North American Review. CXL, 97. (February, 1885.)

BENTON, T. H. Thirty Years' View, or a History of the Workings of the American Government for Thirty Years, from 1820 to 1850. 2 vols. New York, 1854.

BIDDLE, A. SYDNEY. The Work of a Constitutional Convention. Penn. Monthly. (IV, 283.) 1873.

BISHOP, J. L. A History of American Manufactures, from 1608 to 1860. 2 vols. Philadelphia, 1861–1864.

BLACK. H. CAMPBELL. Handbook of American Constitutional Law. St. Paul, 1895.

BLAINE, JAMES G. Twenty Years of Congress: From Lincoln to Garfield. 2 vols. Norwich, 1884.

BORGEAUD, CHARLES. Adoption and Amendment of Constitutions in Europe and America. (Translated by Charles D. Hazen.) New York, 1895.

BRADLEY, J. P. The Constitutional Amendments. A letter on the number of States requisite to ratify an amendment. Washington, 1865.

BROOKS, ADAMS. The Embryo of a Commonwealth. Atlantic Monthly. LIV, 610. (November, 1884.)

BRYCE, JAMES. The American Commonwealth. 2 vols. London and New York, 1888.

BUCKALEW, CHARLES R. The Electoral Commission and its Bearings. North American Review. CXXIV, 16. (March and April, 1877.)

BURGESS, JOHN W. Political Science and Comparative Constitutional Law. Boston and London, 1890.

CALHOUN, JOHN C. Works. VI. 6 vols. New York, 1853–1855.

CHITTENDEN, L. E. Report of the Debates and Proceedings of the Conference Convention. New York, 1864.

CITIZEN, By a. Amendments to our National Constitution proposed, with a Statement of the Reasons which would seem to require their Adoption at the Present Time. Wheeling, W. Va., 1869.

COMMITTEE (A) of the Massachusetts Legislature on Additional Amendments to the Federal Constitution, 1790. The American Historical Review. ii, 99.

COMMONS, J. R. Proportional Representation. New York, 1896.

CONKLING, ALFRED. The Powers of the Executive Department of the Government of the United States, and the Political Institutions and Constitutional Law of the United States. Albany. N. Y., 1882.

COOLEY, THOMAS M. The General Principles of Constitutional Law in the United States of America. Boston, 1880.

COOLEY, THOMAS M. A Treatise on the Constitutional Limitations. 6th edition. Boston, 1890.

COXE, BRINTON. An Essay on Judicial Power and Unconstitutional Legislation. Philadelphia, 1893 [1894].

CURTIS, G. T. History of the Origin, Formation, and Adoption of the Constitution of the United States. 2 vols. New York, 1860.

DANA, JR., RICHARD H. Points in American Politics. North American Review. cxxiv, 1. (January, 1877.)

DAVIS, HORACE. American Constitutions. Johns Hopkins University Studies. 3d series, Nos. ix-x. Baltimore, 1885.

DESTY, ROBERT. The Constitution of the United States, with Notes. San Francisco, 1887.

DU BOIS, W. E. B. The Suppression of the African Slave Trade to the United States of America, 1638-1870. Harvard Historical Studies. i. New York, 1896.

DUPRIEZ, L. Les Ministres dans les Principaux Pays, d'Europe et d'Amérique. Paris, 1893. Tome II.

ELLIOT, JONATHAN. The Debates in the Several State Conventions on the Adoption of the Federal Constitution. 5 vols. Washington. 1836.

ELLIOTT, C. B. The Legislature and the Courts. Political Science Quarterly. (v, 224.)

FEDERALIST, THE. Edited by Henry B. Dawson. 2 vols. New York, 1864.

FISKE, JOHN. The Critical Period of American History, 1783-1789. Boston and New York, 1888.

FOSTER, ROGER. Commentaries on the Constitution of the United States, Historical and Judicial. Vol. I. Boston, 1895.

FROTHINGHAM, JR., R. Rise of the Republic of the United States. Boston, 1881.

GALLATIN, ALBERT. The Writings of. (Edited by Henry Adams.) 3 vols. Philadelphia, 1879.

GARLAND, H. A. Life of John Randolph. 2 vols. New York and Philadelphia, 1850.

GOODE, G. BROWN. The Origin of the National Scientific and Educational Institutions of the United States. Papers of The American Historical Association. iv. Part 2.

HARE, J. I. CLARK. American Constitutional Law. 2 vols. Boston. 1889.

HAMILTON, J. C. Life of Alexander Hamilton. A History of the United States of America as Traced in his Writings and in those of his Contemporaries. 7 vols. Boston. 1879.

HART, ALBERT BUSHNELL. Disposition of Our Public Lands. Quarterly Journal of Economics. I, 169, 2511. January, 1887.

HART, ALBERT BUSHNELL. Introduction to the Study of Federal Government. Harvard Historical Monographs. No. 2. Boston, 1891.

HAYNES, JOHN. Popular Election of United States Senators. Johns Hopkins University Studies. Series XI. Baltimore, 1893.

HILDRETH, RICHARD. The History of the United States of America. 6 vols. New York, 1856.

HINSDALE. B. A. The American Government. Chicago, 1895.

HITCHCOCK, HENRY. American State Constitutions. New York, 1887.

H., J. A. Examination of the Power of the President to Remove from Office during the Recess of the Senate. New York, 1861.

JAMESON, J. A. A Treatise on Constitutional Conventions: Their History, Powers, and Modes of Proceeding. 4th edition. Chicago, 1887.

JAMESON, J. F. Introduction to the Constitutional and Political History of the Individual States. Johns Hopkins University Studies. 4th series, No. VI. Baltimore, 1886.

JEFFERSON, THOMAS. The Writings of Thomas Jefferson. Edited by H. A. Washington. 9 vols. Washington, 1853–54.

JOHNSTON, ALEXANDER. History of American Politics. New York, 1886.

JOHNSTON, ALEXANDER. Representative American Orations. 3 vols. New York, 1884.

KENT, JAMES. Commentaries on American Law. Revised by O. W. Homes, jr. 12th ed. 5 vols. Boston, 1873.

LALOR, JOHN J. Cyclopedia of Political Science, Political Economy, and of the Political History of the United States. 3 vols. (III, 162.) Chicago, 1881–1884. ·

LANDON, JUDSON S. The Constitutional History and Government of the United States. Boston, 1889.

LIEBER, FRANCIS. Amendments of the Constitution Submitted to the Consideration of the American People. New York, 1865.

LOCKWOOD, H. C. The Abolition of the Presidency. New York, 1884.

McDOUGALL, MARION G. Fugitive Slaves. (1619–1865.) Fay House Monograph. No. 3. Boston, 1891.

McKNIGHT, DAVID A. The Electoral System of the United States. Philadelphia, 1878.

McMASTER, J. B. A History of the People of the United States. 4 vols. New York, 1883–1895.

McMASTER, J. B. A Century of Constitutional Interpretation. The Century. XV. 866. (1889.)

McMASTER, J. B. The Political Organization of the United States. Chapter X in Shaler, Nathaniel Southgate. The United States of America. 2 vols. New York, 1894.

McMASTER, J. B. The Third Term Tradition. Forum, November, 1895. XX.

McPherson, Edward. Political History of the United States of America during the Great Rebellion. Washington, 1865.

McPherson, Edward. The Political History of the United States during the Period of Reconstruction. Washington, 1871.

McPherson, Edward. A Handbook of Politics for 1876. Washington, 1876.

Madison, James. Letters and Other Writings. 4 vols. Philadelphia, 1865.

Madison, James. Papers of James Madison: Being his Correspondence and Reports of Debates. 3 vols. Washington, 1840.

Manie, Herny Sumner. The Constitution of the United States. Essay in Popular Government. London, 1885.

Marshall John. Life of George Washington. 5 vols. Philadelphia, 1804-1807.

Mason Edward Campbell. The Veto Power: Its Origin, Development, and Function in the Government of the United States. (1789-1889.) Edited by Albert Bushnell Hart. Harvard Historical Monograph, No. 1. Boston, 1890.

May, Sir Thomas Erskine. Constitutional History of England. 2 vols. New York, 1887.

May, Sir Thomas Erskine. Practical Treatise on Parliamentary Law. London, 1883.

Michigan Political Science Association, Publication of. i. May, 1893.

Morse, Jr., John Torrey. Thomas Jefferson. American Statesman Series. Boston, 1883.

Morton, Oliver P. The American Constitution. North American Review. cxxiv, 341 (May-June, 1877); cxxv, 68 (July, 1877).

Nation, The. Choice of Presidential Electors by Districts. Statistics compiled by John Dickerman. lii, 421-422.

New Englander, The. Amendments to the United States Constitution. iii, 591.

New York State Bar Association, Report of a Committee of the. 1890. Reports of the New York Bar Association. xiii, 140.

Niles' National Register. i-lvi. (1811-1839.) Baltimore, 1811-1839.

North American Review. The Right of a State to Nullify an Act of Congress. xxxi, 487-512. October, 1830.

North American Review. Our Electoral Machinery. cxvii, 383 (October, 1873); cxxiv, 1, 161, 341.

Oberholtzer, E. P. The Referendum in America. University of Pennsylvania. Pub. iv. Philadelphia, 1893.

O'Neil, C. A. The American Electoral System. New York, 1887.

Overland. Thoughts Toward Revising the Constitution of the United States. vi, 388.

Parton, James. Life of Andrew Jackson. 3 vols. New York, 1860.

Pennsylvania. Journals of the Senate and of the House of Representatives of the Commonwealth of. 1800-1850. Lancaster, 1800-1811. Harrisburg, 1812-1850.

PENNSYLVANIA MONTHLY. Powers of Constitutional Convention. (5 : 813.)

PHELPS, E. J. The Choice of Presidential Electors. Forum. XII, 702. February, 1892.

PITKIN, TIMOTHY. A Political and Civil History of the United States. 2 vols. New Haven, 1828.

POMEROY, J. N. An Introduction to the Constitutional Law of the United States. Boston and New York. 1888.

POORE, BEN: PERLEY. The Federal and State Constitutions, Colonial Charters, and Other Organic Laws of the United States. 2 vols. Washington, 1877.

PRESIDENTIAL COUNT, AND OFFICIAL RECORDS, THE. New York, 1877.

PROCEEDINGS OF THE NATIONAL CONVENTION to Secure the Religious Amendment of the Constitution of the United States, at Cincinnati, January 31-February 1. 1872. Philadelphia, 1872. At New York, February 26-27, 1873. New York, 1873. At Pittsburg, February 4-5, 1874. Philadelphia, 1874.

PRYOR, R. A. The Sufficiency of the Constitutional Amendments. Forum (May, 1890). IX, 266.

RHODES, JAMES FORD. History of the United States from the Compromise of 1850. 3 vols. New York, 1893-1895.

RIDDLE, A. G. Recollections of War Times. New York, 1895.

ROBINSON, JAMES H. Original Features in the United States Constitution. Annals of American Academy of Political and Social Science. I, 2.

ROGERS ET AL. Constitutional History of the United States as seen in the Development of American Law. Political Science Lectures, 1889. University of Michigan. New York, 1889.

RÜTTIMAN, Prof. Das Nordamerikanische Bundesstaatsreçht. I. Zurich, 1867.

SALMON, LUCY M. History of the Appointing Power of the President. Papers of the American Historical Association. I. No. 5.

SARGENT, NATHAN. Public Men and Events. 2 vols. Philadelphia, 1875.

SCHOULER, JAMES. Grave Danger in our Presidential Election System. Forum. XVIII, 532. (January, 1895.)

SCHOULER, JAMES. History of the United States of America under the Constitution. 5 vols. Washington, 1880-1889. New York, 1891.

SCHOULER, JAMES. Constitutional Studies. New York, 1897.

SCHURZ, CARL. Life of Henry Clay. American Statesman Series. Boston, 1890.

SMITH, E. P. The Movement toward a Second Constitutional Convention in 1788. In Essays in the Constitutional History of the United States. Edited by J. F. Jameson. Boston, 1889.

SMITH, MELANCTHON. An Address to the People of the State of New York, showing the Necessity of making Amendments before its Adoption. 1788. Reprinted in (Ford, P. L., editor) Pamphlets on the Constitution. Brooklyn, 1888.

SPARKS, JARED. Convention for Adopting the Constitution. North American Review. XXV, 249.

SPARKS, JARED. Life of Gouverneur Morris. 3 vols. Boston, 1832.

SPOFFORD, A. R. The Electoral System of Choosing President: History of its Origin. In an American Almanac, etc. 1878.

STANWOOD, EDWARD. A History of Presidential Elections. 2d ed. Boston, 1888.

STEVENS, C. ELLIS. Sources of the Constitution of the United States. New York, 1894.

STIMSON, F. J. American Statute Law. 2 vols. Boston, 1892.

STORY, JOSEPH. Commentaries on the Constitution of the United States. Edited by T. M. Cooley. Boston, 1873.

SUMNER, W. G. Andrew Jackson as a Public Man. American Statesman Series. Boston, 1882.

TAYLOR, ROBERT S. Danger Ahead. Arena. V, 286. (February, 1892.)

THAYER, J. B. In Harvard Law Review. VII, No. 3.

THAYER, J. B. Cases on Constitutional Law with Notes. Part I. Cambridge, 1894.

TIEDMAN, C. G. The Unwritten Constitution of the United States. New York, 1890.

TIFFANY, JOEL. A Treatise on Government and Constitutional Law. Albany, N. Y., 1867.

THORPE, F. N. Origin of the Constitution. Magazine of American History. XVIII, 130.

TUCKER, J. R. The History of the Federal Convention of 1787 and of its Work. New Haven, 1887.

UNITED STATES. Annals of Congress. (1789–1823.)

UNITED STATES. Congressional Debates. (1823–1837.)

UNITED STATES. Congressional Globe. (1833–1873.)

UNITED STATES. Congressional Record. (1873–1889.)

UNITED STATES. Digest and Manual of the Rules and Practice of the House of Representatives, etc. Compiled by Nathaniel T. Crutchfield. Washington, 1895.

UNITED STATES. Documentary History of the Constitution of the United States of America. Bulletin of the Bureau of Rolls and Library of the Department of State, No. 7. Washington, 1895.

UNITED STATES. Journals of the Senate and House of Representatives. (1789–1889.)

UNITED STATES. Senate Reports, Forty-third Congress, First session. Vol. II, No. 395.

UNITED STATES. House of Representatives Reports, Forty-fifth Congress, second session. Vol. IV, No. 819. Forty-sixth Congress, first session. Vol. II, Nos. 6, 347. Forty-ninth Congress, first session, Vol. VIII. No. 2493. Fifty-second Congress, first-session. Vol. IV. No. 1290. Fifty-second Congress, second session. Vol. II, No. 2439. Fifty-third Congress. No. 1658.

UNITED STATES. Revised Statutes of the United States. Washington, 1878.

UNITED STATES. The Statutes at Large of the United States. (1789–1889.)

UNITED STATES. Treaties and Conventions concluded between the United States of America and other Powers since July 4, 1776. Washington, 1873.

VON HOLST, H. The Constitutional and Political History of the United States. 6 vols. Chicago, 1877–1889.

VON HOLST, H. The Constitutional Law of the United States of America. Chicago. 1887.

VON HOLST, H. John C. Calhoun. American Statesman Series. Boston, 1882.

WASHINGTON, GEORGE, Writings of; being his Correspondence, Addresses, Messages, etc. Edited by Jared Sparks. 12 vols. Boston, 1837.

WEBSTER, DANIEL. Works. 6 vols. New York, 1854.

WILLIAMS, EDWIN. The Statesman's Manual. 4 vols. New York, 1854.

WILLOUGHBY, W. W. The Supreme Court of the United States. Johns Hopkins University Studies. Extra Vol. VII. Baltimore, 1890.

WILSON, HENRY. History of the Rise and Fall of the Slave Power in America. 3 vols. Boston, 1877.

WILSON, WOODROW. Congressional Government. Boston, 1885.

WILSON, WOODROW. The State. Boston, 1889.

WINSOR, JUSTIN. The Narrative and Critical History of America. 8 vols. Boston (1886–1889).

YEAMAN, G. H. Revocation of Ratification of the Fifteenth Amendment. The Nation. x, 84.

INDEX.

431